# The International Theological Commentary on the Holy Scripture of the Old and New Testaments

*General Editors*

Michael Allen
*of Reformed Theological Seminary, USA*

and

Scott R. Swain
*of Reformed Theological Seminary, USA*

Consulting Editors

Mark Gignilliat
*of Beeson Divinity School, USA*

Matthew Levering
*of the University of St. Mary of the Lake, USA*

C. Kavin Rowe
*of Duke Divinity School, USA*

Daniel J. Treier
*of Wheaton College, USA*

# The Pastoral Epistles

Gerald L. Bray

LONDON • NEW YORK • OXFORD • NEW DELHI • SYDNEY

T&T CLARK
Bloomsbury Publishing Plc, 50 Bedford Square, London, WC1B 3DP, UK
Bloomsbury Publishing Inc, 1385 Broadway, New York, NY 10018, USA
Bloomsbury Publishing Ireland, 29 Earlsfort Terrace, Dublin 2, D02 AY28, Ireland

BLOOMSBURY, T&T CLARK and the T&T Clark logo are trademarks of
Bloomsbury Publishing Plc

First published in Great Britain 2019
Paperback edition published in 2025

Copyright © Gerald L. Bray, 2019

Gerald L. Bray has asserted his right under the Copyright, Designs and Patents
Act, 1988, to be identified as Author of this work.

For legal purposes the Acknowledgements on p. xviii constitute an
extension of this copyright page.

All rights reserved. No part of this publication may be: i) reproduced or transmitted
in any form, electronic or mechanical, including photocopying, recording or by
means of any information storage or retrieval system without prior permission in
writing from the publishers; or ii) used or reproduced in any way for the training,
development or operation of artificial intelligence (AI) technologies, including
generative AI technologies. The rights holders expressly reserve this
publication from the text and data mining exception as per Article 4(3)
of the Digital Single Market Directive (EU) 2019/790.

Bloomsbury Publishing Plc does not have any control over, or responsibility for,
any third-party websites referred to or in this book. All internet addresses given
in this book were correct at the time of going to press. The author and publisher
regret any inconvenience caused if addresses have changed or sites have ceased
to exist, but can accept no responsibility for any such changes.

A catalogue record for this book is available from the British Library.

A catalog record for this book is available from the Library of Congress.

ISBN: HB: 978-0-5673-3419-0
PB: 978-0-5677-1661-3
ePDF: 978-0-5676-8943-6
ePUB: 978-0-5676-8944-3

Typeset by Newgen KnowledgeWorks Pvt. Ltd., Chennai, India

For product safety related questions contact productsafety@bloomsbury.com.

To find out more about our authors and books visit www.bloomsbury.com
and sign up for our newsletters.

# Contents

| | |
|---|---|
| General Editors' Preface | ix |
| Preface | xi |
| Acknowledgements | xviii |
| Abbreviations | xix |
| Note on Bible texts and translations | xx |
| | |
| Introduction to the Pastoral Epistles | 1 |
|   The current state of scholarship | 1 |
|   The author | 7 |
|   Paul's apostleship | 15 |
|   The recipients | 19 |
|     Timothy | 20 |
|     Titus | 23 |
|   Paul's key theological principle: The church is God's household | 30 |
|     Jews and Greeks in a 'new creation' | 31 |
|     An ordered society | 35 |
|   The subject matter of the Pastoral Epistles | 38 |
|     Paul's missionary endeavours: His achievements and their limitations | 39 |
|     Paul's co-workers: His relationship and advice to them | 40 |
|     The government and good order of the church | 40 |
|     True and false doctrine | 41 |
|     Difficulties and opposition in the congregation | 42 |
|     Prospects for the future | 43 |
|   Dating the Epistles | 43 |
|   Genre and style | 48 |
|   The history of transmission and interpretation | 51 |
|     Early church commentators | 53 |
|     Medieval commentaries | 56 |
|     Early modern commentaries | 59 |
|     The modern period | 62 |

## 1 Timothy — 69

### 1 Timothy 1 — 71
- 1-2 Paul's opening greeting and salutation — 71
- 3-7 Warnings about false teachers — 85
- 8-11 The law and those who break it — 95
- 12-17 The conversion of Paul — 111
- 18-20 Paul's charge to Timothy — 126

### 1 Timothy 2 — 133
- 1-4 The universal mission of the church — 133
- 5-7 The mediator and his messenger — 150
- 8-15 Men and women in the church — 162

### 1 Timothy 3 — 177
- 1-7 The overseer — 177
- 8-13 The deacons — 191
- 14-16 The mystery of godliness — 198

### 1 Timothy 4 — 211
- 1-5 The danger of false asceticism — 211
- 6-10 Training for godliness — 221
- 11-16 Self-discipline — 229

### 1 Timothy 5 — 241
- 1-2 Relationships within the church — 241
- 3-16 Widows — 246
- 17-22 Elders — 257
- 23-25 Timothy's self-discipline — 269

### 1 Timothy 6 — 273
- 1-2 Slaves and their masters — 273
- 3-5 The character of the false teacher — 281
- 6-10 Wealth — 289
- 11-12 The good fight of faith — 295
- 13-16 Paul's charge to Timothy — 303
- 17-19 The rich — 308
- 20-21 Final salutation — 310

## Contents

| | | |
|---|---|---|
| 2 Timothy | | 313 |
| | | |
| 2 Timothy 1 | | 315 |
| 1-2 | Greeting | 315 |
| 3-5 | Personal testimony | 318 |
| 6-8 | Timothy's spiritual gift | 322 |
| 9-10 | God's eternal purpose in Christ | 328 |
| 11-14 | Paul's confession and example | 336 |
| 15-18 | The faithfulness of Onesiphorus | 345 |
| | | |
| 2 Timothy 2 | | 349 |
| 1-7 | The faithful servant | 349 |
| 8-13 | Union with Christ | 356 |
| 14-19 | Working for God | 370 |
| 20-21 | Worthy servants | 379 |
| 22-26 | The character of God's servants | 382 |
| | | |
| 2 Timothy 3 | | 389 |
| 1-9 | The life and character of the godless | 389 |
| 10-17 | The life and character of the godly | 406 |
| | | |
| 2 Timothy 4 | | 427 |
| 1 | The return of Christ | 427 |
| 2-5 | The preaching ministry | 430 |
| 6-8 | Paul's hope | 444 |
| 9-15 | Personal relationships | 449 |
| 16-18 | Paul's rescue | 453 |
| 19-22 | Final greetings | 455 |
| | | |
| Titus | | 461 |
| | | |
| Titus 1 | | 463 |
| 1-4 | Greeting | 463 |
| 5-9 | The character of an elder | 473 |
| 10-16 | The character and behaviour of the wicked | 486 |

| | | Titus 2 | 499 |
| --- | --- | --- | --- |
| | 1-8 | The behaviour of church members | 499 |
| | | The old men | 502 |
| | | The old women | 505 |
| | | The young women | 507 |
| | | The young men | 512 |
| | | Titus as teacher and role model | 513 |
| | 9-10 | Slaves | 516 |
| | 11-13 | The grace of God in the life of the believer | 520 |
| | 14 | The work of Christ | 527 |
| | 15 | Paul's charge to Titus | 531 |
| | | Titus 3 | 535 |
| | 1-3 | The character of a Christian | 535 |
| | 4-8 | The nature and effect of the gospel | 544 |
| | 9-11 | The divisive person | 557 |
| | 12-15 | Final greetings and advice | 563 |

| | |
| --- | --- |
| Select bibliography | 567 |
| Index of scripture references | 571 |
| Index of ancient and medieval writings | 583 |
| Index of names and places | 584 |
| Index of subjects | 588 |

# General Editors' Preface

The T&T Clark International Theological Commentary series aims to offer interpretation of the Bible that addresses its theological subject matter, gleaning from the best of the classical and the modern commentary traditions and showing the doctrinal development of scriptural truths. In so doing, it seeks to reconnect to the ecclesial tradition of biblical commentary as an effort in *ressourcement*, though not a slavish repetition. Alert to tendencies toward atomism, historicism and scepticism, the series seeks to offer a corrective to the widespread pathologies of academic study of the Bible in the modern era.

In contrast to the modern study of the Bible as a collection of witnesses (fragmented and diverse) to ancient religious beliefs and practices, this series reflects upon Holy Scripture as a common witness from and of the triune God of the gospel. These interpretations will give priority to analysis of the scriptural text as such, reading any given passage not only in its most immediate context but also according to its canonical location, in light of what has historically been termed the *analogia scripturae*. In so doing, however, the series does not mandate any uniform approach to modern critical methods or to the appropriation of classical reading practices; the manner in which canonical reading occurs will follow the textual form and subject matter of the text rather than dictate them.

Whereas much modern biblical criticism has operated on the presumption that the doctrinal resources of the church are a hindrance to the exegetical and historical task, commentaries in this series will demonstrate a posture of dependence upon the creedal and confessional heritage of the church. As Zacharius Ursinus noted centuries ago, the catechetical and doctrinal resources of the church are meant to flow from and lead back unto a cogent reading of the biblical canon. In so doing, the reception history of the text will be viewed as a help and not merely as an obstacle to understanding portions of Holy Scripture. Without mandating a particular confessional position (whether Eastern or Western, Roman or Protestant), the volumes will be marked by a creedal and confessional alertness.

Finally, commentary serves to illumine the text to readers and, thus, does well to attend not only to the original horizon of the text but also to its target audience(s). Unfortunately, much biblical interpretation in the modern academy (from both its more liberal and conservative wings) operates as if a sharp divide should be drawn between the source horizon and the receptive horizon. This series, however, gestures towards contextual concerns regarding how the biblical literature impinges upon, comes into confrontation with or aligns with contemporary questions. While the series does not do the work of homiletics, the commentator ought to exposit with an eye to that end and an ear to those concerns.

In seeking to honor these canonical, creedal and contextual commitments, then, the T&T Clark International Theological Commentary series will include sequential commentary on the totality of scriptural books, though the format of volumes will be shaped by the specific demands of the various biblical texts being expounded. Commentators will provide English translations or make use of widely known contemporary translations of varying sorts, but their exposition will be based ultimately upon the original language(s). Commentators will be selected for their capabilities as both exegetical and dogmatic theologians, demonstrated in linguistic and literary facility, creedal and confessional clarity, and an ability to relate the two analytic exercises of dogmatic reasoning and exegetical reasoning. Through its principles, format and selective criteria for commentators, the series intends to further sketch and, in so doing, show the significance of a theological reading of Holy Scripture in the modern era.

*Michael Allen and Scott Swain*

# Preface

## Theological interpretation: The Pastoral Epistles as Holy Scripture

A desire to see theological concerns return to the heart of Biblical studies has inspired the commentary series in which this volume appears, but it leaves open the question of what a 'theological commentary' is and, in particular, how this approach be understood in relation to the Pastoral Epistles. At one level, everyone agrees that the Bible is primarily theological in its scope and intention, and no commentary can escape that basic fact. But although theology cannot be ignored, it has not been the primary focus of much recent scholarship. At times, reference to it has even been regarded as a form of bias, especially when Christians have interpreted the Hebrew Bible in a specifically Christian way. In New Testament studies, 'theology' is often understood to mean the outlook of the individual writers and/or the communities that gathered around them, with the result that we are now presented with a 'Pauline theology', a 'Johannine theology' and so on – perspectives that can be so distinct that they contradict one another.

With respect to Pauline studies, the problem is further complicated because many scholars have argued that only some of the Pauline corpus is directly attributable to the apostle. They base this conclusion on the evidence of a core of texts which consists of Romans, 1 and 2 Corinthians, Galatians, Philippians, 1 Thessalonians and Philemon. These are the letters that they accept as undoubtedly genuine, making the rest appear to be inauthentic because they do not conform to the norms established by the acknowledged seven. Doubts persist in the case of Ephesians, and occasionally of Colossians and 2 Thessalonians too, but because of their uncertain origin the evidence of those epistles is often excluded from comprehensive studies of Paul's thought. Needless to say, the Pastoral Epistles have suffered from this method of analysis and in many respects may be regarded as its chief victims. It has been confidently asserted that their content (e.g. their emphasis on matters of church order), their allegedly 'advanced' approach to standard Christian themes (like Christology) and the relative absence of references to recognized Pauline subjects (like justification by faith or the work of the Holy Spirit) all suggest that they are not genuine. In answer to this, defenders of apostolic authorship point out that anyone who was trying to pass his letters off as Pauline would have taken care to ensure that they resembled the genuine ones as much as possible. Paul himself would have had no need to do that and would probably not have thought of repeating himself if the matters at hand did not require it. As proof of that we may cite a doctrine like justification by faith, which everyone accepts as quintessentially Pauline, but which is virtually absent from most of his letters, apart from Romans and Galatians. If 2 Corinthians and Philippians are regarded as genuine, despite the fact that they say nothing about justification, why should 1 Timothy be rejected because it is also silent on the matter? Surely Paul did not have to say the same thing over and over again and he had the freedom to alter his approach as circumstances required. This might have meant developing one aspect of his doctrine as opposed to others, so that is not a reason to discredit his authorship of letters that do not conform to a set pattern that has been determined by a consensus of modern commentators and was quite unknown to him.

Recent scholarship on the theology of the Pastoral Epistles has not been extensive, though some of it is of high quality, and it represents a wide range of approaches. From a perspective that accepts their pseudonymity and discounts much of their teaching as sub-apostolic, there is the short but wide-ranging study by Frances Young, *The Theology of the Pastoral Letters* (Cambridge: Cambridge University Press, 1994). Despite her scepticism and rejection of much of what the Pastoral Epistles say, Dr Young nevertheless finds elements of value in them and seeks to emphasize those elements over the many other things that she feels compelled to reject. More ambitious, but at the same time more solidly anchored in the tradition of the church, is the symposium edited by Andreas J. Köstenberger and Terry F. Wilder, *Entrusted with the Gospel. Paul's Theology in the Pastoral Epistles* (Nashville, TN: Broadman and Holman, 2010). This examines pseudonymity in some detail (and rejects it) before going on to discuss the major theological themes that the letters contain in a systematic way – beginning with God the Saviour, and moving from there to Christology, salvation, ecclesiology, Scripture, ethics and mission, in that order. The concluding chapter, by Professor I. Howard Marshall, gives a brief but comprehensive overview of critical scholarship in the first decade of the twenty-first century.

More recently, Thomas G. Long has produced a mid-length commentary in a series that claims to be explicitly 'theological' in its approach (*1 and 2 Timothy and Titus*, Louisville, KY: Westminster John Knox Press, 2016). Written in a semi-popular style, this commentary is strong on references to modern culture and to pastoral situations in which clergy today are likely to find themselves. It emphasizes contemporary 'relevance', as can be seen from the way it compares 1 Tim. 2:8-15 to John Gray, *Men Are from Mars, Women Are from Venus* (New York, NY: HarperCollins, 1992), but whether such 'parallels' are helpful for interpretation may be questioned. Somewhat surprisingly, there is relatively little theological discussion, and what there is tends to be negative. In assessing 1 Tim. 2:8-15, for example, Long accepts modern theories of gender equality without criticism and uses them as a reason to dismiss the value of the text he is expounding for the modern church. To be fair, he does put the 'Pastor' (as he calls the anonymous author) into what he regards as his historical context and does his best to present him sympathetically. But since he believes that any perceived dissonance between modern liberal values and the Biblical text must be resolved in favour of the former, the value of the commentary is severely limited and its 'theological' dimension is often imperceptible.

A truly theological commentary on the Pastoral Epistles cannot wholeheartedly adopt any of the approaches outlined above. Dr Young's assertion, that the Pastoral Epistles must be read selectively, in the hope of salvaging material that can still be used by the church today, suffers from the fact that the criterion for deciding what is (and what is not) still valid is determined by the modern commentator, and not by the nature of the texts or the intentions of their author. Whatever we think about the Pastorals, it is safe to say that their author did not share this view. As far as he was concerned, everything he wrote was relevant and applicable to the church. Whether he took future generations into consideration is unknown, and perhaps his belief in the imminent return of Christ made him think that there would not be many of them. Be that as it may, the church has always accepted the Epistles as God's eternal Word, intended for us as much as for the original recipients. Past commentators may have misunderstood or misapplied them, but they always endeavoured to make sense of the whole text and not just of the parts that appealed to them.

The symposium edited by Drs Köstenberger and Wilder avoids the need to pick and choose what is 'relevant', but it filters the Epistles through a grid that has been artificially imposed on the text. The Epistles are mined for whatever evidence that they can contribute to the construction of a more broadly based systematic theology, and the result cannot be regarded as a commentary on the texts themselves. As the editors acknowledge, the Pastoral Epistles cover only some theological themes and do so unevenly, not because their author lacked a coherent theological vision but because his purpose in writing was limited to certain points that he wanted to make and he never intended to paint a complete picture of his beliefs.

As for Dr Long's commentary, it is clear that his desire to achieve the maximum pastoral relevance for today has determined his exposition to such an extent that it is hardly a commentary at all. Some of his parallels with modern life may be helpful for preachers looking for applications they can make, but this will vary enormously from one context to another and his examples will soon be outdated. A generation from now, readers will be more puzzled by his analogies than by the original text, which gives it a built-in obsolescence that reduces its long-term value.

A truly theological commentary must respect the integrity of the Epistles as they stand, recognizing that their author intended them to be read in the way he wrote them. It must also accept that Paul, his immediate audience and the church ever since believed that they were written with an authority that came from God. Ultimately, this belief is the dividing line that separates the theological from other forms of commentary. Are the Pastoral Epistles human reflections on spiritual matters that have been canonized by the church and so given an authority that they do not intrinsically deserve? Are we therefore entitled to accept, modify or reject parts of them according to our own notions of the divine? Or are they rather a revelation from a Being who stands outside time and space, whose main purpose is to teach us about himself by explaining his plan and purpose for us? Is there a God who became a man in the historical person of Jesus Christ, to whom Christians are united by grace through faith and given a perspective that transcends the limitations of human finitude?

Christian faith has always wrestled with the presence of the transcendent in the imminent, or to put it more concretely, with the incarnation of the eternal God in a particular human being. The Pastoral Epistles are a message in time and space from a God who dwells beyond them and about spiritual matters that are not bound by the limitations of the world in which we live. A theological commentary will respect this dual dimension and indicate how the historical texts, written in transient circumstances that are only partially recoverable, reveal eternal truths that summon us, just as they summoned those who first read them, to submit to their authority.

In this respect, the Pastoral Epistles do not stand alone but are part of a wider canon known to us as Holy Scripture. It will be objected that Paul did not know that he was writing canonical Scripture and that the original recipients of the letters would not have understood them in that way. That is certainly true, but the apostle believed that he was writing under the direction of God, and he expected his addressees to receive them as a divine command. For that reason, Christians were soon treating them on a par with the acknowledged Scriptures, and belief in their divine inspiration has remained the doctrine of the church ever since.

The Scriptural status of the Pastoral Epistles was recognized from a very early time, and that determined the way in which they were read and understood. The significance of this can be seen from the way in which the Jewish Scriptures were used in the apostolic church. On the Sabbath day, Paul was in the habit of going into a synagogue and expounding the Scriptures, explaining how the promises made to Israel had now been fulfilled in Christ. In his view, Jews who examined this claim by searching the Scriptures for themselves were doing the right thing, and if they were sincere, their investigations would convert them to the Christian movement.[1] What we do not know is what Paul and his Jewish interlocutors understood by the 'Scriptures'. Were the Beroeans in Acts 17 looking at the Hebrew originals or at a Greek translation, most likely the one we now know as the Septuagint (LXX)? We do not know. Did they include the extra books, which we call the Apocrypha, in their synagogue readings? Again, we do not know, though there is no sign in the New Testament that Christians used those books to make their theological points. There was certainly a Biblical canon consisting of the Law (Torah) and the Prophets, but the third section, known as the Writings, was more debatable. We do not know whether it included the book of Esther, and there is no sign of the Apocrypha. Its boundaries were somewhat fluid, but the Hebrew Bible as we know it was virtually complete when the Pastoral Epistles were written and its authority was universally accepted by both Jews and Christians.

The curious thing is that the co-existence of different texts and translations of the Old Testament did not matter to the early Christians, nor does it seem to have bothered contemporary Jews. Neither of them doubted that there was only one God, or that he had revealed himself to Israel. Jews and Christians both agreed that the Hebrew Bible is a divine revelation, which asserts that the universe was created by God and is essentially good. They both believed that the entry of evil into the world was the result of the disobedience of spiritual creatures (both angelic and human) and that Abraham had been called by God to be the ancestor of a chosen nation that would bear witness to his revealed truth. Paul did not have to argue for these things, or even mention them very often, because it was not necessary. In the Pastorals, as elsewhere, Paul developed his arguments on the assumption that these beliefs constituted a coherent world view that he and his audience shared. For that reason, a theological commentary on the Pastoral Epistles cannot disregard components of that world view that are not mentioned in the text, because to do so would be to misinterpret them by detaching them from their wider context.

To this uncontested Jewish legacy, Christians added their conviction that in Jesus of Nazareth God had spoken to Israel in a full and final way. Jesus was the Messiah (Christ) who had come to fulfill the promises made to the

---

[1] Acts 17:2-3, 11.

prophets of old, as well as to open the way of salvation to the Gentiles. Christ was the hermeneutical key to the Scriptures, the bedrock on which Paul's teaching was built. In reading his letters, it sometimes seems that he skipped randomly from one subject to another, but the person and work of Jesus Christ governed his thought and linked superficially disparate texts together. The Pastoral Epistles were received by the church as Scripture because they were seen to fit into this bigger picture, and the modern interpreter must always bear that in mind.

The Pastoral Epistles do not introduce teachings that were foreign to what Paul taught elsewhere, but they do emphasize certain aspects of his message that needed restating. In these Epistles, the apostle's focus was on how local churches should govern themselves and continue the work that he had begun. Timothy and Titus were his agents in this endeavour, and in writing to them he shared his strategy and concerns for the ongoing mission of the gospel. It was essential that they should ground his congregations in the correct doctrine, which so often had either been misunderstood by the new converts or corrupted by false teachers. The Christian community had to do everything 'decently and in order', as he wrote to the Corinthians, so that the outside world would see how the lives of believers had changed and be persuaded to turn to Christ themselves.[2]

Christianity was something new in the ancient world and the church had to establish its identity in a clear and compelling way. This was the apostle's main concern in the Pastoral Epistles, and a theological commentary must point out how this aim was expressed in them. Real and potential difficulties had to be identified and overcome, and Paul had a wealth of experience on which to draw. Modern commentators tend to assume that the points he raised correspond to actual problems in the churches he was writing to, but we must be cautious about that. Sometimes he mentioned particular people who had fallen away or who were causing trouble, and in those cases he was undoubtedly addressing a particular situation directly. But quite a lot of his advice is rather vague, concentrating on tendencies rather than on individuals. The deviations he referred to may have existed somewhere and posed a threat to the churches over which Timothy and Titus presided, but perhaps it was a case of 'forewarned is forearmed' as much as anything else. Paul's perspective was rooted in the reality of spiritual warfare which was not limited to his immediate circumstances. It was essentially the same everywhere, and it is still the same today.

Our pastoral priorities are different from Paul's and some of his instructions may no longer seem immediately relevant to us, but we can still

---

[2] 1 Cor. 14:40.

understand where he was coming from and adopt his fundamental approach when addressing the spiritual problems we face. For example, his advice to slaves is superficially redundant in a society where slavery does not exist, but the principle that Christians must fulfil their obligations to employers and superiors remains as valid today as it was then. Just as slaves were not to presume on their spiritual equality with the human masters as an excuse for disregarding them, so we cannot use our spiritual standing before God as a means of escaping our earthly duties. Our circumstances are different, but the sense of obligation inherent in our relationships with both God and other people makes us approach them with the same attitude that Paul wanted the slaves of his day to adopt. We do not need to know much about ancient slavery in order to understand this, and a theological perspective helps us to appreciate that we can still apply apostolic principles despite what in many respects is a vastly different situation.

A theological commentary of the Pastoral Epistles is one that treats them as an authoritative word from God to his people that speaks today with the same compelling power as it spoke when it was first revealed. Human finitude is such that no one can claim to have written the definitive interpretation of that revelation, and there will always be scope for disagreement and improvement. New discoveries and perspectives cannot be ruled out, and these may modify our perceptions by introducing new factors into the analysis that hitherto have been unknown or misunderstood. But experience suggests that there is a constant thread of witness and confession that unites believers across the ages. A theological commentary bears witness to the communion of saints and is a contemporary expression of the truth that unites all who have put their trust in Christ. Its aim is to show why the Pastoral Epistles have survived the passage of time and have retained the canonical authority that they have always enjoyed. *Cor ad cor loquitur* – heart speaks to heart, and the heart of the believer is the dwelling place of God on earth.[3]

---

[3] Gal. 4:6.

# Acknowledgements

I am deeply grateful to the series editors for giving me the opportunity to write this commentary and to those at T&T Clark who made it happen. I am also thankful for the opportunities that I have had to research the topic at Knox Theological Seminary in Fort Lauderdale, Florida, at Moore Theological College in Sydney, Australia, at Beeson Divinity School in Birmingham, Alabama, and at Tyndale House in Cambridge, as well as to Dr Philip Towner, who read the manuscript and made some invaluable suggestions for its improvement, and to Dr Frank Thielman, who allowed me to audit his classes on the Epistles and learn from them.

# Abbreviations

NPNF     P. Schaff et al., eds. *Library of the Nicene and Post-Nicene Fathers of the Christian Church.* 2 series (14 vols each). Buffalo, NY: Christian Literature, 1887–94. Reprint, Peabody, MA: Hendrickson, 1994.

PG     J.-P. Migne, ed. *Patrologia Cursus Completus. Series Graeca*, 166 vols. Paris: Migne, 1857–86.

PL     J.-P. Migne, ed. *Patrologia Cursus Completus. Series Latina*, 221 vols. Paris: Migne, 1844–64.

# Note on Bible texts and translations

This commentary is based on the Greek text as found in the twenty-eighth edition of the Nestle-Aland *Novum Testamentum Graece*, published by the Deutsche Biblegesellschaft, Stuttgart, in 2012. The English translation used for the main text is the New Revised Standard Version (NRSV), supplemented from time to time by the New International Version (NIV) and/or the English Standard Version (ESV) when they give a better or more accurate reading. Generally speaking, Greek words and expressions have a wider range of meaning than any English 'equivalent', and it is necessary for translators to make a choice that will best serve their purpose. For that reason, a commentary must refer to more than one translation, and it is occasionally desirable to suggest further possibilities that no readily available translation has so far adopted. All such instances are noted in the commentary at the appropriate place.

# Introduction to the Pastoral Epistles

## The current state of scholarship

Even a cursory survey of modern Biblical scholarship will quickly show that there is a large body of secondary literature on the Pastoral Epistles (1 and 2 Timothy, and Titus).[1] Though relatively modest by the standards of other New Testament books, there is still considerably more material available than can be digested by the average reader. Much of this literature illumines our understanding of the Pastorals in important ways, but its sheer volume and the often mind-numbing detail of some commentaries can easily distract us from the main purpose and significance of the texts themselves. The Pastoral Epistles are short, but beyond claiming to have been written by the apostle Paul to two of his co-workers, 1 Timothy and Titus are relatively uninformative about the precise circumstances in which they were written. In the first case it seems that Paul was in Macedonia and in the second that he had recently left Crete, but we are told no more than that. In 2 Timothy, on the other hand, we learn that Paul was in prison, apparently awaiting execution. Beyond that, it is generally agreed that if he was its author, it was probably the last letter he wrote before his death.

For over seventeen centuries the Pauline origin of the Pastoral Epistles was universally accepted and they were interpreted accordingly. But since the early nineteenth century, their apostolic provenance has been widely doubted in scholarly circles, and modern commentators cannot take Pauline authorship for granted in the way that their predecessors did. It is true that almost everything said against their genuineness is speculation, based more on silence than on evidence, but this has done little to dampen the spirits of those who challenge their authenticity.[2] Yet in spite of this, defenders of the classical tradition are numerous and undeterred by the weight of what

---

[1] See, for example, D. T. Thornton, *Hostility in the house of God. An investigation of the opponents in 1 and 2 Timothy* (Winona Lake, IN: Eisenbrauns, 2016), pp. 283–302, for a recent list of the most important works.

[2] See T. G. Long, *1 and 2 Timothy and Titus* (Louisville, KY: Westminster John Knox Press, 2016), pp. 11–13.

passes as the scholarly consensus. Whatever we think about their authorship and origin, the Pastoral Epistles are important witnesses to the history of the early church. Those who insist that they are pseudonymous believe that they represent a stage of ecclesiastical and theological development that is too highly developed to have been apostolic. On the other hand, if they are genuine letters written by Paul to Timothy and Titus, they provide us with unique and invaluable information about how the apostle's congregations functioned. Whatever position we adopt regarding their authorship, it remains uncertain whether, or to what extent, they set a pattern of ecclesiastical government for subsequent generations to imitate. The reason for that is that the organization of the church which the Pastoral Epistles assume did not last for long. If it seems to some to be too 'advanced' for the apostolic age, it is certainly too primitive to correspond to what we know came later.

The Pastoral Epistles must therefore be dated somewhere in the century between Paul's missionary activity and the appearance of the monarchical episcopate as the ecclesiastical 'norm'. We cannot say for sure when that form of episcopacy first appeared, but it cannot have been long after AD 100 at the latest, making it probable that the Pastoral Epistles belong to the first century and not to the second. But if that is so, the case for accepting Pauline authorship is strengthened, because there were still people alive who remembered him and who would have known if the letters were pseudepigraphal. Defenders of pseudonymity recognize this, but they usually claim that the recipients of the letters were well aware of the situation and were not bothered by it. As T. G. Long puts it,

> none of the original readers or hearers of these letters would have been fooled into thinking these were letters from the actual Paul. What they received, instead, was a message from the iconic Paul, the Paul of blessed memory, the Paul who would have said this to us were he here to say it.[3]

The main difficulty with an assertion like this is that it is entirely speculative and unsupported by what we know of the early church's reaction to pseudonymity in other cases. There is virtually no chance that the first Christians would have accepted the Epistles as coming from some 'virtual' Paul who was otherwise unidentified, and if they did, it is almost impossible to explain why this knowledge was not communicated to later generations, who were uniformly convinced that Paul himself was the author of the Pastorals.

---

[3] Long (2016), pp. 11–12.

Modern doubts concerning the authorship and date of the Pastorals are to some extent based on their form and content, which seem to many modern scholars to be un-Pauline because of the degree to which they differ from epistles like Romans and Galatians. Their stylistic peculiarities are universally recognized but many factors could account for these – the different subject matter, the fact that the letters are addressed to individuals rather than to churches, and the possibility that Paul used another secretary, or even wrote the Epistles himself.[4] Nobody in the early church picked up on this aspect of the Pastorals, and since they spoke and wrote Greek as a matter of course, their failure to notice anything odd about them is surely significant.

More influential than the literary arguments advanced against Pauline authorship is the understanding of the history and development of the church that so many modern commentators bring to the text. Those who believe that the ecclesiastical structure that the Pastorals reflect could not have been in place before Paul's death will necessarily argue for pseudonymity, whereas those who defend Pauline authorship must claim that the church situation they describe is not anachronistic. The problem is that there is not enough external evidence to decide the matter either way, and so the scholarly debates continue with neither side being able to prove its case beyond reasonable doubt. As P. H. Towner puts it,

> It is not possible to prove the authenticity of the letters to Timothy and Titus. The problems raised are on both the literary and the historical levels. The question is whether a reasonable case can be made that places them within the Pauline orbit.[5]

It is fair to say that at the present time, the default position among scholars is that the Pastoral Epistles are pseudonymous, but as Towner and others have insisted, the reasons for this are far from compelling. As defenders of the Epistles' authenticity, they point out that pseudonymity is an assumption that most of those who assert it have accepted uncritically. When the evidence for it is examined more closely, serious defects appear in their arguments and those who advocate it have failed to give convincing answers to the questions which their opponents have raised. In fact, a conservative approach to the origins of the Pastoral Epistles is neither impossible nor poorly represented in recent literature. It is surely significant that of the four major commentaries on them that have appeared in this millennium, three defend the traditional

---

[4] See P. H. Towner, *The Letters to Timothy and Titus* (Grand Rapids, MI: Eerdmans, 2006), p. 87, who makes this suggestion.
[5] Towner (2006), p. 26.

Pauline authorship and the fourth advocates a mediating position which claims that they were put together shortly after the apostle's death, most likely by disciples who had access to genuine Pauline material which they used to compose them.[6]

Scholarship does not stand still, and every year there is a generous supply of new publications devoted to examining this or that aspect of the Pastorals, but it would be fair to say that so far they have done little more than add particular nuances to these four major commentaries, which for the time being remain collectively the best synthesis of scholarly achievement in interpreting the Epistles. Taking them in chronological order, they are as follows:

1. *The Pastoral Epistles* by I. Howard Marshall (1934–2015), which appeared in the International Critical Commentary series in 1999 and was reissued in 2004 (London: T&T Clark). It is an exhaustive study of the Greek text, which pays particular attention to parallels with other New Testament writings, as well as to links with contemporary non-Biblical literature. The author demonstrates a deep familiarity with twentieth-century scholarship and gives his readers an excellent guide to it. He rejects Pauline authorship, but he also shies away from straightforward pseudonymity. Without drawing hard and fast conclusions, he prefers to locate the composition of the Epistles in the immediate post-Pauline period (late 60s or early 70s) and describes the process by which they came into being as one of 'allonymity', a word that he invented to describe something that seems to be unparalleled elsewhere. According to this theory, Paul's disciples were able to speak in his *persona* and to convey an authentically Pauline message, albeit in a situation that the apostle did not know himself. In common with most other scholars, Professor Marshall regarded 2 Timothy as the last of the three Epistles to have been written, but unlike many of them, he put Titus first, although if his theory of 'allonymity' is correct, all three Epistles must have been composed about the same time and with the same general purpose in view.[7]
2. *Pastoral Epistles* by William D. Mounce, which appeared in the Word Biblical Commentary series (Nashville, TH: Nelson, 2000). The great strength of this commentary is the thorough way in which its author

---

[6] This is the view of I. H. Marshall, *The Pastoral Epistles*, 2nd edn (London: T&T Clark, 2004), which is commended by Towner as preferable to theories of straightforward pseudonymity, though he does not accept it. See Towner (2006), pp. 25–6.
[7] Marshall's view is echoed by T. G. Long (2016), though without specific acknowledgement.

investigates the vocabulary of the Pastoral Epistles. He demonstrates that their apparently unusual verbal and stylistic features do not detract from the likelihood of authentic Pauline authorship. Dr Mounce concentrates on a detailed examination of the Greek text, leaving no stone unturned in his analysis of its grammar and syntax. As with Professor Marshall's work, the commentary contains extensive bibliographies for each section, though on the whole, Dr Mounce interacts somewhat less with other scholars than most other commentators do. On the other hand, he does not hesitate to engage with them on controversial subjects, where he expounds conservative conclusions with his trademark thoroughness.

3. *The First and Second Letters to Timothy* by Luke Timothy Johnson, which appeared in The Anchor Bible Series (New York: Doubleday, 2001). The obvious weakness of this commentary is that it does not cover Titus, except where questions of origin and composition are concerned (and then only in passing), but it offers a detailed and reasoned argument for accepting the traditional Pauline authorship. Of particular importance is Professor Johnson's insistence that the term 'Pastoral Epistles' is misleading, because it assumes that the three letters are more closely connected than they really are. He makes out a good case for reading them independently, as separate works in their own right. This approach undermines theories of pseudonymity, which usually assume that all three epistles were written by the same person (or people) as part of a deliberate programme to promote 'Pauline' teaching in the church. The commentary is strong on Biblical and classical parallels, though some of the author's conclusions are eccentric and unlikely to gain wide assent.

4. *The Letters to Timothy and Titus* by Philip H. Towner, which appeared in the New International Commentary on the New Testament Series (Grand Rapids, MI: Eerdmans, 2006). The gap in time between this commentary and its predecessors allowed the author to engage with them in a way which the other three could not do, and the book is the stronger for it. In many ways it represents a synthesis of their findings and often relies on them for their detailed bibliographies, their thorough examination of Greek vocabulary and their literary references. Of particular interest is the fact that this commentary attempts to follow through Professor Johnson's suggestion that the letters should be read separately, and it would not be too much to say that one of Dr Towner's aims has been to deconstruct the concept of a distinct group of 'Pastoral Epistles' once and for all. He was a student of Professor Marshall's and worked closely with him in the preparation of his earlier commentary, but unlike his mentor, he had more conservative conclusions about the authorship of the letters, which was

one of the factors that propelled him to write his own commentary. Dr Towner has also highlighted the importance of the many allusions to the Old Testament for understanding the Pastorals, an aspect that has often escaped the notice of other scholars, and he has pointed the way towards a deeper consideration of their theological dimension, which others have acknowledged but not developed to any great extent. Dr Towner is also more alert to the possibility that Paul was interacting with political and cultural trends like the promotion of the imperial cult and the sexual liberation of upper-class women, which he saw as a danger to the spiritual health and integrity of the church. As with so much else, suggestions like these must remain speculative, but they open up interpretive possibilities that have been largely ignored in the past. In many ways, and especially in its concern for the importance of theological questions, the present commentary follows on from the agenda set by Dr Towner, building on his insights in much the same way as he built on the earlier works mentioned above.

The appearance of these four major commentaries in less than a decade has led some observers to speak of a 'golden age' of Pastoral Epistles scholarship, and it is certainly true that nothing of comparable significance has appeared since 2006. At the same time, these magisterial works have spawned any number of secondary studies, so it is fair to say that the Pastorals are being more widely read and examined by scholars today than they have been for some time. These writers have developed a number of individual themes that occur in the Epistles, and their conclusions are important for that reason, but the four great commentaries remain foundational to recent study of the Pastorals and must therefore serve as our point of departure.

As far as their presuppositions are concerned, it may be said that the authors of all four commentaries are committed Christians, though it is not easy to say how far their faith has influenced their work. In the most basic sense, it is probably true that they would not have entered the field of New Testament studies without it, but it is not clear what impact this has had on their conclusions. For example, although Howard Marshall was an Evangelical scholar in the tradition of F. F. Bruce, his unwillingness to accept straightforward Pauline authorship of the Pastoral Epistles made him something of a liberal dissenter in those circles and his commentary cannot be called 'Evangelical' in the usual sense of the term. Professor Johnson, by contrast, is a lay Roman Catholic, but he is in no sense subservient to his church and has always worked in an interdenominational (and essentially secular) context. In fact, a number of his fellow Catholics have reacted negatively to his conclusion that Paul wrote the Pastorals. These seems surprising at first sight, since one might think that the Roman Catholic Church would welcome support for the belief that its present ecclesiology can be traced back to the apostles, but that does not appear to be so. What we learn instead is how far modern Catholic scholars are able depart from the official teaching of their church, which Professor Johnson has somewhat ironically ended up defending on secular grounds.

Professor Mounce is a conservative Evangelical and reflects that ethos quite faithfully, though he is concerned to point out that his interpretation is based on the texts and not on his own *a priori* faith commitment. As he sees it, it is the evidence of the texts that has shaped his faith and not the other way round, though it must be admitted that he began with presuppositions that are congenial to what he has concluded. This may be a factor in the reluctance of non-Evangelical scholars to support his defence of apostolic authorship, though so far it seems that nobody has said that openly. Dr Towner takes a conservative stance on authorship, but as a liberal Episcopalian he is theologically more akin to Luke Timothy Johnson than to Professor Marshall. What can be said of all four commentators is that their Christian beliefs have given them an attitude of respect for the texts, which is something that should be expected from any responsible interpreter, whether he shares their faith or not. If they have sometimes inclined towards interpretations that fit their confessional positions, they have done so on the basis of evidence drawn from the texts themselves and have defended their views in a scholarly manner. Others may disagree with them, but they cannot be faulted on this and (so far at least) nobody has been able to refute their conclusions beyond reasonable doubt.

## The author

Who wrote the Pastoral Epistles? On the surface at least, the evidence could hardly be clearer. Unlike the Gospels, Hebrews and the three Epistles attributed to John, which are anonymous, or letters like James and Jude, which were written by men whom it is hard to identify, the Pastoral Epistles bear the name of the apostle Paul, and until the early nineteenth century, the claim that he was their author was all but universally accepted. Nobody in ancient times doubted it, with the possible exception of Marcion, who did not include them in his Pauline canon. Unfortunately, we do not know whether this was because he was unaware of their existence or because, as Tertullian thought, he explicitly rejected them.[8] If

---

[8] Tertullian, *Adversus Marcionem*, 5.21.

he did not know about them, we have no way of determining whether this was because they had not come to his attention or because they had not yet been written. Marcion's ignorance of them is sometimes used by those who insist that the letters are pseudonymous as evidence for their claim, but this is an argument from silence and so must be treated with caution, if not dismissed altogether.[9]

The Protestant Reformers accepted the unanimous witness of the church that the Pastoral Epistles were genuinely Pauline, and that consensus remained undisturbed until the early nineteenth century, when critical methods of a new kind were applied to them for the first time. Under the influence of the so-called Tübingen School in Germany, the Pastoral Epistles were increasingly regarded as witnesses to what they called 'early Catholicism', that is to say, a development in the late or post-apostolic church towards a more institutional (and less charismatic) form of teaching and organization that eventually produced the medieval papacy. Differences in vocabulary and style between the Pastorals and the other Pauline Epistles, which had thitherto gone unnoticed, were highlighted and used as 'evidence' that the Pastorals were not written by the apostle but were probably of late first- or early second-century origin.

That assessment of the Pastoral Epistles has always been contested and there are still many scholars who are unpersuaded by it, but in spite of their efforts, the prevailing scholarly consensus is to reject their Pauline origin and to assign them to a post-apostolic source. Opinions differ as to how close that source was to the apostle himself. Some argue that the epistles were written by one or more of his disciples, who may be presumed to have had a reasonably detailed knowledge of his thought, but others claim that they were later compositions, put together by an anonymous writer who had no personal connection with Paul. But either way, the basic thesis is the same. To those who accept that they are pseudepigraphal, the Pastoral Epistles do not represent the mind of the apostle himself but express opinions that, even if some of them originated with him, have been filtered (in varying degrees) through the lens of a more developed ecclesiology than anything he could have envisaged or espoused.

We shall give detailed consideration of the weight of this evidence in due course, but for the moment let it suffice to say that it is of three types:

---

[9] The Pastoral Epistles are also missing from an early papyrus collection of Paul's letters, known as P 46, which does not contain 2 Thessalonians or Philemon either. We know that the manuscript is missing seven of its pages, which may have contained the Pastorals, but we cannot say for sure, and some have argued that they are too long to have been written on only seven pages.

1. *Literary.* The claim is made that the vocabulary and style of the Pastoral Epistles is sufficiently different from those of the other Pauline letters as to preclude his authorship.
2. *Biographical.* The claim is made that the Pastoral Epistles do not fit into any discernible period in the apostle's career and cannot be harmonized with what is known from the Acts of the Apostles and the uncontested Pauline corpus.
3. *Historical.* Those who deny Pauline authorship assert that the structure of the church and a number of doctrinal positions found in the Pastoral Epistles belong more naturally to a later stage of the church's growth. The author may have been drawing on the apostle's authority (and perhaps on elements of his teaching), but if so, it was in order to give pastoral guidance to a second, third or even fourth generation of believers.

These objections are serious, and given the paucity of evidence for the first-century church, it is impossible to reach any firm conclusion one way or another. In the end, the question hangs on the weight of probability, which commentators will assess differently rather than on objectively demonstrable facts. There is nothing in the Pastoral Epistles that would necessarily exclude Pauline authorship, but those who defend it have to admit that there are significant differences between them and the rest of the Pauline corpus for which there is no obvious explanation. Paul may have used a different amanuensis (secretary) for the Pastorals, though if 2 Timothy was written much later than the others (which is possible) it is hard to account for the scribe's sudden reappearance, especially since he does not seem to have been used for anything else. It is more likely that, given the personal nature of the epistles, Paul wrote them himself, without external assistance, which would account both for their similarity to each other and for the absence of the stylistic flourishes that were typical of a professional amanuensis.

Doubts on this score will always remain, though it must be remembered that the burden of proof lies with those who reject the apostolic origin of the Pastorals and not with those who defend it. In spite of all the criticism, the fact remains that the Epistles themselves state that they were written by Paul, that for more than seventeen centuries this claim was never seriously questioned, and that there are still many scholars of different theological persuasions who are prepared to defend the ancient tradition. If it is to be abandoned there must be good reasons for doing so, and it remains to be seen whether the objections to it can withstand the scrutiny to which they must in all fairness be subjected. The position adopted in this commentary is not only that the traditional view is the correct one, and that the proposed alternatives are both less satisfactory and ultimately untenable on the basis of the evidence available to us, but also that they *must* be of Pauline origin if they are to have any authority as Holy Scripture in the life of the church. The importance of Paul as an individual and the uniqueness of his divine vocation play too important a part in the Epistles for any other solution to be possible. A pseudepigrapher, however well-meaning, could never have claimed the apostle's authority in the way that the Pastorals do, and if he had done so he would have been guilty, not just of impersonation but also – and perhaps more importantly – of usurping a divine commission that had not been given to him.

To sum up, the great weakness of the theory that the Pastoral Epistles were the work of one or more pseudepigraphers is the inability of those who hold that view to offer a credible alternative. Among the questions which they fail to answer satisfactorily are the following:

1. Who would have been sufficiently motivated to impersonate Paul, and why?
2. Why did the pseudepigrapher(s) produce three letters when one would have been enough?
3. If (as many claim) the recipients of the Epistles were not deceived, why was their knowledge so easily lost in the next generation? On what basis did they accept the authority of the true author(s), and was his or their identity known to them? If it was, why did he (or they) resort to pseudepigraphy?
4. Why did the pseudepigrapher(s) include personal details of the apostle, including requests from him, if they and the recipients both knew that he was dead? What would have been the point of that, other than to deceive?
5. Were Timothy and Titus still alive when the letters were written, and if so, what did they make of them?
6. Why did the pseudepigrapher(s) decide to address their letters to Paul's co-workers when the genuine Paul apparently never did that? Would it not have been more convincing if the letters had been sent to churches instead of to individuals?
7. Why did the early church accept the Epistles as genuinely Pauline without dissent, when it is known that it debated the authenticity of several other New Testament books on grounds similar to those which have persuaded many modern scholars to embrace the theory of pseudepigraphy?

Unless and until adequate answers can be given to these questions, the claim that the Pastoral Epistles are the work of the apostle Paul himself, and not of a pseudepigrapher, or even of a close disciple writing after his death, must be allowed to stand as a valid position based on proper scholarly criteria. To put it in judicial language, the Epistles are innocent until proved guilty!

Along with Jesus and Peter, Paul is one of the best-known figures in the New Testament. But unlike the other two, who are known to us mainly from what others said about them, Paul has bequeathed us a number of autobiographical details in his letters which we can set alongside the account of him given by Luke in the Acts of the Apostles. There are some well-known problems in trying to harmonize these two sources, but these are mainly matters of detail where (as always) the scarcity of our documentation makes it impossible to reconstruct a fully coherent picture from the evidence we have. Despite a few loose ends, the main outlines of Paul's life and career are clear and uncontested. He was a Jew born in the diaspora, almost certainly in Tarsus (which he claimed was his home city) and probably sometime in the first decade of the first Christian century, since he was a student in Jerusalem in the early 30s.[10] He was a Roman citizen by birth, most likely because his father or grandfather had been rewarded for his services as a tentmaker to the Roman army, though we cannot be certain of that.[11]

Paul came from the tribe of Benjamin and bore the name of Saul, the king of Israel who was also of that tribe. He saw himself as a strict Pharisee, though whether this was by his own choice or due to his family is not known. It would have been difficult for a diaspora Jew to have practised Pharisaism with any consistency, and perhaps Paul's commitment to it was a reaction against his more easy-going parents, though we have no way of knowing if that was the case.[12] What is certain is that he went to Jerusalem for his education and studied under the greatest rabbis of the time, including the famous Gamaliel.[13] We do not know where he was when Jesus was crucified, but the complete silence of the New Testament on this point suggests that he was not in Jerusalem at the time and did not witness the dramatic events surrounding it. He first appears there not long afterwards, when the deacon Stephen was stoned for his supposedly blasphemous confession of faith in Christ.[14]

After that, Paul worked as an enthusiastic volunteer for the temple establishment, specializing in the persecution of Jesus' followers. His

---

[10] Acts 8.1; 21.39.
[11] Acts 22.25-28.
[12] Perhaps there is a clue in 2 Tim. 1.3, where he talks about the faith of his 'ancestors' but does not mention his parents. Might that imply that they were less devout than their forbears had been?
[13] Acts 22.3.
[14] Acts 8.1.

reputation as a zealous enemy of the new movement seems to have been fairly widespread, but the church was still very small and word would have travelled fast, so that is perhaps not surprising. It was when he was on his way to round up Christians in Damascus that the risen Christ met him on the road and that he was converted.[15] He was then taken to Damascus, adopted by the local Christian community there and instructed in his new faith. His conversion soon became known and he was forced to flee the city by night, after which he either went to Jerusalem, in order to make the acquaintance of the disciples, or to the Arabian desert, where he spent three years in seclusion.[16] The exact chronology is uncertain at this point, but either way, Paul (who now used his Roman name in preference to the Jewish Saul) was soon being accepted as a Christian teacher. The apostles in Jerusalem apparently regarded him as their equal, though this was contested by some members of the church and Paul later had to defend his credentials against those who objected to him and his ministry.[17] One factor that may have played a part in Paul's acceptance by the disciples was his education. Compared to men like Peter, James and John, Paul was an intellectual who knew far more about rabbinic interpretations of the law than they did. For Paul, it was natural to go to the synagogue and preach, but we never hear of Peter or anyone else (except Jesus himself) doing that, perhaps because they would not have been qualified to do so.

After conferring with the apostles in Jerusalem, Paul seems to have gone back to Tarsus for a number of years, perhaps because of family obligations, but we know nothing about his activities during that time.[18] Around AD 48 he set out on his missionary career, which soon saw him taking the Christian message outside the Roman province of Syria. He became known as the 'apostle to the Gentiles' in contrast to Peter, who was designated as the 'apostle to the Jews'.[19] This apparent division of labour must be treated with some caution however, since (on the whole) Paul went to diaspora communities of Jews where he preached the gospel and drew off those who believed his message. They were a mixed bag, consisting mainly of Jews and of Gentiles who had attached themselves to the synagogues as 'God-fearers', though as time went on, there was an increasing number of Gentiles who joined the church without having had any previous contact with Judaism.

---

[15] Acts 9.1-19.
[16] Acts 9.23-31; Gal. 1.16-19. It seems that Luke simply omitted any reference to Paul's sojourn in Arabia.
[17] 2 Cor. 11.21-33.
[18] Gal. 1.21.
[19] Gal. 2.8.

In the course of his active ministry Paul went on at least three missionary journeys that took him over the southern parts of Asia Minor and what is now Greece. He was based for considerable periods of time at Ephesus and at Corinth, but he also made periodic visits to Antioch (his original base) and Jerusalem. This activity is sketched for us in the Acts of the Apostles, but Luke's account, though clear enough as it stands, is a partial and highly selective history of a ministry that stretched over more than a decade (from about AD 48 to about AD 62). The one date that we can pinpoint is AD 51, when we know that he was in Corinth, because he was hauled before Gallio, who was proconsul there in that year.[20] Luke records various times when Paul was beaten and imprisoned for his preaching, but he himself tells us that he led an even more adventurous life and went to places that Luke does not mention. He travelled widely around the Greek world and was shipwrecked several times, though we know nothing about this beyond his own passing remarks.

Around AD 60 Paul was involved in making a collection for the church at Jerusalem, which had fallen on hard times, and he decided to take the funds he had raised to the city himself, despite the many warnings and premonitions of danger that he received. He was duly arrested and put on trial when he reached the city, but he saved himself from almost certain death by appealing to the judgment of Caesar, which as a Roman citizen he was entitled to do. Even so, he languished in gaol in Palestine for a couple of years before the Roman authorities finally got around to sending him to the capital for trial. After an epic journey, recounted by Luke with great verve and colour, he reached Italy. The local Christians knew that he was coming and went to meet him at Puteoli (near Naples), from where they escorted him to Rome.[21]

Paul lived in Rome for two years, during which time he remained active, but after that no more is heard of him. He may have been released from captivity and resumed his journeys, or he may have been caught up in the persecution that followed the great fire of Rome in AD 64. There is general agreement that he was put to death in the reign of Nero (AD 54–68), so that if he was set free it cannot have been for long. He is thought to have been buried at Rome, though this is speculation. Whatever happened, we have no certain knowledge of him following his arrival there from Palestine, a circumstance that has some bearing on the composition of the Pastoral Epistles, as we shall see.

---

[20] Acts 18.12.
[21] Acts 28.11-16.

Paul occasionally travelled alone, but most of the time he was accompanied by a group of supporters and disciples, who included Timothy and Titus, among others. He does not seem to have had a fixed entourage who stayed with him all the time, but what governed their various comings and goings is unclear. We know that at one point he parted company with Barnabas because of a disagreement about what to do with Barnabas' somewhat reluctant nephew Mark[22] and that there were some who deserted Paul later on.[23] But there were a number of other companions, including Luke and Silas (Silvanus), who travelled with him at different times. Where these 'co-workers' went when they were not with Paul is unknown, but they seem to have kept in touch with him through a network of trading contacts in the Mediterranean world. These were the channels that Paul used to send his letters and they were very active. We know that Priscilla and Aquila, with whom Paul lived and worked during his time in Corinth, also resided periodically at Rome and Ephesus, and there is no indication that this was exceptional.[24] In a world where few people ventured very far from home, Paul's friends were highly mobile, and they could have turned up almost anywhere at any time. Except when Paul (or Luke) happen to tell us what their movements were, we know nothing about them, and we cannot assume that they were present with (or absent from) him at any given moment.

Paul's literary corpus consists of thirteen letters, or almost half the New Testament. When they were written is largely unknown. The Acts of the Apostles says nothing about Paul's letter-writing, and only internal evidence allows us to guess when they might have been composed. In most cases we know that they were written sometime after Paul's missionary visit to the city or province to which they are addressed. 1 Thessalonians seems to have been penned only a matter of months after his departure from that city, and Galatians may be similarly early, but the others are harder to pin down. Romans is the big exception to the rule – Paul had not visited the imperial capital and was writing to a church that he did not know personally, though he had connections with several of its members whom he knew from elsewhere.

Matters are complicated by the fact that six of the Pauline letters were formally written by both Paul and Timothy (2 Corinthians, Philippians, Colossians, 1 and 2 Thessalonians, and Philemon) and the two letters to Thessalonica were written by Silvanus (Silas) as well. To what extent did these colleagues of Paul's influence the style and content of his letters? It is

---

[22] Acts 15.37-39.
[23] 2 Tim. 4.10. See also 2 Tim. 1.15.
[24] Acts 18.1-3, 18, 26; Rom. 16.3.

of particular interest to note that Timothy was associated with sending all six, including four that are universally accepted as genuinely Pauline. This presumably means that he was with Paul longer than Silas was, though we cannot be sure about that. We also know that Paul normally used a secretary, or amanuensis, who is occasionally identified. For example, Romans was 'written' by a certain Tertius, who was with both Paul and Timothy at the time.[25] It is also possible that Ephesians and Colossians were 'written' by Tychicus, one of Paul's companions who is mentioned in Titus and 2 Timothy and who probably came from Ephesus, where Timothy spent time ministering to the church after Paul's departure from the city. The impression we get from 2 Tim. 4.12 is that Paul had recently sent Tychicus to Ephesus, presumably with his letter to that church and one to the Colossians, which Tychicus would explain to them when he got there. Added to all this is the possibility that 2 Corinthians (at least) is a composite letter, put together from more than one communication that the apostle sent to the church in that city. As with much else, we have no way of knowing this for sure, though Paul may have written other letters that have not survived, like one to the Laodiceans that is mentioned in Col. 4.16.

## Paul's apostleship

If Paul's letters have a 'typical' signature it is 'Paul, an apostle of Christ Jesus by the will of God', which occurs in that form in 2 Corinthians, Ephesians, Colossians and 2 Timothy and with only slight variations in 1 Corinthians, 1 Timothy and Galatians. There is, however, another 'typical' signature, in which Paul describes himself as a 'servant', which he uses in Romans, Philippians and Titus. In the first and last of these he adds that he is also an apostle, but that is left out of Philippians and is not found in either of the letters to the Thessalonians. No doubt Paul saw himself as both a servant and an apostle, though there is no discernible pattern that determined which of these two designations he would use to describe himself on any given occasion. What can be said is that in ten of his letters, including all three of the Pastorals, he calls himself an apostle, which suggests that he saw this as his primary authority for writing. The three exceptions (Philippians, 1 and 2 Thessalonians) were written in conjunction with co-workers who were fellow servants of Christ but not apostles, which may explain why that designation is omitted. What should be noted is that the salutations in the Pastoral Epistles

---

[25] Rom. 16.22.

do not exhibit a common pattern that would distinguish them as a group and set them apart from the rest of the Pauline corpus. All three are different and closer to one of Paul's other letters than to another Pastoral, a small but perhaps significant sign that they cannot be lumped together under a single heading and labelled 'pseudonymous'.

What is common to all three Pastoral Epistles is that Paul announced himself as an 'apostle of Christ Jesus' (or 'Jesus Christ' in Titus) and that this designation was of special importance, both to him and to the church at large. Paul was not among the original disciples of Jesus and therefore not one of the first apostles, a fact that made him suspect later on in his ministry. He was called by a special divine commission, which he regarded both as equal to the one the other apostles had received and sufficient to dispense him from any need to seek their approval for his ministry.[26] So confident was he of this that he was prepared to rebuke Peter to his face and to tell his congregations about it as evidence of his calling before God.[27]

It is not entirely clear what the word 'apostle' meant in the first generation of the church, though one criterion for claiming the title was being a witness of the risen Christ. Paul had seen Jesus on the road to Damascus, but the other apostles had met him, often more than once, during the forty days immediately following his resurrection. Whether the term could be applied to everyone who saw him in that time is not certain. Paul mentioned 'false apostles' who came from the Jerusalem church and preached that it was necessary for Gentile converts to become Jews if they wanted to be Christians, but who were they?[28] Was he being ironic in using the term 'apostles' or had they been among the five hundred or so people who had seen Jesus before his ascension into heaven?[29] There is also some ambiguity about Andronicus and Junia (Rom. 16.7) who were 'well known to (or among) the apostles'. Were they also in this group of five hundred?

What is certain is that neither they nor the 'false apostles' who troubled Paul's congregations were among the Twelve, and it is to them that the word 'apostle' has traditionally been attached. The Twelve were not merely witnesses of the resurrection but men charged by Jesus himself and given the authority to govern and direct the church. Though he was not one of the

---

[26] Gal. 1.11–2.10.
[27] Gal. 2.11-14.
[28] Gal. 2.4. False apostles also appear in 2 Cor. 11.1-15, where it seems that not only were they preaching a different gospel but also demanding payment for it. In neither case is there any mention of seeing the risen Christ; they seem to have been called 'apostles' because of their preaching and teaching activities, which appeared to imitate those of Paul.
[29] See 1 Cor. 15.6.

original Twelve, Paul's apostleship was equal to theirs in kind and it is in that light that his claims to apostleship must be understood.

Of the Twelve, the only one whom we know referred to himself as an apostle was Peter, who prefaced his letters in much the same way as Paul did.[30] John never referred to himself in that way and neither did James or Jude, who contented themselves with the designation 'servant' and whose precise identity is uncertain. The apostle Matthew's name is traditionally associated with the first Gospel, but there is no indication in the text that he wrote it and we cannot say whether he referred to himself as an 'apostle' or not. Paul, by contrast, used the title on a regular basis. So characteristic of him was this habit that in later centuries, the church spoke of Paul as *the apostle*, without further qualification, since it seemed obvious that the title applied to him in a way that it did not to anyone else.

Paul understood his apostleship as giving him the authority to guide and direct the church in the true meaning of the gospel. This included purely theological teaching, but it went much further than that. Paul believed that his status gave him the right to judge the affairs of local congregations, and he did not hesitate to intervene in disputes concerning the order and good government of the church. He even made it clear that if he appeared in person he would expect to take charge of the local congregation and put right whatever had gone amiss during his absence.[31] He did not try to interfere with the work of his fellow apostles and deplored it when church members sought to pit one of them against another, but just as Peter was not immune to his criticism, so we must assume that the others would not have been either had an occasion to rebuke them arisen.

Paul had a high view of the authority that had been entrusted to him and he exercised it without deference to anyone else. On occasion, he even made pronouncements that he attributed to his own theological analysis and not to a direct revelation from God.[32] Modern commentators have sometimes used this as a way of diminishing the authority of his teaching in those respects, but that is to misunderstand the nature of Paul's self-awareness. He knew that he had been commissioned by Christ and that gave him the right to take decisions concerning church life, whether he had a direct command from God or not. As one who had the mind of Christ, he did not need to wait for specific orders but could use his reasoning powers to determine what the church ought to do in particular circumstances. The passages in which he

---

[30] 1 Pet. 1.1; 2 Pet. 1.1.
[31] 2 Cor. 13.10.
[32] 1 Cor. 7.12, 40.

relied on his own assumptions therefore serve to illuminate the extent and validity of his apostolic commission, not to detract from it.

At a later time, the church relied on Paul's apostolic authority as its justification for including his writings in the canon of the New Testament. It taught that his letters were divinely inspired because of the commission he had received from God, and from a very early time it equated them with the Hebrew Scriptures (2 Pet. 3.15-16). The process of canon formation was a long one, and many of the details are obscure, but 'apostolicity' was an important criterion for inclusion. When there were doubts about this (as there were with Hebrews and Revelation, e.g.), there were disputes about whether the books concerned should be recognized as canonical. The apostolic origin of the Pastoral Epistles was never doubted by anyone in the early church, which creates a problem for those who insist on their pseudonymity. Who would have impersonated the apostle and how likely would it have been for him (or them) to have got away with it undetected? A brief survey of possible candidates will quickly show how serious this difficulty is.

One candidate for pseudonymous authorship is Luke, partly because there are linguistic similarities between the Pastorals and Luke-Acts and partly because there are reasons for thinking that Luke was with Paul at the end of his life.[33] But Luke did not claim Pauline authorship for his own work and neither did the anonymous writer to the Hebrews, who must also have come from his inner circle of colleagues. If they wrote without claiming the authority of the apostle's name and the church was prepared to recognize their works as 'apostolic', at least for canonical purposes, why would anyone close to Paul feel a need to claim to be the apostle himself? Would it not have been enough for him to say that the contents of the letters had been communicated to him by Paul and that he was articulating the master's thoughts? After all, that is what the disciples of Jesus did with his teaching, which they not only paraphrased but also translated for general consumption. Why would Paul's disciples not have done the same with him? Luke did it in Acts, and it is hard to see why he would not have adopted the same approach in the Pastorals (if he was their author).

The strategy of the pseudepigrapher, if there was one, is not altogether intelligible in this respect, and we may legitimately wonder why anyone would have adopted it. The idea that such a person was not intending to deceive anyone must surely be rejected out of hand. Paul's co-workers knew that he would not take kindly to being represented by someone else without

---

[33] 2 Tim. 4.11.

his permission, especially if the message they conveyed could not have come from him because it went beyond what he taught and practised. Such a person would have been anathema in Paul's eyes – and everybody knew it! In the circumstances, there is no word for this other than deliberate fraud, and had that been the case there would surely have been people who would have noticed, just as they noticed that Hebrews did not come from Paul's pen. Perhaps a pseudepigrapher might have got away with this once, but three times would seem to be chancing his luck, and it is hard to see why he would try to repeat the procedure. Could he not have said everything he wanted to say in a single letter? There may be literary and historical problems in assigning the Pastoral Epistles to Paul, but the difficulties raised by the pseudepigraphal alternative are greater still, not least when the significance of Paul's apostleship is taken into account.

If the authority of the Pastoral Epistles rests on the apostolic credentials of their author, as the canonical tradition of the church has always insisted, rejection of those credentials must inevitably entail the discrediting of the letters along with them. No doubt they would remain important sources for our understanding of the early church, just as *1 Clement*, the *Didache* and the *Shepherd* of Hermas are. Much of what they say might be taken as good advice even now, but they would not have the authority of Holy Scripture, they would not command the attention of preachers in the pulpit, and they would not be used to change lives in the power of the Holy Spirit. The importance of the authenticity of their claims to apostolic origin cannot be overstated, because it is on them that their right to a place in the New Testament canon depends.

## The recipients

What we have seen with respect to the author of the Pastorals is equally true of the recipients. On the surface, their identity is clear. Two of the epistles are addressed to Timothy, who was a well-known collaborator and companion of Paul's and was involved in the writing of six of the eleven Pauline letters that are not addressed to him. The other recipient was Titus, less prominent than Timothy and apparently not involved in writing any of Paul's letters but nevertheless a member of the Pauline circle and well known in the early church.[34] We have no way of knowing what prompted Paul to write to them

---

[34] He accompanied Paul on his famous trip to Jerusalem in defence of the Gentile mission. Gal. 2.1-3.

specifically but (apparently) not to any of his other colleagues, who had similar connections with him. We also do not know to what extent the letters were meant to be 'private'. Privacy in the ancient world was not what we would understand by that term today. Paul could not have written to anyone in an entirely confidential manner, and even when his letters were clearly intended for a single recipient in a particular situation (as Philemon was), it was public knowledge and it has been preserved as such for the edification of the whole church. Whether Paul foresaw that or not is beside the point; he must have known that the word would get out, and what was true of Philemon was even more true of Timothy and Titus. Paul's letters to them were not primarily concerned with their personal circumstances, and they include references to the wider church, including greetings to its members. It is possible, perhaps even probable, that in writing to Timothy and Titus Paul was shoring up their authority in the eyes of the congregations where they were ministering and whose decisions he expected them to accept. He was certainly not giving them confidential advice that he did not want others to know about!

## Timothy

Timothy was the son of a Gentile father and a Jewish mother, who had brought him up as a Christian. His name means 'honoured by God' or 'honouring God', which suggests that his mother thought of him as a potential 'God-fearer' from birth, that is to say, as a Gentile who did not become a Jew but who nevertheless worshipped the God of Israel. We can infer from the evidence that his maternal grandmother Lois came from a Jewish family and we know that she was the first one in that family to profess faith in Christ.[35] It seems that she and her husband had no objection to seeing their daughter Eunice marry a Gentile, which means that they must have been fairly liberal Jews. They were almost certainly living in the diaspora at that point, but we do not know how or when they got there. Nor do we know whether Timothy's father was a Roman citizen, though the silence of our sources suggests that probably he was not. What we do know is that Timothy had not been circumcised as a baby, though apparently his father did not object to having his son brought up to believe the Hebrew Scriptures.[36] Timothy seems to have professed faith in Christ during Paul's first missionary journey to Lystra, where his family was then residing. Paul took him under his wing and treated him as a son, which implies that Timothy may have been twenty

---

[35] 2 Tim. 1.5.
[36] In this respect, Timothy resembles Augustine of Hippo (354–430), who was also the son of a Christian mother and a pagan father.

or more years younger, though we cannot say for sure. Children reached maturity earlier in the ancient world (where life expectancy was much shorter than it is today), and Timothy may have been no more than fourteen or fifteen when Paul 'adopted' him. What we do know is that Paul insisted that Timothy should be circumcised, partly because his mother was Jewish and partly because Paul expected him to minister among Jews who would not have paid much attention to a Gentile.[37]

The significance of this should not be underestimated. Paul spent a good deal of his early ministry, particularly in Galatia (where Timothy came from), teaching his congregations that Gentile converts did not need to be circumcised in order to join the church. He also had to struggle against the so-called 'false apostles' who were visiting places like Lystra and saying the exact opposite. For Paul to have Timothy circumcised in those circumstances was to make an important theological statement that could easily have been used against him by his opponents. If keeping the Jewish law was so unnecessary, they might have argued, why did Paul bother having Timothy circumcised? Was he preaching one thing but practising another, even if only to be on the safe side?

We have no way of knowing whether the 'false apostles' knew about Timothy's circumcision, but the risk that they might find out was certainly there, and Paul would hardly have allowed such a hostage to fortune if there had not been good reasons for him to do so. The case of Timothy is a reminder that the apostle could be flexible in the way in which he applied his principles, even though he remained uncompromising on the principles themselves. In another well-known example, we know that in theological terms he saw nothing wrong with eating meat that had been sacrificed to idols, because idols did not exist and Christians were free to eat whatever God had provided for them in his creation. But we also know that he expected them to refrain from doing so if there was a danger that Jewish converts, whose upbringing under the law had made them more sensitive on this matter, would be scandalized and possibly turn away from Christ because of such behaviour by Gentiles who claimed to follow him.[38] Paul's policy was to adapt to the situation – to be a Jew to Jews and a Gentile to Gentiles, because the most important thing was to win people for Christ.[39] This was certainly his motive in having Timothy circumcised. It was not because he saw any need to keep the law for its own sake, though there may have been an element of Judaism in his thinking, since Timothy was half-Jewish by birth.

---

[37] Acts 16.1-3.
[38] 1 Cor. 8.1-13.
[39] 1 Cor. 9.20-22.

An uncircumcised man would not have gained acceptance as a Jew, and Paul wanted Timothy to be beyond any possible reproach in this respect. Rather than have him face endless explanations of why he had not been circumcised by his Jewish mother, Paul preferred to get the potential problem out of the way so that his mission among diaspora Jews could proceed without unnecessary complications. Circumcision, though painful for an adult, was a small price to pay for that.

Timothy accompanied Paul on his missionary journeys in Greece and was present when the apostle wrote his most important letters to the churches. In addition to being the co-author of six of these, he was also with Paul when the latter wrote Romans and 1 Corinthians.[40] In fact, the only letters the apostle wrote in which Timothy did not figure were Galatians and Ephesians. His absence from the former can be explained by the fact that he was himself a Galatian and Paul may not have wanted him to be too closely associated with criticism of his home church. The fact that he is not mentioned in Ephesians can also be explained by his close association with the church in that city. It is possible, and perhaps probable, that Paul wrote to Ephesus shortly after Timothy left his ministry there, and as with Galatia, he may not have wanted Timothy to appear to be too implicated in the internal affairs of the church. Timothy also appears in Heb. 13.23, with the notice that he has just been released from prison and was probably on his way to wherever the author of the book was at the time. Where, when and why he had been imprisoned we cannot say, but it shows that he was sufficiently faithful a disciple of Paul's as to suffer a punishment similar to his.

Timothy's imprisonment is a reminder to us that although he was usually with Paul, he also spent considerable periods of time elsewhere, apparently because one or other of the two men was on a mission. For example, Silas and Timothy stayed in Beroea when Paul left for Athens, where they joined him some months later.[41] Before long, though, Paul sent Timothy back to Thessalonica in order to check on the church there, and some years later it was Timothy who delivered the first of Paul's letters to the Corinthians. The impression we get is that he was still quite young, perhaps a bit bashful and possibly subject to periodic illnesses. Paul had to exhort him not to be afraid of his youth and urged him to drink a little wine for his stomach, which suggests that he was not as robust as young people often are. At some point Paul left Timothy in Ephesus while he went to Macedonia, and it was then that the first of his letters to him was written. This may have been sometime

---

[40] Rom. 16.21; 1 Cor. 16.10-11.
[41] Acts 17.14-15.

in the late 50s, or perhaps after his release from prison in Rome, assuming that he was indeed set free and allowed to travel. Either date is possible, though perhaps the former is more likely, given our lack of knowledge about what happened to Paul after his two-year imprisonment in Rome.

The second letter to Timothy was written later, when Paul was in prison in Rome, though we cannot say whether that was for the first or the second time. It seems that Timothy had left Ephesus and gone somewhere else in Asia Minor, though precisely where is unknown. Legend says that he became the first bishop of Ephesus and that he died there, but there is no evidence to support this story and nothing more is heard of Timothy after this.

## Titus

Titus was another of Paul's trusted companions, but in many ways he stands in contrast to Timothy. First of all he was a Gentile, probably from Antioch. He shared the name of a Roman emperor (AD 79–81), the son of Vespasian (AD 70–79), but there is unlikely to have been any connection between them. Titus accompanied Paul on his famous visit to Jerusalem following his Galatian mission, when the issue of Gentile converts had to be sorted out. Paul had had Timothy circumcised but he refused to do this with Titus, perhaps because as a Gentile with no claim to be even partly Jewish, his circumcision would have done nothing but play into the hands of the 'false apostles'. It is instructive to see how Paul could deal quite differently with two men who in other respects appeared to be similar. Later on, Paul sent Titus to sort out the affairs of the Corinthian church after Timothy's mission had apparently failed. It may have been during this period, when Paul was based in Ephesus, that he paid a visit to Crete and established churches there. All we know is that somewhat later he sent Titus to consolidate the mission on Crete, and the contents of his letter suggest that it was written around the same time as the first epistle to Timothy. When Paul wrote to Timothy again, Titus had gone to Dalmatia, which is the last we hear of him.[42] According to legend, Titus was the first bishop of Crete, but as with Timothy at Ephesus, there is no evidence for that and he disappears from the historical record at this point.

One of the more intriguing aspects of the careers of both Timothy and Titus is that we know so little about them after the end of Paul's correspondence. It is fairly easy to believe that Titus might have vanished into some provincial backwater, but if Timothy was in or around Ephesus it is hard to account for

---

[42] 2 Tim. 4.10.

the complete silence of our sources regarding his subsequent career. Was he known to John, the author of the book of Revelation? It is hard to believe that he was not, but we have no evidence that would prove this and John's letter to the church at Ephesus says nothing that might help us either way. Of course, John did not mention Paul either, which is surprising, given that he must have been well known to the Ephesian church. All we learn from this is that we know very little, even about a church as prominent as that of Ephesus, and that to speculate beyond the evidence is liable to raise more questions than it answers.

It is perhaps to be expected that these gaps in the record have encouraged a number of scholars to assume that the Pastoral Epistles are essentially fictitious. As they see it, Timothy and Titus may have existed as historical individuals but they were not the recipients of the letters that were formally addressed to them. In reply, it must be asked whether a pseudepigrapher could have got away with this if either or both of them were still alive when the letters were written. It would have been impossible to keep the letters from them, and even after their deaths there would be plenty of people around who would have known whether they had received them or not. If the letters had been produced but were clearly fakes they would have gained no credibility – the ancients were not nearly as gullible in this respect as some modern commentators seem to think they were. Then again, the number of letters militates against their inauthenticity, since what might have been possible with a single epistle was unlikely to have been the case with three, especially when two of them were addressed to the same person. There is also the problem that although 1 Timothy and Titus are close enough in content to have come from the same period in time, 2 Timothy does not fit this pattern. Would a pseudepigrapher have written two broadly similar letters to different men and then penned a third to one of them but dated it some years later? No doubt he could have done that, but it is harder to believe that he went to all that trouble than it is to accept that the letters are authentically Pauline and reflect the apostle's changing circumstances.

Theories of pseudepigraphy have serious problems, but it is only fair to point out that defenders of the Epistles' authenticity also have certain enigmas to deal with. One particular problem for them is the Epistles' relation to the churches of Ephesus and Crete. Of the two, Ephesus is far better known, with at least four independent sources of information available to us in the New Testament alone. We know of Paul's mission to the city from Luke's account in Acts, and we have a brief analysis of its spiritual state in Rev. 2.1-7. There is no obvious connection between these two accounts, a circumstance that has been explained in different ways. Some believe that there were two different churches in Ephesus – a Pauline one and a Johannine one – that did not interact with each other. That is unlikely though, if only because the non-Christians who opposed the preaching of the gospel would not have differentiated between them. Even if there had been two distinct churches, they would have been thrown together by their enemies, who in Ephesus were exceptionally active. Furthermore, it would be almost impossible to explain why no memory of that early time has survived. Usually when different congregations exist they either stay apart or else splinter further; if they merge, as they sometimes do, that fact tends to be celebrated. In the case of Ephesus there is no sign of either development, so we ought to conclude that there was only ever one church in the city, though it may have met in different locations as a collection of house churches. The apparently different feel between Acts and Revelation is most likely due to the fact that they were written at different times, Revelation being the later of the two accounts, and with quite different ends in view. We know from Paul's reaction to developments in Galatia that a church could quickly lose its first love, as the Ephesians had apparently done, though in their case there remained enough of the original fervour to mitigate some of John's criticism.

Where Paul's letter to the Ephesians and 1 Timothy fit into this scenario is impossible to say. Most likely 1 Timothy was written before Ephesians, since the latter says nothing about Timothy being there either then or earlier, but that is pure guesswork. Once again, there is little apparent connection between either of these letters and the other accounts relating to the Ephesian church, and the evidence we have is too limited for us to be able to link them together in any convincing way. In particular, none of the Pauline sources (including Acts) says anything about the Nicolaitans, whom the Ephesians are commended for having rejected in Revelation. Who were they? Do they have any connection with the obscure heresies mentioned in 1 Timothy? We have no idea! But Ephesus was a large city with a mobile trader population, and it is not unlikely that false teachers would have visited it. The book of Revelation does not say that they had infiltrated the Ephesian church; on the contrary, they had been rebuffed by it and may have had no impact at all on its internal affairs.[43] If that was the case, neither Paul nor Timothy need have bothered with them and their silence would reflect that they were not a major concern for either man.

The situation in Crete presents a different set of problems, though they are simpler than those posed by Ephesus, if only because of lack of any evidence that would complicate the picture. Crete was not exactly a backwater in Paul's

---

[43] Rev. 2.6. This was in contrast to the church at Pergamum, where some had succumbed to their teachings. See Rev. 2.15.

time, but it did not figure very prominently in Graeco-Roman life either. The ancient Minoan civilization that had flourished there in the distant past had long since disappeared and the island had been politically obscure ever since. Paul stopped there briefly on his way to Rome, but there is no sign that he established any churches at that time, and the circumstances of his visit probably made that impossible in any case. Whether he had been there earlier we cannot say, just as we do not know if he revisited the island after his release from prison in Rome. According to his epistle, he had established churches on Crete and left Titus there to complete the work. That makes it unlikely that he planted congregations in the short time between his two imprisonments, so we probably ought to assume that he had conducted a mission to the island some years earlier. When that might have been we cannot say, but it could have occurred when he was based at Corinth or at Ephesus. He could have gone to Crete for a few weeks or months during one of those extended sojourns, but we have no idea whether he did so or what the result was. On the other hand, it seems most unlikely that a pseudepigrapher would have made the story up. Why Titus, and why Crete? If there had been no churches in Crete that claimed a Pauline foundation, that would have been obvious and the epistle would surely have been dismissed out of hand. If an author had wanted to portray Titus as the one who followed up Paul's missionary endeavours in a remote location, Dalmatia would have been a more plausible choice, since we know that Paul had been to Illyricum and 2 Timothy says that Titus had gone there as well.[44] The only explanation (other than accepting the letter's authenticity) is that Crete was so obscure that nobody would bother to check the details, but that in itself is suspicious. The island was not that far out of the way, and somebody would have known the truth if it was not what the Epistle made it out to be. But nobody ever seems to have questioned the story, so the presumption must be that it is substantially accurate, even if there is now no way that we can verify the details.

The unlikely choice of Titus as a recipient of one of the Pastoral Epistles is further evidence for the authenticity of the letter addressed to him. A pseudepigrapher would almost certainly have chosen someone more prominent, like Silvanus or Apollos, and placed them in a relatively obscure but not improbable location – Laodicea perhaps, or another city of Asia Minor where Paul could easily have been at some point. Indeed, we can go further and suggest that if the Pastoral Epistles were fictitious, they would have taken a different form entirely. Paul normally wrote to churches, not to individuals, and certainly not to his helpers and associates. If a pseudepigrapher had

---

[44] Rom. 15.19; 2 Tim. 4.10. Illyricum and Dalmatia are essentially the same place.

wanted to offer Pauline advice to a particular church, would he not have composed an epistle directed to a congregation and written in a style that everyone would recognize as Paul's? The choice, not only of a relatively obscure location like Crete, but of particular people (instead of churches) as recipients of the letters, represents a departure from the Pauline norm which, if it were spurious, would surely have aroused suspicion. In other words, the very oddity of the Pastoral Epistles is an argument in favour of their genuineness to which too little attention is paid. Equally important for determining their authenticity is the sort of personal detail that the Pastorals include. 1 Timothy is relatively free of circumstantial references and could conceivably have been written by someone who knew little about the apostle's everyday affairs. But why would someone tell Timothy to bring the cloak that Paul had left behind at Troas, as we read in 2 Tim. 4.13, or ask Titus to come to Nicopolis for the winter (Tit. 3.12) if he knew that Paul was already dead? Such embellishments add nothing to the message of the Epistles and would be pointless if they were not true. A pseudepigrapher would have had no need to include them, and if the recipients knew that Paul had passed away, details of this kind would surely have disturbed them or at least made them highly suspicious of the motives of whomever was passing himself off as Paul. The very casualness and banality of such remarks testifies to their authenticity and supports the belief, already justifiable on other grounds, that the Pastoral Epistles were indeed the work of Paul himself.

Modern commentators tend to focus less on Timothy and Titus (whom many of them regard as fictitious recipients) and concentrate instead on the churches to which the letters were presumably sent, but this was not necessarily the approach taken in earlier times. Theodore of Mopsuestia, for example, writing about 400, saw 1 Timothy as a manual for bishops:

> Paul teaches Timothy what he ought to do now that he has entered upon the administration of the churches. For this reason he gives him complete instructions ... he has plainly produced in the letter a complete body of teaching ... Therefore, in my judgment it would be fitting for all bishops to study this letter thoroughly as carefully as possible. For diligently instructed in this way, they would be able to know how either to rule or to administer the churches of the Lord God as is right, by devoting themselves to Paul's laws. For what Paul wrote to Timothy when he left him at Ephesus and put him in charge of all the churches in Asia are rules no one may doubt can be applied to every bishop entrusted with the governance of the churches of God.[45]

---

[45] Theodore of Mopsuestia (2010), pp. 525, 527.

Theodore's understanding of Timothy's appointment is clearly anachronistic, but it is telling that he believed that Paul's instructions were as valid for bishops in his day as they were for their first recipient and that he regarded the epistle as a handbook of ecclesiastical administration generally. Whatever we think of the role played by Timothy and Titus in their respective churches, it is clear that the Pastoral Epistles were addressed to their congregations at least as much as to them personally, and modern research has concentrated heavily on that aspect of the interpretive problem, not least because it deflects the pseudonymity question – at least to some extent. It is assumed that the two letters to Timothy deal with a situation that had arisen in the Ephesian church and that the one sent to Titus found similar problems in Crete. The general consensus of recent commentators is that both churches, but especially the one at Ephesus, were suffering from the activities of people in them who were openly opposed to Paul's teaching. They therefore interpret almost everything in the Epistles as a reflection of this opposition and assume that Paul (or the pseudepigrapher) was writing to counteract it. Defining what exactly the opposition was has thus become a major topic of debate in modern research which has delved more thoroughly into what might loosely be called 'background' material than has ever been the case in the past. As a result, the problems occurring at Ephesus (and to a lesser extent in Crete) are thought to reflect wider trends in Roman society, like the appearance of the so-called 'new woman'. She is supposed to have been a sexually liberated person who was disrespectful, and perhaps even contemptuous, of traditional social norms, and the church is thought to have been suffering from her influence on them.

Alongside that, there were any number of other forces at work too. There were Judaizers who were interpreting the law of Moses in a narrow and often trivial way. There were proto-Gnostics, who were promoting intellectual fantasies as the way to get closer to God. The cult of the emperor was also somewhere in the mix, not to mention the continuing influence of pagan religion in all its many forms. Most scholars freely admit that almost all the texts to which they appeal are vague and general in nature – they might be referring to deviations based on factors like these, but the language used is too vague for us to be able to pin anything down with precision. We are left to assume that the threats to the Pauline gospel were either genuinely embryonic or else that they were portrayed that way by a later generation that had to confront them more directly.

Is this picture true? There is no doubt that Paul faced opponents in the churches to which he was writing. He named several of them specifically and told us something about the nature of the problem. The complete list is as follows:

| | | |
|---|---|---|
| Hymenaeus | 1 Tim. 1.20 | rejection of the faith |
| Hymenaeus | 2 Tim. 2.17 | denial of future resurrection |
| Alexander | 1 Tim. 1.20 | rejection of the faith |
| Alexander the coppersmith | 2 Tim. 4.14 | harm done to Paul |
| Phygelus | 2 Tim. 1.15 | desertion of Paul |
| Hermogenes | 2 Tim. 1.15 | desertion of Paul |
| Philetus | 2 Tim. 2.17 | denial of future resurrection |
| Demas | 2 Tim. 4.9 | desertion of Paul |

It is usually assumed that Hymenaeus is one person who appears twice, and the same may be true of Alexander, though the name is too common for that to be taken as read. Desertion of Paul figures high on the list, but whether that constitutes 'opposition' to his teaching is hard to say, since we do not know why they turned away.[46] They are almost all thought to have been members of the church who grew disaffected for some reason, though Alexander the coppersmith may have been an exception, and so of course was Demas.

Were these people ringleaders of a group, or were they isolated individuals that had to be dealt with before they could establish an organized opposition? And what exactly did they believe? Was there a coherent system of thought that can reasonably be called the 'Ephesian heresy' which may have extended its reach to Crete, or were there just isolated tendencies that had no inner coherence but had appeared more or less independently of one another?[47] Is it safe to assume that everything the apostle warned about was actually present in the church he was addressing? Could he have been pointing to trends that he had observed elsewhere and that he could see coming, even though they had not yet arrived?

Dillon Thornton has examined all these questions and concluded that the opponents can be characterized as follows:

1. They were disaffected members of the Pauline community and not outsiders.
2. They rejected the apostolic gospel.

---

[46] Demas is something of an exception but as he had been one of Paul's companions and was not a member of the Ephesian church, he should probably not be counted in this list.
[47] See Mounce (2000), pp. lxix–lxxxi, who argues for a full-blown heretical movement and interprets the Epistles as a refutation of it. More recently Thornton (2016), pp. 237–79, has fleshed this out further and attempted to reconstruct a picture of what the opponents were like.

3. They had a false eschatology because they were unable to appreciate the subtlety of Paul's approach to this question.
4. They had a special *gnōsis* (kowledge) that trumped the apostle's teaching.
5. They charged for their ministry and won ready hearers, especially among the women of Ephesus.

With regard to the third of these, which in many ways was the most central problem of all, Thornton says,

> For them [the opponents] *anastasis* ['resurrection'] was a purely spiritual event, one that had been fully realized in the present. This notion of resurrection probably led to a confusion of the ages: believing they had been raised, the opponents thought they were living only in the age to come. This eschatological formulation probably stemmed from the Pauline doctrine of the present new life in Christ; the opponents thought the only resurrection was the mystical resurrection that took place at conversion/baptism. Irrespective of what the opponents were saying about Christ's resurrection, immaterialising the believer's resurrection (which was tantamount to denying the future, bodily resurrection) was in Paul's assessment an attack on the apostolic gospel.[48]

Thornton has based himself on the one doctrinal point that is clearly stated in the Pastoral Epistles themselves and interpreted it in a way that seems to do justice to the known facts concerning it. What remains unknown, however, is how far that particular view penetrated the thought of the opponents in general or how central it was to their theological programme, if they had one. Thornton has made out a good case for what is known about at least two of the opponents, but many question marks remain about the others and we cannot build a complete picture of them or their teaching out of the evidence provided for us in the Pastoral Epistles. Ignorance remains, and there seems to be no way that it will ever be overcome.

## Paul's key theological principle: The church is God's household

Paul's key theological principle was that the church is the household of God, a community of believers that stands out in the world as a demonstration of the divine presence in it. It is tempting to call this his 'ecclesiology', but

---

[48] Thornton (2016), pp. 264–5.

that term is anachronistic and liable to mislead us. Indeed, one of the biggest problems in the history of the interpretation of the Pastoral Epistles has been the temptation to read them through the lens of later church structures. Until quite recently many scholars were attached to the idea that the Epistles represent what Ferdinand Christian Baur and the Tübingen school called 'early Catholicism' – the presence in the churches of elements like a monarchical episcopacy that would later mature into the medieval Catholic system. As Protestants, they naturally rejected that system and demoted the Pastorals to a secondary, post-apostolic phase of the church's development in which the free spirit of the first generation hardened into institutionalism. Roman Catholics, of course, rejected this interpretation and saw 'early Catholicism' as evidence that their own ecclesiology could be traced back to apostolic times.

Linked to the Protestant criticism was the view that Paul believed that justification by grace through faith and not by works was the key principle on which, in Martin Luther's words, the church stands or falls. The almost complete absence of that doctrine from the Pastorals was therefore taken as further evidence that they could not be genuinely Pauline. But as more recent research has shown, there is no one idea that can be considered to be the centre of Paul's theology. His gospel was a coherent message grounded in the life, death and resurrection of Jesus Christ, and specific themes like justification or the church as God's household must be understood in relation to that. His epistles were not essays in systematic theology but responses to particular situations that had arisen in the course of his ministry, and he concentrated on them in the light of his overall teaching. In the case of the Pastoral Epistles his focus was on the church – what it was, what it ought to be doing and where it fitted in the wider plan of the salvation that God had revealed in Christ. To say that the doctrine of the church is the underlying theological principle of the Pastoral Epistles is not to minimize or deny the importance of the rest of Paul's teaching. Rather, it is to stress that it was the aspect of that teaching that most needed developing in Paul's letters to Timothy and Titus and that everything else must be understood in relation to it.

## Jews and Greeks in a 'new creation'

In their acceptance of Christ as Lord and Saviour, Jews and Gentiles were brought together in a new body of believers which the New Testament calls the 'church' (*ekklēsia*).[49] The Greek word *ekklēsia* was known from ancient

[49] The English word, which is common to the other Germanic and to some of the Slavic languages, derives from the Greek *kyriakē*, meaning 'dominical'. It is a shortened form of the phrase *kyriakē ekklēsia*, which may be translated as 'the Lord's assembly'.

Athens, where it was used to mean the assembly of the citizenry. Whether (or to what extent) that influenced the Christian use of the term is unknown, but probably not much. Greek words are capable of embracing different meanings according to context, and in the sense of 'convocation' or 'gathering' *ekklēsia* could be used to describe the church without reference to Athenian custom. More relevant to the early Christians was the meaning of *ekklēsia* in the LXX, where it was used to translate the Hebrew *qahal*, a term used to describe the congregation of the people of Israel when they gathered to hear the law being read.[50] But the *qahal* was quite different from the Athenian *ekklēsia* in that it was not a deliberative assembly of the citizenry, and neither word conveyed the New Testament concept of a particular group of people with its own distinct identity and transnational organization.

We can therefore say that although the word *ekklēsia* was used in pre-Christian times, the church of Christ was a phenomenon unprecedented in ancient Israel and foreign to the Greek (Gentile) world. This newness was a fundamental theme of the New Testament proclamation and it stood in sharp contrast to anything found in either Jewish or Greek culture. For all their differences, Jews and Greeks thought alike when it came to defining what we would now call 'society'. In both cases, their national identity was defined by a mixture of blood and culture. Jews believed that they were physically descended from Abraham and they accepted the law of Moses as their national 'constitution', but although they had once spoken Hebrew, they placed less emphasis on the need to speak a common language. By the time Christianity came on the scene, Hebrew was dying out and being replaced by Aramaic or Greek, into which their sacred Scriptures had already been translated. The Greeks were less specific about their human ancestry, but they were bound together by a shared culture and by a language that in the first century was rapidly losing its dialects and becoming 'common' (*koinē*) to almost all who spoke it.

In spite of these differences, however, both Jews and Greeks regarded themselves as superior to other peoples and did what they could to protect their exclusiveness, particularly in the face of cultural pressures that threatened to dilute it. Judaism appealed to a number of Greeks, who appreciated its monotheism and high moral standards, but the barriers to becoming a Jew (circumcision and the adoption of Jewish food laws, e.g.) were too high for many of them and so they remained on the fringes of the synagogue as 'God-fearers'. Jews were not prepared to compromise on this, which is one reason why so many of them objected to early Christian

---

[50] See, for example, Deut. 4.10; 9.10; 18.16; 31.30; Judg. 20.2; 1 Sam. 17.47; 1 Kgs 8.14.

practice. To allow the 'God-fearers' to join the assembly of God's people on equal terms with Jews was to dilute the faith and incur the risk that Jews might disappear entirely, as indeed Jewish Christians did in the second generation. Similarly, Greek culture attracted a number of Jews, but their religion kept them from integrating into the Hellenistic cultural sphere in the way that the Romans did. In truth, few Jews became pagans, just as few Greeks embraced Judaism. The two groups remained quite distinct from one another in spite of widespread contact and frequent interaction.

Belonging to the church was a new departure for those who joined it, whether they were Jews or Greeks, because it transcended these traditional barriers and made them redundant. The church was a society of divine origin, constituted not by physical descent from a common ancestor nor by a shared language and culture, but by a spiritual experience described as 'regeneration' – being born again. The radical nature of this was challenged by some Jewish Christians, who did not want to accept Gentiles into the church unless they became Jews first. Paul never denied the importance of the church's Jewish inheritance, but he rejected the idea that the law of Moses could exercise a controlling influence over its membership. As far as the Gentile world was concerned, the church adopted Greek as its common language but rejected the pagan culture associated with it. As Paul put it, in the church there was neither Jew nor Greek, because they had become one in Christ Jesus.[51] Paul did say that he had become a Jew to the Jews and a Greek to the Greeks, but this was an evangelistic strategy, not a theological principle based on what we would now call 'diversity'.[52] His purpose was the same in every case – to win men and women for Christ, not to legitimize cultural differences in the life of the church.

Belief in the divinity of Jesus Christ as the Son of God the Father forced Christians to expound their doctrine of God in a way that had never been necessary for Jews. This necessity was what gave rise to the discipline of 'theology', which had no ready equivalent in the Jewish world. The rabbis studied the law and discussed how it could be applied in cases that the Old Testament did not explicitly cover, but they did not examine the being and nature of God himself. Theology was a Greek concept. For Plato, who was the first Greek writer known to have used the word *theologia*, it meant what we would call 'mythology', the lore of the gods. But for Christians, theology could only be the knowledge of the one true God, which was

---

[51] Gal. 3.28.
[52] 1 Cor. 9.20-22.

grounded in their experience of him and expressed in his revealed Word. As a discipline, theology was slow to develop among Christians and did not come to maturity until the Middle Ages, but the ingredients that later went to make it up were already present in the New Testament. Christian theology was rooted in the beliefs of Old Testament Judaism and was later expressed in terms derived from Greek philosophy and Roman law, but it transcended all of them. Like Christians themselves, it was a 'new creation' in Christ, whose person and work were fundamental to it from the very beginning.

What the Pastoral Epistles teach us is that the church is the earthly embodiment of God's presence in the world, 'the household of God … the church of the living God, a pillar and buttress of the truth'.[53] The early Christians understood that confessing Christ was a definite commitment to him and to his work for the salvation of the human race. That commitment was the same, regardless of age, sex or national identity. There was not one Christ for Jews and another for Greeks, just as there was not one salvation for men and another for women. Paul and his companions knew about cultural differences, but they were not particularly impressed by them and saw no need to alter their message in order to accommodate them. The church was united, not because of a shared language or tribal ancestry, but because its members had a common experience of God, and it was from that that they drew their theology. It was composed of self-confessed sinners, whose lives had been transformed by the Christ who had died to pay the price of their sins and had risen again to make them a new creation in him.

Jews had an initial advantage in the church because they had received the promises given to the patriarchs of Israel, which Jesus had come to fulfill. They therefore understood the context in which his ministry had taken place, and those who accepted his message could work out its consequences for themselves. Where they had difficulty was that although the principles of the Old Testament law were strengthened by the gospel of Christ, the practices that had accompanied that law were made largely redundant once its purposes had been accomplished. For many pious Jews, letting go of what they had learned from childhood was very painful, and in some cases too difficult, which is why Paul took a pragmatic approach to the continued observance of Jewish practices among his own people. But at the same time, he was often harder on his fellow Jews than he was on Gentiles, precisely because he thought that the Jews should have known

---

[53] 1 Tim. 3.15.

better than to cling to the shadow of things to come once those things had arrived.[54]

For the Greeks, joining the church meant entering a different intellectual world. They could go on speaking their mother tongue but words and concepts they habitually used were set in a new and unfamiliar context. Where Jews were plagued by legalism, Gentiles were threatened by heresies caused by misunderstanding the theological meaning of words like 'flesh', 'world', 'sin', 'faith', 'hope' and 'love'. All these and many more came to mean something more precise than what they had meant before, and the scope for error was great. Paul had to get Gentiles to think with a new mind, a task that was essential if the gospel was to take root among them.[55]

## An ordered society

The church was the place where converted Jews and Greeks came together as equal members of the family of God. It was a society in which the old barriers had been taken away and a new set of relationships had been created. Those relationships were defined by a common relationship to God in Christ, which made everyone equal and fundamentally the same. Church members were different from one another, not because of their ethnic, economic or social background but because they had individual spiritual gifts that were meant to complement each other and build up their common life. Had Christians all been identical there would have been no such complementarity and perhaps no need for cooperation either; it was because the Holy Spirit had apportioned different gifts to individual people that they had to pool their resources for the greater good of the whole.

Both Jews and Gentiles lived in an orderly society that was governed by law and by a hierarchy of authority. This pattern carried over to the new creation that was the church, though the principles on which the church's government was based were different from those which obtained in the secular sphere. The order that prevailed in the church was not based on human achievement or on a sense that some people were more important than others but was anchored in the gifts of the Holy Spirit, which God apportioned to believers according to his sovereign will. The church's 'constitution' was written in the Scriptures, and interpreted by the Spirit's presence in the heart of believers. Its structure was ordained by God the Father, who was the ultimate author

---

[54] This is the argument of Romans 2–4.
[55] 1 Cor. 2.14-16; Gal. 3.1-6; Eph. 4.1-6; Col. 2.8-15.

of the divine plan of salvation. The administration of that plan was delegated to the Lord Jesus Christ, the Father's only Son and the supreme head of the church.[56] Christ appointed delegates to establish and proclaim his kingdom – these were the apostles, of whom Paul was one. The apostles in turn gathered around them helpers and co-workers, whose duty it was to apply their teaching and maintain it in its fullness and purity.

These helpers did not have the authority given to the apostles and so could not add to the deposit of faith that had been entrusted to them, but they could appoint local leaders who would share the apostolic duties of teaching and oversight. This is where the Pastoral Epistles come into the picture. In them, the apostle Paul was instructing his co-workers Timothy and Titus how to establish an ongoing ministry in the church. That pattern would eventually become the norm, though not without many changes and developments along the way. The Father's purpose for the church and Christ's lordship over it are now known and understood according to the teaching of the apostle Paul, which has been preserved for us thanks to the mandate he gave to men like Timothy and Titus. They were not bishops of churches with an apostolic commission that has been handed down through the ages, though many have claimed that. Rather, they were apostolic delegates charged by Paul with forging a permanent system of church government, but one in which their own position, like that of the apostle whom they served, would not be passed on to any successors.

There were many other people in the church who were set apart by circumstances that demanded particular consideration – the poor, the widows, the sick and so on. These people were individuals, of course, but they also belonged to subgroups within the church that had a distinct collective identity. A well-ordered community had to provide for each of them in an appropriate way, and working out how to do that was one of Paul's major reasons for writing to Timothy and Titus. His purpose was to sketch out the ways in which Christians should live together, respecting their human identities but fitting them into the overall pattern of the church as the one body of Christ. What we classify as 'social welfare' was part of the church's mission and therefore part of its theology. Those who rejected it were guilty of blasphemy against God because they were failing in their duty to their fellow human beings, who were created in his image. There was no real distinction in Paul's mind between theory and practice. One led inexorably to the other, and there was no place in the church for those who failed to translate their beliefs into action.

---

[56] 1 Cor. 15.27-28.

Behind the organization of the church which Paul entrusted to Timothy and Titus there lay a coherent understanding of its character and mission. To become a Christian was to pass from the thinking of this world to that of the world to come; it was to have the mind of Christ.[57] That mind was a coherent whole, even if it was not always fully expressed. Circumstances might oblige Paul to focus on one aspect of it – justification by faith alone, for instance, or the resurrection of Christ – but the whole was always there, and it was fundamental to the church's intellectual outlook. The apostles regarded their teaching as a body of belief that they could draw on as and when it was necessary. That belief had to be accepted without question – it was what all Christians professed, even if some of its details had never been explicitly stated. True believers were expected to recognize this underlying pattern of truth and acknowledge that Paul's teachings were an expression of it – the tip, if you like, of a vast but largely submerged theological iceberg.

Neither doctrine nor good works could save – both were dependent on the inner working of the Holy Spirit, who made sense of the one and produced the motivation for the other.[58] It is often claimed that the Pastoral Epistles say less about the Spirit than Paul's other writings do, but this apparent lack of emphasis must be seen in context. Much of what Paul says about the Holy Spirit elsewhere is due to the misunderstandings about him and his work that had arisen in the church.[59] Timothy and Titus did not have to be corrected on that point; rather they had to be encouraged to apply their understanding to practical situations as they arose. Paul's advice to them depended on the Spirit for its application, because without his divine working, nothing would have been achieved. Even when the Holy Spirit is not specifically mentioned, his presence and activity must be factored in if we are to understand what Paul was saying to his fellow workers.

It is against this backdrop that the arguments developed in the Pastoral Epistles have to be interpreted. Most of Paul's letters were written because some aspect of the gospel proclamation had not been properly communicated or understood by a particular congregation. The Pastoral Epistles are somewhat different, because in them Paul takes a more general approach, giving counsel to Timothy and Titus that went beyond their immediate circumstances and was intended to serve as a preparation for their ministry in general. This is not to say that the Epistles do not address the particular situations in which they were written, but that their message

---

[57] Paul developed this theme at some length in 1 Cor. 2.8-16.
[58] This is very clearly stated in the Epistle of James, but the same theme runs through the Pauline Epistles as well.
[59] See especially 1 Corinthians 12–14.

was also geared to the longer-term development of the church and its mission. A pastor who is trained today must be prepared to face situations that may arise in the future, as well as problems that are current now. Paul could not have foreseen much of what would come to pass in the next generation, but his counsels to Timothy and Titus were often framed in terms sufficiently broad that they could be applied to other circumstances without difficulty. For example, they contain warnings about tendencies that we know would later emerge in the so-called 'Gnostic' heresies of the second century, but without the kind of detail that would suggest that the author of the Epistles knew about them. Paul's advice could be applied to a number of different situations, without necessarily reflecting any one of them in particular.

In addition to these general remarks, there is also a good deal of material in the Pastoral Epistles that refers to Paul's immediate circumstances and would make little sense if they were written by anyone other than the apostle himself. His mention of personal friends, of his plans for the future and of belongings that he had left in particular places and wanted to recover, reminds us that spiritual fellowship in Christ is not just a theoretical idea but a lifestyle that has some very practical applications. To be a child of God is to care about other children of the same heavenly Father, and to serve them as best we can, in matters both great and small. The household of faith was created by the Holy Spirit and drew its strength from union with Christ, in whose image it was incarnate in the material world and bore witness there to the saving power of God.

## The subject matter of the Pastoral Epistles

If we take the Pastoral Epistles at face value and assume that they are letters written by the apostle Paul to Timothy and Titus it is fairly clear that each of the Epistles is intended to be a mixture of encouragement and guidance from the older man to the younger ones. Both Timothy and Titus had assumed (or rather been given) authority for managing churches founded by Paul in the course of his missionary activity and the apostle was concerned to ensure that they were continuing along the lines he had laid down from the beginning. It is apparent that the churches were at different stages in their development, with the one at Ephesus (where Timothy was) being already a fairly mature congregation, whereas those on Crete (shepherded by Titus) were still in the first phase of church planting. Not surprisingly, the concerns that Paul addressed and the advice he gave varied from one situation to the other. There is the added complication that 2 Timothy was written while Paul was a prisoner in Rome awaiting probable execution, a circumstance that added a sense of urgency, as well as poignancy, to Paul's letter.

To analyse the subject matter of the three Epistles, it is probably best to consider their content under a number of different headings, as follows:

1. Paul's missionary endeavours: His achievements and their limitations.
2. Paul's co-workers: His relationship and personal advice to them.
3. The government and good order of the church(es).
4. True and false doctrine.
5. Difficulties and opposition in the congregations.
6. Prospects for the future.

If we take these in turn we shall see how the Epistles resemble each other and how they differ. As Luke Timothy Johnson has argued, we shall discover that the Epistles are quite distinct from one another, despite some obvious similarities, and that they are best treated as separate compositions, not as a collection that naturally belongs together.

## Paul's missionary endeavours: His achievements and their limitations

**1 Timothy.** In this Epistle, Paul had established a church at Ephesus and been there long enough to set it on a reasonably solid foundation. The congregation was already big enough to have a number of widows and a functioning eldership. There were a number of families in the church, some of them quite wealthy, and there was also a significant body of household slaves. Having got that far, the apostle knew that it was time to move on, at least temporarily, and he had set off for Macedonia and perhaps further afield, in order to continue his church-planting work. Before leaving Ephesus, however, he was forced to discipline two members of the congregation, Hymenaeus and Alexander, who had been causing trouble, and there were a number of outstanding problems that he left Timothy to deal with.

**2 Timothy.** Paul's active missionary career now seemed to be over. He was chiefly preoccupied with delegation, sending Crescens to Galatia, Titus to Dalmatia and Tychicus to Ephesus.

**Titus.** Paul had just left Crete where he had been church planting, and he expected Titus to stay to finish off the work that he had begun. He himself seems to have gone to Epirus or Dalmatia, since he was planning to spend the winter at Nicopolis, which is in northwest Greece.

## Paul's co-workers: His relationship and advice to them

**1 Timothy.** Paul regarded Timothy as his 'true child in the faith', probably because to all intents and purposes Timothy had received his Christian education from the apostle. He recognized that Timothy was still young and might have difficulties establishing his authority in the congregation, but he trusted him fully and insisted that Timothy should claim the leadership role for which he had been commissioned. Much of his advice to Timothy concerned the ways in which he should deal with different groups in the church whom he might find awkward, in particular those who were considerably older than he was and the younger women who might mistake his interest in them for something other than what it was. He took a special interest in Timothy's physical health as well as in his spiritual growth, perhaps because he was afraid that Timothy might neglect to look after himself properly if he were not reminded of the importance of such things. Finally, Paul insisted that Timothy should teach the faith with complete integrity and protect the gospel message that had been entrusted to him against all attempts to subvert it.

**2 Timothy.** Paul was much more intensely personal in this Epistle than in the others. He was concerned with Timothy's personal development, the content of his preaching and teaching and his ongoing faithfulness in the face of challenges from both inside and outside the congregation. He was distressed that so many of his co-workers were no longer with him, and conscious that some of his erstwhile supporters had apparently abandoned him to his fate.

**Titus.** Like Timothy, Titus is Paul's 'true child in a common faith', though their relationship appears to have been more businesslike than the one Paul had with Timothy. Titus was to expect visits from some of Paul's other co-workers and the apostle saw Titus as a key player in his wider team of travelling evangelists.

## The government and good order of the church

**1 Timothy.** Paul expected Timothy to take charge of appointing the right people to manage the affairs of the church and to ensure that its members lived in a way that was honouring to the gospel. He was especially concerned that the prayer life of the congregation should be ordered in a way that furthered the task of evangelism and that in public worship both men and women should assume their proper place. Timothy was to pay special attention to the widows in the church, and in particular to make sure that those who needed help received it while those who were young and wanted to remarry should be encouraged to do so. His aim was to reduce the financial burden on the church and at the same time to control the potential for disorder that might result if socially active widows were under-occupied. He was also concerned for the elders, insisting that those who taught the congregation should be duly compensated for their labours as a matter of principle. Finally, he wanted the slaves to honour their profession of faith by doing a good job for their masters, so that the gospel would not be brought into disrepute. He did not address their masters as such, but he warned the richer members of the church (many, if not most of whom would have owned slaves) of the dangers that come from putting a false trust in riches, and urged them to pursue spiritual and not worldly gain.

The aim of everyone in the church should be to pursue godliness, by which Paul meant putting the teachings of the faith into practice. This would take different forms according to the circumstances of particular individuals, but the underlying aim would be the same. Nobody was exempt from this requirement, which was the true sign of the spiritual unity of the church.

**2 Timothy.** Paul was mainly concerned with the influence that false teachers were having on the vulnerable and undereducated – in particular on certain women who were prone to follow any novelty they came across. In general, this Epistle is much less preoccupied with matters of church order and government than the others are, but Paul wanted Timothy to train up others who would carry on the work of mission.

**Titus.** This Epistle is broadly similar to 1 Timothy, with Titus being expected to appoint elders in all the churches and introduce good order and discipline in their members. Cretans had a bad reputation for dishonesty, and Paul warned Titus that he would have to deal with that, though he cited no particular examples of individuals who had offended in that way.

## True and false doctrine

**1 Timothy.** Paul was very concerned that Timothy should preach the gospel in its fullness and purity. He was not to allow members of the church to distract others by teaching their eccentric views of the Mosaic law, and he warned against a false asceticism that threatened to discredit the goodness of the created order, which God had given human beings for their enjoyment and profit. Teachers of false doctrine were to be recognized for what they were – men who were depraved in mind and spirit, who were driven by base motives and wanted only to destroy the church. The only way to combat them effectively was by preaching the truth and reminding people that they were waiting for the appearing of Christ in glory. With that perspective in view, they would resist the temptation to fall away in pursuit of merely temporal rewards, and the church would be preserved in its intended purity.

**2 Timothy.** Avoiding false teaching was a major concern of Paul's in this Epistle. He constantly stressed the need to preach the pure gospel and to teach the Scriptures. It was important for Timothy to 'guard the deposit' that had been entrusted to him and to stick to the pattern of sound words that he had received from Paul. Rightly handling the word of truth and avoiding any distraction that might lead to heresy was to be Timothy's top priority.

**Titus.** Paul stressed the need to teach sound doctrine, and this Epistle contains a fuller exposition of the gospel message than either of the others does. False teaching was an ever-present danger, but its effects do not seem to have penetrated the Cretan churches very deeply at this stage in their development. Paul is more concerned to impose right behaviour on an unruly population so that Christians would set an example for others by their way of life and concern for others.

## Difficulties and opposition in the congregation

**1 Timothy.** These appear to have been of two types. First, there were people who thought they knew more about the Law of Moses than they actually did, and who were leading people astray by indulging in trivialities and bizarre interpretations of it. Second, there were others, who may have come in from outside, who were denying the goodness of creation and undermining one of the key pillars of the gospel. It is not clear whether these people were organized in opposition to Paul. The former group may not have seen themselves as his opponents at all, but it is harder to argue that that would have been the case for those who advocated an unnatural asceticism. They seem to have been much more focused in their false teaching and may well have constituted a definite opposition to the apostle's teaching.

**2 Timothy.** Members of the church were in danger of falling into traps set for them by false teachers. There were particular individuals in the church who had set themselves up in opposition to Paul and gone after their own fancies. Spiritual immaturity was a major problem that Timothy had to deal with, maintaining a steady discipline himself and sticking to the gospel message regardless of the opposition he might face.

**Titus.** Most of the problems Titus would encounter came from the indiscipline of church members, which would easily lead them into accepting false teaching if they had the opportunity to hear it. Taming the natural rebelliousness of the Cretans would be Titus' major task, which he would have to accomplish by finding and appointing the right people as elders of the local congregations.

## Prospects for the future

**1 Timothy**. Paul had every intention of returning to Ephesus in the not too distant future. He thought of his Epistle as a stopgap, intended to give Timothy guidance as to how to proceed during his absence.

**2 Timothy**. Paul saw his future as bleak. He was anticipating death, probably by judicial execution, and was mainly concerned with passing his ministry on to Timothy. He also foresaw future problems with false teachers, and opposition from those opposed to his teaching, but there is no sign that he was expecting a general persecution of the church by the state.

**Titus**. Paul envisaged Titus' ministry as short-term and promised to send Titus helpers so that he could leave the work in their hands and rejoin the apostle in a few months' time. There is an eschatological hope to give the people a sense of purpose in their self-discipline, but no particular mention of what to expect in the immediate future and no stated plan for further missionary work on Crete.

# Dating the Epistles

Internal evidence, such as it is, and comparisons with what we know of Paul's ministry, suggest that the Pastoral Epistles must be dated either in the late 50s, when Paul was based at Ephesus and possibly travelling around the Aegean on relatively short mission trips, or else in the mid-60s, after his first Roman imprisonment and during his second period of detention, which probably ended with his execution.

On a pseudepigraphical reading, it is virtually impossible for any of the letters to have been written before AD 64, the year of the great fire of Rome and the first persecution of Christians, when Paul may have been put to death. Scholars have noted that there are verbal similarities between 1 Timothy and the letters of Ignatius of Antioch (d. 118) that appear to indicate some dependence of the latter on the Pastorals, though the evidence is ambiguous and cannot be regarded as conclusive.[60]

The Epistles were almost certainly being quoted by Polycarp, perhaps as early as AD 110 and certainly by 135, so they must have been written a good while

---

[60] See J. H. Bernard, *The Pastoral Epistles* (Cambridge: Cambridge University Press, 1899). The coincidences cannot be denied but the restricted sample of the writing available, and the obvious similarity of the subject matter between the Pastorals and the post-apostolic epistles makes it impossible to prove that there is a definite relationship between them.

before that.[61] The difficulties associated with the pseudepigraphical option(s) are legion, as we have already seen, and Polycarp's testimony compounds them further. He was already an adult by AD 90 and would have known if the Epistles had not been circulating by then. But if they were pseudepigraphal, that leaves relatively little time for their composition, and of course we have no way of knowing who wrote them or in what circumstances. It is one thing to write such letters, but who would have assured their publication and distribution, and how would that have happened? Could they have appeared in churches that had no connection with either Timothy or Titus, and then been accepted by those that did? There are enormous difficulties here, and it must be said that the advocates of pseudepigraphy have not given them enough thought. Whatever 'solutions' they propose are entirely speculative and it is hard to see how any of them could overturn the *a priori* assumption that the Epistles are genuine.[62]

Marcion's failure to mention them must be seen in this context and compared with a statement of Jerome's to the effect that Tatian, another second-century heretic, rejected 1 Timothy but accepted Titus, apparently because the former explicitly condemned the kind of asceticism that Tatian was promoting.[63] Clement of Alexandria (150?–215?) quoted 1 Tim. 6.20, which speaks about 'knowledge so-called', and claimed that because of that the heretics of his day all rejected the Pastorals.[64] Evidence for both knowledge and use of the Pastoral Epistles in the post-apostolic period compares very favourably with that for other New Testament books and it cannot be assumed, as many modern scholars unfortunately do, that their absence from Marcion indicates that they had not yet been written. If Clement was right, his rejection of them was common to others among his contemporaries and need not surprise us.

Two other avenues regarding dating remain to be explored. The first is the relative order in which they were written. Which of the three Epistles was written first? Can we tell? 1 Timothy and Titus are relatively alike and reflect a situation in which Paul was free to travel and minister, so it is not unreasonable to suggest that they were written about the same time. 2 Timothy, on the other hand, was written when Paul was in prison, and the impression we are given is that his days were numbered. It is therefore likely

---

[61] Polycarp's *Epistle to the Philippians*, written between AD 110 and 135, strongly alludes to 1 Tim. 6.10 and conflates it with 1 Tim. 6.7. Other allusions occur as follows: 5.2 (2 Tim. 2.12); 8.1 (1 Tim. 1.1); 9.2 (2 Tim. 2.11; 4.10); 11.3 (2 Tim. 2.25); 12.3 (1 Tim. 2.2).

[62] Polycarp's testimony has been challenged, but see L. T. Johnson, *The First and Second letters to Timothy* (New York: Doubleday, 2001), pp. 298–300.

[63] Jerome, *Commentarium in Titum*, prologue (Migne, PL XXVI, col. 555).

[64] Clement of Alexandria, *Stromateis*, 2.11.

that it was written last, and possibly some years after the other two. Beyond that we cannot go, and it must be stressed that even this much is essentially speculation.

The second important consideration for dating is the nature of the heresies and deviations mentioned in the Epistles. These appear to be of Judaic origin, which supports the belief that the Pastoral Epistles are earlier in date rather than later. Whether there is any Gnostic influence behind these errors is uncertain but improbable. Gnosticism is a term usually reserved for a series of attempts at creating a systematic theology by synthesizing Greek philosophical ideas, Biblical themes and elements associated with Eastern mystery religions. The leading 'Gnostics' were active in the first half of the second century, though Irenaeus traced their origin to Simon Magus, who appears in the Acts of the Apostles, so some connection between the false teachers mentioned by Paul and a Gnostic or proto-Gnostic worldview cannot be excluded. The problem is that the evidence in the Pastoral Epistles is not precise enough to allow us to make clear identifications with the teaching of any one sect or leader. The best solution, which is generally adopted both by those who think the Epistles are genuine and those who think they are pseudepigraphal, is that they reflect a time when heretical teachings had not yet been organized into identifiable systems by particular teachers, even if elements of what was to come later can be detected here and there. That makes a date for their composition prior to AD 100 almost inevitable, and of course those who believe that they are authentic would push it back a generation or so before that.[65]

The Gnostic phenomenon was of a kind that almost presupposes a gestation period in which various trends and ideas came together, and the Pastoral Epistles cannot be dated later than that early stage. There is plenty of evidence from the other New Testament epistles that similar tendencies were emerging elsewhere, and there is no reason to suppose that they were any more developed in the congregations envisaged by the Pastorals than they were in other churches in the 50s and 60s. The fact that Paul's 'opponents' in the Pastoral Epistles are so hard to identify is an indication that the problems the apostle faced or envisaged were still in an embryonic stage. The Nicolaitans who appeared in the late 60s, if not before, were already followers of a particular person, and this phenomenon would become almost universal within a generation. It is we who abstract and group them under the heading of Gnosticism; they identified themselves, and were identified

---

[65] For a detailed exposition of the problem of the 'opponents' of Paul in 1 and 2 Timothy, see the detailed study of the question by Thornton (2016).

by their contemporaries, according to the teacher whom they followed. This tendency was already evident in the Corinthian church, which Paul rebuked because of it.[66] That there is no sign of anything like this in the Pastoral Epistles argues in favour of an early dating, and sometime during the reign of Nero (54–68) fits what evidence there is nicely enough.

Neither 1 Timothy nor Titus shows any sign of persecution or imprisonment, and in them Paul seems to be actively engaged in missionary activity around the Aegean Sea. We know that he was based for several years in Corinth and in Ephesus, and it may be that these Epistles were written sometime during that period, perhaps around AD 56 or 57, when he was on his way from Asia Minor to what is now Greece. Whether he went to Crete from Ephesus or from Corinth is impossible to determine, but either is possible.[67] There is some indication that he spent time in Illyricum, a Roman province in the western Balkans that could be stretched to include Dalmatia and Epirus, and that could explain why he wanted Titus to meet him at Nicopolis (in Epirus) and why Titus later went to Dalmatia, presumably to anchor Paul's mission in much the same way as he had done in Crete.[68]

2 Timothy must be dated later, when Paul was a prisoner in Rome. We know that he went there about AD 62, as is recounted in Acts 28, and that he was under a very mild form of house arrest for two years. Luke concluded his narrative at that point, leaving Paul's subsequent fate unmentioned. It is probable that it was during this time that Onesiphorus went from Ephesus to find him, a task that was made as difficult as it apparently was because Paul was staying in his own rented accommodation. It is even possible that Onesiphorus had a hand in Paul's release, perhaps by agreeing to take him into his personal custody. That could have occurred early in AD 64, allowing Paul to go back to the Aegean region as quickly as he could. A possible reconstruction of his subsequent movements might look as follows:

He may have travelled with a few companions along the well-worn route to Corinth, where Erastus 'remained',[69] before crossing to Troas. There he would have stayed with a certain Carpus before venturing further down the

---

[66] 1 Cor. 1.11-17.
[67] Johnson (2001), p. 137, and Towner (2006), p. 107, both adopt this hypothesis for dating 1 Timothy. In Towner's words, 'Paul's frequent travels back and forth between Asia Minor, Achaia, and Macedonia and his practice of dispatching delegates to churches are clear from his letters, so the kind of assignment envisioned here is not at all unlikely.'
[68] See Rom. 15.19; Tit. 3.12; 2 Tim. 4.10.
[69] 2 Tim. 4.20. Erastus may have accompanied Paul from Rome, but he was originally from Corinth, where he was (or had been) the city treasurer (Rom. 16.23). Perhaps he was going home. It is also possible that he had been in Corinth all along and that Paul had tried to persuade him to travel to Asia Minor with him.

Asian coast. If he arrived in Troas in late spring, that might explain why he left his cloak there – he would not have needed it in the hot weather.[70] He also had a store of books and parchments, but it is not clear whether they were with Carpus or elsewhere, perhaps at Ephesus, where Paul seems to have been welcomed into the household of Onesiphorus. If so, Timothy was not in Ephesus at the time. He may have gone back to Lystra on family business – perhaps his mother or grandmother had died, which might explain why Paul took the unusual step of mentioning them so favourably at the beginning of his Epistle. In any case, Timothy's absence from the city was probably temporary, since by the time Paul wrote to him he seems to have returned there.

Paul could then have moved on to Miletus, where he left Trophimus, who had fallen ill.[71] What may have happened after that is unknown. The fact that Paul had left his cloak at Troas and was clearly intending to collect his library suggests that he was planning to head back up the coast before winter, but that he never made it. Meanwhile, the great fire of Rome, which burned from 18 to 23 July AD 64, had been blamed by Nero on the Christians, and it is possible that Paul, having recently been under arrest in the capital, was detained and returned there in the latter part of the year, charged this time with sedition. He must have been back in Rome for some time, because he did not write to Timothy until after his first defence, which would have been in late 64 or early 65, when Nero's bloodlust and paranoia were reaching their peak.[72] If that was the case, it would explain why Paul said that nobody supported him – they would have been in hiding. Paul must have sent his letter to Timothy sometime in the spring of 65, hoping that his younger colleague could get his things together and reach Rome before the end of the shipping season in October/November. He sensed that the time was short, and it is possible, perhaps even probable, that he died (or was executed) before Timothy could get there. There is no further extant correspondence or word of either Paul or Timothy, so that seems to have been the most likely outcome. However, it should be stressed that although the above reconstruction is plausible, it can be no more than speculative given our lack of detailed knowledge. All that we know for certain is that when Paul disappeared from the historical record, so did Timothy and Titus – for reasons that must remain forever hidden from our eyes.

---

[70] 2 Tim. 4.13.
[71] 2 Tim. 4.20.
[72] It was in AD 65 that the Roman philosopher Seneca, once the young Nero's tutor, was forced to commit suicide, so Paul was in good company.

To sum up, we can be fairly confident that 2 Timothy was the last of the Pastoral Epistles to have been written, but there is no way of knowing whether 1 Timothy precedes Titus or the other way round. Most commentaries ignore the issue and follow the Biblical order in their exposition, a practice that the present volume follows. But some scholars prefer to invert this order by applying their own theories of dating to the collection. Thus we find that I. H. Marshall (2004) puts Titus first, followed by 1 Timothy, whereas W. D. Mounce (2000) starts with 1 Timothy and then moves on to Titus. Both conclude with 2 Timothy in third place. Neither of these solutions can be definitive, and on balance it seems best to retain the traditional arrangement, if only so as not to confuse readers looking for the treatment of a specific Epistle.

## Genre and style

Do the Pastoral Epistles belong together as a subgroup within the Pauline corpus, and can they be categorized according to a particular genre or style? At the most basic level, they are clearly letters addressed to particular individuals, though that is hardly enough for them to be classified as belonging to a specific 'genre'. They also follow certain conventions, like the opening salutation and the concluding personal remarks, that are found in a wide range of ancient letters. They tell us nothing more than that. Paul's salutations differ from the usual secular forms because they include a strong spiritual element, but otherwise they are unexceptional.

More specifically, many commentators have suggested that 1 Timothy and Titus resemble imperial rescripts, known as *mandata principis*, which the emperor sent to provincial governors and the like, with instructions as to how to handle particular administrative problems. There is no doubt that Paul was doing something similar to this in these two epistles, though whether he (or anyone else) was conscious of imitating a particular genre is impossible to say. Perhaps he had *mandata* in the back of his mind as he was writing, but if so, any imitation of them is likely to have been subconscious rather than deliberate.[73] 2 Timothy is universally acknowledged to be different from the others, more exclusively personal and intended as a word of encouragement and exhortation rather than as a *mandatum* in the usual sense. Because of this it is often labelled 'paraenetic', though

---

[73] See the discussion in Towner (2006), pp. 33–6, who traces the origin of this theory back through Johnson (2001) to C. Spicq, *Les Epîtres Pastorales* (Paris, Gabalda, 1948), pp. 35–6. Both Johnson and Spicq affirm the Pauline authorship of the Pastorals.

again, how consciously Paul may have been adopting a recognized genre is impossible to say. On this point there is a significant difference between those commentators who accept the letters as genuine and those who believe that they are fictitious. The former are liable to regard the whole question of 'genre' with a certain scepticism, and treat the letters as occasional productions called forth by circumstances rather than as set pieces that conform to a prescribed literary model. Those who prefer pseudonymity are naturally more inclined to think in terms of a premeditated style which the author adopted, though if that was the case, he did not follow a recognized pattern at all closely. It is probably best to conclude that any resemblances in the Epistles to a given genre are coincidental, and that literary factors played little part in shaping their content. There is certainly no reason to suppose that Paul adopted a particular form of writing because it suited what he wanted to say, or that he was constrained by stylistic considerations from expressing himself as he would have wished. Whatever we say about the genre and style of the Pastoral Epistles, such considerations are of little importance for their content or interpretation.

What does matter is the question of whether the collection possesses an identifiable unity. Everybody recognizes that the three Epistles share certain characteristics that set them apart from Paul's other writings, but whether these are enough to make them a series of their own is another matter. The term 'Pastoral Epistles' is of modern origin, going back no further than to a course of lectures on them given by Paul Anton in 1726 and published after his death.[74] The term was convenient, and it has become especially popular since belief in their pseudonymity has spread. Most people who argue for that think that they were written by a single pseudepigrapher (or perhaps a single group of pseudepigraphers) who produced them at the same time as a distinct collection. That in turn has prompted other commentators to stress the differences among them, and in particular the individual characteristics of 2 Timothy which make it stand out from the others. If 1 Timothy and Titus were intended for congregational use in a way that 2 Timothy was not, it would not be at all surprising if its subject matter was handled in a different manner. There does seem to be a good deal of material in 1 Timothy and Titus that is designed for public proclamation, and to that extent their style may have a particular significance, but it is hard to see how that would have affected the content of the message.

---

[74] The lectures were given at Halle (1726–7) and published by J. A. Maier, *B. D. Pauli Antonii exegetische Abhandlung der Pastoral-Briefe Pauli an Timotheum und Titum* (Halle, 1753). But the idea that the epistles had a pastoral content and intention is much older. See Johnson (2001), p. 13, n. 3.

Great play has been made of the so-called *hapax legomena*, meaning by this words that appear in the Pastoral Epistles but nowhere else in the New Testament. At one time it was thought that most of these words had either been invented by the writer or else did not enter common use until the second century AD, 'evidence' that was naturally used to support the case for pseudepigraphy. Further research has greatly modified this thesis and it can now be said that most of the *hapax legomena* are attested in other texts dating from the first century and even earlier, and would not have struck Paul's contemporaries as odd or unfamiliar. The fact that they do not occur elsewhere in the New Testament is of relatively minor significance, partly because the text sample is very limited and partly because the vocabulary in question is mainly determined by the subject matter, which is not discussed in such detail elsewhere.

More significant than individual words is the occurrence (or non-occurrence) of certain grammatical features that set the Pastoral Epistles apart from the rest of the Pauline corpus. Some of these can be found in Luke-Acts, which are acknowledged to have a particular affinity with the Pastorals. But the resemblance may mean no more than that Paul and Luke worked together at certain periods (as they probably did) and shared a common amanuensis, whose stylistic quirks are reflected in their finished writings. It is significant that nobody in the ancient world thought that the Greek was so unusual as to raise suspicions about the author's identity – a situation that stands in sharp contrast to the doubts expressed (in ancient as well as in modern times) about the authorship of 2 Peter. Ancient readers were well attuned to such matters and would not have missed obvious turns of phrase that struck them as non-Pauline, so their testimony must be taken seriously. As with so much else to do with the Pastorals, we do not know enough to be able to make a definitive judgment and must rely on the witness of those who were better placed in this respect than we are. That witness is unanimously in favour of authenticity, and so objections of this kind cannot be taken as evidence supporting pseudonymous authorship.

One feature of the style of the Pastoral Epistles that most commentators seem to miss is that they are replete with triadic formulae which the apostle uses to make different points. The triad was a rhetorical device and is too common in ancient literature to be classifiable as characteristic of any one style, but its presence in the Pastoral Epistles cannot be ignored. Depending on how the triads are calculated (some are doubled), there are fifteen in 1 Timothy, eight in 2 Timothy and ten in Titus, which is a large number given the relative brevity of the letters themselves.

In general, triads tend to emphasize one of the three elements and subordinate the others to it. Normally it is the first one that dominates, as in 1 Tim. 6.15, where God is described as 'sovereign, king and lord'. His sovereignty is primary and is manifested in his kingship (status) and lordship (function or activity). The range and effectiveness of the second and third elements depend on the first – the greater his sovereignty, the higher the status of his kingship and the wider the breadth of his lordship. Occasionally this pattern is altered in favour of the third part of the triad, and even (very rarely) of the second. As an example of the former, 1 Tim. 6.9 describes the fall of a greedy man into temptation, a trap and ruin. Clearly temptation is the beginning of a process that culminates in ruin, which is definitive and therefore ultimately more serious than either of the others. An example of the third type can be found in 1 Tim. 1.2, where Paul sends the greeting 'grace, mercy and peace', where he has added 'mercy' to what was a standard Christian greeting of the time.

Quite often it is difficult to see that any one of the ingredients can claim a clear priority over the others and they seem to sit side by side as more or less equal. As an example of that, see 1 Tim. 6.16, where God is described as immortal, unapproachable and invisible. It might be possible to argue for the priority of one of these attributes over the other, but the context does not particularly encourage us to do so and it does not seem to make any real difference. Nevertheless, the triadic pattern remains clearly visible in Paul's rhetoric and readers of the Pastoral Epistles need to bear that in mind and be on the lookout for it.

In general, we must conclude that the distinctive features of style that make up the Pastorals may be enough to give them a particular identity, but they are not so markedly different from accepted conventions as to preclude the possibility, or even the likelihood, of Pauline authorship. As we have already suggested, the apostle may have written them himself, without secretarial assistance, in which case their peculiarities can find a ready explanation without having to resort to hypotheses that no ancient witness would support.

## The history of transmission and interpretation

At first sight, evidence for the early history of the transmission and interpretation of the Pastoral Epistles is somewhat disappointing. There are no fragments of the text of 1 and 2 Timothy that can be dated before the fourth-century Codex Sinaiticus, though there are some of Titus in P 32, which was written about AD 200. On the other hand, as we have already seen, there are several allusions to the Pastoral Epistles and even quotations from them that can be dated as far back as the early years of the second century, bringing them within living memory of the apostles themselves. After AD 150, references to them become more definite and it is clear that they were widely regarded as Holy Scripture. For example, both Theophilus of Antioch and Athenagoras of Athens, writing sometime around AD 177, allude to 1 Tim. 2.2, which they cite as authoritative apostolic teaching.[75]

Shortly after that there is ample evidence from Irenaeus (140?-200?) that the Pastoral Epistles were widely known and treated as authoritative Scripture. In his great work against the heresies of his time, Irenaeus quotes them often, and since he came from Smyrna and had known Polycarp in his youth, he was in a good position to know that they had long been accepted as Pauline.[76] Clement of Alexandria, writing about the same time or slightly later, used Tit. 2.11-13 and 3.3-5 as his authority for writing his *Exhortatio*, and he quoted both 1 and 2 Timothy several times in his *Stromateis*.[77]

Eclipsing these however was Tertullian (160?-220?), who quoted the Pastoral Epistles in at least eighteen of his approximately thirty extant works, sometimes marshalling several texts from them in support of a single argument.[78] It was only because he believed that Marcion had rejected them that he did not use them in rebutting Marcion's theology, as he explicitly stated.[79] After Tertullian's time, use of the Pastoral Epistles was constant and widespread across the church, as can be seen from the writings of Hippolytus of Rome (170?-236), Cyprian of Carthage (200?-258), Origen of Alexandria (185?-254?) and Novatian of Rome (210?-280?).[80] Luke Timothy Johnson, who has made a detailed study of the evidence culled from these and other early writers, concludes as follows:

> Most of all, the letters to Timothy and Titus are read together with, and contextualized by, the other letters of Paul. And since the dominant way

---

[75] Theophilus of Antioch, *Ad Autolycum*, 3.14; Athenagoras of Athens, *Legatio*, 32.
[76] Irenaeus, *Adversus omnes haereses*, 1.preface quotes 1 Tim. 1.4 as the words of the apostle. Later on in the same work, he quotes 1 Tim. 1.9 (4.16.3); 2.5 (5.17.1); 3.15 (3.1.1); 4.2 (2.21.2) and 6.20 (1.23.4; 2.pref.1; 2.14.7). He also quotes 2 Tim. 4.10-11 (3.14.1).
[77] Clement of Alexandria, *Exhortatio*, 1; *Stromateis* 1.1; 1.9; 1.10; 1.11; 1.17; 2.6; 3.6; 3.12; 3.18; 4.3; 4.7; 4.16; 5.1; 6.3; 6.9; 6.17; 7.2. See also his *Paedagogus*, where he quoted 1 Timothy four times (2.2; 2.3; 3.11; 3.12).
[78] See Tertullian, *De praescriptione haereticorum*, 33, where he combines 1 Tim. 1.4; 4.3 and 2 Tim. 2.3. Also *Scorpiace* 13 (2 Tim. 1.7-8; 2.11; 4.6). See L. T. Johnson, *The First and Second Letters of Timothy*, p. 21, nn. 21-2, for a more extensive list.
[79] Tertullian, *Adversus Marcionem*, 5.21.
[80] For the details, see Johnson (2001), pp. 22-3.

such early readers appropriated Paul was as a moral teacher, this only made the letters to Timothy seem more obviously his own.[81]

It is clear from these and other sources that the Pastoral Epistles were used both to refute the claims of various heretics and to establish a moral standard for the church. They were frequently cited by the *Apostolic Constitutions*, an anonymous fourth-century canonical collection that was concerned with church discipline, which is one of the main themes of the Pastorals, and later on both Augustine of Hippo (354–430) and John Chrysostom (347–407) regarded them as authoritative for determining what qualities a preacher and teacher ought to possess.[82]

**Early church commentators**

It was not until the fourth century that commentaries on the Pastorals began to appear,[83] though this situation was far from unparalleled in the early church. The first datable one comes from Ephrem (Ephraim) Syrus (306–373) and was written in Syriac, though only an Armenian translation of the original has come down to us.[84] On purely historical matters, Ephrem was no better informed than we are and used the Acts of the Apostles as his point of reference. However, he realized that Paul's opponents were Jewish and thought that the aspiration to the office of an overseer (1 Tim. 3.1) applied to the presbyterate rather than to the episcopate as it was understood in his time. This somewhat anachronistic interpretation shows that he had a sense of historical relativity and was not simply assuming that the church to which Paul was writing was identical to the one he himself knew.

---

[81] Johnson (2001), p. 23, refers readers to an unpublished doctoral dissertation by D. K. Rensberger, 'As the Apostle Teaches: The Development of the Use of Paul's Letters in Second Century Christianity' (PhD dissertation, Yale University, 1981), for confirmation.
[82] Augustine of Hippo, *De doctrina Christiana*, 4.16; John Chrysostom, *De sacerdotio*, 4.8. Augustine did not write a commentary on the Pastoral Epistles, but extracts from his writings that related to them were collected by Bede. They have never been published, but an English translation of them was made by David Hurst and has been published as *Bede the Venerable. Excerpts from the works of Saint Augustine on the letters of the Blessed Apostle Paul* (Kalamazoo, MI: Cistercian Publications, 1999), pp. 295–330.
[83] Extracts from many of these can be found in P. Gorday, ed., *Ancient Christian Commentary on Scripture. New Testament IX: Colossians, 1–2 Thessalonians, 1–2 Timothy, Titus, Philemon* (Downers Grove, IL: Inter-Varsity Press, 2000), pp. 129–308.
[84] It was translated into Latin by Armenian monks in the late nineteenth century. Ephraim Syrus, *Commentarii in Epistolas D. Pauli* (Venezia: Typographia Sancti Lazari, 1893).

Ephrem's commentary was followed by a careful and literal examination of the Pastorals by Theodore of Mopsuestia (350–428). Theodore had a keen sense of context and was remarkably generous to women, both in his interpretation of 1 Tim. 2.11-15 and elsewhere. He resisted the temptation to suggest that women were spiritually inferior to men, accepted the legitimacy of women deacons and interpreted Paul's prohibition against them speaking as referring to prophecy in the church, not to teaching in the home, which he thought was perfectly acceptable.[85]

Theodore's contemporary John Chrysostom (347–407) did not write commentaries in the strict sense but devoted eighteen homilies to 1 Timothy, ten to 2 Timothy and six to Titus, which are particularly valuable for the way in which they connect the Pastorals to the rest of the Pauline corpus. His main theme in his sermons was the importance of right behaviour, guided and governed by the principle of love, something that he thought was noticeably absent from the teaching of heretics.[86]

Theodoret of Cyrrhus (Cyrus) (393–466) also wrote a commentary on all fourteen epistles of Paul (including Hebrews) in which he demonstrated considerable dependence on both Chrysostom and Theodore of Mopsuestia. As a general rule he combined the best of his predecessors' analysis into a single whole, showing considerable historical and critical acumen, thus providing us with what is perhaps the best single commentary from the Greek fathers.[87]

In the Latin-speaking world, the first commentary was written by the so-called Ambrosiaster (fl. 366–384), which covers all Paul's letters but omits Hebrews, which the Western church of the time did not accept as Pauline. Ambrosiaster was especially sensitive to Paul's many references to Jews and the law, which he contrasted (as the apostle did) with salvation in Christ.

---

[85] Theodore of Mopsuestia, *In Epistolas B. Pauli Commentarii: The Latin Edition with Greek fragments*, vol. 2, *1 Thessalonians-Philemon*, ed. H. B. Swete (Cambridge: Cambridge University Press, 1882). An English translation has appeared, edited by R. Greer, *Theodore of Mopsuestia: Commentary on the Minor Pauline Epistles* (Atlanta, GA: SBL Publications, 2010), pp. 524–772.

[86] John Chrysostom, *Homiliae in Epistolas ad Timotheum et Titum* (Migne, PG LXII, cols 501–700). An English translation is available in the *Library of Nicene and Post-Nicene Fathers*, ed. P. Schaff, XIII, pp. 407–543. This translation was revised in 2009 by K. Knight for New Advent and is available online at http://www.newadvent.org/fathers/2306.htm for 1 Timothy, http://www.newadvent.org/fathers/2307.htm for 2 Timothy and http://www.newadvent.org/fathers/2308.htm for Titus.

[87] Theodore of Mopsuestia, *Interpretatio Epistolarum I ad Timotheum, II and Timotheum et ad Titum* (Migne, PG LXXXII, cols 787–870). An English translation by R. C. Hill is available: Theodoret of Cyrus (Cyrus), *Commentary on the letters of St Paul*, 2 vols (Brookline, MA: Holy Cross Press, 2001), II, pp. 208–60.

He stressed the universality of the gospel but also the need for individuals to respond to it, and was negative towards women, even going to the point of saying that they could be saved only if their children believed in Christ, which is an odd interpretation of 1 Tim. 2.15. His commentary is chiefly useful for what it tells us of the state of the Western church in the late fourth century and shows little awareness of any historical development since the time of Paul.[88]

After him came Pelagius (fl. 400–420) whose commentary was recycled under the name of Jerome. A variant of it also circulated under the name of Primasius, though it probably came from the school of Cassiodorus (485–580). Pelagius was condemned for his belief in free will, though nothing of this is apparent in his commentary, which may have been expurgated for conservation purposes. It is possible that he knew at least some of the Greek commentaries, but the chief value of his work is that by extensive use of cross-referencing, it situates the Pastoral Epistles within the wider context of Scripture as a whole.[89]

From the authentic Jerome we have only a commentary on Titus, though he translated all the Pastorals as part of his Latin ('Vulgate') version of the New Testament.[90]

The ancient commentaries all tend to assume that Timothy and Titus were bishops of their respective churches, and they interpret the Epistles in that light. Paul was writing to them to tell them what a bishop should do, and the implication was that what was right for his immediate successors was also relevant for those who lived several centuries later. Most of the commentators were aware that some things had changed in the meantime – for example, they knew that in the beginning *episkopos* ('bishop') and a *presbyteros* ('presbyter', 'priest') had been virtually interchangeable terms, and that there had been an order of female deacons, which had practically disappeared by the fourth century. But these developments did not trouble them unduly and they had no hesitation in applying the advice Paul gave to his co-workers and disciples to the church leaders of their own time, many of whom (as they did not hesitate to point out) were in dire need of it.

---

[88] Ambrosiaster, *Commentarius in Epistulas Paulinas*, ed. H. J. Vogels, 3 vols (Wien: Hoelder-Pichler-Tempsky, 1966–9), III, pp. 249–334. An English translation, edited by G. L. Bray, is available in *Ambrosiaster. Commentaries on Galatians-Philemon* (Downers Grove, IL: Inter-Varsity Press, 2009), pp. 120–60.

[89] Pelagius, *Commentarius in Epistulas D. Pauli* (Migne, PL XXX, cols 875–900). It may be noted that there is also a commentary on Titus alone, written by Jerome (Migne, PL XXVI, cols 555–600).

[90] *Saint Jerome's commentaries on Galatians, Titus and Philemon*, trans. T. P. Scheck (Notre Dame, IN: University of Notre Dame Press, 2010), pp. 277–349.

## Medieval commentaries

Medieval commentaries[91] in the Greek world are attributed to Oecumenius of Tricca (Trikkala) in the tenth century and to Theophylact of Ochrid (Ohrid) in the eleventh century, though this is misleading.[92] They appear to be variants of a common commentary tradition that was handed down from one generation to another and perhaps finally codified by the men to whom they are attributed. They overlap in many places and both contain material that almost certainly comes from a variety of sources, many of which are no longer extant.[93] This inbuilt archaism may account for the favourable attitude towards women that they exhibit, particularly in the matter of allowing them to teach others in private.

In the Latin world, the tendency to copy earlier masters more of less faithfully can be seen in the commentary attributed to Primasius (sixth century), which is just a reworking of Pelagius, and in Bede's collage of excerpts from Augustine. This tradition was carried on by Florus of Lyons (790–860), so much so in fact, that for many centuries his compendium of Augustinian citations circulated under Bede's name.[94] Much fuller that Florus is the commentary of Rabanus Maurus (784–856), which is an encyclopedic collection of patristic sources and cross-references to other parts of Scripture but cannot be regarded as original to him.[95]

Commentaries in the mold of Rabanus, but usually focussed on citing passages from Augustine and Ambrosiaster (regarded as Ambrose), were written by Alcuin of York (735–804),[96] Lanfranc of Bec (1010–1089),[97] Anselm of Laon (d. 1117)[98] and Peter Lombard (1090–1160).[99] They were clearly intended to be reference works for students and others who wanted to know what the tradition of patristic interpretation was. Anselm of Laon's

---

[91] For background on these, see S. R. Cartwright, ed., *A Companion to St Paul in the Middle Ages* (Leiden: Brill, 2013).

[92] Oecumenius of Tricca, *Pauli Apostoli ad Timotheum et ad Titum epistolae* (Migne, PG CXIX, cols 133–262); Theophylact of Ochrid, *Epistolarum Divi Pauli ad Timotheum et ad Titum expositio* (Migne, PG CXXV, cols 9–172).

[93] It is quite possible that much of what they say goes back to lost works of Didymus the Blind of Alexandria (fourth century), and some of it may have originated with Origen.

[94] Florus of Lyons, *Expositio in epistolam I ad Timothem, II ad Timotheum et ad Titum* (Migne, PL CXIX, cols 397–419).

[95] Rabanus Maurus, *Expositio in epistolam I ad Timotheum, II ad Timotheum, et ad Titum* (Migne, PL CXII, cols 580–692).

[96] Alcuin of York, *Tractatus super sancti Pauli ad Titum epistolam*, Migne, PL C, cols 1009–26.

[97] Lanfranc of Bec, *Commentarii in omnes Pauli epistolas* (Migne, PL CL, cols 345–72).

[98] Anselm of Laon, *Epistolae ad Timotheum et ad Titum* (Migne, PL CXIV, cols 623–42).

[99] Peter Lombard, *In epistolas ad Timotheum et ad Titum* (Migne, PL CXCII, cols 325–94).

commentary is generally regarded as having been the most influential in this respect, because it formed the basis for the so-called *Glossa ordinaria* that accompanied most medieval editions of the Latin Vulgate.

The Pelagian tradition, concealed under the names of Jerome and Primasius and unknown to those who followed it, continued to exercise considerable influence in the early Middle Ages. Typical of it is the work of Sedulius Scotus (ninth century), whose main innovation was his statement that the salvation of women referred to in 1 Tim. 2.15 meant that they had to be baptized![100] Better than that are the commentaries of Anton of Verceil (d. 950), which concentrate on theological matters like the meaning of the Mosaic law, the importance of Christ's incarnation and the doctrine of the church. On the other hand, he had a more negative approach to women, which perhaps reflects his own era more faithfully than Sedulius did.[101]

Medieval Latin commentaries in the true sense of the word began with one by Haimo (Aimon) of Auxerre (d. 855).[102] Haimo interpreted the Pastorals entirely according to the practice of the church in his own time and his work shows no awareness of historical development. At the same time, he appeared to have had some knowledge of Greek and of Jewish folklore which he transmitted as faithfully as he could. But Haimo's commentary is chiefly noted for advocating the spiritual reading of the text in addition to the literal one, a feature which makes it typical of the Middle Ages.

Of much higher quality is the carefully argued commentary by Bruno of Cologne (1032-1101), who founded the Carthusian order.[103] Bruno introduced an element of dialogue into his commentary, presenting a Timothy who asked Paul to explain why he had issued particular instructions. This method of commentating is similar to the one that would later dominate the schools of law and theology, and it may be regarded as early evidence for the development of the 'question and answer' style of learning that would characterize scholasticism.

The method was developed in a different direction by Hugh of St Victor (d. 1142),[104] who took out the personal element of dialogue and substituted a more schematic structure instead. Hugh asked theological questions of his text and then proceeded to answer them, whether the answer was to be found in the text or not! He showed no interest in the historical background

---

[100] Sedulius Scotus, *In epistolas ad Timotheum et ad Titum* (Migne, PL CIII, cols 229-50).
[101] Anton of Verceil, *Epistolae ad Timotheum et Titum* (Migne, PL CXXXIV, cols 663-720).
[102] Haimo of Auxerre, *Expositio in Divi Pauli Epistolas* (Migne, PL CXVII, cols 783-814).
[103] Bruno of Cologne, *Epistolae ad Timotheum et ad Titum* (Migne, PL CLIII, cols 425-84).
[104] Hugh of St Victor, *In epistolas ad Timotheum et ad Titum* (Migne, PL CLXXV, cols 593-608).

of the epistles or in Paul's original meaning. More theological still is the commentary by Hervé de Bourg-Dieu (d. 1149),[105] whose work is a classic of the genre. His approach and conclusions were generally Augustinian, with a strong emphasis on love as the fulfilling of the law, though his attitude towards women and their possible place in the church was uniformly negative, in keeping with medieval attitudes generally.

The best of the medieval commentaries, at least from a modern standpoint, was undoubtedly the one written by Thomas Aquinas (1226?–1274).[106] Aquinas employed an intellectual rigour not seen before, and he was the first to recognize a 'pastoral' dimension to the Epistles. He was not afraid to reject traditional interpretations when they seemed to him to be mistaken, and he used his Aristotelian philosophical background to bring out the moral implications of Paul's teaching in a way that had not been seen since ancient times. Unfortunately his systematic approach led to a certain artificiality in places, and his work is of uneven quality. As with most of his contemporaries, he was negative in his approach to women but justified this by citing Aristotle's belief in the natural inferiority of the female sex, which was not at all what Paul was saying.

Aquinas' commentaries enjoy the unusual distinction of having been the basis of a monograph dedicated to the Pastoral Epistles, which aims to bring out their particular characteristics and illustrate their importance for our understanding both of Thomas himself and of the church of his time.[107] According to this, Aquinas was chiefly interested in determining the character and function of an ideal bishop, which is what he believed Paul was outlining in the Pastorals. 1 Timothy was interpreted as an extended exposition of the grace of episcopacy, including both the moral and spiritual qualities desired in a bishop and the various functions that he was required to perform. 2 Timothy was regarded as an exhortation to pastoral oversight so profound that it would lead the bishop to sacrifice his own life for the sake of his flock. Titus was taken to be an examination of the criteria for appointing future

---

[105] Hervé de Bourg-Dieu, *In epsitolas ad Timotheum et ad Titum* (Migne, PL CLXXXI, cols 1403–1506).

[106] Thomas Aquinas, *In omnes Sancti Pauli Apostoli commentaria*, 2 vols (Torino: M. E. Marietti, 1924), II, pp. 183–278. An English translation has been made by Chrysostom Baer, *Commentaries on St Paul's epistles to Timothy, Titus and Philemon* (South Bend, IN: St Augustine's Press, 2007). Another one has recently appeared in the *Latin-English Edition of the Works of St Thomas Aquinas* (Lander, WY: The Aquinas Institute for the Study of Sacred Doctrine, 2012), XL, pp. 239–458.

[107] Michael G. Sirilla, *The Ideal Bishop. Aquinas' Commentaries on the Pastoral Epistles* (Washington, DC: CUA Press, 2017). Readers should note that the author consistently uses 'episcopacy' when he means 'episcopate'.

bishops and of the need for an effective teaching and preaching ministry to counter the activities of heretics.[108]

After Aquinas' time commentary writing went into decline. Nicholas of Lyra (d. 1329) produced a series of comments that he called 'postils', a word of uncertain origin.[109] The postils resembled the *Glossa Ordinaria* and were often substituted for it, being printed in Bibles in the late fifteenth century and thus becoming widely known and influential. On the whole, Nicholas avoided allegory and pioneered an approach to textual exegesis that would be picked up by Martin Luther and used to great effect in the Reformation.

The last distinctly medieval commentary was that of Dionysius (Denys) the Carthusian (d. 1471), which produced some fanciful and non-literal interpretations of the text that were increasingly our of tune with the spirit of his time. They were edited in the early twentieth century but have never been translated or published in a readily accessible form.[110]

Like the patristic commentators before them, the medieval writers focused on the role of the bishop in the church, despite the fact that this had changed considerably from what had been the norm in Roman times. Many of them did little more than cut and paste what they had inherited from antiquity, but those who ventured further usually developed the pastoral aspects of the bishop's ministry, which time and changing circumstances had often compromised. Unlike their forbears, however, the Latin commentators of the middle ages had only an imperfect knowledge of Greek and knew even less about the social and political world in which Paul and his disciples had lived. Their commentaries sometimes contain valuable flashes of insight, but on the whole it is not hard to see why they have been superseded. Either they bore little relation to the texts or when they attempted what we would now recognize as historical-critical analysis, their lack of linguistic skills and practical information about the period they were commenting on makes much of what they had to say unacceptable by modern standards of textual interpretation.

## Early modern commentaries

The Renaissance saw a new departure in commentary writing,[111] which was foreshadowed by the brief notes of humanist scholars like Lorenzo Valla

---

[108] Sirilla, *The Ideal Bishop*, p. 100.
[109] It was supposed to mean 'after those things' (*post illa*). Nicholas of Lyra, *Postilla super epistolas Pauli* (Mantova: Paulus de Butzbach, 1478).
[110] Dionysius the Carthusian, *Opera omnia in unum corpus digesta ad fidem editionum Coloniensium*, 42 vols (Monstrolii, 1896–1913). The commentary on the Pauline Epistles is in Vol. 13.
[111] See R. W. Holder, ed., *A Companion to Paul in the Reformation* (Leiden: Brill, 2009), for useful background to this period.

(1406–1457), Erasmus of Rotterdam (1466–1536) and Thomas de Vio Cajetan (1469–1534).[112] All these writers emphasized the priority of the Greek texts over the Latin translations thitherto in general use and placed a strong emphasis on textual accuracy which led them to criticize the generally low standard of so much medieval commentary writing. This tradition was continued after the Reformation by men like Sebastian Castellio (1515–1563), Isaac Casaubon (1559–1614), John Cameron (1579–1625) and Abraham Scultetus (1566–1625), all of whose comments can be found in the same *Critici sacri* that contains the notes of Lorenzo Valla. The most exhaustive work of this kind was produced in the seventeenth century by Hugo Grotius (1583–1645), who compiled a veritable encyclopedia of sources that still impresses readers today.[113]

Martin Luther (1483–1546) delivered a series of lectures on 1 Timothy and another on Titus in which he combined the learning of Renaissance humanism with the demands of the gospel as he understood it.[114] Luther was particularly insistent that the Pastoral Epistles reflect the typically Pauline understanding of the law and the gospel and saw no theological difference between them and Galatians or Romans. His associate Philipp Melanchthon (1497–1560) wrote a full commentary on the Pastorals in which he developed Luther's persepctive in a more comprehensive and systematic way.[115]

The most detailed and original Reformation commentator however was John Calvin (1509–1564), who wrote a full commentary and delivered a series of sermons on them which are still extant and available in print.[116] Calvin is particularly notable for his careful attention to ancient rhetoric and

---

[112] Valla's notes can be found in *Critici sacri, sive annotata doctissimorum virorum in Vetus ac Novum Testamentum, quibus accedunt tractatus varii theologico-philologici*, 9 vols (Amsterdam: Henricus et Vidua Theodori Broom, 1698), VII. Desiderius Erasmus, *In Novum Testamentum annotationes* (Basel: Johann Froben, 1519). Thomas de Vio Cajetan, *Epistolae Pauli et aliorum apostolorum ad Graecam veritatem castigatae* (Paris: Apud Iod. Badium, 1532).

[113] Hugo Grotius, *Annotationes in Vetus et Novum Testamentum* (Amsterdam, 1641). It was also included in *Critici sacri*.

[114] Martin Luther, *Lectures on First Timothy*, in *Luther's Works*, 55 vols (St Louis, MO: Concordia, 1973), vol. 28, pp. 217–84; *Lectures on Titus*, in *Luther's Works* (St Louis, MO: Concordia, 1968), vol. 29, pp. 4–90.

[115] Philipp Melanchthon, *Enarratio epistolae primae ad Timotheum et dourum capitum secundae, scripta et dictata in praelectione publica* (Wittenberg: Crato, 1561); *Epistola Pauli ad Titum* (Erfurt: Mattheus Maler, 1519).

[116] John Calvin, *The Second Epistle of Paul the Apostle to the Corinthians and the Epistles to Timothy, Titus and Philemon*, trans. T. A. Smail (Edinburgh: Oliver and Boyd, 1964); *Sermons of M. John Calvin on the Epistles of S. Paule to Timothie and Titus*, trans. by L. T. (London: G. Bishop, 1579); facsimile reprint (Edinburgh: Banner of Truth, 1983). The sermons on 1 Timothy have been retranslated by R. Van Neste and B. Denker, *John Calvin's Sermons on* 1 Timothy, 2 vols (Jackson, TN: Union University Press, 2016). Those on Titus have been retranslated by Robert White, *John Calvin. Sermons on Titus* (Edinburgh: Banner of Truth, 2015).

for his firm conviction that the epistles were Pauline in origin. His critical acumen approached modern standards and he is still regarded as a serious dialogue partner in modern commentaries. Like Luther and Melanchthon before him, he saw no difficulty in linking what the Pastoral Epistles say about the law with Paul's teaching elsewhere, and his commentaries are full of cross-references to other parts of Scripture.

Among later commentators in the early modern period, mention should be made of Johann Albrecht Bengel (1687-1752), whose conservative interpretation of the Pastorals was widely accepted in the eighteenth century. His *Gnomon Novi Testamenti*, which is full of careful textual exegesis and terse comments remained a standard reference work for more than a century after his death and can still be consulted with profit today.[117] Roman Catholic commentators of the early modern period were usually very learned in patristic and medieval sources, but their concern to defend traditions with little basis in fact and their tendency to use the Latin Vulgate as their authoritative text seriously compromises their value.[118]

The first scholar to show signs of the 'modern' approach to the Pastoral Epistles was Johann David Michaelis (1717-1791), who accepted their Pauline authorship but focused his attention on the historical setting in which they were written.[119] Michaelis drew attention to what he saw as Paul's desire to strengthen Timothy's authority in the church, an emphasis which led others to question whether that would not have been a post-Pauline development. Whether he intended it or not, Michaelis set the stage for the modern debate about what is now called the *Sitz im Leben* of the text. Do the Pastoral Epistles reflect the situation in the church, especially at Ephesus, in the time of Paul, or must they be placed a generation or more later because the apostolic communities had not developed to the extent that the Pastoral Epistles appear to assume during the lifetime of the apostle? On that question, all future commentaries would be based, and the answer their authors gave to it would largely determine whether they should be ranked among the 'liberal' or 'conservative' guilds of Biblical interpreters.

Commentators of the early modern period generally retained the outlook of their ancient and medieval predecessors but they placed more emphasis on the teaching office of the apostles and their disciples, and therefore on the needs of the congregations to which they ministered. They also stressed the need for commentators to master the ancient languages, which they did

---

[117] Johann Albrecht Bengel, *Gnomon Novi Testamenti* (Tübingen: Fues, 1855).
[118] For a discussion of them and their work, see Johnson (2001), pp. 40-1.
[119] J. D. Michaelis, *Introduction to the New Testament*, 4 vols (Cambridge: J. Archdeacon, 1793-1801), IV.

to an exceptional degree. Modern readers must occasionally dissent from their conclusions but they recognize that the methods they employed were similar to the ones that we still use today and that their interpretations are often respectable by modern standards, even if alternatives are frequently preferred.

## The modern period

Michaelis' emphasis on the need to situate the writings of the New Testament in their historical context soon led to questions being raised about the Pastoral Epistles, and in particular about 1 Timothy. In 1804, J. E. C. Schmidt (1772–1831) pointed out how difficult it was to find an adequate context for that epistle, though he did not express any doubts about its Pauline authorship.[120] But three years later Friedrich Schleiermacher (1768–1834), who launched a full-scale attack on its authenticity, developing arguments that in some cases are still being recycled today.[121] One that is no longer heard was Schleiermacher's conviction that 2 Timothy and Titus were both authentic but that 1 Timothy was too different from either of them to be accepted as Pauline. His approach was entirely literary and linguistic, and it must be admitted that 1 and 2 Timothy are quite different from each other. It is entirely plausible that they were written at different times and in quite different circumstances, but whether that justifies us in saying that they must have had different authors is much less certain. Schleiermacher's claim that the similarities between 1 Timothy and Titus can be explained by saying that the pseudonymous author of the former copied the latter, and did so badly, was pure guesswork on his part and the argument seems to have died with him.

On the other hand, Schleiermacher's belief that there is a distinctive Pauline 'style' of writing that can be identified and used as a criterion for judging the authenticity of the entire Pauline corpus has proved remarkably resilient, despite its many obvious weaknesses. Schleiermacher was untroubled by such considerations as context and the presence (or absence) of an amanuensis, nor did he have the linguistic resources that now allow us to show that the 'unique' vocabulary of the Pastorals is not so strange after all, but none of this has had much effect on those who have swallowed his basic premise. Of course, Schleiermacher also pointed out that the form of

---

[120] J. E. C. Schmidt, *Historisch-kritische Einleitung ins Neue Testament* (Giessen: Tasche und Müller, 1804).
[121] F. Schleiermacher, *Über den sogenannten Ersten Brief des Paulus an den Timotheus: Ein kiritisches Sendschreiben an J. C. Gass* (Berlin: Realsculbuchhandlung, 1807).

1 Timothy is different from most of Paul's letters, in that it was addressed to a single individual rather than to a church (though that was also true of 2 Timothy and Titus!), that it is difficult to determine at what point in his career Paul would have written the letter, and that the details of church order which it contains seem to be too advanced for the first decades of his mission.

There is one important point on which Schleiermacher was absolutely clear. If 1 Timothy was not written by Paul then it was a deliberate forgery and ought not to be included in the canon of Scripture because its author was guilty of moral turpitude. Subsequent generations have continued to wrestle with this problem, because although it has proved to be fairly easy to doubt their Pauline authorship, it has been impossible to dislodge the Pastorals from the New Testament canon. The logical, if somewhat unsatisfactory, result of this is that there is now a widespread tendency to ignore the Pastorals when discussing Paul and to discount them in discussions about what the theology of the early church actually was.

The doubts that Schleiermacher expressed concerning 1 Timothy were soon extended to the other Pastorals by his contemporary, Johann Gottfried Eichhorn (1752–1827).[122] One consequence of this was that Eichhorn disagreed with Schleiermacher about the authorship of the Epistles, maintaining that all three were written by the same person, but that he was not Paul! Eichhorn was followed by Wilhelm De Wette (1780–1849), whose 'brief' commentary on the Pastorals repeated earlier arguments and added that the pseudepigrapher had clearly fallen away from the pure teaching of the apostle – evidence of the decline of the church into a form of legalism that would not be challenged until the Protestant Reformation or fully overcome until the nineteenth century![123]

The growing belief that the Pastoral Epistles represented a post-apostolic and essentially aberrant form of Christianity that would eventually take over the church in the form of 'Catholicism' was fully developed by Ferdinand Christian Baur (1792–1860), the founder and chief ideologue of what became known as the Tübingen School of New Testament interpretation.[124] Baur moved beyond merely doubting the authenticity of the Pastoral Epistles to offering an alternative scenario that could explain their origin. In his mind, they were written at Rome in the middle of the second century as a response to the threat posed by Marcion and the Gnostics of the time and were a major

---

[122] J. G. Eichhorn, *Einleitung in das Neue Testament*, 3 vols (Leipzig: Weidmannische Buchhandlung, 1812). Eichhorn's critique is in the third volume, part 1.

[123] W. M. L. De Wette, *Kurze Erklärung der Briefe an Titus, Timotheus und die Hebräer* (Leipzig: Weidmannische Buchhandlung, 1844).

[124] F. C. Baur, *Die sogennanten Pastoralbriefe* (Tübingen: Fues, 1835). On the Tübingen School in general, see H. Harris, *The Tübingen School* (Oxford: Clarendon Press, 1975).

ingredient in the effort of the Roman church to concentrate authority in its own hands. Working from that presupposition, Baur soon concluded that only four New Testament letters were genuinely Pauline (Romans, 1 and 2 Corinthians, and Galatians). His scepticism opened the door to even more radical denials of Pauline authorship, to the point where Bruno Bauer (1809–1882) was able to claim that the entire corpus of letters was a forgery.[125] That was going too far, and eventually Philippians, Philemon and 1 Thessalonians were reinstated as genuine, at least in the eyes of most scholars. Colossians, Ephesians and 2 Thessalonians found themselves in a grey zone of 'disputed' letters, but the Pastorals continued to be regarded as pseudepigraphal. This compromise position was developed and virtually canonized by Heinrich Julius Holtzmann (1832–1910) whose thorough study of the then available evidence set the standard for the critical approach that has continued to the present day.[126]

Holtzmann was both more thorough in his treatment and more subtle than his predecessors, but in essence he followed them. The supposed opponents of the apostolic teaching were still second-century Gnostics, there were serious inconsistencies between the Pastorals and the other Pauline letters and the church order described in them could not have existed in Paul's time. Holtzmann also saw his critique as part of the nineteenth century battle between Protestants and Catholics over the origins of the church. At a time when Rome was claiming that its ecclesiastical polity went straight back to the apostles and enjoyed an infallible, divine authority, it is perhaps not surprising that Holtzmann's opposition to that was as strong and as welcome in non-Roman Catholic circles as it was. But however understandable his position may have been in the political context of his time, its claim to be scientifically based is no more plausible than the dogmatic assertions of Rome are. In the words of Luke Timothy Johnson,

> The compromise position ... represented a retreat from a genuinely rigorous application of hard criteria applied to all Paul's letters, in favour of a much softer appeal to sensibility, what seemed 'more Pauline' to most scholars. And once 'most scholars' read from within a single construal, arguments are no longer really needed ... An observer is tempted to suggest that the expulsion of the Pastorals [from the Pauline

---

[125] B. Bauer, *Kiritk der paulinischen Briefe* (Berlin, 1850–1852).
[126] H. J. Holtzmann, *Die Pastoralbriefe kritisch und exegetisch behandelt* (Leipzig: Englemann, 1880). On the wider New Testament canon, see H. J. Holtzmann, *Lehrbuch der historisch-kritischen Einleitung in das Neue Testament*, 3rd edition (Freiburg: Mohr [Paul Siebeck], 1892).

Introduction 65

canon] was the sacrifice required by intellectual self-respect if scholars were to claim critical integrity and still keep the Paul they most wanted – and needed.[127]

In other words, rejection of the authenticity of the Pastoral Epistles has now become a critical dogma, justified more on ideological than on scientific grounds, which modern liberal scholars need in order to preserve the kind of 'Paul' they have constructed from the letters they imagine to be genuinely his. It is a sad, and indeed a scandalous, example of how an ideologically motivated position can be defended in the face of all evidence to the contrary and imposed as incontrovertible dogma by those who claim to be operating from a standpoint of academic objectivity.

But although Holtzmann's scepticism has retained the centre ground of New Testament studies for the past century and a half, it is remarkable how many commentators continue to advocate Pauline authorship of the Pastoral Epistles. Indeed, it would not be too much to say that most of the major full-length works on them have come down on the side of their authenticity, and that they have been written from a variety of theological and ecclesiastical perspectives, making it impossible to regard them as special pleading for one particular point of view.[128]

Opposition to the critical dismissal of the authenticity of the Pastoral Epistles is as old as the criticism itself. Schleiermacher was strongly opposed by a number of his contemporaries, who were quick to point out weaknesses and fallacies in his arguments.[129] After Baur's more detailed rejection of the Pastorals there was another round of opposing voices, which demolished his presuppositions and pointed out that it is impossible to define who the opponents censured in 1 Timothy actually were, that Jewish influences in the Pastorals were too strong for a second-century dating to be plausible and that the church organization they reflect is much less structured than Baur and his colleagues had maintained.[130] All these points continue to be

---

[127] Johnson (2001), p. 48.
[128] For lists of these, see D. Guthrie, *The Pastoral Epistles* (London: Tyndale Press, 1957), and Johnson (2001), pp. 49–50.
[129] H. Planck, *Bemerkungen über den ersten paulinischen Brief and den Timotheus* (Göttingen, 1808); J. A. L. Wegschneider, *Der erste Brief des Apostels Paulus an den Timotheus neu übersetzt und erklärt, mit Beziehungen auf die neuesten Untersuchungen über die Authentie desselben* (Göttingen: Apud Röwerum, 1810); M. J. H. Beckhaus, *Specimen observationum de vocabulis hapax legomenois et varioribus dicendi formulis in primam epistolam ad Timotheum obviis* (Lingae, 1810).
[130] M. Baumgarten, *Die Ächtheit der Pastoralbriefe* (Berlin: Dehmigke, 1837); C. S. Matthies, *Erklärung der Pastoralbriefe, mit besonderer Beziehung auf Authentie und Ort und Zeit der*

made by conservative critics of the liberal consensus and if anything, their validity is more easily demonstrated today than it was then. The major difficulty for the conservative side is one of chronology. Can the Pastoral Epistles be fitted in to a defined period in Paul's life? It seems clear that 2 Timothy, which was definitely a prison epistle, must be placed towards the end of the apostle's career, but neither 1 Timothy nor Titus contains any hint of his imprisonment and so cannot be regarded as especially late. The main difference of opinion among conservative commentators today is whether these two epistles should be placed sometime in the late 50s, when Paul was still active in Ephesus and Corinth, or whether they belong to a supposed period of grace in the early 60s, after Paul had been set free in Rome and before his rearrest. That, of course, depends on belief in a second imprisonment, distinct from the one recorded in Acts 28, for which explicit evidence is lacking.[131] But differences of this kind are minor compared to the more fundamental question of Pauline authorship. Whether 1 Timothy and Titus were penned in the 50s or in the 60s, conservatives all agree that they came from the hand of Paul himself, and that is the key point at issue among them. Other questions, like the identity of Paul's opponents and the structure of church government remain of interest and are still debated, but the general consensus seems to be that our relative lack of evidence makes firm conclusions on such matters impossible. Broadly speaking, this is still the state of conservative scholarship today, which if anything is more active and persuasive than it has ever been.

Yet in spite of the strong resurgence of conservative opinion in recent years, the critical position elaborated by Holtzmann continues to hold sway in general surveys of the New Testament, even if they occasionally nod in the direction of the conservative view and acknowledge how strong it is among serious scholars. Few topics in New Testament studies are in more urgent need of revisiting at the present time, and it is the position of this commentary that a theological approach to the questions involved can only help to further the rehabilitation of the Pastoral Epistles as an integral part of the authentic Pauline corpus.

The modern interpretation of the Pastoral Epistles has concentrated heavily on the background that lies behind them. Both conservative and more radical

---

*Abfassung derselben* (Greifswald: Mauritius, 1840); A. Wiesinger, *Biblical Commentary on St Paul's Epistles*, trans. J. Fulton (Edinburgh: T&T Clark, 1851), pp. 147–256.

[131] If there was a second imprisonment, it is generally agreed among conservative commentators that 2 Timothy almost certainly belongs to it and not to the first one, though (as with everything else) that cannot be proved. In any case, the difference in dating would not be very great – AD 67 perhaps, instead of AD 63 or so.

commentators have taken a great interest in what the underlying motive(s) for writing them might have been and they read the texts looking for clues as to the nature of the churches which Paul was addressing through Timothy and Titus. This has led them to espouse theories of social organization which may or may not have existed or been influential in the early church. It has also led some to probe the state of Roman law in the first century, and the nature of the imperial cult, which is supposed to have had a bearing on the composition of the Pastorals. But far more important than either of these has been the ongoing search for the 'opponents' of Paul. In the words of Luke Timothy Johnson,

> Identifying the opponents in the Pauline letters has been one of the enduring preoccupations of scholars working within the historical-critical paradigm. The motivation is straightforward. If Paul's opponents can be connected to some specific group in antiquity about which we have complementary evidence, then his all-too-oblique responses may gain greater intelligibility and the character of the struggles in which he was engaged may become clearer. The methodology used for determining opponents has often left much to be desired, but such considerations have not prevented repeated and repetitive efforts.[132]

It will be apparent from this that the modern quest is elusive and unlikely to reach any solid conclusions, due to lack of evidence, but that there is enough material for scholars to chew on endlessly as they seek to reconstruct their own speculative models of what the churches described in the Pastoral Epistles were like. It may be less obvious, but it is even more significant, that this historical quest serves mainly to distance the Pastoral Epistles from the modern church. The more we claim to understand what was going on in the first century, the more we are liable to think that it is too different from our own situation to have much practical application today. This is particularly evident when it comes to the question of women and the place they occupied in the apostolic congregations. Everyone today recognizes that the role of women in the ancient world was very different from what it is in Western societies today, and most modern commentators have not hesitated to state that the ancients were wrong and we are right, making it not only desirable but necessary to abandon the plain teaching attributed to Paul as a typical, first-century Jew and thus call into question the usefulness of the Pastorals for Christian life and ministry today. Here, perhaps more than anywhere else

---

[132] Johnson (2001), p. 390.

in the New Testament, the disconnect between modern thought and Biblical teaching becomes too obvious to ignore or explain away. The result has often been that the Pastoral Epistles are effectively omitted from contemporary expositions of Pauline thought and often discounted in the affairs of the church, particularly when questions relating to women's ministry come into view. Those who wish to defend the Pastorals and apply them on the ground that they are just as relevant to our situation as they were to that which they originally addressed face an uphill battle in trying to convince both the academic and the ecclesiastical establishment that such 'conservatism' is not only justified but is in fact the only way that we can do justice to what the texts themselves proclaim is God's abiding Word to his people.

# 1 Timothy

## Chapter 1

- 1-2 Paul's opening greeting and salutation
- 3-7 Warnings about false teachers
- 8-11 The law and those who break it
- 12-17 The conversion of Paul
- 18-20 Paul's charge to Timothy

## Chapter 2

- 1-4 The universal mission of the church
- 5-7 The mediator and his messenger
- 8-15 Men and women in the church

## Chapter 3

- 1-7 The overseer
- 8-13 The deacons
- 14-16 The mystery of godliness

## Chapter 4

- 1-5 The danger of false asceticism
- 6-10 Training for godliness
- 11-16 Self-discipline

## Chapter 5

| | |
|---|---|
| 1-2 | Relationships within the church |
| 3-16 | Widows |
| 17-22 | Elders |
| 23-25 | Timothy's self-discipline |

## Chapter 6

| | |
|---|---|
| 1-2 | Slaves and their masters |
| 3-5 | The character of the false teacher |
| 6-10 | Wealth |
| 11-12 | The good fight of faith |
| 13-16 | Paul's charge to Timothy |
| 17-19 | The rich |
| 20-21 | Final salutation |

# 1 Timothy 1

## 1-2. Paul's opening greeting and salutation

*1. Paul, an apostle of Christ Jesus by the command of God our Saviour and of Christ Jesus our hope, 2. To Timothy, my loyal child in the faith: Grace, mercy and peace from God the Father and Christ Jesus our Lord.*

The opening salutation in 1 Timothy is considerably more elaborate that what we find elsewhere in the Pauline corpus.[1] Paul's standard approach, found in the majority of his letters, begins with an assertion of his apostleship 'by the will of God' and then moves on to the addressee(s) and the formal greeting. Here, however, we find him introducing himself as 'an apostle of Christ Jesus by the *command* of God our Saviour and of Christ Jesus our hope'. The somewhat vague term 'will' is replaced by the more specific 'command', and 'God' is defined more precisely as 'our Saviour' along with 'Christ Jesus our hope', a description of him that is not found anywhere else in the New Testament, though the sentiment it conveys is common enough.[2] The salutations at the beginning of letters are important, not only because they identify who is writing, but also because they tell the recipient what he is expected to think about the sender and how he should relate to him. The surprise here is that the greeting is so formal. Since Paul and Timothy knew each other very well, the apostle did not have to explain who he was, and certainly not in such elevated tones as the ones used here. Timothy did not need to be told what Paul's apostleship meant or where it had come from, so Paul's self-description was obviously not intended just for him. The apostle was defining his commission from God as a prelude to his teaching because his message was geared for a wider audience that did not share Timothy's relationship to him and may not have fully understood the nature of his calling, or been so willing to accept his authority. By choosing the terms he did, Paul was looking beyond Timothy to the church for which he had

---

[1] Martin Luther (1973), p. 217, somewhat oddly, seemed to think that it was *less* formal and elaborate than was the norm for Paul.
[2] See, for example, 1 Cor. 15.12-19; Gal. 2.20-21; Eph. 2.12; Phil. 3.10-11; Col. 1.27.

responsibility. He was directing his readers' thoughts to certain aspects of his ministry to which he wanted them to pay special attention, because they formed the foundation for the teaching that he was about to give them.[3]

It hardly needs to be said that the uniqueness and somewhat grandiose nature of this salutation, addressed to a close colleague, is an argument against the case for pseudonymity. A pseudepigrapher would surely either have copied a recognized Pauline greeting taken from another of his letters, or else adopted a much more familiar style, in keeping with the friendship between the two men. From that point of view, the opening lines of 1 Timothy make no sense and would surely have aroused suspicion in its first readers. It is much more plausible that the author was indeed Paul, who wrote in the way he did because he had the freedom to depart from what might have been expected of him in the circumstances and because he wanted to back Timothy up in his ministry. For his part, Timothy would have recognized that underlying intention and been grateful to his mentor for offering him such strong support as he sought to apply the apostle's teaching to a particular congregation.

Paul's claim to be called an 'apostle' is well known and is the basis for what follows. He believed that it was his apostleship that justified and defined the teaching authority that had been entrusted to him, though he did not explicitly say so in this letter. His readers would have known that Paul was not a 'normal' apostle, because he had not been a disciple of Jesus during his earthly ministry nor had he seen the Risen Christ in the forty days between his resurrection and his ascension. They would also have known that although this compromised Paul's claim to apostleship in the eyes of some, he claimed the authority he did because God had expressly commanded him to be his messenger to the Gentiles.[4] Like the other apostles, he was a witness to the Risen Christ but in an unusual way.[5] For Paul, being an apostle was not the natural consequence of having been a disciple of the earthly Jesus but the direct result of a divine intervention by which God had called him for a particular purpose.[6] Perhaps because of that, his letter to Timothy was not a memoir of past experiences but a forward-looking programme of action, which he wanted Timothy and his congregation(s) to receive as a word from God that they were expected to implement.[7] It is this awareness of his calling

---

[3] Calvin (1964), pp. 184, 187, made much of this in the introduction to his commentary and in his remarks on the salutation.
[4] Gal. 2.7-10.
[5] 1 Cor. 15.8.
[6] Gal. 1.15-16.
[7] Compare him with Peter, who did not hesitate to base his apostolic authority on his recollections of Jesus during his earthly ministry. See 2 Pet. 1.16-18.

to a teaching mission that underlies Paul's self-description as an apostle – what he wrote to Timothy was by extension God's instruction to the church. That was the message he wanted to convey and it is for that reason that his letter was preserved and included in the canon of the New Testament.

From his use of the word 'apostle' elsewhere, we can assume that Paul understood that his chief calling was to proclaim the gospel of Christ and to persuade people to submit to it. Ironically, this comes out most clearly in his description of others as 'false apostles'.[8] They were doing the same thing as Paul was, but in the wrong way. The false apostles believed that they were proclaiming the gospel and they were persuading others to accept it; the problem lay in the content of their message. They could not be faulted for lack of zeal or a sense of mission, but they had misunderstood the gospel and were misrepresenting it. They were as dangerous as they were because they looked and acted like true messengers of Christ but were claiming that the only way Gentiles could follow him was to become Jews first. It was that which made their teaching false and which obliged Paul to warn his congregations not to accept a counterfeit as the real thing.[9]

The use of the inverted form 'Christ Jesus' is typical of Paul and may emphasize the importance of the Son of God's Messianic role. It is unfortunate that the Hebrew *Mashiach* (Messiah), which was translated into Greek as *Christos* ('anointed') became fixed in that form as a personal name, which obscures its true meaning and purpose. By reversing what to us is the 'normal' order of the names, Paul may have been reminding his readers that it was the anointing that defined who Jesus was and not the other way round. It may also be a sign of Paul's Jewish background, since for most Jews the general Messianic hope was more important than the precise identity of the Messiah. Many Jews in Paul's day were expecting a Saviour figure who would come to rescue Israel and re-establish the kingdom of David and Solomon on a permanent, and spiritually perfect, basis. This Messiah would have to be a descendant of David, but which one of them he would be and how he would make himself known was uncertain. What we can say for sure though, is that Jesus of Nazareth was not what they were looking for. Those Jews who accepted him as the Messiah had to revise their expectations of what the Messiah should be and do. Jesus was not the warrior king of their imaginations, but a prophetic figure who would sacrifice himself in order to obtain a spiritual kingdom that was not of this world. Furthermore – and this seems to have been a major sticking point – his messiahship would not be confined to the Jewish people but would extend to the whole world.

---

[8] 2 Cor. 11.13.
[9] Gal. 1.6-9; 3.1-2.

Messianic Jews in Jesus' day longed for the regeneration of Israel, but they showed little or no interest in extending that regeneration to anyone outside their own nation.

The Christian claim was that the Son of God had become incarnate as an Israelite, a child of the Mosaic covenant, in order to occupy and fulfill the three great covenant offices of prophet, priest and king. These were identified by the anointing of those who were called to them. It was therefore as the Anointed One that Jesus accomplished the tasks for which the covenant offices were designed, and did so in a way that made them redundant. There were Israelites like Habakkuk who had been prophets and priests, and others, like David, who had been prophets and kings, but nobody had been all three. In particular, no Israelite had ever been a priest-king. The only such person recognized by Israel was Melchizedek, to whom Abraham had paid a tithe, but he was unique.[10] Long before the appearance of Jesus, Melchizedek was acknowledged as a 'priest for ever', without father or mother, and without successors.[11] Jesus was explicitly equated with him because of the exceptional nature of his priesthood, which reinforced the significance of his anointing and joined it to the kingly role that the Messiah was expected to fulfill.[12]

In addition to that, Jesus had performed the duties assigned to the covenant offices in a unique way. The Old Testament prophets had been commissioned to proclaim a word that was not theirs but that came from God. The priests were appointed to sacrifice a spotless lamb for their own sins as well as for those of the people, and the kings were called to rule over a kingdom that was frequently in rebellion against them and that was eventually divided and conquered. But Jesus came to proclaim himself, to give himself as the sin offering, and to rule over God's people by uniting them in his body. He was a prophet who *was* the Word, a priest who *was* the sacrificial victim and a king whose presence *was* the kingdom. In sum, he was the Anointed one in a way that nobody else had ever been or ever could be, and by using the form 'Christ Jesus' the apostle draws attention to his uniqueness in a subtle but effective way.

The name 'Jesus' is significant in its own right, because it is the name of Joshua, the man who succeeded Moses and who entered into the land that had been promised to Abraham. Unfortunately, as with the name 'Christ', the preservation of the Greek form of the name has obscured this connection, at least in English and most other Western European languages.[13] Paul's hearers

---

[10] Gen. 14.17-20. Melchizedek was not an Israelite, of course.
[11] Ps. 110.4.
[12] Heb. 5.6-10; 6.20-7.21.
[13] In Greek, the two men are distinguished as Jesus the Prophet (Jesus Navé), using the Hebrew word *nabi* in a slightly Hellenized form, and Jesus the Messiah (Christ).

however would have understood 'Christ Jesus' as Joshua the Messiah, the designated heir of Moses and the one who brought the promises of the law to fulfillment in the gospel. The theological significance of this connection should not be underestimated. Jesus was the fulfillment of the promises made to Moses, the one who entered the true promised land and took possession of it. Everything in the Hebrew Scriptures pointed to him, and only in that context could they be interpreted properly.

The phrase 'command of God' underlines the fact that God's will is definitive and cannot be disregarded. When he reveals his will to us, it becomes our command. God's will was determined from all eternity, and although it was expressed as coming from the Father, it was common to all three members of the Trinity. When Jesus prayed in the Garden of Gethsemane that the Father's will, and not his, should be done, he did not mean that there was a difference between the will of the Father and that of the Son.[14] What that verse tells us is that Jesus had two wills – the divine will which he shared with the Father and the Holy Spirit, and a human will, which did not want to die. In speaking the way he did, Jesus demonstrated that he was a psychologically normal human being, not someone with a death wish, which would have compromised the nature of his sacrifice. In the Garden of Gethsemane he submitted his human will to his divine one, thereby bringing the two wills into perfect union and setting us an example of how we too must submit our will to God's if we are to be his children.

In relation to the command given to Timothy, John Chrysostom noted that there is no indication anywhere in the New Testament that the Father told Paul what to do; rather it was the Son. But as he went on to remark,

> whatever the Son commands, this he [Paul] considers to be the commandment of the Father, as those of the Spirit are the commandments of the Son ... What then? Does it derogate from the power of the Son, that his apostle was sent forth by the commandment of the Father? By no means. For observe how he represents the power as common to both.[15]

It is the call to obedience that lies behind Paul's use of the word 'command' in this verse. The Greek term *epitagē* can be used of a formal document, and that may be implied here. It was the equivalent of the Latin *mandatum*, the term used by the Romans to describe an imperial rescript. This lends support to the theory that 1 Timothy is a 'mandate letter' modelled on the practice

---

[14] Mt. 26.39, 42; Lk. 22.42.
[15] John Chrysostom, *Homilies on* 1 Timothy, 1.1 (NPNF 13, p. 408).

of the Roman administration, and that the *epitagē* in question is more than just an oral instruction. It must certainly be distinguished from the sort of commands that are given on particular occasions and limited to them; Paul's commission was a permanent one and had serious long-term implications for his authority as a teacher. What he said and did was authorized by the same divine mandate that had been given to him to be an apostle, so that what he taught the church had God's authority whether it is derived from a specific set of instructions or not. Even when Paul told a congregation that what he was giving them was his opinion, and not a message that he had received directly from God, the divine *epitagē* was his justification for doing this, and it constituted the basis of the spiritual authority that his statements had in the life of the church.[16]

However, although there may be some resemblance between Paul's letter and an imperial rescript, the divine *epitagē* cannot really be compared to an instruction from the emperor. The difference between them is greater than any similarity because it is the difference between their respective authors. What God commands is universal and absolute, whereas what the emperor ordered was relative and restricted to the limits of his jurisdiction. Superficial similarities, if there are any, cannot override this fundamental incompatibility, and there would have been no doubt in anyone's mind as to which of the two deserved to be given priority. The urge to find similarities between Pauline practice and contemporary secular usages must not be pushed to the point of suggesting that the apostle was dependent on the surrounding culture for his approach, let alone for the content of his message to the church. If a precedent has to be sought for his behaviour, it is to be found in the commission given to the Old Testament prophets, who were also called and commissioned by God – frequently against their will. Secular equivalents, if there were any, were mere caricatures of that, just as the pagan gods were at best pale imitations of the real one.

The word 'God' is not specified as referring only, or even primarily, to the Father, but the juxtaposition of 'Christ Jesus' steers us in that direction. The point that Paul was making here is that it is *God* who is our Saviour, not just the Son, and not just the man Jesus of Nazareth.[17] The theological implications of this are several:

---

[16] 1 Cor. 7.40.
[17] Towner (2006), p. 97, draws attention to this but claims that by referring to God as 'our Saviour' Paul was *suppressing* the Christological dimension of the title, which is found in the other Pastorals and elsewhere in the New Testament. It seems unnecessary to adopt so extreme an interpretation. More probably, Paul was concerned to emphasize that God the Father is our Saviour, and that he sent his Son as proof of his commitment to us and the basis of our hope that the promise of salvation would be realized.

1. Our salvation is the work of our Creator. There was a temptation in the early church, manifested in the various Gnostic heresies but not confined to them, to say that the Father of Jesus Christ was a Redeemer who was superior to the Creator God of Israel. The logic behind this was that if the Creator God had been the Father of Jesus he would have made a perfect world that would not have needed redemption. But since the world is not perfect, it could not have been made by the supremely perfect God, who instead appeared in the image of his Son as its Redeemer. What Paul says here contradicts that idea, whether it had been consciously expressed in his time or not. No Jew could have accepted such a theology, and Paul was too deeply rooted in the Hebrew Scriptures to have been open to the possibility that there could be a god higher than the Creator who revealed himself in the Old Testament. In his mind, the Creator and the Redeemer were one.

2. The sin of the world does not derive from the creation, but from something that has gone wrong by the will of creatures who had been given the freedom to disobey their Creator. In other words, evil is not intrinsic in nature, but an aberration caused by disobedience. This disobedience began in the spiritual world, with the revolt of Satan and his minions (whom we now call 'demons' or 'devils') and extended to the human race by Satan's success in tempting Adam and Eve to follow him instead of God. The fact that this disobedience was not inevitable but was the result of a deliberate and sinful choice means that both the demons and human beings are responsible for the situation in which they now find themselves. They are not innocent in God's eyes and cannot be absolved from the punishment that their disobedience has incurred. It is to deal with this problem that God the Father sent his Son into the world to take our punishment on himself and so save those who believe in him.

3. Salvation for human beings is possible. By becoming a man and taking our place on the cross, the Son of God paid the price of our sin and opened the way to restoring believers to the divine fellowship enjoyed by the Trinity and the angels that did not rebel. Had 'sin' been an intrinsic part of human nature, there would have been no hope of salvation, because the mere fact of existing would have cut humanity off from God. Salvation would then have been possible only by ceasing to exist as a consciously distinct being, a belief that is common to Buddhism (Nirvana) and to some forms of ancient Greek philosophy, but completely alien to the Christian gospel.

4. Salvation is God's purpose. God did not give Paul his commission (*epitagē*) merely so that the apostle could preach the condemnation and destruction of the world. That was part of his message, to be sure, but it was always accompanied by the promise of redemption and renewal.

5. Salvation is the fruit of God's love for his creatures, however much they may have wandered away from him. As Jesus said to Nicodemus: 'God so loved the world that he gave his only-begotten Son.'[18] Commenting on this, John Calvin said,

> Therefore when we behold our salvation in the person of our Lord Jesus Christ, we must also look to the very head and fountain from which he came to us, that is to say, from this love which God had for mankind. And this is the reason why Saint Paul calls God our Saviour. He is telling us, by this word, that as often as we think upon the profit which Jesus Christ has brought us and we have received by him, we should lift up our hearts higher and know that God, having pity upon the lost state of all the flock of Adam, provided for us and gave us this remedy, namely our Saviour Jesus Christ, who came to draw us out of the bottomless pit of death.[19]

Paul then went on to tell his readers that the *epitagē* of God came also from 'Christ Jesus our hope'. The significance of this is twofold. First, it put Jesus on the same level as 'God' as the co-author of the command. The apostle did not elaborate on this, but the implications are clear. If Jesus had been inferior to God he would not have been able to issue a divine *epitagē*, nor would his name have been associated with it. He might have communicated it to Paul as a messenger from God, but in that case he would have been no different from an angel. Given the importance that the Epistle attaches to Christ's mediatorial role between God and man, his participation in authoring the divine command is a significant commentary on what that role is. He is not a third party mediating between God and mankind but God himself, who conveyed the Father's saving love to us by becoming a man.

Jesus is described as our hope because he is the one who has paid the debt that we owe to God and who pleads for us before the Father's throne. Without his intercession on our behalf we would be without hope in the world, a point that Paul also made elsewhere.[20] On the importance of this for the gospel message and its reception, W. D. Mounce has this to say:

> The promise of hope was one of Christianity's most outstanding features in a world in which hope had little place. Popular belief was dominated by pessimism. The philosophers had dismissed the Olympian gods

---

[18] Jn 3.16.
[19] Calvin (2016), p. 15.
[20] Eph. 2.12.

but had not replaced them with an alternative that provided hope for people. Most could see only the fear and senselessness of chance and the arbitrariness and finality of fate. Stoicism, perhaps the most influential philosophy among the cultured in the first century AD, taught an apathetic determinism in which individual choice and freedom were absent; one must simply accept whatever fate decides.[21]

It is because of Jesus that we have assurance of salvation and some knowledge of what that will mean when we die and go to be with him. The hope of the Christian is not just the forgiveness of sins (which we have already obtained), but the resurrection life that awaits us when we depart this world.[22] We have the promise that, in spite of the fact that we are still sinners, we can live in a way that pleases God here and now and look forward to a life to come that will be better than the one we now enjoy. That Paul should emphasize this in his opening salutation is an indication of what the rest of the epistle is about. He had been sent by God to preach salvation and the hope it gives us in Christ, and it was in furtherance of that mission that he was now writing to Timothy, and through him to the church at Ephesus.

After introducing himself and explaining his commission in this way, Paul moved on to the next item in his salutation – the identity of the letter's recipient. This was his experienced companion and co-worker Timothy, whom he described as his 'true child in the faith'.[23] The word Paul used for 'child' is *teknon*, which might better be translated as 'offspring' because it contains the idea of birth, which the word more commonly used for 'child' (*pais* or its diminutive *paidion*) does not. Of course Paul used *teknon* in a metaphorical sense, to describe the close relationship that he had with the younger man, who was not physically related to him. We know that Timothy learned a great deal from Paul and that Paul cared for him in a fatherly way, but there may have been more to their relationship than that. When writing to the Corinthian church Paul said, 'Though you have countless guides in Christ, you do not have many fathers. For I became your father in Christ Jesus through the gospel.'[24] It is therefore possible that Timothy was converted through Paul's preaching at Lystra, even though his mother and grandmother were already Christians and had brought him up knowing the

---

[21] Mounce (2000), p. 7.
[22] See Phil. 1.21-23.
[23] The NRSV says 'loyal child in the faith', but whereas 'loyal' and 'true' can be synonymous in English, this is not the main emphasis of the original Greek. Both the NIV and the ESV rightly prefer 'true' over 'loyal'.
[24] 1 Cor. 4.15.

Scriptures from birth, though we have no evidence that would confirm that.[25] Whether that was the case or not, there seems to be no doubt that Timothy's life was transformed by his encounter with Paul and the two men remained close for the rest of Paul's life.

Particularly significant here is the descriptive adjective *gnēsion* ('genuine, authentic') which expresses how Paul understood their relationship.[26] The basic meaning of *gnēsion* is readily apparent. Timothy was Paul's 'real' son, the disciple who understood his message, who believed and taught it faithfully and who could be relied upon to stick to it without compromise in the face of adversity. When Paul heard Timothy speak he heard himself – their minds met and they were fully united on all essential matters. This was of great importance to Paul, who had had too much experience of 'helpers' who had fallen away, and of converts who had failed to understand important aspects of his teaching. Knowing whom he could trust was not easy, even within his inner circle of associates, but Timothy stood out from many of the others. Paul did not say that he was the *only* one of his companions that he could rely on – Titus and Luke remained loyal to him through thick and thin and Paul addressed Titus in similar terms – but he was certainly one of a small number and particularly precious to the apostle for that reason.

The use of the words 'true child' also indicates how Paul envisaged the succession to his own ministry. Timothy could not become another apostle because he had not seen the Risen Christ, nor would he ever enjoy apostolic authority in the way that Paul did. This difference between them is made clear in the epistles which the two men jointly issued, where the salutation typically reads, 'Paul, an apostle of Christ Jesus and Timothy our brother.'[27] Timothy's relationship to Paul was close enough that he could be described as a member of the same family, with all the privileges and obligations that such a status conferred in the ancient world, but he could not step into Paul's shoes. He was Paul's colleague and helper, but not his heir, because his apostleship was a uniquely personal commission from God and would die with him.

Timothy's position explains how Paul understood what would eventually come to be called the 'apostolic succession'. That phrase was not used until many centuries later, and then it was in an institutional context far removed from the personal relationship between Paul and Timothy. In the Roman Catholic Church, the bishop of Rome is regarded as the successor of the apostle Peter, who is said to have been that city's first bishop. In Catholic teaching, 'apostolic succession' as applied to the papacy is not merely

---

[25] This point is made by Towner (2006), p. 99.
[26] Paul uses the same word in Phil. 2.20 to describe Timothy's unique relationship to him.
[27] See 2 Cor. 1.1; Col. 1.1; Phlm. 1.1.

historical, but is held to include the inheritance of the full apostolic powers of Peter, including the right to proclaim new doctrine that Christians have to believe in order to be saved.

Nothing like that can be found in the writings of Paul, or anywhere else in the New Testament, for that matter. Paul founded many churches but he was not their bishop in the later sense of that term, and none of his churches ever claimed him as such.[28] The ministry that he passed on to the next generation was not that of an apostle but of a preacher and teacher of the apostolic message. Furthermore, it was personal to individuals like Timothy and Titus and not connected to a particular office that would eventually be filled again by a designated successor. Timothy may have been the 'bishop' of Ephesus at the time the Epistle was written, though what that would have meant in his case is uncertain. He was certainly not the church's *episkopos* because Paul expected him to find somebody suited to that role and appoint him to it.[29] He undoubtedly performed some of the tasks that later bishops assumed, but in Timothy's time it would have been anachronistic to think of an *episkopos* in that way. People would probably have misunderstood what was meant if the title had been used of him, but this hardly matters. Paul delegated his pastoral ministry to Timothy because Timothy shared his beliefs to such an extent that there was no discernible difference between them. It was for that reason that Paul commissioned him to act on his behalf, but that commission was no more inheritable than Paul's apostleship was. This was the nature and extent of 'apostolic succession' insofar as such a term would have been understood in the first century, and only in that sense can it be used of Timothy. It would be better to call him an 'apostolic delegate' since Paul was still alive and Timothy was acting on his behalf, but we do not know whether his authority would have lapsed on Paul's death, as the term 'delegate' might imply. Timothy was certainly more like an ambassador from Paul than a successor to him, though perhaps the apostle saw him as continuing in that role after his own death, when Timothy would become the keeper of the apostolic tradition, or deposit of faith entrusted to him.

The essence of Paul's relationship to Timothy is expressed by the words 'in faith' which Paul appended to his salutation. There is no article in the Greek text, which makes it unclear whether Paul thought of 'faith' as a defined set of beliefs or as an attitude of heart and mind that testified to their shared relationship to Christ. Given that creedal statements did not exist at that time, it is going too far to say that their relationship was rooted in a

---

[28] The same can be said of Peter and probably of the other apostles as well.
[29] Assuming, that is, that there was only one *episkopos* in every congregation, which is not clear.

formal agreement on matters of doctrine, but Paul would not have spoken of Timothy in the way that he did if there was any discernible difference in what they believed. The two men were on the same page theologically, and it was that which determined Paul's attitude towards and shaped his confidence in his younger colleague. Formal creeds became necessary when heresies appeared that threatened to destroy the unity of the church's faith by falsely interpreting the apostolic teaching. In Timothy's case there was no such misunderstanding and therefore no need for a formal statement of belief. Creedal statements are superfluous when people are of one mind, though they serve as useful reminders of what that unity of faith ought to be and have become necessary in a world where the essentials of the Christian faith have been contested and denied, even by people claiming to be members of the church.

Paul concluded his salutation with a blessing similar to those that normally accompanied his letters, though there is the significant addition of the word 'mercy' that must be explained.[30] In his blessing, Paul made it clear that his earlier reference to 'God' referred primarily to God the Father, and he described Christ Jesus as 'our Lord' in the usual form. The use of this title implies that Paul thought of Christ as God, since the phrase 'our Lord' or 'my Lord' was the standard Jewish substitute for the unpronounced name of YHWH in the Hebrew Bible. If Paul did not believe in the divinity of Christ he would never have spoken of him in these terms, although he may have avoided calling Christ 'God' out of deference to Jewish monotheistic sensibilities.

What is really significant here is that the blessing is threefold – 'grace, mercy, peace'. Paul's normal style was to say 'grace and peace', which may have been an adaptation of the standard Greek *chairein* ('greeting') – replaced here by the similar-sounding *charis* ('grace') – and the addition of the Hebrew *shalom* ('peace'), which was (and still is) the standard Middle Eastern greeting. The phrase could then be understood as a combination of Greek and Hebrew that neatly reflected the composition of the early church. Whether Paul connected these two terms consciously is impossible to determine, but as the same formula is found in both 1 and 2 Peter, we should probably conclude that the phrase was in common use among Christians, whether they thought of it in terms of a Hebrew-Greek mixture or not.

The addition of 'mercy' in between these two is not unknown elsewhere – it occurs in 2 John, for example – but its appearance here (and in 2 Timothy,

---

[30] Theodore of Mopsuestia (2010), p. 527, drew attention to this and said that Paul added 'mercy' because of the great affection he had for Timothy.

though not in Titus) was a departure from Paul's usual practice and is probably significant for that reason. Given the standard form of greeting, it may well be that Paul wanted to put a special emphasis on 'mercy' by the rhetorical device of inserting it between two more familiar terms. Readers would have noticed the unusual insertion and perhaps paid special attention to it for that reason. Mercy is certainly a major theme of the Epistles and so it is not unreasonable to suppose that Paul was preparing his readers for that by adjusting his usual form of greeting in this way.[31] Many commentators have noticed the unusual addition of 'mercy' but none has developed the theme as much as Martin Luther, who wrote,

> Why does Paul add 'mercy' here? Every theologian has been established as a bishop of the church to bear the troubles of everyone in the church. He stands on the battle line. He is the prime target of all attacks, difficulties, anxieties, disturbances of consciences, temptations, and doubts. All these hit the bishop where it hurts. Still greater trials follow. The princes of this world and the very learned seek him out. He is made a spectacle for both devils and angels. So then, it is enough to pray for two things for the rest: that they be in grace and peace; yet for a bishop one must add 'mercy' not only that God would deign to give his grace that he might have forgiveness of sins and peace but that he would have constant mercy on him, that he would heap many gifts on him with which to serve his brothers; also, that God would grant his mercy because he constantly endures great tribulation.[32]

It is easy for modern commentators to find fault with this analysis – Timothy was probably not a 'bishop', certainly not in the traditional sense and the word 'mercy' was not added for that reason. But Luther's pastoral insight into the trials of a minister is striking and valid, so even if he is wrong in strictly exegetical terms, his words are true and edifying in themselves.[33]

---

[31] Calvin (1964), p. 1881, read the triad differently. He noticed that the introduction of 'mercy' was unusual, but ascribed it to Paul's extraordinary affection for Timothy. He then added that Paul had reversed the order of grace and mercy, saying that 'the reason why God at first receives us into favour and why he loves us is that he is merciful'. That is doubtless true, but it seems to misinterpret what Paul was really trying to say. Interestingly, he defends Paul's order in his sermon on the text; see Calvin (2016), pp. 19–20.
[32] Luther (1973), p. 219.
[33] Luther may have taken his cue from John Chrysostom, who said of this, 'Teachers stand more in need of mercy.' *Homilies on* 1 Timothy 1.2 (NPNF 13, 409).

Whatever the rhetorical function of Paul's triadic blessing may have been, there is no doubt that it follows a clear theological sequence. Grace is the foundation of the Christian life. Without it there could have been no salvation; indeed, it can be said that the creation itself was a work of divine grace! Mercy is important because it puts the emphasis on forgiveness. It is a reminder that we need that particular application of divine grace if we are to enjoy the kind of fellowship with God that he wants us to have with him.[34] Finally, peace is what results from the work of God's saving grace and mercy. We who were once enemies of God because of our sin and rebellion are now at peace with him, a theme which echoes and re-echoes through the Pauline corpus.[35] Such a theological approach may help us to decide what kind of triad the greeting is. Seen from the 'objective' standpoint of God's plan of salvation, it can be argued that grace is fundamental to the other two, since without it there would have been no mercy and therefore no peace either. But considered from the 'subjective' perspective of human experience, it may be said that grace and mercy are the necessary forerunners of that peace of God which passes understanding and is the special inheritance of those who believe in Christ.[36] Looked at in this way, the triadic greeting can be read according to either or both of the standard patterns. One of them emphasizes the sovereignty of God and the other stresses the practical outworking of that sovereignty in the life of the believer. There is no need to choose one pattern over the other; both are true and they complement one another. Paul may not have consciously intended that, but he would surely have agreed with such an interpretation of his words.

One final point to notice is that Paul's greeting does not mention the Holy Spirit. This apparent omission has sometimes been used as evidence that Paul did not believe in the Spirit's divinity but like all arguments from silence, that can be no more than speculation. To put it in context, none of the New Testament epistles employs a Trinitarian salutation, with the possible exception of 1 Peter, where the salutation is so elaborate that it can hardly be called a formulaic greeting at all. The argument against the existence of a Pauline Trinitarianism is refuted by a number of other texts where the Holy Spirit is clearly mentioned in a Trinitarian context. Most obvious is the closing blessing in 2 Cor. 13.14, but there are others, like Gal. 4.6, Eph. 2.18 and so on. Paul's doctrine of the Holy Spirit, including belief in his divinity,

---

[34] This point was made by John Calvin (2016), pp. 19–20.
[35] See especially Rom. 8.1.
[36] Phil. 4.7; Rom. 8.1.

must be based on a thorough study of his writings and not decided merely on the basis of the absence of any reference to him in the formulaic greetings at the beginning of his epistles.

It may also be said that Paul was moved by the Holy Spirit to write to Timothy, but that the Spirit spoke as the messenger of the Father and the Son without drawing attention to himself. In reading the words of Paul, Timothy was hearing the voice of the Spirit, pointing him to the command of God the Father and the Son. For that reason, the Epistle was (and is) regarded as Holy Scripture on a par with the already recognized canon of the Hebrew Bible, which had been given to Israel in a similar way.[37]

## 3-7. Warnings about false teachers

*3. I urge you, as I did when I was on my way to Macedonia, to remain in Ephesus so that you may instruct certain people not to teach any different doctrine, 4. and not to occupy themselves with myths and endless genealogies that promote speculations rather than the divine training that is known by faith. 5. But the aim of such instruction is love that comes from a pure heart, a good conscience, and a sincere faith. 6. Some people have deviated from these and turned to meaningless talk, 7. desiring to be teachers of the law, without understanding either what they are saying or the things about which they make assertions.*

This section gives us the main reasons why Paul decided to write to Timothy. He tells us that he left Timothy behind when he went on a journey from Ephesus to Macedonia, but there is no indication of how much time had elapsed since then. It is reasonable to assume from what the text says that Paul had not yet returned to Ephesus or met up with Timothy elsewhere, and that he was not planning to do so in the near future, since if he were, sending him a letter would have had little point. What we do not know is whether he was writing from Macedonia or had already moved on to somewhere else. Perhaps the latter option is preferable because Paul sent no greetings to Timothy from any of the Macedonian churches, which Timothy already knew well from his own missionary journeys with the apostle. Paul may have gone on to a place where Timothy had never been (Illyricum?) which would explain why there were no such greetings for him to send, but of course this is no more than speculation. What is certain is that his message to Timothy

---

[37] See 2 Pet. 1.21.

was based on their shared mission in Ephesus which he had now entrusted to his junior colleague but in which he continued to take a personal interest.

Theodore of Mopsuestia makes the interesting point that Paul 'asked' (or 'urged') Timothy to stay at Ephesus and work there on his behalf – he did not order Timothy to do so, as he might have done by pulling rank on the younger man. As Theodore saw it,

> the saints were zealous to summon all people to the work of true religion by entreaty, so that they might produce eagerness in them together with a certain delight of the mind. This is because an entreaty surely can animate even those who are quite indolent, while the weight of the command seems often to have made sluggish even the person grasped by eagerness.[38]

Paul reminds Timothy that he is merely repeating what he had told him before his departure, so it is clear that the apostle was well aware of the difficulties that Timothy had to face. He must have sensed that they were of a serious nature and would not be quickly resolved, which would explain why he felt obliged to repeat his counsel in writing. Timothy would have heard it all before, but by putting it in a letter Paul was speaking not only to him but to the church in general, reminding them that he had already shared his concerns with Timothy personally and encouraging them to support him in his efforts to resolve the difficulties that the Ephesian church was encountering.

The basic problem was that there were false teachers in Ephesus who were leading people astray, and Paul wanted Timothy to put that right. It does not seem that their errors involved heresy in a strictly doctrinal sense.[39] As far as we can tell, the false teachers were not denying the divinity of Christ or the message of the gospel. Instead of attacking the fundamentals of Christian belief, they were distracting the congregation by getting them caught up in secondary matters that led to endless (and pointless) discussions that helped nobody and solved nothing. Paul was concerned that church members might be led to think that the study of genealogies was of the essence of the faith, when in fact it was peripheral at best and fanciful at worst.

---

[38] Theodore of Mopsuestia (2010), p. 527. John Chrysostom, *Homilies on* 1 Timothy 1.3 (NPNF 13, 409) said much the same thing.

[39] Calvin (1964), pp. 188–9, analyses the Greek word *heterodidaskein* ('to teach differently') into form and substance. The false teachers may have altered the form of their presentation, or changed the content – or both. In fact, it may have been neither. What they appear to have been doing was teaching something else that was not germane to the subject, whether it was true or false in itself.

Interest in genealogy is a widespread phenomenon and is particularly common in oral cultures, where the deeds of the ancestors are passed on from one generation to another in the form of myths and legends. The Maori people of New Zealand, for example, all know what canoe their ancestors arrived in, and consider themselves to belong to that *waka*, as they call it. They may be right about this, but it is hard to say for sure, though the *waka* continues to play an important part in their social structures. The Somalis of East Africa also trace their ancestry back through many generations, and it forms an important part of their social and political life. The ancient Israelites were similar to this in some ways. Paul knew what tribe he belonged to (Benjamin) and most Jews of his time could trace their ancestry back a long way.[40] It was often not a simple matter, either. The two recorded genealogies of Jesus show that they could be based on different principles and contain apparently conflicting information without anyone being unduly concerned about this. Today we have lost the key to interpreting them, but the early Christians knew that there were different ways of calculating Jesus' ancestry and were not bothered by that. The genealogies made sense to those who composed (or transcribed) them, and that was what mattered most, though the differences between them were fertile ground for speculation by those who took an interest in such things.

The Hebrew Bible pays considerable attention to genealogy, both in Genesis and in 1 Chronicles, because Israelite religion was rooted in the nation's descent from Abraham. It was not as peripheral a subject to them as it might appear to us. It was by means of genealogy that the Jews established their identity as the people of God and that they determined what their relationship was to the surrounding nations. Historical accuracy in the modern sense was not their main concern, and dates are rarely given, so that it is impossible to reconstruct a connected narrative of the past on the basis of the genealogies alone. But they do describe how the different peoples of the Middle East were related to one another and they explain the origins of the well-known historical animosities between them. The Edomites, for example, were descended from Esau, Jacob's brother, who had robbed him of his birthright. The intimacy of the link recurs in the prophecy of Obadiah, who condemned Edom for not coming to the aid of its brother Judah,[41] and the Herodians who ruled in Judaea in the time of Jesus were also of Edomite (Idumaean) origin. It could therefore be argued that genealogy had a practical significance which made it important for people to study.

---

[40] Phil. 3.5. The two genealogies of Jesus remind us of this. See Mt. 1.1-17; Lk. 3.23-38. But note that Jesus is the only New Testament figure whose genealogy is recounted.
[41] Obad. 1.10-14.

There was also considerable interest in the ancient patriarchs, whose somewhat shadowy appearances in Genesis 4–11 led to considerable speculation about them. Enoch was a particular favourite, and a book attributed to him circulated widely in New Testament times, so widely in fact that it was quoted by Jude in his epistle.[42] The stories told about these men were legendary rather than historical (as we would now understand that term), but they were not necessarily fictitious. They may have had some factual basis that had been overlaid with other themes, rather like the stories of King Arthur. Paul used the Greek word *mythos* to describe these legends, but although he clearly disapproved of them, we should be careful not to equate this term with 'myth' as that word is popularly used today. He was not denouncing them because he thought they were *false* but rather because he considered them to be *irrelevant*.[43] The Christian gospel had not sidelined the ancient legends and genealogies by introducing a more accurate or scientific view of the past, but had made appeals to them redundant by altering the theological basis on which the identity of God's people was constituted.

This change of perspective went to the heart of the difference between Judaism and Christianity. The former remained rooted in the human ancestry of Israel but the latter distanced itself from that by welcoming people of every language, nation and tribe into its fellowship. Paul expended a great deal of energy expounding this – 'in Christ there is neither Jew nor Greek'.[44] What he was claiming in 1 Timothy was that those who focused on genealogy as if human ancestry made a difference to God had missed the point of the gospel. His qualification of the genealogies as *aperantoi* ('endless' or 'boundless') is a rhetorical exaggeration, but it reflects his sense of frustration at the colossal waste of time that tracing them was. There would always be lateral lines to follow, and gaps in the records that would be impossible to fill. Since the Christian's standing before God depended on his faith, not on his physical descent, working out the family tree was a waste of time and also self-indulgent, because it would allow some people to boast of their own immaculate pedigree and give them an excuse to look down on others who had apparently come from nowhere. Given that Jewish Christians were often tempted to think of themselves as superior to Gentile converts, promoting the study of genealogy would only feed their pride. It was therefore potentially

---

[42] Jude 1.14-15.
[43] Towner (2006), pp. 109–10, points out that the Greeks used *mythos* to describe tales that were both false and deceptive, and assumes that this is what Paul meant here. He may be right, but if so, the context suggests that the myths in question were elaborations on genealogies, which were not necessarily false or deceptive in nature.
[44] Gal. 3.28.

divisive and dangerous, quite apart from the fact that it made no difference to anybody's spiritual standing before God.

Paul warned Timothy that genealogical research would lead to *ekzēteseis*, a word that is perhaps best translated here as 'controversies'.[45] This phenomenon is familiar to anyone who has engaged in scientific investigation. Data are discovered that in themselves are objective facts, but they have to be interpreted in relation to other facts and according to criteria that may not be immediately obvious. Scholars constantly dispute the findings of their colleagues, by questioning not their existence (which is usually irrefutable) but their significance, and the large amount of genealogical data available, not least in the Old Testament, was fertile ground for this sort of argument. Paul was afraid that believers would miss the wood for the trees, and this fear explains what he said next.

As he expressed it to Timothy, people were in danger of quarrelling over trivial details rather than concentrating on the *oikonomia* of God in faith. *Oikonomia*, from which the word 'economy' derives, has a broad range of meaning in Greek. It is a compound of *oikos* ('house' or 'household') and *nomos* ('law') and its primary meaning was something like 'household management'. From there its range was extended to cover many forms of planning and governance, and in later times it was the word used to correspond to Latin *dispositio* or *dispensatio*. In the present context we should probably not take it quite that far, especially if we think of 'dispensation' in the covenantal sense in which it is most often encountered in theology today, but Paul's usage was certainly headed in that direction. For him, God's *oikonomia* was the plan, purpose and intention for which he had given the law in the first place. Even the Biblical genealogies were there for a reason, but their true meaning could only be understood in relation to faith. Hebrews 11 is the outstanding example of the outworking of this principle, but it is also intrinsic to Paul's argument about the significance of Abraham in Romans 2–4. The true children of Abraham were those who believed as he did, whether they were his physical descendants or not.

Modern commentators have had a good deal to say about the *oikonomia Theou*, putting great stress on the etymology of the term and linking it closely to household governance. There are differences of opinion as to whether the term refers more to the actual management of the house or to the underlying plan and purpose of God which decided the way that management would actually work out, but there is no need to make such a distinction here.

---

[45] And not merely 'speculations' as both the NRSV and the ESV have it. The NIV is better here.

A plan that was not implemented would have been useless, but so would activity that lacked a clear purpose. The two things must go together and we ought to retain both in our interpretation.[46]

The genealogical records preserved in the Bible are there to remind us of the faithfulness of past generations who preserved God's revelation to them and passed his promises on intact to their successors. As Christians, we have inherited those promises and must be grateful for that. When we read the Old Testament we must be aware of our debt to, and of our spiritual fellowship with, those who have gone before us and prepared the way for the coming of Christ. But to get caught up in obscure genealogical details is to be led astray by something that may appear to have a point but that in fact is a waste of time. As Paul knew only too well, *genealogia* could easily turn into *mataiologia*, the study of vanity, and those who got caught up in it found themselves being distracted from what really mattered.

It is important to emphasize that Paul was attacking the abuse of an essentially harmless and even edifying subject, rather than condemning something that was wrong in itself. This proves that what he objected to was unrelated to any of the Gnostic heresies of the second century which were much more serious threats to the church. The Gnostics created fantastic cosmologies which had a genealogical element but which went far beyond anything found in the Old Testament and were quite different in character. Hebrew genealogies had odd features that were hard to explain but they were dealing with real human beings. The Gnostic constructions were entirely fanciful and purported to describe the interrelationships of various supernatural phenomena, including what was really a family of divinities. Had Paul been confronted with that he would certainly have taken a much harder line than he did here, so it is unlikely that they had developed by the time he was writing. 1 Timothy predates Gnosticism, even if much of what it says could be used to counteract it once it appeared.

What was happening at Ephesus was typical of a phenomenon that repeats itself with depressing frequency in the life of the church. Open heresy is relatively rare, but subtle distractions are quite common. Those who are led astray in this way are convinced that they are doing something worthwhile, and superficially they may seem to be justified in this. After all, the Ephesian

---

[46] Marshall (2004), p. 367, puts the emphasis on actual management, whereas Johnson (2001), pp. 163–4, opts for the underlying order on which that management is based. Towner (2006), p. 113, sympathizes with Marshall but eventually sides with Johnson, as he says, 'the first thought is not of administration as ministry and responsibility, but of the shape of things and the ordering of life to be achieved through the various activities of ministry and service.' That may be true, but the first thought does not exclude a second one, which is equally important!

genealogists could claim to be following the example of Scripture and doing no more than interpreting it. In itself, this was no more evil than playing Scrabble using only words found in the Bible. It could even be argued that it sharpened the mind to perceive details that might otherwise be overlooked. But at the same time, this kind of activity lost the plot because it had no conception of the underlying purpose for which the law had been given. Because of that it was basically pointless and ultimately harmful, in that it obscured what really mattered and lost the heart of the gospel message in a mass of trivial footnotes, as we might say today.[47] John Calvin expressed the heart of the matter well when he said,

> all who do not apply the Word of God to good profit and use show contempt for and falsify good and wholesome doctrine. To be brief, the Word of God is profaned and made vile unless we apply it profitably, that we receive from it good instruction leading to our salvation. And so all that is uttered and delivered without bearing fruit, and serving nothing to the salvation of those who hear us, is said to be like a fable … God will not waste time with us in this way, nor be seen as an actor or entertainer.[48]

Paul commissioned Timothy to warn the Ephesians of this danger, but he made it clear what the purpose of the warning (*parangelia*) was. God never condemns something without saying why, and his ultimate purpose (*telos*) is always a positive one. So it is here. The warning was intended to produce an atmosphere of love (*agapē*) which, as Paul said in 1 Cor. 13, is the focal point of Christian faith. We are so familiar with this concept now that it is easy to forget how important it is. As W. D. Mounce has said,

> The concept of love runs throughout Scripture. God's love is the basis of redemption (Jn 3.16) and of a person's own love for both God and for others. The beauty of the word *agapē*, 'love', has often been pointed out. As a defined in Scripture, this love offers itself freely to someone who does not deserve it; this love does not seek to possess the beloved. There is little evidence for its secular use before the LXX, and whatever meaning it may have had is enhanced by Christian usage. It is a word that can be defined only within the context of Biblical theology.[49]

---

[47] This was the view of Ambrosiaster (2009), p. 121.
[48] Calvin (2016), p. 33.
[49] Mounce (2000), p. 23.

Love in this Christian sense would only be genuine and fruitful if it were based on three fundamental pillars. Once again, we see a rhetorical triad at work, based this time on an ascending sequence.[50] The three necessary ingredients of love are the following:

1. A pure heart (*kathara kardia*)
2. A good conscience (*agathē syneidēsis*)
3. Unfeigned, or sincere faith (*anhypokritos pistis*)

Paul began with the need for a 'pure heart', a theme that goes back to the Old Testament and is familiar to us from the Beatitudes in the Sermon on the Mount.[51] The pure in heart are those who will see God, said Jesus, and no doubt Paul had similar thoughts in his mind when he wrote this. The heart was considered to be the seat of the mind as well as of the emotions, and its purity was gauged by the conformity of a person's thoughts to the will of God. Paul wrote about this in 1 Corinthians, and it was clearly a subject that was very dear to him, as it was to Jesus.[52] To the pure, all things are pure, but if we do not start with that, then nothing will ever come right.[53] Thomas Aquinas put it well when he said,

> Is a pure heart required for charity? The answer is yes; for it is impossible for an impure heart to be prompt in regard to charity: because a thing loves that which is in conformity with it. But an impure heart loves that which conforms to it among the passions.[54]

A good conscience is one that is free from any feelings of residual guilt, which means that the person who has it has been forgiven for his sins and has no outstanding spiritual debts to pay. The use of the word *agathē* for 'good' (as opposed to *kalē*) suggests a spiritual quality similar to *kathara* ('pure'), which is no doubt the sense that Paul wanted to convey. Much has been written about Paul's use of the term 'conscience' (*syneidēsis*) and there is a lively debate about whether it is meant to be understood as a principle in its own right, equivalent to the 'heart', or as the means by which the subject takes possession of his heart and applies its purity (or corruption!) to his life.[55]

---

[50] Towner (2006), pp. 114–16, agrees with this but does not notice the triadic structure.
[51] Mt. 5.8.
[52] See 1 Cor. 2.6-15; 8.1-13; 13.1-13.
[53] Tit. 1.15.
[54] Thomas Aquinas (2012), 1.2.15 (p. 247).
[55] See Towner (2006), pp. 117–19, for a detailed discussion of this.

Given that a 'good conscience' builds on a 'pure heart' and leads to a 'sincere faith', it would appear that, in this instance at least, the conscience is meant to be understood as the means by which the basic principle of a believer's purity of heart is applied to the demands of his life of faith. That 'conscience' can have other meanings need not deter us from accepting that here it is this one that is primarily intended, because the context makes this plain. As elsewhere, the Greek (and Hebrew) mind was more inclined to synthesis than to the modern penchant for analysis, and we should interpret these terms as overlapping and mutually reinforcing rather than as conceptually distinct in any exclusive sense.

Finally, an 'unfeigned faith' is one that is sincere in all respects and that maintains its integrity in the face of the challenges and temptations that inevitably afflict those who believe. It is not a good-time feeling but an inner conviction that withstands the tests it has to face and triumphs over adversity. It also implies, as the word 'faith' always does in this Epistle, a correct understanding of the truth of the gospel, or what would now be called 'orthodoxy'. The terminology to describe that had not yet been developed but the sentiment was there. Paul drew attention to the fact that it was for want of these things that some people had lost their sense of direction and fallen into useless discussions. What a person is not only shapes what that person does but guards him or her against errors of this kind. Adherence to the truth without reservation is not an optional extra but is the indispensable foundation of everything we do. We go astray when we are not properly prepared for the challenges we have to face, and when that happens, we suffer the consequences of our inadequate training.

The logic of the text suggests that a pure heart, a good conscience and an unfeigned faith are the stepping stones that lead to a life of love. But as Martin Luther pointed out, it is an unfeigned faith that creates a pure heart in us and gives us a good conscience. In his words,

> it is the nature of faith that it establishes a good conscience toward God and all men; for it teaches me that I must trust in Christ alone as Saviour, because his suffering has redeemed me. where this condition exists, purity of heart follows shortly after.[56]

The end result of combining a pure heart, a good conscience and an unfeigned faith was an outpouring of love, which was the true manifestation of the power of the gospel at work in the life of the church. Love is not a

---

[56] Luther (1973), p. 226.

tolerance of ignorance, sin or even of eccentricity. It is rooted in truth and can only exist when the members of the Christian community have received and maintained the gospel in purity of both content and application. Turning a blind eye to deviance of any kind is not an act of love but the very opposite, even if maintaining the right spiritual discipline may cause hurt and division in individual cases. Believers cannot put their faith in anything that falls short of the truth, because if they fail in this, their message will lose its saving power and divine authority.[57]

The tragedy of those who were indifferent or susceptible to false teaching was that they thought they were doing the right thing. Many of them were probably sincerely convinced that their approach to the law was the correct one, and they were unable to look beyond the superficial details to consider the underlying spiritual issues. They thought of themselves as 'teachers of the law' (*nomodidaskaloi*) but in fact they had no coherent grasp of what they were saying and knew nothing of the true meaning of the things they asserted with such confidence. That confidence was misplaced, but they did not realize it, with the consequence that they were trapped in a blindness that prevented them from correcting their mistaken behaviour and ultimately made everything worse. As Ambrosiaster put it, they did not understand that the law and the prophets were fulfilled in Christ, and were therefore redundant after his coming. Because they insisted on maintaining the law, even in its more recondite details, the *nomodidaskaloi* had 'wandered away into vanity, because they wanted to teach what they did not understand.'[58]

That Paul was against these false teachers and their activities is obvious, but to what extent can they be regarded as his 'opponents'? What does that term, widely used in current commentary literature to describe the people whose teaching he was criticizing, actually mean? It is not at all clear from the evidence that they were consciously or deliberately attacking Paul and his teaching, and in that respect they may have been rather different from the false apostles whom Paul had to deal with in Galatia, for example. Nor is it certain that they were organized in any formal way. There could have been many individuals who thought along similar lines and whom Paul therefore grouped together, but who did not see themselves as a fellowship of anti-Pauline sentiment. Paul gives no indication that there was a leader directing their activities, or that there was anyone who specifically preached

---

[57] See Thornton (2016), pp. 32–48, for a detailed analysis of Paul's teaching on these matters.
[58] Ambrosiaster (2009), p. 121.

against him in the church.[59] It is even possible, if unlikely, that some of them (at least) had no idea that Paul disapproved of what they were doing! That may be going too far, but the impression we get is that the self-appointed *nomodidaskaloi* were a nuisance within the Ephesian church rather than a defined party in declared opposition to Paul, or still less a breakaway group.[60] Of course, that did not mean that they were any less dangerous. On the contrary, the fact that they were so hard to identify probably made them more, rather than less of a threat to the well-being of the Christian community, since the lines of what was and what was not acceptable teaching had not been clearly drawn.

## 8-11. The law and those who break it

*8. Now we know that the law is good, if one uses it legitimately. 9. This means understanding that the law is laid down not for the innocent but for the lawless and disobedient, for the godless and sinful, for the unholy and profane, for those who kill their father or mother, for murderers, 10. fornicators, sodomites, slave traders, liars, perjurers, and whatever else is contrary to sound teaching 11. that conforms to the glorious gospel of the blessed God, which he entrusted to me.*

Paul insisted that the law of God is fundamentally good.[61] It is easy to portray his approach to the Christian life as freedom from the law's demands, but this freedom must be understood in its proper context. It is not the law itself that is bad but the people to whom it has been given. The law is good if it is correctly used, but the problem is that sinful human beings are incapable

---

[59] Thornton (2016), p. 34, notes that Paul often referred to false teachers who opposed his message in vague terms. Compare what he says about them in 1 Cor. 15.12; 2 Cor. 10.12; Gal. 1.7, 2.12; Phil. 1.15.
[60] How closely they were connected to the main body of the Ephesian church is unknown and probably varied in individual cases. G. D. Fee, *1 and 2 Timothy, Titus* (Peabody, MA: Hendrickson, 1988), pp. 39-40, thought that some of them were actually elders in the church who fancied that they were competent to teach when they were not. But as Thornton (2016), p. 35, points out, that is probably going too far. Nevertheless, it seems clear that they had not broken away from the church but remained within it, perhaps somewhere on the fringes.
[61] Rom. 7.12; Gal. 3.7-11. For a discussion of what the word 'law' means here, see Johnson (2001), pp. 175-6. Johnson concludes that here 'Paul seems to be thinking of Law in the sense of moral commandments rather than the entire spectrum of biblical legislation' but the mention of genealogies suggests that this perspective is too limited. More likely, Paul was thinking of the Torah in general, especially since the *nomodidaskaloi* would not have confined themselves to its moral precepts alone.

of doing that. To do the right thing it is necessary to have the law written on one's heart, so that obeying its precepts comes naturally. It is difficult to convey this properly in translation, especially since Paul made a play on words here. The law (*nomos*) must be used 'lawfully' or 'legitimately' (*nomimōs*), which means that it must be understood and applied in the right spirit. Those who are not in tune with it will find it irritating at best and a hindrance at worst, because their desires are headed in the opposite direction. Such people need to have their minds corrected so that they can think straight, and then keeping the law will not be a problem at all. In a sense, this may be compared to the need for wearing glasses. Those whose eyesight is poor need glasses so that they can see properly, but those whose eyesight is good do not. A person with poor eyesight will need glasses as long as his short-sightedness persists. He may have it corrected by laser surgery or the like, which may be compared to conversion by the Holy Spirit, and if that happens, the glasses will no longer be needed. They are good (and even necessary) for the purpose for which they are intended, but ideally they should not be needed at all.

The ancient commentators laid great emphasis on two aspects of the law. First, they said that its primary purpose was to point us to Christ, and that after the Saviour had come the law was redundant.[62] Secondly, they distinguished between those parts of the law that ceased to have any force once Christ had come, and those that were of eternal value because they corresponded to natural morality. Theodoret of Cyrrhus (Cyrus) gives the fullest explanation of this:

> [Paul] indicated that the basic requirements of the Law are consistent and in harmony with the gospel, these basics being, You shall not commit adultery, You shall not kill, You shall not steal, and the like. The obsolete requirements, on the other hand, are those to do with sacrifices, days, corpses, lepers and suchlike.[63]

In the Middle Ages, Thomas Aquinas divided the law into its moral and ceremonial aspects, and insisted that it was only the latter that ceased to be relevant after the coming of Christ. The moral precepts retained their validity, and Aquinas stressed that it was important to read and apply them for the purposes for which they had been given. In his words,

---

[62] Theodoret of Cyrrhus (Cyrus) (2001), p. 210, expresses this most clearly, but the same idea underlies what Ambrosiaster (2009), p. 121, has to say. Theodore of Mopsuestia, surprisingly, passes over this in silence.

[63] Theodoret of Cyrrhus (Cyrus) (2010) p. 210.

The proper use of these [moral] precepts is that a man not attribute more to them than is contained in them. For the law was given in order that sin be recognized (Rom. 7:7). Therefore the hope of justification must not be placed in them, but in faith alone (Rom. 3:28).[64]

Martin Luther's comment on this passage is of particular interest, given his well-known opposition to the law as a means of salvation. He wrote,

> Use the Law as you wish. Read it. Only keep this use away from it, that you credit it with the remission of sins and righteousness. Beware of making me righteous by the Law. Rather, use it to restrain. You must not give the Law the power and virtue to justify. But you are teaching this – that there is a righteousness of works and of the Law ... It is a spiritual misuse of the Law if anyone wants to make men righteous by it, if anyone teaches that men can be justified by the Law and by works. The Law is abused when I assign to the Law more than it can accomplish. Good works are necessary and the Law must be kept, but the Law does not justify.[65]

The practical difficulty with the law is that there is nobody who can claim to be righteous to such an extent that it is made redundant. The translation of the word *dikaios* as 'innocent' is an attempt to interpret what Paul is saying in the context of criminal activity, which is certainly one aspect of what is meant here.[66] But innocence in this sense is hardly restricted to believers – very few people actually commit the crimes that Paul goes on to list, and if the law was intended only to condemn those who do such things it would have been largely irrelevant to most pagans, as well as to Jews and Christians. Yet as Jesus pointed out, criminal behaviour is only the outward manifestation of lawbreaking. In his teaching, everyone is guilty, not because they have committed crimes but because they have had evil thoughts in their hearts, which are just as reprehensible and far more widespread.[67]

Righteousness cannot be reduced to mere innocence in criminal justice terms. It is a divine attribute that belongs exclusively to God and has been manifested in his Son, who makes it available to us by the power of his Holy Spirit. We can be clothed in his righteousness and so delivered from the penalties of the law, but we can never dispense with the law altogether

---

[64] Thomas Aquinas (2012), 1.3.21 (p. 251).
[65] Luther (1973), pp. 231–2.
[66] Calvin (1964), p. 193, adopts this interpretation.
[67] Mt. 5.17-48.

because we cannot become righteous in ourselves. Christians ought to understand what the law is and know how to apply it because they are in tune with its spirit. The law does not disappear from the Christian life but finds its true vocation as a guide and a light to those who know what it is for. When we get to heaven we shall be fully righteous and then the law will disappear because it will no longer be needed.[68]

In the meantime, the law has been given to us as a standard and deterrent to sin. Here Paul expresses what the later Reformed tradition would call 'the third use of the law'. This means that in addition to its primary purpose, which was to reveal God's standards, and its secondary purpose, which was to condemn human failure to live up to them and point to the need for Christ, there is a third use to which the law can and must be put. It is a guide to the Christian life, pointing out what we must avoid and indicating the path that we must follow. Keeping it is not a way of earning salvation, but of demonstrating the new life that we have received by the grace of God in Christ. Christians are holy people because they have been chosen for salvation, and this means that they must lead holy lives. The law is a guide to what that means in practice, and if this is understood, then it can be used *nomimōs*, as Paul has indicated that it should be. How believers ought to react when they hear the law was summed up by John Calvin as follows:

> although the faithful know that the law of God cuts them to the quick, yet they find such sweetness in it, that the bitterness does not stop them from tasting it. They would rather have God chastise them, threaten them and point out their wretchedness, than to be left buried by their own corruption. And thus the faithful, although their fleshly appetites cry out to be satisfied, nevertheless want to be corrected by the law of God, and offer themselves willingly to it, and receive its admonitions meekly and patiently.[69]

In this passage Paul defined sin as the behaviour of sinners, and outlined a general catalogue of different types that can be found. The list is by no means exhaustive, but it gives us an indication of the kinds of people we must expect to find in a sinful world. It is divided into two parts, though these are

---

[68] Towner (2006), pp. 124–5, misses this and mistakenly concludes, 'The sins [listed here] portray graphically a depth of depravity so clearly different from Christian godliness that the irrelevance of the law (as Paul is thinking of its usefulness here) for believers is immediately felt.' He seems to think that Christians are righteous in themselves, and not merely by the imputation of Christ's righteousness to them.

[69] Calvin (2016), p. 71.

not distinguished by any formal indication. The first part describes the inner spiritual state of sinners. This state is not the *result* of actual deeds, but their *cause*. It expresses how their relationship to God and to their fellow human beings has been broken. Paul set out six types of these that we are likely to encounter. Perhaps he was influenced by the practice of ancient Greek theatre, which personified different characteristics and created figures that incarnated them in a particularly striking way, though the idea was not to separate the human race into defined categories based on individual failings, but to make people aware of their faults and alert them to the need to correct them.[70]

The theatrical characterizations were deliberately exaggerated for didactic purposes, and Paul may have been doing the same thing here. The particular types are not mutually exclusive, and in real life we are likely to find them present to some extent in virtually everybody, even if one of them appears to be more prominent in a particular person. The ones Paul listed are abstractions of tendencies that are present in everyone who is separated from God. They are outward manifestations of an inner spiritual malaise that is common to all human beings. Depending on the circumstances, we may manifest any or all of them in different ways and to varying degrees, but the spiritual malady they reflect is the same in every case. In common with his contemporaries, Paul did not use abstractions in the way that we do. He did not speak of 'lawlessness' (*anomia*), though the word existed and is found elsewhere in the New Testament.[71] Rather, he personified the different manifestations of sinfulness, reminding us that sins are not abstract ideas but acts committed by people who are in the wrong relationship to God. The 'types' of sinful people that Paul described are as follows:

1. The lawless (*anomoi*). This term refers primarily to those who consciously flout the law rather than to those who are merely ignorant of it. Paul knew that there were Gentiles who kept the law in their hearts even though they did not know what it was, and he praised them, holding them up as an example that contrasted with the faithless Israelites, who knew the truth but refused to follow it.[72] Those who are lawless have rejected any standard or constraint, and so they are potentially capable of anything.

---

[70] This was all laid down by Theophrastus (371?–287? BC), whose manual *Characters* was a guide to the stock figures of the Greek theatre.
[71] Mt. 7.23; 1 Jn 3.4.
[72] Rom. 2.12-16.

The catalogue of specific sins that follows is a mere appendix of detail that illustrates this fundamental principle of lawless sinfulness.

2. The insubordinate (*anhypotaktoi*). These are people who recognize no authority but their own. Insubordination was the essence of Satan's sin and it is characteristic of all those who imitate him in his rebellion. Of course it is highly ironic, because such independence is an illusion – nobody, not even Satan, is exempt from the sovereignty of God. It is rooted in pride, which is the fruit of spiritual blindness and the poor judgement that results from it. The effects are catastrophic because legitimate authority is overturned, and with it the order that is inherent in the universe. If there is no order there is no security, and if there is no security there can be no peace. Salvation involves the restoration of divine order which requires the conquest of insubordination by a spirit of submission and obedience. Jesus demonstrated this by submitting to his Father in the Garden of Gethsemane: 'Not my will but your will be done.'[73] The writer to the Hebrews picked this up and explained it by saying that although Jesus was the Son of God, 'he learned obedience through what he suffered, and being made perfect, he became the source of eternal salvation to all who obey him'.[74] Subordination is also an important virtue in the Pastoral Epistles, being enjoined, for example, in 1 Tim. 2.11 and 3.4, and also in Tit. 2.5, 9 and 3.1.

3. The impious (*asebeis*). In the first instance, these are people who take God's name in vain and who mock rituals and places dedicated to worshipping him. The religious foundation is still present in Paul's use of the word, but the context suggests that for him it had a wider range than that. Today we sometimes say that there are people for whom nothing is sacred, meaning by this that they treat nothing with special deference or respect, and it seems that this is what Paul meant here. We live in a world where 'investigative journalism' is promoted as a way of uncovering scandals that powerful people would otherwise hush up and so we have become accustomed to a certain kind of public irreverence. How far can that be justified? What did Paul have in mind when he included 'impiety' among the signs of rebellion against God?

There is no doubt that Christians thought of 'piety' in a way that was quite different from prevailing attitudes in the ancient world. Both Jews and Greeks measured it primarily by external criteria. A Jew who ate non-kosher food

---

[73] See Mt. 26.39.
[74] Heb. 5.8-9.

would have been 'impious', as would a Gentile who robbed a temple. Both these things happened often enough, but if the guilty party was subsequently afflicted by some misfortune, there was a ready explanation at hand – his discomfiture was the direct result of his 'impiety', or misbehaviour. Christians did not think in that way. They did not go around deliberately showing disrespect to other religions, though Paul was accused of having done that in Ephesus.[75] For Christians, 'piety' and 'impiety' were spiritual concepts, more closely connected to attitudes of heart and mind than to particular actions. Of course, what people did was the result of what they believed, so it was right to think that bad behaviour pointed to something deeper. The real problem, as Paul said elsewhere, was that 'there is no fear of God before their eyes'.[76] Interestingly, the quotation originally referred to Jews, though when Paul picked it up he explicitly extended it to cover Gentiles as well.

'Impiety' in this sense means that there is no awareness that there will come a day of reckoning. It is characteristic of evildoers that they seldom pause to think that there might be consequences to their actions. Their 'devil may care' attitude can easily lead them to do things that a wiser person would avoid, because their minds have been darkened by their pride. This takes us to the heart of the matter – sinfulness is the fruit of pride and however it manifests itself, pride is always 'impious' by definition.

4. The aberrant (*hamartōloi*). This is the word normally used for 'sinners' in general, but in this context it must be more specific than that. Those who go astray do so because there is something in them that causes them to rebel against the will of God. As with the *anomoi*, this rebellion can lead to anything, and so the word is often used to mean 'sinners' in general. What seems to be envisaged here is what we might call 'willful disobedience'. There are some people who are contrarian by nature. In some contexts that might be a good thing, since conformism is hardly commendable if it means keeping quiet in the face of injustice. But most of the time, aberrancy for its own sake is harmful. Laws and procedures exist for a reason, and even if they are sometimes inconvenient, going against them sets a bad precedent and can easily land people in trouble later on. Paul was the last person who could have been accused of legalism, but while he deplored a slavish subservience to the letter of the law, he also insisted that everything should be done decently and in order.[77] Breaking the rules merely to demonstrate one's 'freedom' was a denial of the very thing it was trying to affirm, and therefore sinful.

---

[75] Acts 19.26.
[76] Rom. 3.18, quoting Ps. 36.1.
[77] 1 Cor. 14.40.

5. The unholy (*anhosioi*). These are people whose behaviour does not conform to their profession of faith and who therefore pervert the things of God by their attitude and behaviour. The word used here is essentially synonymous with *anhagios* ('unholy'). If there is a difference, it is that *anhagios* refers primarily to the character of God, which can be extended to places, people and things where he is present, whereas *anhosios* stresses the work of human beings who are trying to conform to God's will. In practice, of course, it is not possible to be *hosios* without first being *hagios* because nobody can do the will of God without the presence of the indwelling Holy Spirit. But it was sadly true that although all Christians were *hagioi* by virtue of their baptism in Christ, not all were *hosioi*, because many of them failed to live up to the demands of their profession of faith. Indeed, it is not too much to say that Paul wrote the greater part of his letters for precisely this reason – those who were called to be holy were not working out their salvation in fear and trembling![78]

Today it is not unusual to hear people claim that all baptized members of the church must be accepted as equals, regardless of their behaviour. It is particularly common for practising homosexuals to justify themselves on this basis, and insist that for the rest of the church to reject their activities is unloving and contrary to the Spirit of Christ. What they have not understood is that although a sinner can be *hagios* because he has been set apart by God, he must also be *hosios* if that calling is to have any meaning.[79] This is why even Jews and the children of Christian parents have to be converted – holiness by association is good as far as it goes, but it does not go far enough.

6. The profane (*bebēloi*). These are the people who live 'without God in the world' and who do not mind saying so openly.[80] The term is broad enough to encompass a wide range of unsavoury activities that insult the name of God. It is easy to attach a term like this to people like the money changers in the temple, for example, but that is simplistic. What they were doing was wrong, but it was not necessarily in open contempt of God as far as they were concerned. The real *bebēloi* were the authorities who permitted such activities, because they were authorizing something that they knew was wrong and possibly even profiting from it in some way.

Even today, 'profanity' is something that it is easy to condemn when it is superficial but hard to spot when it is not. The person who swears by the

---

[78] Phil. 2.12.
[79] Paul did not hesitate to say that the children and spouses of believers were 'holy' (*hagioi*), although they were certainly not automatically *hosioi*. See 1 Cor. 7.13-16.
[80] Eph. 2.12.

name of God, often without thinking, is thought to be vulgar and rude, but ministers of the gospel who use their position to extract donations from gullible listeners are harder to deal with. Yet it is clear that the first type of person harms nobody but himself and does little, if any, damage to the church, whereas the second type can cause real harm and bring the gospel into disrepute. The former are thoughtless but the latter are cynical, which is far worse. Neither is right, but in passing judgement on such behaviour we must learn to distinguish the superficial from the substantial, and direct our condemnation accordingly.

Is there a particular reason why Paul chose these six categories to illustrate his point? They seem to bear a vague resemblance to the first four commandments of the decalogue, but they are too general to be classified under specific ones. However, they are followed by a further seven or eight categories that describe particular sins and follow the order of the Ten Commandments much more obviously.[81] This can perhaps be explained by saying that Paul concentrated on the second table of the law, which addresses love of neighbour, rather than on the first, which speaks more directly about our relationship with God, though it is impossible to separate one from the other. The people he has in his sights are breakers of the following five commandments:

1. The fifth commandment. These are the 'father-beaters' (*patrolōiai*) and the 'mother-beaters' (*mētrolōiai*). It is interesting to note that we do not have terms that correspond exactly to either one of these. We speak of 'wifebeaters' and of 'childbeaters' but not of father or mother beaters! This is the only place that these words appear in the New Testament, but Paul did not invent them. They can be found in classical Greek literature going back at least to the fifth century BC and would have been familiar to his readers. Greek mythology knew of this activity, which often led to the murder of a parent.[82] Even to pagans, that was one of the most heinous crimes that anyone could commit and something that was sure to call down the wrath of the fates. Hebrew culture seems to have been less troubled by this problem, but if that is true, it is only because the Israelites found such crimes even more unspeakable and so the social taboo against abusing one's parents was more effective. Their attitude can be gauged from the curse of Noah against his youngest son Ham, who had seen his father naked and drunk but done nothing about it and even

---

[81] Marshall (2004), pp. 378–9, gives an extensive list of parallels with the Ten Commandments and comes to much the same conclusion as the one offered here. Towner (2006), pp. 124–5, follows him in this, but with less detail.

[82] The NRSV and the NIV take that for granted and translate the words accordingly, but the ESV is (rightly) more cautious.

broadcast the fact to his brothers.[83] If disrespect of that kind was enough to incur a curse, it was hardly necessary to delve into anything more serious.

Whether Paul intended these terms to be understood only in the literal sense is hard to say. Jesus had interpreted the sixth commandment ('You shall not kill') in a way that applied it to malicious thoughts that one might harbour against another person, and it is possible that Paul thought in the same way.[84] Parricide is rare, but many people turn against their parents without harming them physically. For a child to rebel against his parent's teaching and reject his authority is a form of murder, because it implies that the parent either does not exist or does not have any right to exercise the disciplinary function over his children that has been given to him by God. Parents are not perfect, of course, but children who notice that should do what they can to shield them and protect them from disgrace, as Shem and Japheth did with their father Noah. Shaming them in public, as Ham did, dishonours God as well as them.

Reticence in this respect is by no means always easy. Josef Stalin's daughter, Svetlana Alliluyeva, had to live with the knowledge that her father was a mass murderer, and the same was true of the children of many of Adolf Hitler's chief supporters. But even in those extreme cases, the children by and large said nothing against their parents. If that was true of them, how much more should it be true of us? Two wrongs do not make a right, and a parent's bad behaviour is no excuse for the children to retaliate by doing the same in reverse.

2. The sixth commandment. These are the murderers (*androphonoi*). This is straightforward and man-killing has been recognized as a criminal offence in almost every culture, unless there are specific circumstances that intervene to legitimate it. In modern times, these exceptional cases would include warfare and judicial executions, which have usually been perceived as the lesser of two evils. Until fairly recently it might also have embraced the so-called 'honour killings', where people have murdered those who have insulted their families and the like, though that was always more controversial and the practice is now generally discredited, at least in most developed countries. Judicial executions have also gone out of favour in many places, though some Christians continue to defend them. It is still debated whether warfare is a legitimate form of killing, but whatever we think about that, everyone should be able to agree that Paul would not have called a soldier on active duty an *androphonos*. His condemnation of murder cannot really

---

[83] Gen. 9.22-27.
[84] Mt. 5.21-26.

be cited in support of pacifism, however desirable it may be to keep the peace whenever possible. What was wrong in Paul's eyes was the blatant disregard for human life that we see among those who kill for the sake of killing. How such people should be dealt with may be hard to decide in particular cases, but that their behaviour cannot be condoned is surely obvious and ought to be accepted by everyone as wrong.

3. The seventh commandment. These are the adulterers (*pornoi*) and practising homosexuals (*arsenokoitai*). The meaning is fairly clear, though modern commentators have expended considerable energy and ingenuity in an attempt to excuse forms of sexual behaviour that they either practise themselves or do not object to, however much those things may be condemned in the Bible. 'Adultery' seems to be obvious to us, but defining it can be trickier than most people realize. What it means here is the deliberate breaking of the norms of sexual behaviour in any given context. In the Old Testament there was widespread polygamy, even among God's people, and extramarital concubinage was by no means unknown. By modern standards, Abraham, Jacob, David and Solomon would all be guilty of adultery, but apart from the case of David and Bathsheba, none of the great men of the Old Testament was punished for it. Even in David's case, it was the fact that his sexual desires led to the death of Bathsheba's husband Uriah which condemned him at least as much as the adultery itself.[85]

This relatively lax attitude to sexual promiscuity had disappeared by New Testament times, when lifelong heterosexual monogamy was the desired goal among both Jews and Gentiles. This was not only seen as an improvement on what had gone before, but was also regarded as God's will from the beginning. The general view was that although polygamy and concubinage had been tolerated in ancient times, they did not reflect the creation order established in the Garden of Eden.[86] Jesus and the early church did not explicitly reject them because they did not have to. Instead, they focused their attention on divorce, which in their minds was just as much a breach of the creation order as polygamy, and one that they actually had to deal with. Jesus was very clear on the subject – a man who divorced his wife and married another committed adultery, unless his wife had had an extramarital affair that justified his repudiation of the marriage.[87]

Few teachings of Scripture have been more controversial than this one, especially in modern times. Divorce is once more widespread, with the inevitable result that marriage has been devalued and the commitment to

---

[85] 2 Sam. 11.1–12.23.
[86] Mt. 19.3-9.
[87] Mt. 19.9.

stay together 'for better and for worse' has been widely ignored. The concept of 'no fault divorce' has entered the law in order to make divorce easier and less costly, but in spiritual terms there is no such thing. The tragedy of our times is that many Christians have been sucked into this form of immorality and the church has turned a blind eye to it, with the consequence that the malady has spread even further. The teaching of the Bible has been wished away by those who find it inconvenient, and the spiritual health of the body of Christ has suffered as a result.

What is true of adultery is also true of homosexual practice. It is often claimed today that the Bible knows nothing of homosexual *orientation*, the assumption being that if it did, homosexual *practice* would not have been condemned. This is false. The Biblical writers did not use the term 'orientation', but they knew what it was – they called it the 'lusts of the flesh'.[88] All human beings suffer from an orientation towards sin which we distinguish from particular acts by calling it 'sinfulness'. Homosexual desire was understood just as much as heterosexual desire was, and among pagans, it was even regarded as superior.[89] But pagans often practised a double standard in sexual matters that tends to be overlooked by their apologists nowadays. Just as a man could have as many women as he wanted without suffering for it but a woman could not so much as look on a man who was not her husband, so an active homosexual was tolerated in a way that a passive one (a *malakos* in Greek) was not. The hypocrisy of this is obvious to us, as it was to the early Christians, who condemned all forms of sexual activity outside lifelong heterosexual monogamy, but it was deeply entrenched in ancient society and vestiges of it survive to this day. The Greek word *arsenokoitai* does not distinguish between active and passive homosexual behaviour. It probably inclines towards the former since it appears alongside *malakos* in 1 Cor. 6.9, but used on its own it would almost certainly include both. By extension it would also cover women who indulged in same-sex acts. They are not distinguished from the men, not because lesbianism was acceptable (or unknown), but because it was common for prohibitions applying to both sexes to be expressed only in the masculine. This was true, for example, of the degrees of kindred and affinity that precluded marriage – nobody ever suggested that what was prohibited to men was allowed to women![90] As is usual in these circumstances, the masculine embraces the feminine unless the latter is specifically excluded, and we must read the text in that way.

---

[88] Gal. 5.16-26.
[89] Plato wrote a whole dialogue about it, the *Symposium*.
[90] See Lev. 18.6-23.

4. The eighth commandment. These are the slave traders or 'people-robbers' (*andrapodistai*) who sold their captives into slavery. How common this was is hard to say, but it is interesting that Paul mentions them rather than the more ordinary kinds of thief. Stealing things was obviously wrong, but things are less important than people, and Paul may have wanted to stress that. The ancient world operated on slavery, repugnant as that is to the modern mind. Slavery was an economic system that was sometimes used as a way of paying off debts, and was even accepted by many for whom it was the only form of social security available to them. In the modern world, condemnation of the practice is all but universal, but it is only fair to consider why it was not attacked more severely in ancient times than it was, and also recall that it did not disappear until industrialization made alternative forms of labour cheaper and preferable.

That being said, even in the ancient world, slavery was not 'normal' and slaves often wanted their freedom. This could sometimes be bought, and was frequently granted by a master in his will. Furthermore, it was not uncommon for domestic slaves to be castrated as eunuchs. They could not have children and so the institution of slavery died with them. The long-term consequence of this was that slavery was always in decline, and for the system to function, new slaves had to be found. The most obvious way of getting them was by enslaving prisoners of war, and that was a common practice. But as the *pax Romana* spread across the Mediterranean world, wars became less frequent and so there were fewer prisoners to enslave. There was a demand needing to be supplied, and this is where the 'people-robbers' came in. Pirates would capture ships and seize their crews. Brigands would attack remote villages and carry off the inhabitants. On the imperial frontiers, and particularly in the Black Sea region, raiders would go to barbarian tribes in what is now Ukraine and grab anyone they could find.

In short, the *andrapodistai* were tolerated as a necessary evil. Like the middlemen who encourage illegal immigration today, they were performing a service, however distasteful their methods may have been. Paul could not collude in this situation. People-snatching was a sin regardless of the circumstances. If it was justified by the need to provide slaves, then so much the worse for slavery – modern readers may not realize it, but Paul's condemnation of the practice was in its own way a form of abolitionism and would have been widely understood as such at the time.

5. The ninth commandment. These are the liars (*pseustai*) and perjurers or 'oath-breakers' (*epiorkoi*), whose behaviour is a false witness. In a world where documentation was unreliable and hard to come by, much store was placed on verbal testimony. Even today, perjury is a serious offence, and this was even more the case in ancient times. It is true that there are

circumstances in which lying, and even oath-breaking, can be justified as the lesser of two evils, but Paul was not referring to them. An obvious example is the case of Rahab of Jericho, who hid the Israelite spies who had taken refuge in her house and was commended for it.[91] Her behaviour answers the question that is sometimes put today – if you had been hiding Jews in Nazi-occupied Europe and the police knocked on your door, would you have confessed to them? The right answer ought to be no, because although we are not supposed to tell lies, in a case like that there would be no choice, since turning innocent people over to certain death is far worse than lying to save their lives.

Of course, circumstances like those of Rahab are exceptional and cannot be used to establish a general rule for every situation. A 'liar' is not someone who chooses the lesser of two evils in a morally ambiguous situation but someone who refuses to tell the truth as a matter of habit, even of principle. It should be said that this kind of lying can take many different forms, one of which is a selective and misleading use of the truth. For example, if a person loses his job because he has reported misconduct among his co-workers and this is then justified by saying that he did not get along with people, or did not 'fit in', that is a lie, even if at one level it may be perfectly true! This is why those who take an oath in court have to swear that they will tell 'the truth, the whole truth and nothing but the truth', since only that can fully escape the charge of falsehood.

Oath-breaking is different from lying to the extent that whereas lying is bearing false witness about others, oath-breaking is a form of false witness against oneself. Those who promise to do something and then go back on their commitment may disappoint other people but they do not shame them. Instead, they bring discredit on themselves because those who experience such behaviour will not trust the person concerned again. As with lying, there may be times when oath-breaking can be excused, even if it is still unpleasant. For example, a person may promise to donate a certain sum to a worthy cause only to discover that he has not got the money and cannot do it. The promise may have been made in ignorance or circumstances may have changed in the meantime, but either way, the expressed intention has not materialized. Sometimes an oath may be extracted under duress, or from a person who is incompetent to swear it. This was often the case in medieval times, when young children were put in monasteries and forced to take an oath of chastity, even if they were not entirely sure what that was. The classic Old Testament example of a wrongful oath is that of Jephthah, who swore

---

[91] Josh. 2.1-21; Heb. 11.31.

that he would sacrifice the first thing that came out of his house when he returned victorious from battle, only to discover that it was his daughter! But tragic as that was, Jephthah's daughter insisted that the oath should be kept in order to save her father's reputation, which she did.[92] We are horrified by this today, but the story serves as a warning not to trifle with oath-taking, because the consequences may be more serious than we imagine.

There is no reference to the tenth commandment in this list, but that may be because Paul thought he had said enough.[93] He was certainly not in favour of covetousness! That he knew that he had not covered everything is made clear by the way in which he rounded off his list with the general phrase 'and whatever else conflicts with sound teaching'.[94]

The Greek word *hygiainousa*, translated here as 'sound', conveys a sense of healing and cleansing, which is what true teaching will do for the mind and spirit of the believer. Every Christian needs to have his heart and mind renewed by the power of the Holy Spirit, and the Spirit works through teaching (*didaskalia*). The Greek word has a broader range of meaning than its English equivalents because it includes both factual truth and moral discipline, in that order. Intellectual assent to the Christian message is essential, because without it we can have no understanding of its true meaning, but by itself it is not enough. It must be accompanied by a change of behaviour that turns a believer away from the sinfulness of his former life to a way of thinking and acting that conforms to the expectations of Christ. The transformation of our thinking must be accompanied by a corresponding transformation of our lifestyle, so that what is healthy in theory becomes health-giving in practice.

The content of this sound teaching is spelled out in the latter part of the sentence. Paul defines it as being in accordance with 'the gospel of the glory of the blessed God, which I have been entrusted with'. This is the first mention of the gospel in this Epistle, so it is important to consider carefully how Paul described it. To his mind the gospel revealed 'the glory of the blessed God'.[95] We know that the Father sent his Son into the world to save sinners, and in the next paragraph Paul would go on to talk about that, but he began with this phrase because the primary purpose of the saving message of the gospel is to glorify God. God is glorified by the salvation of sinners because it shows both his desire and his power to forgive them. God wants

---

[92] Judg. 11.29-40; Heb. 11.32.
[93] In Rom. 13.9, Paul omitted the ninth commandment, most likely because he was only giving a random sample of prohibitions and not a complete list.
[94] Towner (2006), p. 129.
[95] Almost all commentators read the text this way and attribute the word 'glory' to God, but Theodoret of Cyrrhus (Cyrus) (2001), p. 210, attached it to the gospel, claiming that Paul 'referred to the message, since it promises the believers the glory to come'.

those who have rebelled against him to repent and return to his embrace, and he has the power to make that happen. He is glorified by this because it reveals his character as a loving Creator and life-giving Redeemer. It shows that if he wants to do something, he can and will do it. To us these are three different steps that do not always follow on from one another. We can want to do something but be unable to do it, so nothing happens. Sometimes we are able to do something but are unwilling to, so again, nothing happens. In God, however, these distinctions mean nothing. If he wants to save us (as he does), he can save us and he will save us – one thing leads inevitably to the others.

The believer has experienced God's saving power and recognizes that he owes his life to him. Paul describes God as *makarios*, a word that we translate somewhat misleadingly as 'blessed'. The problem is that the English word suggests that God has received a blessing of some kind from us, which is obviously impossible. To use 'blessed' as a description of God seems strange to us, but that is only because our language is inadequate to express the original meaning. God is not 'blessed' by someone else (in the way that we are), but he possesses and manifests all the outstanding qualities and characteristics with which he blesses us.[96] For us to call him blessed reflects an attitude of thanksgiving on our part for his gracious gift of those qualities to us which is supremely expressed in the nature and content of our worship. We approach God with thanksgiving for the blessings he has bestowed on the undeserving, and it is for this reason that he is described here as *makarios*.

Paul tells us that he had been entrusted with this gospel, which was another way of asserting his apostolic authority.[97] He used the passive voice of the verb *pisteuō*, which is normally translated as 'believe', though 'trust' is also implied. In this case 'trust' is the only possible translation, since the passive form of 'believe' would make no sense. What Paul meant is that God had entrusted his saving message to him, knowing that he would preach and proclaim it faithfully to all who would listen. It is a reminder to us that God has chosen to work through human servants who can only accomplish the tasks assigned to them by the presence of his grace at work in them. Left to his own devices, Paul could have done nothing to further our salvation and neither can we. To be entrusted with a task is to be strengthened by the Spirit in order to accomplish it, and it was to that outworking of God's plan that Paul now turned.

---

[96] Marshall (2004), p. 383, makes this point.
[97] Paul is known to have spoken elsewhere in this way about his commission from God. See, for example, 1 Cor. 9.16-17; Gal. 2.7; Rom. 2.16; 1 Thess. 2.4.

## 12-17. The conversion of Paul

12. *I am grateful to Christ Jesus our Lord, who has strengthened me, because he judged me faithful and appointed me to his service,* 13. *even though I was formerly a blasphemer, a persecutor, and a man of violence. But I received mercy because I had acted ignorantly in unbelief,* 14. *and the grace of our Lord overflowed for me with the faith and love that are in Christ Jesus.* 15. *The saying is sure and worthy of full acceptance, that Christ Jesus came into the world to save sinners – of whom I am the foremost.* 16. *But for that very reason I received mercy, so that in me, as the foremost, Jesus Christ might display the utmost patience, making me an example to those who would come to believe in him for eternal life.* 17. *To the King of the ages, immortal, invisible, the only God, be honour and glory for ever and ever. Amen.*

Having praised God for entrusting him with the gospel message, Paul went on to thank Christ Jesus for having empowered him to proclaim it, expressing himself in a way that indicates that he regarded Christ as fully divine, since he had just said much the same thing about 'God'.

For 'I give thanks' Paul used the phrase *charin echō* instead of *eucharistō* ("I thank'), which may be a Latinism (*gratias ago*) that he picked up from popular speech. Whether that tells us anything about the letter's origin is hard to say. Latinisms were common in Greek, particularly in the international business milieu in which Paul moved, and the phrase could have come more naturally to him than it would have to a pseudepigrapher. In any case, the meaning is clear. God is to be approached with thanksgiving, which should always be the first part of intercessory prayer. Without this grateful attitude of heart and mind there would have been no spiritual empowerment and Paul would not have been entrusted with his ministry. In the Gospels there is a story of ten lepers who were healed by Jesus, but only one returned to thank him for it, a reminder of just how rare gratitude is in human life.[98] These opening words are therefore not to be overlooked, because their insistence on having the right approach of gratitude to God is the key to everything that follows.

The word for 'strengthened' is derived from *dynamis* ('power' or 'potential'), which must be carefully distinguished from *energeia* ('energy'). God is full of *energeia*, which characterizes his ever-active being, but he has no *dynamis* in himself. The reason for this is that in him, power and potential

---
[98] Lk. 17.11-19.

are fully realized and there is nothing that remains undeveloped or unused. God is fully who and what he is, with no room left for growth or change in himself. Human beings are very different from him in this respect. When God empowers us, his divine *energeia* gives us spiritual *dynamis*, a potential that remains to be activated and realized. Paul's gift was not a reward for good service but an incentive that made such service possible. He could not have fulfilled his ministry without it, nor could any activity on his part have been a justification for receiving it. Just as an electronic device cannot operate unless it is plugged in, so we can do nothing unless we are connected to God and he is at work in us. We may be structurally suited to do the work that God has ordained for us, but without his empowerment we can do nothing. What is more, as Paul goes on to explain, our sinfulness has made us unsuitable for the tasks he wants his people to carry out. To illustrate this point, he uses himself as an extreme example of a principle that, one way or another, applies to us all. As Calvin put it,

> Saint Paul shows us here that not only the preachers of the gospel should humble themselves and acknowledge the grace that is bestowed on them, not lifting themselves up proudly and presumptuously, but also that all the faithful should consider that when the gospel is preached to them, it does not come from man but from a greater Master.[99]

Paul described Christ Jesus as 'our Lord', a designation that is not only evidence that he believed in Christ's divinity, but that also reminded Timothy and his congregation that Paul's relationship to the Lord Jesus was fundamentally the same as theirs, although it worked itself out in a different way. Paul recognized that he has received a special, personal commission from God, but he also acknowledged that this commission has been given to him in the context of Christ's universal lordship, which embraces every member of the church. His ministry had been given for their benefit, and they must hear and accept it as an act of obedience to their common Lord. Failure to do this would be the fruit of disobedience, either because Paul would have disobeyed God by not delivering his message, or because the people would have rejected it – or both. Paul's preaching of the gospel and the church's reception of it were equally subject to the sovereign will of God, who has distributed gifts to his people without any 'respect of persons'.[100] Paul did not feel that he deserved more than others or that he had been justly given

---

[99] Calvin (2016), p. 85.
[100] Acts 10.34; Rom. 2.11.

more than they had. But he also knew that the congregations whom he was called to serve were called to hear and receive his message as a word that came not from him but from God. He approached them as a servant but he came with the authority of the one whom he served.

Paul knew that God had judged him to be trustworthy (*pistos*) and so had appointed him for service (*diakonia*), but the ultimate reason for this divine choice was a mystery to him. Objectively speaking, not only did he have nothing to offer to God, but there was a great deal in his past that by rights should have counted against him.[101] Before his conversion Paul had been a blasphemer (*blasphēmos*), a persecutor (*diōktēs*) of the church and a bully (*hybristēs*) to boot.[102] Once again we find a triad of descriptor nouns, each of which illustrates the others. The first and greatest of Paul's sins was that of blasphemy. The formation of the church was a work of God that even some Jewish leaders recognized could not be stopped by human means.[103] To oppose it was to reject what God was doing in and through his Holy Spirit, who had descended on the disciples of Jesus on the day of Pentecost. Jesus had told them that the sin against the Spirit would not be forgiven (not that it *could* not be forgiven!) though Paul made no mention of that.[104] Even so, it is clear that his blasphemy came close to being unforgivable, which reminds us both of the seriousness of his behaviour and of the miracle of God's grace in reaching out to him in spite of it.

Paul's blasphemy was rooted in his spiritual rebellion and what he did expressed that. Persecuting Christians was the outward and visible result of an inner separation from God that would have manifested itself in some other way if the circumstances had been different. As it was, Paul was authorized by the Jewish high priest and his council to undertake his persecuting activities, but he was a willing and eager participant in their plans, which is why they entrusted him with the task. This is a reminder to us that persecution of the church is never just a legal activity carried out by neutral officials who are only obeying orders. It is a spiritual force, motivated by an inner rebellion against God. In recent times there has been a great deal of discussion about this in the wake of the persecution of Christians and others by totalitarian regimes around the world. One of the arguments often made to excuse those who are engaged in this is that the persecutors have no animosity towards

---

[101] Paul often referred to his life of sin and rebellion before his conversion. See, for example, 1 Cor. 15.8-11; Gal. 1.13-16; 2 Cor. 4.1-6; Phil. 3.4-11; Rom. 1.1-7; Eph. 3.7-8.
[102] The NRSV translates 'man of violence', the NIV 'a violent man' and the ESV 'insolent opponent'. All these renderings are possible but they are not as accurate or as evocative as 'bully'.
[103] Acts 5.34-39.
[104] Mk 3.29.

Christians – they are only doing what they have been assigned to do by their superiors. Of course that may be true as far as it goes, but it does not mitigate or excuse the responsibility of those who carry those orders out. It takes great courage to disobey a superior, but this is where conscience comes in, and as we have already seen, conscience is a vital ingredient of the Christian life. Those who have a good conscience cannot act in a way that they know to be wrong, even if they are ordered to do so. There is a price to pay for defiance, but the Christian is called to take up the cross and the servant is not greater than his Lord. If Jesus came to die for us, then we must be prepared to die for him, though mercifully it does not often come to that. Ridicule and demotion are the more frequent outcomes, which for some people may be as hard to bear as death, but there can be no doubt that a willingness to die is what is expected of the faithful witness to the gospel of Christ.

Finally, Paul had been a bully as well as a blasphemer and a persecutor. We know from accounts of Nazi and Soviet death camps that there were some people in them who excelled in their zeal to persecute others, and who took advantage of the authority given to them to humiliate and denigrate their charges above and beyond the call of duty. Very often they were people of little or no account themselves, but by what appeared to be an accident of fate, they ended up being in charge of intellectuals, professionals and rich people who were being deliberately degraded by the power ranged against them. Resentful of their own inadequacies, camp guards and others took advantage of this situation by doing whatever they could to belittle and demean those whom they knew to be better than themselves. Paul was not the social inferior of those whom he persecuted, but he was young and would not normally have been given the authority to persecute others which he evidently possessed. He made the most of the opportunity though, and ended up as a bully who was convinced of his own superiority over those whom he attacked. One thing led to another, and before long Paul was as bad as anyone who opposed the will of God could be, and a good deal more active in his opposition than most.

After giving this somewhat sordid account of himself, Paul suddenly changed track with the astounding assertion that in spite of everything, he had been shown mercy (*eleos*). Greek possesses a verb to describe this (*ēleēthēn* as it appears here), which most other languages do not, and its use in this context serves to accentuate the miraculous nature of what happened to him. Paul could not say *why* mercy had been shown to him, but not to others who were far less guilty than he was. He does not comment on that, but focuses instead on the fact that mercy was granted to him because he had acted in ignorance. We are reminded of the words of Jesus on the cross, when he asked the Father to forgive his persecutors, because they did not know what they were doing.[105]

Paul's unbelief (*apistia*) was not a deliberate rejection of the truth but a blindness that prevented him from seeing it in the first place. This is an important distinction, because if he had understood what he was doing he might not have been shown mercy, and the punishment due to those who blasphemed against the Holy Spirit might have been meted out to him in full measure.[106] This distinction was picked up by Ambrosiaster, who commented,

> Paul had not done that [*i.e.* persecuted the church] out of malice but in error, which is easy to admit and repent of. Someone who knows that what he denies is true is not acting from error but out of malice, and his wound is incurable because he is forced by jealousy to say that what he knows to be true is actually false.[107]

John Calvin gave a clear explanation of how Paul's ignorance and unbelief differed from that of the Pharisees:

> Although Paul also had an evil disposition in some measure, with him it was thoughtless zeal that carried him away, so that he thought he was doing what was right. Thus he was not a deliberate enemy of Christ, but only so by error and ignorance. On the other hand, the Pharisees who accused Christ falsely and with a bad conscience were not altogether free of error and ignorance, but their motives were self-seeking and a perverse disinclination for sound teaching, in short, a furious rebelliousness against God, so that out of malice and quite deliberately, they set themselves against Christ.[108]

Here we must be careful not to be too dogmatic. Although Paul tells us that it was because of his ignorance that he received pardon, he does not say that he would not have received it otherwise. God shows mercy on those whom he has chosen, regardless of what they have or have not done.[109] It was his

---

[105] Lk. 23.34.
[106] On the cross Jesus asked the Father to forgive his persecutors, because they did not know what they were doing (Lk. 23.34). Elsewhere Paul made the point that if the rulers of this world had understood what they were doing, they would not have crucified the Lord of glory (1 Cor. 2.8). Ignorance may not have been an excuse, but it was certainly a mitigating factor in God's judgement.
[107] Ambrosiaster (2009), p. 122.
[108] Calvin (1964), p. 197.
[109] Exod. 33.19, quoted by Paul in Rom. 9.15.

will that Paul should be called and converted. Paul understood that in his case this was due to his ignorance but he did not make that a general rule for everyone, not could he have done. Jesus forgave people who knew they had sinned as well as those who were ignorant, and sometimes he did so in dramatic circumstances.[110] But whether we have sinned consciously or not, what we do not know is why God has reached out to us and forgiven us. We describe this as his mercy and experience it as his love, but we cannot explain it beyond that. There is a mystery in God's purposes that is beyond our understanding, but when we experience his presence in our lives we are filled with awe and wonder, which is the attitude we should always have in our relationship with God.

What Paul's remark does tell us is that he knew nothing of what Christianity stood for before his conversion, a fact that is borne out by the account given of that in Acts 9. When Jesus appeared to him on the road to Damascus, Paul did not recognize who he was. Even after he was told, he still knew nothing about the faith he had been attacking and had to be instructed in it by members of the Christian community in Damascus.

The difference between knowledge and ignorance is still observable today among those who persecute Christianity. There are some who know a good deal about it, who have studied it and who may even have been brought up to believe it, as the young Josef Stalin was. People like him are unbelievers but they are by no means ignorant of what they are attacking. However, there are also other people, and we can perhaps include most Islamic terrorists among them, whose antipathy towards Christianity is based on prejudice and a vague sense that Christians are enemies who threaten them in some way, but who have no real understanding of what they are attacking. The young Paul was a persecutor of this type. He knew that Christians were disrupting Jewish communities by their preaching, and that threat was all he needed to oppose them. It is for that reason that he described himself as ignorant (*agnoōn*) and for that reason that mercy was shown to him. He waned to do the right thing but did not understand what was required of him. Like the rich young ruler, Paul did what he thought was right, but unlike him, when he found out the truth, his zeal was channelled in the right direction and he became one of the greatest apostles of the Saviour whose followers he had ignorantly persecuted.[111]

Looking back on his conversion many years later, Paul realized that the grace of God, whom he referred to here as 'our Lord', had overflowed

---

[110] See Lk. 23.39-43; Jn 8.1-11.
[111] Cf. Mt. 19.16-22.

in relation to him, along with faith and the love that is in Christ Jesus. In one sense this was an exaggeration, of course. Paul did not receive any more grace, faith or love than any other Christian. Salvation is the same for everyone, and nobody is more gifted with it than others. There are certainly different callings within the body of Christ and each believer is equipped with the spiritual power that he or she needs for the task entrusted to them, but at the basic level of faith there is no distinction – all are one in Christ Jesus.[112] Paul was not claiming that God had blessed him more than other people, and he never rested his apostolic commission on that. This verse has to be understood not as an objective fact but as a subjective reaction to God's work in his life. In other words, it is not so much what God had done for him as how he felt about it that he was stressing here.

There is however another aspect to this, which applies to every Christian. As John Chrysostom observed,

> mercy was not confined to this, that punishment was not inflicted; many other great favours are implied by it. For not only has God released us from the impending punishment, but he has made us righteous too, and sons, and brethren, and heirs, and joint-heirs. Therefore it is he says that 'grace was exceeding abundant.' For the gifts bestowed were beyond mercy, since they are not such as would come of mercy only, but of affection and exceeding love.[113]

In describing his conversion, Paul had recourse to yet another a triadic formula, one which in this case is clearly structured. It is grace, accompanied by faith and love – in that order. It is tempting to think that love must be the greatest of these three (as Paul stated in 1 Cor. 13), and the juxtaposition of 'in Christ Jesus' might lend weight to that idea, but even if that is true, it is not the emphasis here. Rather, Paul saw everything in the context of grace, which is the foundation of our salvation. Grace is entirely a work of God, and although it is present in human activity, it cannot be recognized by those who lack spiritual discernment. Unbelievers may see the faith and love of Christians, but whatever they make of them, they cannot understand that these things are rooted in underlying divine grace, because they have no knowledge of that. It is there but they cannot see it, and so they do not give glory to the One who has made the visible faith and love of believers possible.

---

[112] Gal. 3.28.
[113] John Chrysostom, *Homilies on* 1 Timothy 3.14 (NPNF 13, p. 418).

Faith naturally precedes love, as it does also in 1 Cor. 13, because it is the context in which love is manifested. This does not mean that Christians are called to love only those who have faith, but that the love we show to others is rooted and grounded in the faith that we have in God and the assurance that we have received from him. Even in our relationship with him, we love whom and what we know and believe, because apart from that, our love would have no objective content. Whether the words 'in Christ Jesus' apply only to love, or to both faith and love together, is a question that is sometimes asked, and the Greek is ambiguous. The rules of grammar require a singular article before the phrase, and its form is governed by the preceding word, which is why we read the feminine singular *tēs*, corresponding to the feminine *agapēs*. *Pisteōs* is also feminine, so *tēs* could also refer to it, but it is not clear whether it does so. In theological terms it scarcely matters, because it is impossible to imagine a love for (or from) Christ Jesus that is not based on faith in him! The two concepts go together and cannot be separated, although they are distinct from one another. In the words of I. H. Marshall,

> Here faith and love are those qualities which must be shown 'in Christ', i.e. in a way determined by the death and resurrection of Jesus. Faith is related to the saving event as faith in the crucified and risen Saviour, and love is determined by the pattern of self-giving love displayed in Christ ... In the present context, the peculiar form of expression may well be determined by the need to contrast the Christian way of salvation and genuine Christian existence, with its basis in the authorized, apostolic gospel, with competing claims to spirituality.[114]

By attributing to God the most extravagant generosity towards him, Paul was emphasizing his deep sense of his own unworthiness, and it is this humility, not some unwarranted pride in God's special gift, that is the mark of a true Christian. Not coincidentally, it is here that, for the first time in this epistle, he tells us what the gospel actually is. It is the reliable claim, that ought to be accepted without reservation, that Christ Jesus came into the world to save sinners, of whom Paul himself was the greatest. This is admittedly a somewhat free translation of the text, which literally says, 'The saying is sure and worthy of full acceptance', but it conveys the spirit of what the apostle means. The message of the gospel is true and objective fact, equally valid for everyone. Every sinner can trust Christ for salvation, and there is nobody who has sinned so greatly that he or she cannot be forgiven by God.

---

[114] Marshall (2004), p. 396.

# 1 Timothy 1

Modern commentators have laid great emphasis on the set phrase 'the saying is sure' (*pistos ho logos*) which is filled out here with the addition of 'worthy of full acceptance'. It recurs several times in this Epistle, and has often been regarded as a signature statement of the author, whether he was Paul or a pseudepigrapher. It does not occur in any of the Pauline writings apart from the Pastoral Epistles, a fact which raises the question of their authorship, but with the usual dilemma – does this uniqueness mean that a hand other than Paul's was at work or is it an indication that the apostle himself wrote the letters? Would a pseudepigrapher have introduced so characteristic a phrase and used it several times when it was not authentically Pauline, or does it appear here because that is exactly what Paul often said when he was preaching and trying to emphasize his point? Perhaps the best way to look at it is to suggest that this is an authentic Pauline expression, which he frequently interjected into his lectures (or sermons?). Perhaps it is best reproduced in English by a phrase like 'You had better believe it', which modern teachers and preachers could easily use in similar circumstances. If that is the case, the extensive discussions about whether the phrase refers to what follows it or to what precedes it would take on a new look – as in English, so in Greek, it could be used either way.[115]

Oddly enough, ancient commentators either did not notice this phrase as being anything out of the ordinary, and sometimes interpreted it differently from what would be customary today. For example, Theodore of Mopsuestia did not see 'worthy of full acceptance' as simply confirming 'the saying is sure' but interpreted it as referring to the response expected of the hearer. In his words,

> [Paul] surely said *worthy of acceptation* because everyone, whoever he may be, will receive it if he believes that God saves people by mercy, since they are sinners because of their weakness. And God's kindness is especially acceptable to all because it has forcefully been made great and much more ample toward us.[116]

Contrast this with the words of I. H. Marshall, who wrote,

> The account of the theological rationale of Paul's conversion is confirmed by reference to a traditional saying which indicates that what has been said rests on a firm basis of church teaching and is in line with it; thus

---

[115] For discussions of the phrase and its significance, see Mounce (2000), pp. 56–7, Marshall (2004), pp. 326–30, and most recently Thornton (2016), pp. 140–3.
[116] Theodore of Mopsuestia (2010), p. 543.

implicitly any other way of salvation – for example, by the law or by an arcane interpretation of it – is ruled out.[117]

Marshall's interpretation, which is in line with what most modern commentators would say, is surely to be preferred over Theodore of Mopsuestia's, but it is curious that the latter failed to see the true meaning of the phrase in this context.

Paul declared that Christ had come into the world to save sinners, raising in some minds the question of whether the incarnation would have taken place if Adam and Eve had not sinned. The logical answer to that is that it would not have done, and that is what the church fathers generally concluded, though as Thomas Aquinas remarked,

> this question is not one of great importance, because God decreed the plan according to which things are to occur. And we do not know what he would have decreed, if he had not foreseen sin. Nevertheless, the Scriptures seem to state expressly that there would have been no incarnation, if man had not sinned.[118]

Many commentators have debated what Paul meant when he described himself as the 'chief' of sinners, partly because the Greek word *prōtos* also means 'first', but most of this discussion is surely beside the point.[119] Paul certainly did not mean that he was the first sinner in time or importance, nor is there any objective reason to suppose that what he had done was any worse than the crimes that others commit. His expression here must be taken as a form of self-awareness that led him to adopt a position of extreme humility in the presence of God. Subjectively speaking, what Paul meant is that the one who preaches the gospel message must recognize that he is preaching first of all to himself, and regard himself as the one most in need of the message – the chief of sinners in effect. There is no place in Christian ministry for pride. It is necessary to say this, because so many ministers of the gospel give the impression that they are somehow better than other people. They may not intend to do that, of course, but it is certainly how they are often perceived – both positively and negatively – by the wider world. A higher standard is (rightly) expected of them, but all too often people take this to an extreme. Either they believe that ordained clergy are better than

---

[117] Marshall (2004), p. 397.
[118] Thomas Aquinas (2012), 1.4.40 (p. 256). Modern commentators do not usually engage with this kind of question.
[119] See Marshall (2004), pp. 399–401.

other people and look up to them accordingly, or they go the other way and regard them as colossal hypocrites who preach to others what they are not prepared to practise themselves. Paul knew this, and was well aware of the danger of trying to win others at the price of losing his own soul.[120] That is why his outlook on the world was governed by this perspective. He was the worst person he knew, and although he did not explicitly say so, he believed that all Christians should think of themselves in the same way, even if our sins do not match Paul's persecution of the church. Only then will we be conscious of the superabundant grace of God, and only then will we attribute our salvation entirely to his glory and not to anything that we might have done to deserve it.

Having established his own unworthiness to receive the grace of God, Paul turned to the question of why he was shown mercy. His only explanation for this was that God had decided to use him to show the world just how merciful he could be. In other words, Paul continued the theme of his own exceeding unworthiness in order to compare and contrast it with the superabundant grace of God. As throughout this passage, Paul's reasoning was subjective, not objective. Objectively speaking, there was no reason why he should have been chosen and not someone else. Subjectively though, he felt that he had been selected, not only because of his own unworthiness but also because he believed that God wanted to use him for the benefit of others. At no point did he make any claim to a superior inheritance among the saints, or anything that might reflect positively on him personally. Instead, he said that he had been saved so that Christ could demonstrate his all-embracing (*hapasa*) lovingkindness, for the benefit of those who would later come to faith. If God could save Paul, his argument ran, he can save anybody, so nobody should feel excluded from the grace of God because his or her sins are greater than Paul's.

Paul described himself as an 'example' (*hypotypōsis*) for others to take heart from, but note that the word he used for this is less definite than *paradeigma*, the usual term for 'example'. He did not mean that others must conform precisely to his situation and experience, which is what *paradeigma* might imply. Each person is different but all need the same salvation, which comes to them in ways geared to meet their particular circumstances. This flexibility is better conveyed by *hypotypōsis*, which is a less definite word and can mean something more like 'sketch' or 'faint impression'. It is hard to know whether Paul intended there to be an explicit nuance of this kind, but we can at least say that we do not have to conform

---

[120] 1 Cor. 9.27.

to him in every detail, and most people do not. The average Christian did not persecute the church before being converted, but that does not make his or her conversion any less precious or authentic in the sight of God. It is not our salvation that is a pale reflection of Paul's but the sinful state from which we have been rescued which is analogous to his. Paul's conversion dramatizes principles that apply equally to everyone. All have sinned and come short of the glory of God; all stand in need of a Saviour.[121] There may be a sense in which some can be said to need him more than others, but his grace is the same for all of us and we are united in him, whatever we may have been or done in the past.[122]

Translators tend to make heavy weather of the phrase *tōn mellontōn pisteuein*, rendering it as 'those who were to believe' or something similar, when it is best simply to say 'future believers'.[123] It is not as though there was a group of sceptics waiting to see what would happen to Paul before committing themselves to Christ. Paul's example was intended to be the pattern for all future conversions, including those that take place today, and the text should be translated in a way that reflects this. Paul understood that his apostolic commission was foundational for the life of the church and that his example would serve as a model and reference point for future generations. So it has been. We do not copy him exactly, but the principles that govern our Christian experience are no different from those that governed his. Like Paul, we must be converted from our former life. Christ must be the centre of our faith and the source of a new life in him. And we must change. We cannot continue as we were before, but must become a 'new creation', entirely dedicated to Christ in everything we think, say and do. Ambrosiaster adds a nice touch that illuminates the significance for us of the mercy that Christ showed to Paul:

> By his patience and generosity towards Paul, Christ could then show others that he was as merciful to his enemy as he would be in the future to those who came running to him.[124]

The fruit of belief in Christ is eternal life (*aiōnios zōē*). The next verse clarifies what this means. Eternal life is not ongoing life as we now experience it, a suspension of death that is never lifted. Rather it is a transformation to a new *kind* of life, a life that is governed by the being of God and not

---

[121] Rom. 3.21-26.
[122] 1 Cor. 6.11.
[123] No modern translation does so, however!
[124] Ambrosiaster (2009), p. 123.

by the limitations of the created order. This is clearly stated by the Greek but very hard to capture in translation. It is always difficult for human language to express concepts of which people have no direct experience, and 'eternity' is a classic example of this problem. The Greek way of doing it, borrowed from Hebrew, is to take the word *aiōn* ('age'; it has given us the word *eon*) which is essentially a time-related concept, and then transcend it by making a grammatical nonsense of it. Eternal life is literally 'age life' and God is described as 'the king of the ages', that is to say, the one who is sovereign over time. His transcendence is confirmed by the phrase *eis tous aiōnas tōn aiōnōn*, translated into Latin as *in saeculum saeculorum* but seldom (if ever) rendered in English as 'to the ages of ages'. We just say 'for ever and ever', which conveys the same idea but loses the sense of paradox which the Greek phrase encapsulates. In strictly literal terms, 'ages of ages' makes no sense, which is precisely why it is used to define something that surpasses human knowledge and experience. It is not just 'never-ending' but is outside the time and space continuum altogether. God dwells in another dimension of reality, and when we are converted we are called to dwell in it too.

It is important to notice that this is one of the few places in the New Testament where divine attributes are specifically listed. As so often, the pattern is triadic – God is 'immortal' (*aphthartos*, which literally means 'indestructible'),[125] 'invisible' (*aoratos*) and 'unique' (*monos*). It is not immediately clear why it is these characteristics that have been singled out or why they are listed in this order, and variants in the manuscripts suggest that the ancients puzzled over this too. Some have *athanatos* ('immortal') instead of *aphthartos*, which is understandable, but also *sophos* ('wise') instead of 'invisible', which is not so easily explained.

If we accept the majority tradition as the most likely one, the triad should probably be read as one of ascending order, like 'faith, hope and love' in 1 Cor. 13, describing his relationship to time, space and being. First comes God's enduring existence, which cannot be removed or destroyed because it is not bound by time. That is followed by his invisibility, which places him outside the material world and underlines the fact that his immortality is not ongoing temporal life but something of a different kind altogether, not bound by space. Finally, his being is unique. Not only is he the one God (*heis theos*); he is the *only* God (*monos theos*). If monotheism was not clearly stated in the Old Testament, so that it is possible to claim that although the Jews

---

[125] Oddly, Calvin (1964), p. 199, omits the word, but mentions it in his sermon (2016), pp. 114–16.

believed in one God he was not necessarily the only God whose existence they acknowledged, this was no longer the case in the early church. The one God of the Christians is the only God that there is, a theological statement with profound implications at every level.

For a start, it means that there can be only one Creator, and that he must also be the only true Redeemer. It also means that the Father, the Son and the Holy Spirit have to be understood as identities (*hypostaseis*) within the one God, and not as three separate deities, making what we now call Trinitarianism an inevitable theological development.[126] It also means that there is no reason to fear any other gods because they are all fictitious, a belief that in New Testament times had practical consequences for such everyday things as eating meat that had been sacrificed to idols.[127] What was a real controversy in the early church came to seem bizarre and pointless as this monotheistic doctrine took hold, with the result that we now have to stop and think when we meet the problem in the New Testament and wonder whether it has any relevance to us now. The ramifications of Christian monotheism were many, and if some of the questions it raised in ancient times seem remote from us now, that is usually a sign of how triumphant it has been in the development of human intellectual history.

Since it is God who rules over (and dwells in) the 'ages of ages', the phrase 'eternal life' must be understood as 'the life of God', a life in which time and space concepts cease to have any meaning. Paul describes God as the 'king' (*basileus*) which is immediately comprehensible to us, though it should be remembered that the Roman emperor (like the Persian shah before him) was generally referred to in this way, at least in the Greek-speaking east of the empire. No Latin speaker would have called the emperor a *rex*, because the kings of ancient Rome had been overthrown in 509 BC and since that time, the city had been a 'republic', at least on paper. The emperor was referred to as the *princeps* ('first citizen'), a word that did not really exist in Greek, though the Latinate form *prinkipos* could be found and eventually became common in the sense of 'prince'. He could also be called the *imperator* ('commander', of which the word 'emperor' is a corruption), for which the Greek equivalent was *autokratōr* ('autocrat'), a word which is not found anywhere in the New Testament though it became standard in later Greek usage.

---

[126] See Heb. 1.3, where Christ is described as the image of the Father's *hypostasis*.
[127] 1 Cor. 8.1-13; Rom. 14.1-23.

Paul's use of *basileus* is probably best understood in the sense of 'emperor' and was not directly linked to the covenant kingship exemplified in David and in his Son, Jesus Christ. But the two concepts were not unconnected, and what we find here may be a blending of the Roman and the Biblical pattern of authority that would eventually come to fruition in the medieval Christian idea of kingship. Paul saw all earthly rulers, however exalted, as subordinates appointed by God to maintain law and order on earth.[128] Considering that many of them thought of themselves as divine and expected their subjects to worship them, relativizing them in this way was deeply subversive of the ancient political order. God alone was the supreme ruler, and even the Roman emperor was no more than a client king, rather like the Herods in Judaea. Eternal honour and glory belonged to God who was the only one worthy to receive it, and Paul concludes this section with what amounts to a prayer of praise to him.

The doxology is addressed to 'God' and in it monotheism is stressed to a degree that is unusual in the New Testament, though certainly consonant with universal Jewish tradition. It has usually been assumed that Paul was addressing God the Father, but some commentators have seen a Christological dimension in it as well, especially since Christ was also acknowledged as the king of the ages.[129] But Theodoret of Cyrrhus (Cyrus) took a different line, making Christ the centre of the doxology and relating the other persons of the Godhead to him:

> Since he [Paul] had presented Christ the Lord as source of those good things, he wanted to make clear that they were made with the good pleasure of God the Father and the co-operation of the divine Spirit, so he moved from the one person to the commonality of nature, and offered the hymn to the Trinity, not mentioning the persons but celebrating the divine nature ... immortality and invisibility are proper both to the Son and to the Spirit. With these matters clarified in this way, the term *God* is a term truly applied to the Trinity alone: beyond it no one else is God by nature.[130]

No doubt Theodoret was reading too much into the text as far as the persons of the Trinity are concerned, but his words remind us of the important truth that the natural attributes of God apply equally to all three of them, and

---

[128] Rom. 13.1-7.
[129] See, for example, 1 Cor. 15.1-28.
[130] Theodoret of Cyrrhus (Cyrus) (2001), p. 212.

so their presence cannot be dismissed as irrelevant to the meaning of the doxology.

## 18-20. Paul's charge to Timothy

> 18. *I am giving you these instructions, Timothy, my child, in accordance with the prophecies made earlier about you, so that by following them you may fight the good fight, 19. having faith and a good conscience. By rejecting conscience, certain persons have suffered shipwreck in the faith; 20. among them are Hymenaeus and Alexander, whom I have turned over to Satan, so that they may learn not to blaspheme.*

Having taken us through the history and meaning of his own calling, Paul returned to a theme that we last saw in v. 5 – the apostolic command that he has been given by God, which he was now entrusting to Timothy, almost as a kind of inheritance. He spoke directly to the younger man, calling him his 'child' (*teknon*) once more, and addressing him in the vocative, a form that he rarely used. It must be said that this has nothing to do with any favouritism on the apostle's part. Timothy was a loyal disciple and fully capable of exercising the charge being entrusted to him, but that was not the primary motive for Paul's action. Rather, he was delegating a part of his ministry to Timothy because of prophecies that had been made about him some time before. We do not know what the content of those prophecies was or who made them, though we occasionally meet prophets like Agabus who played a part in Paul's life.[131] It is very possible, and perhaps probable, that there were people who prophesied Timothy's future at the time of his birth, a practice that is not unknown elsewhere and recalls what the aged Simeon said about the baby Jesus.[132] We do not know what happened, but we must remember that Paul and Timothy lived in a world where prophecies at the time of a child's birth were not uncommon, and that they were taken more seriously then than they probably would be today.

Ambrosiaster did not hesitate to link the prophecies to predestination, though he appears to make a distinction between them, the prophecies coming before Timothy's calling by Paul, which in Ambrosiaster's eyes was the moment at which his predestination was made plain:

> Timothy was predestined from the moment he was chosen by the apostle for this task, so that he might be ordained and judged worthy to become

---

[131] Acts 21.10-14.
[132] Lk. 2.25-35.

a future bishop and thus fulfill his gospel service in faith and with a pure conscience.[133]

Whatever the circumstances or content of the prophecies was, Paul's purpose in mentioning them was to encourage Timothy to 'fight the good fight'. We would normally expect to find the word *agōn* used for 'fight' (as it is in 2 Tim. 4.7), or perhaps the word *machē* ('battle'). Instead, Paul chose a term that more clearly reflects organized warfare; it was a *strateia*, something that would normally be waged by a *stratos* ('army'). There may not be much significance in this, although it suggests that Timothy's warfare would not be haphazard, but would be planned and directed by a divine strategy. The sovereignty of God is not mentioned as such, but the implication of it lies not far beneath the surface and must be taken into consideration as we read and interpret the meaning of this passage.

Martin Luther interpreted the good fight as the work of teaching the people the truths of the gospel. As he put it,

> He who teaches well is a good soldier. In the Word the ignorant are taught, the sluggards aroused, foes overcome and consoled ... these are very burning, powerful words.[134]

In this, Luther was followed by John Calvin, who put it quite bluntly,

> The devil cannot abide that they [i.e. the preachers] should preach the Word of God purely; instead he will resist it and work to have a thousand devils against it, attempting all he can. Therefore we must be ready to fight ... wherever the Word of God is preached, by and by there must be troubles and much sedition.[135]

The weapons of this warfare are spiritual of course, and Paul mentioned faith and a good conscience in particular. Faith is obviously essential, because without clear convictions and a deep trust in God no resistance to the forces of evil is possible. To this, Paul added the necessity of a good conscience, which was vital if the plan of battle was to succeed. Conscience is a major theme of the New Testament and it may be described as the individual's

---

[133] Ambrosiaster (2009), pp. 123-4. In common with his contemporaries, Ambrosiaster assumed that Timothy became a bishop in the sense in which that office was understood in his own time.
[134] Luther (1973), p. 251.
[135] Calvin (2016), p. 127.

appropriation of the gospel message and his sense of responsibility towards it. A good conscience is one that has received the faith taught by Christ and put it into practice; by contrast, a bad conscience is one that has heard the Word but failed to apply it. Somewhere in between was the 'weak' conscience, which might be defined as that of a person who has accepted the truth of the gospel but found it difficult to put into practice in a consistent or coherent way.[136] In this context, P. H. Towner sums it up well:

> the 'good conscience' is an ethical description of what the Spirit does within the believer to apprehend God's law. The condition of the conscience is determined by one's disposition toward the gospel (by conversion).[137]

Martin Luther said much the same thing but in more striking language, with a clear focus on faith in God:

> Faith is to believe in God and thus have a conscience secure in Christ. You will not produce a good conscience by being a soldier. You will be a soldier by teaching, etc., but watch out that your good conscience is not on account of these; yet you will have a good conscience in this service as a soldier ... a good teacher is very pleasing to God and very displeasing to the devil.[138]

Unfortunately, it is not uncommon for a person to have faith but to be troubled in his conscience, particularly if his actions do not match his words. How many preachers and teachers have we seen whose private lives make a mockery of their profession? Sometimes they are caught out, and the resulting scandal brings their ministry to an inglorious end, often doing considerable damage to the church and its members in the process. This seems to be what Paul had in mind when he spoke of suffering 'shipwreck in the faith'. Commentators have made surprisingly heavy weather of this phrase, debating whether the shipwreck refers to the gospel mission or to the spiritual disaster suffered by the rebels themselves.[139] It seems unnecessary to be so precise in distinguishing one from the other, because in all likelihood both suffered the consequences, as is usually the case in similar situations today. At the same time, it can be argued that a setback to the gospel mission

---

[136] See 1 Cor. 8.7, 10, 12.
[137] Towner (2006), p. 158.
[138] Luther (1973), p. 252.
[139] See Marshall (2004), p. 412; Towner (2006), p. 159.

can be repaired over time more easily than the personal damage caused to the rebels. Whatever harm they may have done to the cause of Christ, the suffering they have inflicted on themselves in the process is deeper and more lasting.

Something like that seems to be what had happened to Hymenaeus and Alexander.[140] They forgot that they had to act with integrity and so made shipwreck of their faith. Like a good pastor, Paul kept his confidences and he does not tell us (or Timothy) what they actually did, but we do not need to know. Timothy probably knew both them and their story, but that knowledge has vanished with time, so that now we can say no more about them than what we find here. But the precise details do not matter. If we knew what they were, we might be inclined to distance ourselves from them, since whatever they had done might seem remote from the sorts of things that we are tempted to do today. Whatever the details may have been, the basic fact is that they had gone wrong and something had to be done about it.

Paul's solution to the problem strikes many people today as strange. He said that he had given them over to Satan, so that they might be taught not to blaspheme. The gist of his remarks is fairly clear. 'Given them over' is metaphorical; it means only that Paul had left them to stew in their own juice and had no intention of interfering in their affairs.[141] The reference to Satan is more troubling. Should we read this as purely symbolic and translate the text in some other way? Does 'Satan' mean no more than 'their own devices'? Or do we have to embrace the full implications of a spiritual reality that is wholly evil, whom God allows to rule over his creatures? There can be no doubt that that is what Paul believed, as did the early church. To them, Satan was very real – indeed, for some people he was more real than God! Today many people discount the existence of a personal devil or at least brush it aside, but this is not the Biblical picture. For Christians Satan is not just a convenient name for an abstract idea or impersonal force. He is a personal angelic being who is fully capable of tempting and ensnaring the human race, as he has in fact done. To ignore him is to ignore the spiritual reality we live in, and much of the weakness of the modern church is due to this. As Don McLean sang in his classic *Miss American Pie*, 'Satan was laughing with delight, the day the

---

[140] The identity of these two men is uncertain. A Hymenaeus appears in 2 Tim. 2.17 and may be the same man, since the name is unusual. Alexander may be the coppersmith mentioned in 2 Tim. 4.14 or the man mentioned in Acts 19.33, if that Alexander was a different person, but these are all conjectures that are not supported (or contradicted) by any external evidence. Calvin's confident equation of him with the Alexander of Acts 19.33 must be regarded as purely speculative. See Calvin (2016), p. 142; (1964), p. 203.

[141] Calvin (1964), p. 203, equated their punishment with excommunication, which was certainly part of it, but somewhat anachronistic in the context of 1 Timothy.

music died.' In the modern world, the music of the spheres has all too often died, or at least been drowned out by an array of competing noises, and we may be sure that Satan is rubbing his hands with glee at his success in getting our contemporaries to write him off as a piece of outdated mythology.

Today, most people would probably expect Paul to pursue men like Hymenaeus and Alexander in the hope of putting them right, and would find his apparent willingness to abandon them somewhat hardhearted and cruel. But Paul knew what the limits of his ministry were, and he realized that he could not let himself be caught up in the affairs of one or two miscreants to the neglect of other things. He also understood that some people have to learn the hard way, and that trying to make life easier for them will not work in the long run. It cannot have been an easy decision for him to take, but in the circumstances it was the best one for all concerned. Modern pastors (and parents) know that there comes a point when they have to let go, and this is what we find here.

The verb *paideuomai* can be translated as a passive ('be taught') or as an active ('learn'), but the meaning is the same. It is not immediately clear who will teach Hymenaeus and Alexander – will it be God or Satan? – but this probably matters less than might appear on the surface. Satan cannot act without divine permission, and the fact that Paul had handed these men over to him does not mean that God had abandoned them. On the contrary, Paul understood it as a way of showing God's love and mercy towards the offenders. Martin Luther put it very well when he wrote,

> Our chastisement ought to be a medicine, for the kingdom of Christ is one of mercy. It does not chastise to destruction but to salvation. It does not kill. It holds no sword except a spiritual one. It keeps a man under Satan, yet it does not deliver him farther than to recover him from the snares of Satan. It wants to have him chastised in such a way that he returns.[142]

Job of course is the classic example of someone whom God handed over to Satan, though that was for a limited time and with a particular purpose in view. God allowed Satan to do his worst with Job (or almost – Satan was not allowed to kill him!) but the trials of Job only served to reveal his inner godliness, and in the end, he was compensated many times over for his sufferings. Hymenaeus and Alexander were not righteous like Job was and so would not have been justified in the way that he was, but it is at least possible

---

[142] Luther (1973), p. 455.

that they might be brought to repentance and welcomed back into the church that they had deserted. We do not know what happened to them in the end, but at least we can say that Paul did not give up on them completely. However sceptical about them he may have been, he continued to hope that they would learn from their mistakes and be restored to the fellowship of Christ. God knows more than we do, and can speak to people in ways that we cannot. Hard as it may be for us to understand, consigning Hymenaeus and Alexander to Satan was as much an act of faith on Paul's part as passing on his charge to Timothy was. The circumstances were very different, but the power and the sovereignty of God were just as applicable in the one case as in the other.

One final point to note here is that Paul categorizes the sin of Hymenaeus and Alexander as 'blasphemy', which gives an added seriousness to the charge laid against them. Blasphemy suggests that they had offended God, and not just the apostle or the church, but how they had done this is not stated. P. H. Towner connects them with the false teachers who were propagating myths and genealogies, but there is no evidence for that.[143] It is also thought that they were false teachers, but the text does not tell us that either.[144] Given that Paul contrasts their behaviour with Timothy's, it may be best to suppose that they were potential co-workers who had turned against him, a phenomenon that was not unknown in the apostle's experience.[145] What they may have done in practice is a secondary matter; the root of the problem was that they had turned away from God and done harm both to Paul's mission and to themselves. It was for that that they were being disciplined, in the hope that they might one day realize the error of their ways and repent. After all, Paul knew that he too had once been a blasphemer, as he had just recalled in v. 13, and if he had been rescued from his sin, there was hope for Hymenaeus and Alexander too.

---

[143] Towner (2006), p. 162.
[144] Marshall (2004), p. 415.
[145] See the case of Demas, in 2 Tim. 4.10.

# 1 Timothy 2

## 1-4. The universal mission of the church

*1. First of all, then, I urge that supplications, prayers, intercessions, and thanksgivings be made for everyone, 2. for kings and all who are in high positions, so that we may lead a quiet and peaceable life in all godliness and dignity. 3. This is right and is acceptable in the sight of God our Saviour, 4. who desires everyone to be saved and to come to the knowledge of the truth.*

In the second chapter Paul begins his exposition of the checklist of things that he was writing to Timothy about. The first of these was the need for prayer for 'all people' (*pantes anthrōpoi*), something that he made a specific priority. He listed what appear to be four different kinds of prayer – 'supplications' (*deēseis*), 'prayers' (*proseuchai*), 'intercessions' (*enteuxeis*) and 'thanksgivings' (*eucharistiai*). The last of these is clearly somewhat different from the others, but it is difficult to see what distinguishes the other three.[1] Even with 'thanksgivings', it is not certain what Timothy was expected to thank God for. Was it just the existence of other people? That would seem strange. Was there some reason to be grateful for them, and if so what was it? The context suggests that Christians ought to be thankful for outsiders who respected the church's legal rights and left it alone to preach the gospel unhindered.[2] But Paul did not forget that they too needed a Saviour and he emphasized that point in his request for prayers to be said on their behalf. We must be grateful for services rendered by unbelievers but never forget that the best thing that we can do for them is to lead them to Christ and pray for their salvation.

There does not seem to be any reason to analyse the four different terms for 'prayer' particularly closely, and it is probably best to conclude that Paul wanted to make his point by repeating it in as many ways as he could. Nevertheless, there is some indication that the ancients perceived a difference in the words of the kind that is brought out by Theodore of Mopsuestia:

---

[1] The same terms, except for 'intercessions' (*enteuxeis*) appear together in Phil. 4.6.
[2] This is the interpretation given by Towner (2006), pp. 162–8.

by saying *prayers, entreaties, requests*, he [Paul] used the change of names in accord with different sorts of requests. For we ask either that good things be given us from God – which he called *prayers* – or release from evils – which he named *entreaties*. Now when he said *requests*, he surely meant it to come in logical order before all... because he said *thanksgiving*, it is clear that it is a different sort of prayer, since it is something other than a request for what is usually lacking; a thanksgiving is made for what has already been bestowed.[3]

Theodoret of Cyrrhus (Cyrus) also distinguished the different types of prayer, but in a somewhat different way. He wrote,

> A *petition* is an entreaty offered for release from some trouble, a *prayer* is a request for good things, an *appeal* is a charge against wrongdoers. Our struggle is not against flesh and blood but against the rulers, against the authorities, against the cosmic lords of this age, against the spiritual forces of wickedness in the heavenly places. For right judgment against these we make our appeal, and we beg righteous assistance. *Thanksgiving* is offered to God for the good things already won.[4]

Centuries later, Martin Luther also distinguished the different types of prayer, stating that the first were 'supplications' in which we pray to be spared from evil, the second are requests for good things to be given to us and the third are intercessions, which he equated mainly with praying for our enemies.[5] John Calvin followed Luther's categories but rejected oversubtle distinctions between them. As he put it,

> not to dwell disproportionately long on a matter of no great importance, Paul is in my view simply saying that whenever public prayers are offered, petitions and supplications should be made for all men ... Paul seems to me to use three words with the same meaning on purpose, the better to commend and the more urgently to press upon us earnestness and constancy in our praying.[6]

---

[3] Theodore of Mopsuestia (2010), pp. 549, 551. It is especially noteworthy that Theodore devotes considerable space to the different types of prayer but says virtually nothing about rulers and their responsibilities.

[4] Theodoret of Cyrrhus (Cyrus) (2001), p. 213. Like Theodore of Mopsuestia, he has little to say about prayer for secular rulers, but he does suggest that Paul asked the church to pray for them because he had their conversion in view.

[5] Luther (1973), pp. 257–8.

[6] Calvin (1964), pp. 205–6.

Calvin's view is now the generally accepted one. As he understood, what is significant is that prayer was Paul's first priority in his missionary work. Without a heart for the lost souls to whom he was called to preach, Paul's words would have been ineffective, but even more importantly, without the assurance of divine guidance and support in his endeavours, there would have been no fruit at all. Prayer can and does take many forms, and elsewhere believers are told to 'pray without ceasing', which can only mean that every opportunity for it must be used.[7] What form(s) these prayers took in the church is not explained, most likely because that would have been obvious both to Timothy and to the congregation at Ephesus. There may have been a liturgy of sorts that would have justified Paul's use here of different words for 'prayer', but we are not told this and have no way of knowing it for certain.

Probably the pattern of worship at Ephesus was similar to what might have been observed in a Jewish synagogue, if only because people would then have recognized what constituted 'prayer', but even that is a guess. Once again we are reminded of how little we know about the early church, and especially about its worship. There can be no doubt that prayer lay at the heart of it, as these verses remind us, but the New Testament nowhere spells out the details of how a church service was (or should be) conducted. It is only when things went wrong, as they did at Corinth, for example, that Paul wrote to correct the congregation's mistakes and we get a glimpse of what should have been going on. But even then, we do not have enough information to be able to reconstruct a typical service.

Paul asked that these prayers should be made 'for all people'. The reason for this, as he made clear in v. 4, is that he saw the gospel as a message of salvation for them, because it was God's will that Gentiles should be saved, and not just Jews. On the surface, this statement seems obvious and uncontroversial, but it has given rise to considerable debate and its meaning must be analysed in the light of what the rest of the Bible teaches about the proclamation of the gospel and God's will regarding the salvation of the human race.

First of all, there is the question of what Paul meant by 'people'. The Greek term *anthrōpoi* is clear and refers to all human beings, both male and female. Traditionally it has been translated into English as 'men', which is ambiguous, since the English word can refer to the human race (as it does here) or simply to its male members. This ambiguity also existed in Greek to some extent, but it did not cause a problem because when it was

---

[7] 1 Thess. 5.17.

necessary to specify 'males' Greek could (and did) use *andres* instead.[8] The most famous example of that is the standard opening of speeches made in Athens, where the speaker addressed his audience as *andres Athēnaioi*, which was appropriate because women did not participate in public gatherings.[9] Latin made a similar distinction between *homines* and *viri*.[10] But as the modern Romance languages developed in the early Middle Ages, the purely masculine *viri* disappeared and *homines* came to stand for both males and human beings in general, as is still the case today.[11] English follows this pattern, perhaps under the influence of French, but other Germanic languages make a distinction analogous to that of Latin and Greek.[12]

In recent years, this ambiguity has caused increasing concern, at least in English-speaking countries, thanks to the rise of feminism.[13] Not wishing to cause offence, a number of translators have replaced the traditional word 'men' with something else, and 'people', a singular noun generally used as the plural of 'person', seems to many to be the most satisfactory option.[14] It is the word that comes naturally to most English speakers and is not artificial or awkward-sounding in the way that 'humans' or 'human beings' is, though it too can be ambiguous. Care must be taken not to misconstrue its proper use as a singular (plural: 'peoples') as in a phrase like: 'Let all the people say, Amen', which occurs in the Old Testament.[15] In that case, the Greek word for 'people' would be *laos*, not *anthrōpoi*, the difference being that a *laos* is a singular word referring to a particular group of human beings that is distinguished from the rest of humanity by certain shared characteristics (language, religion, etc.), whereas *anthrōpoi* is plural and generic to the entire

---

[8] But *andres* has an ambiguity of its own, because it can mean either 'males' or 'husbands'.
[9] See Acts 17.22.
[10] As a matter of interest, the English word 'man' is etymologically related to *homines*, as can be seen from the adjective *humanus* – just drop the ending -*us* and the first syllable *hu-*! It is also worth noting that Hebrew can make a similar distinction between *adam* and *ish*, which has a feminine form *isha* when the need arises.
[11] Cf. Italian *uomini*, French *hommes*, Spanish *hombres*, Portuguese *homens*, Romanian *oameni*.
[12] German and Dutch, both of which are sister languages to English, distinguish between *Mensch/mensch* and *Mann/man*. Note that in English, the feminine of 'man' is the compound 'wife-man', which has been abbreviated to 'woman'. Neither German nor Dutch has any equivalent to this.
[13] To gauge how modern this concern is, consider that as recently as 1967, the world's fair held in Montreal boasted the theme *Terre des hommes* in French, which was translated into English as 'Man and his world'. Nobody complained.
[14] Somewhat surprisingly, Mounce (2000), p. 78, opts for this translation, despite its unsatisfactory nature.
[15] See, for example, Ps. 106.48.

human race.[16] A translator or interpreter must also be careful to avoid using the word 'persons' here, because a person is not necessarily a human being. In the Trinity, the Father, Son and Holy Spirit are all persons but they are not humans – a point that may seem arcane but which is important in view of what Paul says in v. 5. In conclusion, it must be stressed that the original Greek text is perfectly clear and unambiguous – Paul was asking the church to pray for all human beings, male and female. The ambiguity, such as it is, is found only in translation.

Paul did not recognize any male-female distinction in this context, but somewhat surprisingly to the modern ear, he seems to have qualified his description of 'all people' in what we would now call class terms. He singled out 'kings and all who are in high positions' as deserving of special prayer, which raises a number of questions. Why did they matter more than anyone else, and who precisely were they? What was the church expected to pray *for*, in their case? Was it their conversion, or simply that they should do the job assigned to them in a responsible manner?

Paul and Timothy lived in the Roman Empire, where there was only one 'king' (*basileus*) – Caesar. Why then did he use the plural? It is true that emperors often had an associate co-ruler, but this was not the case at the time the letter was written and that idea would probably not have occurred to Paul. It is possible that he was thinking of the client kings who still ruled in the east – the Herods, for example, with whom Paul is known to have had dealings during his ministry.[17] That would have made perfect sense if Timothy had been in Syria, but he was at Ephesus, where there were no client kings, and for Paul to ask him to pray for them would have seemed strange and irrelevant.

Modern minds might suppose that he was thinking in general terms of future rulers, but that is the least likely possibility of all. Leaving aside Paul's expectation of the imminent return of Christ, those who live in a monarchy know that it is not done to speak of a successor to the reigning sovereign. The wise men who went to Herod asking about the one who had been born to be king of the Jews found that out in a particularly grisly fashion, though it is hard not to think that they should have been more sensible in the first place.[18] In ancient times, the standard royal greeting was 'O king live for ever!'[19] Even today, that thought is not far from the minds of the subjects of a monarch like Queen Elizabeth II, for example. Consider the words of the royal anthem:

---

[16] The Latin for *laos* is *populus*, from which the English word 'people' is derived.
[17] Acts 25.13–26.32.
[18] Mt. 2.1-18.
[19] Dan. 3.9; 6.21.

> God save our gracious queen
> *Long live* our noble queen
> God save the queen!
> Send her victorious
> Happy and glorious
> *Long to reign* over us
> God save the queen!

Everyone knows that the longer she reigns the sooner the end will come, but nobody says that openly or expresses any desire to see it happen. If such thoughts are still regarded as unpatriotic today, they would have been downright treasonable in ancient times (as they were in most European countries until only a few centuries ago). Even the Jewish leaders, who were not known for their loyalty to Rome, were careful to stress that they acknowledged no king other than Caesar, since to have done otherwise would have brought punishment down on their heads.[20] Paul, a Roman citizen, would certainly have understood that!

Most probably, Paul's use of the plural *basileis* ('kings' or 'emperors') was a subtle way of keeping his distance from any particular ruler. By ancient standards, Rome was quite modest in the claims that it made for its emperors. The Pharaohs of Egypt had always been worshipped as gods, as had many other eastern monarchs, but the Romans looked down on this practice and refused to adopt it. When Julius Caesar married Cleopatra VII of Egypt, her status as a living goddess did him no good back home, and was one of the reasons why he was assassinated. A century later, Rome had become more accustomed to having some sort of imperial cult, but even then it took the form of a post-mortem deification of the emperor. This allowed his successor to call himself the 'son of a god' and claim divinity by association, but it never went any further than that.

Christian prayer for the emperor(s) could not be confused with any kind of pagan deification, however nuanced that deification may have been. Prayer for Caesar might easily have been misunderstood, and so Paul had to tread carefully. The emperor could not be worshipped, but it was necessary to pray for him, as well as for all who exercised civil authority, because it was on the right performance of their vocation that the freedom to preach the gospel depended.[21] In later times Tertullian would remark, somewhat ironically, that 'the blood of martyrs is the seed of the church', but that was not Paul's

---

[20] Jn 19.15.
[21] Rom. 13.1-7.

perspective.²² He did not invite persecution as a means of encouraging church growth, but the very opposite. In his mind, the gospel would be preached most effectively if Christians were allowed to live in peace, and it was the duty of the secular rulers to ensure that they could do so. He did not go into as much detail here as he did in Rom. 13.1-7, where he justified the power of secular rulers to restrain ungodliness and assured the Roman Christians that if they obeyed the law and paid their taxes they would have nothing to fear, but the thought is much the same.

Prayer for pagan rulers was common among Jews who were subjected to their rule and it had been enjoined on the Babylonian exiles by Jeremiah.²³ As I. H. Marshall noted,

> Such prayer was meant to ensure the welfare of God's people under pagan rule and came to be regarded as a sign of loyalty; it avoided the necessity to pray to the rulers themselves or acknowledge them as worthy of divine honours.²⁴

It seems that Paul must have been writing this before AD 64, when state persecution of Christians began, after Nero blamed Christians for having started the great fire of Rome. Until then, opposition to the preaching of the gospel came mainly from Jews, who saw it as a threat to their own community, and from pagan merchants who earned their living from the sale of idols – a problem that was particularly acute at Ephesus.²⁵ Paul might not have changed his mind once official persecution started, but it is hard to believe that he would have said nothing about it. People who were being put to death merely for professing the name of Christ would not have been happy to be told that they ought to pray for their rulers as if they were always wise and just, doing no more than what God expected of them!

Paul's inclusion of 'all in authority' reflects the reality of Roman rule, which was delegated to governors, city officials and occasionally town councils. Most of the time his brushes with the law never went beyond local officials of this type, who had the power to hinder his mission or to further it. Jesus himself suffered and died 'under Pontius Pilate', not 'under Tiberius Caesar' (AD 14–37), who almost certainly had no idea what was going on in his name. We know that this was true of Paul's experience when he was arrested in

---

²² *Apologeticum*, 50.1.
²³ Jer. 29.7.
²⁴ Marshall (2004), pp. 421–2. Marshall references Johnson (2001), p. 129, in support of his statement.
²⁵ Acts 19.21-41.

Jerusalem, and that had he not appealed to Caesar, he would probably have been set free by the Roman governor.[26] There was no guarantee of that of course – Jesus was even more innocent than Paul was, but he was not liberated for political reasons, and Paul could easily have suffered a similar fate. It was not that Roman justice was arbitrary – it usually was not – but that it could be influenced by considerations that had little or nothing to do with the case in question. In recommending prayer for the authorities, Paul would certainly have had this in mind. He expected the emperors to do their job and to do it in the right way – two aspects of the same thing, perhaps, but not identical.

Even after the end of persecution and the recognition of the Christian church as first a legal, and then the official religion of the Roman Empire, Christians preserved a sense that church and state were distinct. Ambrosiaster, for example, writing about AD 370, had this to say:

> They [i.e. Christian leaders] are to pray for the rulers of this world, that they would be able to keep their people subject to them, so that left in peace, we might serve our God in tranquillity of mind and quiet. They are also to pray for those to whom supreme power has been entrusted, that they might govern the state in righteousness and truth and supply all things in abundance, so that the disruption of rebellion might be taken away and happiness put in its place.[27]

Ambrosiaster's view may be taken as typical of most commentators through the ages, but there was one major exception – Martin Luther. Somewhat surprisingly for one who stood up against the might of the Holy Roman Empire, Luther said,

> The first moral work of love among Christians is toward civil office. True Christians therefore do not say no to a public officer, even though he is an unbeliever, much less to a Christian one ... On this subject Paul speaks in great detail. We must note every syllable. The first fruit of love is to be that you Christians respect every public officer in the world and that you pray for them, because you hear what it means to keep the realm in peace. When a good magistrate fails or is upset, then nothing good is left in this life ... We must forget about all fruits of love if public offices do not stand firm in peace.[28]

---

[26] Acts 26.32.
[27] Ambrosiaster (2009), p. 124.
[28] Luther (1973), p. 256.

John Calvin, for his part, was less deferential to secular rulers. In one of his sermons on this passage, he proclaimed,

> Truly our Lord Jesus Christ ruled in the world in spite of the princes ... and religion must not be grounded upon them. For when they would lift up themselves against it ... Jesus Christ does bruise them and beat down their rebellion with his spiritual sceptre, as with a rod of iron, and treads them under his feet, and confounds and brings them to shame in their rage and fierceness. Nevertheless, if the magistrates do their duty as they ought, we shall see that what they do, and the order of the kingdom of our Lord Jesus Christ, agree very well together.[29]

In their different interpretations of this passage we can see the germ of the different historical trajectory of Lutheranism and Calvinism with respect to secular authority. Where Lutherans would typically be submissive to secular rulers, even to a fault, Calvinists would subject them to the bar of Christ's judgement – and if they fell short, feel free to rise up in rebellion against them.[30]

Paul believed that if the rulers of the empire did what was expected of them, Christians would have a quiet life and live 'in all godliness (*eusebeia*) and respectability (*semnotēs*)'. To us, this sounds like a picture of the middle-class suburban church culture with which we are familiar nowadays, but that did not exist in ancient times. We have to read Paul's words in context. His language meant that the church should have been able to live peaceably and mind its own business, without being molested or interfered with by those who did not like it. Paul was not saying that Christians ought to set the moral tone for the neighbourhood, though he knew they would have contributed much to that if they had been tolerated as he wanted them to be.[31] The reality that he and the churches he founded had to face was one of popular suspicion that could easily lead to open opposition. Jews did not like the way he preached in their synagogues and then departed with a sizeable number of the congregation, who had accepted the gospel message. Pagans were unhappy when they started losing business because converts to

---

[29] Calvin (2016), p. 168.
[30] Calvinists rebelled in the Netherlands (1566), in England (1640) and in America (1776). There is no Lutheran equivalent to this.
[31] Jesus told his disciples that they were to be the salt of the earth and the light of the world. See Mt. 5.13-16. Paul told the Corinthians that a believer sanctified his or her entire family. See 1 Cor. 7.14-16.

Christianity were no longer buying idols or contributing to the upkeep of the local temples.[32]

In many parts of the world today Christians face a similar situation, whether they are active in evangelizing their neighbours or not. Even in traditionally Christian countries there are worrying signs that increasing secularization is leading to previously unknown discrimination against Christians which is likely to get worse as time goes on. Governments are increasingly less inclined to defer to Christian moral and spiritual sensitivities, and the rise of militant Islamic fundamentalism has persuaded some that all religions are intrinsically dangerous to society. Paul's prayers for a quiet life under God-fearing rulers are far from being out of date in the modern world!

There are two Greek words used for 'life', *zōē* and *bios*. Normally Paul uses the former, which puts the emphasis on the inner life of the soul – life as opposed to death. But here he chooses *bios*, which fits the context better. *Bios* is outward, social activity, which is what is meant here. Paul was not expecting secular rulers to provide Christians with peace of mind – that was the work of God the Holy Spirit. What the authorities were called to do was to provide the conditions for a peaceable life in the world – protection against enemies, justice in the courts and so on.

Much has been made of the words *eusebeia* ('piety' or 'godliness') and *semnotēs* ('respectability'), both of which were in common use in the ancient world.[33] What they meant in practice depended on what was expected by the particular religious and social observances of the different places in the empire – Rome was remarkably tolerant and pluralistic in this respect. The exact nature of Christian 'godliness' could only be determined by Christian doctrine and discipline, which might easily be misunderstood by those who had no understanding of that. Pliny the Younger's famous letter to the Emperor Trajan in AD 111 is a prime example of this – Pliny knew that the Christians had some strange rituals but had no idea what they meant and found them barbarous.[34] But Pliny also believed that Christian practices were harmless, and Paul no doubt thought that reasonable people would share that view. Many people today find the religious behaviour of some ethnic minorities odd and even incomprehensible, but although they may be disconcerted by it, few would go so far as to say that they are harmed or offended by what they see.

---

[32] Ephesus was a particular hotbed of this kind of opposition. See Acts 19.21–41.
[33] See Marshall (2004), pp. 135–44, and Towner (2006), pp. 171–5, for lengthy discussions of *eusebeia* and what it meant in different contexts. Both commentators come to the conclusion adopted here, as far as Christian 'godliness' is concerned.
[34] Pliny the Younger, *Epistulae* 10.96.

Respectability is somewhat more complicated, because it moves beyond mere tolerance to de facto acceptance by wider society.[35] How far Christians were likely to achieve that is hard to say, and the evidence of the early centuries is not encouraging, at least if the polemics of men like Tertullian are to be taken at face value. Was it really true, as he claimed, that every time there was a natural disaster people blamed it on the Christians? Were they social outcasts to that extent?[36] It is impossible to be certain about this, and doubtless practice would have varied according to circumstances. As far as Paul's meaning is concerned, it is safe to say that he *wanted* Christians to appear to be respectable in the eyes of their pagan neighbours, and that he *expected* this to happen because their behaviour was law-abiding and should not have given any offence. Whether this goal was achieved or not, of course, was not up to him to decide.

Verse 3 is somewhat ambiguous. Was Paul saying that it was good and acceptable for Christians to pray for their rulers regardless of what they did, or did he mean that he expected them to act in the way that he thought they should? Probably it is the first of these meanings that Paul had in mind here, but we are not obliged to choose between them, since both were good and right. Christians ought to pray for their governments, even if they are bad ones, but those in authority ought to behave correctly too. Paul nowhere suggested that the church should target the secular rulers as potential converts, and it never did so. In the second century there were Christians who wrote 'apologies' for the faith, which were usually addressed to the emperor, but their primary aim was to get him to tolerate them, not to convert him personally. The two things could not be so easily separated however, as we see from Paul's encounter with King Herod Agrippa II. When the king asked Paul to explain his faith, he did it so persuasively that Agrippa remarked that it was almost enough to make him become a Christian.[37] Paul had not specifically targeted him for conversion, but when the opportunity to bear witness to Christ arose he took it and treated the king as a man who was just as much in need of the Saviour as anyone else. He did not seek to pervert the course of justice by distracting his judges, or make them feel guilty for trying him, but in defending himself he did not hesitate to insist that what he was saying had implications for them personally.

---

[35] See Marshall (2004), pp. 187–9, for a discussion of this.
[36] This is the main theme of Tertullian, *Apologeticum*, written in or around AD 197. Tertullian was concerned to refute the charges against Christians, which he regarded as absurd, but it seems highly likely that he exaggerated his presentation of them for rhetorical effect.
[37] Acts 26.27-29.

No ruler or judge is abstractly impartial or able to administer the law irrespective of his or her own convictions, and in urging Timothy to pray for them, Paul undoubtedly had that dimension in mind. Christians who hold political power often have hard decisions to take and they can easily become targets for the hatred or jealousy of their rivals. Many people think that Christian politicians are insincere in their faith, while others are afraid that they may let it intrude into their work in a way that is detrimental to their calling. Accusations of this kind may be unfair, but they are far from being unknown and Christians have to pray especially hard for those who are trying to live out their faith in the public arena.

The phrase Paul used was taken from Deuteronomy, where it occurs several times to describe behaviour that was consonant with the law and therefore acceptable to God.[38] Prayer for secular rulers was not to be judged by its results, nor were its intentions meant to go beyond the secular sphere of duty allotted to the rulers in question. What mattered was that Christians should fulfil *their* responsibility to pray, regardless of whether the people being prayed for deserved it, or even understood what was being done on their behalf.

Here again, Paul calls God our Saviour as he did in his opening salutation. He reminds Timothy that the salvation that had been worked out in the death and resurrection of Christ was part of an eternal divine plan in which the Father and the Holy Spirit also had an essential role to play. At the heart of that plan was God's desire that all people (*anthrōpoi*) should be saved and come to a knowledge (*epignōsis*) of the truth (*alētheia*). There is general agreement that by 'knowledge' Paul meant understanding and acceptance of the truth, since mere information would hardly have been sufficient. It is also agreed that by 'truth' Paul had in mind the message of the gospel, which he had already expounded in part and which he was going to elaborate on further in the next few verses.[39] Controversy has focused on the phrase 'desires all people to be saved', a statement that can be understood in different ways.[40] What did Paul mean? There are basically three possibilities, which can be broken down as follows:

1. God wants everyone to be saved and they will be, even if they do not profess faith in Christ in this life.
2. God wants everyone to be saved but individuals have the freedom to refuse this offer and some do, so God's will is not fully realized.

---

[38] Deut. 12.25, 28; 13.19; 21.9. See Marshall (2004), p. 424.
[39] See Marshall (2004), p. 428; Towner (2006), pp. 178–9.
[40] For parallel statements, see Rom. 3.27-31; 11.26-32.

3. God wants all *kinds* of people to be saved, not just Jews. Only some are chosen, but they come from every tribe and nation.

These different options can be analysed as follows:
  1. God wants every human being to be saved by faith in Christ, as v. 5 states. In fact, of course, not everybody believes, and so we are left to consider other possibilities. Will God's will be realized in a different way, perhaps by giving them another revelation, or by speaking to them about Christ after their death? There have always been those who believe that people are saved by being true to their own convictions, whatever they may be. Paul thought that a Gentile who did not know the law of Moses could please God by obeying his conscience, so perhaps there was some scope for such an idea in his thought.[41] But he was talking about Gentiles before the coming of Christ. Once the gospel had been revealed there could be no salvation apart from belief in him. Jesus had appointed the apostles and the church as the bearers of his message, so Paul could not have accepted that there is any way to heaven other than through Christ.[42] Peter tells us that after his crucifixion, Jesus went to preach to the souls of those who had been imprisoned in the days of Noah, so there may be some basis for thinking that people might hear the gospel after their death, but the circumstances he described were very specific and have no equivalent in the post-deluge world.[43] However we understand a passage like that, there are no grounds for thinking that anyone can be saved by following a non-Christian religion or philosophy, so this interpretation has to be rejected for lack of evidence to support it.[44]

But despite the difficulty in accepting this interpretation, it continues to have an appeal to some, especially to those who would be on the more 'liberal' spectrum of theology. For example, T. L. Long has written,

> The text simply says that God *desires* the salvation of all, not that all are saved, but as many theologians have observed, if God desires it but does not achieve it, this has implications about the power of God. The New Testament as a whole is somewhat ambiguous about whether every human being will be redeemed, and we should be cautious about going beyond what we are given. The main thrust, however, of this and

---

[41] See Rom. 2.12-16.
[42] Rom. 3.21-26.
[43] 1 Pet. 3.18.
[44] Marshall (2004), p. 426, notes that this interpretation is impossible because faith is necessary for salvation.

other texts, is toward a God whose mercy is wide and whose saving love embraces the whole of creation.[45]

2. An alternative reading of this verse accepts that God wants everyone to be saved, but that his will is thwarted by rebellious human beings.[46] According to this way of thinking, God wants me to be saved, but if I reject him, I shall not be. I do not have the ability to procure my own salvation, but I can refuse the one on offer and God will respect my choice because I possess free will. What happens to those who are unable to exercise their free will – children who die in infancy, for example, or the mentally handicapped – is not usually discussed, but the assumption seems to be that they will be saved, because they have no ability to reject God's will for them. This is a difficult position to maintain, because it suggests that people who are mentally unformed or disabled are better off than those who are not. There is nothing in the Bible to support that view and like the preceding one, it suffers from twisted logic. In both readings, we are left with the assumption that ignorance is better than knowledge, which cannot be right. If that were the case, preaching the gospel would be irresponsible because it would put people at risk of losing a salvation that they might have obtained if they had remained ignorant of it! We can be quite certain that Paul did not think like that.

But despite possible objections to this view, it has been widely held in one form or another throughout Christian history. Ambrosiaster discoursed on it at some length, though he emphasized the rebelliousness of the human heart and its consequences:

> God wants everyone to be saved, but only if they come to him. He does not want this if it means that people are saved when they do not want to be. He only wants them to be saved if they also want this. Just as he gave the law to everyone, so he excludes no one from salvation ... It is faith which gives salvation, and unless the mind accepts it with total willingness, it will not only do him no good, it will also harm him.[47]

3. The third possibility is that when Paul refers to 'all people' he is speaking out of an essentially Jewish context. Jews may have been unclear about the nature of God's salvation, but whatever it was, they believed that it was meant for them and for nobody else. They were the chosen people, and only those

---

[45] Long (2016), p. 62.
[46] This is the solution preferred by Marshall (2004), pp. 426–7, who regards it as virtually beyond doubt.
[47] Ambrosiaster (2009), p. 125.

who became Israelites could inherit the promises that God had made to Abraham and fulfilled in Christ. We know that there were Jewish Christians who thought like that and that Paul spent a good deal of time and energy refuting them, so there are grounds for assuming that it was this background that he was addressing. In contrast to Jewish exclusivism, Paul argued that God wants all kinds of people to be saved, and not just Jews. This was one of the main themes of Paul's gospel message and it recurs in v. 7. It may also have been the case that the Ephesian church, though theoretically sound in its theology and open to the possibility of fresh conversions, was actually hardening into a social club and losing its zeal for evangelism. Outsiders were not turned away if they approached the church, but not much effort was being made to reach out to them and they could easily have felt unwelcome in practice. That seems to have been John's assessment of the Ephesian church in Rev. 2.1-7, and signs of its diminishing ardour may have been apparent when Paul was writing to Timothy. It is certainly a common phenomenon in many churches today, which often have to be reminded that God is reaching out to people beyond their particular community, and it would be no surprise if Paul was aware of this tendency. On balance therefore, and in line with the broader teaching of Scripture concerning election and the covenant, it seems that it is this interpretation, rather than any of the others, that is the most likely.[48]

At the heart of these differences of interpretation lies the question of the nature of God's sovereignty. Is it absolute, or has he voluntarily relinquished some of his power in order to accommodate the free will of the creatures to whom he has given it? It would have seemed strange to Paul to think that he had the option of rejecting the will of God for his life. He told the Galatians that God had chosen him from the womb, although he did not know it and spent his youth in rebellion, even as he thought he was doing God's will.[49] At no point could he have been described as a seeker, and when he went on the road to Damascus the last thing he wanted was to become a Christian. God intervened in his life in a dramatic and decisive way, and when that happened, there was nothing he could do to resist it. Of course Paul's conversion was extraordinary and he did not expect others to follow the same path, because he understood that God's plan was to prepare him for an equally extraordinary life of service later on. But although the drama and the details of Paul's case were unusual, the underlying principles of his conversion

---

[48] So Towner (2006), p. 178. Marshall (2004), p. 427, acknowledges that this is the reading preferred 'by scholars who find a doctrine of particular election underlying the New Testament', but he adds that 'nothing in the context suggests such a limitation'.
[49] Gal. 1.15-16.

were the same for every believer. Paul did not recount his own experiences in order to tell others that what had happened to him was unlikely to happen to them. On the contrary, he used his own life as a dramatic example of what could and should be their experience as well, even if it would normally be in a more subdued way. A spiritual birth, like a natural one, may be difficult or it may be smooth, but the basic pattern is the same in every case.

Furthermore, Paul could not have accepted a concept of divine sovereignty that was less than absolute, as that would have been inconsistent with his monotheism (which is stressed yet again in the next verse). Even if God were somehow to allow his creatures to make their own decision about whether or not to accept his offer of salvation, he would still be in ultimate control because that 'freedom' would depend on his permission. It would also have encouraged rebellion on the part of the creature, since otherwise it would be impossible for anyone to know whether he was truly free. Attempts to solve the problem of divine sovereignty in this way run into contradictions that make the whole thing nonsensical, and Paul certainly would not have fallen into that trap.

The only solution that takes adequate account of all the data is the third one. When Paul said that God desires the salvation of all people, what he meant was that the gospel had to be proclaimed to every tribe and nation, and not just to Jews. That was a major question in the church of his day, and it explains the vehemence with which he defended the Gentile mission. It was neither an affirmation of universal salvation nor an admission that God was not all-powerful. Both these options, however attractive they may appear to be on the surface, must therefore be rejected.

Having said that, we must note that Paul's emphasis in these verses was on the need to pray for everyone without discrimination. It is not for us to know the secrets of God's will, and we cannot know in advance whom he will save. Just as the sower in the parable cast his seed wherever he could, so the Christian evangelist must do the same with the word of the gospel, to which the seed is compared.[50] A real planter would not do that. He would prepare the ground first and then sow his seed where it was most likely to bear fruit. Many Christians are tempted to think in the same way and target certain individuals or groups accordingly. Even worse, they are also tempted *not* to pray for certain people because they think that they are beyond redemption. It was this that Paul's words were designed to combat. To the early Christians, it may have seemed very unlikely that the Roman authorities would accept the message of Christ and be converted, but that was no excuse to give up

---

[50] Mt. 13.1-9, 18-23.

on them. It would take more than two and a half centuries, but the empire eventually surrendered to the gospel and the rulers who had persecuted it became its staunch defenders instead.

Preaching after Christianity had become the only official religion of the Roman state, John Chrysostom did not hesitate to interpret this verse as a call to Christians to show love to all, whoever they might be and whatever they might believe. In his words,

> Fear not to pray for the Gentiles, for God himself wills it; but fear only to pray against any, for that he wills not. And if you pray for the heathen, you ought of course to pray for heretics also, and not to persecute.[51]

This was also the approach taken by Martin Luther, who distinguished between eternal and temporal salvation, and concluded that in this verse it must have been the latter that Paul had in mind. Who is saved in eternity depends on the predestination that is hidden in the mind of God and not revealed to us. But in this world, deliverance from enemies and relief from suffering ae granted to believers and unbelievers alike. The blessings of this life are not reserved for those who know Christ as their Saviour, and we must not limit our prayers in that way. Just as the sun shines on everyone, so the message of the gospel has gone out into the whole world. It is our duty to preach it without discrimination and in that sense to pray for every human being, even though we know that not all have been chosen for salvation.[52] John Calvin took a similar approach, though he was more precise in the distinction he made between groups of people and individuals. As he put it,

> the apostle's meaning here is simply that no nation of the earth and no rank of society is excluded from salvation, since God wills to offer the gospel to all without exception. Since the preaching of the gospel brings life, he rightly concludes that God regards all men as being equally worthy to share in salvation. but he is speaking of classes and not of individuals.[53]

Both Reformers said essentially the same thing. Individuals are chosen for salvation according to the hidden will of God, but the command to preach the gospel is issued to all nations, because whatever God's criteria for election

---

[51] John Chrysostom, *Homilies on 1 Timothy* 7.4 (NPNF 13, p. 430).
[52] Luther (1973), pp. 262-3.
[53] Calvin (1964), pp. 208-9.

may be, they are not dependent on human factors and therefore do not permit us to discriminate among different types of people.

### 5-7. The mediator and his messenger

> 5. *For there is one God; there is also one mediator between God and humankind, Christ Jesus, himself human,* 6. *who gave himself a ransom for all – this was attested at the right time.* 7. *For this I was appointed a herald and an apostle (I am telling the truth, I am not lying), a teacher of the Gentiles in faith and truth.*

That Paul was speaking in the context of Jewish-Gentile relations when he said that God desires that 'all people' should be saved becomes clearer in the following verses, which speak about the role of Christ as the 'mediator' between God and the human race. Theologians have paid little attention to the statement that there is 'one God', probably because they have assumed that this is obvious, but they have discoursed at great length on the term 'mediator' (*mesitēs*) and on what it means to say that Christ Jesus was a man (*anthrōpos*). To appreciate the nature and the force of Paul's argument, we must take it one step at a time.

First of all, there is the apparently banal assertion that there is 'one God'. In the context, the meaning of this is that he is everybody's God, and that his will embraces the entire world. This seems natural to us, but it was not so in ancient times, where people tended to assign different nations and/or tasks to different gods, rather in the way that Roman Catholics parcel out the saints as patrons of particular people or causes. In this scheme of things, Israel's God was good enough for Israel but irrelevant to everyone else. In theory, Jews could not believe that and be consistent with the teaching of their Scriptures, but to some extent they played along with it by emphasizing their uniqueness and by cutting themselves off from Gentiles as much as they could. Given that situation, Paul's first concern was to challenge Jewish prejudices by pointing out that their monotheism ought to give them a concern for other nations besides their own, because nobody could be outside or beyond the reach of the one God.[54] As I. H. Marshall put it,

> Since there is only one God and not several, there can therefore only be one way of salvation. If there were many gods, there could be different

---
[54] So Towner (2006), p. 180.

ways of salvation for their worshippers, but since there is only one, the possibility is excluded.⁵⁵

Once that principle was established, Paul's next step was to explain how we gain access to the one God. The answer to that was that we can do this only in and through Jesus Christ. What Paul was saying here is what Jesus told his disciples in Jn 14.6: 'I am the way, the truth and the life. No one comes to the Father except by me.' Great play has been made of the word 'mediator', but everyone agrees that its fundamental meaning is that Christ is the only way for human beings to reach God.

The choice of the word 'mediator' to describe the role of Christ in our relationship to God gave rise to much speculation in the early church. Basically there were two models for understanding it, one of which was ontological and the other juridical. According to the ontological scheme, Christ was an intermediate being who was neither fully God nor merely man. He was divine and sinless enough to be able to connect with God, but at the same time he was finite enough to appear as a man, though in fact he was something in between. As the mediator he provided a link between man to God without being identified fully with either. This model was popular among many whom we would now describe as 'Arians'.⁵⁶ Many people wanted a Saviour who could rescue them from the limitations of their creaturely existence, but at the same time they wanted someone whom they could understand (at least to some degree) and relate to. They thought that if Christ were fully God he would not be a distinct person in his own right, because there is only one God. Nor, if he had been God, could he have become a man, because God is invisible, immortal and so on. But they also believed that if Christ were fully man he would be the same as we are and no more able to save us than we are to save ourselves.

The basic problem was that most people thought in terms of being or 'substance' when they used words like 'God' and 'man'. As beings, the Creator and his greatest material creature were incompatible. The only link between them was provided by angels, who were spiritual creatures who appeared on earth as messengers of God but who could not be mediators in any real sense. They were ambassadors sent to reveal God's will, not counsellors who were somehow meant to enter into dialogue with human beings or take our

---

⁵⁵ Marshall (2004), p. 429.
⁵⁶ The Arians were named after Arius (256–336), who believed that the Son was a divine creature. His followers, and many others who held similar views, were prominent in the fourth century, when they were combatted by Athanasius (296–373) and those of like mind to him, who are now recognized as the orthodox party in the church.

concerns to God. Angels were not on intimate terms with their divine Master but did his will as and when he revealed it to them. It was not for nothing that the writer to the Hebrews insisted that Christ the Son was infinitely greater than they were, and there is no reason to suppose that Paul would have thought any differently.[57] For him there was only one God and one mediator – a uniqueness that excluded any identification of Christ with an angel. But if there were good reasons for not relegating the mediator to the status of an angel, it was not so obvious that he was not a spiritual creature of some other kind. The difference between him and an angel would then have been one of dignity and role rather than one of substance or being, and the integrity of both divinity and humanity that made them mutually incompatible would have been preserved.

Regarding the mediator as an intermediate being between God and man seemed to many to be the best solution to the problem, and was attractive for that reason. But what those who advocated this position failed to realize is that a Christ who was neither God nor man would be unable to bridge the gap between them. As an intermediary he would hover over the abyss that separates the creature from the Creator but without touching either one. In fact, of course, he would have to be confined to the side of the creature, because to be anything other than the Creator is to be inferior to him and therefore unable to connect with his being. It was this realization that finally persuaded the early church that a solution based solely on an ontological principle was unworkable. There was no middle ground between the Creator and the creature – you had to be one or the other. Since God is our Saviour, it followed that Christ our Saviour must be God, and that became the cornerstone of orthodox Christology. Once that happened, the ontological model had to be reinterpreted because it could not account for the mediatorial role of the Son. In the words of John Chrysostom,

> this is the property of a mediator, to be in close communion with each of those whose mediator he is. For he would be no longer a mediator if he were connected with one but separated from the other. If therefore he partakes not of the nature of the Father, he is not a mediator, but is separated. For as he is partaker of the nature of men, so is he partaker of the nature of God, because he came from God. Because he was to mediate between two natures, he must approximate to the two natures; for as the place situated between two others is joined to each place, so must that between two others be joined to either nature.[58]

---

[57] Heb. 1.5-14.
[58] John Chrysostom, *Homilies on 1 Timothy*, 7.5 (NPNF 13, p. 430).

Better than the ontological model was the juridical one of mediation which relies not on a union of natures but on a personal relationship, which is the only effective way in which God and man can be connected. But it must be stressed that the theologians of the early church remained wedded to ontological categories and some of them preferred to speak in terms of the union of two natures, the divine and the human, rather than emphasize the oneness of the mediator. Theodoret of Cyrrhus (Cyrus) was an example of this:

> He [Paul] spoke of Christ as *human* since he called him *mediator*: by becoming man he acted as mediator … by uniting humanity to the divine nature he brought about entire and indissoluble peace. If, on the contrary, according to Arius and Eunomius, he has no share in the being of the Father, how is he a mediator? While he is united with us in so far as he is one in being with us in terms of humanity, he is not likewise united with the Father if, in their view, he is removed from that nature. But the divine apostle called him *mediator*. Consequently, he is united both with the Father in divinity and also likewise with us in humanity.[59]

Ambrosiaster, on the other hand, while he shared the ontological framework of Theodoret, gave greater weight to the unity of Christ's person and therefore to his activity as the mediator:

> Because the Father and the Son are one, not in person but in their undifferentiated nature, the Son of God took on flesh and was born as a man, in order to be the arbiter between God and men … If he had stayed within the unity of God he could not have been called the mediator between God and men, because as God only he would have been an alien being calling people who had turned away from him back to grace. But as a man who had not sinned against the law which had been given, he became the arbiter between the one who had sinned and the one who knew no sin.[60]

By the time we come to Martin Luther, the ontological question was no longer in the forefront, and had been replaced by the mediator's work of salvation. This, Luther interpreted according to his earlier distinction between temporal and eternal salvation. As he expressed it,

---

[59] Theodoret of Cyrrhus (Cyrus) (2001), p. 214.
[60] Ambrosiaster (2009), p. 125.

> There is a true God, who saves all men with a general salvation; and Christ the mediator, who saves with an eternal salvation which also comes from God but through Jesus Christ. After all, Christ was not incarnate to have kingdoms, wives, and children. We have those gifts without the death of Christ. In those prior things God is our Saviour without Christ. However, in our eternal salvation God is not our Saviour without the mediator. You see that Paul is speaking about salvation in general. This he then divides into temporal and eternal salvation.[61]

The juridical concept of a 'mediator' is one of a third party who stands in between the other two and tries to reconcile them. In a quarrel between two human beings, a mediator has to be compatible with them to the extent that he must be able to communicate with them and understand where they are coming from. He must also be able to explain the view of each side to the other and to do so in a way that enables both disputing parties to find a satisfactory solution to their differences. Reconciliation does not mean that one party must surrender and become inferior to the other, but that both will find a way to live together in peace, respecting their differences but not allowing them to become a source of unnecessary friction.

At first sight, this model is much closer to the way in which Paul envisaged Christ's work than the ontological one is, and it makes greater sense to most people today. One important advantage of it is that it puts the emphasis on the personhood of those involved. Christ is a personal mediator between God and man, both of whom are personal beings. It is this shared personhood that makes it possible for us to communicate with God, and it is as persons that we are saved. Flesh and blood cannot inherit the kingdom of God, so it does not matter whether we are ontologically compatible with the divine or not.[62] In the resurrection life of heaven we shall have spiritual bodies that are unlike the ones we have now, a point that Paul did not hesitate to expound at length in 1 Cor. 15.35-58. But as persons we shall remain the same, because if that were not the case, salvation would have no meaning. The 'person' who came back from death in a spiritual body would be somebody else, which would hardly be the salvation of the one who had died!

But if the juridical model of a mediator is closer to what Paul intended than the ontological one is, it raises questions of its own. In human terms, a mediator normally assumes that each party in the negotiations has some

---

[61] Luther (1973), p. 263.
[62] 1 Cor. 15.50.

right on his side and understands that his task is to ensure an equitable distribution of whatever is in contention to both parties. In the case of God and man, however, it goes without saying that God is in the right and man is in the wrong. Salvation is not a compromise between two essentially equal parties, but the triumph of the superior one over the other. If the wrong were to defeat the right or even establish some sort of compromise with it, the result would not be salvation but destruction, which would make a mockery of any mediation. The right must win out over the wrong and that can only happen in one of two ways. The first is that the wrong would be annihilated, wiped out of existence altogether. That might have been possible, but as with the triumph of the wrong over the right, the result would have been destruction, and not salvation. Somehow, the party who was wrong had to be brought over to the side of the one who was right and reconciled to him. His wrongness must be eliminated, but without losing his identity or his relationship with God in the process.

This can only be done satisfactorily by distinguishing man's wrongness from his being. Man is not a sinner because ontologically he is a creature and not the Creator. He is a sinner because he has disobeyed God and been cut off from fellowship with him. What is required is the elimination of that disobedience and its consequences, not the transformation of a lesser being into a higher one that would no longer suffer from a partiality to sin. Once that principle is grasped, the true nature of Christ's mediation can be understood. It is basically 'juridical' but not in the usual sense of that term. Christ is not a compromiser, a referee setting out to give each side in the argument its due on the assumption that they are both essentially equal. Rather, he is the one who has reconciled man to God by eliminating what is wrong in man and by restoring him to the fellowship with God which he forfeited by his primordial disobedience.

In order to accomplish this, Christ could not be an intermediate being along the lines of an angel, but had to be a man himself. Elsewhere Paul called him the new or 'last' Adam, and contrasted his obedience with the disobedience of his ancient prototype.[63] Unless Christ was what we were originally meant to be and what he wants us to become once more, he could not have effected the necessary change in us. If he had been some other kind of being, we would not know what he would expect of us. Would he want us to become like him, even if that meant being something quite different from what we were originally intended to be? How would that be possible? As it was, it was in his humanity that Christ was the model of what he wants us

---

[63] 1 Cor. 15.42. See also 1 Cor. 15.22; Rom. 5.12-21.

to be, which is why Paul insisted that he was a human being (*anthrōpos*). At the same time, the mediator had to deal with the problem that has cut us off from God. God cannot just overlook our sinfulness or pretend that it is not there. He is unable to live with iniquity and must eliminate it. Because we are sinners – not just people who have done bad things but people who are incapable of doing anything good – he must destroy what has gone bad in us and start again. This is why Paul said elsewhere that Christ became sin for us. He became a curse on our behalf, so as to pay the price for our wrongdoing.[64] That price was death, but it was followed by resurrection and restoration. 'I am crucified with Christ', said Paul, 'nevertheless I live; yet not I but Christ in me, the hope of glory.'[65]

Christ took our place and paid the price for our sins, so that we might be reconciled to God. Paul did not specifically state that he was God, but he did not have to. It was inherent in the logic of his argument. Christ had come from God and returned to him, taking us with him and reconciling us with our heavenly Father. But for that to happen, the one who was God had to become man. In the words of I. H. Marshall,

> First, it is as a human being that he [i.e. Christ] 'mediates' between God and humanity. Second, it is in his humanity that he carries out his redemptive mission which culminated in his self-offering. There is a strong link between the suffering and humanity of Christ in the early church, and this link may be sufficient for an understanding of the phrase.[66]

This price is what Paul here called the 'ransom' (*antilytron*) with which Christ has purchased our salvation.[67] In Greek, the word is connected to 'redemption' (*apolytrōsis*), a word whose basic meaning is 'buying back'. But to whom was the ransom paid? In secular affairs, a ransom is normally a sum of money given to a kidnapper or some other enemy in return for the release of the captive being ransomed. If this analogy is applied directly to the salvation of mankind, it would seem that Satan was the recipient of the

---

[64] 2 Cor. 5.21; Gal. 3.13.
[65] Gal. 2.20.
[66] Marshall (2004), p. 430. Marshall cites Phil. 2.7-8, Gal. 4.4-5, Rom. 8.3 and Heb. 2.14 for evidence of his assertion regarding the link between the suffering and humanity of Christ.
[67] Paul uses *antilytron hyper* instead of *lytron anti*, found in Mk 10.45, both meaning 'ransom for'. There may be a case for arguing that *antilytron* is more forceful than *lytron*, but if so, it is a nuance with no real significance. Quite possibly *antilytron*, with its additional preposition, was replacing *lytron* in everyday use at this time, as frequently happened with other Greek words.

ransom, but this makes little sense. What would Satan have done with the ransom he received? He could not have kept Christ captive for long. Some theologians in the early church tried to resolve this problem by saying that the ransom was a trick that God played on Satan. Christ offered himself to the devil, they said, rather in the way that we might bait a fish. Satan took the bait but found that he was ensnared in the process.[68] In this way the death of Christ supposedly accomplished two things – it saved mankind and defeated Satan at the same time. This was a good result, but if this analysis of what happened were to be accepted, it was achieved by devious means than many (rightly) thought were unworthy of God.

The bait theory of the ransom therefore never got very far, and most commentators soon realized that if there was a ransom at all, it could only have been paid to God. At first sight, this might seem strange, but in the context of sin and rebellion, it is God, and not Satan, who is our 'enemy'. He is the one who holds us 'captive', not in a superficial way but in the deeper sense of keeping us bound to the power of Satan until we are set free by Christ.[69] When the Son of God paid our ransom to the Father, we were released from our captivity and united with him. Satan was not so much 'defeated' as made irrelevant – a far more humiliating fate. A vanquished enemy may still keep his honour and mystique, as Napoleon did in his exile on St Helena, but one who is forgotten and ignored just fades away in ridicule and indifference. This is what has happened to Satan. He is still around, as Paul recognized when he consigned Hymenaeus and Alexander to him, but his seductive power over believers is gone for good. He will not make a comeback, because those whom he thought he controlled have been set free by the ransom paid on their behalf by the one mediator who was capable of doing it.

There is, however, another dimension to the ransom concept that must not be overlooked. This is that Christ's death was a sacrifice that enables him to intercede with the Father on our behalf. John Calvin expressed this plainly:

> The mention of redemption in this passage is not superfluous, for there is a necessary connection between Christ's sacrificial death and his continual intercession (Rom. 8: 34). They are the two parts of his priestly office, for when Christ is called priest (Heb. 7:17) the meaning is that once by his death he made expiation for our sins to reconcile us to

---

[68] Gregory of Nyssa, *An Address on Religious Instruction*, 24. Gregory seems to have been following Origen, who also thought that the ransom was paid to the devil. See his *Commentary on Matthew*, 16.8.
[69] The early Christians were familiar with this picture. See Rom. 8.7; Jas 4.4.

God, and now, having entered the heavenly sanctuary, he appears in the presence of the Father for our sakes that we may be heard in his name.[70]

The fact that Christ gave himself as a ransom 'for all' (*hyper pantōn*) has been the source of yet another controversy, this time over whether he died for everyone or only for those who are destined for salvation. The nub of the matter is once again the sovereignty of God and whether it is possible for human beings to resist his will. We have already seen that Paul could not have accepted such a conclusion, but he certainly did not believe that Christ died for every human being in the sense that they are all saved. What this must mean therefore is that there is nobody who cannot be saved by Christ. His atoning death and the ransom he paid are sufficient and fully adequate for everyone who believes in him. Nobody can commit a sin that is beyond Christ's power to forgive. Even blasphemy against the Holy Spirit *can* be forgiven, as we have already seen; what Jesus said was that it *would not* be forgiven, which is quite different.[71] In this sense, Christ's death is universal and needs no supplement or alternative to deal with cases that it cannot cover.

Martin Luther wrestled with this, and interpreted the 'for all' in the framework of the distinction he made between temporal and eternal salvation. As he put it,

> It is not clear whether this 'for all' means for all men or for all those who are redeemed. It sounds as if he [Paul] were speaking only about the faithful, because he seems to be making a distinction between temporal and eternal salvation. that is, he seems to say that all who are redeemed are redeemed through him [Christ] and not another. Whoever wants to argue may go his own way. He [Paul] appears to be making a distinction here between faithful and faithless men.[72]

'Christ died for both Jews and Gentiles' is Paul's message and this is how he understood the 'all'. At the same time, his death only has meaning, and therefore applicability, within the context of the household of faith. Just as the atoning sacrifices made by the high priest in the Jerusalem temple were intended for Israel and not for the Gentiles, so the sacrifice of Christ is intended only for the new Israel, for those who believe in him. They in turn have been chosen from before the foundation of the world, as Paul testified

---

[70] Calvin (1964), p. 212.
[71] Mt. 12.31; Mk 3.29.
[72] Luther (1973), p. 264. Calvin (1964), p. 210, repeated what he had said earlier: 'The universal term "all" must always be referred to classes of men but never to individuals.'

of himself.[73] We cannot predict who these people are, or force-feed potential converts into the church. God knows those who are his. His sheep hear his voice and follow him, but the goats do not, however much they may look like sheep to the superficial observer.

Verse 6 concludes with a somewhat mysterious line that may be translated as 'the testimony at the proper time'. The problem is that although there is no doubt about the meaning of the word *martyrion*, which is translated 'testimony' or 'witness', it is not clear what it is referring to. Is it the ransom that is the witness, or the advent of the mediator? At one level the two are clearly connected, since the ransom could not have been paid before the mediator appeared. But if we have to make a distinction between them, it is probably better to say that it is the ransom that is the witness, and not the incarnation of Christ. By itself, the incarnation of the Son of God does not tell us much beyond the fact that he could and did become a man. Important though that was, it does not explain the reason behind the event and so does not actually bear *witness* to anything. It is the ransom that speaks of God's saving power at work, and we must focus our attention on that.

In theory, the incarnation could have happened at any time in human history, but is the same true of the ransom? Paul says that it was revealed 'at the right time', though it might be better to translate this phrase as 'at particular moments' (*kairois idiois*) since it is plural in Greek and refers to specific points in time, suggesting that there were more than one of these. We should probably not press this detail too far, but there is a tendency to restrict the saving work of Christ to his atoning death on the cross, and fail to see that it is broader than that. His death cannot be separated from his subsequent descent into hell, or from his resurrection, ascension and heavenly session at the Father's right hand. There was a process at work here, revealed in and by a sequence of events that culminated in the presentation of the ransom to the Father in heaven. The word *idios* is ambivalent. It can mean 'proper' or 'right' but it can also mean 'particular', and the context suggests that this is a better translation here. The specific time which God chose to reveal his plan of salvation was of course the right time, but while we can appreciate the former we cannot really explain the latter. Why was it the right time? We do not know. All we can say is that it happened when it did, and that those historical events form the basis of our faith and of our experience of salvation by God in Christ.[74]

---

[73] Gal. 1.15.
[74] Calvin (1964), p. 213, places great emphasis on the hidden counsel of God in determining the right time and challenges doubters with the following words: 'Those who are not content with the answer that God has ordered the succession of times by his own secret wisdom, will one day discover that he was using the time they think wasted in getting hell

This was the message that Paul was appointed to proclaim. Once again, there is a triadic structure to the way his vocation is defined, though the interjection in the middle of the verse obscures this somewhat. Paul was called to be a herald (*kēryx*), a missionary (*apostolos*) and a teacher of the Gentiles (*didaskalos ethnōn*). As is often the case with such triads, the first element sets the tone for the rest. Paul was a herald because he was called to preach. A herald does not proclaim his own message but conveys what has been entrusted to him. Those who hear him know this, and would never expect him to start telling people what his own opinions about the message he has been sent to proclaim are. Other words could have been used to describe this function, but they would have been more ambiguous. For example, Paul could have said that he was an *angelos* ('messenger') from God, but that would have suggested that he was a supernatural being, because the word *angelos* was by this time being restricted, especially in Christian usage, to the spiritual messengers whom God sent to proclaim his purposes, and was no longer readily used of human beings.

The other word in common use for this was *prophētēs* ('prophet'), but that also had specialized connotations that made it ambiguous. Paul was not proclaiming a word from God that he had received for a particular occasion, but the message of the gospel that had been revealed and was meant to be preached in its fullness for all time. There was nothing about it that was previously unknown or not readily accessible to everyone. *Kēryx* was a term that avoided these distracting and irrelevant connotations and concentrated instead on what was essential, and that probably explains why Paul used it here.[75]

*Apostolos* is another potentially ambiguous word. Paul was certainly an apostle in the fullest sense, but here the term seems to have a more restricted meaning. In this context he is not primarily concerned with his authority but with his mission. The Greek word embraces both meanings without difficulty, but it is the second of these that stands out in this triad. It was the duty of a herald to spread the word, and that is what Paul did, by travelling around the Roman world preaching to anyone who would listen. Paul took this aspect of his ministry very seriously, explaining that he became a Jew to the Jews and a Gentile to the Gentiles, so that by all means he might

---

ready for the over curious!' In saying this, of course, he was echoing words of Augustine (*Confessions*, 11.12) to the same effect.

[75] Marshall (2004), p. 434, notes that the word is unusual in Christian usage, but thinks that it is no more than the noun connected with the verb *kēryssō* ('preach') and of no particular significance.

win some to the faith.⁷⁶ This is what his missionary commission led him to do, and it was an essential complement to his preaching. It is unfortunately possible to say the right thing in the wrong way and so fail to communicate the message, and Paul did all he could to avoid that. Without going so far as to say that the medium was the message, he nevertheless knew how to adapt his presentation to the audience he was addressing, and that was a key part of his calling.

Also very important was the teaching that he was called to undertake. His preaching had to have content, and that content had to be of use to those to whom he spoke. His target audience was the Gentiles, because God had called and appointed him to direct his mission to them. In actual fact though, he often spoke to Jews first, especially in the diaspora synagogues where he usually went to preach when he arrived in a new city. But he did not go to the Jews in order to reinforce their distinctiveness from the rest of humanity. On the contrary, his intention was to show them how the promises made to their ancestors had been fulfilled in Christ, and fulfilled in such a way as to make them valid for everyone who believed. The Gentiles had to be taught the Jewish world view. They too were children of Abraham by faith, and the promises were meant for them as much as for the Jews. They had to accept that there was only one God, that his creation was good, and that he had saved his people through the sacrificial death of his Son in accordance with the law of Moses. In other words, they had to be grafted into the tree of Israel, as he said to the Romans.⁷⁷ Those who were not Jews by birth had to become Biblically minded people by receiving the proper instruction, and that was Paul's specially appointed task.

An important theme of these verses is truth (*alētheia*). Not only did Paul use the word three times in only two verses (4 and 7), but he insisted on it by interjecting the phrase, 'I am telling the truth, I am not lying.' Did anyone suppose that he might be? Possibly, because this kind of interjection is found elsewhere, 'in contexts where Paul's claim to be the apostle to the Gentiles, or to authority, was being challenged'.⁷⁸ Whatever the case, the unusual intensity of this statement shows how important the concept of truth was to him. For Paul, as for the early Christians in general, the truth was found in Christ, and in Christ alone. To preach the truth was to preach Christ. To know the truth was to know him. The devil was the father of lies (Jn 8.44), and by clinging so insistently to the truth, Paul was distancing himself from

---

[76] 1 Cor. 9.20.
[77] Rom. 11.13-24.
[78] Towner (2006), p. 188, who cites Rom. 9.1, 2 Cor. 11.31, 12.6 and Gal. 1.20 as other examples of the phenomenon.

Satan and his deceptions. The world was full of false teachers who appeared to offer something very attractive but who were doing nothing but leading the innocent astray by their apparent cleverness. Paul would not do that. His message was simple, even foolish-sounding, as he told the Corinthians, but it was also the power of God and the wisdom of God that changed people's lives.[79]

Paul concluded his exposition with the reminder that he was fulfilling his mission 'in faith and truth'. Earlier on he spoke of faith and love in similar terms, and although 'truth' is a different concept, it is very close to 'love' in many ways. Not to tell people the truth is not to love them; to love them is to tell them the truth. Of course it is possible to speak the truth in an unloving way, and Paul wanted to avoid that, but it is not possible to love people and avoid telling them the truth. Many people think that it is, and they justify their view by saying that they do not want to hurt others. Their motive sounds good and it may be sincere, but in the end they are not doing anyone a service and they are not showing them real love. If I have only six months to live, I do not want to be told that I am in robust health and have no need to worry for the foreseeable future. All human beings are dead in trespasses and sins, and to pretend that they are good people with a bright future ahead of them is a lie. They need to know the truth, and the truth is that Jesus Christ has paid the ransom for their sins so that they can live as God intended, and enjoy the fruits of a salvation that is unimaginable without him.

## 8-15. Men and women in the church

*8. I desire, then, that in every place the men should pray, lifting up holy hands without anger or argument; 9. also that the women should dress themselves modestly and decently in suitable clothing, not with their hair braided, or with gold, pearls, or expensive clothes, 10. but with good works, as is proper for women who profess reverence for God. 11. Let a woman learn in silence with full submission. 12. I permit no woman to teach or to have authority over a man; she is to keep silent. 13. For Adam was formed first, then Eve; 14. and Adam was not deceived, but the woman was deceived and became a transgressor. 15. Yet she will be saved through childbearing, provided they continue in faith and love and holiness, with modesty.*

---

[79] 1 Cor. 1.20-25.

Having given an account of his own mission, Paul now moved on to consider the composition and structure of the church. He began with brief remarks about the men in the congregation, followed this with a much fuller treatment of the role of women, and finally moved on to discuss the function and appointment of church officers.[80]

Regardless of any differences there may have been in local conditions, it was Paul's wish that the men (*andres*) in every congregation should pray. Once again we see the importance of prayer in the life of the church, partly because it comes first, partly because it is meant to be universal and partly because it should be common to all the men. Paul did not expressly say so, but the context makes it plain that the prayers were meant to be audible. The men were to raise their hands in a respectful way, avoiding anger or argument.[81] This can only mean that they were to take turns, not jostling for position, and that they were not to criticize one another. Many men have a competitive spirit, and some are convinced that they can do things better than others, but that attitude was to be avoided. Worship was not a time to show off or to pick quarrels. Paul does not tell us what the men might have been arguing about but that hardly matters. It was the negative attitude that produced such behaviour that worried him, and it is just as prevalent today as it was then. Churches often divide over forms of public worship and people can feel very strongly about their particular preferences. In the Corinthian church, for example, there were people who insisted on praying in tongues, even at times when that was inappropriate and helped nobody.[82] Paul wanted to avoid this, and just as he admonished the Corinthians, so he counselled Timothy to restrain those who had a tendency to do that kind of thing.

The manner of praying followed traditional Jewish custom. Men were meant to stand and lift up their hands, a posture that would immediately indicate to everyone what they were doing. When advising Timothy on this, Paul was simply following established practice; he was not prescribing it as the only way that anyone could or should pray. In a world that lacked voice amplification there were advantages to being conspicuous, especially if the

---

[80] Some commentators have interpreted 'men' and 'women' as 'husbands' and 'wives', which is possible but not required by the text and on balance unlikely, since the commands would surely have applied to unmarried men and women as well. See Marshall (2004), p. 444, for a brief discussion of the question.

[81] Rather curiously, Theodore of Mopsuestia (2010), p. 555, claimed that 'anger' referred to hatred of a neighbour, whereas 'argument' signified disagreement with Christian teaching. He therefore interpreted Paul to be saying that the men must be at peace with both God and their neighbours. Theodoret of Cyrrhus (Cyrus) (2001), p. 215, adopted the same interpretation, which seems to have been a common place in the Greek church.

[82] 1 Cor. 14.20-33.

prayers being offered were meant to be shared by an entire congregation, but it could easily become a hypocritical ritual and Paul certainly did not want to encourage that.[83]

The phrase 'in every place' would appear to be straightforward and of little significance, and most commentators have passed over it accordingly. However, Theodoret of Cyrrhus (Cyrus) thought that Paul added these words to emphasize that Christians could pray anywhere, and not merely in the temple at Jerusalem, as he thought the Old Testament prescribed.[84] Martin Luther thought that Paul was enjoining uniformity of practice across the church as a whole – a typical sixteenth-century concern.[85]

The hands are described as 'holy' (*hosioi*), a transferred epithet that is meant to indicate that the men concerned have consecrated themselves to the service of God. The hands themselves could not be made 'holy' by some form of ritual cleansing, though it is quite likely that some church members of Jewish origin (and possibly many Gentiles as well) thought in that way.[86] Holiness was not a matter of external acts but of internal disposition, so that 'holy hands' really meant the hands of men whose hearts were pure in the sight of God.[87]

The assumption that all the men had the duty to pray might also have been seen as a rejection of Jewish notions of priesthood, where acts of worship were confined to a particular class of people, but this is uncertain. Such a democratization of religious activity was already present in the synagogue (as opposed to the Jerusalem temple) and so it cannot be regarded as a Christian innovation. Paul does not say that all the men had to pray, and his counsel to the Corinthians suggests that he did not expect that to happen as a matter of course. Any of the men could pray, but circumstances might dictate that only a certain number of them would actually do so on any given occasion.[88] Paul did not say whether women were allowed to pray out loud or not, but from what he said elsewhere it seems that he expected them to do so. His only

---

[83] See Jesus' criticism of the Pharisees in Mt. 6.5-6.
[84] Theodoret of Cyrrhus (Cyrus) (2001), p. 215. John Calvin (1964), p. 214, said something similar.
[85] Luther (1973), p. 271: 'the congregations should pray at the same time and should help each other with prayers for each other, so that there should be no place which prays against another place.' The same thinking can be seen in the various Books of Common Prayer issued in England and enforced by corresponding parliamentary Acts of Uniformity.
[86] It was standard practice to wash one's hands when entering a sacred place. See Exod. 30.19-21.
[87] See Marshall (2004), p. 445.
[88] See 1 Cor. 14.27-31.

concern was that they should be properly dressed, a theme to which he would return in this epistle.[89]

Paul devoted a considerable amount of space to the place of women in the church, which was a matter of great importance, not only for him but also for the life of the congregations in general. In the Jewish world, women were segregated from men in public worship, and something of this may have persisted in the church. It is quite likely that the women sat apart from the men, as is still the case in many Middle Eastern congregations today. But if customs like that were hard to abandon, the fundamental equality of men and women in the eyes of God was affirmed by Paul and translated into church practice as far as was practicable. The commands that he gave specifically to women did not touch on the question of their equality with men but on the natural differences between the sexes, which also had to be respected in the life of the church.

The first of these differences dealt with the question of dress. Some men pay a lot of attention to their appearance, but on the whole this is a matter that interests women more than it does the average male. Rightly or wrongly, women are usually more concerned than men are with the way they look, and are more ready to criticize other women if what they are wearing seems inappropriate to them. It is true that women's attire can attract (or repel) men, which may be one reason why Paul spent so much time on it, but as often as not, it is the women themselves who bother about such things and who want to appear their best in public, whether the men notice them or not. Cultural attitudes may have influenced their behaviour to some extent, but the phenomenon is so universal, even in these days of so-called 'gender equality', that it is hardly necessary to mention them as a contributing factor to Paul's exposition of the subject.[90]

Paul tackled the question head on by saying that while it was essential for women to dress appropriately, their guidelines should be drawn from a desire

---

[89] See 1 Cor. 11.5, 13.
[90] Towner (2006), pp. 191–210, discusses the place of women in the church at great length, and relies heavily on B. Winter, *After Paul Left Corinth: The Influence of Secular Ethics and Social Change* (Grand Rapids, MI: Eerdmans, 2001) and *Roman Wives, Roman Widows: The Appearance of New Women and the Pauline Communities* (Grand Rapids, MI: Eerdmans, 2003). Winter argues that there was a section of upper-class Roman society in which women pushed the boundaries of sexual freedom, and that this was influencing the behaviour of church members in Corinth and Ephesus. Whether this was so or not, the evidence that it lies behind Paul's comments here is not forthcoming. It is far more likely that Paul was dealing with a situation in which the fundamental equality of men and women in Christ had to be balanced with what was acceptable in the social context of the time. There is no need to introduce extraneous factors as an explanation for Paul's counsels on this matter.

to serve God and not to show off to their neighbours, whether male or female. The principle that Paul stated was that a woman's clothing should be suitably modest and that she should avoid ostentatious or expensive decoration that would attract notice and distract others from the proper business of worship. Many commentators have assumed that Paul was against the wearing of clothes that betrayed the wealth or status of those wearing them, but while there may be some truth in that, it is not the whole story. There may have been occasions when the wives of prominent officials (for example) would have been expected to appear in finery that matched their station, and failure to do so would have had a negative effect. A governor's wife who dressed like a fishmonger would certainly have aroused comment, and it is hard to believe that it would have been approving, even if somebody explained that it was a form of modesty assumed for religious reasons![91]

Interestingly enough, Paul did not describe what he thought 'modest' attire was, and perhaps it is just as well, since fashions and styles change so much. Quite possibly he would have preferred something resembling the Muslim *hijab* or a traditional nun's habit, and he would certainly have expected women to cover their hair.[92] But we really do not know how far he would have taken this, and it is best not to speculate. Every culture has its own norms of modesty, and as long as they are observed, it seems that Paul's injunctions can be followed without difficulty. As usual, he was more interested in the principle than in the details and would probably have been quite flexible on the latter as long as the former was kept firmly in mind.

What Paul was really interested in was not women's clothing but their spiritual attitude.[93] A woman who wanted to impress others with her devotion (*theosebeia*) would do this by good works, and there are plenty of examples from the Bible that illustrate this. In the ancient world, many businesses were family-run and hospitality was a major activity of great social importance. In the home, the woman reigned supreme and her influence was enormous. People who imagine that Paul's advice to Timothy was oppressive towards women do not understand the context in which they were living. In their world, women played a vital role in the economy and in all forms of social interaction, most of which took place in the household. There were no factories or offices in the modern sense, and it was in the home that the sincerity and ability of a Christian woman would be most clearly seen by those who came there to transact their business. Visitors to a house, whether guests or clients, would quickly feel the woman's touch and be impressed

---

[91] Luther (1973), p. 274, recognized this and made a specific exception for weddings.
[92] 1 Cor. 11.6.
[93] Calvin (1964), p. 216, insisted on this and used it to cut the discussion short.

by her faith, if she was the kind of person who was acting in the way that Paul recommended here. The classic New Testament example of this is that of Priscilla and Aquila, a husband and wife team who worked and ministered together and with whom Paul was closely associated.[94]

The church was one of the few places that women would be seen in public and allowed to interact with men to whom they were not related. How they behaved in that context was therefore of particular importance, and the comparative rarity of the phenomenon meant that there were few established social customs to guide them. In providing guidance in this area Paul was meeting a social need that would determine how the church would be seen in the world to which it was called to bear witness. The church could not afford a situation in which that witness might be compromised by behaviour that would be, or would be understood as, an abuse of the unusual degree of freedom given to women by the gospel. Paul had to teach people that with freedom came responsibility, and it was how to achieve that balance that he was expounding to Timothy. Ambrosiaster understood this very well:

> Humble dress suits a good profession of faith, because then it will not be thought to be anything other than what it is. The woman who wants to be seen all dressed up in the house of God is not doing this for God's sake, but for that of other people. She gets what she wants from them ... but she will not get anything from God.[95]

Verses 11-12 describe the conduct that Paul expected of a woman in church. Its leading theme is 'silence' (*hēsychia*), which is consonant with what he told the Corinthians.[96] Paul's admonition to women consists of two parts. A woman was

1. To learn and not teach.
2. To be submissive and not to exercise authority over a man (*anēr*).

These two things are connected but they are not identical. First of all, a woman was called to learn. To many people today this sounds somewhat demeaning, and is often explained by saying that girls did not receive the same education as boys and so needed to catch up with the men in this way. There may be some truth in this, but a woman was told to learn and not

---

[94] Acts 18.2-3, 18-19, 26; Rom. 16.3; 1 Cor. 16.19; 2 Tim. 4.19.
[95] Ambrosiaster (2009), p. 126.
[96] 1 Cor. 14.33-35.

teach, which suggests that she was capable of the latter. If so, Paul's advice was not based on her supposedly inferior achievements, and there is nothing in the text to suggest that it was.

Did Paul think that learning was inferior to teaching? Not necessarily. Learning was something that all Christians were called to do. We must remember that the word Paul used here (*manthanō*) is the same as that used to describe the disciples (*mathētai*) and there can be no higher honour than to be, and to be called, a disciple of the Lord. Very often it is through silent meditation and reflection that we learn most about our faith, and the best teachers are the ones who are constantly learning. John Calvin was particularly insistent on this:

> This is not only for women that they should learn, but men have their part in it also. He who thinks himself to be so wise that he has no more need to learn is a fool, yes, a crazy person. For this is our true wisdom, to know that we are ignorant, so that we may be daily more and more confirmed in good doctrine … let us not think that men and women differ herein.[97]

The fact that women were told to learn in the church does not mean that they could not teach outside it, and many of them must have done so, especially in the home.[98] Mothers taught their children, and older women instructed the younger. Priscilla is even known to have explained the word of God more fully to Apollos, although it is clear that Apollos was the preacher and that her instruction took place in private.[99] To imagine that Paul thought that women would not have a ministry in the church is therefore mistaken; quite probably, their quiet guidance and encouragement did more than the words of even the most compelling preacher to bring the congregation to maturity in Christ. It is apparent that his main concern was that they should behave in a way that was appropriate to the circumstances so as not to hinder the preaching and teaching of the gospel.

Submissiveness (*hypotagē*) is another quality that a woman was expected to show, and its true meaning is not always properly appreciated today. By being submissive she would gain respect and perhaps even be sought out

---

[97] Calvin (2016), p. 258.
[98] Luther (1973), p. 276, made this point. He also said that the prohibition refers to wives – single women could (and sometimes did) have a public ministry, as was clear from a number of cases in the Old Testament (Huldah, Deborah and Jael in particular) and the four unmarried daughters of Philip, who were prophetesses (Acts 21.9).
[99] Acts 18.26. It should be said that she did this in conjunction with her husband, though there is no indication that she took a lesser role – if anything, the reverse!

quietly for counsel and advice. The public teaching ministry was given to men, but women did not receive instruction for nothing and they could make use of it in the right context. It is here that Paul returned to the question of teaching and told Timothy that he did not entrust that to women if men were on the receiving end. It is clear from what he said that by 'teaching' he meant exercising authority of some kind. In other words, women were not to be put in a position of telling men what to do. There is nothing surprising or unusual about this command, which is paralleled in 1 Cor. 14.34-35, though without any mention there of a women having authority over a man:

> The women should keep silent in the churches. For they are not permitted to speak, but should be in submission, as the Law also says. If there is anything they desire to learn, let them ask their husbands at home. For it is shameful for a woman to speak in church. (ESV)[100]

The meaning of *authentein* ('to exercise authority') has been questioned, but the context makes it clear.[101] *Authentein* stands in contrast to *hypotagē* and should be read as its complementary opposite. Men and women stand in a hierarchical relationship to one another, a theme that Paul developed much more fully in 1 Corinthians.[102] Attempts to make it mean something like 'domineer', and to dismiss its relevance for ministry in the church must be rejected.[103] There is no sign that Paul was reacting to a disorder at Ephesus caused by domineering women, though such people were known to exist elsewhere.[104] What he said here was meant to be understood as a general principle to be applied at all times and in all places. This is borne out by what follows. The reasons for the restrictions that Paul placed on women were two:

1. The order of creation. Adam was made first and then Eve.
2. The nature of the fall. Eve was deceived first and then Adam.

---

[100] See Towner (2006), pp. 193-4, for a discussion of the parallel. Against his own inclination towards 'gender equality', Towner concludes that 'it is not really necessary to posit anything more than that in two different situations involving the public speaking of women Paul took a similar tack in restricting women from engaging in a public behaviour that had reached a level of abuse and was causing disruption.'
[101] See the lengthy discussion in Mounce (2000), pp. 120-30. His conclusion (p. 130) is that 'Paul is prohibiting two separate events: teaching and acting in authority. The relationship that exists between the two is that of a principle and a specific application of that principle.'
[102] 1 Cor. 11.3-16.
[103] See Marshall (2004), pp. 456-60, who goes into this at great length, without coming to a definite conclusion.
[104] Rev. 2.20-22.

The importance of these two principles can scarcely be exaggerated. First of all, Paul said that the roles of men and women in the church are determined by the order of creation, a point that he also made to the Corinthians.[105] This is what God intended from the beginning, and in the Christian community, which represents the new creation in Christ, the same pattern must be followed. The submission of the woman to the man was not an aberration caused by sin and it must not be understood in that way. At the same time, it is a fact that sin entered the world through the woman, who believed Satan and deceived her husband. That did not make her more guilty than Adam was, and the long tradition of 'Christian' misogyny that portrays Eve as the gateway to hell must be firmly rejected.[106] Elsewhere in the New Testament, it was the sin of Adam that caused the fall of the human race and Eve was not mentioned.[107] In interpreting this text, Martin Luther sought to absolve Adam from blame, but John Calvin was more forthright. As Calvin saw it, Adam believed Satan's lie just as much as Eve did, and cannot be excused on the ground that he was only trying to keep her happy.[108]

This is as it should be. If Adam had rejected his wife's persuasion, he would not have fallen and nor would she. Her fall was tied to his, and it was his responsibility to rescue and protect her from the wiles of the devil. But if the serpent had approached Adam first and he had succumbed, Eve would have been dragged down into his fall because of her subordinate position in the created order, even though she had not sinned herself. That would have been unjust, and in those circumstances the subordination of the woman to the man would have been quite unfair. As it was, they both had a responsibility for the fall, and so the punishment they received was justly shared by each of them. But although both men and women have fallen, the consequences have worked out in different ways because the hierarchy established by creation has not been overturned. The man remains the 'head' of the woman and must take responsibility for her. But it was by means of the woman that God would bring salvation to his people because she was the one who would play the greater part in the propagation of the human race. In the case of our Saviour's birth, that predominance would become absolute, since there was no male participation in it at all.[109] As Paul pointed

---

[105] 1 Cor. 11.7-10.
[106] See Theodore of Mopsuestia (2010), pp. 561, 563, and Theodoret of Cyrrhus (Cyrus) (2001), p. 216, both of whom rejected any idea that women have inherited a curse from Eve.
[107] Rom. 5.12-14; 1 Cor. 15.22.
[108] Luther (1973), pp. 278-9; Calvin (1964), p. 218.
[109] Gen. 3.15; Isa. 7.14; Mt. 1.20-23; Lk. 1.26-35.

out to the Corinthians, male and female are complementary, and one cannot be saved without the other.[110]

This is what Paul meant when he wrote that a woman would be saved 'through childbearing'. To avoid any possible misapplication to one particular woman (Mary the mother of Jesus?), he then lapsed into the plural: 'if *they* continue in faith, etc'. What is true of individual women is true of all of them.

Some people have claimed that by saying that a woman would be saved through childbearing, Paul was saying that a woman would be protected from harm when giving birth. Even today, the dangers inherent in that are real, and many women suffer severe pain in the process. Complications can easily arise and everyone is relieved when the stress is finally over. Paul knew that, and it is quite likely that his hearers thought in those terms when they first heard his message. The difficulty with such an interpretation is that while there is some truth in it, there are obvious difficulties that make it impossible. First of all, it cannot be said that women are *invariably* kept safe through childbirth. Are we to say that those who die in giving birth (or shortly afterwards) have been unfaithful in spiritual affairs? That would be a monstrous conclusion, and the church has never accepted such an idea. Second, not all women can or do have children. In ancient Israel this was regarded as a misfortune and there were women who desperately tried to conceive.[111] But whatever the popular feeling about this was, the prophets never succumbed to it. The Old Testament is full of comfort for the 'barren woman', who will receive a spiritual reward even greater than the one who is the mother of many children.[112] Whatever Paul meant here, he cannot have limited himself to the physical aspect of the matter alone.

That feeling is confirmed by what he said about the role of faith, love and holiness in the lives of women, whether they have borne children or not. The first thing to notice here is that Paul once again used a triad that demands interpretation. Does faith govern the love and holiness that follow or is there some other organizational principle at work? It would be unlike Paul to think of love as an aspect of faith – elsewhere, it is faith that leads up to love and not the other way round.[113] Nor would he normally have placed love in the middle between two other concepts. The precise meaning of *hagiasmos* ('holiness') is also uncertain. The root *hag-* suggests that this is a God-given quality rather than something that human beings have devised as an offering to him (which would be probably expressed by some derivative of *hosios*), but

---

[110] 1 Cor. 11.11-12.
[111] Gen. 25.21; 30.1; 1 Sam. 1.5-20; 2 Kgs 4.14-17.
[112] Ps. 113.9; 127.3-6; Isa. 54.1-17.
[113] 1 Cor. 13.13.

it does not appear to be the culmination of faith and love, nor does it sound like an expansion of the idea of faith.

The solution seems to lie in the phrase *meta sōphrosynēs*, translated as 'with modesty' but perhaps better rendered as 'with wisdom' or even 'with common sense'. What is required is a balanced mixture of all three things together. Faith, love and God's holiness all have a part to play in the well-ordered Christian life, and if these things are kept in their proper place and respected as they ought to be, salvation will be assured.

That brings us back to the question of what is meant by 'salvation' and what its relationship to childbearing is. There is no reason to think that Paul was using the word 'salvation' in anything other than its usual sense. The context of the fall strongly suggests that he was referring to the way in which the consequences of that unhappy event were put right, and that means that he was talking about eternal life in Christ. What has childbearing got to do with that?

It can hardly mean that having a big family is a guarantee that the mother will go to heaven, though there have been forms of Christian piety that have come close to suggesting such a peculiar idea. Logically speaking, there would be little point in having children at all if this meant only that the parents were bringing more sinners into the world. Bearing children must have a more positive consequence than that, and indeed it was part of the creation mandate given to Adam and Eve before their fall.[114] By continuing to reproduce the human race, even in its fallen state, women were reclaiming the original promise of creation, and in this way they were wisely applying the gifts of faith, love and holiness that were given to them by the grace of God.

Given the controversy that has surrounded this text over the years, it is especially interesting to note how Ambrosiaster understood it. He rejected the idea that a woman would be saved through physical childbirth, perhaps because evidence to the contrary was all too prevalent. Instead, he interpreted it spiritually, as follows:

> Paul says that she *will be saved through bearing children*, as long as she maintains faith, love and a pure life. Paul says that those who are born again by faith in Christ are these children, because if they persevere in their regeneration she will be delivered along with them and rise from the dead. It is not that she will be delivered by them, but by their [new] birth. When those who are destined for eternal life believe, it amounts

---

[114] Gen. 1.28.

to a resurrection from the dead, and she will be saved if they believe and lead a pure life.[115]

For most of the history of the church these verses were uncontroversial and the exposition given above was accepted by virtually everyone without comment. Until the 1960s it was usually taken for granted that women should not exercise pastoral authority in the church and almost everyone agreed that Paul's teaching on the subject was straightforward, at least in its essentials.[116] It is only since the rise of modern feminism that this traditional position has been widely challenged. Those who reject it do not usually do so because they disagree about what the text says, but because they regard its interpretation as a hurdle they must overcome in order to establish the validity of the full inclusion of women in the ordained ministry of the church.

The more consistent of Paul's modern opponents agree with the traditional interpretation of these verses but argue that they have no relevance for the church today. In their view, Paul was simply wrong about male-female relations, an error that they ascribe to the prejudices of the time as much as to anything else. Less consistent in their approach are those who maintain that Paul's views were valid in their own context, because anything else would have been socially unacceptable and misunderstood, but that had he lived in a different culture (such as ours!) he would have approached the question differently. Sometimes commentators lay particular emphasis on the fact that when Paul spoke of not allowing women to teach, he did so personally, as if this were his decision (and therefore potentially reversible) and not a command from God that must stand for all time. Those who take this view seek to uphold the divine inspiration of the text, while at the same time offering a rationale for disregarding its teaching today.

In practice, the more consistent and the less consistent objectors arrive at the same conclusion. They both agree that whatever Paul said and meant, his words do not carry any authority for the pattern of the church's ministry now. Unfortunately, this view comes unstuck when we consider the reasons that Paul gave for maintaining his stance. The creation and fall were not ancient prejudices or limited understandings of human nature that time has shown to be irrelevant. If we reject Paul's teaching on women, we must also reject the Biblical view of the world on which it was based. Indeed, it is hard to think of any other piece of pastoral advice which the apostle gives that has such a

---

[115] Ambrosiaster (2009), p. 126.
[116] This also applied to most of those who thought that the epistle was pseudepigraphical, though some thought it was a sign of the increasing institutionalization which went under the name 'early Catholicism'.

solid theological underpinning as this one has. We are not dealing here with a mere personal opinion about something that was expedient in one cultural environment but not necessarily applicable to others. On the contrary, Paul was teaching that the relationships between men and women in the church are grounded in fundamental principles that are valid for all time and that touch the very heart of the gospel's saving message.

Defenders of the traditional interpretation sometimes lapse into sentimentality about the supposed 'inferiority' of women, but they cannot be faulted on the ground of Biblical exegesis and exposition, where their view is clearly what Paul meant and taught.[117] The problem for them comes when it is asked whether it is still valid and if so, how it ought to be applied today. Those who believe that the Bible is God's Word and that it speaks to the situation of the church in every age therefore find themselves going against the mainstream current of modern society. It is certainly true that women today perform tasks that only a generation or two ago were largely reserved for men, and that most people, including conservative Christians, are happy about that. There are many excellent female scholars and administrators who have placed their talents at the service of the church and who are greatly appreciated. Missionary societies in particular have always relied more heavily than the rest of the church on female ministry and almost nobody would claim that the gospel has suffered because of it. The facts on the ground appear to speak for themselves and even those who argue for the traditional position are seldom inclined to dispute them.

Nevertheless, it has to be accepted that Paul based his argument not on cultural considerations but on the basic doctrines of the creation and the fall, neither of which has changed in the slightest. The suitability of a woman to serve in a ministerial role in the church is not determined by current social norms or by the educational attainments of the woman concerned, both of which may easily favour female appointments. Rather it is grounded in a theological outlook that many people today misunderstand or reject but that remains fundamental to the Bible, and not just to the Pastoral Epistles. To abandon it is to give up any claim to Scriptural authority because on this point the teaching of Scripture is clear, consistent and unequivocal.

Matters are further complicated because the ministerial structures of most churches are out of line with the teaching of the New Testament to one degree or another. Reforming them is a matter of urgency for almost

---

[117] Even Calvin (1964), p. 218, allowed himself to say that 'the weakness of her sex makes woman more timorous and timid'. Such comments, innocent though they probably were, must be rejected and are not to be found in Paul's argument.

all the major Christian bodies, but to do this on a coherently Biblical basis would mean dismantling many of the institutional patterns that we have grown accustomed to over the centuries. Instead of that, modern reformers have usually preferred to extend the current system to cover people who were not previously included in it. The central role given to the pastor/minister/preacher/priest has changed remarkably little; the only difference is that women are now being admitted to the office alongside men. This is not promoting women's ministry as a distinct form of service in the church. All it is doing is expanding the traditionally male pattern of ministry by opening it to women and absorbing them into it. In other words, it is not reform at all. The women who have been co-opted in this way are often among the staunchest defenders of the system because for them it is the achievement of a status for which they have struggled for at least a generation. The result is that what is presented as a radical change is in fact a deeply conservative reaction against any serious restructuring.

As far as appropriating this text for the modern church is concerned, we may perhaps turn to the opinion of Luke Timothy Johnson, who is himself in favour of modern 'gender equality' but who recognizes the difficulties which that places on our interpretation of the ancient text. Johnson sympathizes with the modern feminist perspective but concludes,

> contemporary assumptions concerning family structures and power relationships are not themselves absolute, but are relative and culturally conditioned in a way not unlike Paul's own assumptions. We may prefer them; we may regard them as superior to Paul's; we may even hope that they represent growth toward God's will for the relations between the genders. But we cannot be so parochial as to think that further growth is not possible or even necessary.[118]

That is the view of someone who reads the text in its secular context, who thinks that modern critics of Paul need to remember that their perspectives are just as time-bound as they believe his were. Christians, of course, cannot be content with that. However much Paul may have been addressing the church of his time, he was also proclaiming God's eternal word to his people. The fundamental principles of creation and the fall into sin have not changed – they are just as relevant today as they were when he was writing. The precise details of how men and women should relate to each other vary from time to time and from place to place, but the theological foundation on which their relationship rests does not change. There may be disagreements

---

[118] Johnson (2001), p. 211.

about how that relationship should be worked out in terms of ministry in a congregation, but whatever solution is adopted, the parameters laid down by the apostle ought to be respected by those who claim to be faithful to his teaching. The message of 1 Tim. 2.11-15 is clear enough; the challenge is to apply it in a way that will carry conviction in the church today.

# 1 Timothy 3

## 1-7. The overseer

*1. The saying is sure: whoever aspires to the office of a bishop desires a noble task. 2. Now a bishop must be above reproach, married only once, temperate, sensible, respectable, hospitable, an apt teacher, 3. not a drunkard, not violent but gentle, not quarrelsome, and not a lover of money. 4. He must manage his own household well, keeping his children submissive and respectful in every way – 5. for if someone does not know how to manage his own household, how can he take care of God's church? 6. He must not be a recent convert, or he may be puffed up with conceit and fall into the condemnation of the devil. 7. Moreover, he must be well thought of by outsiders, so that he may not fall into disgrace and the snare of the devil.*

The opening phrase of the first verse is ambiguous because it is uncertain whether it belongs with what precedes or with what follows it. The chapter division, which was determined around the year 1200, puts it with what follows. Most translators and commentators have acquiesced in this decision, but the Nestle-Aland Greek text disagrees and its judgement has been accepted by a number of modern scholars.[1] The phrase has already occurred in 1.15, where it is obviously connected with the subsequent statement, but here such clarity is lacking. Matters are not helped by the fact that although the Greek *pistos ho logos* seems fairly straightforward, finding the right way to translate it is not. The *logos* may be an established saying (i.e. a known catchphrase which Paul was merely repeating) or a fresh statement of his own. *Pistos* means 'trustworthy' or 'reliable', but why the apostle should have felt the need to insist on that here is unclear. Was he confirming an already existing popular opinion, or was he stating something new and reinforcing it

---

[1] Marshall (2004), p. 475, and Towner (2006), p. 248, both opt for the view that it refers to what follows, though Towner is more tentative in drawing that conclusion. Johnson (2001), p. 203, however, goes the other way, as did John Chrysostom, *Homilies on 1 Timothy*, 9.3.1 (NPNF 13, p. 436). The question remains open.

in this way? If the phrase looks back to what precedes it, we should probably choose the second option, because few people would have thought much about the relationship between childbirth and salvation. But if Paul was referring to the statement that comes next, people may already have been thinking along those lines. As we might say today – 'the episcopate is a good job if you can get it.'

Perhaps we do not have to choose between the two and can allow the ambiguity to stand, since both statements are reliable in their different ways and both need to be emphasized in church life, albeit for different reasons. It is important for the promises made to women to be properly understood, but it is equally important for the role of the overseer (or 'bishop') to be recognized and honoured. Each has a part to play in the life of the community, and there is a tendency to underestimate (and therefore undervalue) both of them. What we can say for certain is that at this point in his Epistle, Paul had dealt with the role of women and was turning his attention to those men who had been called to particular ministries within the congregation.

The first of these ministries was that of the *episkopos*. Paul began by repeating the saying that anyone who aspires to the episcopate, or ministry of oversight, desires a 'good work' (*kalon ergon*). The NRSV, the NIV and the ESV all translate this as 'noble task' but although that is doubtless correct, the link with 'good works' (*agatha erga*) in 2.10 and elsewhere should not be obscured. To serve God in this way is indeed a 'good work' in the spiritual sense and it should be recognized as such.[2] There is no appreciable difference between *kalon* and *agathon*; it was customary in ancient Greece to refer to great men by using both terms together – *kalos k'agathos* was a set rhetorical phrase from the classical period onwards.[3]

Episcopacy, whatever it involved in practice and by whatever name it was called, was an honourable vocation, but Paul did not say that it should be actively sought by members of the congregation. To desire it is to desire a good work, but it does not mean that the desire itself is to be encouraged (and still less rewarded) if there is no objective basis for it. We do not know what the process of appointment was, but we can be sure that it was not an

---

[2] Theodore of Mopsuestia (2010), p. 563, commented, '[Paul] rightly said "work" and not "office". For ecclesiastical services are not offices but a work, because each one of them is appointed for the benefit of the community, whether it is the episcopate or the diaconate or anything else.' In this he was followed by Calvin (1964), p. 222, who said much the same thing.

[3] There was a tendency for *kalon* to mean 'outward beauty' and for *agathon* to be understood as 'inward purity', but in the case of works the difference is minimal and both aspects are important. A good work should proceed from a pure heart and also appear to be something positive and useful.

election in the modern sense, where candidates present themselves as worthy of the office to which they aspire and ask the voters to agree with them. It does seem that there was a selection process and it may have taken the form of an election, perhaps by the elders of the congregation, but anyone who actively campaigned for it would probably have been disqualified, if only for that reason. Suitability was something that others ought to recognize; it was not to be claimed by the man himself. In this Epistle, Paul was counselling Timothy to seek out such men and appoint them; he was not addressing potential candidates and advising them how to apply for the job!

The word *episkopos* has been the focus of much comment and the subsequent history of the church has skewed our perception of what it meant in the first century. The word has entered the vocabulary of most European languages where it has been corrupted into the forms with which we are now familiar – 'bishop' in English, *évêque* in French, *obispo* in Spanish and so on. In these forms a 'bishop' has normally been understood as a president who exercises spiritual oversight in a given territory or jurisdiction, known from Roman imperial usage as a 'diocese'. In later times, the episcopate constituted a distinct order of ministry that was superior to that of a deacon or a priest (presbyter). When general synods of the church were held, it was the bishops who were summoned to attend and it was they who voted. The bishop embodied the presence of Christ in the congregation and represented it to the outside world. This did not mean that he was infallible; on the contrary, bishops were exposed to the danger of heresy and schism, and were occasionally deposed on that account. The episcopal office was too important to be left to unworthy occupants, and church history is full of disciplinary measures that were taken at different times against unsatisfactory bishops.

By the second century, the episcopate had taken on its classical 'monarchical' form which in some churches has continued to the present day.[4] Bishops were (and technically still are) elected by their congregations and the system seems to have worked reasonably well most of the time. As always, the problem is that we hear mainly about the exceptional cases, where something had gone wrong and had to be corrected. This distorts the picture and encourages us to think that the episcopate was a corrupt institution that had long since distanced itself from its New Testament origins.

---

[4] The earliest evidence we have for this comes from the letters of Ignatius of Antioch, which can be dated to AD 118. See especially his letter to the Ephesians (3.2; 4.1-2; 5.1-2; 6.1), to the Magnesians (3.1-2; 6.1; 7.1), to the Trallians (2.1-2; 3.1), to the Philippians (3.2; 4.1) and to the Smyrnaeans (8.1-2; 9.1). This spread indicates that a monarchical episcopate was already in place and accepted in Asia Minor in the early second century, but there is as yet no sign of it in 1 Timothy. See Mounce (2000), pp. 186-92, for the evidence from the early church.

It was for that reason that monarchical episcopacy, which by 1500 had been the universal norm in both Eastern and Western churches for well over thousand years, was challenged by the Protestant Reformation. Some Protestant churches retained it, others modified it and still others abandoned it altogether. Whether Anglican or Lutheran episcopacy can be equated with that of the early church is a matter of debate, even within their respective communions. Other Protestant bodies have found it impossible (or undesirable) to maintain an episcopal order in the traditional sense and have devised various ways of replacing it. Some have opted for a college of presbyters, with a moderator who serves for a fixed term but who does not belong to a separate order of ministry. Others have preferred to situate episcopacy in the local congregation, where it is the head pastor who assumes the duties and responsibilities which episcopal oversight entails. Arguably, this model comes closest to what obtained in the New Testament, with the important proviso that there are no longer apostles to supervise them and provide a link with the wider church.

The difficulty that the modern commentator faces is that all these groups claim Biblical authority for their chosen pattern of church government and point to texts like this one as justification for their practices. They cannot all be right, but each of them may reflect elements of the original forms of episcopacy, so that one cannot claim to be authentic in a way that excludes the others, even if that is the official position of the Roman and other 'episcopal' churches. This historical situation makes it difficult to approach the original texts with any claim to objectivity, but in reading them we must remember that Paul knew nothing of later developments and make an effort to understand what he was saying on his own terms.

What can be said with some degree of certainty is this:

1. Every congregation had at least one *episkopos*. He would have been in charge of the church's affairs, ensuring that everything was done decently and in order. Whether he did this himself or shared particular responsibilities with others is unknown, but no doubt much would have depended on circumstances. Many local congregations would have been small and lacking in experienced leaders, so the *episkopos* probably ran them more or less on his own. On the other hand, larger churches seem to have had a collective leadership and it is uncertain where the *episkopos* fitted into it. If there was only one of them in a given locality he would doubtless have acted as a coordinator between various house churches of the kind that existed in Corinth and (probably) in Rome. But perhaps each house church had its own *episkopos* who may have liaised with others in the same city to maintain a wider sense of unity among the Christians there.

An *episkopos* was appointed by an apostle or by an apostolic delegate like Timothy or Titus. There is no sign that he was elected, either by the congregation as a whole or by a group within it, like the 'presbyterate' or 'eldership'. *Episkopos* and *presbyteros* could be used interchangeably for the same position, and it stands to reason that the *episkopos* was an elder, since it is hard to see how he could have functioned otherwise.[5]

What is less clear is whether every elder was also an *episkopos*. The word *episkopos* described a particular activity, whereas *presbyteros* put the emphasis on status, but whether it was possible to possess the status without exercising the role associated with it we cannot say.[6]

2. The character of an *episkopos* was more important than his function(s). Paul was insistent about the former but had nothing much to say about the latter. Furthermore, the qualifications for an *episkopos* are very similar to those for deacons (*diakonoi*) and even for widows who are to be supported by the church as a whole. This strongly suggests that the church's unity was found, not in the people's loyalty to the *episkopos* as their head, but in the transformation of all church members into the likeness of Christ. How they then functioned in the life and ministry of the church was a secondary consideration. We cannot assume that there was no clear division of labour, since the evidence from elsewhere suggests that the different functions emerged for precisely that reason.[7] But however it worked out in practice, the most important thing for Paul was that Timothy should choose the right kind of people for the tasks at hand and worry about the details later.

Having said that, it appears from the text that Paul had a clear idea of the ministerial function of oversight (*episkopē*) and that he expected the *episkopos* to perform it. He evidently assumed that the duty of oversight is an integral part of the church's life and that it would be exercised by a man who was chosen because he had the particular qualities needed for that. From the standpoint of later historical developments, it is interesting to note that Paul said nothing about any relationship between the function of *episkopē* and the apostleship that he himself possessed. There is no sign of a 'laying on of

---

[5] Acts 20.17, 28; Tit. 1.5, 7. Theodoret of Cyrrhus (Cyrus) (2001), pp. 216–17, recognized this and claimed that the bishops of his day (fifth century) had been called 'apostles' in the first generation of the church. That supports the theory that the *episkopoi* filled a vacuum left by the apostles when they died.
[6] For an extended discussion of the relationship between *episkopos* and *presbyteros*, see Marshall (2004), pp. 170–81. Marshall rightly concludes (p. 180), 'Given the complexities regarding the possible use of traditional materials and the general uncertainty about the development of church order, any solution offered must be tentative.'
[7] Acts 6.1-6.

hands' or anything equivalent to that which might be understood as a mark of 'apostolic succession'.

There is also no indication that an *episkopos* received a special grace from God in order to be able to perform his tasks, so that as long as he was appointed in the right way and by the right people, his suitability for the office could be assumed. On the contrary, everything in the passage suggests the exact opposite. Paul was saying that nobody should assume (or be given) the *episkopē* unless he has *already* been tried, tested and found suitable for it. In principle at least, any adult male member of the church could be eligible for the post, as long as he could meet the criteria that Paul laid down.

It should also be noted that the qualifications listed for *episkopē* were not primarily theological or academic. No doubt Paul would have insisted that the man appointed must hold the right doctrine, which he would have received from an apostle or from an intermediary like Timothy, but that was not where he put his emphasis. The future *episkopos* was examined for his personal maturity in both spiritual and secular affairs, with a strong emphasis on his behaviour and ability to manage his household in a way that gained him respect among those outside the church. He was expected to be able to teach his congregation, but there is no mention of his ability to preach or evangelize. Did Paul assume these things and so not bother to mention them? Perhaps, but the complete absence of any requirements of that nature must make us wonder how Paul conceived of *episkopē*. The evidence strongly suggests that for him it was mainly a matter of pastoral oversight and administration, and that the ministries which Paul outlined in 1 Corinthians 12 and elsewhere were more widely distributed among the members of the congregation.[8]

Historically, it was long assumed that the *presbyteroi* were a lower order of ministers, who were essentially delegates of the *episkopos* working under his direction. That is certainly the pattern that we find from the second century onwards, but whether it can be traced back to the New Testament is controversial. In the nineteenth century, J. B. Lightfoot (himself an Anglican bishop) 'proved' that in the early church there was no distinction between an *episkopos* and a *presbyteros*, so that the later differentiation was initially one of function and not of status.[9]

---

[8] 1 Cor. 12.4-11, 28-30; Rom. 12.6-8.
[9] John Chrysostom, *Homilies on 1 Timothy*, 11.8 (NPNF 13, p. 441), said that there was no great difference between a bishop and a presbyter, so that what Paul said about the former could apply equally to the latter. Thomas Aquinas (2012), 2.3.87 (p. 275), went even further and said the two orders were only nominally distinct. These examples show that the ancient perception that *episkopoi* and *presbyteroi* were essentially the same was never entirely lost.

This view has been challenged by those who have pointed out that there is no example of the word *episkopos* being used in the plural, to describe a college of ministers, as there is of *presbyteros*, but whether this was intentional or simply an accident of transmission is impossible to say. Certainly their functions overlapped to a large degree, and if the author of 2 and 3 John was the apostle, there is even evidence that the word *presbyteros* could be used of them. This is not the case with *episkopos*, and it is noticeable that John seems to have been writing to officials in a local church, using his status as a *presbyteros* in a way that gave him authority over them.

What this evidence means can be (and has been) endlessly debated, but it should make us very cautious about trying to rank the *episkopos* in an ecclesiastical hierarchy that may not reflect the historical reality. But whatever an *episkopos* did, and however many there may have been in any given congregation, we can say with some certainty what kind of man he was expected to be. On this point at least, Paul spoke with great clarity. An *episkopos* was a man who was

1. 'irreproachable' (*anepilēmptos*)
2. 'the husband of one wife' (*mias gynaikos anēr*)[10]
3. 'temperate' (*nēphalios*)
4. 'self-controlled' (*sōphrōn*)[11]
5. 'respectable' (*kosmios*)
6. 'hospitable' (*philoxenos*)
7. 'able to teach' (*didaktikos*)
8. 'not a drunkard' (*mē paroinos*)
9. 'not violent' (*mē plēktēs*)
10. 'gentle' (*epieikēs*)
11. 'not quarrelsome' (*amachos*)
12. 'not a lover of money' (*aphilargyros*)

That there should be twelve criteria in the list is almost certainly not accidental, but there is no obvious connection to the twelve apostles or to the twelve tribes of Israel. The number belongs to the rhetorical tradition and should probably be understood as representing the completeness of character that was expected from those who would be called to exercise *episkopē* in and over the church. There was little scope for flaws that cancelled out particular virtues. For example, a man might be able to teach yet at the same time be

---

[10] The NRSV paraphrases this as 'married only once'.
[11] NIV and ESV. The NRSV has 'sensible'.

quarrelsome and greedy for financial gain, but an *episkopos* could not afford to be like that. He had to be godly in every respect, so as to be able to deal with the wide variety of circumstances that were bound to come his way.

The list has to be read in Greek for us to appreciate its true meaning. One reason for this is that many of the words do not have exact equivalents in translation. Greek tends to contain more concepts in a single word than most modern languages do, and having to choose one of these in preference to others can easily lead to an impoverished understanding of what is meant. A good example of this is *sōphrōn*, which the NIV and ESV have translated as 'self-controlled' and the NRSV as 'sensible'. No doubt it is both those things, but it is much broader in scope than the English words convey. *Sōphrosynē* is wisdom, common sense, discernment, the ability to take the right decisions, to avoid compromising entanglements and to maintain a mental balance in all situations. It is a quality that embraces the whole of life and that represented an ideal in ancient Greece to which all aspired but which relatively few attained.

Much the same can be said for several of the other qualities listed here. It is symptomatic that modern languages do not have words for many of them but have to resort to paraphrases, even when it is clear what they mean. In some cases however, the clarity is more apparent than real. *Philoxenia* means 'hospitality', but in the ancient world this was a much more far-reaching concept than anything that goes by that name today. It meant welcoming people into the home, feeding and lodging them, attending to their needs and sending them on their way rejoicing.[12]

When it was practised it attracted favourable comment from the beneficiaries, who saw it as a gift from God, but when it was ignored, the guilty parties were virtually banished from respectable society. Today, a cup of coffee and a chair to sit on while we wait for whatever we have come for may be appreciated, but they are nowhere near to matching what the ancients expected to find when they arrived in a strange place for the first time.

There does not appear to be any discernible order or logic in the order in which the different qualities are listed, though it may be fair to say that there is a tendency to put the individual, essentially internal ones at the beginning, and then moving on from there to a stronger emphasis on the social and external ones towards the end. It must be stressed however that this is a tendency rather than a definite progression, and that in every case, the qualities listed are rooted in the heart of the person concerned and move outwards from there. I. H. Marshall has suggested that the first of them,

---

[12] See 3 Jn 1.5-8; 1 Tim. 5.10.

translated here as 'irreproachable' 'represents the general basic requirement to be fulfilled by the overseer, for which the remaining qualifications in the list will provide concrete definition.'[13] That interpretation fits with a common tendency to start with a generic (but fundamental) requirement which is then illustrated in its different aspects, and may be accepted as a plausible explanation of the structure that Paul has adopted.

Perhaps the most difficult of the qualities to interpret is the one that superficially appears to be the easiest to understand. This is that an *episkopos* is supposed to be 'the husband of one wife'. Like many languages, Greek does not have special words for 'husband' and 'wife' but uses simply 'man' and 'woman'. But whereas in English 'man of one woman' would not necessarily imply marriage, in Greek it does. Partly this was because ancient marriage was less demanding than its medieval and modern counterparts have been, not least because Christian influences introduced obligations and depths to the relationship that had not previously existed. The language never caught up with this, however, and the Greek capacity to allow one word to mean many different things made such precision less necessary than it might otherwise have been.[14]

But if that much is clear, why did Paul express himself in the way he did? It is doubtful that he was going out of his way to reject polygamy, if only because polygamy was rare to the point of non-existence in his day and it is extremely unlikely that there would have been anyone in the church who practised it.[15] It might conceivably mean that he expected a man to remain unmarried after his wife's death, an interpretation that is applied to the priesthood in the Eastern Orthodox Church to this day.[16] But although such cases occur from time to time, they are rare and it seems unlikely that Paul would have made an issue out of them. Widows were permitted to remarry, and actively encouraged to do so if they were under sixty, so it is hard to see that Paul

---

[13] Marshall (2004), p. 477. Martin Luther (1973), p. 284, injected a note of realism into his comment on this when he said: 'Before God no one is above reproach, but before men a bishop is to be so.' Absolute perfection is unattainable, but the *episkopos* must not lay himself open to accusations of hypocrisy in his profession.

[14] Interestingly, Theodore of Mopsuestia (2010), pp. 565–75, was greatly exercised by the 'one wife' question, particularly because in his time there was a tendency to reject men who had lawfully married a second wife while turning a blind eye to others who had only one spouse but were sexually promiscuous. Theodore apparently thought that polygamy was practised in Paul's time but offers only Old Testament evidence for that assertion. In this he was followed by Theodoret of Cyrrhus (Cyrus) (2001), p. 217, again without any evidence to support his assertion.

[15] Calvin (1964), pp. 223–4, mistakenly thought this, though he said that he was following John Chrysostom, who was equally mistaken on this point.

[16] However, it should be noted that the Eastern Orthodox discipline was not established until the Council *in Trullo* (pp. 691–2) and so cannot be traced back to apostolic times.

would have denied the same privilege to a widower.[17] Nor is it likely that he was censuring adultery, a sin that was too obvious for it to be expressed in such an oblique way and which the language does not fit. A concubine was not a wife – an important distinction that was observed throughout the Old Testament and in New Testament times as well. If that had been the issue at stake, Paul would certainly have said so and not pretended that he was dealing with bigamy.

The most probable explanation of this phrase is that it refers to divorce and remarriage. In the Roman world, divorce was very easy and there were many cases of men changing their spouses when it suited them to do so. Women did not have the same freedom to abandon their husbands, of course – the double standard was just as operative then as it has been ever since. But the Christian church did not allow divorce, except in cases of infidelity, and that could apply to either party.[18] A man whose wife cheated on him could divorce her, and was even expected to do for the sake of his honour. In that case he was free to remarry and his previous commitment would not be held against him. But a man who divorced his wife for any other reason was regarded as an adulterer, particularly if he then remarried. That kind of man was definitely excluded from church leadership, not least because his multiple marriages would have created a series of relationships that could not be easily ignored and that might have involved him in particular obligations which the artificial end of a marriage would have made more difficult to fulfil. Divorce and remarriage were socially disruptive back then to a degree that is less usual now, though they are no more acceptable for Christians today than they have ever been.

An *episkopos* was called to set an example, and lifelong faithfulness to a single spouse was a major part of that.[19] Of course, Paul did not insist that every *episkopos* should marry or have children. He himself was single and preferred that state because it left him free to minister to the church, and it would have been the height of hypocrisy if he had denied that option to an *episkopos*. His point was that an *episkopos* must have his domestic affairs in order, whatever they might be, so that they would not distract him from the task to which he had been called.

The fact that an *episkopos* should be able to teach (*didaktikos*) is an indication of what at least one of his functions was, and the emphasis of the

---

[17] 1 Tim. 5.14.
[18] Mt. 19.9.
[19] Thomas Aquinas (2012), 3.1.96 (pp. 277–8), said that the rule was introduced not only for sexual reasons but because of 'what marriage represents, namely, the union between Christ and the church. There is one spouse, Christ, and one church.'

word suggests that what Paul had in mind was what we would today call his 'communication skills'. An *episkopos* not only had to know the truth of the gospel but he had to be able to put it across in a convincing way so that other people would be persuaded by it. This was a very important quality in the ancient world, where so much of life was conducted orally in the public arena. Public speaking was a highly prized art and young men studied it as a central ingredient of their education. For an *episkopos* the ability to present well, both in appearance and in speech, was an important element of his leadership, and virtually essential for communicating with the outside world. An *episkopos* who could not do that would have made a very bad impression and left outsiders wondering what the church had to recommend it to society.

Having described the character desired of the potential *episkopos*, Paul then went on to list three things that would be essential for him to have in order to be able to do his job properly. First of all, he had to demonstrate that he could manage his own household well. Nothing betrays a man's true character more than the way in which he governs his family, and Paul rightly saw this as the key to determining how he would handle the church and its affairs. An *episkopos* had to show that he was able to attract loyalty from his children, who must in turn be advertisements for his suitability. If a man could not do this, he would not be able to manage the affairs of God's house. Inevitably, we are reminded of the tragic figure of Eli, the high priest in Samuel's youth, who could not control his rebellious and immoral sons. In the end, both they and Israel paid a high price for this failure, when the tabernacle was destroyed and the ark of the covenant fell into the hands of the Philistines.[20] Paul did not mention that precedent, but it cannot have been far from his mind as he thought about what a good *episkopos* ought to be like and what the consequences would be if he were not.

We know, of course, that sin is all-pervasive and that there are cases where children are a great grief to their parents, even when the parents have done nothing to deserve that. It is an unenviable situation to be in and hard choices may have to be made. Every once in a while we read of prominent men and women who give up their careers because they need to spend time with their children and set a good example to them. Sometimes this awareness only comes after a child has got himself into trouble and the parents have to pick up the pieces. In a few tragic cases, the realization comes too late, and distraught parents find that their child has committed suicide, been killed in an accident or landed in prison. A pastor must not neglect his family for the sake of his ministry, and yet that happens more often than we like to admit.

---

[20] 1 Sam. 2.12-36.

It is a hard thing to do, but a father who gives up his job for the sake of his family is admired, whereas one who buries his head in the sand and carries on regardless is merely pitied.

Of course, there are limits to what parents are required to do and they cannot be blamed for the misbehaviour of their adult children who are fully responsible for their own actions. Paul was speaking to parents who had children under their control, not to those whose offspring had left home and struck out on their own. He did not address the question of what to do when the adult children of Christian leaders dishonoured their parents, but we may confidently assume that he would not have been happy with such a situation. Whether he would have expected a Christian leader in that position to resign we cannot say, but he would almost certainly have had to distance himself from the child in question. There is no more effective way of undermining church discipline than by allowing those in responsibility to tolerate ungodly behaviour in the name of family loyalty. How often do we meet people who have come to accept divorce, homosexual practice and other such things because their children have landed up in such situations and they cannot distance themselves from them? Whatever sympathy we may have with those who are caught in such a dilemma, surrendering to the way of the world on grounds like these undermines the church's witness and cannot be accepted without doing serious harm to the body of believers.

Another essential requirement for an *episkopos* was spiritual maturity. He must not be 'a recent convert' (*neophytos*) because of the danger of pride that often goes with inexperience and leads to disaster later on. We sometimes come across bright young men who show enormous promise and are put forward in the church as potential leaders because of it. Occasionally they may be given great responsibilities at a young age, and even start congregations of their own. But as the years go by, their inexperience and immaturity start to show. Without proper training and a good grounding in the basic principles of godliness, they may easily lose their way and the ministry which they originally seemed to be so good at fizzles out. It may not always end in scandal or embarrassment, but it loses its shine and ceases to attract others in the way that it initially did. Leadership requires maturity alongside enthusiasm, and when that maturity is missing the results can be painful to behold.

It is interesting to observe that this question perturbed the ancient commentators more than anything apart from the need for an *episkopos* to be the husband of only one wife. The nature of the comments suggests that they had first-hand experience of the problem, which had probably been induced by the rapid growth of the church following the legalization of Christianity in AD 313. There must have been a good number of men who sought a career in the church and who were appointed to high office without having proved themselves worthy of it. Theodore of Mopsuestia was particularly trenchant on the subject:

> someone who is a recent believer and has received the grace of baptism and has not yet furnished proof of his own purpose or been taught in order about what is fitting for him, if he should be advanced to this position so that he would himself teach others, lifted up by this very ordination, he will greatly lose his senses.[21]

Finally, the *episkopos* must be well thought of by outsiders. In the ancient world this would have been relatively easy to determine, partly because the church was too small to subsist as a self-contained community and partly because people lived in close proximity to one another and knew each other very well. If a church leader were a less-than-respectable member of his local village or city, this would be generally known and the reputation of the church would suffer accordingly. Even today, when a prominent church leader falls into scandal, the effect rubs off on everyone because the outside world tends to bracket all Christians together – 'that is what those church people are like'! Paul knew this and was determined that Timothy should do everything he could to avoid such a situation. To him, such slanderous attacks on God's people were a snare of the devil designed to undo the work of evangelism that was so essential for the salvation of souls.[22]

If those who were charged with the primary responsibility for ensuring the church's reputation were themselves behaving in ways that hindered their mission, then the devil would have gained an important victory in his ongoing struggle against the forces of light. The *episkopos* must not fall into such a trap but be protected against the wiles of Satan by the soberness and propriety of his own character and conduct.

It is clear from Paul's remarks that the *episkopos* represented the public face of the church to outsiders. His was not the only ministry in the congregation and there was plenty of scope for others, including women, to serve in different capacities. But it was the *episkopos* who held it all together

---

[21] Theodore of Mopsuestia (2010), pp. 583, 585. For similar remarks, see Ambrosiaster (2009), p. 127; Theodoret of Cyrrhus (Cyrus) (2001), pp. 218–19.

[22] Whether the word *diabolos* should be translated as 'Satan' or as 'a slanderer', meaning a human critic, is debated. Luther (1973), pp. 291–5, accepted the traditional interpretation of 'Satan', though he was somewhat unhappy with it and preferred 'slanderer', but Calvin (1964), pp. 227–8, disagreed. Marshall (2004), pp. 482, 484, clearly prefers 'the devil', as do most modern commentators.

as the one who was specially charged with the pastoral care of the church.[23] If he were to fail in his task the whole church would suffer, which is why Paul placed such great importance on his calling to the ministry of oversight.

Was there any particular reason why Paul devoted so much space to listing the qualities of an *episkopos* at this point in his Epistle? Modern commentators have persuaded themselves that this must reflect a situation in the Ephesian church where false teachers had imposed themselves and had to be ejected. In the words of P. H. Towner,

> In all of this, it is not hard to see the failure of the false teachers behind these qualifications for leadership. If indeed some of them had been young teachers in the church, overcome by pride or arrogance and led astray into ungodly behaviour in one way or another, Paul's concern is to shore up the church's leadership and protect the church's testimony in society. Replacements would have to be found who could undo the damage done by the apostates to the church and its reputation. For those leaders who have not fallen, the instructions warn of the danger, but also positively encourage perseverance in the standard of behaviour and administration that will project a winning testimony in society.[24]

The main difficulty with this kind of interpretation is that it is entirely speculative. If there really were false teachers who had erred because of their youthful arrogance then the explanation offered here would make sense, but there is no evidence that such people had ever been in control of the church or that they even existed. Who would have appointed them? If they were in charge, how would Timothy (who was also youthful, if not arrogant) ever have got his foot in the door or been able to make the kinds of changes that would have been required? Would anyone at Ephesus have listened to Paul if they had been led astray in this way? The assumption that there must have been a group of false teachers hostile to Paul's mission whose activities provoked these remarks goes beyond the known facts and the list itself never suggests that there was opposition in the church to what Paul was proposing. The most we can say is that something like that *may* have been the case, but it is a dubious hypothesis on which to build an interpretation of the passage as a whole.[25]

---

[23] Acts 20.28.
[24] Towner (2006), p. 260.
[25] It is indicative of how doubtful this is that Thornton (2016), who details the 'opponents' of Paul and his gospel, does not discuss this section at any length.

## 8-13. The deacons

*8. Deacons likewise must be serious, not double-tongued, not indulging in much wine, not greedy for money; 9. they must hold fast to the mystery of the faith with a clear conscience. 10. And let them first be tested; then, if they prove themselves blameless, let them serve as deacons. 11. Women likewise must be serious, not slanderers, but temperate, faithful in all things. 12. Let deacons be married only once, and let them manage their children and their households well; 13. for those who serve well as deacons gain a good standing for themselves and great boldness in the faith that is in Christ Jesus.*

After dealing with the *episkopos* Paul moved on to consider the deacons. This office was known from the Jerusalem church, because from the very first days after Pentecost the apostles chose seven men to perform the administrative and pastoral tasks of the congregation, leaving them free to preach the gospel.[26] From the evidence in Acts, it appears that deacons were a significant part of the church, and that they were by no means restricted or prevented from preaching and evangelizing. The first major sermon recorded by Luke was that of Stephen, a deacon who was the first man to be put to death for his faith in Jesus.[27] Later on we discover that Philip the deacon had a roving evangelistic ministry and his witness to the Ethiopian eunuch is recorded in a way that the activities of most of the apostles are not.[28]

How long this overlap continued we cannot say.[29] Paul assumed that Timothy and his church already had a number of deacons whose ministry was fairly well defined and distinct from that of an *episkopos*. The fact that he discussed the requirements for becoming a deacon more briefly than those for an *episkopos* suggests that it was a 'lower' kind of ministry, but that is to think in the hierarchical categories of a later time.[30] Of course, our information is limited and incomplete, but there is nothing in Scripture to suggest that *episkopoi* inherited the mantle of the apostles or were expected to function like them. The 'apostolic succession' claimed by the historic episcopate was

---

[26] Acts 6.1-7.
[27] Acts 7.1-53.
[28] Acts 8.26-40.
[29] See Mounce (2000), pp. 207-12, for a detailed presentation of the evidence regarding the role of deacons and deaconesses in the early church.
[30] They may have been assistants to the *episkopos*, as several commentators suggest, but that is an inference from the position reference to them occupies in the text and is nowhere stated as such.

a later invention, as was the idea that deacons were necessarily subordinate to it.[31]

Did Paul believe that a deacon was inferior to an *episkopos*? From the evidence presented here, it is hard to believe that he would have accepted a man as a deacon if he did not measure up to the standards demanded of an *episkopos*. The proximity of the two offices in the text and the similarity in the requirements demanded of them must have encouraged readers to take the demands made on each one individually as applicable to both. Nevertheless, the list of characteristics desirable for a deacon is shorter and somewhat different from what we find for an *episkopos*, and we must ask whether there is any significance in that. In Paul's mind there were four qualifications needed in a deacon. He was to be

1. 'serious' (*semnos*)
2. 'not double-tongued' (*mē dilogos*)
3. 'not addicted to much wine' (*mē oinōi pollōi prosechōn*)
4. 'not greedy for dishonest gain' (*mē aischrokerdēs*)

The last two of these appear to be repetitions of words already used for the *episkopos* and little more need be said about them. The term *semnos*, translated 'dignified' in the ESV,[32] is rather like *sōphrōn* in that the general idea is clear enough but its range of meaning is so broad that it is hard to find a single word to translate it. The basic idea is that a deacon must play the part assigned to him. If he is to minister the Word of God he must convey the seriousness of what he is doing, and he must behave in a way that is consistent with that. He must be perceived as trustworthy if he is to operate in a way that is honouring to his calling. What that means in practice will vary from one situation to another, but every deacon must recognize that he is a servant of his divinely appointed mission, and act accordingly.

The word *dilogos* is also clear but again somewhat difficult to translate in a single word. It means someone who says one thing to one person and another to another, or else one thing at one time and something else later on. It is a common failing and one that is particularly dangerous in a church officer, because it destroys the trust that needs to be there between him and the members of the congregation. It should be said that a man may be *dilogos* without intending to be deceptive, even if that is often the result. Some

---

[31] Mounce (2000), p. 196, supports this view: 'There is no suggestion in the text that the deacon is subordinate to the overseer. Both performed vital functions in the church, and it is the deacon who is expressly told that a reward awaits those who serve well.'
[32] The NIV paraphrases this as 'worthy of respect'.

people like to keep others happy and so tend to agree with them, regardless of whether that makes them inconsistent or not. Everyone knows that there are some supervisors who accede to the demands of the last person who speaks to them, and how demoralizing that can be. The intentions may be good to start off with but they are unprincipled, and the end result of such behaviour is often catastrophic.

Deacons were also expected to 'hold the mystery of the faith with a clear conscience'. Once again, the general drift is clear but the precise meaning is hard to pin down. Having 'a clear conscience' means that a deacon must be sincere and convinced of the truth of the message he is called to preach, but if what has been said about conscience earlier in the epistle has any relevance here, it would also include living it out in practice.[33] It is unfortunately all too easy to say one thing and do another, a failing which is particularly serious when it comes to giving pastoral advice. If the minister does not follow it himself, how can he expect others to do so?

More problematic though is the phrase 'mystery of the faith'. In later centuries, the word *mystērion* was used to mean the equivalent of the Latin *sacramentum* and applied to the rites of the church, in particular to baptism and the Lord's Supper.[34] It does not seem possible for the word to bear that meaning in this context, but we must still ask why Paul does not simply say 'hold the faith'. Most probably he wanted to go beyond intellectual assent to points of doctrine, though that is by no means excluded. He wanted deacons to understand the spiritual significance of their faith, to experience its transforming power in their lives, and to insist on the need for that in the conversion of every believer. This is a *mystērion* because its nature is not publicly revealed and readily accessible to every enquirer. Only those who 'taste and see that the Lord is good' can understand the mystery of his saving presence in their hearts.[35]

The content of the 'mystery' is, however, clear – as P. H. Towner puts it, it is 'the revelation of salvation in Christ as proclaimed in his [Paul's] gospel.'[36] The need for this spiritual dimension of faith to be present may help to explain what Paul meant when he insisted that deacons must be tested before being allowed to serve. He did not say what the test might consist of, but it was not an academic examination in the modern sense. More probably the prospective deacon was expected not only to be able to give an account of his faith but to show that he could put it into practice and communicate it

---

[33] This is the view of Marshall (2004), p. 491, picked up by Towner (2006), p. 264.
[34] It seems that Cyril of Jerusalem (fourth century) was the first to do this consistently.
[35] Ps. 34.8.
[36] Towner (2006), p. 264.

to others before being formally commissioned to do so. This requirement may also indicate that deacons were often closer to ordinary church members and more involved in teaching them than an *episkopos* was. If the deacons performed the administrative tasks assigned to them in Acts 6, they would have come into contact with a wide range of people at the point of their need. A lot is demanded of someone in that position, because the church cannot afford to make too many mistakes at the pastoral level. If the confidence of the people in their ministers is lost, the ministry itself will falter, and it is probably for that reason that Paul was so concerned with the need for testing. Martin Luther captured this well:

> We must not call a deacon because of his appearance or because he is friendly. We do not test him in this way. If, however, we try to find out from testimony whether he is good, serious, diligent, and the kind of man who gladly pursues piety and is happy to listen to preaching, then we are testing him. One will be able to determine this from the testimony of his brothers and neighbours. We must not take people into the ministry unless they have this testimony.[37]

Paul seems to have assumed that the deacons would normally be men, but we know that women also occupied this position in the early church and there is no reason to think that they were excluded from it here.[38] Female deacons were expected to be 'serious' (*semnai*), which presumably means that they had to conform to the social norms that governed what they could and could not do in public. It is hardly possible to imagine how they could be regarded as 'serious' or 'dignified' if they did not do that. They were also expected not to be 'slanderers' (*diaboloi*). This is one of those rare occasions where the word normally reserved for Satan, the Great Slanderer, is used in its original meaning and with a much broader application.[39]

---

[37] Luther (1973), p. 298.
[38] Johnson (2001), pp. 228-9, Marshall (2004), pp. 492-5, and Towner (2006), pp. 265-7, all prefer the interpretation 'women deacons' as opposed to 'deacons' wives'. The same was true of John Chrysostom, *Homilies on 1 Timothy*, 11.11 (NPNF 13, p. 441), Theodore of Mopsuestia (2010), p. 603, and Theodoret of Cyrrhus (Cyrus) (2001), pp. 219-20. Ambrosiaster (2009), p. 128, on the other hand, thought that female deacons were a sign of Montanism and (wrongly) found no evidence of them in the New Testament, and in this he was followed by Thomas Aquinas (2012), 3.2.118 (p. 285). Luther (1973), pp. 298-9, simply assumed that the reference must be to deacons' wives, as did Calvin (1964), p. 229. Some modern commentators like Mounce (2000), pp. 202-5, follow them in this, but the suspicion must be that it is because they have objections to women's ministry in the church today and not because they are convinced that there were no female deacons in the first century.
[39] Compare the way the same word is used in vv. 6-7 above.

It is hard to know just what Paul had in mind here, and it is unwise to try to pin his thoughts down too precisely. No doubt slander would have included gossiping about others, but it may have gone much further than that. In male-dominated societies, women who had a relatively large degree of freedom could easily have appeared as threatening. Potiphar's wife, for example, in the story of Joseph, used her position to slander him, and the latter could do nothing to protest his innocence.[40]

It would have been better for him if Potiphar's wife had been in seclusion, since then the encounter recorded in Genesis 39 could not have taken place. Something like that may have been in Paul's mind when he looked at the position of female deacons. They were privileged in their standing in the church, but could abuse that if they moved about too freely and gave the wrong impression to other members of the congregation. It is all too easy to imagine how a woman caught in a compromising situation might blame it on the other party, and like Joseph, the latter would have found it difficult or even impossible to speak up in his own defence.

Female deacons were also expected to be 'temperate' (*nēphalioi*), just as an *episkopos* was, and 'faithful in all things'. The word *pistai* here might be better rendered as 'trustworthy'. They were not just expected to attend to their duties in a reliable way but also to keep confidences and show loyalty to the church.

Moving on from the female deacons, Paul repeated what he had already said about the *episkopos* in that male deacons were to be the husbands of one wife, and to demonstrate their ability to keep their families under control. Deacons who did well in shaping their own families and ruling their affairs would lay a firm foundation (*kalos bathmos*) for their ministry and gain great freedom (*pollē parrhēsia*) in their Christian faith. Once again, the general idea of what Paul was saying is clear but the words he used are difficult to translate exactly. The primary meaning of *bathmos* is 'depth' and the emphasis is on building a foundation that would go so deep that it could not be moved. It is a rootedness that cannot be detached, either from the soil or from the visible structure of ministry that can be seen by the wider church. People would sense that here was a man who lived out what he preached, and his reputation would grow accordingly.

It is this that leads to the secondary meaning of the phrase, which is 'good standing' in the sense of having a high reputation, or as we might say 'top marks'.[41] Someone who performed well in the diaconate would

---

[40] Gen. 39.6-20.
[41] The word *bathmos* is used for a mark or grade in the academic sense and this may well be what Paul means to imply here. The deacon who performs well will get top marks!

be respected for his labours, though Paul did not specify whether this respect would come from others in the church, from outsiders, or from both. In the case of an *episkopos*, it was those outside the church whose good opinion was being sought, which suggests that he was meant to act as the public face of the congregation when that was required. Deacons functioned mostly within the congregation, and so it was probably in that context that their reputations would be enhanced. Few outsiders would have known what a deacon did, so it is hard to see how they would have admired him for it, though obviously if they did, Paul would not have objected!

It is the knowledge that he had served well that would give a deacon much 'boldness'. The word *parrhēsia* is difficult to translate but both the NIV's 'assurance' and the ESV's 'confidence' seem to be inadequate to convey the meaning. It can best be imagined as the freedom that an actor or musician who is deeply disciplined and trained can acquire in interpreting the play or piece of music which engages him or her. Supreme mastery of the techniques involved permits a kind of freedom that enhances the meaning of the subject without distorting or spoiling it. Similarly, the deacon who has complete control over himself and who is comfortable in his ministry may also feel free in the way he exercises it, perhaps going out of his way to show compassion or concern in situations where less confident people might feel inhibited and unable to act.

Needless to say, this kind of 'boldness' is not license for the deacon to do as he pleases. Its limitations are not stated but they are implied by the 'faith in Christ Jesus' which sets the boundaries within which those who are called to serve him are entitled to act. Unusual behaviour may occasionally be necessary and justified by circumstances, and a deacon should not feel inhibited from exercising his ministry merely by fear of what others might think. Jesus healed people on the Sabbath even though this was disapproved of by some, and ministers of the gospel have a similar freedom when it is required. But freedom in Christ must never become a cloak for immorality, as it sometimes has been when an unscrupulous pastor has been able to persuade others to trust him to do as he pleases without ever calling him to account. Every ministry takes place in a wider context and those called to exercise theirs in a public position are not dispensed from the standards and obligations that apply to everyone, regardless of their particular circumstances.

The benchmark against which a deacon's ministry was to be measured was (and could only be) the faith which is found in Christ. This is first and foremost the personal relationship that all Christians must have with their Lord and Saviour. That is the context in which everything else takes place. In practical terms it has two major consequences. The first is adherence to the truth that Christ revealed. A deacon could not rely on his position, or even on his accomplishments, as a guarantee of spiritual soundness. He also had to know the truth and believe it, because it was the truth that had set him free in the first place.[42]

Second, he had to live in accordance with it. Every Christian, but especially every minister and preacher of the gospel, must act in a way that is consonant with the message he proclaims. Nothing does more harm to the church than the perception that its officers are hypocrites, and that must at all costs be avoided. The believer who loves Christ and puts his faith in him will naturally want to tell the truth about him and follow it to the best of his ability. That desire, planted in us by our relationship with him, is the ultimate guard and protector of our ministry and the guarantee of the good reputation that ought to accompany it.

Before we move on to the next section, something ought to be said about the relationship between Paul's teaching concerning the *episkopos* and the deacons, on the one hand, and the development of the ordained ministry on the other. Taking Paul's remarks about each of them together, what we find is a remarkably 'primitive' view of church order. Given that for the past two centuries the Pastoral Epistles have been regarded as evidence of 'early Catholicism', that is to say, of a departure from the pure apostolic teaching in the direction of a hierarchically organized church, and that this has been used as evidence that the author was a pseudepigrapher and not Paul himself, this finding is very significant. The picture painted in this chapter cannot be located in the post-apostolic age, and certainly not in the second century, by which time the main features of what was to become the classical form of church government were already far advanced.[43]

The specific signs of early composition are as follows:

1. There are only two orders of ministry, the *episkopoi* and the *diakonoi*. The *presbyteroi* are not mentioned. It is probable that Paul saw no real difference between an *episkopos* and a *presbyteros*, but even if he did, it has no bearing on the pattern of ministry in the church.
2. The *diakonoi* are probably similar to the deacons mentioned in Acts 6, but the *episkopoi* are not linked to the apostles in any way. There is no sign that they performed any apostolic functions and no indication that they had to be appointed by an apostle.

---

[42] Jn 8.32.
[43] On this subject, see Marshall (2004), pp. 497–504.

3. Character was more important than function. In many respects there was no difference in the qualifications demanded for an *episkopos* and those required for a *diakonos*. What they did mattered less than what they were like.

All of this points to a flexibility of practice within a defined pattern of ministry that fits the apostolic age but that was quickly and significantly modified in the next generation. A post-apostolic pseudepigrapher would have been concerned to justify those changes by reading them back into apostolic times, but the Epistle does not do that. On the contrary, it preserves the memory of a structure that had already been superseded in the first post-apostolic generation and that nobody at that time would have had an interest in portraying as normative. None of this can prove that Paul wrote the Epistle, but that it reflects a pattern that he would have recognized is undisputable and greatly increases the likelihood that it is a genuine letter of his.

## 14-16. The mystery of godliness

*14. I hope to come to you soon, but I am writing these instructions to you so that, 15. if I am delayed, you may know how one ought to behave in the household of God, which is the church of the living God; the pillar and bulwark of the truth. 16. Without any doubt, the mystery of our religion is great: He was revealed in flesh, vindicated in spirit, seen by angels, proclaimed among Gentiles, believed in throughout the world, taken up in glory.*

Verse 14 interrupts the main argument, but it is important as a witness to the letter's origin. Here Paul tells Timothy that he is writing to encourage him to hold the fort until he comes himself, which he hopes will be soon. Wherever Paul was, he was clearly not on a long-term missionary journey and was intending to get back to Ephesus as fast as he could. This is important because it is just the kind of detail that it is hard to imagine a pseudepigrapher interjecting at this point. It might be conceivable for a polite fiction of this kind to appear at the end of the epistle, along with other salutations made up for the occasion, but why put it here? The simplest explanation is that Paul wrote the letter himself and was conscious of its stopgap nature. We have no way of knowing how long it would have taken him to get back to Ephesus. Given the slow and erratic nature of so much ancient travel, it may have been as much as a year, especially if he had to winter somewhere en route. He evidently thought it was worth his while to write before setting out on the return journey and that Timothy would have time to make good use of his advice before he arrived. Paul envisaged the possibility that he might be delayed, and wanted to assure Timothy that, if that happened, there was plenty that he could be getting on with in the meantime.

Paul took this opportunity to explain to Timothy what he expected the younger man to do with the Epistle once he received it. Translators often complicate matters by failing to see that the subordinate clause used here is a substitute for the imperative, a form that was often avoided in highly irregular verbs like *oida* (know). What Paul meant is that if he was delayed, Timothy would know what to do 'in the house of God', which was 'the church of the living God, the pillar (*stylos*) and ground (*hedraiōma*) of truth'. The imagery here is reminiscent of the Jerusalem temple, but as it is applied to the Christian church, which was not a building made with hands, we must go beyond that obvious precedent in order to determine its true origin and meaning. Like everything that derived from the law of Moses, the temple was the outward expression of a spiritual reality that went back to the faith of Abraham, Isaac and Jacob, and it is to them that we must look for the spiritual principle that lies behind the imagery.

The idea of 'the house of God' can be traced back at least as far as Jacob's vision of heaven in Genesis 28. When he awoke from his sleep, Jacob named the place Bethel ('house of God') and even set up a stone there, which he called a pillar and named 'God's house'.[44] There seems to be little doubt that this is what Paul was thinking about when he wrote to Timothy, and that Jacob's vision was the foundation of what Israel later believed about the role of the temple in Jewish religion and society. To go to the temple was to go to the house of God. To profane it was to profane God's dwelling place. It was because the temple was what it was that only Jews were allowed into it – and so on. It was a holy place and a witness to the presence and activity of God among his people.

With the sending of the Holy Spirit at Pentecost, God's presence was no longer manifested in a building made with stones but in the hearts and minds of believers. They were the living stones that were being built up into a new temple, which was appropriately called 'the church of the living God'.[45] Once we understand this, the meaning of the words 'pillar' (*stylos*) and 'ground' or 'foundation' (*hedraiōma*) becomes clear. Scholars are in some doubt as to what part of the building's structure the *hedraiōma* actually was, because the

---

[44] Gen. 28.10-22, esp. vv. 17-19.
[45] See 1 Pet. 2.5.

word is rare and ambiguous in the original Greek, but that hardly matters in this context.[46] Phrases like this are common in Hebraic usage – consider, for example, 'the image and likeness of God' – and there is no appreciable difference between the two terms. It was the Hebraic custom to express a single idea by using two slightly different words for it, and this appears to be what Paul was doing here.

The comparison with Genesis 28.19-22 also gives us a clue as to how it should be interpreted. The pillar/ground is a *witness* to the truth of God's self-revelation in Christ and it exists for that reason.[47] It is not the *source* of truth, as many later interpreters would claim. The logic of this interpretation is easy to see once it is examined closely. The living God is present in and through his church, which manifests his divine power at work in many different ways. The church is a fellowship of believers called together under the headship of Christ, but it is not a single entity that possesses some kind of decision-taking power of its own. Later generations would maintain that it had the authority, in and through its ministers, of whom the bishop of Rome (the pope) was the chief, to issue decrees governing doctrine and all aspects of the Christian life. In theory, these ministers would not act independently, but merely articulate what 'the church' in its wisdom has always believed. The argument is circular of course, because once the definition has been made, only those who agree with it can be regarded as members of the true church!

Ambrosiaster placed special emphasis on the church as a vehicle and repository of the truth. In his words,

> The whole world is in transgression because it is convulsed with different kinds of error. Therefore it is necessary for a house of God to be set apart, where the truth will be respected according to his will. His servants confess what he himself has been pleased to teach them, and so that his words will not be nullified, he has confirmed them with miracles which cannot be done by anyone else, so that the unbelief of which they are accused is inexcusable and perishes. These signs and wonders are the pillar and ground of truth.[48]

---

[46] The question is discussed exhaustively – and exhaustingly – by Mounce (2000), pp. 222-4, but it is hard to see that the meaning is seriously affected whatever choice of definition one finally makes.
[47] Calvin (1964), p. 231, wrote of this, 'The church is the pillar of the truth because by its ministry the truth is preserved and spread ... is not the church the mother of all believers, because she brings them to new birth by the Word of God, educates and nourishes them all their life, strengthens them and finally leads them to complete perfection?'
[48] Ambrosiaster (2009), p. 129.

To argue that the church is the *witness* to the truth rather than its *source* alters our perception of its identity and function. There is no 'church' that acts as an agent in its own right. The church consists of people and it is the people in it, in this case its most prominent spokesmen and representatives, who determine how the truth it holds in trust should best be expressed. It is not infallible, because it is not the truth itself, but it is a reliable guide as to where the truth may be found and what it is. Just as Jacob's pillar reminded those who saw it of the house of God and gateway to heaven, so the church points people to the truth of Christ, which the next verse outlines.

Before turning to that, we must remember that the 'house of God' was always more than just a building – it was also a community of people. That was evident in the Old Testament, where even in the days of the tabernacle, it was possible for Hannah to dedicate her son Samuel to its service and to see him grow up in the household of the priests and levites.[49] At the time of Jesus' birth we also discover that there were people like Simeon and Anna living in the temple because of their great piety.[50] The church was a great fellowship of believers who had dedicated their lives to the Lord and who, like Simeon and Anna, were eagerly awaiting his coming.[51] What had previously been true on a small scale was now the norm, a development made possible by the fact that the church was not a building made with hands and therefore not spatially limited in the way that the Old Testament temple was.[52] The significance of this is even greater when we recall that Jesus saw himself as the temple, and the church was regarded as his body.[53] By extension, each Christian is also a temple of God, because the Holy Spirit dwells in our hearts by faith.[54] We are therefore called to live holy lives, not just because of our association with the wider church, but also because we are ourselves the living stones that go to make up the bigger edifice.[55]

It is this perspective that underlies what Paul was teaching in these verses. The individual believer is part of a wider whole – contributing to it and drawing strength from it. It is not necessary to draw a clear distinction between the material and the spiritual – both belong together in the wider perspective of the fellowship of God's people. As I. H. Marshall put it,

---

[49] 1 Sam. 1.21–2.11.
[50] Lk. 2.25-38.
[51] For the second time, of course!
[52] Calvin (1964), p. 231, put it nicely when he wrote, 'There are good reasons why God should call the church his house, for not only has he received us as his sons by the grace of adoption, but he himself dwells in the midst of us.'
[53] Jn 2.19; cf. Mk 14.58; 1 Cor. 12.27.
[54] 1 Cor. 6.19.
[55] 1 Pet. 2.5.

the church is God's dwelling and household. Ethical and theological implications come together in these images. On the one hand, within God's household there is a standard of behaviour and responsibilities which must be acknowledged. On the other hand, where God dwells there is salvation.[56]

What the church exists to do is to confess and to bear witness to 'the mystery of godliness' (*to tēs eusebeias mystērion*). We have already considered the meaning of the word *mystērion*, but here it is tied not to *pistis* ('faith') but to *eusebeia* ('godliness'). It is possible to distinguish these two terms by saying that 'faith' is a more objective concept, stressing the truth of the beliefs it possesses, whereas 'godliness' is more subjective and practical, putting the emphasis on how we live out the things we believe. Perhaps that is the case, but it is hard to see that there is any real difference between them in practice. The mystery of faith and the mystery of godliness may not be exactly the same thing, but they go together.[57] Indeed, the sixfold description of what 'the mystery of godliness' is proves that the objective content of faith is fundamental to it, since that is what Paul focuses on, to the exclusion of anything else. He defines the mystery as

1. the appearance [of Christ] in flesh
2. the justification [of Christ] in Spirit
3. the vision [of Christ] by angels
4. the preaching [of Christ] among the nations (Gentiles)
5. the acceptance [of Christ] in the world
6. the ascension [of Christ] in glory

The first thing we notice about this list is that although it is clearly built around the person and work of Christ, he is never explicitly mentioned. It is the mystery of godliness that reveals him as the truth, which manifests itself in these various ways. The similarity to Jn 14.6 ('I am the way, the truth and the life') is unmistakable, and this verse can easily be read as a fuller exposition of what Jesus meant when he was proclaiming himself to his disciples. The truth is not an abstract set of propositions, even if it can be described to some extent by using them, as is the case here. Rather, the truth is Jesus Christ and the mystery of godliness cannot be explained or understood apart from him.

---

[56] Marshall (2004), pp. 509–10; see also pp. 512–21, for an extended discussion of this theme.
[57] Marshall (2004), p. 523.

At first sight this list looks like the Christological section in a proto-creed and there are certainly elements in it that point in that direction. It begins with the incarnation and ends with the ascension, which strongly suggests a creedal framework centred around the earthly life of Jesus, but the intervening stages are not coordinated with the first and last ones in a historical sequence as they would be in the classical creeds. Items four and five, in particular, did not occur until *after* the ascension, when Jesus told his disciples that these things would happen and that they were to wait in Jerusalem for the Spirit to come upon them and equip them for that task. As for Christ's justification in the Spirit and the vision that the angels had of him, it is not at all certain what historical events Paul was referring to, if any. It is just as likely that he was talking about the heavenly glory of Christ, which followed his ascension but preceded the preaching of the gospel and the ingathering of the Gentiles.

Although it was probably not a proto-creed, the list has a formulaic character that suggests that it may have been a kind of mnemonic device used by the church as a way of inculcating the main ingredients of its faith in Christ to new or young believers. In a culture where relatively few people could read (and even fewer had books), easily memorized phrases had a particular importance, and this is probably what we are dealing with here. If that is the case, Paul cannot be held responsible for the order of the statements being made; he was simply picking up something that was already in circulation and using it as a way of reminding people what the 'mystery of godliness' was.

It is therefore best to interpret these statements as a logical progression from one thing to another, but one that is not directly dependent on the chronological unfolding of historical events in the life of Jesus. The six items listed appear to have been put together in contrasting pairs. In the first pair, the contrast is between flesh and Spirit. In the second one, it is between angels and human beings. In the final one it is between earth and heaven.[58] Let us look at each of them in turn.

First of all comes the contrast between flesh and Spirit, which is a common New Testament theme and fundamental to Christ's identity and mission. The statement that Christ appeared in the flesh is an implicit affirmation of the fact that he had previously existed in a purely spiritual form.[59] As this would later be expressed, the divine person of the Son of God became a man in Jesus Christ. As it is found here, it could be (and to some extent was) misread in terms of a divine apparition. There were those who claimed that

---

[58] For other possible constructions, see Marshall (2004), pp. 500–2. Marshall concludes that the hymn is too complex in its structure to be amenable to simple analysis.

[59] Cf. Jn 1.14.

Christ merely appeared to be a man, rather like the appearance of angels in the Old Testament, and that he was not a genuine human being. This view is nowadays known as 'docetism' from the Greek verb *dokei* ('it seems'). It was not identified as such in ancient times and never constituted an organized heresy linked to the teaching of one particular man, but the phenomenon can be detected in a certain tendency to exalt Christ's divinity at the expense of his humanity.[60] The fact that nothing is said here about Jesus' suffering and death could lend weight to the accusation of docetism, because a phantom human being would not experience such things, but that is an argument from silence and must be treated with extreme caution. We know that Paul did not believe anything like that, and the contrast with 'Spirit' in the next line makes it clear that for him, the flesh of Christ was a material reality. The crucifixion is admittedly not mentioned but neither is it denied, and the claim that this line is therefore 'docetic' does not stand up to examination.[61]

For Paul, the appearance of Christ 'in flesh' was an incarnation of the Son of God in our 'sinful flesh', and that could have only one purpose – atonement for sin.[62] That this is what he thought is subtly revealed by the next line, where we are told that he was *justified* in the Spirit. That would hardly have been necessary if there was nothing in him that needed to be justified, and the phrase only makes sense when we read it in the context of Paul's discussion of justification elsewhere, and especially in Romans. Christ was justified in the Spirit because he put our sins to death in the flesh. He was raised again for our justification, and that is what the use of the word 'Spirit' implies here.[63] His justification was not a physical, material or merely human thing based on good works and self-sacrifice. On the contrary, it was a work of the Holy Spirit who raised him from the dead and revealed in him the only kind of life that can triumph over sin and death.[64]

To be justified in the Spirit is to be vindicated by the power and presence of God. It was not the degree or even the quality of Jesus' suffering and death that justified him, but the work of the Spirit in the whole process. It is important to say this, because although a death even more horrible than that of Jesus can be imagined, a person who suffered it could not thereby claim to have brought a greater redemption to the world. Christ's passion is not to be compared with anyone else's suffering, because its meaning and efficacy

---

[60] Theodore of Mopsuestia (2010), p. 611, associated this heresy with Simon Magus who 'was saying that the Lord had appeared in flesh only as a phantom'.
[61] Marshall (2004), pp. 523–5.
[62] Rom. 8.3.
[63] Rom. 4.25.
[64] Rom. 1.4.

depend not on human considerations, but on the plan and purpose of God that were revealed in Christ's vindication – his resurrection in the power of the Holy Spirit.

The pairing of flesh with Spirit makes sense when we think that the work that Christ began when he came into the world was brought to completion when he took it back into his heavenly glory and sent the Holy Spirit to bear witness to all that he had done. Martin Luther interpreted the phrase with respect to the preaching of the gospel, which is proclaimed to everyone without exception, but which only bears fruit in those who have been touched by the Spirit of God. In his words,

> To be sure, Christ's work is published everywhere; however, it does not justify everywhere, it is not accepted everywhere, and not all people believe in it ... Christ is revealed to the carnal eyes of all men, but he is not received except where the Holy Spirit is.[65]

John Calvin takes a different approach, saying that 'justification' in this context means 'an acknowledgment of divine power', a statement that he backs up by referencing various Scriptural passages where the term is used in that way.[66] That naturally leads to the work of the Holy Spirit, which (like the fathers of the early church) he finds in the resurrection of Christ.[67]

The next contrasting pair is formed by the angels and the Gentiles.[68] The incarnate Son was revealed to the angels and proclaimed among the Gentiles, neither of whom had previously known anything about God's plan to save his people in that way. The angels were servants of God whom he sometimes used to reveal his purposes, but they were not privy to what God was doing in his Son and did not participate in his saving work, at least not directly. It is true that the angel Gabriel was sent to announce his coming to Mary, but when the time came Jesus was conceived by the Holy Spirit, not by an angel, and angels played little part in his earthly ministry.[69] They were eventually told what the Son was doing, but this may not have happened until after his resurrection, which is the first time that we hear of their involvement in Christ's saving work.[70] Peter was rescued from prison

---

[65] Luther (1973), p. 306.
[66] Calvin (1964), p. 233. He cites Pss. 19.9; 51.4; Mt. 11.19; Lk. 7.29, 35 in support of his definition of justification.
[67] Calvin (1964), pp. 233–4. He quotes Rom. 1.3 in support of this interpretation.
[68] Johnson (2001), pp. 233–4, argues that 'angels' refers to human 'messengers', but although this is technically possible, it makes little sense in the context and is rejected by Marshall (2004), pp. 526–7, and Towner (2006), pp. 281–2.
[69] Lk. 1.26-38; Mt. 1.20. On the role of angels in Jesus' earthly ministry, see Mt. 4.11.
[70] Mt. 28.2; Mk 16.5-7; Lk. 24.4; Jn 20.12-13.

by an angel, and John tells us that each church had a guardian angel of its own.[71] How would that have been possible if the angels had not seen what the Son had done?

The fact that Christ was preached among the Gentiles was dear to Paul's heart.[72] Just as the angels had no prior knowledge of God's saving purpose, so the Gentiles had been kept in ignorance until the work of Christ had been accomplished. One point to notice is that while the angels *saw* the glorified Christ, the Gentiles only *heard* about him. The difference between seeing and hearing is brought out in the story of Thomas, who refused to believe in the resurrection of Jesus unless he saw it.[73] Jesus rebuked him for his unbelief, and used the incident to underline the superiority of faith over sight, a message that is repeated elsewhere in the New Testament. Faith comes by hearing, said Paul to the Romans.[74] In Revelation 1 John heard a voice behind him, but it was only when he turned that he saw the one whose voice it was.[75] Turning is an image for conversion, so from that we learn that it is when we believe the message we hear that our eyes are opened to see the one who has brought salvation to us.

The last pair focuses on the contrast between earth and heaven. The claim being made here is that the preaching of the gospel 'in the world' has led to widespread belief in Christ. What this means is not immediately obvious. On the one hand, we know that Jesus commanded his disciples to go into the world and preach the gospel, which to some extent they had done.[76] It could also be said that on the day of Pentecost the world had come to them, because over three thousand people from all over the Roman Empire had turned to Christ when they heard Peter preaching about him.[77] As a result of that, there were Christians in many parts of the Mediterranean world even before the apostles got there, a fact that impressed many who found it hard to understand how such a movement could spread so far and so fast. But as we know, there was still a long way to go and it is only in recent times that we can fairly say that virtually the whole world has had the opportunity to hear the gospel of Christ.

Paul knew more than most people what the past successes and remaining challenges of the Christian mission were and did not take the progress that the gospel had made as a reason to claim that all the nations had already

---

[71] Acts 12.7-11; Rev. 2.1–3.22.
[72] Eph. 3.8-10.
[73] Jn 20.24-29.
[74] Rom. 10.5-17.
[75] Rev. 1.10-13.
[76] Mt. 28.19; Acts 1.8.
[77] Acts 2.8-11.

believed in Christ. He did not discount the geographical spread of the church, but from what he says in his other epistles, we know that his concept of the 'world' was not limited to what might be found on a map. To him, the 'world' was a spiritual reality that was hostile to God. It was governed by Satan, who had led it into rebellion against its Creator.[78] Christians had to arm themselves for spiritual warfare against this evil power, who was far more dangerous than mere flesh and blood.[79] That this hostile environment should show evidence of belief in Christ was a miracle. It was the first and greatest sign that his victory over sin and death was penetrating the ranks of the enemy and rescuing men and women from his clutches. It was also an indication that the gospel message of salvation was triumphing over other conceptions of what was in store for the human race.

The traumatic upheaval that belief in Christ would produce among those who live 'in the world' was demonstrated to great effect in the church's mission to the Jews. At one level this should have been easy, since the Jews were waiting for the coming of the Messiah and it was only to be expected that they would believe in him when he came. Indeed, the evidence of the New Testament is that the early Christians, who were themselves Jews, were deeply disappointed that so many of their countrymen had not accepted Jesus for what he was.[80] The reason, of course, was that the majority of Jews thought like men and women of the world, in spite of the fact that the revelation of God had been entrusted to them. Their picture of the Messiah was a worldly one, which made it impossible for them to recognize the truth when they encountered it. It was because the Jews failed to understand that the promises made to them had been fulfilled in Christ that the apostles turned to the Gentiles, who knew nothing of those promises and so were even more deeply mired in the 'world' than unbelieving Jews were.

Yet it was among these ignorant Gentiles that the preachers of the gospel were successful to a degree that they could hardly have imagined possible. Why would barbarians who were strangers to the ways of God's people suddenly turn around and accept a Jewish Messiah as their Saviour? Jews were not much liked in the Roman world and few Gentiles had a high opinion of their culture or civilization, which paled by comparison with those of Greece or Egypt. Yet before anyone was fully aware of what was happening, Gentiles all over the Roman Empire were turning to Christ. It was not a mass movement by modern standards, but the fact that it was happening at all was

---

[78] 2 Cor. 4.4; Eph. 2.2-3.
[79] Eph. 6.11-12.
[80] Jn 1.9-11; Rom. 11.1-24.

what impressed the early Christians, and this is reflected in the statement we have here.

At the same time, the success of the Christian mission was due to the fact that Christ had been taken up into glory. He did not preside over his new kingdom on earth in the way that David or Solomon had done, even though he was their acknowledged heir. The persistent misunderstanding among the Jews about the nature of the Messianic kingdom was definitively challenged by his ascension into heaven. It was there, and not on a reconstituted throne in Jerusalem, that Christ was glorified, and from there that he sent his Spirit into the world to proclaim the gospel message of salvation. Jesus' kingdom was not of this world. He had been crowned on the cross where he had been proclaimed to the Jews as their king, but what emerged from that was a heavenly and not an earthly kingdom. It is from his throne in heaven that the king rules over his people on earth, and it is from there that he will come to judge the world at the end of time.

What Paul was saying to Timothy was that a Christian does not understand Christ unless he shares this perspective; it is ultimately what the 'mystery of godliness' is all about. To be godly is to be spiritually minded. Even the disciples of Jesus found it hard to grasp this. Some wanted to have a special place in his kingdom, imagining that it would be an earthly state that would rival and replace the Roman Empire.[81] After his resurrection, these same disciples wanted to know whether the moment of their triumph had finally arrived, and it appears that they were still thinking in earthly and material terms.[82] Only slowly, and in the light of Pentecost, did they come to see what Jesus really meant when he said that his kingdom was not of this world, and only then were they set free to preach him as he truly was.

It is in the light of this that we are called by Paul to understand what the identity of church really is. It is the house of the living God, not a building made with hands, nor an institution bound together by rules and hierarchies, but a spiritual creation that owes its existence to the risen, ascended and glorified Christ, who has been justified by the Holy Spirit whom he has sent to dwell in the hearts of everyone who believes in him. This church cannot be tied down by material things or confined to worldly categories. It is not another 'religion' or philosophy that is trying to explain the mysteries of the universe in its own terms. On the contrary, it is a spiritual phenomenon, given by God and sustained by him through the indwelling presence of the Spirit who justified the sacrificial work of Christ by raising him from the dead

---

[81] Mt. 20.21; Mk 10.4.
[82] Acts 1.6.

and taking him up into heaven. Those who know that Spirit know what Paul was talking about here. Those who do not can see the outward manifestations of the Spirit's work – the buildings, the congregations, the spiritual culture of the ages – but they cannot understand its inner workings. The mystery of godliness, as Paul would have expressed it, has simply passed them by.

# 1 Timothy 4

## 1-5. The danger of false asceticism

*1. Now the Spirit expressly says that in later times some will renounce the faith by paying attention to deceitful spirits and teachings of demons, 2. through the hypocrisy of liars whose consciences are seared with a hot iron. 3. They forbid marriage and demand abstinence from foods, which God created to be received with thanksgiving by those who believe and know the truth. 4. For everything created by God is good, and nothing is to be rejected, provided it is received with thanksgiving; 5. for it is sanctified by God's word and by prayer.*

At this point Paul moved on from general statements about the church that could be applied to any congregation to address particular problems that had arisen at Ephesus. Many commentators have seized on the evidence of these verses and constructed an entire heretical movement out of them, but although we come closer to that here than anywhere else in the Epistle, we do not have enough information about the false teachers (as opposed to the false teaching) to be able to draw any definite conclusions about them.[1]

Those who believe that the Epistle was written by a pseudepigrapher naturally see this passage as evidence of a post-apostolic development. The pseudepigrapher would have been concerned to attack the false teaching and retrojected his strictures onto the apostle, who was credited with having foreseen what would be coming. It would presumably have been easier for to combat these false ascetic tendencies if the authority of the apostle could be invoked in support, and so that is what the pseudepigrapher did. The text's explicit reference to 'later times' lends plausibility to this argument, since if Paul were the author of the Epistle, his words here would be interpreted as prophetic. Foresight is not impossible, of course, but the detailed description of the false teaching being denounced makes a critical reader suspect that

---

[1] For a balanced assessment of the evidence, see Thornton (2016), pp. 55–70.

the author is talking about an actual situation known to him and not merely predicting something that would occur at some later time.

What can we say about this? First of all, there is no reason to suppose that the danger of false asceticism was linked to a recognized heretical movement. If it had been, it would surely have been identified in the way that the Nicolaitans were in John's letter to Ephesus.[2] Asceticism was a widespread phenomenon in the ancient world, especially among philosophers, where Platonists, Stoics and Cynics all practised some form of it. Their motivation was clear – they were trying to get away from the corrupting effects of the material world and were repelled by the vulgar devotion to sex and gluttony that characterized so much pagan religion. To these intellectuals, high ideals and asceticism went together, and so it would have been perfectly natural for Christians, who also had high ideals, to think that asceticism was a natural accompaniment to them. The connection would have been an easy one to make, and Gentile converts would not have found it incongruous. On the contrary, many of them may have found it harder not to associate the two things – how could you be spiritually minded if you were indulging in material pleasure at the same time? That dichotomy was not the teaching of the Bible or of the New Testament church, but it is not hard to see how it could have caught on and spread without any prompting from a heretical source.

Furthermore, the content of the false teaching is unknown apart from the two ascetical elements mentioned in the Epistle. There may have been more to it than that, but if so, it does not seem to have had any impact on the church. It is therefore more likely to have appeared as a form of spiritual discipline rather than as a coherent doctrine that explicitly denied or challenged Biblical principles. How influential it was is impossible to say, but from what we are told it sounds as if it was of Gentile origin and therefore more alien to the Scriptures than a Jewish aberration would have been. Paul had already dealt with the latter, in the form of an inordinate interest in the minutiae of genealogies, and it is noticeable that his approach here is quite different. In the earlier case, he regarded the aberrant behaviour as frivolous and absurd but did not attach any spiritual significance to it. Here, however, he sees the error as profoundly spiritual in nature, which also suggests that it was of Gentile (pagan) origin and not simply an odd interpretation of the Mosaic Law.

What Paul seems to have feared was the emergence of a heresy rooted in Greek philosophical concepts. Jewish sectarians did not normally reject

---

[2] Rev. 2.6. See also v. 15.

marriage and their dietary restrictions were tied to the law of Moses, which Paul did not mention. There was a certain tendency among Jews and Christians to regard pagan deities as lying spirits, but Paul does not seem to have been talking about that and he probably regarded the Olympian gods as non-existent rather than as demons in disguise.

In the pagan Greek world what passed as 'spiritual' was mainly in the mind, and to a large extent, that was the preserve of the philosophers. Not all of them to be sure – the Epicureans, for example, embraced matter, for which they were denounced as hedonists. The Stoics were also materialists, at least in theory, but their attitude towards what they thought of as the grosser forms of materialism were similar to those of their bitter enemies, the Platonists, and Paul would probably have seen little to choose between them. On balance, it seems most likely that he was thinking about some form of Platonism that might see itself as akin to Christianity and seek to pervert the gospel by claiming to have the right understanding of it.[3]

For Paul, the battle against asceticism was quite unlike the exaggerated interest in genealogy that he dealt with at the beginning of the epistle. Paul denounced that as a waste of time, but he did not suggest that it was intrinsically evil. In this case, however, his tone was quite different. What was happening at Ephesus was a falling away from the gospel that had been expressly (*rhētōs*) predicted by the Holy Spirit, which made it more serious. Furthermore, the Spirit had warned the church that this aberration was the activity of demons whose purpose was to lead people astray. We know that not all error was motivated by evil spirits. Some of it was due to simple misunderstandings, in which case those who had been led into it should have been open to correction from those who knew better. That was the case with Apollos, for instance, and with those who had received only John's baptism, because they had not heard of anything else.[4] But Paul did not bracket this particular deviation from the truth in the same category. He warned Timothy that false asceticism was the product of a spiritual force that could not be repulsed by education alone. It had to be fought in the power of the Holy Spirit, who is the only one able to deal effectively with that kind of error.

---

[3] Ambrosiaster (2009), p. 130, did not hesitate to connect these false teachings to the Marcionites, the Patricians and (above all) the Manichees, all of whom were still active in his own time. Theodore of Mopsuestia (2010), p. 615, writing a generation later, said the same thing, as did Theodoret of Cyrrhus (Cyrus) (2001), p. 221, who was writing still later. We can safely say that by AD 400 these heresies had become a commonplace of ancient commentators, whether they had any direct knowledge of them or not. Calvin (1964), pp. 238–9, picked up on them as well, though modern commentators are generally agreed that they are all too late (with the possible exception of Marcionism) to have been teachings that either Paul or a pseudepigrapher would have known.

[4] Acts 18.24-26; 19.1-7.

When did the Holy Spirit speak about this future apostasy? That we cannot say for sure.[5] Falling away from God was something that was almost endemic in Israel, and can be traced at least as far back as the making of the golden calf in the desert.[6] At the very moment when Moses was receiving the law of God, the people were turning away from it. The speed with which this happened was breathtaking. As God said to Moses when he was still up the mountain, 'They have turned aside quickly out of the way that I commanded them.'[7] The subsequent history of Israel was one of constant backsliding and was almost always associated with the worship of false gods. It is hardly surprising therefore that what began as recorded fact was transformed into predictive prophecy – the past would repeat itself in the future.[8] Jesus warned his disciples to expect this as a sign of the last days.[9] It was also a typical theme in early Christian preaching, as we can see from a wide variety of New Testament references.[10] Perhaps the Holy Spirit had spoken to Paul directly, although he did not say that, or perhaps he was referring to the past history of Israel as paradigmatic of what happens to God's people in every age. All that we can say for sure is that he believed that the Spirit had made it plain that this kind of trouble would come, and he was writing to counteract it.

What Paul meant by the phrase 'in later times' is not entirely clear, though it seems most likely that he was referring to his own time not to an unknown future.[11] In his thinking, the coming of Christ into the world marked the 'last days' of God's revelation in human history and there were many signs of demonic activity that accompanied that.[12] From the beginning of his earthly ministry, Jesus had to deal with Satanic attacks that ranged from direct temptation by the devil to more subtle attempts to persuade his followers to do what they could to thwart his mission.[13] The Son of God came into the world not only to pay the price for human sin but also to gain victory over the evil that has caused it, and so spiritual warfare with the devil and his

---

[5] Recent commentators seem to be agreed that it is most likely that the message had come either through Christian prophets or directly to Paul himself. In either case, it is clear that Paul believed that the Spirit of prophecy was still very much active in the church. See Towner (2006), p. 288.
[6] Exod. 32.1-10. Calvin (2016), vol. 2, p. 17, brought this out in a sermon on this text.
[7] Exod. 32.8.
[8] See Dan. 7.25.
[9] Mt. 24.4-12; Mk 13.22.
[10] 2 Thess. 2.3-12; 2 Pet. 3.3; 1 Jn 2.18; Jude 1.18.
[11] This interpretation has widespread assent among modern commentators. See Mounce (2000), p. 234; Marshall (2004), pp. 537-8; Towner (2006), pp. 288-9. It is also accepted by Thornton (2016), p. 57.
[12] Heb. 1.2.
[13] Mt. 4.1-11; 16.23.

agents was never far from the surface during his earthly ministry. Casting out demons was also a feature of the apostolic mission in which Paul was directly engaged.[14] Furthermore, Paul had personal experience of apostasy from the faith occurring almost immediately after his own preaching for conversions, as his anguished letter to the Galatians testifies.[15] He did not attribute this to the work of Satan but he did see it as a turning away from the Holy Spirit and therefore as a spiritual rebellion that could easily have been seen as the work of the devil.

That the danger of apostasy would only grow with time stands to reason. As the events of the life, death and resurrection of Jesus grew more distant and the ever-expanding church had fewer eyewitnesses to the key moments of the gospel proclamation, opportunities for deviating from it were bound to increase. The supposed 'true meaning' of what Jesus had taught could be expounded by unscrupulous (or merely inventive) teachers with less fear of contradiction, and teachings that would have been impossible to propagate in the immediate aftermath of Pentecost could have gained a hearing that they would not have had earlier.

Paul believed that the passage of time would lead to an increased desire to turn away from the faith. There may have been many reasons for this, but the root of apostasy was spiritual. People grew tired of hearing sound doctrine, and their itching ears were ready to accept any novelty that might come along. It might be argued that this was not surprising, since Jews who had accepted the gospel could have been accused of having done the same thing. Rather than stick with the tried and true traditions of Judaism, they had turned to the message of Christ and gone off after something new and untested. There probably were people in the churches who were temperamentally disposed to do that, and who would be eager to follow any new teaching when it emerged. There were certainly converts who fell away, and some of them may have been of that type.

What is clear is that the false teachers that Paul had in mind were not people who had come into the church from outside, but church members who had professed the true faith but then turned away from it. Paul does not digress on the subject of whether their faith had been sincere or not, but if it was, it was like the seed that fell on stony ground, in the words of Jesus' famous parable of the sower. Whatever genuineness it may have had, it was not solidly grounded and in due course those who professed it turned away from the truth.[16]

---

[14] Acts 16.16-18.
[15] Gal. 3.1-3.
[16] See Mt. 13.20-21.

It was as they turned away that they began to pay attention to 'deceiving spirits and the teachings of demons'. We are not told whether this was the cause or the consequence of their defection, and the ambiguity may reflect different ways in which people rejected Christ. Some would have been enticed away by the attractions of a rival teaching; others may have already rebelled against Christ in their heart and so been open to the blandishments of the evil spirits. Both scenarios are plausible, and we know from our experience of similar things today that it is often virtually impossible to tell one way or the other. Nor does it matter very much in the end. What is important is that, however it had happened, people were turning away from Christ and being attracted to false teaching.

The sources of this teaching are described as 'deceiving spirits' and as 'demons'. The first thing to notice is that there were many of them. Paul did not exclude the possibility that they were all working under the authority of Satan, but that was not what mattered to him in this context. To his mind, the diversity of sources was itself an indication of the falsity of their teaching, since all truth is one. No doubt the truth could have been communicated by more than one spiritual being, but that would have been pointless, and elsewhere Paul stressed the fact that there is only one Spirit, who proclaims the gospel message in its fullness.[17] Those who heard that message might absorb it in different ways, but they would all have acknowledged a common source and ascribed any differences between them to their own mental and spiritual limitations, not to any diversity in the message itself.

The aim of these evil spirits was to deceive, which suggests that they were more than just straightforward liars. Much of what they said was probably true in itself, but either it was not the whole truth or it was misconstrued in some way and misapplied. The most successful heresies usually contain a large measure of truth, but it is either mixed in with alien ideas or else taken out of context.

Whether the 'spirits' (*pneumata*) and the 'demons' (*daimonia*) are the same is unclear. They functioned in much the same way so it probably does not matter very much, but if the heretical tendency was of Platonic origin it is possible that the *daimonia* were the spirits of the philosophers themselves. Socrates, who had inspired Plato, spoke of his inner *daimōn*, which most modern interpreters equate with the 'conscience'. That may support the theory of a Platonic origin for the use of the term here, especially since Paul refers to the conscience in the same sentence. If that is right, the 'teachings of demons' would be the ideas of the philosophers, which both they and Paul

---

[17] 1 Cor. 12.4-6; Eph. 4.3-6.

would have seen as spiritually inspired. Certainly we must be careful not to equate *daimonia* with 'demons' in the modern sense, which are invariably evil and malicious. No doubt in Paul's usage the word's meaning was rapidly heading in that direction, but Timothy may not have reacted to it quite as negatively as we would today.

The deceiving spirits and 'demons' did not act directly but through human intermediaries. Paul did not call them 'false apostles', perhaps because they made no such claim for themselves, and he said nothing about who they were or how they presented themselves in the church. Instead, he concentrated on their character and on the nature of their teaching. Once again, we see how the inner state of a man governs and guides what he will say and do. In line with the rest of the Scriptures, who and what a person is will be known by what that person says and does. If elements of his teaching are false, that will indicate that the teacher is a false prophet, even if some of what he says happens to be true.

Paul described the agents of the deceiving spirits as *pseudologoi*, a term that can be translated as 'liars', though that word risks conveying a misleading impression. To our minds, a 'liar' is someone who knows the truth and conceals it by uttering falsehoods, but it is probable that the *pseudologoi* whom Paul has in mind were more sophisticated than that. It was not so much that they got their facts wrong, though that may sometimes have been the case, but that they twisted the truth by constructing a false system of belief out of discrete facts that were true in themselves. For example, a *pseudologos* might have said that a Christian must be fully devoted to serving God, that our eternal destiny is in heaven and not on earth, and that if we are really sincere in our faith we would be doing our best to imitate Christ as closely as possible. All those things are true, but if we conclude from that that we must reject marriage because it is a thing of this world and Jesus himself was celibate (as was Paul), we have drawn an erroneous conclusion on the basis of true data. That is what a *pseudologos* probably did, and why his deception was so dangerous.

Paul did however add that the *pseudologoi* were not innocent. It is not that they were ignorant of certain aspects of the truth which, if they had been aware of them, would have corrected their false teaching. Rather, they were acting *en hypokrisei* ('in insincerity'). Their grasp of the truth may have been inadequate, but they knew enough to realize that what they were saying was wrong. They should therefore have been able to change their tune, or at least desist from teaching their faulty doctrine, without external prompting. The reason they did not do this was that they had 'seared their own conscience'. Today we would probably use a different image to describe this – 'blunted' perhaps, or even 'anaesthetized' – but the point is clear. The sensitivity to wrongdoing which their conscience should have had had been lost. They knew that they were doing the wrong thing but they had become inured to it and were no longer capable of repentance.

This phenomenon is unfortunately very common and many modern examples can be cited to confirm it. Those who sent Jews and other 'undesirables' to their deaths in Nazi concentration camps were people in this depraved state. They were aware that what they were doing was evil, but they were living, as we would now put it, 'in denial'. At a less exalted level, there are many people like this all around us. They cut corners where they can, cheat on their employers or on the government, and fail to practise what they preach in any number of ways. There are even professors of theology who write books on subjects like 'holiness' or the inerrancy of Scripture, but who have divorced their wives and run off with a teaching assistant. People like these are not especially 'wicked' but they are blind to what they are doing because their consciences have been 'seared', as Paul put it. They have grown so used to a double standard that they no longer recognize it, and may even be offended if this is pointed out to them.

In the particular case that Paul was dealing with here, the *pseudologoi* were preaching that a true believer would forbid marriage and reject certain kinds of food. This was not the same thing as remaining celibate or fasting from time to time. Paul preferred celibacy to marriage and assumed that fasting was a normal practice. Indeed, he even thought that a married couple could legitimately refrain from having sexual intercourse when they were setting aside time for prayer![18] The problem was not with the practices but with the precepts that were wrongly derived from them and made compulsory for members of the church.

In Paul's mind, celibacy and fasting were useful as means to an end, but they were not ends in themselves. A celibate person could devote himself (or herself) to God and to things that married people could not. Paul did this himself. He was a travelling evangelist because he did not have family responsibilities to worry about. He never encouraged married men to desert their wives and families on the excuse that they were serving God, and we can imagine what he would have said to anyone who did that. Similarly, he thought of fasting as a discipline making room for prayer, but he explicitly said that this should be for a limited time only. He never forbade marriage, and even encouraged it when he saw that the consequences of an unspiritual celibacy would be worse.[19] For him, it was always possible to prefer one thing

---

[18] 1 Cor. 7.5.
[19] 1 Cor. 7.36.

without turning his back on the other, and that is what he did in the case of celibacy and marriage.

With the *pseudologoi* it was very different. They wanted to impose celibacy and abstinence from food. What Paul saw as a blessing for those who were called to it, they saw as a rule to be forced on everyone. The result, as always in such circumstances, is that a discipline intended for good became a curse. This was more or less what had happened with the law of Moses, though the details were different. The Pharisees would never have imposed celibacy and the Jewish food laws had little to do with abstinence, but the spiritual attitude was similar. Once a gift hardened into a regulation it lost its charisma, as it were, and became a burden for those who were wrongly subjected to it.

The history of later times bears this out. It was not until 1123 that the Western Church managed to impose celibacy on its clergy, a rule that the Roman Catholic Church still observes. The resulting distortions are well known and continue to plague the church today. Artificially celibate clergy are liable to have mistresses or leave the ministry in order to marry. Some turn to homosexuality or paederasty as an outlet for their unbridled sexual passion. But in spite of many scandals, the church authorities cling to their unjustified regulation and must be held responsible for the moral quagmire that so often results from it.[20] Compulsory fasting is now much less common in the Christian world than it once was, but it remains a fundamental tenet of Islam, with comparable results. During the holy month of Ramadan faithful Muslims are expected to abstain from food during the day, but can eat as much as they like during the night. The result is a complete distortion of the normal diet and many people actually gain weight during the fast, because they eat too much (and the wrong things) as soon as the restriction on eating is lifted. What is intended to be a spiritual blessing quickly becomes a curse, and people who live in Muslim countries often testify to the negative effects of fasting during Ramadan.

It is interesting to note that while Paul paid no attention to the prohibition against marriage, other than to condemn it, he commented at some length on the food restrictions. We do not know why this was so, but perhaps it was because the food laws touched everyone on a daily basis in a way that the marriage laws did not. The principle he was trying to enunciate was the same in both cases, and so perhaps he felt it best to elaborate on the error that was more common and more far-reaching. But what was it about this asceticism that made it the work of evil spiritual forces?

---

[20] Luther (1973), pp. 312-17, unsurprisingly, makes considerable play of this. What is interesting is that he saw the same misunderstandings among the radical 'Protestants' of his own time as he found in the Roman church.

The fundamental reason for saying that was that banning food (and marriage) was an offence against the created order. It is noteworthy how often Paul came back to the goodness of creation in his exposition. Far from being called to reject the material world as fundamentally evil, the redeemed person has been set free to enjoy what God has made for us. The food which the *pseudologoi* were condemning had been made to be eaten, and in refusing it they were breaking God's law by going against his original intention.

Of course, Paul hastened to add, the consumption of food must be understood in the wider context of man's relationship to God. This meant that it had to be received 'with thanksgiving', a reminder that the gifts of God, while generous, must not be taken for granted. Second, the food was meant for the faithful, who had learned and understood the truth. Eating is a human necessity but it is also a divine privilege and responsibility. Gluttony was a sin to be avoided and the consumption of food ought to be regulated by human needs, not by human desires. It was a microcosm of the Christian life, which we are called to live for the glory and service of God and not for our own pleasure. Knowing the truth, here as elsewhere, is knowing Jesus Christ who is the Truth, and doing what he would have us do in each and every particular circumstance.

In the next two verses (4-5) Paul extended this principle to cover the whole of creation. Everything created by God is good, a belief that goes back to the creation narrative in Genesis 1. Nothing is to be rejected, but rather it must be received with thanks, because it is made holy (*hagiazetai*) by the 'word of God' (*logos Theou*) and 'prayer' (*enteuxis*).

Note first of all that when Paul (and Genesis) spoke of the creation as 'good' this word is not meant to be understood in a moral or spiritual sense. Matter is 'good' because it is not faulty or corrupt; it is what God intended it to be. Even poisonous substances are good in this sense, but it would obviously be silly to suggest that Christians are free to eat and drink poison! It is only certain things that were made edible and suitable for physical sustenance, and it is those things that a Christian was expected to receive with the appropriate gratitude. Food that is naturally suitable was to be consecrated to God in prayer, after which it would be sanctified by his Word.

This all seems clear and logical, so much so that we are liable to overlook what it really means. First of all, it was possible for created things to be made holy, not by some form of ritual purification but by divine decree. Food could and did become a sign of God's presence not because of what it is or was in itself, but because it had been set aside for the purpose of glorifying him. To make it a matter of prayer was to lay it before God as a just thanksgiving for his bountiful mercy, and the promise was given that if this was done with the right intention God would accept our prayers and bless the food we eat.

Quite what Paul meant by the term *logos Theou* ('word of God') is unclear. In another context, Christ himself was the *logos Theou*, but this can hardly be the meaning here. Nor should we expect a divine intervention of the kind that occurred at Jesus' baptism – the heavens do not open when we give thanks and there is no voice proclaiming God's word in the literal sense. We probably ought to interpret *logos* here as referring to the promise of God made to those who pray to him in faith. He has given us his Word and he will keep it when we pray in conformity to his known will and purposes.

The mention of 'holiness' is a reminder of the presence of God, which cannot be taken lightly. If we do not receive our food with the right attitude (that is to say, 'with thanksgiving') then it will not be sanctified to our use. Its physical effects may be no different, but its spiritual dimension will be obscured, with potentially disastrous results. Few things are as potentially harmful as doing the right thing in the wrong way or for the wrong reason(s), and the abuse of God's creation is no exception. Instead of succumbing to that, we are called to promote the holiness of the material world by treating it as part of God's plan for our well-being and seeing in it his presence at work, in fulfillment of his purposes for us.

## 6-10. Training for godliness

*6. If you put these instructions before the brothers and sisters, you will be a good servant of Christ Jesus, nourished on the words of the faith and of the sound teaching that you have followed. 7. Have nothing to do with profane myths and old wives' tales. Train yourself in godliness, 8. for, while physical training is of some value, godliness is valuable in every way, holding promise for both the present life and the life to come. 9. The saying is sure and worthy of full acceptance. 10. For to this end we toil and struggle, because we have our hope set on the living God, who is the Saviour of all people, especially of those who believe.*

Verse 6 is a transition from the condemnation of the *pseudologoi* to an exposition of Timothy's role as a true minister of God's Word. Most editions and translations place it at the head of the next paragraph, but in fact it is a conclusion to what has gone before and a preparation for what Paul had to say to Timothy as a leader of the church. Before developing that theme, he reminded Timothy of his duty to pass the apostolic teaching on to his congregation. He regarded the Christians at Ephesus as his 'brothers', the first of a series of images based on the model of the family which he would use to expound his teaching about pastoral ministry.

A brother is someone who is fundamentally an equal in every respect. He shares the same parentage, which in this case means the privilege of being adopted by God as his child. That adoption links him not only to all other believers, including the apostle Paul, but more importantly to Jesus Christ himself. The one who is the Son by nature has adopted us into his family and made us co-heirs with him by sending his Holy Spirit into our hearts.[21] That is the basis of our brotherhood, and not some physical relationship. A brother is someone that we can treat with both familiarity and respect. We do not have to be polite to him in the way that we would have to be with strangers, but neither can we ignore him or disregard his interests. What happens to him happens to the whole family, whether it is good or bad. If he rejoices, we all rejoice. If he suffers, we all suffer. If we see him doing the wrong thing we go to the rescue in that powerful mixture of rebuke and assistance that only family members can give to one another. We do not excuse him or let him off lightly, because his behaviour affects the well-being of everyone, but at the same time we forgive and restore him when he repents and comes to his senses, because he is a member of our family and we cannot disown him or watch him perish.

It is in this light that Timothy is being called on to present Paul's teaching to the congregation. His ministry to his 'brothers' is really a service to Christ Jesus. If Timothy performs his task well, he will demonstrate what a good servant of the Master he is. It is Paul's reminder that whatever we do in the service of the church we do in the service of the Lord, and it is that dimension which counts above all else. Timothy will not be praised for what he has done for the Ephesian Christians, but for what he has done for God, and Paul reminds him that it is that awareness that must guide his whole approach.

Paul points out to Timothy not only that he is capable of this ministry, but that he is ideally suited to it. He has been nourished (*entrephomenos*) on the 'words of faith' (*logoi tēs pisteōs*) and on the good teaching (*didaskalia*) that he has accepted (*parakolouthō*). The words Paul uses here are heavy with meaning. First of all, Timothy has been fed the right doctrine. Paul has just been talking about the use and abuse of food, and so it is highly significant that he stayed with this metaphor when he turned to the spiritual preparation that Timothy had received for his ministry. The feeding of the mind and the spirit is just as important as the feeding of the body, and as a person matures, it becomes considerably more important. The body will eventually wither and die, however much good food it receives, but the soul will not. The words of faith will produce a strong and mature believer who will not weaken and

---

[21] Rom. 8.15-17; Gal. 4.6.

fail with old age, but who will go on to reign with Christ in his glory. In a very real sense, there is a progression through life from one kind of food to the other. A child needs physical nourishment in order to grow, and in his first years spiritual things are beyond his comprehension. But as he develops and matures, spiritual things become more important and physical growth becomes less so. Within the realm of faith, believers must go from the early stages, described as the milk of the Word, to the more developed ones, which are described as meat or solid food.[22]

Timothy had been well nourished on the words of faith. The Greek phrase implies both direct sayings and the logical structure that undergirds them. As a child he probably memorized large chunks of Scripture, just as Jesus and Paul would have done. But he also learned what they meant and how they should be applied. This was the 'good teaching' that he had received and accepted. The Greek word conveys both ideas. Timothy had not only received the best theological education available to him but he had also taken it to heart. Unlike so many who were experts in the letter of the law, Timothy understood its spirit, and that mattered more.

Paul reinforced his praise for Timothy with a reminder that he must turn away from 'profane myths and old wives' tales'. This little appendix is a reminder to interpreters not to assume that everything Paul said corresponds to an actual problem that he was being forced to deal with. There is no sign that Timothy was prone to believing false tales, and perhaps he wondered when he got the letter why Paul was warning him away from things that he had no interest in. In one sense, the admonition was unnecessary, as Paul himself recognized. After all, if Timothy had been indulging in the things that Paul was condemning, it is highly unlikely that he would have chosen him for the mission which he had entrusted to him.

The warning must therefore be interpreted not as something that applied to Timothy personally but as a reminder of the danger that was facing the church. Here we return to the problem that the apostle was addressing in the first chapter. Timothy was not guilty of falling for these myths, but there were others in the church who had not had his sound upbringing and who lacked his spiritual maturity. They were potentially more vulnerable and some may already have succumbed. It is not necessary to look for evidence of that in order to appreciate the potential danger. There are always people who have done nothing wrong but who are unsure in their minds and have not had a chance to think things through properly. They may not be particularly interested in myths, but they do not know much about them

---

[22] 1 Cor. 3.1-2; Heb. 5.12-14.

and may therefore be more open to listening to them than they ought to be. By telling Timothy to have nothing to do with them, Paul was telling the Ephesian church to wake up and realize the danger these things posed before it was too late. Timothy's obvious resistance to their apparent charms thus appears, not as a personal quirk that has no application to anyone else, but as an example for everyone to follow. Timothy was staying away from them because Paul had told him to, and if Paul's words were good enough for him, then they were good enough for everybody in the church.

Having given his opinion of the false asceticism that he feared would soon be promoted by people who were determined to misinterpret the gospel and turn the freedom given to Christians into a new form of bondage, Paul went on to focus on Timothy. He was well aware of the danger of preaching to others while neglecting his own walk with the Lord, thereby running the risk of losing the very gift that he was proclaiming, and he did not want Timothy to make that mistake. Following the general principle that what a person does reflects who that person is, he concentrated first on Timothy as an individual in the sight of God and then went on to outline what was expected of him as a minister of Christ in the church.

In making his appeal to Timothy, Paul treated him as a typical young man. That is to say that he started with physical exercise and what today would loosely be called 'sport'.[23] The ancient Greeks were just as passionate about athletics as many people (and especially men) are today, but the nature of their recreational interests was different. In the modern world, team games play at least as important a role as individual athletic prowess does, and in some cases (like cycling and swimming) the two dimensions overlap, so that it is sometimes hard to say where the individual effort gives way to the team and vice versa. In ancient times though, things were much simpler because team games as we understand them did not exist. Almost all competition was individual – who could throw the discus furthest, who could ride the fastest chariot and so on. This in turn demanded intense physical training, since when the competition came, there was no way that the weakness of one member of the team could be compensated by the strength of another. Each athlete was on his own, and so he had to be good at everything connected with his particular sport. It was also the case that athletes usually competed

---

[23] Calvin (1964), p. 243, missed this point. He wrote, 'By the exercise of the body he [Paul] does not mean hunting or racing or digging or wrestling or manual labour, but rather all outward actions undertaken for the sake of religion, such as vigils, long fasts, lying on the ground and such like.' It is a relatively rare instance in which Calvin failed to see the anachronism of his remarks and misinterpreted the original context.

in the nude, so that their bodily strength and skill could be used to maximum effect with the minimum of extraneous hindrance.

The Greek word for exercise (*gymnazō*) literally means 'strip naked', and that is what the athletes did. We have no way of knowing how sporty Timothy was, and perhaps his intense study of the Scriptures left him little time for athletics, but this is beside the point. Paul was using Timothy as an example and through him appealing to all young men who might be called to God's service, speaking to them in a language that they would appreciate and take to heart. First of all, Timothy was to strip himself down, not to physical nudity but to spiritual godliness! Modern minds do not usually think of nakedness in that way, but Paul was making an important point here. He did not want Timothy to be encumbered by added extras, by useless and frivolous things that would stand in the way of his service to God. For the man who is born again in Christ, his whole being is a temple of the Holy Spirit, and to hide it behind something that represents a compromise with the world is to obscure its natural beauty. Just as the true athlete takes care of the way he looks and wants every muscle to be toned in just the right proportions, so the spiritual warrior ought to want his soul to be equally well prepared for the struggles it will have to face. Modern prudishness about nakedness must not let us shrink from learning this lesson, which Timothy and his friends would have understood perfectly.

Paul then went on to extend the comparison in order to bring out the point of what he was saying. Bodily exercise (*gymnasia*) has its uses 'for a while' (*pros oligon*) but godliness is good for ever (*pros panta*).[24] Modern translators and commentators sometimes miss the force of the Greek idiom here, by translating *oligon* as 'little' and *panta* as 'everything', making the imagery spatial (to do with quantity) rather than temporal, which is how it should be understood. Perhaps this is because few of them are athletes themselves! Anyone who is a sportsman knows that he will reach his peak at a certain point and will then be able to maintain it for only so long before he starts to decline. If we look at champion tennis players for example, we find that seven or eight years is the maximum that any one of them is likely to go undefeated, and even that is exceptional. The tragedy of the athlete is that once he ceases to win competitions, his fame declines and his life no longer seems to have any meaning. A man of thirty can be knocked out

---

[24] Marshall (2004), p. 551, recognizes that this interpretation is possible for *pros oligon* but rejects it because he does not accept it for *pros panta*, although it is a standard Greek idiom. Other commentators either pass over the text or make the same mistake, as Thornton (2016), p. 138, does.

by a lad of eighteen and discovers that his career is over just as most other people are beginning to get stuck into whatever they plan to do for the rest of their lives.

This is what Paul had in mind here. Olympic glory is fine while it lasts, and staying in shape is advisable for as long as it is a practical possibility. But sooner or later physical strength will decline, and then what? Godliness stands in sharp contrast to this. It contains a promise (*epangelia*) not only for now, but for ever! It can do for the soul in this life everything that physical exercise can do for the body, and what is more, it carries on into the life to come. Flesh and blood cannot inherit the kingdom of God, so swimming laps or walking the treadmill will get us nowhere once we are no longer physically able to do such things.[25] But the time we spend in prayer, in studying the Scriptures and in ministry will prepare us for the life of heaven in a way that nothing else can. We cannot earn our way into glory by such means, because salvation is by grace through faith and not by works, but they are useful (*ōphelimos*) in getting our minds and spirits accustomed to the climate that will greet us when we get to heaven.

Paul was not enthusiastic about wasting time with athletic activities, but he did not regard them as spiritually dangerous, which is somewhat surprising. Today we seldom associate sports with religion, but in the ancient world the two things were closely connected. The Olympic Games, for example, were a pagan religious ritual, and when Christianity was made the official state religion in the late fourth century, they were suppressed for that reason. But although Paul (and everyone else) knew that, he made no mention of it in his remarks to Timothy. Perhaps he realized that the religious element was basically irrelevant to what he wanted to say and so left it out. Maybe it was so residual, even in the minds of most pagans, that it never occurred to him to mention it! But it was there nevertheless and serves as a reminder to us that Christians were not as cut off from the world as we might imagine. Jews never took part in pagan athletic activities unless they were apostates from their ancestral religion, but Christians do not seem to have been under such constraints. They were certainly not encouraged to join in, but neither were they forbidden to have anything to do with them on the ground that they were spiritually incompatible with the gospel.

Ambrosiaster followed the literal sense of Paul's remarks but he added an ascetic dimension to them:

---

[25] See 1 Cor. 15.50.

Carnal people exercise their bodies in one way and spiritual people do it in another. Carnal people feed their bodies by wining and dining, and so hasten to their damnation, but spiritual people control their bodies by fasting and abstinence, so that the pledges they make about their desires may be worthy of the coming resurrection. The spiritual person beats his body for the sake of his future hope, whereas the carnal one has no hope of the future and so pampers it for the time being, thereby encouraging it to sin.[26]

In v. 9 we come across the same formulaic saying that we saw earlier in 1.15. It is sure (*pistos*) and worthy of full acceptance. The problem is to know whether Paul was stating this as a conclusion to the preceding remarks or as an introduction to what follows.[27] In most of the other instances where it occurs, the reference is forward-looking, and so we must begin with that presumption here, but a moment's glance at the context will show us that such a reading is awkward and unlikely. Almost certainly it points us back to what has just been said, though it is not clear how far back we should take it. Some would include the whole of v. 8, while others would restrict it to the second half of the verse only. The most natural reading would suggest that it is the second part of v. 8, which sounds like a proverb of sorts, is more likely, but it does not make much difference in practice. As P. H. Towner remarks, 'In either case, the force of the faithful saying formula is to underline both the need to pursue godliness and the instruction's apostolic authority.'[28] We may safely leave it at that.

Verse 10 is another story. Paul often spoke of his mission as hard work, and it is natural to see this verse in that context.[29] It is not clear whether the struggle was mainly spiritual or physical, nor whether it was individual or collective. In other words, was Paul referring primarily to his own inner battles against lethargy and discouragement, or was he talking more about the opposition that he encountered in his preaching and teaching efforts? Probably it is unnecessary to make such distinctions.

---

[26] Ambrosiaster (2009), p. 132.
[27] Luther (1973), p. 324, was happy to accept either interpretation, since to his mind both what came before and what followed were of equal importance. Calvin (1964), pp. 244–5, and (2016), vol. 2, pp. 89–90, takes the phrase as referring to what comes in the next verse.
[28] Towner (2006), p. 309.
[29] Marshall (2004), p. 555; Towner (2006), pp. 309–10. For examples of Pauline usage, see Rom. 16.6; 1 Cor. 15.10; 16.16; Gal. 4.11; Phil. 2.16; Col. 1.29; 1 Thess. 5.12.

The fact that the passage comes immediately after a short discourse on the value of athletic training suggests that it is both physical and spiritual, individual and corporate. The ancients did not separate body and soul in the way that we might do today; for them, it was a case of a sound mind in a sound body (*mens sana in corpore sano*), so both dimensions were of equal importance.

Having said that, there is no doubt that Paul's focus was spiritual. He had his mind set on the living God, who is both spiritual and active in the affairs of humankind.[30] Everything he does is in response to him, and it is clear from what he says next that the preaching of the gospel is in the forefront of his mind. God is our Saviour, and that message, which he picks up from 2.3-4 must be taken to the whole world. The reason for that missionary imperative is clearly expressed by saying that God is the Saviour of all people, a statement that must be taken as referring to every tribe and nation, and not only to Jews.[31] Some confusion has been caused by a tendency to translate the Greek word *malista* as 'especially', though as I. H. Marshall correctly observes, it would be better to render it as something more like 'by which I mean'. If we read it like that, the possible contradiction between a universal and a definite atonement disappears. Marshall himself thought that the gospel is offered to everyone on the ground that all human beings are potential believers, even though only some actually believe, and he saw this apparent discrepancy as the cause of the spiritual warfare that Paul and Timothy were engaged in.[32] But for Paul, it would surely be better to say that salvation belongs only to those who believe, although such people are to be found all over the world, which is why his missionary work was necessary. Like Jesus during his earthly ministry, Paul was out to gather in the lost sheep of the house of Israel, not to try to turn goats into sheep.[33]

---

[30] Marshall (2004), p. 556, says that Paul speaks of God as 'living' because 'he gives the promise of life' as v. 8 tells us. No doubt that is part of the truth, but there is no need to restrict the adjective in this way. God is living in himself, quite apart from the promises he makes to us.

[31] Calvin (2016), p. 93, interpreted the text to mean that God is the preserver of all mankind. As he put it, 'this word *Saviour* is not taken here in its proper and nearest signification ... in respect of everlasting salvation which God promises his elect, but for a deliverer and defender'. See also Calvin (1964), p. 245, where he said the same thing more briefly, though he admitted that believers would be especially protected.

[32] Marshall (2004), p. 557: 'because God is potentially the Saviour of all but only those who believe are saved, there arises the necessity for the spiritual battle to which the apostle and his co-workers are committed'.

[33] Mt. 10.6; 15.24; 25.31-46.

## 11-16. Self-discipline

*11. These are the things you must insist on and teach. 12. Let no one despise your youth, but set the believers an example in speech and conduct, in love, in faith, in purity. 13. Until I arrive, give attention to the public reading of Scripture, to exhorting, to teaching. 14. Do not neglect the gift that is in you, which was given to you through prophecy with the laying on of hands by the council of elders. 15. Put these things into practice, devote yourself to them, so that all may see your progress. 16. Pay close attention to yourself and to your teaching; continue in these things, for in doing this you will save both yourself and your hearers.*

Having spoken to Timothy about how he should prepare himself for his ministry, Paul then moved on to describe what that ministerial task would involve. First of all, Timothy must 'command and teach these things'. Timothy was required by the apostle to take charge of the community that he was called to serve. He had an authority given to him by God and he was expected to exercise it. But it is important to note that he was not just appointed to give orders; he was also expected to teach what Paul had communicated to him. Commands without teaching were useless and would probably be counterproductive, since few people want to obey rules that they do not understand. The commands that Paul gave Timothy were not arbitrary instructions. They were based on a deep theological logic, rooted in the relationship between the Creator and the creation, between the Saviour and those whom he had chosen for salvation. The congregation had to learn this so that it would accept the rationale behind the counsels that Timothy was to give them.

Timothy was still a young man and liable to be disregarded by at least some members of the church for that reason.[34] Young people are often idealistic and inexperienced, and Timothy's energy and enthusiasm might have been interpreted in that way. To counteract this, Paul told him that he must become a model (*typos*) of what was expected of believers, and then listed five different ways in which this was to be done:

1. In speech
2. In conduct
3. In love
4. In faith
5. In chastity or purity

[34] Paul's concern that Timothy might not be well-received is evident from what he wrote in 1 Cor. 16.10-11, though there is no mention of his youth in those verses.

As always, the order is important. First of all, Timothy must speak in a way that would bring credit on him and his ministry. Paul did not specify what this would involve, but we can surmise from what he said elsewhere that he expected Timothy to be serious in his conversation, to be focused on his mission, to avoid coarse language and jokes, to eschew gossip and critical remarks about others that were unhelpful (even if true). In an oral culture like that of the ancient world, the way a man spoke said a great deal about his character and he would be judged accordingly. Moreover, speech was at the heart of Timothy's ministry. He was called to preach, to teach and to bear witness to the Word of God. If his own speech fell short of this, his ministry would be compromised and he would lose the respect of his congregation. On the other hand, if he watched what he said, and spoke to the point (and only when and as required), others would respect him for his wisdom and self-control, and they would admire him for being wise beyond his years. It was in every respect a key element in making a good impression on those whom he was called to serve.

Next, there came behaviour. Timothy had to practise what he preached. This is obvious but also very hard to do in a consistent way. As a minister, he was on a pedestal and carefully watched by everyone in the church. If he acted in ways that belied his message that would soon be observed and everything he said would be taken with a pinch of salt. Worse still, he might encourage others to indulge in grandiloquent rhetoric which bore no relation to their lives. There could be nothing worse than saying the right thing but evacuating the words of any meaning. If that were to happen, the gospel would become an empty formula, a ritual to be repeated but not a transforming power in anybody's life. The church could not afford that, and so Paul moved from speech to conduct as a matter of course.

Third in the list comes love. Words and behaviour are important, but they must be directed to a purpose, and that purpose was the salvation of unbelievers and the edification of the congregation. This practical application was, and had to be seen to be, an act of love. If Timothy had said and done all the right things but lacked this essential ingredient, he would have been like the sounding gong or brass cymbal that Paul mentioned in 1 Cor. 13.1. A rigid orthodoxy in belief and a cold superiority in behaviour would easily have led to Pharisaism and undermined Timothy's ministry by alienating people from it. Love meant applying the truth by word and deed to each member of the church in the way that was right for them. The people had to be cared for and cherished as the children of God that they were, and especially so when hard things had to be said.

Following love there is faith. In this context 'faith' probably meant having a positive attitude as much as anything else. Timothy had to believe that his mission had a purpose and that God would bring it to fruition. There are many disappointments in ministry and it is easy to get discouraged. Paul himself recorded how many of his companions and associates turned away, and most of his letters would not have been written if things had been going well in the churches he had founded. Faced with such obstacles, a minister must not only have faith in his calling but must be able to communicate that faith to others. During the Second World War Sir Winston Churchill won the respect and loyalty of people all over the world, not so much for anything he did as for the faith he had in the darkest extremity that his cause would prevail in the end. He was able to communicate that faith to others and inspire them, even when the outward situation looked dire in the extreme. This quality is what Paul wanted Timothy to have – the faith that can move mountains and win others to follow in his footsteps.

Next comes chastity (*hagneia*), often translated 'purity' because 'chastity' has come to have too narrow a meaning to fit the context. Nevertheless, there should be no doubt of the centrality of sexual continence in this command.[35] Timothy was dealing with people, often at the most emotional moments in their lives. Many would have shared their deepest thoughts with him, cried on his shoulder and looked to him for guidance and support. Ministers today know how easy it can be for such charged relationships to cross a line from what is deep and helpful to what becomes complicated and problematic. Many have gone into situations trying to be of help only to discover that they have been caught up in an emotional web from which they cannot extricate themselves. A young man, in particular, might reasonably be assumed to have a heightened sense of feeling and could easily mistake pastoral care for something else that, if pursued, could lead to scandal and ruin his ministry completely. Could the congregation trust Timothy to maintain the right kind of relationship with everyone in the church? Would he be more inclined to develop a counselling ministry to pretty young girls than to old men who had lost their teeth? That may be putting it somewhat crudely, but it is the sort of temptation that chastity (or purity) is meant to counteract. Failure here could be – and all too often has been – catastrophic, and it is no accident that Paul puts *hagneia* at the end of a checklist of virtues that he expected Timothy to manifest in his ministry.

Ambrosiaster's comment on this bears repeating,

> Timothy was a young man in terms of his age, but in terms of his morals and behaviour he was old and mature. Paul therefore urges him to grow

---

[35] Towner (2006), pp. 315–16, supports this view.

so that he will be an example of all good works. That way a wonderful and very mature discipline would appear in a young man, so that his acts would belie his age and he would be regarded not as a young man but as an elder. People older than he was would be ashamed if they did not behave like him ... whereas young people would have a teacher who was the same age as they were.[36]

Paul then went on to tell Timothy that he must continue in three activities that would constitute the backbone of his ministry. These were

1. Reading
2. Exhortation
3. Teaching

Paul prefaced his instructions with a brief note that Timothy was to occupy himself with these things until he came, another reminder that Paul saw Timothy's ministry as a kind of stopgap and gave his counsel with that in mind. But the principles he laid down for the short term were valid for the long haul as well. There is no fundamental difference between what Timothy was expected to do while he was filling in for the apostle and what any minister would be called upon to do on a more permanent basis. Circumstances will inevitably have an effect on the way a ministry is exercised, but the principles remain the same. The visiting preacher or the teacher who is taking a short intensive course must act in fundamentally the same way as someone with full-time responsibilities in a given situation, which is what Paul was saying here.

First on the list is 'reading' (*anagnōsis*). Translations usually interpolate 'the public reading of Scripture' for this word, which is probably what it means, even though it does not explicitly say so.[37] In ancient times reading was an oral activity, as even the English word implies.[38] In the context of ministry in a church, to read could hardly be anything else than the public reading of Scripture, as the modern word 'lesson' (or 'reading') indicates when it is used in that context. The Greek term for this is interesting, because, unlike its English or Latin equivalents, it does not imply speech. Instead, it

---

[36] Ambrosiaster (2009), p. 132.
[37] By 'Scripture' it was the Hebrew Bible that was meant, but some commentators think that specifically Christian material would have been read as well. If that was the case, then parts of what later became the New Testament were already functioning as Scripture in the first generation of the church. See Marshall (2004), p. 563.
[38] Its German cognate is *reden* ('to make a speech') and a similar connection can be found in other languages as well.

means 'recognition', which is a different analogy, implying the affirmation of knowledge. Books were held to contain knowledge, and to declaim them out loud was to recognize this. The Bible is the supreme source of knowledge for both Jews and Christians, and proclaiming its contents was a form of encounter with God in public worship. This is the true measure of its importance and it was not an accident that it came first in Paul's list of things to do.

The public reading of Scripture was a solemn activity that served a didactic purpose quite apart from any sermon that might have followed it. The practice was probably adapted from that of the Jewish synagogue, though this can only be speculation. P. H. Towner captures something of what the experience must have felt like:

> In response to the new realities presented by exile and eventual resettlement in the land, weekly synagogue readings ... served to tell and retell the story that kept Israel's faith and identity alive. The function of Scripture reading in the NT era within the Christian movement undoubtedly served the same basic purpose. Again, new realities are absorbed into the growing story of Israel's salvation. Now regular public reading of Scripture also served to locate the new identity in Christ.[39]

This needs to be restated today, because in a world where virtually everyone is literate, it often happens that untrained people are asked (sometimes without prior notice) to read the Scriptures in church. Unfortunately, what frequently comes across is their lack of training for this – they can reproduce the words but not the cadences that make them both meaningful and memorable. The public reading of Scripture is not something that everybody can do well; it is an art that must be cultivated. Furthermore, it is not something that can be delegated to just anybody. Its importance at the centre of public worship should be demonstrated by giving it to a recognized minister, who by his very presence will remind the congregation that this is a significant and indeed fundamental part of public worship and ministry.

The reading of Scripture is the controlling element in the triad of tasks that the apostle gave to Timothy. Exhortation (*paraklēsis*) follows 'reading' and is based on it. What Timothy was expected to do was to make the words of the Biblical text bear on the lives of those who heard it read. It was what would now be called a sermon, though one that was clearly an exposition of the text(s) that had been read. The Greek term is the same as *paraklētos*

---

[39] Towner (2006), p. 320.

('Paraclete'), the name given by Jesus to the Holy Spirit whom he would send to take his place in the lives of his disciples, and we may be certain that Paul had that in mind. There could be no genuinely spiritual 'exhortation' without the work of the Paraclete behind it, and this is what the Holy Spirit was commissioned to do. He was not himself the Word, but he brought the Word to bear on the lives of believers by convicting them of sin, righteousness and judgement.[40] Without that, the mere reading of the text would have no effect.

Following exhortation and closely tied to it is 'teaching' (*didaskalia*). Elsewhere in the Epistle, 'teaching' tends to refer primarily to the content of what is taught, the body of doctrine that constitutes the bedrock of the Christian faith. Here, however, the apostle focused on the activity by which that body of doctrine is communicated. It was the role of the minister to do this, either himself or by appointing suitable people to represent him. The content of the message was the controlling factor, of course – the minister had no authorization to teach anything that was not contained in the Scriptures that he read in public. But the manner in which it was put across was equally important. Timothy had a privileged position. What he said was taken seriously and mattered to people in a way that might not have been the case if the same thing had been uttered by someone who was not in his shoes.

The threefold nature of this exhortation is paradigmatic for the reading and application of Scripture in the church. Today we might talk about exegesis, exposition and application, a distinction that goes back to Thomas of Chobham, writing about 1215, and that is exemplified in the works of John Calvin – exegesis being his commentaries, exposition his *Institutes* and application his sermons. The Pauline triad was less sophisticated than that, but the same pattern is recognizable. In the public reading of Scripture would have come exegesis – explaining the meaning of the text. In the sermon there would have been the exposition of that text. And in the teaching, Timothy would have been applying the text to the needs of the church to which he was called to minister. The form changes over time, but the substance of the minister's calling remains the same across the centuries.

Along with his ministerial position came the gift (*charisma*) that Timothy had received. Paul did not specify where the gift had come from, but it is clear from what he says elsewhere that the source must have been the Holy Spirit.[41] Unfortunately, the office and the gift do not always go together, but both are essential for an effective ministry. Whether Timothy was really in danger of

---

[40] Jn 16.8.
[41] 1 Cor. 12.4-11.

neglecting his gift is hard to say, but it is possible that at times he was so caught up in ministry that he failed to consider what had been given to him. As Paul describes it, it had come by two different (though complementary) routes. First of all, he had received it through prophecy. In a way that both he and Paul must have known but that is hidden from our eyes, Timothy had been singled out for greatness, possibly even from birth.[42] The implication is that his ministry had been foretold by people who had been enlightened by the Holy Spirit. It was certainly a spiritual gift that could come from no other source, and it was recognized as such by the church. This recognition took the form of the laying on of hands, which Paul here described as the *epithesis tōn cheirōn* rather than by the shorter word *cheirotonia*, which later became the standard term for 'ordination'.

The laying on of hands followed the prophecy and was not a substitute for it. In later centuries there would emerge a doctrine of 'apostolic succession' which maintained that it was necessary for a minister to have hands laid on him by people who stood in a direct line that could be traced back to the apostles themselves. The belief was that this laying on of hands was *by itself* the guarantee of spiritual *charisma*, which it alone could convey. This false interpretation produced a situation in which there were many ordained clergy who had no real vocation but who were permitted to exercise spiritual functions because they had received this external qualification and were therefore empowered to do it. Sadly, belief in the spiritual efficacy of this ritual still persists in some quarters, with the result that the ministry is seriously compromised and may even be a scandal and a hindrance to the true preaching of the gospel.

At the other end of the spectrum are the freelance preachers who claim the *charisma* but who have not received (and who see no need for) any outward recognition by the church. In some cases they may have a valid ministry, especially when the institutional church is weak or corrupt, when it may be a necessary corrective to a situation that has been allowed to deteriorate to that point. But it is also often the case that unrecognized ministries do more harm than good, and that people who feel called by God in a way that allows them to operate independently of the church will lead others astray because they have not got the backing they need. Official authorization cannot replace the *charisma*, but the *charisma* can benefit by being publicly recognized and supported. The church is a body of believers, not a collection of individual(ist)s, and both aspects need to be present for a ministry to be balanced and effective.

---

[42] It may perhaps be compared with Simeon's prophecy concerning Jesus. See Lk. 2.27-35.

The laying on of hands was performed by the *presbyterion*, another word that looks familiar but whose meaning is hard to define precisely. It is obviously the same as our word 'presbytery' but whether it was anything like what we would now understand by that term is debatable.[43] Given the context, it seems unlikely that the *presbyterion* included members from outside the local congregation, and so it cannot be equated with the modern Presbyterian use of the term.[44] It is more likely to have been the eldership in the church where Timothy was commissioned for ministry, though where that was is uncertain. It may have been in Ephesus, where Timothy then was, or in another city of Asia Minor, perhaps even his home town of Lystra. Paul did not elaborate on this and we do not know any more about it than what he has told us. In particular, he did not say whether he himself had been one of the elders who had laid hands on Timothy. This is important, because in 2 Tim. 1.6 Paul said that he had laid hands on the younger man – though when and for what purpose is not stated. Of course we are not dealing here with ordination in the modern sense, so there is no reason why Timothy should not have received the laying on of hands more than once, depending on the ministry to which he had been called at a particular time.

What is certain is that there was an eldership in the local church and that it took responsibility for the ministry there. We must assume that there were several elders, since the word *presbyterion* would not make sense if it referred to only one person, so it may be significant that Timothy had hands laid on him by a group of people and not just by one other (Paul or perhaps an *episkopos* if there was only one of these in a congregation). What we now call ordination was a collective, if not exactly a community affair, which in turn suggests that Timothy's gift was affirmed by a representative group of mature and responsible people. This was important, not just because it was good for the minister to have widespread support in the congregation, but because it was important for the church to be governed by a group of experienced people who could pool their expertise and share their wisdom. No one person can do this effectively for long, and collective responsibility seems natural for the body of Christ, in which the different parts are called to coordinate their activities and work together in harmony.

V. 15 is clear in its meaning but somewhat difficult to translate succinctly. Paul instructed Timothy to 'study' (*meletaō*) what he had just told him and to

---

[43] Theodore of Mopsuestia (2010), p. 629, understood that it was different from the presbyteries of his own time, but he mistakenly equated it with the company of the apostles, who (he thought) had laid hands on Timothy along with Paul.

[44] But as Marshall (2004), p. 569, notes, 'if the passage is to be applied to later times, it supports presbyterian rather than episcopal ordination'.

'be' in them, using the somewhat odd imperative form of *eimi*, the verb to 'be'. As often in Greek, the verbs are capable of carrying a range of meaning that is impossible to capture in translation. The verb *meletaō* stands in contrast to *amelei* ('neglect') in the preceding verse, and may be taken to mean its opposite. Timothy was expected to put what he has been taught into practice, to test it and to bring out its hidden implications as they became apparent in the course of his study. At the same time, Paul told him to 'be' in them, that is to say, to make them so much a part of himself that everything he thought, said and did would naturally reflect them. The Greek verb 'to be' has a notion of permanence about it that reflects the eternal 'be-ing' of God. Timothy's gifts were intended to define not only his character but his identity, which they could only do if they were so deeply ingrained that it would be impossible to imagine him without them.

This is what Paul meant when he said that the purpose of Timothy's concentration on these things was so that his 'progress' (*prokopē*) might be clear to everyone. Once again, we are faced with a clear statement whose meaning seems obvious but that is in fact difficult to capture. Paul saw Timothy's personal development was the maturing of a young man into the role of a congregational leader and (in some sense at least) his own delegate. The results of his efforts were meant to be visible to everyone, but what exactly would others see in him? No doubt part of it would have been an increased confidence in his ministry. Much of what Paul said implies that Timothy was shy and conscious of his youthfulness, but this may reflect modern perceptions more than the ancient reality. In New Testament times young people were almost never taken seriously unless they were child prodigies (like the twelve-year old Jesus in the temple) or had been propelled into prominence by dynastic accident, as some of the Israelite kings had been.[45] Timothy was called to be wise beyond his years, and whether he was could only be known by the unfolding experience of his ministry.

Paul rounded off this section of his Epistle by telling Timothy to protect himself and the teaching that had been entrusted to him. In the apostle's mind, these two things went together. What Timothy said was validated by what he was; what he was gave him the freedom and the authority to say what he did. The man and his message effectively fused into one, and so it was important to ensure that there was no discrepancy between them. It is easy to think that Timothy was a special case, and that as Paul's representative he was called to a higher degree of consecration than the average pastor would be, but there is no sign of that in the Epistle.

---

[45] Lk. 2.41-51; 2 Kgs 11.4-21; 2 Chron. 23.1-11.

Of course, in some respects Timothy was unique, but so is everyone who is called into the ministry of the church. The principles that applied to him were valid for everyone, as the rest of this sentence makes clear. Timothy was not an oddity, a one-off phenomenon that could never be repeated or replaced, but an example for others to imitate and to measure themselves against. That is why Paul wrote to him and why his letter has been preserved. Had Timothy been unique, and had his experience been so special that nobody else could share it, it is unlikely that we would have heard so much about it and it would hardly have been preserved as a model for others to follow.

Paul counselled Timothy to remain firm both in his calling and in his doctrine. Both are essential for an effective ministry. He had to be confident that he was doing the right thing in the right place at the right time, even if the challenges he faced were sometimes overwhelming. A minister of the Word is a target for opposition, much of which appears to those affected to be senseless and unjustified. But opponents of the gospel know that one of the most effective ways to silence it is to undermine those who are called to preach it, and that one of the best ways of doing that is to attack their self-confidence. Timothy had the prophecies about him and the affirmation of the elders to rely on, and those two things could keep him going in the hard times.

Keeping the teaching pure was equally important. It is always tempting for a preacher to go soft at the edges, to lose his focus or to get distracted by some pressing but ultimately secondary problem that commands his attention. It can also be tempting to compromise with opponents in the hope of either winning them over or at least neutralizing their impact. But if Timothy were to humour them, perhaps by letting one of them teach a class on genealogy, for example, on the assumption that it would not do any harm, the floodgates would be opened. The congregation would not know what to think, the guest speaker might assume that he had a green light to go on and teach further, and his own ministry might be compromised in unforeseen ways. How would Timothy have been able to denounce such frivolity, as Paul was urging him to do, if he had shown some sympathy with it?

Perils of this kind are probably what explain Paul's closing remarks in this passage. Do this, he says, and 'you will save both yourself and your hearers'. Yet again, we are faced with a Greek verb, in this case *sōizō* ('save') that has many different meanings according to context. In this instance it can hardly refer to salvation in the spiritual sense, because Paul would never say anything that might suggest that Timothy (or anyone else) could save himself or others. It must have a less intense meaning than that. Most likely it means something like 'you and those who hear you will be safe', that is to say, protected from the dangers and embarrassments that can hinder a ministry.

It was Timothy's duty as a pastor to keep his flock safe from harm, and that is almost certainly what the apostle is referring to here.

The role of the pastor in protecting his congregation from harm must never be underestimated, but this text has received surprisingly little attention from most commentators, perhaps because they think that what it says is too obvious to need further elaboration. An exception to this general pattern was John Calvin, who gave the matter considerable attention. He wrote,

> Paul has good reason to urge Timothy to give heed both to himself personally and to his teaching for the general advantage of the church. Once again, he commends constancy to him, that he may never grow weary, for many things happen which can divert us from the right course, if we do not firmly set ourselves to resist them.[46]

Calvin also believed that pastors would be greatly encouraged in their work if they felt that their salvation and that of their flocks was directly connected to their devotion to their ministry. As for the relationship between the saving power of God and the work of the minister, Calvin had this to say,

> Nor should it seem strange that Paul ascribes to Timothy the work of saving the church, for all that are won for God are saved and it is by the preaching of the gospel that we are gathered to Christ. And just as the unfaithfulness or negligence of a pastor is fatal to the church, so it is right for its salvation to be ascribed to his faithfulness and diligence. It is indeed true that it is God alone who saves and not even the smallest part of his glory can rightly be transferred to men. But God's glory is in no way diminished by his using the labour of men in bestowing salvation. Thus our salvation is the gift of God, since it comes from him alone and is effected only by his power, so that he alone is its author. But that does not exclude the ministry of men, nor does it deny that that ministry may be the means of salvation.[47]

The best defence against trouble, Paul implied, is a firm and consistent reliance on the calling of God and on the teaching that he has given in his Word. Stick to them, trust in them and live in the light of them, and all will be well. Paul does not give us the impression that he thought that Timothy was in serious danger, but he knew that it was better to enunciate the principles

---

[46] Calvin (1964), p. 248.
[47] Ibid., pp. 248–9.

of effective ministry when things were going reasonably well, rather than wait until there was trouble. It is a reminder to us that the teaching we have received in Scripture is designed not just to meet the needs of the moment, but to prepare us for the trials and temptations that may come our way. Forewarned is forearmed, and Paul was determined to ensure that Timothy and those who modelled themselves on him would be fully prepared for the battles they would be called to face. W. D. Mounce sums it up well:

> This paradigm of Christian ministry, directed specifically to Timothy but applicable to ministers of all times, stands in judgment on those who neglect the teaching of Scripture, consume themselves with arguments about words devoid of godliness, bring reproach upon the church by their sinful lives, refuse to immerse themselves in the things of God, and as a result are destroying not only themselves but also those who listen and follow their example. Conversely, it is a word of encouragement and hope to those who are faithful to the apostolic example and teaching of the gospel.[48]

---

[48] Mounce (2000), pp. 266–7.

# 1 Timothy 5

## 1-2. Relationships within the church

*1. Do not speak harshly to an older man, but speak to him as to a father, to younger men as brothers, 2. to older women as mothers, to younger women as sisters – with absolute purity.*

As is often the case in Paul's letters, the last chapters of 1 Timothy are devoted mainly to pastoral matters affecting the congregation to which he was writing. In this case, his concerns were mediated through the ministry of Timothy to the church at Ephesus but they are more general in tone. We cannot assume that the Ephesian church was afflicted by all of the problems he raised or that it was in greater need of his advice than others were, though no doubt many of the issues he raised confronted Timothy in his ministry. What we should notice is that Paul left the details to Timothy and concentrated instead on the principles that make his advice universally relevant, even to situations that are far removed from the one he was addressing.

Paul's first concern was the nature of the relationships that Timothy ought to have with members of his congregation. This is always a delicate matter for a pastor, but Paul confined himself to certain broad categories – old and young, male and female. He dealt with the men before the women and gave priority to the older over the younger, but too much should not be made of that. In his context that must have been the natural order in which to proceed and it does not indicate that Paul thought that one group was more important than another. Paul also addressed the older men in the singular, while using the plural for the others. Again, too much should not be made of this. There must have been more than one old man in the church, and there is no reason to suppose that he was singling out the leader of the congregation, that is, the *episkopos* or *presbyteros* of later ecclesiastical order.[1] The use of

---

[1] Paul's use of the word *presbyteros* here naturally raises the question of whether he was referring to an elder, as opposed to merely an old man, but the context suggests that it is age rather than status that he had in mind. This is confirmed by his use of *presbyterai* for the older women in the next verse. Towner (2006), p. 330, remarks, 'It is germane here to point out that probably part of Timothy's task in Ephesus was to correct the

the singular in this case is most easily explained by the nature of the advice Paul was giving. Timothy was told not to rebuke an older man, and because a rebuke would probably have been directed towards an individual rather than a group the singular seemed more appropriate. Paul then went on to speak about the others, and it is probable that the more general nature of his remarks made using the plural seem more natural since he was referring to them collectively.

It is not clear how Timothy was supposed to decide who was 'older' and who was 'younger'. This vagueness reflects a common uncertainty that persists to this day. At what point does a young person stop addressing his elders by a title like 'Mister' or 'Mrs' and adopt their first name instead? Sometimes older people have to give younger ones permission to do this, precisely because the boundaries are unclear. In Timothy's case we can be fairly certain that a man or woman who was old enough to be his father or mother would have belonged to the 'elder' category, and Paul's advice as to how to relate to them bears this out. Those nearer his own age he could easily have regarded as brothers and sisters, as Paul recommended, and there would probably have been little problem with that. It is the middle group in between these extremes that causes the uncertainty, but Paul does not acknowledge their existence, perhaps because trial and error was the only way to decide who belonged in what category.[2]

To some extent it would have been easier for Paul to distinguish between older and younger women than between older and younger men, because with women the natural dividing line was menopause. As long as a woman could bear children she would be considered 'young', but when her childbearing years were over she would become 'older', if not necessarily 'old' in the absolute sense. We know from what he says about widows in v. 9 that he did not think of them as 'old' until they had reached sixty, which creates a gap that we might describe as 'middle age', and it is this group, both male and female, that Paul passed over in silence. Perhaps we should conclude from this that his categorization of church members by age was not intended to be comprehensive. He may have been concerned only with exceptional cases – those who were older or younger than the 'norm'. We do not know what was in his mind, but it is otherwise hard to account for the fact that he overlooked the generation that must have formed the backbone of the church.

---

leadership, which had come under the influence of false teaching. That leadership would have consisted of men drawn from the age range above Timothy's.' This is a possibility, but there is no need to read it into the text and it remains pure speculation.

[2] The ancients tended to think of forty as the age at which a young person became 'old', but of course this was only a rough guide and there must have been many cases of uncertainty.

It may be noted in passing that Paul made no mention of children. We can probably assume that Timothy was not married, though we have no idea whether this was because he was still very young or because he had resolved to remain celibate as Paul was. Either way, the apostle gave him no advice as to how to deal with those who were underage, though there must have been a fairly large contingent of them in the church. Probably the reason for this is that Paul did not imagine that Timothy would have had any direct relationship with them. Whatever contact he had with children would have been in and through their parents and he would not have dealt with them outside their family context. The upbringing of children was a family responsibility, and Timothy would have had to respect that. In some of his other epistles Paul did address the children directly, so the possibility that Timothy might have had a ministry to them cannot be completely discounted, but it is likely to have taken the form of general exhortation from the pulpit rather than one-to-one counselling of the kind that characterized his relationship with the adult members of the church.[3]

At the heart of Paul's advice regarding older people was the duty of the young to respect them, which was as universal in ancient society as it is in many parts of the world today.[4] The fifth commandment tells us to honour our father and mother, and Paul extended that principle to include all the older members of the congregation. They may not have expected such treatment, of course, especially not from Timothy. His role as Paul's representative might have given him a status in their eyes that would have excused him from showing the customary deference to the elderly, but Paul would not have accepted that excuse or tolerated such behaviour in a church leader. Regardless of Timothy's position, he was still expected to maintain the customary attitudes of honour and respect due to older people.

This was particularly evident in the approach that Timothy was told to adopt towards the older men. That would have been the most difficult kind of relationship for him, because both he and they would have been conscious of the difference in their ages. Paul's warning to Timothy not to let others despise his youth is a reminder that some of the older men probably found it hard to take him seriously.[5] Some may even have gone out of their way to disregard him, if only to show that they were not going to let a young upstart tell them what to do. In a case like that, Timothy would have had to assert his authority or lose it, but everything depended on how he did this. If he confronted the older men directly he would have alienated them by going

---

[3] Eph. 6.1-4; Col. 3.20-21.
[4] Martin Luther (1973), pp. 332–3, made this the focal point of his comment on this text.
[5] See above, 4.12.

against accepted social convention – young people did not speak to their elders like that, and if Timothy had done so, he would have confirmed their suspicion that he really could not be accepted as their leader.

Instead of tackling them directly, Paul recommended another approach. Timothy was to disarm them by encouraging them, rather than by censuring them for their attitude towards him. By valuing them and showing them how much they mattered both to him and to the church, Timothy could turn a potentially hostile group of people into his staunch supporters and allies. It was all a matter of respecting them and making them feel wanted for the experience and advice they could offer, even if they were no longer strong enough to take charge of things in the way that they had once done.

As for the younger men, Timothy was to treat them as brothers. Paul had already spoken of the entire congregation in this way (4.6), but here the reference is more specific. Human nature suggests that this group is the one that Timothy would have related to most easily. They would have had common interests, a similar experience of life and comparable hopes and expectations for the future. They would also have had the energy to get things done, and if teamwork was to form a vital part of Timothy's ministry, it would have been from these men that most of his team would have been drawn. The relative absence of men in this age group in modern congregations is a sign of the church's weakness, widely acknowledged as such and difficult to alter. Getting the men involved is a challenge that many pastors have to face, and for Timothy, treating them as brothers – equals and co-workers in the ministry – was a vital start to the process.

In dealing with the older women (*presbyterai*), Timothy was to treat them as if they were his mothers. Here again, we see how Paul was able to use human psychology in order to further the peace of the church. Older women generally like younger men who pay attention to them. One of the ironies of modern feminism is that many women who have risen to high positions are more inclined to promote junior men than junior women. There are doubtless many reasons for this, but the mother-son relationship, whether it is biological or not, is one of the strongest human bonds. By treating the older women as his mothers, Timothy was not only honouring them but also reinforcing his own position – we can only imagine how they would have reacted to anyone who was unkind or disrespectful to 'our Timothy'!

At the same time, the son-mother relationship was also a very strong bond, highlighted for Christians in the relationship between Jesus and his mother Mary.[6] In the gospels, Joseph is a remote figure whose relationship to his 'son'

---

[6] See especially Jn 19.26–27.

is left unexplored, but Mary appears often, a fact that has been immortalized in countless paintings, prayers and works of devotion. Although Paul did not say so, the bond between Timothy and the older women was almost certainly the deepest one in the church, and would have influenced the conduct and outcome of Timothy's ministry more than any other.

Finally, Timothy was to treat the younger women as sisters, 'in all purity' (*hagneia*). Here the sexual dynamic was prominent, as we might expect when dealing with people of marriageable age and of the opposite sex. The modern reader is inclined to see Paul's advice in individualistic terms – Timothy was not to get romantically involved with a woman in his church. No doubt that was true, but there is another dimension to this that tends to get overlooked nowadays. It is not just that Timothy was expected to keep a respectful distance from these women; he was also expected to defend their honour if it were to be challenged by someone else. Women who found themselves the objects of unwanted attention from other men had to be protected from them, and here the brother-sister relationship would be most clearly revealed. As we shall see later on, there were a number of young widows in the church who were free to marry without parental permission. Some of them may have been highly desirable catches, especially if they were financially well-off, and there was no guarantee that their suitors would be the right kind of men. Timothy had his work cut out with these sisters!

It should be remembered that the brother-sister relationship was the one most frequently used to describe the Christian fellowship in general. Paul frequently addressed his congregations as 'brothers' or 'brethren', and used the word 'sister' when referring to particular women.[7] He did this because we are all children of the same heavenly Father, making the sibling relationship the most appropriate one to use in that context.[8] In this situation however, he respected the age differences within the congregation and used the brother-sister image in a more restricted sense, one whose meaning in this case was determined by Timothy's own relatively young age. This indicates a more pastoral and individual approach, that takes the human circumstances of particular people into consideration. The principle that all Christians are brothers and sisters is not denied, but it is adapted to conform to widespread human sensitivities about relative age. Paul had no desire to overturn the natural order of society in the name of an abstract theological principle. Instead, he chose to adapt that principle to the circumstances, preserving the truth it contained in a way that would be understood and respected by those to whom it was being communicated.

[7] Rom. 16.1.
[8] Gal. 4.6.

In summing up this section, Ambrosiaster had this to say,

> When somebody sees that he is being persuaded to accept things that contribute to a good life without arrogance, he will agree to be humble and defer to the person advising him. Things are often obtained by persuasion which cannot be had by laying down the law. When the baser instincts are stitrred up, they usually succumb to gentle treatment.[9]

It is a wise observation and one that is as pertinent today as it was when it was first written.

## 3-16. Widows

*3. Honour widows who are really widows. 4. If a widow has children or grandchildren, they should first learn their religious duty to their own family and make some repayment to their parents; for this is pleasing in God's sight. 5. The real widow, left alone, has set her hope on God and continues in supplications and prayers night and day; 6. but the widow who lives for pleasure is dead even while she lives. 7. Give these commands as well, so that they may be above reproach. 8. And whoever does not provide for relatives, and especially for family members, has denied the faith and is worse than an unbeliever. 9. Let a widow be put on the list if she is not less than sixty years old and has been married only once; 10. she must be well attested for her good works, a sone who has brought up children, shown hospitality, washed the saints' feet, helped the afflicted, and devoted herself to doing good in every way. 11. But refuse to put younger widows on the list; for when their sensual desires alienate them from Christ, they want to marry, 12. and so they incur condemnation for having violated their first pledge. 13. Besides that, they learn to be idle, gadding about from house to house; and they are not merely idle, but also gossips and busybodies, saying what they should not say. 14. So I would have younger widows marry, bear children, and manage their households, so as to give the adversary no occasion to revile us. 15. For some have already turned away to follow Satan. 16. If any believing woman has relatives who are really widows, let her assist them; let the church not be burdened, so that it can assist those who are real widows.*

---

[9] Ambrosiaster (2009), p. 133.

After dealing with Timothy's relationship to the younger women in the church, Paul went on to consider the widows, of whom there appear to have been many in his congregation.[10] It is one of the ironies of human life that men usually marry younger women even though women on average live longer than men do. This is understandable because a man may want to establish himself economically before taking on the responsibility of a family, and he will then probably want a wife of childbearing age. It is a common pattern that makes good practical sense but it inevitably leads to a situation in which there are almost always more widows than widowers, not only in the church but in society generally. So much was this the case in ancient times that Paul never mentioned widowers at all; there may have been one or two in the church, but they were not a significant constituency and apparently no special provision had to be made for them. It was presumably taken for granted that they would marry again if they wanted to, or be cared for by their female relatives if they chose to remain single. As far as we can tell, Paul looked after himself or relied on the hospitality of the people with whom he lodged, and he probably assumed that other men in his position would do the same.

Widows were another matter. The duty to take care of them was embedded in the Old Testament and taken over by the early church as a matter of course.[11] In so far as there was a social welfare system in ancient times, widows seem to have been its chief beneficiaries because they were more vulnerable than other members of society. Orphans could be adopted and the disabled either had relatives to care for them or earned their living by begging. But in a male-dominated society, widows were particularly vulnerable, and given the fact that many women married men much older than themselves, they were also quite numerous. A rudimentary structure providing relief was therefore in place for them in both the synagogue and the church. But as anyone who has ever been involved in charitable work of this kind knows, not everybody needs help to the same degree and benefit fraud, as we think of it nowadays, is all too common. It was in order to deal with this while maintaining the proper level of care for those in need that Paul wrote to Timothy in the way he did. The length of the passage dedicated to widows shows us how important this problem was, and the criteria that Paul laid down for dealing with it remain instructive for the church today.

---

[10] Some feminist writers have interpreted this passage as an attempt by the pseudepigrapher to suppress a nascent feminist movement within the church, but this is implausible. See Johnson (2001), pp. 270–2, for a mildly sympathetic but basically negative assessment of such claims.

[11] Deut. 10.18; 24.17; Isa. 1.17; Acts 6.1; Jas 1.27.

As Paul saw it, widows had to be assessed according to three criteria – family, age and character. First of all, there were those whom he regarded as 'genuine' widows. These were the elderly women who had nobody to look after them and who depended on the charity of the church. They were probably a minority of the overall total of widows but they were the ones in greatest need and so the church had to give priority to them. Next there were the older women who had children or other close relatives who could look after them, and Paul expected them to relieve the church of the burden.

Finally, there were the younger widows, whom Paul defined as those under sixty. This is rather surprising, since even today sixty is a considerable age and people lived shorter lives in ancient times. A sixty-year-old woman in those days would have been quite elderly! One aspect of this that we do not often think of is that it would have been difficult to prove the age of many of these women because records were not kept in the way that they are now. People would have had a rough idea of how old they were, but it is worth bearing in mind that the only person in the New Testament whose age is mentioned is Jesus, and even he was described only as being 'about thirty' when he was baptized![12] Many of these widows' ages would have been known only approximately; it is hard to imagine a 59-year-old woman having to wait until her next birthday before being put on the roll of the church (as would be the case with pensioners today). Given that a rough guide was often the only one available, much must have depended on common sense and on decisions taken in particular cases, so that what appears to us as a fixed 'rule' would probably have been more flexible in practice.[13]

Having said that, it is clear that the younger widows were a real problem. From the tone of his remarks, it is apparent that Paul was most exercised by the status and behaviour of this group, which he saw as potentially disruptive for the life of the church as a whole.

After briefly mentioning the 'genuine' widows, Paul paused to deal with those who had families that could take care of them. In particular, he urged their children and grandchildren to honour their own household and repay their elders for their upbringing. Paul's language here is almost untranslatable, but it reflects a viewpoint that was very commonly held in the ancient world. The official Roman state religion was essentially an ancestor cult, and preserving the honour of the family was always high on the agenda of every solid citizen. When Paul described this as *ton idion oikon eusebein* ('to honour one's own household') he would have been immediately understood

---

[12] Lk. 3.23.
[13] Marshall (2004), p. 593, supports this view, concluding, 'it must be remembered that these instructions are probably more in the nature of ideals than precise regulations.'

by anyone with a Greek or Roman education. Underlying his words would have been the thought that if pagans honour their forbears, how much more should Christians do the same? Most of the time, of course, Paul rejected pagan customs and he would certainly not have encouraged worship of household gods and the like. But sometimes pagan traditions reflected God's will and, in those cases, Paul believed that Christians ought to replicate them, and if possible, improve upon them. When it came to respecting the elderly, Paul did not hesitate to appeal to the Gentile world and urge Christians to demonstrate a similar devotion.

Social welfare within the family has always been important, and even in our modern age primary caregivers are often relatives who offer their services free of charge. This is part of being a family – the young should take care of the elderly, just as they were once taken care of by them. For the widows, it was literally payback time – the Greek word *amoibē* which Paul used here means 'salary' or 'wage'. This was not something to be rejected along with pagan culture in general, but rather to be adopted and pursued because it is 'acceptable' (*apodekton*) to God. God's standards are high, and the duty to look after aging parents was one that both Jesus and his disciples emphasized as the right way to fulfil the fifth commandment. There was a tendency among some Jews to back out of this responsibility by claiming that they had given their money to the service of God and were therefore dispensed from aiding their parents.[14] James condemned this.[15] Paul did not mention it, but he was certainly aware of the remarkable example of Ruth, who not only took care of her aged mother-in-law Naomi, but converted to the faith of Israel in order to do it.[16] And of course Jesus himself made provision for his mother even as he was dying on the cross.[17] With precedents like that, Christians who were able to take care of their parents had no excuse not to do so.

Paul then paused to deal once more with the 'genuine' widows, before returning to the relatives whose responsibility it was to look after their family. In v. 8 he left his hearers in no doubt. People who did not take care of their relatives, especially those who lived under the same roof, had denied their faith and were worse than unbelievers. This is very strong language, but it reminds us of the consequences of being a Christian. Faith is not just belief in the truths of the gospel, important and foundational though they are. Faith is also a way of life. 'Charity begins at home' as the saying goes, and Paul made that point here. Those who are close to us are our responsibility, and we must

[14] Mt. 15.3-6; Mk 7.8-13.
[15] Jas 1.27.
[16] Ruth 1.16-17.
[17] Jn 19.26-27.

look after them first, before we range further afield. Of course, he was not against wider missionary activity, which is what he himself engaged in. But he was free to do that because he did not have the same family responsibilities that others had. Those who were tied down in that way he expected to fulfil their obligations, and we may be certain that if anyone had tried to get out of them by following him around the world instead, he would have sent them home immediately.

The people Paul denounced in v. 8 were in his opinion worse than unbelievers. This is not an objective statement of fact, but a subjective conclusion that circumstances had led him to. In purely objective terms, unbelief was the greatest of sins and would lead inexorably to eternal damnation. But for a believer, the worst sin was hypocrisy. Those who knew the truth and refused to obey it were guilty, not just of ignoring God but of insulting him. Having seen the light, they preferred the darkness and in doing so they sealed their own fate. An ignorant unbeliever might always come to faith and change his behaviour, but someone who had once tasted the heavenly gift and then fallen away would prove to be irredeemable.[18] Paul had no time for such people because they had knowingly refused what was best for them, and the strength of his language shows clearly how he felt about them.

Meanwhile, Paul had also been meditating on the predicament of the 'genuine' widow. This was a woman who had been left all alone in this world but who had the time and the inclination to devote herself to a life of prayer. Paul saw this as an opportunity for her to bring great blessing both to her personally and to the church. To understand this, we must remember that in his mind prayer was the most important activity in which God's people can be engaged. He wanted believers to pray without ceasing. But of course, the practicalities of everyday life made that hard for many people to do. In an age that lacked modern household conveniences, ordinary chores could take up a lot of time and women were the ones who organized and ran the households. Even if they had servants to help them, they still had a lot of planning to do, and housekeeping was a full-time occupation.

Paul also recognized that it was right for a wife to devote herself to her husband, just as a husband was expected to take care of his wife. In the natural course of events she was likely to outlive him, and be free, in the last years of her life, to devote herself to other things. Leisure was rare in the ancient world, but widows were more likely than most other people to enjoy it. Their own needs were few, and after shouldering the burden of running an entire

---

[18] Heb. 6.4-6.

household, having nobody to take care of but themselves must have seemed like a kind of holiday. The question then was what to do with their spare time. Essentially they could choose one of two options. Either they could live for the service of God, or they could please themselves. In Middle Eastern countries today, it is customary for widows to wear black in recognition of their status and in mourning for the husbands they have lost. However, there are always some widows who do not do this. Instead, they wear gay clothing and behave as if their widowhood means little or nothing to them.

Paul had little time for this second type of widow. As far as he was concerned, such a woman was spiritually dead even though she was still physically alive, because she was not putting God and her responsibilities, which included remembering her dead husband in an appropriate way, first in her life. A real widow must be like the *episkopos*, irreproachable (*anepilēmptos*) in everything she did. The association of this word with two quite different types of church member serves to underline the common responsibility that each of them had. The *episkopos* exercised a public administrative role, but the widow was just as central to the well-being of the church, and in ways that from God's point of view were sometimes more important. This is because the *episkopos*, like a married woman, had to take care of the things of this world, while the widow was free to devote herself to God. This order of priorities may not appeal to the modern age, where having a job and earning a salary are often taken to be the measure of a person's worth, but Paul's point was that the true believer should not think in the world's way. From a Christian perspective, the widow's freedom to worship God places her on a higher plane, and to spurn that for the pleasures of this life is as ungodly as failing to take care of relatives in need.

From what Paul said, it appears that there was a roll (*katalogos*) in the church on which widows were registered.[19] In his mind, there were three qualifications for being put on the list:

1. The woman must be sixty years old or more.
2. She must have been the wife of one man.
3. She must have a reputation for good works.

---

[19] Towner (2006), p. 345, remarks, 'While the implication here is that a formal list or roster and related enrollment procedure already existed, which Paul sought to adjust, nothing in the term itself reveals *how* formal the procedure was or in what sort of group the process determined membership.' Probably the system, such as it was, had been copied from the synagogue and so its existence cannot be taken as evidence that the Epistle must be post-apostolic on the ground that no such procedure had developed in apostolic times.

The first of these was the basic qualification that governed the others. It would be perfectly possible for a woman to satisfy the second and third conditions but not the first, and if so, she was not to be enrolled. What exactly Paul meant by saying that she must have been the wife of one man is not clear, though it parallels the requirement for an *episkopos* or a deacon to be the husband of one wife.[20] The conditions imposed on the male officers of the church were the same as those imposed on the widows, because both had a recognized standing in the congregation. Having said that, the principle must have been applied in slightly different ways. For example, an *episkopos* or a deacon would have been still married, whereas a widow obviously was not. How she might have had more than one husband is also not immediately clear. Presumably she would not have been like the Samaritan woman whom Jesus met in John 4, who had had 'five husbands', but none of them was legitimate![21] That kind of interpretation seems to be impossible here. Perhaps a widow's first husband had died, and she had remarried. In that case, she would probably still have been counted as the wife of one man, because remarriage after the death of a spouse was universally recognized as legitimate and was even encouraged by Paul himself in this very passage.[22] Almost certainly, the prohibition is meant to exclude women who had divorced and remarried, but that too is difficult, especially in the ancient world, where a man could send his wife away against her will and there was nothing she could do about it.

To our minds, it is hard to understand why someone in that position would not have been free to remarry, but that seems to have been the case. Even if she had been the injured party in the divorce, that divorce was still illegitimate and she was not free to marry again. Marriage was the joining of two people into one flesh, and as long as the other party to it was alive, that union endured. To many people today, that sounds unfair, but it was the standard expected of both women and men. Divorce, except in the case of adultery, was simply un-Christian and the church could not be seen to be tolerating it, however indirectly.[23]

The woman must also have a reputation for good works, examples of which are listed by the apostle as follows:

1. She has brought up children.
2. She has shown hospitality.
3. She has washed the feet of the saints.

---

[20] See above, 1 Tim. 3.2, 12.
[21] Jn 4.17-18.
[22] See below, 1 Tim. 5.14.
[23] Mt. 19.9.

4. She has cared for the afflicted.
5. She has devoted herself to every kind of good work.

The first of these seems obvious enough, though it must be set against the provision that family members must take care of their own relatives. If the widow in question had brought up children, it was their responsibility to look after her in her old age and she should not have been enrolled on the widows' list in the church. But there were probably cases where a widow's children were unable to look after her, perhaps because they had died or had gone away elsewhere. There are always complex situations for which there are no fixed rules, and a range of possibilities must be considered. It may also have been the case that the children she brought up were not her own. Many young women worked as nannies, and some did so without ever having children of their own. They had brought them up but the children had no responsibility to look after them in old age. In cases like these, a widow's child-rearing experience had to be taken into account in any fair assessment of her qualifications for assistance from the church.[24]

Hospitality is another very important part of life, and this was especially in the ancient world, where (as the Greek word that Paul used here suggests) it involved having people to stay, sometimes for considerable periods. The apostle Paul himself was often the beneficiary of such hospitality, and it is mentioned elsewhere in the New Testament as well.[25] We should also not forget that in a world where churches met in houses, this role could be very important, and Paul referred to the congregations that met in the houses of women like Lydia and Chloe.[26] Were these women married? We do not know, but to some extent it did not matter. The house was their domain, and so the church that met there was identified with them, even though they were not *episkopoi* or *presbyteroi*. Hospitality was a widely recognized virtue in ancient times and the church placed great store on it.[27] It was a service that Christians were expected to offer even to strangers, some of whom might turn out to be messengers from God.[28]

Washing the feet 'of the saints' was a form of hospitality that demonstrated a humble, yet at the same time noble, attitude of service. Paul would have

---

[24] Marshall (2004), p. 595, highlights this possibility and regards it as quite likely, 'since by definition the widow has no children or grandchildren to look after her'. Towner (2006), p. 347, however, tends to discount this aspect, without excluding it entirely. Both opinions, it must be stressed, are purely speculative.
[25] See 3 Jn 1.5-6.
[26] Acts 16.14; 1 Cor. 1.11.
[27] Rom. 12.13; 1 Pet. 4.9.
[28] Heb. 13.2; 3 Jn 1.5-8.

known about Jesus' washing his disciples' feet, but the custom was a common one and he probably felt no need to refer to that specifically.[29] More important would have been the willingness of a person of some status to undertake a task normally reserved for servants, and it was this spirit that Paul expected to find in widows if they were to be recognized as deserving of recognition by the church. Women also played an important nursing role, and Paul mentioned that as his third qualification for a widow in receipt of a church pension. Illness and other forms of suffering were common in the ancient world and medical care was rudimentary, so caring for the afflicted was a vitally important social ministry.[30] Finally, the pious widow should have been devoting herself to every kind of good work. Paul could not specify everything, and there must have been many acts of kindness that women could perform above and beyond those listed here. His main concern was to emphasize the attitude of selfless service that a widow should have, not to single out particular activities as deserving of special reward. No doubt some things were more important than others, but Paul was more interested in people who had the right spirit than in those who made a great success of their ministries.

Up to this point, Paul's advice to Timothy sounds reasonable and routine, the sort of thing that we could expect from anyone at any time and not a response to any kind of crisis in the church. It is only when we turn to the situation of the younger widows that we realize that Paul thought that Timothy had a serious problem on his hands. In Paul's eyes, these younger widows were likely to

1. cool in their ardour for Christ
2. lay aside their faith
3. want to marry
4. indulge their love for gossip and troublemaking

The apostle was of course speaking in general terms and there must have been some who were not like that, but in his eyes those exceptions would have proved the rule. Most of the young widows were not ready to settle into a comfortable old age, with nothing to do except pray and build up the church. It was by their desire to do those things that Paul measured people's

---

[29] Mt. 26.14-39; Jn 13.1-17.
[30] There is no reason to include persecution as a form of suffering, though Marshall (2004), p. 597, mentions it as a possibility. But even he recognizes that persecution is not mentioned anywhere else in this Epistle, and when it comes up in 2 Timothy (1.8; 2.3) it affects only Paul and Timothy, not their congregations.

passion for Christ. When interest in them faded, Paul concluded that their longing for Christ did so too. In his mind, if a widow was drawn away from a life of prayer to an interest in remarrying, it was a step backwards and worthy of condemnation, if not of punishment. By barring the younger widows from the church roll, Paul may have been trying to protect them from such an outcome. He did not want them to take on unduly heavy commitments, only to discover that they subsequently reneged on them because other more worldly desires intervened. By not binding their consciences in the first place, Paul could let the younger widows pursue their wishes without putting them at fault, and so his strictures about keeping them off the widows' roll, although at first sight they might appear to be unjust, were actually an act of kindness on his part.[31]

Paul also saw the younger widows as being prone to idleness and gossip. They were likely to travel from house to house, minding other people's business and causing trouble by saying things they ought not to say. Idle hands are the devil's playground, and that was as true of women in this situation as it is of people everywhere. Ambrosiaster sums it up very well:

> It is better to work for a living and keep one's self-respect than to do nothing and wait shamelessly for handouts. In that way Satan finds an opportunity to undermine ill-advised souls who claim to be godly but act unjustly, for nothing is more dangerous than if one's deeds belie one's profession. Satan does not go after open evil in order to rejoice in it. It is when he sees somebody trying to practise deception that he acts to show that such a person is his child and not God's, and God does not intervene to prevent this.[32]

It was particularly difficult for the early church to deal with widows, because they enjoyed an unusual freedom in ancient society. They were no longer under the care of their parents, and their husbands were dead. There was therefore nobody to tell them what to do or to try to keep them in line. It was a situation that was ripe for trouble and it seems that some of the women fell into the trap all too readily. Paul did not explicitly say so, but we can assume

---

[31] Both Marshall (2004), pp. 599-600, and Towner (2006), pp. 350-1, suggest the possibility that the younger widows might have been tempted into sexual sin, though there is no reason to think that from what Paul said in the text. It is obviously not possible to speak for every case, but if promiscuity had been an issue surely the apostle would have mentioned it. It must be said in this connection that modern commentators tend to exaggerate the predicament of widows in ancient society and to speculate about them in ways that are not justified by the evidence.
[32] Ambrosiaster (2009), p. 136.

that if they were hindered from fulfilling their desires, things would get even worse. If they were trapped in a life of singleness that they did not want, they would almost inevitably seek an outlet for their frustration, and the sorts of unhelpful activities that Paul mentioned would be obvious avenues for them to explore.

In order to forestall the possibility of having unhappy women disturb the peace of the church, Paul counselled Timothy to encourage the younger widows to marry, to have children and to manage their households. In other words, he wanted them to go on doing what they would have been doing in any case had their first husbands not died. It may not be immediately apparent but this advice reveals an age gap, in that it was generally believed that forty was the maximum age for childbearing, but widows could not be enrolled in the church until they were sixty. There must have been a considerable group that fell between these two ages, but what was supposed to happen to them? Paul did not consider that question, though it was implied in the advice that he gave to Timothy. His primary concern was that there should be no occasion given to 'the adversary' (*ho antikeimenos*) for slander, although he had to admit that there were already some who had gone off after Satan.

We must assume that the 'adversary' and Satan were one and the same, and that the following he had attracted among some of the younger widows was a weapon he could use to mock the church. To Paul's mind, the problem of these widows was part of the spiritual battle that God's people were waging against Satan, who would use every device at his disposal to disrupt the fellowship of the saints. It was to prevent this that he gave the advice he did, and this was his principal concern. If, by repelling Satan, he could also satisfy the desires of the younger widows, so much the better, but that was a secondary matter. The main thrust of his argument was spiritual, and it was in that context that he spoke in the way that he did.

Paul ended the section on widows by repeating his advice that those who had them in the family ought to take care of them and not burden the church with the responsibility, so that the church could look after the ones who had real needs.[33] The only difference from what he said earlier is that here he placed the burden of caring for these widows on believing women in the church. Evidently he expected them to take the primary role in caring for their less fortunate sisters and that was at least partly in order to avoid scandal. It was not a task that a man could easily have undertaken without

---

[33] Ambrosiaster (2009), p. 136, complained about continuing abuses in his own time and speculated as to the cause. His conclusion was insightful: 'Sometimes this happens by negligence, but sometimes it occurs because those who want help are very persuasive.' How true!

arousing potentially salacious comment, and wisdom dictated that just as it was important to marry the younger widows off so as to avoid the snares of the devil, so it was necessary to take care of the widows in a way that would not lead to unhelpful gossip. Getting women to look after other women was the best way forward, and this was what Paul suggested to Timothy as he concluded his remarks on the subject.

Applying a passage like this one to modern church life is problematic for a number of reasons. The social context is very different, and today women have much greater freedom than they did in the past. There is also a greater sense of individualism, so that few congregations would have a recognized group of 'widows' that would require special consideration as such. There is also the feminist critique which, even if it is misguided, is bound to intervene in any discussion of the principles Paul was enunciating. Nevertheless, as L. T. Johnson eloquently reminds us, the text is about more than appears on the surface, and its wider message needs to be heard today as much as ever. In his words,

> Where else in the New Testament is the tradition of community support for the poor, and the mutual responsibility of households and of the *ekklēsia* for such support, as a manifestation in faith itself, so clearly stated? It is not Paul's success in solving the problems of the ancient Ephesian church that gives this text its perennial importance. It is that Paul witnesses to the prophetic demand of caring for those who have no other hope, and struggles with the deep ambiguities that any such commitment involves within every cultural context.[34]

## 17-22. Elders

*17. Let the elders who rule well be considered worthy of double honour, especially those who labour in preaching and teaching; 18. for the Scripture says: 'You shall not muzzle an ox while it is treading out the grain', and: 'The labourer deserves to be paid.' 19. Never accept any accusation against an elder except on the evidence of two or three witnesses. 20. As for*

---

[34] Johnson (2001), p. 276. Calvin (2016), vol. 2, p. 150, was very aware of the deficiencies of the church in his day in this respect. He said, 'If we should compare our time with that which Saint Paul speaks of, have we not better occasion ... to maintain this order which he appoints and sets down here, than they had in those days? For the poor Christians were persecuted ... having nothing certain. Therefore if we compare the charity that was then with the charity of these days, we may be greatly ashamed.'

*those who persist in sin, rebuke them in the presence of all, so that the rest also may stand in fear. 21. In the presence of God and of Christ Jesus and of the elect angels, I warn you to keep these instructions without prejudice, doing nothing on the basis of partiality. 22. Do not ordain anyone hastily, and do not participate in the sins of others: keep yourself pure.*

After dealing with widows, Paul moved on to consider the role of the elders in the congregation. From the tone of his remarks we can assume that both he and Timothy knew exactly who these elders were and what they did, though neither of these things is immediately obvious to modern readers. Nor is it clear what links the elders may have had with the *episkopos* whom Paul mentioned at the beginning of the letter. Were there separate offices or were *presbyteros* and *episkopos* just different names for the same men, as most modern commentators assume? There is also the question of what the relationship was between the *presbyteroi* who had a role in governing the church and the old men to whom Timothy was expected to show respect and even deference. Were they the same people, and if not, how much overlap was there between them? How young could a ruling *presbyteros* be? And what was Timothy supposed to do with old men who were not official *presbyteroi*, in a culture where old age commanded a certain status whether there was any responsibility attached to it or not?[35]

To answer these questions, and others related to them, it is best to begin with the word *presbyteros* itself. In the world in which Paul and Timothy lived, there was clearly a connection between authority and status on the one hand, and old age on the other. This is a phenomenon found in many, perhaps most, cultures and was well attested in the ancient world. The senior council in Sparta was called the *gerousia*, from *gerōn* ('old man') and the Roman *senatus* was named from the Latin *senex* ('old man'). Over time however, these institutions came to be distinguished from what they supposedly represented. Rome never had really young senators, but many of them were far from being 'old' in the conventional sense of the word. One might almost say of them that whereas originally, old age had conferred status and authority in government affairs, as time went on, it was that authority and status that conferred honorary old age!

---

[35] These questions, and the impossibility of coming to any definite conclusion regarding them, are set out clearly by Marshall (2004), pp. 610–12. Towner (2006), pp. 361–4, claims that the distinction Paul was making was between those who had exercised the duties of an elder properly and those who had failed, but this is speculation that is not supported by the text, and seems unlikely. If some elders had failed, Paul would surely have said so and not merely suggested to Timothy that the good ones should receive double compensation for their efforts!

Something analogous to this process happened in the Jewish, and later in the Christian world as well. Elders were by definition not particularly young, but nor were they necessarily 'old', and it was certainly not the case that every old man was an 'elder' in the official sense. One of the main underlying themes of this Epistle is that at Ephesus a young man had been put in charge of the elders. This fact is brought out with particular clarity in this passage, and Paul was outlining the ways in which both he and they had to deal with what was superficially an anomalous situation.

It is also clear from this text that the official elders, who must have constituted the *presbyterion* mentioned in 4.14, were the 'rulers' (*proestōtes*) of the church. But was this true of all of them, or only of some? Here Paul's words are tantalizingly unclear. He says that the good ruling elders were worthy of 'double honour' (*diplē timē*), which raises more questions than it answers. Were there also 'bad' ruling elders, and if there were some who were not doing their job properly, why were they not removed? Was the 'double honour' a reward for special achievement, and if so, how was that to be measured? It seems clear from what Paul said that only some of the elders were engaged in preaching and teaching, but how were they selected and what did the others do? What percentage of the total number belonged to this superior category? We have no idea! Even more intriguingly, was the eldership a paid position? The Greek word *timē* is ambiguous; it can mean 'honour', but it can also mean 'price' or 'value', and the next verses, which quote directly from the Hebrew Bible and the words of Jesus, are explicitly connected with wages. Thus, the natural meaning would be that all the elders were paid a salary, but those who did especially well deserved double, though whether they actually received it, either in cash or in kind, is not stated. Perhaps it was because they were *not* getting what they deserved that Paul spoke in the way that he did, in order to encourage the church to adopt a 'fair reward' policy.

At the very least, it seems likely that those who preached and taught were compensated for their labour, though perhaps not as generously as they should have been. The spiritual principle on which Paul rested his case was taken from the Torah, which says, 'You shall not muzzle an ox when it treads out the grain.'[36] This is a classic example of Jewish *pesher* exegesis, in which Paul had been trained and which he used to great effect in his ministry. The Torah contained a number of similar precepts which had a literal meaning that, in many cases, was inapplicable as such. Those who had oxen were bound to respect the text, but they were few and the Word of God was expected

---

[36] Deut. 25.4.

to have a relevance to everyone. This was found not in the circumstances it describes but in the principle that underlies the command. This principle was, quite simply, that the labourer is worthy of his hire, as Jesus put it.[37] Jesus' words were clarifying the meaning of the Old Testament text, and there is no reason to suppose that anyone trained in the study of the Torah would have disagreed with him on this point.[38]

In the example given by Jesus, it can be argued that the precept is based on sound economics, since nobody will work voluntarily if he is not properly compensated for it.[39] But the quotation from the Torah, which the words of Jesus were used to expound, is not so obviously based on a purely economic rationale. No doubt it was a good idea to feed the oxen since they would not have functioned for long without some nourishment, but this particular form of it was not necessary for that need to be fulfilled. Rather, what we see here are two quite different principles at work. One is that the labourer is an integral part of the labour that he is offering. To compensate him for it is not to discharge him from responsibility, but to include him in the overall project. It is in his interest, as much as anyone else's, for the work to be done well and in a timely manner. The second principle is that of love. The ox was allowed to graze on the corn because God is generous and loving towards those who do what he expects of them. So it should be with the elders who perform their tasks in the right way.

The question of material compensation is always a delicate one, but not nearly as delicate as what Paul went on to discuss next – the problem of discipline in the eldership. People who minister to a congregation expose themselves to criticism from those whom they are called to serve. This can be motivated by any number of factors, some of which may be justified but many of which are not. It is very difficult to keep everybody happy, and if personal jealousy or other similar factors enter in, those in responsible positions may find themselves the objects of attack. How should the church leadership deal with this?

---

[37] Lk. 10.7; Mt. 10.10.
[38] Commentators disagree about the origin of Paul's quotations here. Most accept that his interpretation of the Old Testament passage was in line with contemporary rabbinic exegesis and therefore not surprising, but how he came by the words of Jesus is more debated. His words correspond exactly to what we find in Lk. 10.7, which has led some scholars to think that Luke may have written the Epistle either as Paul's *amanuensis* or as the executor of his will. But the sayings of Jesus must have been circulating in the church long before the gospels were written and there is no reason to suppose that Paul was unaware of this one. See Marshall (2004), pp. 616–17; Towner (2006), pp. 366–7.
[39] Ambrosiaster (2009), p. 136, made this point and concluded with a memorable judgement: 'The preacher of the kingdom of God ought to receive a salary which he can neither complain nor boast about.'

Paul tackled this question by appealing to the Torah once again. In Deut. 19.15 it says that two or three witnesses are required for an accusation to be taken seriously *against anybody*, and Paul repeats that elsewhere.[40] Here he applied this universal principle to the particular case of the church elders, who might have been more exposed to such charges because of their prominence. For some reason, there seems to be a general assumption in many quarters that if people are well known enough, any accusation made against them must be taken seriously. Of course, the mere fact that they have been accused is bound to compromise their reputation to some extent. They have more to lose than others who are relatively obscure and unknown, which is one reason why the fairness of the law must be extended to them with special emphasis.

What exactly the Deuteronomic precept meant is a matter of interpretation. It is phrased in a rather loose way – 'two or three'. Is a third witness to be sought out when there is already a second one, or is one simply to be added to the list if he happens to be around? If there are more witnesses, should they be included as well, or should only two or three be selected to represent the others? And what if the second or third witness is related to the first, or dependent on him in some way that might compromise the value of his testimony? In modern times, when two witnesses or guarantors are required for some legal purpose, it is often stated that they should not be related to each other, or to the person to whom they are witnessing, so as to respect the intention behind the requirement of asking for more than one witness in the first place. Did this principle apply in the case that Paul mentioned here?

Once again, we cannot answer these questions with certainty. We may assume that a man and his wife would not have constituted 'two' witnesses, but that was at least as much because the testimony of a woman was not considered equal to that of a man as for any other reason. Would two brothers have passed the plurality test? What about an employer and his employee? Modern readers, accustomed as we are to vast and sometimes oppressive bureaucracies, are often highly sensitized to the possibility of abuses and Paul must have been aware of them, not least because he was so often on the receiving end himself. But he did not go into the details here, probably because the point he was trying to make was clear enough. An accusation made against an elder must have some credibility if it is to be admitted, and no doubt Timothy and the other elders would have been sensitive to that. After all, their turn could be next and it was in their own interest to make the procedure as fair and as transparent as possible.

---

[40] 2 Cor. 13.1. See also Deut. 17.6, which also mentions the same principle.

One oddity, at least from the modern point of view, is that Paul does not seem to have recognized any presumption of innocence. Today we are used to the idea that an accuser must not only state his case but prove it beyond reasonable doubt, and that unless he can do so, the accused person is innocent. In the Roman system, things worked differently. An accused man had to demonstrate his innocence, which (to our minds at least) seems grossly unjust. It was for that reason that Paul was arrested, detained for several years in Palestine and then finally sent to Rome for trial, where he had to wait for at least another two years. That would be a serious miscarriage of justice if it were to happen today, but it was par for the course for the Romans and it was often easier just to take the punishment and be done with it. Paul made himself awkward by demanding a proper trial, and from one point of view, his determination could be said to have been unwise. After all, if he had just been beaten and then released, as had happened to him on several other occasions, he would have recovered and carried on. As it was, he spent years in detention before coming to trial, a loss of potential earning time that could have ruined a businessman.[41]

Paul could do nothing to change the secular law, but it is somewhat disconcerting to the modern mind to discover that he did not challenge it within the church either. Perhaps this was because people would have thought that for the church to have adopted a procedure different from the one used in the secular sphere would have been wrong. There are certainly cases of guilty people going free today because there is not enough evidence to convict them, and people who know this often feel that the accused has benefitted unjustly from the system. If Paul had advocated the modern approach, to which people were not accustomed, that feeling would undoubtedly have been much stronger, and the morale of the congregation could have been seriously undermined. For all its faults, it was better to follow the procedure people were familiar with, so as not to undermine their sense of right and wrong.

Paul said nothing about how Timothy should proceed to investigate charges made against an elder. There was presumably some consultation, at least with the *presbyterion*, but that is not stated. What was probably a restraining influence on everyone concerned was the need to pronounce judgement in public. If the accusation made against someone was clearly unfair, or at least was thought to be so by a sufficiently large group of people, there would be a real risk that opposition would be expressed at the time the judgement was made, and the assembly could have dissolved into disorder.

---

[41] Acts 26.32 makes this point.

Nobody would have wanted that, which strongly suggests that Timothy would have done his best to ensure that he was on firm ground before taking such a drastic step.

It is interesting to note that when Paul spoke of punishing the accused, the word he used to describe the victim was *hamartanōn* ('sinning one'). He did not use the word *hamartōlos* ('sinner'), perhaps because in theological terms, we are all sinners deserving of punishment. Here Paul was thinking not so much of 'sin' in the spiritual sense as of 'wrongdoing' in the context of church life and responsibility. But it is still significant that he saw such wrongdoing as a form of sin, and that he assumed that this had been recognized by all those involved.

Paul had no doubt that when someone was accused and convicted, he must be punished by being publicly rebuked. There were limits to the kind of sanction that Timothy could have imposed, because the church was not a legal organization and had no power to punish anyone according to the law. Presumably the 'sinning one' could have walked away from the congregation, and there would have been nothing anyone could have done about it. Verbal rebuke, accompanied in severe cases by exclusion from the fellowship, was virtually the only form of discipline open to the church leadership, and it was doubtless for this reason that it figured so prominently in Paul's advice-giving. Nevertheless, we must not underestimate the impact that such a rebuke could have. Shame was a potent force in the ancient world, as it still is in many societies today. Even unbelievers might well hear of what had happened and adopt a negative attitude to the accused as a result. People seldom bother much about the details of such cases; often, the mere fact of being named in an accusation is enough to blacken a person's reputation. In the small-town and village culture of the time, word would have spread quickly, and an accused man's ability to escape the consequences of his misdeed would have been considerably diminished. Justice could be done, and be seen to be done, with relatively little cost and no outward 'punishment' at all, which is probably what both Paul and Timothy would have regarded as the best outcome.

Paul's sense of justice comes across most clearly in v. 21, where he urged Timothy to act fairly and to avoid any show of partiality in his judgements. The extreme seriousness of this is brought out by the fact that he swore (*diamartyromai*) before God, Christ Jesus and the elect angels! Today, a declamation like this would probably sound like an empty formula that serious people might avoid lest it be taken as injurious to the name of God, but this was not so in Paul's case. He was well aware that all human activity, and especially the behaviour of ministers of the gospel, was under God's judgement, and so ought to be conducted with reverence and fear.[42]

---

[42] The word for 'swear' literally means 'bear witness' and in its participial form

Paul was actively expressing his faith when telling Timothy how to behave in disciplinary cases, since he knew that God requires of believers that they should do justice, love mercy and walk humbly with him.[43] Human behaviour was righteous only to the extent that it reflected the divine character, and it was this that Paul wanted to bring out in the advice that he was giving here.

First of all, he mentioned 'God' without specifying the name of the Father, though the context makes it clear that this must be what he meant. The Father is the supreme judge, whose standards have been given to the world as a measure of what is required of us, and before whom we must one day give account of ourselves. It is therefore particularly appropriate that Paul should recreate this scene, if only verbally. He pictured himself bearing witness before the judgement-seat of God because he was aware that what he did in this life reflected that reality and would come back to affirm (or to haunt) him when that great day came. We might even say that this was a 'dry run' for the heavenly judgement that we shall face at the end of time, and that the same expectations apply to us now as will be used to assess our conduct then.

Christ Jesus follows immediately after God (the Father), not because he is inferior but because he is one with the Father both in expectations and in judgement. In terms of expectations, he is the one who has satisfied the Father's demand for justice, not only for himself but also for us. He has fulfilled the Father's expectations and if we are united to him we benefit from that. What we cannot do for ourselves he has done for us, so his witness on our behalf is not to be taken lightly or regarded as an added extra. It is fundamental to our own standing before God and so it is no surprise that it should occupy the central position in this triad of spiritual authorities.

Finally, Paul mentioned the 'chosen angels'. We might have expected to find the Holy Spirit here, but the context does not really fit that. Paul was bearing witness to the Father and the Son, and also to the chosen angels, but he was doing so *in* the Holy Spirit and not *to* him. Without the indwelling presence of the Spirit in his heart he would not have been able to bear witness before God, because he would not have had the spiritual power to do so. God accepted Paul's testimony *in the Spirit* but not otherwise. The Holy Spirit is therefore present in this remark, but as the agent and not as the co-recipient of the testimony.

Who the elect angels were and why they appear to have taken the place of the Spirit is a matter about which we can only speculate. It seems obvious that they were angels who had not followed Satan in his rebellion against

---

(*diamartyromenos*) is now used to mean 'Protestant', because a Protestant is a person who bears witness ('pro-tests') his faith. This gives us a sense of the verb's meaning here.

[43] Mic. 6.8.

God, but whether they included all of them we cannot say. Were there angels who remained obedient to God when Satan fell, but who were not among the elect? What would that mean for their eternal destiny? And were they obedient because they were elect or was it the other way round? It seems that they must have been chosen first and then demonstrated their election by being faithful when the temptation came, since otherwise they would have earned their elect status by their obedience, which can hardly be right. It is also hard to imagine how there could be obedient angels in heaven who had *not* been chosen by God, since they could hardly stake a claim to being there apart from his will. If there is one thing we can be certain of, it is that the obedient angels did not surprise God by showing unexpected faithfulness, so the only real alternative is to say that they had been set apart from the beginning and that it was the others who fell in the rebellion of Satan.

But it is one thing to establish their status and identity and quite another to explain why they should be included among the witnesses of Paul's command to Timothy. The elect angels had not established the criteria by which Paul's work would be judged – that was the work of the Father. Nor had they accomplished the Father's will in a way that made it possible to incorporate Paul into their pattern of obedience – that was the work of the Son, Christ Jesus. The angels were present both because they were witnesses to the working out of the relationship between God and the apostle, and because they had a special role to play in keeping watch over believers, including Paul. This is the phenomenon of the 'guardian angel(s)' that were assigned to every church and seemingly to every believer as well. It is pointless to speculate on how many of them there were. Revelation 2–3 gives us the impression that the seven churches of Asia each had a single guardian angel, but there are other texts where it appears that whole hosts of angels were given individual human beings as their particular charges.[44] In later tradition, the idea grew up that every Christian had his own guardian angel, which may be true even though there is no textual evidence that supports the idea unequivocally. Such questions are the stuff of speculation but they make no difference in the end. What counts is that the elect angels were observing the proceedings, and that as witnesses, they might at some point be sent to confirm the divine decree with regard to Paul and his requests, or to exact the punishment appropriate for anyone who has rejected the saving grace of God.

Paul's command to Timothy was that he should 'keep' (*phylassō*) the pattern of rules that he had laid down. His word is a strong one, invoking the image of a guard (*phylax*) who was charged with special responsibility

---

[44] Ps. 91.11; 1 Cor. 11.10; Gal. 3.19.

for doing the right thing and who would be answerable to God if he failed. Justice and due process were not things that could be taken for granted, or expected to flow naturally from the hearts and minds of good-natured people. They were precious gifts that had to be carefully guarded by taking care to avoid prejudice (*prokrima*) and partiality (*prosklisis*).

The theory was good and virtually everybody agreed with it in principle, but putting it into practice was another matter. In a sense, it could be said that God manifests *prokrima* because he knows what the punishment for our sins will be even before we commit them, and by the death of his Son in time and space he has passed judgement on them even before they have occurred. The individual believer knows what God's verdict on his sins will be before he commits them and that there is no way it can be avoided.

But there is a huge difference between God's foreknowledge of our sins and human *prokrima* in judging others. God's vision is absolute and his standards are applied equally to everyone. He does not condemn us because he does not like us or because he thinks that there is no way that we can ever avoid doing the wrong thing, even when we have not yet done it. He is not prejudiced in that way. On the contrary, he condemns us because he knows that every child of Adam has sinned and fallen short of his glory. Dwelling outside time and space, as he does, there is no '*pro-*' in his *krima* because everything has happened within the compass of his eternal knowledge. Human beings, on the other hand, are finite creatures with limited understanding. We are all burdened with the weight of our own sins and prone to let them influence our judgement. To some extent we are all swayed by our preconceived ideas and are liable to exercise our discernment in the light of them. How could it be otherwise?

The result, unfortunately, is that our human verdict is almost bound to err on one side or the other. Either we shall be too lenient in excusing faults, or too strict in attacking them. There will be hidden motives in our actions, some of which may be so deeply concealed that we are unaware of them ourselves. In particular, it is highly unlikely that we shall judge matters in a way that is to our own detriment, even if we may sometimes be prepared to confess a degree of fault on our part. We are also prone to categorize others according to race, gender or ethnicity in ways that may have some superficial credibility but which are deeply unfair to particular individuals. It is reasonable to suppose that an Arab student is more likely to be an Islamic terrorist than an Icelandic fisherman is, so that our natural inclination will be to blame the former for a bomb attack rather than the latter, but however justified such generalizations may appear to be, they are still catering to prejudices of one kind or another and are relatively impervious to the facts, unless (of course) those facts support the conclusions we have already drawn. Some degree of distortion in our judgement is almost inevitable, which is all the more reason why we must be on our guard against it. Timothy was no exception to this rule, and neither was Paul. If they were different from us, it was only because they understood their own limitations better than most of us do, and were careful to take steps against them so that they would not succumb to the pressure of their own weaknesses.

Closely tied to prejudice (*prokrima*) is partiality (*prosklisis*), which Paul also condemned. The main difference between them seems to be that prejudice is negative and general, directed against groups of people, whereas partiality is positive and usually personal, showing favouritism to particular individuals. When these individuals are family members, the danger of partiality towards them is so well recognized that there are often legal safeguards against it. It would be almost unthinkable, for example, for a judge to preside in a case involving one of his children or his wife, because even if it is not stated, the danger of partiality is obvious. We do not know whether Timothy had his favourites in the church, but even if he did not, others would have had them and the principle remains a valid one. Natural inclinations are very hard to combat, but the first step must always be a frank admission of their existence. Paul was not concerned with whether they were understandable or not; in matters of church discipline they were out of place. The reputation of the leadership, as well as the health of the congregation, depended on fairness in matters of judgement, hard as that is to achieve.[45]

Paul concluded his section on elders by warning Timothy not to lay hands 'hastily' (*tacheōs*) on anyone, nor to take part in the sins of others. This combination of prohibitions may seem strange at first sight, but there was probably a connection between the two. There is sometimes a temptation to appoint people to responsible positions without undertaking a serious investigation of their suitability first. The reasons for this may be many and varied. In some cases, there is a felt need for so-called 'affirmative action'. If women and minorities (for example) are under-represented in church leadership, there will be calls to appoint them whether they are properly qualified or not. Sometimes there may be churches without pastors or

---

[45] Towner (2006), p. 373, is particularly emphatic about this. He writes, 'the human agent of God is clearly to emulate the divine objectivity in the administration of church discipline, without jumping to conclusions before the evidence has been heard, and without discrimination based on personal relationships.'

teachers, and available people may be sent there without adequate preparation. Occasionally it may be thought that no investigation is necessary. A person who has graduated from a well-known theological college or seminary may be accepted on the strength of that, without further enquiry. In each of these cases the appointment will appear to those who make it to have been justified, but afterwards the negative consequences of inattention and taking shortcuts may become apparent. 'If only we had known ... ' is a lament too often heard after things go badly wrong with church leaders whose credentials have not been properly verified.

In this context, the 'sins of others' may refer primarily to the willingness of some people to overlook deficiencies in ministerial candidates, again for a variety of reasons. For example, some people may say that a man who has been divorced and remarried ought not to be barred from pastoral ministry on that account, and that the church should show love and compassion (i.e. tolerance) to those in that position. There are always hard cases, admittedly, but nowadays the tendency is to err on the side of leniency and acceptance, opening the door to trouble further down the road and to a lowering of standards across the board. Faced with such a situation, what is a man of God supposed to do? Should he go along with such leniency, even when he knows it to be wrong, or should he resist it, even when it may mean that he has to resign his own position?

Paul's advice is clear. The man of God must not associate himself with the sins of others, but stand out against the crowd even when it is costly to do so. His duty is to keep himself 'pure' (*hagnos*), a word that is associated with sexual chastity and may indicate what the nature of the sins in question usually were. The command is clear enough but the difficulties involved in obeying it were as great in Timothy's day as they are now. Nevertheless, there is no option for those who would be leaders of the church, who must be chaste in their behaviour in a way that reflects the purity demanded by God of all his servants. The misdeeds of one member of the church, and particularly of someone with responsibility in it, affect everyone – as Paul said to the Galatians, 'a little leaven leavens the whole lump', or as we might put it today, we are all tarred with the same brush.[46] Church discipline of prominent individuals is not a private matter, but something that must be exercised publicly, fairly and thoroughly. The failure of so many churches today in this respect, and the resulting shame and discredit that undisciplined miscreants bring on the church, is ample evidence of what happens when this principle is ignored.

---

[46] Gal. 5.9.

## 23-25. Timothy's self-discipline

*23. No longer drink only water, but take a little wine for the sake of your stomach and your frequent ailments. 24. The sins of some people are conspicuous and precede them to judgment, while the sins of others follow them there. 25. So also good works are conspicuous; and even when they are not, they cannot remain hidden.*

After dealing with church order, Paul turned to Timothy's own self-discipline. First in his mind was the need for Timothy to take care of himself physically. This is something that everyone knows to be true but that many find hard to make time for, especially if they have busy schedules that do not allow for much regular exercise or control of diet. Out-of-shape pastors harm not only themselves but the church as well, and it is not a sign of piety to neglect the needs of the body as long as we are called to minister in it.

In Timothy's case, he seems to have had too simple a diet. He drank water instead of wine, which was not a bad thing in itself but which in his case was not doing his health any good.[47] Paul was not advocating alcoholism, of course. He told Timothy to take 'a little wine' (*oinos oligos*) for his stomach, and since in ancient times wine was normally diluted with water, it would have been difficult for him to have had enough to get drunk. Bearing that in mind, there are certain principles that can be drawn from Paul's advice here.

First of all, abstinence from strong drink is not necessary or even particularly virtuous in itself. God has given wine for the enjoyment of the human race and there is no reason to reject it.[48] At the Last Supper Jesus took a cup of wine to symbolize his blood and passed it round for the disciples to drink from it. The wine was already there – we are not told that Jesus made it out of the available water in the way that he did at the wedding feast of Cana. Churches today that substitute grape juice for wine as a matter of general principle are not obeying the Lord's command, and their pseudo-piety ought to be exposed for what it is.

---

[47] It is not known why Timothy drank only water, though Marshall (2004), p. 623, claims that it must have been for religious reasons. He cites several commentators who have argued that abstinence from alcohol was an ascetic practice typical of Paul's supposed opponents, and that Timothy ought not to do anything that might lead people to think that he was on their side in some way. As so often in these chapters, such suggestions are purely speculative and go far beyond anything that can be demonstrated from the text itself.

[48] Ps. 104.15. See G. H. Kreglinger and E. H. Peterson, *The Spirituality of Wine* (Grand Rapids, MI: Eerdmans, 2016). Calvin (2016), vol. 2, p. 255, thought that Timothy's intentions were good but that he had gone too far and needed to be more balanced in his approach to food and drink.

At the same time, health considerations must always be paramount. There was nothing wrong with water, but if Timothy needed more than that, he ought to stop drinking it alone and do what was best for him. Similarly, although it is not stated here, people with an addiction to alcohol must refrain from using it, and the church should do all in its power to assist them. There can be no excuse for forcing wine down the throat of someone who is physically unable to take it without doing harm to himself, and potentially to others as well. Discernment is required here, and in Timothy's case it was his proneness to illness that dictated Paul's approach. We do not know what Timothy suffered from, but stomach and intestinal weaknesses of various kinds are very common, and the relatively poor diet in ancient times meant that chronic illness (and a shortened lifespan) were much more frequent than they are today. The advances of modern medicine are a gift from God that we must use with gratitude, and our ability to control our diet by eating fresh foods that were not available in earlier times must be exploited to the full. Yet the reality is that an alarming proportion of the population in most developed countries is clinically obese and the churches seldom seem to be doing much about it. Pastors and congregations desperately need to be educated in this area and provided with the resources necessary for creating a healthy pattern of living that can be enjoyed by everyone. That is what Paul wanted for Timothy, and it is what we should want for all who profess the name of Christ in the world today.

Paul concluded by reminding Timothy of the way in which sins and good deeds tend to appear in the world. In the case of sins, there are some that are obvious from the start and lead directly to judgement, while others take time to appear. In the case of good works, some are equally conspicuous from the beginning, but those that are not will not remain hidden for long. The message here is simple. Whether we do what is right or wrong in our lives, the truth will come out sooner or later. Sooner may be preferable, both so that wrongdoing can be identified and condemned, and so that good works can be recognized and rewarded. But even those who conceal what they are doing, whether it is good or bad, will not be able to do so for ever. Sins that emerge in the course of time will suffer the same condemnation as those which have been known from the start, while good deeds will also reveal themselves in the end, even if those who have done them prefer to remain anonymous.

The difficulty of judging between the bad and the good is particularly serious when it comes to appointing people to a ministerial function. Paul did not relate his remarks to that circumstance directly, but the fact that he had just discussed the behaviour of elders gives it a certain relevance at this point in his exposition. John Calvin certainly thought so, and lamented the frequent failure of the church to exercise adequate discernment in this matter:

> We often fail in choosing ministers, for unworthy men steal in by craft, and the right men are unknown to us; or, though we ourselves judge rightly, we cannot bring others to accept our judgment, so that the best men are rejected in spite of all our efforts, and evil men either insinuate or force themselves forward. In these circumstances the state of the church and our own situation inevitably give rise to great anxiety.[49]

The moral here for Timothy was clear. He could not conceal either his own behaviour or that of others, whether it was bad or good. If it was bad, that fact would emerge eventually and the behaviour would be censured. If it was good, that too would come out in the end and be rewarded. The wise man will concentrate on doing good without publicizing it (which is not necessary) but without concealing it either (which is ultimately impossible). It is by our fruits that we shall be known, and we have the promise that when others see our good works they will glorify God, who will honour us for our faithfulness to him in all things.[50] That is what Timothy was told to aim for and where Paul left him to work out his own salvation in fear and trembling.[51]

---

[49] Calvin (1964), p. 268.
[50] Mt. 7.16; 5.16.
[51] Phil. 2.12.

# 1 Timothy 6

## 1-2. Slaves and their masters

*1. Let all who are under the yoke of slavery regard their masters as worthy of all honour, so that the name of God and the teaching may not be blasphemed. 2. Those who have believing masters must not be disrespectful to them on the ground that they are members of the church; rather they must serve them all the more, since those who benefit by their service are believers and beloved. Teach and urge these duties.*

Having dealt with widows and elders, Paul turned next to slaves, who were evidently numerous enough in the congregation at Ephesus to warrant special consideration. Domestic slavery was an everyday reality in the circles in which Paul moved, and the letter to Philemon gives us a good insight into his approach to it. Today slavery is so strongly disapproved of that it is almost impossible for us to imagine how anyone could have looked favourably (or even relatively indifferently) on it, and there is no doubt that the apostle's willingness to tolerate it has become a stumbling block for many of our contemporaries. How, they ask, was it possible for him to preach freedom and new birth in Christ while at the same time refusing to do anything about the physical and material bondage he saw around him? This is so disturbing to many people today that they react by arguing that Paul was subtly attacking the institution of slavery by laying down principles that would eventually overthrow the institution. It is a comforting thought, and it is true that many nineteenth-century abolitionists were Christians who were guided by Biblical principles, but it is too much to claim that Paul foresaw that. As far as we can tell, he accepted slavery as a fact of life that would endure as long as the governing classes in our fallen world derived some benefit from it. That is certainly what happened in practice; it was only when it became cheaper and more efficient to use machines instead of forced labour that slavery finally disappeared, at least from the developed world. We must be glad that Christians were involved in that process but we also have to recognize that, much as the church disliked slavery and tried to restrict it whenever it could, abolition was not a practical possibility for a long time and most people tolerated it as a necessary evil.

In this respect, Paul's approach was governed by the general outlook of his time. How much personal contact he had with slaves is uncertain, but it may not have been all that much. We do not meet slavery in the Israel of Jesus' day, at least not in the circles in which he moved, and the question never arises in the Gospels. Nor do we hear much about it in the diaspora communities in which Paul ministered. Priscilla and Aquila, for example, were business people who might well have been slave owners, and the same must have been true of Lydia and several others whom we come across in the Acts of the Apostles, yet nothing is said about any slaves they may have had. There is no mention of them in his epistles to the Romans, the Corinthians, the Galatians, the Philippians or the Thessalonians. Were there really no slaves in any of those churches? Silence tells us nothing, of course. We only hear about Philemon because Paul was sending his runaway slave Onesimus back to him; otherwise we would know nothing about them either.

In a world where there were no labour-saving devices, household help was necessary, and virtually every well-to-do person had a number of people on hand to do the daily chores. Some of these may have been their own children, some were probably free people who were sheltered (if not paid) in return for their labour and some were slaves. There were also vast numbers of slaves who toiled on the great estates (*latifundia*), in the mines and on the ships, but apart from the exceptional circumstances of the shipwreck recorded in Acts 27, we do not hear of Paul having any contact with them. We might add a further category that consisted of gladiators and other 'performers' in the arena, who were encouraged to slaughter each other for the amusement of the masses, but they were relatively few in number and did not usually mix with the general public. The slaves Paul knew were almost family members, and probably most of them were fairly well treated. Certainly it seems from his epistles that masters who abused their slaves were more like men who abused their wives or who mistreated their children than like the brutal overseers of legend (and probably of reality in the cases mentioned above).[1] Quite apart from anything else, it would have been much easier for household slaves to have belonged to a church than for any of the others, and their presence in the congregation suggests that they were relatively free to live their own lives on a day-to-day basis.

How somebody like Onesimus became a slave in the first place is not recorded. Usually, slaves were captives in war, and if the alternative to slavery

---

[1] Eph. 6.9; Col. 4.1.

for them was death, their fate may not seem quite so awful. Some free men sold themselves into slavery for economic reasons. There was no social welfare system in the ancient world, and slavery was a way of keeping body and soul together and of being looked after in a secure employment situation. Free people who were left to starve often envied slaves, who seemed much better off, even if they were not able to do whatever they liked. We do not have to approve of this situation, but we should at least try to understand that for many of those who were caught up in it, the realistic alternatives might easily have been worse. Moreover, diligent slaves could often earn money and save up to buy their freedom, which was frequently granted on the death of a master. Slaves were usually not distinguished by their race, so once they were set free (or had run away successfully) they could melt into the general population and few people would have known their background. After a few years, all memory of their past would have been lost. In this respect, ancient Roman slavery was different from its modern American counterpart, where even generations after emancipation, it is still relatively easy to tell who comes from a slave background and who does not, a situation which has the effect of prolonging some of the evil effects of the institution long after it has officially disappeared.[2]

None of these mitigating factors will justify slavery to the modern mind, but they should at least be taken into consideration when Paul's attitude towards it is being examined.[3] The Greek word *doulos* can be 'labourer' or 'servant' as well as 'slave', which may be why Paul specified that he was talking about those who were in bondage, or 'under a yoke' (*hypo zygon*). He never discussed whether the yoke was justified, nor did he offer suggestions as to how it might be removed. Instead of that, he identified himself with the slaves' situation by calling himself a *doulos* of Jesus Christ who was in bondage to his spiritual master. Paul saw physical slavery as a picture of the spiritual service that Christians owe to God, and it is in spiritual terms that he addressed the behaviour of those who were enslaved.

The first requirement of slaves, according to Paul, was that they should regard their masters as 'worthy of all honour'. In practice, of course, this meant that they should obey those who owned them, something that would be much easier to do if they respected them. Here we see a principle which

---

[2] Mounce (2000), pp. 330–1, makes reference to American defenders of slavery in the antebellum South, many of whom professed to be Christians acting according to Biblical principles. Mounce calls this abuse of the Bible 'exploitation of the gospel', but accepts that such arguments have been made in the past and may someday be made again.

[3] Mounce (2000), p. 331, comments, 'The fact of the situation is that Paul had a different agenda from what many have today. His ministry was governed by a passion to spread the gospel, and the cause of the gospel took precedence over all else.'

can be applied *mutatis mutandis* to modern forms of employment. To work for another person is to do what they say, according to the authority given to them, but that pattern only works well if it is based on respect. If an employee knows that his employer is dishonest or not doing his job properly, there is a real danger that he will not respect him (or her) and so be inclined either to disobey orders or (perhaps more commonly) to do the minimum necessary not to be dismissed. Shirking on the job is a common phenomenon in modern life, and it was far from unknown among slaves in ancient times. Indeed, one of the persistent criticisms of slavery through the ages has been that it is economically inefficient, because the enslaved have no real motivation to do what is expected of them and are liable to cheat their masters whenever they can.

Paul insisted that Christian slaves should not adopt that attitude, not because their masters were good people nor because their situation was reasonable and they ought to be content with it, but because if they failed to do so, 'the name of God and the teaching' would be blasphemed. In other words, a disobedient or recalcitrant slave would not only attract adverse comment against himself, but discredit the faith that he claimed to profess. In Paul's mind, slaves were not working for an earthly master so much as for a heavenly one, and the way they carried out their obligations bore witness to the validity of the beliefs they held. We have no way of knowing whether their masters appreciated this – perhaps some did, but probably most did not. Nor can we say whether any master was converted to Christ by the example of one of his slaves, though that may have happened from time to time. Above all, there was no expectation that a slave might be set free for good behaviour, which (if it had been a real possibility) might have been a reasonable case for Paul to have made. If slaves thought that their lot would improve significantly if they behaved well, they might have responded to the incentive and done as Paul asked, but he never approached them on that assumption. Instead, he appealed to the honour of God and the likely reaction to the validity of the gospel if they did not do what was expected of them.

This may sound strange to us, but there is a principle here that can be easily replicated in modern conditions. An employee who is always taking time off in order to attend church meetings or work at evangelistic campaigns is unlikely to make a favourable impression on his employer, who is not paying him for that purpose. If an employer thinks that someone he has hired is indulging in outside activities during office hours, and the employee justifies those activities by an appeal to 'faith', there is every chance that the employment will be terminated and that nobody else who has such inclinations will be taken on in future. Employers who have been cheated in this way are very likely to turn against 'religion' and see it being used as an excuse for laziness and corruption, thereby bringing the name of God and the message of the gospel into disrepute. Such things may not happen very often, but they are sufficiently common to make us be aware of the danger and do our utmost to combat it, as Paul was doing here.

The other problem that Paul dealt with is the one that arises when spiritual and secular matters overlap. It is probable that many Christian slaves worked for Christian masters because they had become believers in that way. Paul or another evangelist may have preached the gospel in a household, which then turned to Christ as a body, and the slaves could easily have been included in that.[4] In Christ, as we know, human barriers were broken down. There was no more Jew and Gentile, no more slave and free man.[5] Before the throne of Almighty God we are all equal, and in the worship of the church, which usually took place in households, that insistence on spiritual equality must have had a considerable impact. This was exactly the situation that Paul addressed in his letter to Philemon. The slave Onesimus had not become a Christian in his household, but he was going back as one, and Paul wrote to his master to ensure that he was given a welcome and treated properly. Their relationship would henceforth be on a different footing because of their common faith in Christ, but how would that affect Onesimus' place in the household?

Paul was quite clear about that – Onesimus (whose name means 'useful') had not been much good to Philemon before, but now he would be truly useful! In other words, Onesimus' conversion would make him a better slave, not a free man. What Paul said to Timothy about Christian slaves serving Christian masters was basically the same as this. A slave must not be disrespectful to his master on the ground that they were brothers in the faith (though of course they were that) but redouble his efforts to be of service because their masters were both believers (*pistoi*) and 'beloved' (*agapētoi*). The statement that they were believers in Christ is clear enough, but the significance of 'beloved' is not so obvious. Did Paul mean that they were beloved by God, that they were (or should be) beloved by their Christian slaves, or both? He must have meant that the masters were beloved by God, at least in the first instance, but that was true of the slaves as well. Probably Paul was implying, if not actually stating, that the slaves should love their masters if they shared a common faith, and serve them for that reason, as well as because of their legal obligation to do so because God loved them both equally.

---

[4] Acts 16.31-34.
[5] Gal. 3.28.

Curiously, Paul did not add the opposite – that masters ought to love and respect their slaves if they are fellow-believers, though in other epistles he was careful to make the master-slave relationship one of mutual respect and obligation.[6] It is dangerous to attempt to argue from silence, and there is no reason to believe that he thought that Timothy did not have to consider a master's attitude towards his slaves. Perhaps there was a particular problem in the Ephesian church, involving slaves who thought that their faith exempted them from menial service or allowed them to talk back to their masters; we do not know. Whatever the reason for his silence, there is no doubt that Paul put his emphasis on making sure that slaves respected their existing relationship with their masters, and went no further than that.

It is very difficult for us to appreciate Paul's outlook when it comes to the question of slavery because our approach to it is so different. Paul did not deny that all human beings are fundamentally equal in the sight of God, but the conclusion he came to was not that slavery should be abolished but that we must *all* become slaves in Christ's service if we are going to be truly free. From his standpoint, 'freedom' in the human sense was often synonymous with disobedience, rebellion and anarchy. Human slavery was a consequence of the fall in which everyone was implicated, masters as well as slaves. Manumission might be a blessing in individual cases, but although Paul encouraged slaves to take their freedom when it was offered, he knew that it could not solve the deeper spiritual problem of the human race.[7] A slave who was set free in this life would not be truly free until he became a slave of Christ, and the same was true of his erstwhile master. There are many testimonies from people who have been unjustly imprisoned or otherwise badly treated, who have overcome that by achieving an inner, spiritual freedom that gives them a moral victory over their oppressors. That does not justify the treatment they have received but it shows what the limitations of human sinfulness are. We may be victimized by it but we cannot be conquered because as spiritual beings we have a resource and a relationship to God that transcends our human circumstances. That is what the slaves in the Ephesian church had to learn, and by learning it they set an example for those who were legally 'free' to follow.

In fact, by doing their duty to their masters out of love for God, the slaves were turning the moral tables on those who owned them. That this may have been Paul's intention is supported by a similar passage in the writings of his Roman contemporary Seneca (d. AD 65) who said,

---

[6] Eph. 6.2-9; Col. 3.22–4.1.
[7] 1 Cor. 7.21-22.

just as a hireling gives a benefit if he supplies more than he contracted to do, so a slave – when he exceeds the bounds of his station in goodwill towards his master by daring some lofty deed that would be an honour even to those more happily born, a benefit is found to exist inside the household.[8]

If a noble pagan could think like that, how much more would the same not have been true of a Christian like Paul? We have no way of knowing whether Paul knew of Seneca's *dictum* or whether the similarity in their thinking was purely coincidental, but at least it shows that the apostle's teaching might not have come as a complete surprise to his contemporaries. As P. H. Towner puts it,

> Paul has turned the tables. The slaves serve, but in God's surprising *oikonomia* they do so from a position of power; nobility and honour, the rewards of benefaction, are accorded here implicitly to the slaves. In all of this, the privileges of honour which that culture reserved for well-to-do patrons, benefactors and slave owners are not denied; nor are the obligations of slaves to their masters trivialized. But the meaning and value of life lived at that level are relativized by the more fundamental reality of the universal Lordship of Christ within God's *oikonomia*.[9]

In the modern world our economic and professional relations are very different in some ways, but the principle that Paul laid down for slaves has a wider application. Martin Luther interpreted it to mean that 'no one has the right to disturb the peace – not even the chosen people of God', an application that had a particular relevance in the years following the peasants' revolt in Germany, when there was widespread insurrection against the secular rulers by those who thought they had been 'liberated' by the gospel.[10] John Calvin also gave the passage a political significance, and interpreted the fact that rulers and ruled shared a common faith as follows:

> It is no small honour that God has made us equal to the lords of this earth in the thing that matters most, for we share with them the same adoption. This should be a powerful inducement to bear servitude with patience. Besides, servitude is more endurable under mild masters who

---

[8] Seneca, *De beneficiis*, 3.33.1 (Loeb).
[9] Towner (2006), p. 390.
[10] Luther (1973), p. 363. The peasants' revolt broke out (and was suppressed, with his approval) in 1525 and Luther delivered his lectures in the first few months of 1528.

love us and whom we love. For the bond of faith reconciles those of very different rank and status.[11]

Today we would most naturally apply this counsel to employees and others with contractual obligations, who must respect their commitments and not expect special consideration from their employers merely because of a shared faith. Equality in the church does not cancel out the internal structures of a business, whatever they may be. It might even happen that an employee becomes an elder in his church whereas his employer does not, creating a sort of 'role reversal' in the spiritual sphere that might be awkward during the work week. What if, as an elder, the employee was called upon to discipline his boss for some failure at church? This may seem far-fetched, but it could happen, and for many centuries slaves were not allowed to hold church office, at least partly for that reason.[12]

Paul's primary concern here was with personal relations and the way they might impact everyday life, but the principle that Christians ought to be more responsible to their employers and others because of their faith, and not less, is one that needs to be reiterated in any number of contexts. Often Christians think that they do not need to sign contracts, take out insurance policies, or keep proper accounts if they are dealing with fellow believers. They think that because they are brothers in the faith, they ought to be able to trust them and that they will do what is right. Unfortunately, this is by no means always the case, and when things go wrong (possibly quite independently of the relationship in question) there needs to be clarity about who is responsible for what, and some way of insuring that everyone lives up to his or her obligations. Christians demonstrate the quality of their faith, not by dispensing with such safeguards but by demonstrating that they are more careful than others in ensuring that every eventuality is accounted for. It is by doing the right thing in the right way that believers commend their faith to others, not by cutting corners or ignoring responsibilities on the excuse that 'we are all Christians'. The believer is still a sinner, and the devil is still active in this world, doing his best to set brother against brother and destroy the work of Christ in any way that he can. Christians do not need to help him in this, but should be wiser than the serpent and build defences that will ensure that everyone is treated fairly and with the Spirit of Christ.

The last sentence in v. 2 is now usually taken with what follows, in conformity with the pattern found earlier in the epistle (4.11; 5.7) but as

---

[11] Calvin (1964), p. 271.
[12] The official excuse was that they were not free to be employed as the church might dictate.

with similar sentences elsewhere, this one is a transition from one thought to another and could go equally well with either. In this case, it might be argued that it fits better with what has gone before, because Paul had issued direct instructions that could be taught and insisted upon as he desired.[13] What follows is not advice at all but a description of those who did not agree with his teaching. There is nothing there for Timothy to 'teach and urge' as Paul had asked him to do, though of course it can be argued that he was contrasting Timothy's obedience (which he took for granted) with the rebellious spirit of others. Even so, the word 'these [things]' (*tauta*) seems to be too concrete and definite to fit well with the next few lines, and so it may be better to resist the modern consensus and suggest instead that these words should be regarded as a coda to what precedes them more than as an introduction to what comes next.

## 3-5. The character of the false teacher

*3. Whoever teaches otherwise and does not agree with the sound words of our Lord Jesus Christ and the teaching that is in accordance with godliness, 4. is conceited, understanding nothing, and has a morbid craving for controversy and for disputes about words. From these come envy, dissension, slander, base suspicions, 5. and wrangling among those who are depraved in mind and bereft of the truth, imagining that godliness is a means of gain.*

After dealing with the situation in which slaves found themselves, Paul moved on to address one of the greatest problems confronting the church – the danger that false teaching would creep into it. He did not specify one particular form of error, and perhaps he was referring back (at least in the first instance) to what he had just said about the proper behaviour of slaves. But whether he was thinking in such specific terms or not, his words here are so generally applicable that they cannot be limited to a single instance. False teaching is harmful both to those who give it and to those who receive it, whatever it is and whoever they are. It is this bigger picture that we must keep in mind as we examine the import of what Paul said on this subject to Timothy and the church at Ephesus.

---

[13] Marshall (2004), pp. 637–8, adopts this position but nevertheless still places the phrase with what follows!

First of all, Paul appears to have invented a word to describe what he was talking about. *Heterodidaskalia* is a term that can be fairly easily understood, but the verb, which would be literally rendered as 'to otherteach' is apparently a neologism.[14] We are inclined to translate it as 'to falseteach', which is undoubtedly what it means, but we must understand that this is because for Paul, difference implied falsehood in a way that it does not for us. We can imagine somebody teaching something different without it necessarily being wrong, because we are sensitive to things like perspective, varieties of interest and approach and so on. But Paul did not think like that. As far as he was concerned, anyone who did not teach what he taught, who did not adhere to 'the pattern of sound words' as he gave it, was mistaken. It was not just a set of ideas that he was handing on to Timothy to play with as he liked, but a way of understanding and expressing those ideas as well.

Let us take an example of this that will illustrate the point. Why do we pray to God as 'Father, Son and Holy Spirit'? God is not a human being (and still less three human beings), so why should he be addressed in words that suggest not only humanity, but masculinity as well? Is it not equally possible to speak to him as Mother, Daughter and Holy Spirit, or even better, as totally non-sexual Creator, Redeemer and Sanctifier, or some equivalent of those terms? Theologians and those who like intellectual discussions may be prepared to concede the case in matters like this, and some have even devised prayers using such different names for the persons of the Godhead. But however justified they may think they are, they are departing from what has been given in the Bible and accepted down through the ages without question. Even if it makes little or no difference, as those who advocate such policies insist, it is still a departure from what has been taught and received, and therefore it lacks the authority which the Bible has given to the traditional form of words. The risk of misunderstanding, and eventual heresy, is there, even if it is far from the intentions of those who have rejected the customary formula.

In the ancient world, Christianity stood out from the different forms of Greek philosophy, and even from Judaism, by its terminological and conceptual precision. Christians had definite beliefs about God, the creation, judgement and salvation. Jesus told his disciples, 'I am the way, the truth and the life. No one comes to the Father except through me.'[15] They did not believe that there were many ways to God, or to the discovery of the truth; everything depended on Jesus Christ and his teaching. This is why Paul said

---

[14] Our limited knowledge of ancient Greek makes it impossible to say this for sure, but the word is not attested in any earlier document.

[15] Jn 14.6.

here that a genuine teacher is one who 'agrees with the sound words of our Lord Jesus Christ and the teaching that is in accordance with godliness'.

Agreeing to the words of Christ was taken literally, and his sayings were frequently quoted and used by his followers, as they were earlier in this epistle (5.18). The fact that the Son of God had become a human being in the individual man Jesus Christ, a Jewish boy from Nazareth who was a descendant of the great King David, tied divine revelation to a particular time and place. What he had taught his disciples was part of his incarnation, the verbal expression of his divine mission of salvation. It was in those words, and in those words alone, that the secret of eternal life could be found. The Greek word *hygiainō* is impossible to translate simply, because it has so many different layers of meaning. Physically, it refers to the health of the body – the words of Jesus could be taken as words that cleansed and restored people to a sound mind and spirit. For this reason, the word is often translated as 'sound'. It can also refer to spiritual regeneration, in which case 'saving' would capture the meaning more accurately, and that is what the ESV prefers, because the context is referring primarily to spiritual, rather than to physical, well-being. But whatever word we prefer, it is important to remember that in the Biblical world view, the two things go together.

What is significant here is that it is not the *touch* of Jesus that heals (as it often was during his earthly ministry) but his *words* that bring salvation. The teaching that accords with godliness is that which exalts Jesus Christ – his life, death and resurrection. It is a teaching that reflects the mind of God in its content and that gives new spiritual life to the people of God by its power. It is not possible for someone to receive it without being transformed in the process. The person who is taught by Christ is one who is convicted of sin, of righteousness and of judgement.[16] In the ancient world there were many people who liked to dabble in intellectual ideas, and Paul met some of them when he went to preach in Athens.[17] Today this tendency to indulge in meaningless intellectual arguments is, if anything, even more widespread than it was in Paul's day. Modern discoveries and technology have now made it possible for everyone to claim some knowledge and express an opinion about a wide range of things, and the advances of science lend plausibility to the idea that we know far more about almost everything than the ancients did. That Jesus was a good man with some interesting and important things to say is still readily admitted by most people, but that he was God in human flesh, the man who had the only answer to the human dilemma, is not. The

---

[16] Jn 16.8-10.
[17] Acts 17.16-21.

result is darkness pretending to be light, confusion masquerading as freedom and 'diversity' claiming to be godliness. Paul's words about the false teachers of his day are therefore just as relevant and meaningful to us as they were to Timothy and the church at Ephesus back then.

Characteristically, Paul moved straight from the false teaching to examine the character of the false teacher(s). What a person says and does reflects who and what that person is, and Paul gave Timothy a straightforward analysis of what to expect when he encountered people who were teaching another gospel. Employing the usual triadic structure as the framework for his analysis, he highlighted three things that stand out in the character of such a man:

1. He is 'puffed up' and conceited.
2. He understands nothing.
3. He loves controversies (*zētēseis*) and arguments (*logomachiai*).

These typical characteristics of a false teacher belong together and follow one another in logical sequence. At the root of his false doctrine is his pride. The man who will not be persuaded by another is convinced not only that he is right, but that he is superior to everyone else and has nothing to learn from them. The true sign of a great teacher is his humility with respect to the limits of his own knowledge and his willingness to learn from others. We meet this conceit in the Gospels, when Nathanael greeted the news about Jesus with 'Can any good thing come out of Nazareth?'[18] Jesus was despised not just for what he said but because he was a Galilaean and presumed to be theologically uneducated. How could someone like that know better than the Jerusalem élite that spent its days immersed in the Torah? Intellectual humility is the mark of a truly great mind, of which there are relatively few, even in academic circles. In 2008, Michael Reiss, then the secretary of the Royal Society in the United Kingdom, was forced to resign because he suggested that creationism should be discussed in the classroom as one theory about the origins of the world. Richard Dawkins, a leading atheist, led the charge against him and under pressure the governing body of the Society caved in to his demands. When the scandal became public, however, the general reaction was one of disbelief. How could a body dedicated to the advancement of science try to suppress *discussion* of a particular theory, even if it was one that challenged the cherished beliefs of the scientific establishment?[19] The pretensions of the

---

[18] Jn 1.45-46.
[19] It should be said that Professor Reiss, who is also an ordained minister of the Church of England, is not a creationist and did not want to advocate that view, but he thought it should be discussed and refuted in a reasonable and reasoned way.

so-called 'learned' to omniscience were exposed and ridiculed, as they should have been. Yet all too often, people with solid (if relative) achievements in different fields become oracles on subjects of which they know little or nothing, confident that their expertise in one area gives them the right to pontificate across the board. A true scientist, by contrast, will doubt even his own theories and discoveries, not because they are meaningless but because they are never more than partial explanations of things that ultimately lie beyond our grasp. His mind will always be open to exploring new approaches and considering different options because he knows that the truth is bigger than he is. Only someone who is 'puffed up' and conceited would think otherwise.

The result of such conceit is that the man who is confident that he knows best ends up understanding nothing. This is one of the greatest dangers of our time. Experts can express their opinions based on the data that they have researched, but that is not the same thing as understanding how the information they have acquired ought to be used. This is a particular problem when scientists are able to perform certain medical procedures which to others appear to be unethical and potentially dangerous. Should they be allowed to proceed in the interests of 'science' or prevented from doing so because they have not grasped the bigger moral picture?

Paul's description of the false teachers chimes in well with this modern phenomenon. His false teachers were men who had a lot of advice to give but who lacked any understanding of what it was that was required. They could rhapsodize for hours on myths and genealogies, and no doubt their mastery of such things would dazzle the uninitiated, but they had no idea what they were doing because they lacked a framework of understanding that would make sense of their supposed 'knowledge'. A glance at the main opinion-formers in the world today will soon convince us that nothing much has changed on this score.

The third characteristic of the false teachers is that they loved a good debate. Nothing delighted them more than to seize on a disputed topic, even one of considerable importance, and demolish their opponents by clever arguments. Today we often come across this in church controversies of various kinds. Some people love to argue over things like infant baptism, church government, or the details of eschatology that are supposedly set out in the Book of Revelation. They will discuss these things at the drop of a hat, but show much less interest in the central teachings of the gospel. Seldom will they mention sin and judgement or point to the shed blood of Christ at Calvary as the only answer to the human predicament. Churches will split over something like women's ordination, oblivious to the fact that neither the arguments nor the outcome has led anyone to Christ. The best way to distract people is to make them think that what they are talking about is so important that it cannot be set aside, and to persuade them that their opponents are ungodly people who ought to be censured or even driven out of the church. In this way, arguments over secondary matters are allowed to shape the nature of the fellowship, which is led astray even as it thinks that it is doing the Lord's will.

Paul went on to point out that the results of such behaviour are not love, joy, peace and the other virtues that come to the fore when the saving words of Christ are given their proper weight, but something else altogether. As he saw it, there were at least five different outcomes, none of which is desirable and all of which are harmful to the life of the church. They are

1. Envy (*phthonos*)
2. Strife (*eris*)
3. Slanders (*blasphēmiai*)
4. Evil suspicions (*hyponoiai ponērai*)
5. Constant friction (*diaparatribai*)

Anyone who has ever worked in an organization where beliefs shape policies will recognize this scenario. First of all there is envy, the hidden evil that results from pride and that people often fail to detect until it is too late. One of the most fundamental teachings of the Christian church is that its members are united in one Holy Spirit, who distributes different gifts to them according to his sovereign will. In 1 Corinthians 12 Paul describes the church as a body. Christ is the head, and its members represent different organs, each with its own capacities and functions. The eye cannot tell the ear that it can dispense with its services, nor can the hand function without reference to the rest. There is no room for jealousy in this, because there is no sense of competition. Each part of the body does what it is assigned to do, contributing to the others and receiving from them what it lacks. That, at least, is how things ought to work.

In practice, of course, they seldom do. One person is given a particular gift and the others wonder why. Instead of congratulating the recipient and benefitting from his good fortune, they look for ways of cutting him down to size. In Australia and New Zealand this is called 'the tall poppy syndrome', by which outstanding people are pilloried and brought down to the same level as everyone else, but the habit is universal, even if it lacks a name elsewhere. It is particularly obvious when one pastor or church does well and others appear to struggle. Where does such success come from? Very few people are content to rejoice in the blessing of God bestowed on someone else; instead, they prefer to find other explanations. The church in question may be preaching a false gospel, designed to emphasize growth in quantity rather than in quality. The pastor may be relying on an attractive personality or on particular gimmicks that attract a crowd, and the style of worship may be tailored to appeal to people who like having a good time but are less concerned with spiritual growth. 'Explanations' of this kind are far from uncommon and they all agree on one thing – the success of the other person or place is suspect and ought to be discounted rather than praised.

Out of envy comes strife. If other people are successful, the suspicion may arise that it is probably because they have had an unfair advantage somewhere along the line. Perhaps they had family connections or money that eased their pathway. In some cases, they may have relied on good looks or an attractive personality. To correct such 'unfairness' countermeasures may need to be taken. Accusations of favouritism may be made, and the value of what a colleague is doing may be questioned. Why spend money supporting a project if it can be shown that the project is of little or no value? Demonstrating something like that may be hard to do without engendering arguments, and people will be encouraged to take sides, often for reasons that have no relation to the matter being discussed. Before long, an organization or church will be divided into opposing camps, each one supporting its own candidates for office and hoping that the favouritism supposedly being shown to the other side will be reversed.

One way of facilitating this process is to discredit opponents, and this can often do immeasurable harm with minimal effort – or proof. How often do we find in committee meetings that one person proposes a name for consideration as an office holder, only to be countered by someone else, who objects on the ground that the nominee is unsuitable, though often without specifying why? The mere objection may be enough to destroy a candidate because unanimity about his fitness for the task at hand cannot be achieved, even though the grounds for that assertion may not have been stated, let alone examined. In the historic Polish Commonwealth this practice was actually enshrined in law – a single member of the parliament (*sejm*) could object to whatever was being proposed and the whole initiative would collapse. It was called the *liberum veto* and regarded as a cherished right by the nobility who possessed the privilege and who were able to abuse it at will. The end result of this was that the Commonwealth disintegrated. It was partitioned three times (in 1772, 1793 and 1795) and Poland disappeared from the map of Europe for over a hundred years. What happened on a grand scale in a major European country can easily be replicated in any number of organizations, where cooperation becomes impossible because everyone is busily trying to find fault with others rather than cooperate to build up the whole. Christian churches are not free of this vice; on the contrary, they can sometimes be among its worst exemplars!

When such an atmosphere emerges, it leads naturally to 'evil suspicions' because even before the accusations are made, people start to wonder where the next one will come from and why. They become convinced that others are plotting against them, an attitude that has a destabilizing effect on relationships and undermines the fellowship of those who ought to be working in a common cause. The result is 'constant friction' (v. 5) because every word and every suggestion is regarded as something potentially hostile that must be combatted.

These things occur because the people involved in them have turned away from God. As Paul saw it, they were

1. depraved (*diephtharmenoi*) in their minds
2. deprived (*apesterēmenoi*) of the truth
3. deluded into thinking they will gain something by a show of godliness

Once again there are three elements in Paul's analysis that flow logically from one to the next. The false teachers are depraved in their minds, which is where the problem started. What and how we think determines what we do and how we act. A Christian has the mind of Christ, which is the essential prerequisite for discipleship.[20] For all the emphasis that there must rightly be on feelings and experience, it is in the mind that repentance and regeneration take root, and it is by his Word that God accomplishes this. The fallen mind is not something peculiar to the false teachers. It is common to everyone who does not know Christ as Saviour and Lord, but the problem becomes particularly acute when it is confronted with the truth and is unable to absorb it. Instead of illuminating the thought and actions of the recipient, the light ends up being refracted into a thousand different hues, none of which is pure and unadulterated. The rainbow effect may be pretty and attractive to some, but it is useless as a guide to knowledge and its inherent instability means that it is never clear what the person in question understands, if anything.

Such a mind is inevitably deprived of the truth, not because the truth has been withheld but because it cannot be properly analyzed and absorbed. John expressed it very well when he said that the light came into the world but that people preferred the darkness, because their deeds were evil.[21] The truth hurts those who cannot take it, and anyone whose mind is corrupt and

---

[20] 1 Cor. 2.16.
[21] Jn 3.19.

whose behaviour is ungodly will inevitably find themselves in that position. This is obvious from the fact that such people believe that godliness, or at least a show of it, is the way to riches and success in this world. The false teachers of Paul's day were earning a living by preaching what people wanted to hear, regardless of whether it was true or not.[22] What they said sounded good but it led nowhere and in the end it did more harm than good. Today there are all kinds of people who do similar things, playing on the widespread thirst for spirituality by offering something that looks like the gospel but falls short of it in crucial ways. They have turned the things of God into a business opportunity, and when the fraud is exposed, as it often is, the cynics are encouraged to rail against 'religion' yet again. An imitation of the truth is far more damaging than an outright lie, because when its inadequacy is discovered it has a way of alienating observers from the real thing and confirming them in their blindness.

## 6-10. Wealth

*6. Of course there is great gain in godliness combined with contentment; 7. for we brought nothing into the world, so that we can take nothing out of it; 8. but if we have food and clothing, we will be content with these. 9. But those who want to be rich fall into temptation and are trapped by many senseless and harmful desires that plunge people into ruin and destruction. 10. For the love of money is a root of all kinds of evil, and in their eagerness to be rich some have wandered away from the faith and pierced themselves with many pains.*

Having analysed the doctrine of 'godliness' preached by the false teachers, Paul continued by setting out the correct interpretation of this important but contested theme. 'Godliness' is indeed a good thing and very profitable to those who seek it, provided it is done 'with contentment' (*meta autarkeias*). This is clearly meant to stand in contrast to what has gone before and we must interpret it in that context. *Autarkeia* is another Greek word that has many possible meanings. In this verse it is traditionally translated as 'contentment', but it could equally well be rendered as 'self-reliance' or 'self-sufficiency', both of which were regarded as virtues by many ancient Greek

---

[22] Paul defended himself against such charges. See 1 Thess. 2.5. It was common in the ancient world for 'teachers' of different kinds to sell their services to anyone who would pay for them. The young (pre-Christian) Augustine earned his living in Carthage this way, and moved to Rome because the opportunities there were greater. He was not alone!

philosophers.[23] In the late nineteenth and early twentieth centuries this last meaning was adopted by economists to describe the policy of some countries which wanted to become self-sufficient in economic terms. They believed that if they could feed their people and provide adequately for them, they would not need the help or resources of other states. To them, that was a good thing because it would mean that they had no incentive to make war on others in order to gain more territory and resources, and autarky, if it was achievable, would thus contribute to international peace.

Christians cannot adopt that meaning of the word, at least not if it is taken to extremes, because members of the church are expected to rely on each other for spiritual as well as material needs. We cannot live in isolation from the body of believers. But there is another sense in which the idea of self-sufficiency can and does apply to Christians. This sense is captured to some extent by the term 'contentment', which is the recognition that believers receive what they need from God and do not have to be jealous of others or anxious to acquire gifts that they have not been given. Each of us must accept that what we have is what is right for us, and not be covetous of what God has given to someone else. We may benefit from the gifts given to others, but we do so when those gifts are freely shared (as they ought to be) and not because we have tried to grasp them for ourselves. In particular, there is no point in trying to wrest financial benefit out of ministering to others, as the false teachers were apparently trying to do.

John Calvin struck the right balance when he remarked on 'contentment':

> This may refer either to an inner disposition or to a sufficiency of wealth. If it is understood as a disposition, the meaning will be that the godly who desire nothing but are content with their poverty have obtained a great gain. But if it is taken to mean a sufficiency of possessions ... it will be a promise like that of Psalm 34:10: 'The lions do lack and suffer hunger; but they that seek the Lord shall not want any good thing'. The Lord is always present with his people and, according as their necessity requires it, he bestows on each his portion from his own fullness. Thus true blessedness consists in godliness and this sufficiency is as good as an increase of gain.[24]

---

[23] See Marshall (2004), pp. 644–5, who quotes Diogenes Laertius on the subject. Diogenes discovered this virtue in Socrates, the Stoics, the Epicureans and the Cynics – a broad range! But as Marshall points out, it is by no means certain that this tradition influenced what Paul was saying here, because Christians are not self-sufficient – they depend on God and not on themselves or on other human beings, which is what Paul was trying to say.

[24] Calvin (1964), p. 274.

It was this aspect of the matter, more than anything else, which determined Paul's remarks here. In what appears to be an allusion to Job 1.21, Paul reminded Timothy in v. 7 that 'we brought nothing into the world and can take nothing out of it'. Here we see the perversity of the human mind at its most glaring. Everyone knows that Paul's argument was based on true, simple logic, which everyday experience demonstrates time and again. Jesus warned his disciples not to lay up treasure on earth, and spoke of the rich man who died and went to hell because he had not taken care of his soul when he was alive. What does it profit a man if he should gain the whole world but lose his own soul?[25] The message is clear and the moral is obvious. Yet the reality is that many people, including many otherwise godly Christians, act in a way that contradicts this simple observation. The great Scottish-American philanthropist Andrew Carnegie once said that it was a disgrace to die rich, a conviction that he had learned from his Christian upbringing. Unfortunately it is a lesson that too few believers have really grasped, and the hold that earthly possessions continues to have over so many is one of the greatest pastoral problems that the church faces. It is a form of idolatry that is all the more powerful because it is seldom recognized as such and therefore it escapes the condemnation that it deserves.

Paul's answer to those who think that they need material goods to survive was to say that as long as we have enough to eat and to clothe ourselves, we should be content. The allusion to Jesus' teaching in the Sermon on the Mount is obvious, and on the basis of it we might reasonably extend the meaning of 'clothing' (*skepasmata*) to include shelter as well, since our dwelling places also keep us 'clothed' against the elements.[26]

Those who reject such advice are all too easily recognizable, and Paul sketched their character in his customary triadic manner. According to him, people who want to get rich fall into temptation, into a trap, and into many senseless (*anoētai*) and harmful (*blaberai*) desires that 'plunge people into ruin and destruction'.

Paul put temptation first, since that is where the way of destruction begins. Temptation is not by itself a sin, and everyone, including Jesus, is tempted one way or another.[27] It is part of the subtlety of the phenomenon that we are always tempted to do something that is possible. We are confronted with a choice between right and wrong that we have to make. Nobody can claim to have been forced into it, not is it possible to blame God for it. What is important is not that we should try to avoid it, because that is impossible,

---

[25] Mt. 6.19-24; Lk. 16.19-31; Mk 8.36.
[26] Mt. 6.25-34.
[27] Mt. 4.1-11; Heb. 4.15; 1 Cor. 10.13.

but that we should not fall into it when it comes our way. Here Paul used language which is of special importance for our understanding of original sin and the bondage of the human will. Sin is not the result of a decision taken by Adam and Eve independently of anything or anyone else. They did not wake up one morning in the garden and determine to disobey God, just to see what would happen.

On the contrary, sin was the consequence of their response to a temptation that came to them from Satan, who had already rebelled against his Creator and who was enticing them into the same rejection of divine authority. They were presented with a choice and knew perfectly well that they should have declined Satan's offer. Indeed, initially Eve did so, and it was only after repeated attempts that Satan broke her resistance down.[28] This too is a warning to us, not to take our initial refusal to be tempted as definitive. It often happens that when we are confronted with evil for the first time, we instinctively rebel against it because we know that it is wrong. But our resistance can be broken down over time, and that is what happened in the Garden of Eden. Temptation can often be more persistent than we realize!

Paul also used the verb 'fall into' (*empiptō*), which shows that he understood what happened to our first parents, and what happens to us all when we yield to temptation, can rightly be described in those terms. Today there are many people who deny the concept of a 'fall' and who insist that the human race was never any better than it is now. They reject the concept of sin and speak instead of 'failure', 'inadequacy' or whatever word can account for the obvious imperfections of the human race, without assigning personal responsibility for them in the shape of disobedience to God. But as Paul insisted, there was indeed a fall (*ptōsis*), mankind is responsible for yielding to temptation, and there is no easy way back from the dilemma that has resulted from that.

This is because yielding to temptation leads us into a trap (*pagis*), from which there is no escape. By promising Adam and Eve freedom from the dictates of God, Satan was luring them into submission to him. What was true of the big picture of sin and death repeats itself over and over again on a smaller scale. Once trapped, a person's mind is no longer able to reason properly. Instead of taking sensible decisions, it is overwhelmed with desires that are both senseless and harmful. Elsewhere, Paul referred to them as the 'lusts of the flesh', not because they spring naturally from our material nature but because the devil makes us put earthly things first in our lives and in doing so distorts our understanding of God and his purposes for us.[29]

---

[28] Gen. 3.1-6.
[29] Gal. 5.17. See also 1 Jn 2.16.

Fleshly desires are senseless because they produce no benefit and are often quite unconnected to any real need that we have. We can live quite happily without the things we long for, but because our minds are trapped we lack the ability to understand this and make the correct decisions. Almost inevitably, the results turn out to be harmful, if not always physically, then certainly mentally and spiritually. Mentally, we may be persuaded that we cannot do without whatever it is that we desire, and so we find ourselves caught up in what amounts to a form of addiction. Spiritually, we are distracted from the service of God and we are turned instead towards the idolatry that such desires represent.

The result of all this is that we are plunged into a pattern of ruin and destruction. Once again, Paul employed the concept of a fall by his use of the word 'plunge' (*bythizō*). The context was almost certainly spiritual, because he used the terms 'ruin' (*olethros*) and 'destruction' (*apōleia*) which both point to a catastrophe that is final. All human beings experience physical death, whether they have fallen into this kind of error or not, but here Paul was talking primarily about eternal damnation. Adam's fall was definitive, and once it happened, there could be no turning back to the paradise that he had lost. We who are his spiritual descendants have inherited that alienation from God, and there is now no way that we can overcome it on our own.

Paul intended his remarks to apply to everyone, but Ambrosiaster focused more specifically on church leaders:

> There is nothing more bitter or more dangerous than if a churchman, and especially one in a high position, is concerned with the riches of this world, because then he is a hindrance not only to himself but to others as well. He sets a bad example for other people, for there will certainly be many who will copy him to their own destruction.[30]

In v. 10 Paul summed up his discussion by telling Timothy that 'the love of money' (*philargyria*) is a root of every kind of evil. Traditional translations have suggested that it is *the* root of *all* evil, as if nothing bad comes from anything else, but this is not what Paul meant here. Of course, sin exists even when there is no money to be gained. Paul did not advocate a kind of Shangri-La in which a perfectly spiritual form of communism would replace all earthly desires and therefore make sin both impossible and irrelevant. Rather, he singled out one particular form of sin and said that succumbing to it is liable to produce many different kinds of evil. Some people will do

---

[30] Ambrosiaster (2009), p. 139.

almost anything to get rich, and the temptation to go for 'easy pickings' (as we might say today) can often be overwhelming. Greed has produced an almost infinite number of scams, forgeries and other deceptions, not to mention open robberies and murders. People have been known to kill others for a pittance, and every day people who are put in charge of money steal it (or some of it) thinking that they will never be caught. Some get away with this, of course, but many do not, and if they are exposed they lose everything. Yet in spite of many examples of this, people still succumb to the temptation. It is an appetite or craving (*orexis*) that is strong enough to make people turn away from the faith and harm themselves with many 'pangs' (*odynai*).

Martin Luther put it well when he said,

> the greedy man deprives himself of eternal life, because his heart is swollen with many concerns. Because he has all these worries, he is forced to fear the dangers of fire and of water. As many worries threaten him as there are grains of sand on the seashore. Thus he destroys this life as well as that which is to come ... Greed is the worship of idols ... greed worships money, but godliness worships God. The greedy man is uncertain and is deprived both of this life and that which is to come.[31]

In these words of Paul we recognize what today we would call an addiction. Those trapped by the love of money cannot escape from it and are led into forms of behaviour that are both irrational and destructive. It is irrational to turn away from the faith that alone can save them, and destructive to pierce themselves with self-inflicted wounds, yet so great is their craving that they cannot do otherwise. We must note here that Paul lays the blame for this squarely on the addicts themselves. They have not been forced into such behaviour by any outside power, but have voluntarily surrendered their wills to it. They may now be trapped in a way that permits no escape, but if so, they are the authors of their own misfortune and must bear the responsibility for the evils that happen to them as a consequence of their bad choices.

A particular point of interest about this passage is that it was quoted by Polycarp of Smyrna (AD 70–156) in a letter that he wrote to the Philippians, probably about AD 130. Among other quotations from the apostle Paul's letters, he wrote, 'the beginning of all evils is the love of money. Knowing therefore that we brought nothing into the world and we can take nothing out of it.'[32] The words Polycarp used are not entirely identical with those of

---

[31] Luther (1973), p. 372.
[32] Polycarp of Smyrna, *Ep. ad Philippenses*, 4.1.

this text, but they are close enough to be a clear allusion to it. L. T. Johnson has examined the question most thoroughly and concluded that Polycarp was indeed quoting a passage that he believed came from an authentic Pauline letter, and given his dates and location in Asia Minor, it is reasonable to suppose that he was in a position to know.[33]

## 11-12. The good fight of faith

*11. But as for you, man of God, shun all this; pursue righteousness, godliness, faith, love, endurance, gentleness. 12. Fight the good fight of the faith; take hold of the eternal life, to which you were called and for which you made the good confession on the presence of many witnesses.*

Turning away from his vivid description of the false teachers led astray by their love of money, Paul now reached the crescendo of his Epistle in a moving plea to Timothy himself. The true servant of God was to be the spiritual opposite of the men whom he has just described. As always, Paul began with who Timothy was and then proceeded to outline what he must do in order to live up to what God expected of him. The fundamental truth about Timothy was that he was 'a man (*anthrōpos*) of God'. This meant that he had been called by God, and that his whole life must be worked out in a pattern of service to him. Everything he said and did ought to reflect his calling, so that those who saw him would see the presence of God in him and respond accordingly. The man of God must be unwavering in his commitment, and he must not draw undue attention to himself. God works through his chosen messengers, not in order to glorify them, but in order to glorify himself. The true man of God knows that he is only a servant, called to bear witness to the one who has sent him but in no way expected to claim honour and status for himself, as the false teachers did.

There has been considerable debate about the meaning of the term 'man of God', which may refer to people who have been called and chosen for a particular task, like the prophets of the Old Testament, or (at the other end of the spectrum) to any Christian.[34] Without denying this, and without suggesting that ordinary Christians are exempt from the requirements Paul laid down for Timothy, the context implies that what the apostle said is of particular relevance to someone in a position of leadership and authority.

---

[33] Johnson (2001), pp. 298-300.
[34] See Marshall (2004), pp. 656-7, who examines the full range of possibilities and whose conclusion is followed here.

Others in the church would look up to him for guidance, and so the example that he set would be of particular importance. He would be seen and recognized by others as 'a man of God', and in that perspective it was essential for him to set a good example of how a Christian ought to behave.

Paul told this man of God that he must 'flee' the things that have ensnared the false teachers. It is not enough merely to be different from them; he must actively reject what they stand for and what they do. He must not imagine that he is impervious to the allure of the temptations that have seduced others. Given the right circumstances, what overtook them could bring him down as well, and he must recognize his natural human weakness. A man of God is not someone who is immune to temptation, but someone who has recognized it for what it is and has turned away from it. In this case flight is not an act of cowardice but of wisdom, and it is in demonstrating his wisdom that the man of God will reveal his true character.

Fleeing evil is the first but not the only task that the man of God must perform. He cannot simply reject what is wrong, but must put a positive alternative in its place. All too often we know what people are against but have no idea what they are for. The man of God must not be like them. He can and must condemn evil, but at the same time he must actively pursue what is good and concentrate his mind and his efforts on that. Unusually, Paul explained what he meant by using not one triadic construction but two. Instead of listing only three main qualities that the man of God must cultivate, Paul here doubled the dose to six, perhaps as an indication that the man of God, like Elisha, was expected to have a double portion of his master's Spirit.[35] It is hard to say whether the six items he listed can be broken down into two groups of three, or whether they all follow naturally in a sequence that depends on the first quality mentioned. If a subdivision is possible, then it seems that the first triad concentrates on the man of God's inner character, while the second stresses its outward manifestation. In any case, the two things are closely linked and cannot be separated from one another.

The six qualities that Paul mentioned are righteousness (*dikaiosynē*), godliness (*eusebeia*) and faith (*pistis*), followed by love (*agapē*), endurance or patience (*hypomonē*) and gentleness (*praÿpathia*). Righteousness is a major theme of Paul's epistle to the Romans and most commentators believe that it is central to Paul's theology generally, although it is seldom mentioned in most of his other letters. That does not prove anything, however, because in Romans Paul developed this theme so thoroughly that it is impossible to imagine that it was not fundamental to his preaching of the gospel. In his

---

[35] 2 Kgs 2.9-10.

other writings he had to address specific concerns that did not usually require a restatement of his basic position on the subject, though it was assumed in the teaching that he gave about other things. Here we find that he put it first in his list of qualities to be highlighted, and that speaks for itself as far as its basic importance is concerned.

Righteousness was a theme that was particularly important to Paul because it was so often misunderstood. Many people thought of it as something they had to aim for, rather than as a gift from God, and at first sight it might appear that this popular view is what the apostle embraced here. To pursue righteousness could be understood to mean living a life of good works that God would recognize and reward, even though that interpretation would be contrary to what he said elsewhere. The broader context, however, shows us that if we interpret the word in this way here we would be separating it from what follows, which is both a logical and a spiritual impossibility. The righteousness that Timothy was told to pursue was one that would lead to godliness and faith, neither of which he could have achieved by his own efforts.

What Paul meant here is that Timothy had to put righteousness, by which we must understand conformity to the mind, will and character of God, first in his order of priorities. Everything else flows from that. Furthermore, such righteousness must come as a gift from God, because only he can communicate his attributes to others. To pursue it must therefore mean to seek it from God by a life of prayer, submission and obedience, and not by human activities that are designed to please him in some way. The man who has received the gift of righteousness will respond with 'godliness', which is the reflection of God's character in him. In some ways, righteousness and godliness are two sides of the same coin and can be regarded as more or less identical, at least in the way that they manifest themselves. They are distinguished from each other, not by their innate quality but by the nature of the relationship that God establishes with us. His righteousness comes as a gift and godliness is the evidence that the gift has taken root in us. It is our response to it, but of course, it is also (by its very nature) a gift from God as well.

The chief manifestation and consequence of this is our faith, which Paul elsewhere describes as the means by which we are made righteous in God's eyes. Our faith is both belief in who God is and trust in what he has done, is doing and will do for us. We believe that he is the Almighty Creator and Sovereign Lord of the universe, who has made all things for our enjoyment and who protects us from harm in this world. We also believe that he has sent his Son to pay the price for our sins and to restore the relationship with him that we have lost by our disobedience. Finally, we believe that this restored relationship with him has initiated a process of growth in his grace, or 'sanctification', which will come to fulfillment when we are taken up into his glory, either at our death or when he returns in judgement. Some of the details may be unclear, but the general drift is unmistakable. To have faith in God is to believe that he has a plan for our lives that will fulfil the promises that he has made to us in his Word. Those promises are sealed by the double gift of righteousness in his sight and godliness in the eyes of the world around us.

In the second triad, love comes first, and follows on naturally from faith. Love does not create faith but it is the means by which faith is manifested. The two things go together in practice, and it is hard to imagine one without the other, but the order is important. Faith is our commitment to what is objectively true and trustworthy. When we put our trust in God we are committing ourselves to the service of our Creator and Redeemer, not because we love him but because we submit to the truth of what we know about him and believe in the promises that he has made to those who do so. It is when we do that that God puts his love in our hearts and enables us to respond accordingly. With respect to God, love sets the seal on our relationship to him. That relationship is not just an intellectual conviction of the truth of what he has said and done. It is also an active participation in his life that involves an ongoing connection. Love is revealed in action. Our behaviour, towards him in the first instance and towards others in the second, is the demonstration of this and it is those things that constitute the word's true meaning. Our love for God is most clearly demonstrated by our submission and obedience to his will. It is when we do what he says that we come to appreciate more deeply who he is and what he has in store for us. A 'faith' that does not result in deeds born out of love is dead, just as the deeds by themselves have no meaning if they have not been done for the right reason. There is an order to be observed here, and it is one which is tailored both to our needs and to the destiny to which we have been called.

In relation to other people, our love for them is a manifestation of what God has done for us. We cannot give to others what we have not received ourselves. Nor must we confuse this divine love with natural affections, even if they can be used to further it. It is normal to feel a special attachment to family and friends – non-Christians do the same. But Christian love is something that goes beyond that and treats all human beings as creatures of God whom we must respect and love. This does not diminish the affection that we have for those who are particularly close to us, but rather extends and transforms what comes naturally to what can only be a divine gift. The church is a brotherhood, a family to which we belong and which we invite others to join. It is not a closed circle, but a dynamic community of those who have known the love of God and who seek to spread it by the way in which they extend that love to others.

Steadfastness is the logical consequence of love and is often the way in which it is perceived. The Greek word *hypomonē* means 'patience' and its importance can easily be seen when we look at the love of God towards his rebellious creatures. Instead of destroying them for their disobedience, God endured it and was patient with them through all the many ups and downs of human and Israelite history. From the human standpoint, our relationship with God has been punctured by failure and restored by repentance, but from his side there has been only steadfastness. He has not wavered in his love for us, nor has he turned away or rejected us. When we are called to share his love with others, we are called to assume this attitude too. We must be patient with those around us who all too often treat us in the way that we have treated God. There may be many times when we will be tempted to give up, or feel hurt that our love has not been received or reciprocated. But just as God has not abandoned us, so we must not abandon those whom he has given to us. It is our persistence and perseverance in this which is the true test of our love, which in turn reflects the nature of our faith, the quality of our godliness and the meaning of the righteousness that we have received. It is a chain reaction that takes us right back to the source of our relationship with God.

Finally there is 'gentleness'. This is the quality that manifests itself in the way that we treat those who have sinned against us, and once again it reflects the way in which God has behaved towards us. If God had treated us as we deserve, we would have been destroyed. The Bible is full of warnings of his severity towards those who have rejected him and of the punishment that awaits those who do not repent. But the wonder of the gospel is that God has not dealt with us in that way. On the contrary, he has been gentle with us, in the way that parents are gentle with their children, even when they know that they have done wrong and must be corrected. God does not ignore our sins or tolerate them, but he handles us sinners with gentleness. He corrects us without breaking us in the process. He restores us and guides us along the way that he has carved out for us, even when we cannot see it for ourselves. When we fail, as we often do, he picks us up, dusts us off and puts us back on the road. He knows that without his grace we can do nothing, and he treats us with all the care and consideration needed to perfect those who are destined to dwell with him in eternity. Part of this preparation is sharing that gentleness with us, so that we can show it to others. For someone like Timothy, who was called to be the leader of a church, that quality of gentleness must have been needed to an exceptional degree, and its presence would have been felt most deeply at those times when he was called to rebuke and discipline his congregation. It was then, above all, that the ultimate fruit of righteousness would be seen most clearly and that it would be used most effectively to build up the people of God to whom he, the man of God, was called to minister.

The significance of Paul's counsels here has been well summed up by P. H. Towner, who writes,

> Timothy is to pursue a life that ... exhibits genuine godliness and compassion for those in error ... Paul does not isolate elements of human conduct from matters of ministry, but rather seeks to integrate belief and behaviour into a holistic pattern of existence. It is not accidental that he began this restatement of Timothy's commission from an ethical perspective: the starting point for ministry is a manner of life that is visibly different from that patterned after the values of the world, which keeps faith and love/conduct bound tightly together.[36]

The aims of the Christian life are clear but we must not suppose that they can be achieved without a struggle. Both in ourselves and in the world around us we are confronted by a host of obstacles that we must overcome if the goal is to be reached. This is not salvation by works. Our salvation has been given to us by God; now we are called to work it out in practical terms, applying it to the challenges of life as they occur. Paul expresses this to Timothy in the memorable phrase 'fight the good fight' (*agōnizou ton kalon agōna*).[37] There is no pretense here – the struggle is real. But at the same time it is 'good' because its purpose is to glorify God.

It is one of the paradoxes of Scripture that language of violence and warfare is often used of the spiritual life. We are accustomed to think that spiritual people should be peaceful, and indeed there are many texts that tell us that.[38] The kind of aggression that accompanies envy, as well as strife and contention, is routinely condemned as ungodly and Christians are warned to stay away from those who behave in that way.[39] Yet there is another sense in which the language of violence can be adopted to express something that is necessary if the state of peace that we long for is to be achieved. It goes without saying that this struggle is spiritual. Paul was very clear about that

---

[36] Towner (2006), p. 410.
[37] The analogy may be either military or athletic. Towner (2006), pp. 410–12, opts for the latter, which seems to fit the context better, but Calvin (1964), p. 276, preferred the former. However, as Marshall (2004), pp. 659–60, remarks, either is possible and it makes little difference in practice.
[38] Mt. 5.9; Heb. 12.14; Jas 3.18; 1 Pet. 3.11.
[39] Prov. 20.3; Tit. 3.9; Jude 1.17–23.

in his letter to the Ephesians, where he counselled them to put on the whole armour of God, so that they could fight against sin, the flesh and the devil.[40] His description there of the body armour that a believer was meant to put on is strongly reminiscent of the qualities that he outlined to Timothy, and we may regard his intention here as identical to what he wrote there, even if some of the details are slightly different.

Paul added that the good fight is a fight 'of [the] faith', which sounds obvious but whose meaning is hard to interpret precisely. Did he mean 'the faith' in the sense of a body of doctrine or 'faith' in the sense of a trusting relationship with God?[41] The appearance of the definite article in the Greek has led some to prefer the former interpretation, but that seems somewhat limited in its scope. The article would normally be used in such a construction and there is no reason to suppose that it has any special force here. Christian faith must always be grounded in the truth and confession comes naturally to it, but it is more than just an agreement with a set of propositions that express what we believe. The life of faith is commitment to a spiritual struggle, and it seems almost certain that this is what Paul wanted to emphasize here. On the other hand, it is clear that professing the Christian faith was potentially dangerous and liable to lead to persecution, as Paul himself had experienced on many occasions. Those who persevered in spite of everything were making 'the good confession' or as we might say today, they were putting their money where their mouth was.

The language here is suggestive of what would be understood in later times as the confession made by those who were put to death for their faith. The good fight of faith would become the experience of martyrdom, which was rewarded with the crown of eternal life.[42] Each martyr knew that in going through this he was making 'the good confession' which had been well-defined by those who had preceded him and which he was himself making in the presence of many glorified martyrs in heaven, who had been through the same experience. The similarities between this and what Paul says to (and about) Timothy are so strong that we should not be surprised that it has been used as evidence that the Epistle was written a century or so after Timothy's time. But a full-blown theology of martyrdom did not emerge until the late second century, and we know that it was in hindsight a theologian like Tertullian interpreted this text in that way.[43] That does not invalidate the application of the text to martyrdom, but it is hard to see how it could have

---

[40] Eph. 6.11-13.
[41] Oddly enough, modern commentators seem to pass over this ambiguity in silence.
[42] Rev. 2.10.
[43] Tertullian, *De praescriptione haereticorum*, 25. See also Justin Martyr, *Apology*, 1.4.

been written in response to it, or even in expectation of it. Timothy was called to pursue spiritual virtue and keep the commandments with no suggestion that he would be exposed to persecution and suffering as a result.

In this connection, it is important to note that when Paul mentioned Jesus in the next verse, he said that he made 'the good confession' before Pontius Pilate, not specifically on the cross.[44] Nevertheless, we must remember what John Calvin had to say about that:

> Christ made his confession before Pilate not in many words but in reality, that is by his voluntary submission to death. For although Christ chose to keep silent before Pilate rather than speak in his own defence... yet in his very silence there was a defence of his teaching no less magnificent than if he had pleaded his case with a loud voice. For he ratified it with his own blood and with the sacrifice of his death better than with any words.[45]

The language must reflect the mid- to late first century, before persecution had become a major problem for the church, but when the martyrdom of Jesus was still fresh in everyone's mind. People knew what they could expect from the enemies of their faith and they had to be on guard against them. It is possible that Timothy had been forced to confess his faith in a public forum and had suffered because of it, but we cannot be sure about that. This may reflect the occasion when he was put in prison, from which he had been released shortly before the epistle to the Hebrews was written.[46] We have no way of knowing this, but Paul certainly realized that despite his relative youth, Timothy would not be spared the suffering that was the lot of every faithful Christian. Whether he had already encountered persecution, or whether he had done no more than preach the need for repentance and regeneration in Christ in a way that had been recognized and received by 'many witnesses', Timothy's record was a good one and would stand him in good stead, whatever the future might hold in store for him. Martyrdom was certainly a possibility, but the evidence of the text suggests that it had not yet become the expected result of his faithfulness to the message of Christ.

---

[44] The Greek phrase *epi Pontiou Pilatou* can mean either 'before Pontius Pilate' or 'in the time of Pontius Pilate'. The former interpretation is more accurate in the context and is therefore to be preferred, but the problem is really one of translation. The original readers would probably not have perceived the distinction.
[45] Calvin (1964), p. 278.
[46] Heb. 13.23.

## 13-16. Paul's charge to Timothy

*13. In the presence of God, who gives life to all things, and of Christ Jesus, who in his testimony before Pontius Pilate made the good confession, I charge you 14. to keep the commandment without spot or blame until the manifestation of our Lord Jesus Christ, 15. which he will bring about at the right time – he who is the blessed and only Sovereign, the King of kings and Lord of lords. 16. It is he alone who has immortality and dwells in unapproachable light, whom no one has ever seen or can see; to him be honour and eternal dominion. Amen.*

Whatever may have been the case in the past, Paul's immediate concern here was to encourage Timothy to go on in the faith, using his experiences as evidence that God could and would protect him from harm. He therefore charged the younger man with the responsibility to maintain his convictions and to be prepared to die for them, if necessary. The God who bore him witness was the one who gives life to all things, an important reminder that even if Timothy were called upon to lose this life, he would not be cut off from the life-giver, who could (and would) restore him to eternal life in Christ, who is also present in Paul's thinking and who had made the good confession just before he was put to death.

Timothy was charged to keep the 'commandment (*entolē*) unstained (*aspilos*) and free from blame (*anepilēmptos*)'. It is not altogether clear what Paul meant by the 'commandment'. It does not seem to have been like one of the Ten Commandments, because nothing of that kind is mentioned here. It is much more likely to refer to something similar to the *epitagē* ('mandate') that Paul had received from God to preach the gospel in season and out of season – in other words, whether it was welcome or unwelcome to those who heard it. Moreover, it seems obvious from the context that it was the content of the commandment itself that Paul was concerned about, since otherwise it is hard to see why he would have talked about it as 'unstained' and 'free from blame'.

The first of these words probably refers to sin, which was perceived to be a kind of stain on the soul.[47] This presumably means that the commandment was not to be corrupted from within. Nor was it to be treated in a way that might bring reproach on it, even if it had suffered no internal corruption. It can sometimes happen that the way things are done brings a procedure into

---

[47] Cf. the Greek term *aspilos syllēpsis* which is used to translate the 'immaculate conception' (of Mary).

disrepute even if there is nothing legally wrong with it. For example, it might be possible to preach the gospel in a tavern or casino without corrupting the message, but the nature of the venue might raise eyebrows and the excuse that the evangelist merely wants to go where the people are might ring hollow in many people's ears. The principle here is that it is not enough to do the right thing; it must also be done in the right way if it is to carry conviction.

Timothy's charge to preserve the commandment undefiled was intended to last until the return of Christ in glory. The second coming was a vivid expectation in the early church, and many scholars believe that Paul thought it would be imminent. We now know that this did not happen, and so we tend to downplay such eschatological references as part of the disappointed hope that supposedly dampened the enthusiasm of the first generation of Christians. We have no way of knowing what Timothy and his congregation thought about this, so it is impossible to evaluate the full impact of these words on those who first heard them. But it is important to note that Paul qualified his remarks by saying that Christ would return 'at the proper time', leaving it open as to when that time would be. Paul knew that in God's eyes a day is as a thousand years, and he immediately entered into a litany of praise that reinforces that point.

Commentators throughout the ages have tended to downplay the eschatological dimension of Paul's remarks here, and this is still true today.[48] But John Calvin was a remarkable exception to the rule. Not only did he appreciate the mind of the early church, but he understood that what was said to them is just as relevant to us:

> It is impossible to over-emphasize the necessity at that time for all godly men to have their minds fixed entirely upon the day of Christ, since innumerable offences were taking place all over the world. They were being attacked on every side, everyone hated them and cursed them, they were exposed to general mockery and every day they were opposed by fresh afflictions: and meanwhile no fruit of all their many toils and troubles could be seen ... But the same reasons hold equally today with us. Satan shows us so many things that, apart from this hope, would a thousand times draw us away from the right course ... The only remedy for all these difficulties is to look forward to Christ's appearing and always to put our trust in it.[49]

---

[48] Towner (2006), pp. 416–18, has an extended excursus on what he calls the 'epiphany concept', but even he seems to avoid the eschatological implications as far as he can.
[49] Calvin (1964), pp. 278–9.

The litany consists of six lines, which may be subdivided into two groups of three. In the first group are the titles by which God is known, and in the second group are some of the essential qualities that he possesses. According to the first triad, God is

1. the blessed and only Sovereign (*dynastēs*)
2. the King of kings
3. the Lord of lords

The terminology here is reminiscent of Rev. 17.14, and reminds us that Paul was moving in the same mental universe as the author of the Apocalypse, who may have been the apostle John. It also reflects language used in 2 and 3 Maccabees, which means that it may have become something of a commonplace in the inter-testamental period.[50]

First of all, God is hailed as the Sovereign, who is by definition 'blessed' (*makarios*) and unique (*monos*). These two attributes are characteristic of his sovereignty. A sovereign is one who owes no allegiance to anyone else and is free to do what he wants. It is because he is not subject to outside influences and has no obligations to others that he is 'blessed'. He is also unique because nobody else can usurp his sovereignty, which by definition can belong only to him. This is a reminder that our God is above and beyond every other power, and that nothing can touch him or diminish his ability to rule. Everywhere we go, he is there, and everything we do, he ultimately controls. We cannot escape from him, either physically or spiritually.[51]

It is his universal sovereignty that explains why God is 'king of kings' and 'lord of lords'. We have become so accustomed to this phrase, not least thanks to the Hallelujah Chorus in Handel's *Messiah*, that it is now almost impossible to produce a more precise translation of the Greek, but we should probably attempt this as far as we can. Paul did not actually write 'king of kings and lord of lords' but rather 'king of those who rule as kings' and 'lord of those who rule as lords'. The difference is that while his kingship and lordship are a permanent status, the rule of others is a function that does not belong to them as of right. That does not make their rule illegitimate, but it does suggest that it is a temporary phenomenon and dependent on the will of the one who is the eternal lord and king. There have often been rulers in this world who have tried to oppose God and even denied his existence, but they have come and gone.

---

[50] 2 Macc. 3.24; 3 Macc. 5.35. See Marshall (2004), p. 666, for further discussion.
[51] Ps. 139.7-12; Rom. 8.38-39.

In contrast to them, God remains the same for ever, and there is nothing that even his most powerful enemies can do to change that. Whether they recognize it or not, the rulers of this world are what they are only because God has allowed them to do what they do. They have no legitimacy apart from him, and their tenure of high office is likely to be short, even by human standards. A king or earthly ruler who declares himself a God and demands worship from his subjects will not last long, and Christians who are impressed or afflicted by earthly powers must always bear that firmly in mind. In God's eyes, even democratic states that have repudiated earthly theocracy have no legitimacy apart from him and a majority vote for sin is no reason for Christians to go along with it.[52] After all, everyone has sinned and fallen short of God's glory, so we should be neither surprised nor persuaded by that.[53] We owe allegiance to a higher power, and if the rulers of this world ignore him the loyalty that we normally owe them cannot be used as an excuse to follow suit.[54]

The second triad expounds some of the attributes of God that accompany his sovereignty and help us to understand the full extent of its reach. According to Paul, God is

1. the only one who possesses immortality (*athanasia*)
2. the one who dwells in 'unapproachable' (*aprositon*) light
3. the one whom no human being has ever seen or can see

It is not often in the New Testament that we find a list of the divine attributes, and what Paul wrote here cannot be regarded as a systematic list of them. We can deduce from what he said that God is immortal, 'unapproachable' and invisible but there does not seem to be any inner logic that would explain why he referred to these characteristics of the divine being rather than to others which might be equally pertinent. It must also be said that later theologians, while they have been quite happy to describe God as 'immortal' and 'invisible', have usually avoided saying that he is 'unapproachable', though the same idea has been conveyed by terms like 'transcendent'. God is above and beyond us in objective, physical terms, but thanks to the coming of Christ and the indwelling presence of the Holy Spirit in our hearts, he is no longer 'unapproachable' in the way that he was in the Old Testament.[55]

---

[52] To take a recent example, the legalization of same-sex marriage by the state is not a reason for Christians to accept it.
[53] Rom. 3.23.
[54] See Rom. 13.1-7.
[55] Eph. 2.18.

Looking at each of these in turn, Paul did not describe God as 'being immortal' but as 'possessing immortality'. Perhaps there is little or no difference between these two forms of expression, but the feeling they convey is not quite the same. Paul seems to have been saying that immortality is something that God possesses, not only in the sense that he is himself immortal but also in the sense that it is something that he can give to others if he wishes to do so. His immortality is something that he shares with us in the gift of eternal life. Of course, our eternal life is not the same as his because it is a work of divine grace and not an attribute of our human nature, but once it is given it is something that we share with him on a parallel, if not entirely equal basis. We shall never be sovereign or almighty in the way that he is, but we can participate in his immortality by his gift of eternal life. At the same time, immortality is a possession that is unique to him and we cannot get it from anywhere else. Whatever eternal life we have can only come from God and it is in that context that we must understand and appreciate it.

That God dwells in unapproachable light is a theme that frequently recurs in the Scriptures. Sometimes it comes in the form of fire, as God came to Moses in the burning bush.[56] At other times, it may come in a vision of light, like the one of Jesus on the mount of transfiguration, or his famous appearance to Paul on the road to Damascus.[57] Either way, it is impossible for those who encounter him to approach him too closely, which is a reminder of how far above us he is. His invisibility reinforces this, and reminds us that the extent of his being is not limited by human perception or definition. God can be present and active in ways of which we are unaware, and often is. His sovereignty extends further than what we can perceive and covers vast areas of life that are above and beyond us. It is a reminder to us to have faith that he can (and does) do what is impossible, and even unimaginable, for us, whether we see him at work or not.

There has been much discussion as to whether Paul's paean of praise to God is meant to refer to the Father or to the Son. The fact that Christ has just been mentioned in v. 14 and that he is called 'king of kings and lord of lords' in Revelation[58] encourages us to think of the Son, but the insistence on his eternal transcendence and unapproachability points us to the Father. In cases of doubt it is usually best to prefer the Father, since he is the person of the Trinity who is regarded as representing God as he is in himself. This was clear to Ambrosiaster, who commented,

---

[56] Exod. 3.2.
[57] Mt. 17.1-13; Mk 9.2-13; Lk. 9.28-36; Acts 9.3.
[58] Rev. 17.14; 19.16.

the light of the Father is in the Son, but because nobody has seen the Father, he dwells in inaccessible light. There is no way to see God other than through Christ. The one who is of God sees God. Because the Son does everything, he is the one who is said to appear and be seen.[59]

Paul ends his litany of praise with a fairly standard phrase in which God's honour and eternal power (*kratos*) are invoked. Once again, there is a fundamental distinction between being and doing. God is honoured for who he is, and his eternal power is a reminder of what he does. Unlike earthly creatures, his strength does not wax and wane with time, but is always the same. It is a matter for both praise and thanksgiving, and so Paul concluded with a liturgical *amen* which reinforces his sense of devotion and commitment to the God whom he has revealed here to Timothy.

## 17-19. The rich

*17. As for those who in the present age are rich, command them not to be haughty, or to set their hopes on the uncertainty of riches, but rather on God who richly provides us with everything for our enjoyment. 18. They are to do good, to be rich in good works, generous, and ready to share, 19. thus storing up for themselves the treasure of a good foundation for the future, so that they may take hold of the life that really is life.*

Before signing off, Paul devoted a final paragraph to the question of the rich. It is possible that this originally belonged to an earlier part of the Epistle, where it might have fitted in better – perhaps at the end of chapter 5. But it is also possible that it was a kind of afterthought in his mind, of the sort that often occurs to people when they are writing letters. Whatever the truth may be, although the verses stand on their own in this Epistle, in their spirit they coincide perfectly with what the rest of the New Testament teaches about wealth and those who possess it.

Rich people are not necessarily lovers of money in the way that the false teachers were. Many of the ones that Paul mentioned had probably inherited their wealth and thought little of it, though they must have known that others were not as well off as they were. Some probably believed that their wealth was a sign of their innate superiority, because why else would they have been

---

[59] Ambrosiaster (2009), p. 141.

so blessed? But it is not necessary to suppose that they were greedy; they did not need to be! At the same time, there was something about their riches that they needed to understand, and this is what Paul had pointed out in 1 Tim. 6.7. Whatever riches a person possesses, they are for this life only. You cannot take them with you when you die, and so there is no cause to be proud of them. Riches are also notoriously fickle. They can vanish as easily as they have appeared, and those who have not earned them are probably more likely to lose them through inadvertence than those who have struggled to get them and who know the value of money.

In any case, it is foolish to rely on material possessions for security. There are things that money cannot buy, and the most important qualities of life are among them. The only one we can really rely on is God, who will supply our needs and give us plenty to enjoy, if we trust him for his provision. Instead of worrying about that, the wealthy ought to concentrate on doing good, on being rich in good works, generous and community-spirited, sharing their goods with others according to their needs. People who do this are storing up for themselves treasure in heaven, which is the only real security (*kalon themelion*) for the future and the surest guarantee that they will inherit eternal life.[60] The close parallel here with the teaching of Jesus is unmistakable, and there is no reason to suppose that Paul thought any differently from his Lord.[61] The redefinition of what constituted 'wealth' was fundamental to early Christianity and was rooted in the prioritizing of spiritual over material things.

One aspect of Paul's statement that is easily overlooked is his reminder at the end of v. 17, that God has richly provided us with everything for our enjoyment. Christians are not meant to be greedy or to abuse the wealth that God may have given them, but there is no need to renounce earthly things as if they are somehow evil. God has made the world for our benefit, and we are meant to make use of it to that end and to take delight in what he has provided for us.[62] The essential goodness of creation is a theme that runs through this entire Epistle, but perhaps nowhere is it more clearly seen than in Paul's approach to earthly riches and his advice to those who possess them. Responsible use of what we have been given, rather than outright rejection of it is his watchword, rooted in the goodness of the Creator but mindful always of the ultimate goal of a better life beyond this one.

---

[60] The Greek *kalon themelion* may be either neuter (more common) or masculine, as it is in 1 Cor. 3.11-12, in which case the nominative form would be *kalos themelios*.
[61] Mt. 6.19-21; 19.16-30.
[62] Johnson (2001), pp. 314–15, stresses this more clearly than most other commentators.

## 20-21. Final salutation

*20. Timothy, guard what has been entrusted to you. Avoid the profane chatter and contradictions of what is falsely called knowledge; 21. by professing it some have missed the mark as regards the faith. Grace be with you.*

In his final salutation Paul made a strong personal appeal to Timothy, reminding him again of his main purpose in writing and begging him to 'guard the deposit (*parathēkē*)' that had been entrusted to him. Scholars have debated where this 'deposit' came from – was it given to Timothy directly by God, did it come to him *via* the apostle Paul or was it part of a wider inheritance common to the church as a whole?[63] In practice it makes very little difference and all three possibilities can be held together. The ultimate depositor is of course God, who spoke through the prophets over many generations and in the last days, through his Son Jesus Christ.[64] The message of salvation had been entrusted to Paul, among others, but he made no claim to originality and on occasion stated quite clearly that he was passing on teaching that he had himself received from elsewhere.[65] Timothy received the message from a variety of sources – his mother and grandmother, the eldership of his church and of course Paul. But it was the same message, entrusted to him for the same purpose, and it was that that he was told he must protect.

Timothy was not charged with the responsibility of proclaiming fresh doctrine as if he were a second-generation apostle. On the contrary, his task was to protect what he had received and make sure that it was not diminished or contaminated by false teachers. The 'deposit' to which Paul referred is the commandment, the mandate and the content of the faith that he had preached and taught, and that then became the foundation of the church's spiritual life.[66] Timothy could only guard it successfully if he

---

[63] See Marshall (2004), p. 676.
[64] Heb. 1.1.
[65] See 1 Cor. 11.23.
[66] Johnson (2001), p. 316, maintains that the 'deposit' is not a set of beliefs but a way of life that is based on the way that God has created the world and saved it, a way of life that is not to be debated but to be received by faith. He is certainly right to draw attention to the dimension of Christian living that must inform our confession of faith, but too great a contrast between these two things is unhelpful and not what Paul intended. The message of this Epistle is that right behaviour will flow from right belief; the two things belong together. Calvin (1964), p. 283, read it as referring to the grace that Timothy had been given in order to discharge his office, but that seems to be inadequate to account for Paul's words.

avoided the 'godless babblings' (*bebēloi kenophōniai*) and contradictions of the counterfeit (*pseudonymos*) 'knowledge' that some people had professed and that had taken them away from the faith.[67] Here again, it is tempting to read the situation of a later time back into the Epistle on the ground that the circumstances described here did not exist in Paul's lifetime.[68] In the early second century there were a number of false teachers who claimed to have a hidden spiritual knowledge (*gnōsis*) which they communicated to their followers, and today they are usually lumped together as 'gnostics'. Irenaeus (d. AD 200?) was very exercised by their teachings and wrote a major treatise against them, but his analysis and condemnation of the phenomenon is a long way from what Paul was saying to Timothy. It may be that the people whom Paul had in mind were the precursors of what would become full-blown Gnosticism in the second century, but when this Epistle was written that had not yet happened.

The existence of people who claimed to possess esoteric teaching was not new, nor was it confined to Christianity. Those who cultivated the study of myths and genealogies were already prominent in Jewish circles well before the time of Jesus, and the influence of such 'oriental' ideas was penetrating the Graeco-Roman world as well. The Sibylline Oracles, for example, were of pre-Christian origin, and there is evidence that the Romans were looking for mystical experiences and other similar things quite apart from any Christian influence. The gospel appeared as a message from on high, to be sure, but there was no secret about it – anyone could have access to its truth and the church was open to people of all backgrounds. The false apostles that we meet in the New Testament were not claiming secret knowledge of teachings that Jesus had hidden from the church. Instead, they were demanding that Christians should conform to the law of Moses, the contents of which were well known. The knowledge being spoken of here may not have been 'secret' at all, because if it were, it is hard to see how Paul could have denounced it as internally contradictory. He must have had some idea of what it was in order to be able to criticize it as he did.

Paul's final words are noteworthy at least partly because the word 'you' (*hymeis*) is plural. Evidently, the letter that was officially addressed to Timothy

---

[67] Some manuscripts read *kainophōniai* ('novelties') as opposed to *kenophōniai*, a confusion that results from homophony in Greek. Either reading is possible, but most modern editions and commentators concur with Calvin's judgement (1964, p. 284) that *kenophōniai* fits the context better.

[68] See Marshall (2004), p. 677, who discusses this possibility but is hesitant to see any reference to later gnosticism in this Epistle. But Theodoret of Cyrrhus (Cyrus) (2001), p. 230, linked what Paul said here to the heresy of Simon Magus, whose followers called themselves 'gnostics'.

as an individual was intended for the benefit of his companions, and probably for his congregation as well. It is a reminder to us that the minister belongs to his people and is not cut off from them. He has a special role to play in the church and therefore he has been given particular instructions related to that, but those guidelines come in the context of a wider fellowship and are meant to be understood and accepted by everybody. When Paul wrote to Timothy he was writing to the church at large, including us today as much as those who sat under Timothy in Ephesus. It is a timeless message, the Word of God given by Paul to his disciple and preserved for the edification of future generations who are called to benefit from his teaching as much as Timothy did.

In concluding, Paul wished 'grace' (*charis*) to be with them all, but he did not specify what he meant. In particular, he did not mention God, which might suggest that his word of farewell was a mere convention with no real meaning of its own. That is possible, but given that the whole epistle comes as a mandate from God, it is unlikely. Paul inhabited a mental universe that was governed by grace. He was what he was by the grace of God, and he never forgot it. Both his relationship to Timothy and Timothy's standing before God were signs of grace. The church whose problems and prospects he was addressing lived by grace and could not have survived otherwise. Paul did not have to specify where that grace came from – everyone knew that God himself was its only possible source. A pseudepigrapher would no doubt have written a more elaborate farewell, recalling what Paul said to some of his churches, but we do not find that here. It was not necessary. Everyone understood what Paul meant, and he could sign off without the flourish of a grand signature at the end. This simplicity supports our belief in the Epistle's authenticity, and reassures us that in this letter we have the genuine words of the apostle being conveyed to his disciple in the faith and intended successor in the leadership of the Ephesian church.

# 2 Timothy

## Chapter 1

| | |
|---|---|
| 1-2 | Greeting |
| 3-5 | Personal testimony |
| 6-8 | Timothy's spiritual gift |
| 9-10 | God's eternal purpose in Christ |
| 11-14 | Paul's confession and example |
| 15-18 | The faithfulness of Onesiphorus |

## Chapter 2

| | |
|---|---|
| 1-7 | The faithful servant |
| 8-13 | Union with Christ |
| 14-19 | Working for God |
| 20-21 | Worthy servants |
| 22-26 | The character of God's servants |

## Chapter 3

| | |
|---|---|
| 1-9 | The life and character of the godless |
| 10-17 | The life and character of the godly |

## Chapter 4

| | |
|---|---|
| 1 | The return of Christ |
| 2-5 | The preaching ministry |

6-8   Paul's hope
9-15  Personal relationships
16-18 Paul's rescue
19-22 Final greetings

# 2 Timothy 1

## 1-2. Greeting

*1. Paul, and apostle of Christ Jesus by the will of God, for the sake of the promise of life that is in Christ Jesus, 2. To Timothy, my beloved child: Grace, mercy and peace from God the Father and Christ Jesus our Lord.*

Paul's second letter to Timothy is markedly different from the first and stands out among the Pastorals for a variety of reasons. First of all, it is a 'prison' epistle, which the others are not. Perhaps for that reason, Paul's particular circumstances figure more prominently than in the others, where the emphasis lies more on the recipients and their congregations. 2 Timothy is also more personal in another way, in that it focuses on Timothy's spiritual development more than on that of the church where he was ministering. It is possible, perhaps even probable, that Timothy was no longer in Ephesus, though it seems from the instructions that Paul gave him that if he was not there, he was probably somewhere else in Asia Minor, perhaps ministering in a church that was somehow dependent on Ephesus. That would not be surprising. The book of Revelation gives us a sense that there was a circuit of seven churches in the province, and it is possible that Timothy had gone to minister in one of those for a time, but that is no more than a guess.[1] Some scholars who believe that the Pastoral Epistles are pseudepigraphical have been willing to admit that this Epistle may be genuinely Pauline in a way that the other two are not, but that too is impossible to prove.[2] The date of its composition is also difficult to determine. It cannot have been written before AD 62 or so, when Paul was first imprisoned in Rome, but whether it comes from the two-year period mentioned by Luke at the end of Acts or from a second imprisonment a few years later is unknown.

---

[1] Revelation 2-3.
[2] This is the view of Michael Prior, *Paul the Letter Writer and the Second Letter to Timothy* (Sheffield: JSOT Press, 1989) and of Jerome Murphy-O'Connor, '2 Timothy Contrasted with 1 Timothy and Titus', *Revue Biblique* 98 (1991), 403-10.

If it was the work of a pseudepigrapher it would obviously have been later in date, but in that case we have no way of knowing when it might have been written or in which of Paul's imprisonments (if there were two) it was theoretically situated. That would probably not matter very much, since the pseudepigrapher is generally thought to have penned all three Epistles at the same time, merely varying the apparent circumstances in which they were written so as to give them an air of authenticity. Of course, that theory raises the question as to why anyone would go to so much trouble, and there is no satisfactory answer to that. In fact it is easier to believe that Paul himself wrote this Epistle as he was awaiting execution and that it has no connection with the other Pastorals beyond the identity of the author and the addressee.

As in the first Epistle, Paul described himself as an 'apostle of Christ Jesus', which was his standard form of greeting. He then expanded on this by adding that it was 'by the will of God according to the promise of the life in Christ Jesus' which was somewhat different from what he said in 1 Timothy and quite unlike the opening salutation in Titus.

In 1 Timothy, Paul had explained that his apostleship derived from the 'command' or 'mandate' (*epitagē*) of God, but here he spoke instead of God's 'will' (*thelēma*). The use of the passive noun *thelēma* instead of the active *thelēsis* or *boulēsis* suggests that by 'will' Paul meant the fixed and eternal plan of God rather than a particular decision taken by God in relation to him. Of course, in the case of God, those two aspects of his will are not very different from each other, but it may reflect a particular perception on Paul's part. Given that he was called to be an apostle in a highly individual way, a fact that he made much of elsewhere,[3] he may have been concerned to emphasize that, in spite of its unusual aspects, his calling was nevertheless part of God's eternal will and plan. *Thelēma* is also a less specific term than *epitagē*, because whereas a command is given on one occasion for a particular purpose, God's settled will is a wider dispensation that includes many other things as well.[4]

Given that the Epistle is highly personal in nature, it may be that Paul wanted to stress this broader perspective at the beginning. What had happened to him particularly (and by extension, what had happened to Timothy also) had to be understood against the backdrop of a bigger picture. That would have been especially important when Paul was in prison facing execution, since it would have been easy for his disciples to have scattered and abandoned the cause of the gospel once he was gone. That had happened at the time of Jesus' death, and it took his resurrection and the subsequent

---

[3] Gal. 1.11-24. See also 2 Cor. 11.21-33.
[4] See Marshall (2004), p. 685.

descent of the Holy Spirit to turn things around. Paul was not Jesus however, and he would not be returning after his death. Hence, there was all the more need for him to emphasize that although God is deeply concerned about particular individuals and fully involved in what they are doing, his will is bigger than they are. People come and go, but God's purposes remain unchanged.

The fact that he was in prison may also explain why Paul put an unusual emphasis on the promise of 'the life in Christ Jesus'. The construction here is quite specific. It is not simply the promise of life in general, which might be taken to mean that Paul expected to be set free, but of the particular kind of life that only Jesus Christ can bring. A prisoner might always hope for release, but if Paul had ever thought like that, he no longer did so. He expected to lose his physical life in the foreseeable future (as he would have done eventually, even if he had been set free), but in spite of that he held on to the promise of eternal life in Christ. That promise was available to all who believe and was not unique to him because he was an apostle, but it is noteworthy that Paul saw his calling in that context. It was because the promise was made to all mankind, and because God had determined that it would be preached to the Gentiles by specially commissioned representatives, that Paul had been called to be an apostle in the first place. The will of God for him in particular was situated within the promise made to believers in general, and it was in that broader context that his evangelistic mission had to be understood and interpreted.

In addressing the letter to Timothy, Paul repeated much of the phraseology he had used in the first Epistle, but with the difference that whereas earlier he had referred to the younger man as a 'true child in the faith', here he said only that Timothy was his 'beloved child'. Too much should not be made of this, though his greeting is undoubtedly less specific – after all, neither Paul nor Timothy had to be a Christian for the one to refer to the other as 'beloved'. It may be, of course, that there is an added dimension here. Timothy was not merely loved by Paul; he was also loved by God in Christ, and Paul's love for him was grounded in that deeper relationship which they both shared. Given the context and the nature of the case, it is unwise to make a distinction between these two superficially different loves. The one is the reflection and result of the other, and if Paul stood *in loco parentis* to Timothy, it was only because their heavenly Father had placed him in that role. The two men were connected by their faith and calling in Christ, not by any blood relationship, but God's purpose in bringing them together was stronger and of greater long-term significance for the church than any physical descent would have been. Ambrosiaster caught this dimension well when he wrote,

The best servants are those who by their own faith and initiative increase the possessions of their masters. Paul writes to Timothy as to his most beloved son, so that he may be an imitator of these things and hand them on to others, so that through his agency Timothy may be a good and faithful teacher, who will preach the truth and win many to the promised life.[5]

John Chrysostom was more personal still:

> where love does not arise from nature, it must arise from the merit of the object. Those who are born of us, are loved not only on account of their virtue, but from the force of nature; but when those who are of the faith are beloved, it is on account of nothing but their merit, for what else can it be?[6]

Medieval and modern commentators naturally recognize the nature of Paul's relationship with Timothy, but for whatever reason, none seems to capture its personal dimension to the degree that the ancients did.

## 3-5. Personal testimony

> *3. I am grateful to God – whom I worship with a clear conscience, as my ancestors did – when I remember you constantly in my prayers night and day. 4. Recalling your tears, I long to see you so that I may be filled with joy. 5. I am reminded of your sincere faith, a faith that lived first in your grandmother Lois and your mother Eunice and now, I am sure, lives in you.*

In his first Epistle, Paul moved on from the initial greeting to talk about Timothy's commission to act as his deputy when he was away from Ephesus. In this Epistle however, both his tone and his approach were different. He said nothing about either his commission or Timothy's, but focused entirely on the younger man's spiritual inheritance and gift. First of all, he thanked God as he remembered Timothy without interruption (*adialeiptōs*) night and day in his prayers, and reminded him that he worshipped with a clear conscience just as his pious ancestors had done. Given that elsewhere Paul told his churches how he broke with his inherited tradition when he turned to Christ,

---

[5] Ambrosiaster (2009), p. 142.
[6] John Chrysostom, *Homilies on 2 Timothy*, 1.1 (NPNF 13, p. 476).

this confession is remarkable.[7] Paul knew that his own family had always been devoted to the service of God, as he too had been before he became a Christian. It had been that very devotion that drove him to persecute the church, because he sincerely believed that the Christians had perverted the Mosaic inheritance which he was determined to promote and safeguard.

What is particularly interesting here is that Paul honoured this pre-Christian inheritance, not because his ancestors were actively looking for the coming of the Messiah – we do not know whether they were or not – but because they worshipped the true God with a clear conscience, just as he himself had always done. They followed the light that had been given to them, and he was grateful for their example. This testimony is especially precious because it is the only evidence we have of Paul's upbringing. Whether he got his personal devoutness from his parents is unclear. Perhaps they had brought him up in strict observance of the law, but it may also be that he had reacted to their relative liberalism and had chosen a more orthodox path, reaching back into his family's more distant past for affirmation. Whatever the truth, it is only here, where he spoke about Timothy's background, that he said anything about his own family, and the vagueness of his remarks is telling. We know that Paul had Christian relatives, but they seem to have been fairly distant.[8] Of his immediate family we know nothing and can only presume that they did not profess faith in Christ as he had done, even though he seems to have spent several years with them in Tarsus following his conversion.[9]

Paul's Greek is strangely Latinate. This may have been the result of his incarceration in Rome, where his language may have been influenced by the dominant tongue. For example, he wrote *charin echō* for 'I thank', instead of *eucharistō* which he normally employed elsewhere. *Charin echō* is calqued on the Latin *gratias ago* ('I give thanks'), which is the standard way of saying 'I thank' in that language. There may also be a Latin influence behind his use of the conjunction *hōs*, which sounds very much as if it is equivalent to the Latin *ut* in this particular sentence. It is not necessary to suppose that Paul knew Latin to the extent that his Greek was subject to interference from that language.[10] That may have been the case, but there was a considerable amount

---

[7] Cf. Phil. 3.5-6. It may be remembered that Philippians was also a prison epistle and may have been written not too long before this one. At the same time, Paul never renounced his Jewish inheritance or denied its significance. See Acts 26.4-21; Rom. 9.1-5; 11.1; 2 Cor. 3.4-5;11.22.
[8] Rom. 16.7, 11.
[9] Cf. Acts 9.30. The chronology is uncertain.
[10] We know that he was bilingual in Aramaic and Greek and perhaps Aramaic was his mother tongue (see Acts 26.14). As a student in Jerusalem he must have been proficient in Hebrew but we do not know whether he had any knowledge of Latin, in spite of the fact that he was born a Roman citizen.

of bilingualism in the circles in which he moved, and the two languages were sufficiently similar for influences of this kind to manifest themselves.[11] These apparent Latinisms have been used to support the theory of pseudepigraphy on the ground that the 'real Paul' would not have spoken in that way, but as is usually the case with such evidence, the opposite can also be claimed, since a pseudepigrapher would probably have tried to make himself sound as much like Paul as possible. The simplest solution is to say that this is Paul's authentic voice, speaking the street language of his time and unconcerned about the niceties of formal grammar.

Some modern commentators have made heavy weather out of the apparent aimlessness of Paul's thanksgiving. What, they ask, was Paul giving thanks for, and why?[12] The sentence is undoubtedly convoluted and rambling, but it is clear from reading it carefully that Paul was thanking God for Timothy's loyalty and faithfulness, not only to him personally but (more importantly) to the cause of the gospel that they both served. It emerges from this passage that Paul placed a high value on steadfastness, even apart from the gospel message. His ancestors had kept their faith without knowing how it would be fulfilled in Christ, and Timothy came from a similar background. Both men were following in the footsteps of those who had gone before, and this was a good thing, even though the coming of Christ had in some ways radically affected the content of the faith they were professing.[13] Continuity of intention and purpose was what mattered most, and in that respect Paul and Timothy were cut from the same cloth.[14]

Paul longed to see Timothy because he remembered the young man's tears, and said that when his desire was realized he would be filled with joy. The longing to reconnect with an old colleague and friend is natural, and it is easy to imagine why Paul would have been happy to do so. What we do not know is when and why Timothy had shed tears for him. It was probably at their last parting, but when had that been, and in what context?[15] It was

---

[11] Compare the popular American use of a phrase like 'much different', which appears to be influenced by Spanish '*mucho diferente*', in sentences where English-speakers would normally say 'very different' instead.

[12] On this subject, see the discussion of Towner (2006), pp. 45–447, who sensibly concludes that the problem lies in the difficulty of translating the complex Greek syntax and not in the substance of what Paul was trying to say. At the same time, most commentators note that Paul's opening thanksgiving is closer to what we find in his other letters than it is to 1 Timothy or Titus.

[13] Johnson (2001), p. 340, stresses this point.

[14] The importance of ancestral faithfulness among the Jews was reinforced by Heb. 11.1-40, which sets out very clearly and at great length how this was perceived and honoured by the early Christians.

[15] See Marshall (2004), p. 693, who says the same thing but recognizes that we cannot say when they had last seen each other or where.

normal for ancient people to express emotion when saying farewell to one another, not least because long-distance contact was difficult and the hazards of travel meant that there was a real chance that people would not see one another again. Even today, similar scenes are common, especially when emigrants leave their native countries for new homes on the other side of the world and are unlikely to return, so we can hardly say that the phenomenon was rare or unexpected. But why had a fairly common occurrence made such a deep impression on Paul? Timothy's tears in this case seem to have been an indication of something deeper than the usual parting emotions, but Paul has not told us what that was.

Most probably it had something to do with the quality of Timothy's faith and the close fellowship which the two men had enjoyed when they were working together. Certainly it was Timothy's faith that sprang to mind when Paul thought of him, and it is interesting to note that he linked it directly to the faithful witness of his mother Eunice and of his grandmother Lois. How Lois had become a Christian is unknown, but it cannot have been long before Timothy's birth, if indeed it went that far back. Lois must have been among the very first Christians, but we know no more than that. Her husband was probably Jewish because her daughter was, but when Eunice was converted is unknown. Did she become a believer shortly after her mother? Women married and had children young, so Lois could easily have been a grandmother before she was forty. It seems likely that Eunice was also a Christian by the time Timothy was born, which must have been sometime in the mid-30s, only a few years after the death and resurrection of Jesus. The time frame here is extremely short, but Paul's remarks remind us of just how little we know about the early church. Lois may even have been one of those who professed Christ on the day of Pentecost and then returned home to her city of Lystra.[16] She would probably not have been able to share her faith in the synagogue, because she was a woman, but there was nothing to stop her from doing so at home.

What is important about this inheritance is that Timothy owed so much to the faith of his mother and grandmother. Of course they could not have forced him to become a Christian, and given that his father almost certainly was not, other influences were not absent from his life. Eunice

---

[16] There is always the possibility that Lois and Eunice were pious Jews, not Christians (at least not before Paul's mission to Lystra), which is what Calvin (1964), p. 292, thought. In that case, there would be no problem with the chronology, and the women's faithfulness would tie in with Paul's mention of his own forbears, who were certainly not Christians. See Marshall (2004), pp. 694–5, who discusses this but concludes that the narrative adopted in this commentary is the more likely scenario.

sounds like the kind of woman whom Paul mentioned in 1 Corinthians 7, who sanctified her unbelieving husband and her children by her faith.[17] Whatever Timothy's father was like, he clearly did not interfere in his wife's religious education of her son. We are reminded very much of the young Augustine (354–430), who was taught Christianity by his mother Monica, despite his pagan father, though of course the overall situation was very different then. Augustine grew up in a world where Christianity was the rising force, and his father eventually succumbed to its persuasive power, but that was certainly not the case in Timothy's day. Timothy's mother did not teach him to follow the growing (and soon to be official) religion, but neither did the young man rebel against her and go his own way, as Augustine did for so many years. In a very real sense, Eunice was counter-cultural, and Timothy seems to have responded to that, apparently quite willingly. Whatever the case, Timothy was not a dramatic convert in the way that Paul was (or that Augustine would be), and we might almost say that he was brought up in a Christian family without any prehistory of paganism.

Paul's emphasis on personal and family relationships as contributory to the faith and commitment seen in Timothy (and indeed in himself) strikes a note that is not always heard in our modern individualistic society. As P. H. Towner notes,

> Loyalty or faith in modern Western culture often operates more on the intellectual than the interpersonal level, and this puts us at a disadvantage when we seek to understand a passage like this. It boils down to this: authentic faith in God requires more from us than simply adherence to doctrinal ideas.[18]

### 6-8. Timothy's spiritual gift

> 6. *For this reason, I remind you to rekindle the gift of God that is within you through the laying on of my hands; 7. for God did not give us a spirit of cowardice, but rather a spirit of power and of love and of self-discipline. 8. Do not be ashamed then, of the testimony about our Lord or of me his prisoner, but join with me in suffering for the gospel, relying on the power of God.*

---

[17] 1 Cor. 7.14.
[18] Towner (2006), p. 455.

Paul's reason for recalling Timothy's inheritance of faith, and the sincerity with which he had embraced it was to encourage him to 'rekindle' (*anazōpyrein*) the gift (*charisma*) of God which he had received by the laying on of Paul's hands. The ritual of the laying on of hands is a familiar one and it served many purposes, so we should not be surprised to find Paul mentioning it as the source of Timothy's gift and calling to serve God. What is striking though, are the differences between what he said to Timothy in this letter and what he wrote in his first Epistle. There Paul had said that although Timothy's gift had been recognized by the laying on of hands of the entire eldership, it had originated in prophecy, which the ritual merely confirmed.[19] In this Epistle however, Paul spoke of having laid hands on Timothy himself, said nothing about the eldership and did not mention prophecy. Less strikingly different, but also noteworthy, is the fact that in the first Epistle he had told Timothy not to neglect his gift, whereas in this one he told him to rekindle it, which suggests that it had somehow faded. What are we to make of this?

In principle there need not be any contradiction between the laying on of hands by the eldership and the laying on of hands by the apostle. It is perfectly possible that Paul was present with the elders on that occasion and that he participated in the event, but whether that is true or not, the intention was presumably the same. Paul's failure to mention prophecy on this occasion may just have been a simple omission without any significance. As an apostle, Paul would not have needed any additional prophecy as his justification, something that would not have been true of the eldership.[20] But at the same time, there is an important distinction between the two accounts of the laying on of hands that probably does make a difference.

The elders laid hands on Timothy in order to commission him for a special task, but it is not clear what that meant for him. Did Timothy become an elder himself? There is no mention of that, and given his youth it seems unlikely. In any case, he did not remain in the congregation at Lystra, so even if they had made him an elder there, it would not have had much effect elsewhere. At the same time, the elders could hardly have given him an authority greater than their own. It is possible that they gave him a *lesser* authority, but if that was the case it must have been superseded at a later stage, because Paul had left Timothy in charge of the elders at Ephesus. It is hard to believe that they would have accepted his authority if it was based on something less than what Paul was claiming for him, and we might have expected the apostle to refer to a subsequent (and higher) commissioning. That he did not do so must make

---

[19] 1 Tim. 4.14.
[20] See, for example, Eph. 2.20, where the apostles and prophets are classed together as foundational to the church.

us suppose that the elders' laying on of hands was a recognition of Timothy's equality with them, even if it did not mean that he was automatically enrolled in the local eldership.

But when Paul spoke of his own laying on of hands, it was something different. He may have considered himself one of the elders, but he was also an apostle. In laying hands on Timothy, he was commissioning the younger man to a ministry that was not identical to his own but 'inferior', in the sense that it was more limited, but was not the same as that of an elder either. As far as we can tell, Paul was not ordaining Timothy as either an elder or an *episkopos* (if that was something different), but rather setting him apart for a special mission that stood somewhere between his own and that of the eldership in general. What this was, and how it should be described, is hard to say. It might appear that Paul was making Timothy a 'bishop' in the modern sense, giving him authority over the elders (presbyters), but this is unlikely because Timothy was also charged with the duty of appointing the *episkopos*, whether he was a presbyter like the others or not. Timothy might be described as an 'apostolic delegate', which is certainly how he functioned in the Ephesian church, but if so, his commission was a temporary one, limited to the period of Paul's absence. What we find here though seems to be something more permanent. Paul's laying on of hands was not an occasional assignment to a specific task, but a permanent appointment which involved receiving a special *charisma* from God. If that was the case, as it appears to have been, the gift and calling of God were irrevocable,[21] so it would not have been limited to a particular mission in the way that a temporary delegation was.

This leaves us with the problem of trying to decide how best to describe Timothy's ministerial commission. He occupied a rung on the ecclesiastical hierarchy that seems to have been unique to him – somewhere below the apostles but above anyone else in the church. In this respect he does not seem to have had any successors, and perhaps he could not have had any. If his role depended on a direct apostolic commission, the disappearance of the apostles would have made future appointments to that 'office' (to use an anachronistic term) impossible. The category of ministry to which Timothy apparently belonged would have died out with him and his colleagues. For that reason, if for no other, it seems inappropriate to use this example of laying on of hands as a prototype of the so-called 'apostolic succession' in the ministry of the church, which it clearly was not.

When Paul told Timothy to 'rekindle' his gift, what did he mean? It is possible that Timothy was only subconsciously aware that he had a divine

---

[21] Rom. 11.29. The context is different but the principle surely applies in both cases.

gift and that he may have neglected it at times, causing it to atrophy in some way. Whether a spiritual presence could be diminished is a hard question to answer, but it could certainly be ignored. Paul wrote many of his epistles to congregations which were guilty of doing just that, so we cannot rule out the possibility that Timothy may have been in a comparable situation when Paul wrote to him. On the other hand, Paul's warning to Timothy not to 'neglect' his gift does not necessarily mean that he was doing so; it may have been more of a potential danger than a reality. Telling him to 'rekindle' it though does suggest that it may have subsided in some way. Perhaps it was still present but invisible, having been submerged under a weight of responsibility, a fear of persecution or some other impediment. Timothy may have grown weary in well-doing, as sometimes happens to faithful men who labour for many years but see little fruit over the course of time.[22] But it may also be that Paul was afraid that Timothy might be unduly discouraged by the fact that his mentor was in prison and likely to die for his faith in the not too distant future. Paul's fate could easily have been a major blow to Timothy's self-confidence, and Paul wanted to guard against that. By telling him to 'keep calm and carry on', as we might say today, he was guarding against that eventuality which, if it were to materialize, would harm not only Timothy but Paul's ministry as well.

We do not know what caused Paul to speak in the way he did, but it is a reminder to us that spiritual gifts cannot be taken for granted. Those who have received them are under an obligation to take them seriously and exercise them for the edification of the church. Failure to do so may not remove the gift, but it will obscure it and render it ineffective for the purpose for which it was given, which in practical terms is almost as bad as losing it altogether.

What Paul had in mind seems to be explained by what he said next. He told Timothy that God has not given us a spirit of fear (*deilia*), but one of power, love and 'self-discipline' (*sōphronismos*), another polyvalent Greek word which might also be translated as 'discernment'. From this, it appears that Timothy had a tendency to hold back from exercising the authority given to him, and even to run away from his responsibilities, out of fear as to what might happen to him if he stuck his neck out. To what extent Timothy was prone to this must remain uncertain, but Paul's remark is applicable to any number of people in similar situations and it would hardly be surprising if Timothy was among them. It is not enough to give someone authority; the person who receives it must know how to use it and not be afraid to do so when the need arises. Fear is a very potent deterrent, especially when there

---

[22] See Gal. 6.9.

are good reasons for it, and Timothy's youth may have made him particularly sensitive on this point.

Unfortunately, history shows us that failure to exercise authority at the right time often means that a worse situation develops and that the latter state is worse than the first. Would a world war have broken out in 1939 if the Western powers had acted earlier to contain the rise of Adolf Hitler in Germany? Most historians think that it would have been better to have intervened sooner, but at the time those with the ability (and responsibility) to do so were afraid of unleashing a bloodbath similar to the one they had been through in 1914–18 and preferred 'peace at any price'. In the end, as we know, world war is what they got, along with the senseless murder of millions of innocent Jews and others. Of course the scale of that disaster was exceptional and unlikely to be repeated very often, but minor versions of the same scenario can occur in churches today, just as they occurred in Timothy's time. A reluctance on the part of the leadership to grapple with heresy, or with some other problem in the congregation, is often the cause of greater trouble later on, but those whose duty it is to act usually claim, with some justification, that to do what is necessary would provoke division and perhaps even destroy the work that has been established. To say, as we often can with the virtue of hindsight, that this would have happened anyhow is cold comfort after the event, but Paul understood what the stakes were and did not hesitate to counsel Timothy against temporizing when action was needed.

As he often did, Paul used a triadic formula to describe the nature of the 'spirit' which had been given to Timothy and by extension has been bestowed on every Christian. He did not explicitly say that this is the Holy Spirit, but it is hard to see what else the word could refer to in this context and virtually all commentators accept that interpretation. The 'spirit of fear' is presumably an attitude of heart and mind rather than a demon; what Paul is really saying is that the Spirit given to us is not one of fear, so we should not read the text as if there were somehow two different spirits in contention. There is only one Spirit, and it is his nature and activity that is the subject of Paul's remarks here.

The Spirit who has been given to us is one of power (*dynamis*), love (*agapē*) and 'self-discipline' or 'discernment' (*sōphronismos*), three qualities that follow one another in logical sequence. First of all, the Spirit is one of 'power'. The Greek word *dynamis* which is used here must be distinguished from its apparent synonym *energeia*, which is 'power' in a different sense. *Dynamis* is more precisely what we would call 'potential', whereas *energeia* is 'realized potential' or 'energy'. The difference this makes can be seen when we consider that God has *energeia* but not *dynamis*, because in his perfect being his potential is fully realized. But when he is at work in the lives of believers, the power that is perfect in him is necessarily potential in us. God's Spirit gives us the ability to act but his presence in our lives is not by itself the fulfillment of that action. He comes into our hearts not simply to be there but to do things in and through us.[23] This is not to deny the importance of contemplation in the Christian life, or of waiting on God to show us the way ahead. We must know who the Spirit is before we consider what he does, since the latter depends on the former, but we must not fall back into a form of quietism that uses the indwelling presence of the Spirit as an excuse for not doing anything at all. If he is truly present in our lives he will be active both in transforming us, and in using us to transform the world around us.

The power of God is manifested supremely in and through love, which is why Paul puts it next in the list. It is not possible to show the love of God to others if we have not received it ourselves, and we cannot experience that love unless his power is at work in our lives. Paul does not elaborate on the objects of our love, though they obviously exist – we love God, we love other people and we love the things that God has given us. This love will manifest itself in different ways according to the nature of the recipient(s), but its guiding spiritual principle is the same. Love must be exercised with discernment, which is why that is the third quality that Paul mentions as a gift of the Holy Spirit. It requires real wisdom to know when and how to show love, and in ministering to a congregation this gift is essential.

Paul therefore encouraged Timothy not to be embarrassed by the witness of our Lord, or by the fact that he was a prisoner for Christ's sake. Once again, we cannot know for sure whether Timothy actually was embarrassed by this, or whether Paul was using him as an example in order to encourage others to stand up and be counted. Most probably Paul's appeal here was a general one, expressed in the first instance to Timothy but applicable by extension to everyone in the church.

The phrase 'the witness of our Lord' (*to martyrion tou Kyriou hēmōn*) is potentially ambiguous and has been interpreted in different ways. The NRSV and the ESV both translate it as 'the testimony about our Lord', leaving it unclear as to whose testimony it is.[24] More probably, given what follows, the phrase refers to the witness of Jesus himself in his suffering and death. By learning obedience to death on the cross, Jesus witnessed a good confession and set an example for believers to follow.[25] They were to take up their cross

---

[23] Gal. 4.6; Rom. 8.26-27.
[24] The NIV paraphrases slightly but says much the same thing.
[25] Phil. 2.8; Heb. 5.8.

and follow him, which is essentially what Paul had done and why he was now in prison.[26] Timothy was invited to share in their suffering (*synkakopathomai*) for the gospel, 'according to the power of God' (*kata dynamin Theou*), a phrase which points us back to what Paul had just said about the nature of the Spirit who has been given to us. The *dynamis Theou* is not the power inherent in the divine being but the inner strength of purpose that he communicates to us, making it possible for our lives to bear witness to his glory. If God is at work in us, we shall have the strength to partake of Christ's sufferings. Paul believed that he had been given the grace to fulfil in his body the sufferings of the Lord Jesus, and this is almost certainly what he is inviting Timothy to share in.[27] Suffering for Christ is not a burden to bear but a joy and a privilege to be enjoyed by those who are called to follow him. P. H. Towner puts it well when he writes,

> The presence of the Spirit of power provides a guarantee of the strength, endurance, and courage needed to face the situation ... it is the very presence of the Spirit in the life of the community and the observable characteristics of the life he produces in God's people that promises suffering. What the Spirit provides is power to endure the stress that comes from bearing witness to God, not removal to some safe place.[28]

## 9-10. God's eternal purpose in Christ

*9. Who saved us and called us with a holy calling, not according to our works but according to his own purpose and grace. This grace was given to us in Christ Jesus before the ages began, 10. but it has now been revealed through the appearing of our Saviour Christ Jesus, who abolished death and brought life and immortality to light through the gospel.*

Having stated the principle that union with Christ involved sharing in his suffering, Paul went on to elaborate on it by a series of comparisons and contrasts that illustrate what God has done and is doing for his people. These can be set out as follows:

---

[26] Mt. 16.24; Lk. 9.23. See also Phil. 2.5-11.
[27] Col. 1.24.
[28] Towner (2006), p. 466.

| | |
|---|---|
| He has saved us | He has called us with a holy calling |
| Not according to our works | According to his own purpose and grace |
| Given to us in Christ Jesus before all ages | Now manifested to us by his appearing |
| Abolishing death | Bringing life and immortality through the gospel |

These principles can be read from left to right (as they are presented in the epistle itself) and also from top to bottom. The four pairs go together and follow one another in a logical sequence, which suggests that they were intended to be memorized as such.

The first pair asserts that God has saved us and called us with a holy calling. The two things belong together and reflect the order in which we experience them. The Christian first comes to a knowledge of salvation and then to a realization that he has been called by God. Later on, as his understanding grows, he comes to see that from God's perspective the order is reversed. We have to be saved before we can appreciate that we have been called, but he called us first and then reached out to us with his saving power. It is a 'holy calling' because not only does it come *from* God but it points *to* God as well. We have been called by the Holy One so that we too may become holy.[29] To be saved is to be rescued from the sins of this world, but it is also to be transformed into the likeness of God in Christ. We do not remain what we were before, nor do we return to the state of Adam and Eve in the garden. Our destiny as believers is to be raised to a higher plane, to become like God in so far as that is possible for a finite creature. Holiness is a divine attribute that can be shared with us, and it is God's will, Paul told the Thessalonians, that we should be made holy, just as he is holy.[30]

What does this mean in practice? To be holy as God is holy means above all to think the way he thinks. What we do depends on what our minds tell us, and if our minds are transformed by the presence of God in our lives then we are more likely to act in a way that can be described as 'holy'.[31] Holiness is defined as obedience to the will of God, not as conformity to his nature. We cannot cease to be human, and whatever we think, say or do will be governed

---

[29] Marshall (2004), pp. 704–5, and Towner (2006), p. 468, both note that the phrase 'holy calling' is ambiguous in the Greek, because it can mean either that God's calling is itself holy or that the life we have been called to live must be a holy one. In fact there is no need to choose between these two possibilities, since both are true and the second proceeds naturally from (and is dependent on) the first.
[30] 1 Thess. 4.3.
[31] Rom. 12.2; 1 Cor. 2.14-16.

by the limitations of our created finitude and the legacy of sin that we have inherited from Adam. This is why, even after we have done our best, we are still 'unprofitable servants'.[32] The Pharisees were condemned by Jesus because they imagined that they could be holy by observing the law of Moses. That was not possible. Even if they had succeeded in their attempt, they would not have been truly holy, because their achievement would have been relative to their limited abilities and would not reflect the absolute being of God.[33] For a human being, holiness is only attainable in and through a personal relationship with God that requires salvation from the kind of life that we live here on earth. That will eventually be obtained by our death and resurrection to a new life. In the meantime we enjoy the 'first-fruits' of the Spirit, whose presence in our hearts makes it possible for us to think God's thoughts and act in a way that reflects them, in spite of our finite nature and inherent sinfulness.

The holiness to which we have been summoned is in no sense the fruit of our own works. There is nothing that we can do in and of ourselves to get closer to God, because by nature we are not like him. Even Adam and Eve in the garden, before they fell, could not have risen above what they were created to be. Indeed, it was the suggestion that they could become like God that constituted Satan's temptation, and caused them to fall away from the relationship that God had intended them to have with him.[34] What Paul meant by 'works' is unclear, but it does not really matter. Whether he was talking about obedience to the law of Moses, or about something broader than that – our behaviour in general, for example – the limits of our ability to do God's will remain the same. We are called to do good works of all kinds; Paul's denial of their value expresses their inability to save us but does not detract from their desirability in themselves. The good works of a Christian are an important manifestation of God's saving power at work, but they do not contribute to the outpouring of that power and are certainly no substitute for it.

Our salvation is worked out 'according to his own purpose and grace' (*kata tēn idian prothesin kai charin*), a reminder to us that it conforms to his eternal plan and is put into effect as he chooses. The *prothesis* is what he has laid down in advance. As Paul said to the Galatians, he had been formed in his mother's womb for the purpose of preaching the gospel, even though there was a time in his early life when he had persecuted the church of God.[35]

---

[32] Lk. 17.10.
[33] Gal. 5.3; Jas 2.10.
[34] Gen. 3.5, 22.
[35] Gal. 1.11-15.

Our salvation belongs to God himself, which means that it reflects his mind and thoughts which are far above ours and often incomprehensible to us.[36] We must not suppose that we can always appreciate what God has in store for us, because he sees things that we cannot see and is preparing us for a life with him that we can only dimly imagine. His purpose may involve suffering; it may even involve a time of rebellion and unbelief, as was the case with Paul himself. But in the end, its logic will be revealed and we shall understand why God has brought us to himself in the way that he has.

It is obvious from the context that Paul was speaking to Christians about their calling by God. He did not mention the fate of unbelievers or suggest that everyone on earth was called. This was typical of his approach to the eternal plan of God for mankind, and we must not extrapolate from what he said here to include the entire human race in his analysis. The calling of God is something that makes sense only to those who have heard and responded to it; others are unaware of it and have no idea what its implications for them might be. Paul placed his emphasis on the eternal plan of God in order to teach us that we have made no contribution to our salvation, which is entirely his doing. Why that eternal plan chooses some and rejects others is a mystery that is apparent from the very beginning of God's self-revelation to Israel, and serves to remind us yet again that whether we live or die, we are entirely in his hands.[37]

God's purpose is revealed by his 'grace' (*charis*), which is the means by which it is worked out and the way we experience it. Grace is a free gift of God that we have done nothing to deserve. It is the spirit in which we have been saved and called to a life of holiness. Without it, neither our salvation nor our sanctification would have been possible. To put it another way, it is the means by which God is working out his plan (*prothesis*) for us, the subjective application of the objective purpose towards which we are headed.

The grace and purpose of God are not an abstraction. They have been embodied in Christ Jesus and given to us 'before all ages' (*pro chronōn aiōniōn*). This is an extraordinary statement that needs to be analysed closely in order to appreciate its full significance. First of all, Paul says 'Christ Jesus' and not the Son of God. This can only mean that God's eternal purpose included the incarnation of the Son from the very beginning. The whole history of Israel was a preparation for his coming, prophesied as far back as Abraham, who 'rejoiced to see his day', as Jesus himself put it.[38] The incarnation of the Son in Christ had been planned 'before all ages', a phrase

---

[36] Isa. 55. 8-9.
[37] Mal. 1.3, quoted by Paul in Rom. 9.13. See also Rom. 14.8.
[38] Jn 8.56.

that attempts to translate something that is literally untranslatable. The Greek says 'before times eternal', which is a contradiction in terms. Time cannot be eternal; the two things are by definition incompatible. Later on, this phrase would be incorporated into the Nicene Creed as 'eternally begotten', another paradoxical statement that was needed in order to do justice to the reality of God's self-revelation. The possibility that Paul might have been speaking about infinitely extended time is ruled out by the preposition 'before'; if time were never-ending it would also be never-beginning, and so there could have been no such thing as 'before' it.

The use of a logically incoherent phrase like this one draws our attention to the limitations imposed by our human finitude. We have to think in time and space categories, even when we are talking about God, because our minds were designed to function within them and cannot transcend them in a consistent or sustained manner. Some people object that because of this, all talk of eternity must be meaningless because there is no reference point in time by which it can be measured, but although that is true, it does not rule out the possibility of our relating to the world of eternity. The reason for that is the fact that we have been created in the image and likeness of God.[39] There is something about us that is not bound by the time and space dimension, even if it is naturally manifested in it. The reality of this is expressed in our language by the use of the present tense in the verb. Strictly speaking, there is no such thing as the 'present' – only the past and the future. But in spite of this, we have a concept of the 'present' that we impose on time in order to define it as either 'past' or 'future' and this concept is a reflection of the image of God in us. He is the eternal 'I am' who reveals himself as such in time and can do so because we have the capacity to understand that and relate to him accordingly.[40]

The so-called 'present' is the indispensable concept by which we measure time, yet it is not itself a temporal reality. It is an idea in our minds that determines our self-consciousness, but in reality it functions outside time. We always live in our 'present' but it moves through time from the past into the future. The context in which it expresses itself changes, but it remains the same from the moment we are born until we die. God, who was not born and who does not die, is always present – *today* is the day of salvation.[41] This is why Paul said 'now' and not 'a generation ago', which would have been more accurate in purely temporal terms. Jesus Christ is the same, yesterday, today and for ever, so that what is revealed to us now is what has always been

---

[39] Gen. 1.26-27.
[40] Exod. 3.14-15.
[41] 2 Cor. 6.2.

and always will be.⁴² He is the one who is, who was and who is to come, the Almighty.⁴³ This is the mental universe in which Paul was operating when he said that the eternal plan of God has 'now' been manifested to us by Christ's appearing on earth. The use of 'now' is a reminder that God uses the present tense to express eternal realities. As Jesus put it, 'Before Abraham was, I am.'⁴⁴

Though he was unable to find words to express it adequately, Paul was undoubtedly saying that the plan of God for the salvation of his people was known in eternity long before it was revealed in time and space. Just as remarkably, it was 'given' to us in eternity as well. Before we ever existed in earthly terms we were known to God, and had received the blessing of eternal life in Christ.⁴⁵ It is impossible for human minds to grasp this fully, because we are limited to the time and space framework and cannot think beyond it. We have no words that are adequate to express this truth, though we can affirm it as part of our faith in Jesus Christ, who has revealed it to us. In the ancient world there were pagans who criticized Christians for what they perceived as the 'novelty' of their faith. How could something be true, they asked, if it had not been known all along? Theodore of Mopsuestia saw Paul's statement here as an answer to that question:

> if by the outward fulfillment of its affairs the gospel is perceived to be new, yet by the decision of its giver it is ancient. For God had long ago given his approval that these things should be done in Christ; therefore, when Christ himself has now appeared to us, he has brought the gospel forth in actual deed.⁴⁶

Theodoret of Cyrrhus (Cyrus) went even further, seeing in this text proof that the Father and Son worked together from the beginning in order to further our salvation:

> while the God of all determined these things even before the ages, he now puts into effect what had been determined. In planning them he had Christ the Lord to concur with him, and in effecting them he had him as collaborator: through his coming he brought the work to completion. Now, in this he clearly brought out as well the eternity of the Son.⁴⁷

---

⁴² Heb. 13.8.
⁴³ Rev. 1.8.
⁴⁴ Jn 8.58.
⁴⁵ See Rev. 13.8.
⁴⁶ Theodore of Mopsuestia (2010), p. 695.
⁴⁷ Theodoret of Cyrrhus (Cyrus) (2001), p. 238.

The coming of the Son of God into the world as Jesus Christ has brought about the abolition of the power of death. The meaning of the word 'death' in Scripture is complex, and this is a good example of how hard it can be to interpret it correctly. The Biblical picture is that death came into the world when Adam and Eve sinned.[48] Does this mean that human beings were immortal until that time? No. When the angels sinned they did not die, because they were immortal by nature. Had that not been the case, Satan and his demons (as we call the angels who fell with him) would not now exist. Adam and Eve, on the other hand, were always mortal, and physical death was part of the original creation. That was necessary, partly because some animals only survive by eating others, and partly because if our first parents had fulfilled the divine command to be fruitful and multiply but had not died, the world would have been hugely overpopulated a long time ago. It makes no sense to argue that human beings would simply have gone on for ever – when would they have stopped growing? What would the state of their unending life have been like? We cannot answer such questions, but it seems most probable that Adam and Eve would eventually have passed out of this world, whether by physical death or by some kind of bodily assumption into heaven, similar to that recorded of Enoch and Elijah.[49]

Furthermore, when Adam and Eve fell and were driven out of the garden of Eden, they did not die physically, but were condemned to reap the consequences of their mortality, because the protection which they had enjoyed in the garden was removed.[50] They were dead spiritually because they were cut off from God and enslaved to Satan, but their physical death seems to have followed the course of nature and was not an immediate punishment for their sin. Similarly, when people become Christians today they inherit eternal life but they still have to die a physical death, and Paul reminded the Corinthians that 'flesh and blood cannot inherit the kingdom of God'.[51] He saw himself as crucified with Christ and dead to sin, but nevertheless alive, not in his own strength but in the life of Christ which had been given to him.[52] He did not worry about what might happen to his physical body, because spiritually he was alive for ever in Christ.[53]

This must be what Paul meant here. Christ has abolished death, not because we are now going to live for ever in this world, but because spiritually

---

[48] Rom. 5.12.
[49] Gen. 5.24; 2 Kgs 2.11-12.
[50] Gen. 3.16-19.
[51] 1 Cor. 15.50.
[52] Gal. 2.20.
[53] Phil. 1.19-22.

speaking we have already died with him and been born again to a new and eternal life. This is why he said that Christ brought life and immortality – the two things go together. The Greek word translated 'bring' literally means 'lighten' (*phōtizō*) and has no exact equivalent in most other languages. It can only be understood by equating death with darkness and life with light. By the coming of Christ, we have been delivered from the darkness of death and ushered into the light of eternal life. Light represents the being and dwelling place of God.[54] It is a world in which there are no secrets and no hidden dangers. Everything is clear, everything is right and everything shines with the glory that reflects the presence of God himself. What Paul meant by 'immortality' was *aphtharsia* ('indestructibility') rather than *athanasia*, though he used that word elsewhere.[55] Indestructibility emphasizes not only ongoing life but ongoing strength as well. We might imagine living for ever in some weakened state, not unlike old age here on earth. But God's gift of immortality is not weakness but power, and it will thrive in its fullness in his eternal kingdom.

The means by which God achieves this is the gospel. That is the key to everything and the reason why preaching its message must always be central to the identity of the Christian church. Without it there can be no life because without it there is no light. The gospel is the light that gives life. It diagnoses what is wrong with us, indicates how that can be corrected and establishes us on a new footing with Almighty God. The gospel is the answer to the human dilemma in a way that nothing else is or can be. Furthermore, the gospel was God's eternal plan, manifested in time and space by the coming of Christ but by no means confined to that temporal revelation. As John Calvin eloquently expressed it,

> God has called us through the gospel, not because he has suddenly taken thought for our salvation but because he had so determined from all eternity. Christ has appeared for that salvation now, not because the power to save has but recently been conferred upon him, but because this grace was laid up for us in him before the creation of the world. The knowledge of these things has been revealed to us by faith. In this way the apostle wisely connects the gospel with God's most ancient promises, so that its supposed novelty might not bring it into contempt.[56]

---

[54] 1 Jn 1.5-7.
[55] 1 Cor. 15.53-54.
[56] Calvin (1964), p. 297.

Paul did not go into the question of how much the men and women of the Old Testament knew about the coming salvation in Christ, but it is clear from other New Testament passages, and in particular from the Epistle to the Hebrews, that they knew that God would one day fulfil his promises to them and therefore had at least some understanding of what was to come.

Paul naturally assumed that Timothy knew what the gospel was, and that the members of the church understood it also. It was the good news of eternal salvation in Christ, and in mentioning it here Paul was taking his readers back to the fundamental principle that underlies the very existence of the church. Christians are those people who have been redeemed by the coming of the Son of God into the world in order to abolish death and give us the gift of eternal life. He did not put any emphasis on the sacrifice for sin by which Christ made atonement for us on the cross, though he obviously knew all about that and did not hesitate to stress its central importance elsewhere.[57] Why did he leave it out here? It is dangerous to argue from silence, but perhaps he omitted it because he wanted to focus on the truly miraculous dimension of the saving work of Christ. Dying to pay the price of sin was something only he could have done efficaciously, but it was not miraculous in the way that coming back from the dead was. The Christian experience is not just the good news that our sins have been paid for, important as that is, but also the promise of new life. It is by the way in which that new life works out in us that we know the truth of the message that the apostles proclaimed and that we continue to share with the world to this day. It is the confirmation of the reality of our salvation and the test that we must apply to determine whether we have really been called by God. If Christ has not risen from the dead then nothing has changed and our preaching is in vain.[58] This is the gospel that makes the difference, and it is those who have experienced that difference who make up the church that Paul was writing to and that Timothy had been called to pastor.

## 11-14. Paul's confession and example

*11. For this gospel I was appointed a herald and an apostle and a teacher, 12. and for this reason I suffer as I do. But I am not ashamed, for I know the one in whom I have put my trust, and I am sure that he is able to guard until that day what I have entrusted to him. 13. Hold to the standard of*

---

[57] 1 Cor. 1.23; 2.2.
[58] 1 Cor. 15.14-17.

*sound teaching that you have heard from me, in the faith and love that are in Christ Jesus. 14. Guard the good treasure entrusted to you, with the help of the Holy Spirit living in us.*

When he turned to the exposition of the gospel, Paul recalled that he had been appointed as its herald (*kēryx*), messenger (*apostolos*) and teacher (*didaskalos*). Here we meet the same triad, presented in the same order as the one that is found in 1 Tim. 2.7. Given that there are many differences between the two Epistles, the repetition of this key phrase takes on special importance because it was obviously central to Paul's conception of his own ministry. First of all, he had been chosen to preach and proclaim the gospel. Second, he had been sent to spread it as far and wide as he could. Finally, he had been appointed to teach it, so that those who had responded to his preaching might be firmly grounded in their faith.

Each of these things is essential and must take place in the order Paul has laid down. Without preaching there is no gospel at all, since faith in it is impossible if has not been heard and received.[59] Without widespread diffusion, the gospel would lose its meaning. Jesus told his disciples to preach the Word to the nations of the world, a command that required the sending out of all those who had been called to proclaim it.[60] Finally, the sowing of the seed required careful tending to ensure that it would grow in the right way and in the right conditions.[61] Paul's ministry embraced all three dimensions but he did not necessarily emphasize them all on every occasion. Usually he preached first, because most of the time he was in a pioneer situation where that was the only option available to him. He also travelled constantly and had a vision for going where no evangelist had been before, though circumstances did not always allow him to fulfil his plans in the way that he had envisaged.[62] Often he left men like Timothy to teach the congregations that he had brought into being, since otherwise his own itinerant ministry would have been impossible, but on at least one memorable occasion he taught a congregation that he had never preached to or even visited.[63] Paul's practice was flexible and often governed by circumstances, but the guiding principles of his ministry remained unchanged throughout his career.

In this Epistle he did more than just repeat the familiar triad by adding to it the explanation that it was because he has been given this mission that he

---

[59] Rom. 10.14-18.
[60] Mt. 28.19; Acts 1.8.
[61] 1 Cor. 3.5-9.
[62] Rom. 15.20; 2 Cor. 1.15-24.
[63] This was the church at Rome to which he wrote his longest epistle.

was suffering 'these things' (*tauta*), by which we are meant to understand his arrest and imprisonment. The underlying message is clear. Paul was suffering, not because he had done anything wrong but because the world hates the message he had been called to bring. The reason for that is that those who are in the grip of Satan will do his bidding, and the devil has no desire to let his captives go free. The good news of liberty in the gospel is not one that he wants to see spread, and the best way to prevent that from happening is to silence those whose calling it is to preach it. Paul did not say all that in this Epistle, perhaps because it would have been dangerous for him to have been so specific. The Roman authorities were reasonably tolerant, but anything that might have been construed as an attack on the imperial regime could have been used against him. At the very least, his letter might have been censored and so a detailed explanation of the spiritual forces at work behind his imprisonment was best avoided. That does not mean that he did not know what was going on behind the scenes though, and we have evidence from his other epistles that he was well acquainted with the struggles that a preacher of the gospel had to face.[64]

Paul understood what the consequences of his mission would be for him personally, and he was not ashamed or embarrassed by that. The reason was that he knew whom he had believed and was persuaded that Christ was able to guard his 'deposit' (*parathēkē*) 'until that day' (*eis ekeinēn tēn hēmeran*).[65] The image was taken from secular life and in that context it is easily understood. Paul's 'deposit' uses the image of a safe deposit box at the bank, and because he trusted its keeper he knew that it would be there when he came to collect it. The task of the reader is to transpose that image onto the relationship that Paul had with God in Christ and to interpret the nature of the 'deposit' accordingly.

First of all, Paul has told us that the relationship he had with Christ was foundational to everything else in his life. He knew whom he had believed, not only in terms of the historical facts of Jesus' life, death and resurrection, but at the level of personal trust and commitment as well. To know Christ in this sense was to trust him and to rely on him to keep his promises. Paul was convinced that Jesus would not abandon him or make him settle for less than he had been promised. Note that the verb 'believe' (*pisteuō*) is in the perfect tense, when the use of the present might seem to be more appropriate. The use of the perfect emphasizes both that his belief began and was established in the past, and that the effects of that belief have continued ever since. In other

---

[64] 2 Cor. 11.23-33; Eph. 6.11-20. See also Mt. 5.11-12.
[65] The phrase picks up on what Paul said to Timothy in 1 Tim. 6.20. See below.

words, Paul professed faith some time ago, and it was at that moment that he received the promises in which he was now trusting. Subsequent experience had confirmed the truth and reliability of his commitment, making it even more significant than it would otherwise have been.

He had also been persuaded (*peithō*) that Christ has the ability to perform what he has promised and to keep his word. Whether this belief came to him at the time of his conversion or grew over time he did not say, but perhaps it does not matter very much. Paul undoubtedly grew in his faith, and his conviction of Christ's reliability must have grown with that. He never seems to have doubted it, which is interesting in itself. Doubt is a problem that many Christians wrestle with. Is that wrong? Was Paul exceptional in this respect, or is his confidence the norm that we should all expect to experience ourselves? When doubts arise, who is responsible for them and how should we deal with them?

Paul did not enter into the complexities of that discussion in these verses. We should not jump to the conclusion that he thought that all forms of doubt were sinful and that Christians should therefore not have them. The problem seems to be that when doubts arise they are usually focused on the self. I wonder whether I am really a Christian, whether I am obeying God, whether I am feeling the power of the Holy Spirit at work in my life and so on. I am looking at myself rather than at God. But if I escape from that trap and look at him instead of at myself, I may see quite a different picture. His death and resurrection have set the seal on my faith for all time. What I cannot do for myself (and that includes believing) he has done for me. Paul's assurance was grounded in objective fact, not in subjective feelings that could easily be ones of failure and abandonment, especially in a prison context. He reminded Timothy of this in order to encourage him and his congregation by setting them an example of how to react when things go wrong.

If his mission had been crowned with honour and success, Paul would have had little to say about this. It was because things had turned out differently that he was forced back onto his basic principles. He had trusted in God to keep him, and in the past God had done so on numerous occasions. Those experiences had grounded him in his faith and convinced him that what had happened before would happen again. At the end of his life he knew that whatever was coming next, God would be with him to guide him and help him overcome whatever danger he might face. Persecution is the lot of every faithful Christian, and it is a measure of Paul's confidence in Timothy that he was prepared to share these details of his own spiritual journey in the expectation that what was happening to him would one day happen to the younger man as well. In the providence of God, Paul's confession of his own faith to Timothy has been preserved for the edification of subsequent generations, who have been called to bear witness to the grace of God in very different circumstances.

The interpretation of this imagery seems to be relatively straightforward and simple, but difficulties arise when we try to interpret the phrase 'to guard my deposit' (*tēn parathēkēn mou phylaxai*).[66] What was Paul talking about? Was his 'deposit' something objective like a suitcase or a sum of money? Obviously not! If it were like that it would have had nothing to do with his salvation, because it would have been no more than an attempt to make his own contribution to the work of Christ. Why would Paul have wanted to leave his own works and reputation in the care of Jesus, and why would Jesus have agreed to guard something that even Paul thought was of no value?[67]

That kind of explanation cannot be right. What Paul committed to Christ was not anything that belonged to him, but the promise of forgiveness and redemption that he had received. In other words, Christ was guarding something that belonged to him already, although it had been extended to Paul by his grace. The treasure that Paul had stored up in heaven was not something that he had earned but something that he had been given. As Paul saw it, Christ was clearly able to protect what was his to begin with, and so he had no difficulty in putting his confidence in him to do what he had promised he would. It was not the content of his teaching nor his faithfulness to his apostolic calling that constituted the 'deposit', but Christ's promise that he would bring to fruition the good work that he had begun in his servant Paul. In other words, Jesus Christ would not let him down in the end, however much his earthy sufferings might lead some people to conclude the opposite. John Calvin hit the nail on the head:

> our salvation is in God's hand, just as a depository holds in his hands the property we entrust to him for safe keeping. If our salvation depended upon ourselves, it would be continually exposed to very many dangers; but being committed to such a guardian it is out of all danger.[68]

---

[66] For the many different ways in which this word has been interpreted, see Marshall (2004), pp. 710–12, who, followed by Towner (2006), pp. 475–6, concludes that most likely Paul was referring to the gospel that he preached. But for the reasons given here, that interpretation seems to be unlikely. Johnson (2001), p. 357, comes closer to the truth when he says that the deposit 'means remaining loyal to the God who has saved them [Paul and Timothy] and called them with a holy calling', but even that puts the emphasis on the work of men rather than on the promises of God, where it belongs.

[67] Phil. 3.8.

[68] Calvin (1964), p. 300.

To return to the image of the 'deposit', Paul said that it would come to maturity on 'that day', which can mean either the day that he died or the day of judgement at the end of time. The latter interpretation fits the context better, but it makes little difference in practice. When a Christian dies he leaves the world of time and space and is taken up into eternity, where the judgement is already given. Paul sometimes talked as though there were an intermediate state between death and the final judgement, and from the human standpoint it must look like that.[69] But he also talked about dying and going to be with Christ, which he assumed would happen immediately and not after centuries of repose in some storage area, waiting for the judgement eventually to come.[70] To those who experience it, death is a transition from one reality to another, from the world of time to the realm of eternity. The judgement that we await in time is already settled in heaven, and Paul knew that when he got there he would be able to claim the inheritance waiting for him. This was his *parathēkē* and that was what he would claim when he stood in front of the judgement seat of Christ.

After discussing his own situation, Paul turned to Timothy and applied the same principles to him. Timothy was commanded to hold onto the blueprint (*hypotypōsis*) of the healing (or saving) words that he had heard from Paul. This was nothing other than the message of the gospel which he had received and understood. It was that pattern of salvation that he must conform to and rely on. By God's provision, Paul had been the herald of the message and Timothy had heard it from him, but the message itself was one and the same. It did not matter to Paul where it came from or who preached it, as long as it was communicated in its fullness and believed by those who had been chosen for salvation. Timothy was not meant to exalt the preacher but the gospel, which came to him as it comes to every believer – as a blueprint or framework for life. Each individual must work out his own salvation, but the underlying pattern is the same for all.[71]

The question inevitably arises as to what constitutes 'holding on' to the pattern of sound words. Does it mean that we should keep the substance of what we have received from Christ and the apostles, but not worry too much about the form in which we express it, or do we have to stick to the actual words found in the Bible and not deviate from them in any way? There is no easy answer to that question. The very fact that we translate the message from the original Greek (not to mention the Aramaic substratum that lies behind it) shows that we are not bound to a fundamentalist literalism. On the other

---

[69] 1 Thess. 4.13-17; 1 Cor. 15.51-55.
[70] Phil. 1.21. See also Rom. 8.38-39.
[71] See Phil. 2.12.

hand, if we try to express what the New Testament teaches in our words, there is a danger that we shall inadvertently omit or distort something. Not infrequently, even keeping the words themselves can be misleading – consider, for example, how 'God is love' can be, and has been, misunderstood and used to support all kinds of beliefs and behaviour that are clearly out of line with the gospel. John Calvin preferred to stick as closely as possible to the actual text, but in a theologically responsible way. His words deserve to be quoted:

> Paul knows how prone men are to rebel and fall away from true doctrine and for this reason he carefully warns Timothy not to depart from the form of teaching which he has received, and to regulate his method of teaching by the rule laid down for him – not that we should be unduly scrupulous over words, but it is exceedingly harmful to corrupt doctrine even in the smallest degree.[72]

According to Paul's testimony, Timothy had accepted the gospel message in faith and in the love which is found only in Christ Jesus. As so often, he coupled faith and love together, and this is natural, because in many ways they are two sides of the same coin. Faith without love would be no more than intellectual assent to a series of doctrines, and not a relationship with God in Christ. Conversely, love without faith would be a feeling with no content, and it is virtually certain that it would be misused in potentially catastrophic ways. The key to understanding what faith and love are, and how they are interconnected, lies in the phrase 'in Christ Jesus'. He is the deciding factor, the object of both our faith and our love. We place our trust in him and love him, because he gives us the strength to do both. To concentrate on him is to put the gospel at the centre of our lives and to interpret faith and love in relation to that.

Verse 14 is somewhat surprising. In it Paul repeated a phrase that he had just used of Christ in v. 12 and applied it to Timothy. 'Guard the good deposit' (*tēn kalēn parathēkēn phylaxon*) was the command that Paul gave to him, even though he had just said that this was what he trusted Jesus to do for him! Some commentators and translators resolve this paradox by translating the phrase differently in the two instances, but they are so close together that it seems impossible to distinguish them from each other in this way. However we understand it, there must be a parallel between what Christ was doing for Paul and what Paul expected Timothy to do for himself. What is it?

---

[72] Calvin (1964), p. 301.

The two verses can be harmonized if we understand *parathēkē* to mean 'inheritance'. Jesus Christ was guarding Paul's inheritance until the time when he would claim it for himself. Paul told Timothy to watch over *his* good inheritance, which was the same promise of eternal life in Christ, but the context was different. What Christ was doing in heaven, Timothy was told to do on earth. There is no contradiction here, because both things are necessary in the Christian life. Our inheritance in heaven can only be guarded by Christ; there is nobody else with the power or the authority to do it. But where earthly things are concerned, we are given the responsibility to look after that same inheritance in the circumstances in which we are placed. In heaven, there is little for Jesus to do except maintain it until we arrive, since there is no way that it can be stolen or disappear. But on earth there is the constant danger that it may be frittered away by negligence or corrupted by false teaching, and so believers must be on their guard. The difference is that between the church triumphant in heaven and the church militant on earth. As long as we are in this life we are engaged in spiritual warfare and the danger that our enemy will try to abscond with our treasure is very real. If he can escape with what is most precious to us there is every likelihood that we shall lose the will to fight. If that happens, surrender is just around the corner, and the struggle to remain faithful to Christ will be lost.

We must be on our guard against such an outcome and make sure that the gospel that we are teaching and preaching here below is a faithful reflection of what awaits us in heaven. There can be no discrepancy between heaven and earth in the matter of salvation. The new life in Christ that we now enjoy is (and must be) a foretaste of the life that awaits us in the eternal presence of God. If it is not, then what we claim as our inheritance here on earth is not genuine. This was the problem that Paul detected in the false teachers that he criticized. They were offering Christians a spiritual experience here and now that did not correspond to what awaited them in heaven. Their horizons were bounded by time and space, which is why keeping the law of Moses was so important to them. They did not see that the Jewish law was a stopgap designed for a time, and that when the Messiah came it would be made redundant. As Paul proclaimed the gospel, the Messiah had come and so the temporary provisions of the law were no longer needed. Instead there was a direct correspondence between what Christ had done on earth and what he is now doing in heaven, because he had gone from one realm to the other and taken his spiritual victory over sin and death with him as he did so.[73] Their teaching was therefore misleading and essentially false.

---

[73] Eph. 4.8-10.

The only way for Timothy to avoid falling into that trap was to guard the deposit of the gospel with the help of the Holy Spirit who dwells in us. The doctrine of the indwelling Spirit is one that is common in Paul's teaching. 'Because you are sons', he says, 'God has sent the Spirit of his Son into our hearts, crying "Abba! Father!"'.[74] Much of Romans 8 is taken up with this theme. There the Holy Spirit is described as the Spirit of adoption, who unites us to Christ. 1 Corinthians 12–14 is another extended discussion of what amounts to the same thing – the power of the Holy Spirit in the individual believer and in the common life of the church.

The notion of an experience that is common to all is indicated here by Paul's use of the term 'in us' (*en hēmin*). Timothy was expected to guard the deposit as an individual, but the Holy Spirit on whom he had to rely in order to do so is given to all believers. This means that Timothy could not understand his commission in a way that would separate him from the shared witness of the church. The Holy Spirit does not say one thing to one person and something quite different to another, at least not where the nature of the Christian's spiritual 'inheritance' is concerned. It might be quite different with something like the strategy of mission – Paul was sent to the Gentiles and Peter to the Jews, for example, but the message they took with them was essentially the same. Perhaps it had to be packaged differently in order to deal with specific problems, as with Jewish sensitivity to eating meat that had been sacrificed to idols. But even then, it was not the basic doctrine that was at stake, but the way in which it was to be applied in order to take account of the 'weaker brethren', as Paul called them. That consideration presumably remained valid even when there were no particularly tender consciences to contend with, but the doctrine itself, the good *parathēkē*, was the same for all. Timothy's interpretation of it had to conform to an apostolic norm, even when circumstances might suggest that it would be wiser to adopt a pattern of application that was particular to them. The church frequently has to wrestle with the question of how far it can adapt its message and approach to fit specific conditions, but whatever latitude we may have been given, the basic message must stay the same if it is to be recognized as the gospel and be blessed by the Holy Spirit.

Just as Christ guarantees the unity of faith and love, so the indwelling Holy Spirit preserves the oneness of the deposit. There is not one salvation for Jews and another for Gentiles, as some (both in New Testament times and since) have thought. Nor can we say that as long as people sincerely follow their own consciences and convictions they will have nothing to fear from

---

[74] Gal. 4.6.

the judgement of God. It is possible to be sincerely wrong, as the Pharisees usually were, and as some of the false teachers may also have been. Paul knew that their teaching was self-contradictory and hypocritical, but they may not have understood that themselves. There were certainly people like Apollos who were teaching an inadequate gospel because that is all that they knew, though in that case he corrected himself when he was put right and went on to be a reliable co-worker of Paul and his companions.[75] The Holy Spirit has been given to us so that we can protect the deposit that we have received, but if someone betrays or contradicts the gospel, it is clear that the Spirit is not at work in him. We cannot accept the view that a person who has been baptized and who is a church member is therefore automatically integrated into the life of the Spirit. It is not by such outward acts but by the fruits that proceed from a pure heart that we know who belongs to Christ and who does not, and it is by those fruits that we must judge them.[76]

## 15-18. The faithfulness of Onesiphorus

> *15. You are aware that all who are in Asia have turned away from me, including Phygelus and Hermogenes. 16. May the Lord grant mercy to the household of Onesiphorus, because he often refreshed me and was not ashamed of my chain; 17. when he arrived in Rome, he eagerly searched for me and found me – 18. may the Lord grant that he will find mercy from the Lord on that day! And you know very well how much service he rendered in Ephesus.*

The concluding verses of the first chapter give us an insight into the complex nature of personal relationships in the Pauline circle and their churches. Paul first informed Timothy that 'everyone' in Asia[77] had deserted him, including Phygelus and Hermogenes. The statement appears to be simple enough at first sight, but it raises questions that we are unable to answer. First of all, did Timothy not know this already given that he was based in Ephesus, and if he did, why was Paul telling him about it? He used the present indicative form of the verb *oida* ('know'),[78] which gives the impression that Timothy was already

---

[75] Acts 18.24-28.
[76] Mt. 7.16.
[77] The term refers to the Roman province, which covered the western part of what is now Turkey.
[78] It is actually the perfect tense of a highly irregular verb and could perhaps be translated as 'I have realized'.

aware of the situation, but this is probably a mistaken interpretation. It seems more likely that the phrase 'you know' is being used here as a substitute for the imperative, which was often awkward and rarely used in irregular verbs like this one. As in modern speech, colloquial usage interjected a 'you know' in order to underline a point that was not known at all, and this seems to be the case here.

What Paul meant by 'all' is also somewhat problematic. Was he thinking of every single person, of church leaders, or of those whom he regarded as his close associates and companions? We can probably work backwards and conclude that it was the last of these that he was primarily referring to. What he meant was that there was nobody left in Asia on whom he could rely. It is most unlikely that he was referring to whole congregations, or even to the local leadership in all of the churches, because he went on to talk about people who remained loyal to him. Probably there were many ordinary church members who respected Paul and his teaching but who were not in direct contact with him and would not have known anything about the inner tensions in the leadership. This is often the situation in churches today and it is reasonable to suppose that things were not very different in ancient times. However, this must remain speculation, because, as so often, there is no evidence that would allow us to decide the matter either way.

When Paul spoke of 'Asia' he was referring to the Roman province of that name. This was the former kingdom of Pergamum, that had originally been carved out of Alexander the Great's disintegrating empire and had been ceded to the Romans by its last king, Attalus III, on his death in 133 BC. That much is clear, but how many churches in the province were within Paul's orbit at this time is unknown. We may surmise that he was referring to Ephesus, Laodicea and Colossae at least, but beyond that it is hard to say. There is no evidence that he had any direct contact with the other five churches of Asia mentioned in Revelation 2–3, though judging from what John says about them, it would not be surprising if Paul was unwelcome in most of them.[79] That however, must remain speculative. Nor do we know who Phygelus and Hermogenes were. The fact that they are mentioned by name suggests either that they had been particularly prominent supporters of Paul, so that their defection from his mission was both surprising and painful, or that they were known to Timothy and had been trusted by him. Timothy apparently knew who they were but he had to be told that they had abandoned Paul, which suggests that either it was a recent occurrence or that these two men were not based

---

[79] There would have been eight churches in the province of Asia, but Colossae was destroyed by an earthquake in the AD 60s, shortly after Paul wrote to it.

in Ephesus and therefore not in regular contact with Timothy. Beyond that we are reduced to speculation once again. It might be added in passing that the mention of people like them is an argument in favour of the authenticity of the Epistle and against pseudepigraphy. One would have expected a pseudepigrapher to have mentioned well-known people and not to have invented characters of whom nobody had ever heard. But if this report of the situation is genuine then such obscurity is understandable because these people were real to the correspondents, even if they were unknown to most others.

In sharp contrast to them, and incidentally as a reminder to us that not everyone in Asia had abandoned Paul, the apostle moved on to praise Onesiphorus, a member of the church at Ephesus, who had often entertained him and was not at all embarrassed by his status as a prisoner. Perhaps Onesiphorus was wealthy and prominent enough to be able to get away with such charity. He certainly went to visit Paul in Rome, which suggests that he was a man of some means and most probably a member of the merchant class. This is what people like Priscilla and Aquila might have done, and it seems natural to associate him with them, at least in socio-economic terms.

But having said that, Paul seemed to think that Onesiphorus was demonstrating a degree of solidarity with him that was unusual and went beyond what he expected. Not only had Onesiphorus shown him hospitality on many occasions and paid no attention to his imprisonment but he had even gone to Rome in order to seek him out, presumably to make sure that he was all right and to express his support for him in such unfortunate circumstances. Rome was then a city of about a million people, so finding Paul might have been more difficult than we imagine, especially if he was under a form of house arrest. Paul took the trouble to inform Timothy that Onesiphorus had searched diligently for him, which means that he must have been impressed by his efforts. He did not suggest that Onesiphorus was putting himself in any personal danger by doing this, but it is quite likely that his search had taken up to a year and had cost him quite a lot in material terms.

Paul hoped that God would show mercy on Onesiphorus' household, which raises some interesting but ultimately unanswerable questions. Were they Christians? What sort of 'mercy' was he talking about? The question becomes more pertinent in v. 18, where Paul was more specific. Now he hoped that Onesiphorus would find mercy in the Lord's presence 'on that day', by which we must surely understand the day of judgement. Was this just a pious way of speaking or did Paul have something specific in mind? Was Onesiphorus dead at the time Paul was writing, which would explain why he asked for God's mercy on his household and spoke of his activities in the past tense?[80] It is unlikely, but perhaps possible, that Onesiphorus was not a Christian, but a kind of Nicodemus figure, who supported the church from outside without committing himself to it. More probably though he was a believer, and Paul thought that he would receive a special reward from God on the day of judgement, because of how he lived on earth. Either way, the expression he used is intriguing. We long to know more about Onesiphorus and his circumstances, but we are not told.[81] All that Paul said is that Timothy knew better than he did how Onesiphorus had served the church in Ephesus, which strongly suggests that his behaviour during Paul's imprisonment, though outstanding, was not exceptional for him. John Calvin commented that although Onesiphorus was on his own in his search for Paul, his faithfulness led the apostle to pray for a blessing on his whole family. Calvin then claimed that this sets a pattern for others because, in his words, 'God's blessing rests not only on a righteous man himself but on his whole house.'[82]

What we can say is that the example of Onesiphorus demonstrates that it is when we find ourselves in trouble that we also discover who our true friends are. They are not many, but their loyalty is all the more precious for being genuine. Onesiphorus had no hope of reward for his services, and if anything, he ran the risk of being arrested himself. Yet in spite of that, he stuck by Paul and the apostle's words, whatever their real meaning may have been, demonstrate how grateful he was for that.

It may be added in passing that the personal nature of these remarks is further evidence that the epistle was written by Paul and not by a later pseudepigrapher, who would have had no motive in recording such details. What we read here about Paul's circle of friends and associates has a ring of authenticity about it that would have been very difficult, as well as pointless, for anyone else to try to replicate. As always, definite proof is lacking, but here the weight of probability argues in favour of the letter's authenticity.

---

[80] Most modern commentators take that view, though it is not confirmed by the text itself. See Marshall (2004), pp. 715–21.

[81] This desire seems to have been felt in the early church as well. An apocryphal work, the *Acts of Paul and Thecla*, says quite a bit about Onesiphorus, claiming that he came from Iconium and had remained loyal to the apostle when others in his circle were deserting him. It is impossible to say whether this apocryphal text contains elements of historical truth or not, but if there is any connection between it and this Epistle, it must be one of the *Acts*' literary dependence on it. See Johnson (2001), pp. 362–3.

[82] Calvin (1964), p. 303.

# 2 Timothy 2

## 1-7. The faithful servant

*1. You then, my child, be strong in the grace that is in Christ Jesus; 2. and what you have heard from me through many witnesses entrust to faithful people who will be able to teach others as well. 3. Share in suffering like a good soldier of Christ Jesus. 4. No one serving in the army gets entangled in everyday affairs; the soldier's aim is to please the enlisting officer. 5. And in the case of an athlete, no one is crowned without competing according to the rules. 6. It is the farmer who does the work who ought to have the first share of the crops. 7. Think over what I say, for the Lord will give you understanding in all things.*

The second chapter begins with a direct appeal from Paul to Timothy. The phrase 'my child' (*teknon mou*) was commonly used to indicate a certain intimacy, but it was essentially unconnected with a family or other kind of relationship. In this case, of course, it repeats the form of address at the beginning of the epistle, and to that extent it reinforces Paul's sense of spiritual paternity with respect to Timothy, but too much should not be read into it. Even today older people can address younger ones in this way without implying any personal connection, and the same was true in the ancient world. We know that in this case there was a bond between the two men, but we cannot say that it was necessarily for that reason that Paul addressed Timothy as he did here.

The verb translated 'be strong' (*endynamō*) could perhaps be rendered more accurately as 'be empowered' since it is clearly connected to *dynamis*, but the meaning is much the same. It recalls what Paul said earlier about the work of the Holy Spirit in the life of the believer, as well as the ability of Jesus Christ to guard Paul's deposit in heaven. The source of this power was the grace (*charis*) of God. Later generations would objectify the concept of grace and turn it into a kind of medicine that, if taken in the right dosage, would supply the power required. Grace, however, is not a thing that can be administered or withdrawn in this way. It is rather God's attitude towards his people, from which spiritual power then flows. That attitude is one of acceptance and forgiveness. It was while we were still dead in our sins that the Father sent his Son to save us, not because of anything we had done or deserved, but because he loved us and wanted us to share in the blessing of eternal life with him.[1] We do not know why God acted in this way; all we can say is that it was his decision and that he acted on it. He has shown us his grace and as a result has given us something of his power. The reverse of this, of course, is that if God decides not to bestow his grace on someone, his spiritual power will not be given to that person.[2] Grace is the precondition for the gift of God's power, but it is distinct from the power itself and precedes it.

In the spiritual experience of the Christian, God's grace is given to enable us to believe in Christ and it cannot be understood otherwise. There is a sense in which every creature experiences God's grace merely by existing, but although this is true, it is a theological deduction made by those who already believe in Christ and is not recognized as such by those who have no knowledge of him. Furthermore, Christ is both the means by which God's grace comes to us and that grace itself. He not only assures us of God's favour towards us but reveals that he is himself the supreme expression of that favour. It is in and through union with Christ that the grace of God is given to us and that those who receive it exercise the spiritual power that he bestows because of it. It follows that the power we receive by the grace of God will be used to further the cause of Christ, which in practical terms means that it will be given in order to spread the gospel and build up the church.

Having laid down the general principle that everything depends on the grace of God in Christ, Paul then proceeded to give specific examples of how that works in practice. His primary concern was to ensure the faithful transmission of the gospel message. He talked first about what Timothy had heard from him 'through many witnesses' (*dia pollōn martyrōn*). This probably means 'in the presence of many witnesses' which is the ESV rendering, though it may also mean that many witnesses acted as agents in transmitting Paul's message to Timothy. The problem with that interpretation is that it is hard to see what it would signify in practice. After all, Timothy and Paul knew each other and worked together for lengthy periods, so there was no need for intermediary agents to relay what one was doing to the other. What the phrase does suggest is that Paul did not teach Timothy in private, an important consideration given that heretics in the next generation would claim that there was a 'secret gospel' that Jesus had transmitted to the apostles but not revealed to the church in general. There is no suggestion of that here,

---

[1] Rom. 5.8; Jn 3.16.
[2] Mt. 24.40; Lk. 17.26-37.

but if Paul's teaching had been given to Timothy *without* witnesses, questions might well have been raised about its authenticity. Timothy could have been accused either of making it up or of misunderstanding what the apostle had said, but nobody would have been able to prove anything one way or the other. With many witnesses to call on, that danger was eliminated.

Who those witnesses were, we do not know. Presumably they would have included Paul's travelling companions, whom Timothy joined for significant periods of Paul's ministry. They may also have embraced the elders of the local church(es) where Timothy served, or even entire congregations. It seems that 1 Timothy was addressed as much to the church at Ephesus as to Timothy personally, so that may be what the apostle had in mind here. Keeping things secret would have been very difficult in the ancient world in any case, and if Paul and Timothy were lodging in people's houses, they would have had little privacy. Even if Paul were instructing Timothy specifically, there would probably have been others listening in, and if he was commissioned by the entire eldership it is likely that he would have submitted to some form of examination by them. At the very least, they would have known what Paul had said to Timothy and been assured that Timothy understood and accepted it.

What Paul was now recommending was that Timothy should repeat the process of training disciples to minister to the next generation in an expanding church. Paul told him to seek out 'faithful people' (*pistoi anthrōpoi*) and pass the message along to them, so that they in turn might become teachers. It is not entirely clear who Paul had in mind when he spoke about 'faithful people'. We may rest assured that most (if not all) of them would have been male believers, but Paul was probably looking for more than that. By *pistoi* ('faithful') he probably meant 'reliable' people who could be trusted to grasp what he was saying, to keep it free from extraneous influences and to pass it on to others. The real question for us is whether he would also have included women in this designation, at least in principle. The word *anthrōpos* is gender-neutral, making this a theoretical possibility, but the context does not favour such an interpretation. Women teachers were rare to non-existent in the Jewish and Christian worlds, and while it is conceivable that Paul or Timothy might have accepted them if there had been any around, it is unlikely that either man would have sought them out deliberately. That sort of thing did not happen in the ancient world, where employment outside the home was a male preserve. We should therefore not be surprised to discover that when Paul illustrated his point, he used three examples that were taken from different aspects of secular life, all of which referred to exclusively male occupations.

His first example was that of the soldier, the second that of the athlete and the third that of the farmer. Soldiers were a familiar sight in the Roman world, and Paul used military imagery to make his points.[3] Athletes were less common in everyday life, but they were heroic figures in their communities and highly admired, much as they are today. Farmers were ubiquitous outside the cities, but since the early church was mostly an urban phenomenon, they may have been the least familiar of the three to the majority of Christians, including Timothy. For example, it is possible that his father was (or had been) a soldier and that he himself had been an athlete, or had had some athletic training as part of his education, but it is unlikely that he had ever been a farmer, or known anyone who was. He did not move in those circles, and as far as we can tell, neither did any of the leaders of the early church.[4] It might also be said that the illustrations Paul chose all emphasized physical as opposed to intellectual strength. He did not use philosophers or even builders as models for Timothy, but men who relied to a large extent on physical fitness for their success.

Paul put the soldier first, perhaps because what he represented was more fundamental to his purpose than the others. The soldier operates in a team, even when he is engaged in hand-to-hand combat, and the minister of the gospel cannot function effectively on his own. He must work with others who are called to the same profession, and that involves sharing in the dangers to which that calling will expose him. Like the preacher, the soldier is likely to suffer if he does his job properly. A church leader can no more shield himself from danger than can an army commander. The morale of his men demands that he should lead them into battle, which in turn means that he must expose himself to the worst that the enemy can do. Jesus, who is the author and object of our faith, went to his death on a cross in order to save us from destruction.[5] To follow him is to be willing to suffer in his wake, as a good solider in Christ's army is expected to do.

The soldier is also set apart from everyday life in order to be able to function more efficiently. Here, too, his calling and training is a model for the preacher and teacher. Bi-vocational ministry is often necessary for economic reasons but it is not the ideal and should be avoided if at all possible. The idea of doing a job five days a week and then being a pastor at the weekend may appeal to some people, but it diminishes both the prestige and the efficacy of the office to which the preacher is called. The soldier's first loyalty is to his commander, whom Paul described as the man who enlisted him in the first place. That is no longer true for soldiers nowadays, but it remains the case for the Christian minister. His enlisting officer is none other than Jesus

---

[3] Eph. 6.11-20 is the classic example.
[4] Even the disciples of Jesus were mostly fishermen, not farmers.
[5] Heb. 12.2.

Christ himself, and it must be the good preacher's aim to please him first and foremost. It is to enable him to fulfill that purpose that he should not be distracted by other pursuits, however legitimate and justifiable those pursuits may be.

The 'business of life' (*hē tou biou pragmateia*), as Paul described civilian affairs, is essential in its own right, but it is not proper for a soldier to engage in it. It is clear from this that, in this context at least, Paul saw full-time ministers of the gospel as soldiers of Christ in a way that others are not. Elsewhere, he commanded every believer to put on the whole armour of God and warned the church that we face a spiritual battle merely because we are Christians, but here he went one step further and imposed a soldier's discipline on the church's leadership to a degree that did not apply to others.[6] This should not be interpreted as creating a kind of hierarchy of virtue in the church. Leaders and laymen are engaged in the same task, but the former are subject to a stricter discipline because they have to fulfill a calling that is not given to others in the same way or to the same degree.

John Calvin saw that Paul's image of the soldier, while primarily directed to the Christian preacher, has relevance for all believers:

> Here Paul is addressing the pastors of the church in the person of Timothy. His statement is of universal application but is specially suited to ministers of the Word. First, let them see the things that hinder them in their work and let them free themselves from them and follow Christ. Next, let other men also see, each in his own station, what keeps them from Christ, that our heavenly commander may have as much authority over us as any mortal man claims over the soldiers of the world who have pledged themselves to his service.[7]

The next image Paul mentioned was that of the athlete, who is not crowned unless he competes according to the rules (*nomimōs*). Paul said nothing about athletic skill here – that was evidently taken for granted, since the athlete would not be in the competition otherwise. But however good he may be, he will not be declared the official winner if he breaks the rules. Today we are very familiar with this problem. Athletic achievement is so highly regarded in some circles, and so well rewarded financially, that competitors are often tempted to take performance-enhancing drugs or engage in forms of corruption like 'match-fixing', in order to win. More than one athlete has

---

[6] Cf. Eph. 6.10-20.
[7] Calvin (1964), p. 307.

been given a trophy or a gold medal, only to be forced to return it when it has been discovered that he has cheated.

The temptations facing a Christian minister are different, but in their own context they can be just as powerful and dangerous. Preachers may be persuaded that they have to attract a large following, and that it is legitimate to employ almost any tactic in pursuit of that aim. Like the Pharisees whom Jesus criticized, they may affect a form of godliness but not submit to Christ either in their devotional lives or in their off-stage behaviour. It is all too possible for Christian leaders to go through the motions without being fully committed in mind and spirit to the message they are proclaiming, and those who try to fool the church by this can be sure that they will not reap the reward they think they have been promised. The crown is not just for high-achievers but for those who have reached the top in the right way.

Finally, Paul looks to the industrious farmer (*ho kopiōn geōrgos*) for his third example. Farmers and farming do not figure very much in the New Testament, and when they do, they are not always presented in a way that a real farmer would recognize. The classic example of that is the sower in the parable of Jesus.[8] That sower casts his seed everywhere he can, with unsurprisingly varied results. Of course, no real sower would ever do that. First, he would scout the ground, then prepare it for sowing and only after that plant the seed. When Jesus told his parable it must have struck any real sower as being quite different from what he actually did, but one of the points that Jesus was making was that spiritual sowing is not the same as its physical counterpart. The preacher is called to proclaim his message to anyone he can but is warned that his efforts will only bear fruit if the ground has already been prepared by God.

Paul was not trying to contrast the behaviour of a farmer with that of a preacher but to demonstrate in what ways they were similar. A farmer who works hard ought to get the first share of the crops he has sown. A preacher who dedicates himself to his labours ought likewise to be the first to benefit from them. What does that mean in practice? It can hardly be true to say that the most industrious preacher has the right to choose which converts will join his congregation, in order to ensure that he gets the pick of the crop! Nor is it right to assume that the most successful preacher is entitled to the lion's share of the numbers. Pastors of megachurches are not necessarily more committed to their work than others, and it is wrong to judge spiritual success in that way. Paul may have meant that the hard-working pastor would be given a deeper insight into the things of God and have a more effective

---

[8] Mt. 13.1-9; 18-23.

ministry as a result. Experienced teachers know that they often learn more from their lessons than the students they are teaching do, and preachers are similar in this respect. By going into their subject more deeply and dedicating themselves to it more completely, it is inevitable that they will benefit from it in a way that others will not. But while that is true, it does not seem to be what Paul was getting at here. More likely, given the overall context, he was saying that the faithful pastor will be the first to be compensated for his labours in the kingdom of heaven. This is partly in recognition of his service, but it is also a confirmation of the value of the blessing that will be given to everyone and that he has proclaimed in the course of his ministry. If a chef does not get the first taste of the meal he cooks, others may legitimately wonder whether the food is worth eating. Similarly, by tasting his own crop first, the farmer is demonstrating his confidence in the fruit that he has produced, and that in itself is an encouragement to others to share in it too.

These were words of encouragement for Timothy to ponder, and the secular examples that Paul gave were intended to give concrete expression to what he expected of those who are fully engaged in the service of God. They are models for the preacher to ponder and to emulate in his own calling. How this would work out in practice, Paul left for the preacher himself to discover. He told Timothy to put his mind to it and promised him that God would give him 'understanding' (*synesis*) 'in everything'. Notice that he said 'understanding' (*synesis*) and not 'knowledge' (*gnōsis*), because it is unfortunately possible to know a great deal yet understand very little. That was the problem with so many of the false teachers that Paul was combatting. They had a great store of factual information about all kinds of things, but they did not understand what they were supposed to be doing with it because the gospel of Christ was not central to their concerns. If the focus was wrong or distorted, the ministry would be skewed and suffer as a result.

It is possible for the faithful preacher to receive understanding in all things because he has the mind of Christ. When Paul added that this understanding would be given to Timothy 'in everything' he did not mean that Timothy would know all that there is to know but that he would be given discernment and sound judgment in every situation that he would encounter. For Paul, understanding was never just an intellectual exercise but was always a practical tool for effective ministry, and the pastor needed wisdom to know how to deal with whatever might crop up. It is that, rather than encyclopedic knowledge, which he must have and which God will give him if he is faithful in his calling.

In considering the examples that Paul gave here for the encouragement of preachers, we must remember that rewards for faithful service are not to be confused with justification by works. The preacher was not trying to earn the favour of God by doing his best but rather to fulfill his ministry in the way that would best honour the one who had given it to him. Those who benefitted from his labours were expected to thank God for his faithfulness and not start a cult of hero worship that would be the antithesis of what God intended. Unfortunately there are preachers who build up a personal following and glory in it, but when they pass from the scene their ministry collapses. That was not what Paul wanted to see. Just as the soldier served a higher master, so the preacher was called to be faithful to the one who had called and commissioned him. If he did that well, that would be all the reward he would ever need or seek.

## 8-13. Union with Christ

> 8. Remember Jesus Christ, raised from the dead, a descendant of David – that is my gospel, 9. for which I suffer hardship, even to the point of being chained like a criminal. But the word of God is not chained. 10. Therefore I endure everything for the sake of the elect, so that they may also obtain the salvation that is in Christ Jesus, with eternal glory. 11. The saying is sure: If we have died with him, we will also live with him; 12. if we endure, we will also reign with him; if we deny him, he will also deny us; 13. if we are faithless, he remains faithful – for he cannot deny himself.

Having given three examples taken from secular life as to how to exercise a spiritual ministry, Paul now focused on the ultimate model – Jesus Christ himself. The imitation of Christ is a Pauline theme, but it is more complicated than it might appear at first sight. Jesus is not our model in the sense of being an example of self-sacrifice that we ought to follow. If we pursued that idea to its logical conclusion, we would end up trying to save ourselves by copying him as closely as possible. The danger would be that we would forget that he came into the world to do something for us that we cannot do for ourselves, so following in his footsteps can only go so far. Orthodox Christians recognize the limitations of such an idea, but it is more popular and more widespread than we might think.

First of all, there are secular examples of martyrdom to which Christ might be compared. The most obvious of these in the ancient world was Socrates, who was put to death because of his philosophical and theological beliefs. Jesus could perhaps be regarded as a Jewish Socrates, a man who challenged the religious pieties of his time and paid the price for it. But Jesus was not Socrates, or any other martyr for truth. He may have had some teachings or beliefs in common with them, but in crucially important ways he was quite different.

Unlike Socrates or any other 'martyr for truth', Jesus had 'risen from the dead'. That was the single most important fact about him and it set him apart from any possible rivals. If Christ had not risen from the dead, wrote Paul to the Corinthians, we would be preaching a lie and would be the most miserable of people, because we would have been deluded into putting our trust in a mirage.[9] In this connection it is important to remember that an apostle was not someone who had known Jesus in the days of his earthly ministry but someone who had seen him after he had risen from the dead.[10] It was not so much what Jesus taught his disciples during his time on earth that the evangelists recorded in the gospels, as what parts of it he recalled to their minds after the resurrection and before his ascension.[11] Of course, what Jesus said then coincided with what he had taught earlier, but the resurrection gave it a new focus and provided the criterion for deciding between what he had said and done in passing and what was of eternal value. It was the resurrection that guided the disciples in selecting from the teaching that Jesus had given before his death, so that it was a kind of prism or filter through which it was refined for the subsequent preaching of the gospel.[12]

Certainly there could have been no uniquely Christian message without his resurrection. Even today there are many people who admire Jesus for his wisdom and sympathize with his sufferings but who do not believe that he rose from the dead and do not accept that he has a claim on their lives as their Lord and Saviour. They are so near to the kingdom of God in one sense, and yet at the same time they are far from it. Paul was therefore right to make the resurrection fundamental to the gospel message.

Another way in which Jesus was unlike any Christian today is that he was 'of the seed of David'. Perhaps somewhere there are still people who are descended from David, but if so, they do not know it any more than we do. The ability to trace our genealogy back that far has been lost – a matter of some importance for a religion like Judaism, in which ancestry plays such an important part and for the false teachers who angered Paul by their inordinate interest in the subject. But such aberrations aside, the fact that Jesus was descended from David in human terms is important for several reasons:

---

[9] 1 Cor. 15.12-19.
[10] 1 Cor. 15.5-9.
[11] Lk. 24.44-49.
[12] Jn 21.25.

1. God had promised David that there would always be a king in Israel who was descended from him.[13] Now that the Davidic line has disappeared, that promise cannot be fulfilled because there is nobody to whom it could convincingly be applied. Jesus came into the world at a time when it was still possible to establish a credible genealogy that stretched back to David. After the fall of Jerusalem in AD 70 and the destruction of the temple, the records disappeared and the tradition was lost. If the promise has not been fulfilled in Jesus it never will be. It is therefore part of our belief in the faithfulness of God that he accomplished what he had said he would, and that in Christ we have a descendant of David who rules over his people for ever.
2. Jesus was a real human being, because the fact that he was descended from David means that he shared David's humanity. He was not an angel who had come down to earth in human form.[14] Jesus' human descent from David recognized the fact that God would fulfill his promise to Israel by drawing on Israel itself and not by imposing some other kind of being as the ruler of his people. Our king is not someone who has no real connection with us but someone to whom we can be united and owe allegiance precisely because he shared the same human nature that we have.[15] It is because of that link that we can approach the divine throne of grace and find the help that we need for our salvation.[16]
3. Jesus was physically connected to the covenant that God made with Israel. As a descendant of David, he occupied a particular place in a real history. His gospel was intended for every nation, but it was also rooted in a time and place that God had set apart for his glory. To believe in him is not to deny Israel or to go beyond it but to accept that it has fulfilled its historical purpose. It has given birth to the Messiah within its own royal family, tying its own covenant inheritance to the universal promise of salvation. In Christ, those who are not part of Israel by blood have been grafted into its covenant by faith. In and through him we are linked to the whole counsel of God that has been revealed since the time of Abraham and brought to fruition in the life, death and resurrection of Jesus, the son of David.
4. Jesus is the king to whom all Christians now owe allegiance. As he told his disciples, his kingdom is not of this world, but it is not divorced from it either.[17] It is a spiritual presence in a material universe and touches

---

[13] 2 Sam. 7.12-16; 1 Kgs 11.36; 2 Chron. 13.5; Ps. 89.20-37; Jer. 33.17.
[14] Heb. 1.5-14.
[15] Heb. 4.15.
[16] Heb. 4.16.
[17] Jn 18.36.

everything with its transforming power. Those who are servants of this king are no longer under the power of the rulers of this world, who cannot claim God's people as their subjects. At the same time, the subjects of the heavenly king are beholden to him as their ruler and guide; they cannot claim to belong to his kingdom without demonstrating their affinity with it by obeying its laws and furthering its interests. The kingdom of Christ is an expanding spiritual empire, seeking new converts and integrating them into its life and witness. What had been revealed to David as a future promise, and partially realized in the reign of his son Solomon, has now become a permanent reality – a king greater than Solomon is here.[18]

Many modern commentators are puzzled by the fact that Paul mentioned the resurrection before saying anything about Jesus' descent from David.[19] Some have posited a two-stage Christology, in which belief in the resurrection was supplemented by an affirmation of Jesus' descent from David, probably in order to counteract a docetic tendency that was supposedly manifesting itself in the early church.[20] However, as I. H. Marshall comments,

> it is the combination of the two facts – resurrection and descent – that qualify Jesus as the Messiah, and there is no indication that the two descriptions are to be separated in order to suggest two stages in the development of the status of Jesus … It follows, then, that the order is immaterial. The One who was resurrected is he descendant of David and this confirms that the latter is the Messiah. The hypothesis adopted by most commentators, namely that the phraseology used here reflected a two-stage Christology, should be abandoned.[21]

It is above all in the preaching of the gospel that we see what the connections between Jesus and ourselves are. Paul never claimed to be divine, nor did he grasp at any form of kingship, but he did say that he had been crucified with Christ.[22] Given that the context in which he mentioned the gospel was that of his own suffering, which he was encouraging Timothy to embrace,

---

[18] Mt. 12.42; Lk. 11.31.
[19] In contrast to the order found in Rom. 1.3-4.
[20] Theodore of Mopsuestia (2010), p. 703, believed this and was followed by Theodoret of Cyrrhus (Cyrus) (2001), p. 241. Even Calvin (1964), p. 309, expresses the same idea, though in more general terms.
[21] Marshall (2004), p. 735. Towner (2006), p. 500, follows Marshall in this without further comment.
[22] Gal. 2.20.

this is of the utmost relevance to us and to our interpretation of what he was saying here. The gospel is the message that our sins have been paid for and forgiven by the shed blood of Christ. His suffering and death were not a meaningless failure but a triumphant success because they achieved what nothing else could have done. Jesus could easily have been a descendant of David (as many others were) and even risen from the dead (as Lazarus had done) without being our Lord and Saviour. The fact that he was David's 'son' made him a particularly appropriate person for the task he was assigned, and his resurrection from the dead set the seal on his achievement, but neither of these things can be separated from the gospel, which gives them their particular meaning.

It must also be remembered that it was not because he *believed* in the resurrection of Jesus that Paul was suffering, still less for his claim that Jesus was a 'son' of David. He was suffering because he was *preaching* the gospel, which included those things but went beyond them. It was because of his calling to preach the message of eternal salvation that he was privileged to bear in his body the sufferings of Christ, or as Jesus himself put it, to take up his cross and follow him.[23] This is how the preacher imitates Christ, and it is a privilege that is open to any Christian. Nevertheless, the preacher is the one more likely to be persecuted because he is the one who stands up to proclaim the unwelcome message. Members of the church who observe this ought to be drawn closer to their leaders, not driven away from them. As John Calvin remarked,

> all godly men should take courage when they see ministers of the gospel attacked and insulted by adversaries, so that they do not for that reason reverence their teaching less, but rather may give God the glory when they see how by his power the gospel can break through all the hindrances the world puts in its way.[24]

Paul was deeply affected by his sufferings, and not least by their inherent injustice. The full effect of this is not easily conveyed in translation. The Greek word for 'suffering' is not the simple *pathō*, as we might expect, but *kakopathō*. The addition of the word *kakos* ('bad') suggests not only the severity of the punishment but its innate iniquity. What had Paul done to deserve this fate? In legal terms, the answer was 'nothing'. All he had done was to preach a message of salvation. Some people had objected to it for a

---

[23] Gal. 6.17; Mt. 16.24; Lk. 9.23.
[24] Calvin (1964), pp. 309–10.

variety of reasons, but none of them should have justified taking legal action against him. Yet there he was, bound in chains like an 'evildoer' (*kakourgos*), or common criminal.

The irony of this was not lost on him. The secular authorities probably thought that by disposing of Paul they could silence his message. It is a common error, and one that the Athenians had made in the case of Socrates centuries before. The Romans should have known that they were unlikely to succeed by resorting to this tactic, but officialdom rarely sees beyond the confines of its own legalistic outlook. In a modern example, the British government condemned the leaders of the 1916 Easter Rising in Dublin to death because what they had done was treason in time of war. The law was on its side, and its action was justified. But as we know, the rebels wanted to be martyrs and it is as martyrs that they have been remembered. Rightly or wrongly, it is now generally thought that Britain lost the south of Ireland because of the way it overreacted to the Rising, making its response counterproductive in the end.

Paul had not committed treason, of course, and his imprisonment could not be justified on that ground, but the counterproductive effect of locking him up would be much the same. Paul realized that, even if he did not live to see it, and he attributed his eventual vindication to the sovereignty of God, against which no earthly power could prevail. As he put it, the 'word of God' is not bound! Paul's language here is ambiguous, perhaps deliberately so. For a start, what did he mean by the 'word' (*logos*)? This could have been the message of the gospel, or the underlying plan of God that was eternally present in his mind, or the incarnate Christ ... It could even have been the Bible, though the New Testament did not yet exist and he would probably have referred to the Old Testament as the 'Scripture' (*graphē*), not as the *logos tou Theou*.[25] The context would suggest that it is the message that he preached which Paul had at the forefront of his mind, but that does not exclude the other possibilities. In fact, it may be best to take them all together as parts of a wider phenomenon, which might be described as the revelation of God's plan and purpose. However we understand it, there can be no doubt that Jesus Christ, the word (*logos*) become flesh, is at the heart of the matter, and every other form that the *logos* takes focuses our attention on him.

If the language of imprisonment which Paul used is to be taken to its logical conclusion, we could say that it is not messages or books that are arrested and thrown into gaol – people are. It was not the Bible that died on the cross for our sins, but the Son of God. The message of salvation could not

---

[25] See 2 Tim. 3.16 for an example of that.

be locked away as Paul was, and it spread in spite of what was happening to him. Yet at the same time we must not forget that we are dealing here with something more than the power of an idea. People may have some notion of what Socrates died for, but it is uncertain how far the philosophy that is attributed to his inspiration reflects what he actually thought and taught. There has certainly never been any suggestion that it might be possible to have a personal relationship with him after his death. The same could be said, *mutatis mutandis*, of similar martyrs ever since. Paul never supposed that anybody would worship him after his unjust death, nor did he want that to happen. He was a preacher of the word of God, but the word itself was quite independent of him. It had existed before he was born, had triumphed over him when he opposed it and would survive his demise. Nor would it change its character over time, as the teaching of Socrates had done. The reason for that is that the word was incarnate in Jesus Christ, who is the same, yesterday, today and for ever.[26] The Romans, and whoever else opposed the word of God, were opposing the man who had risen from the dead, the descendant of David who had come into his kingdom, the Almighty Son of God incarnate. They did not stand a chance.

It was because he knew this that Paul had the inner spiritual strength that he needed in order to endure the pain and suffering to which he was so wrongly subjected. His imprisonment was of a piece with everything else that he had been through and that he catalogues elsewhere – the beatings, the shipwrecks, the losses of various kinds. None of that mattered to him, because he knew that it was all part of a greater divine plan in which he had been privileged to share. This plan was nothing less than the salvation of the elect, for whose sake his entire mission had taken the shape that it had.

The implications of this are of cosmic importance. Paul understood his own life and experiences in the light of the destiny of the 'elect' (*eklektoi*). Few concepts have been (and still are) more contested than this one. Most people recognize that Israel had seen itself as the chosen people of God. Whether they were right to have done so is a secondary question, which for many is of little direct relevance for Christians. Either Israel was wrong to have been so chauvinistic, and Christ came to break down their pride and mistaken self-analysis, or it was right, but the extension of the gospel message to the whole earth has made Israel's election no longer as important as it had previously been. If anything, those who think like this would probably argue that talk of Israel's election is now a hindrance, at least to the extent that it persuades many Jews (and Christians) to regard it as somehow exempt from

---

[26] Heb. 13.8; Rev. 1.8.

the demands of the gospel, which it is not. What a tragedy, in their view, to think that Israel may be cutting itself off from salvation by insisting that it has inherited an election that sets it apart from the rest of the world.

The question gets even more complicated for Christians, who have identified themselves with Israel and the promises that God made to it but interpret them in a purely spiritual way. The result is that there has always been a tension between those who claim that the gospel is meant for everyone, and those who say that Christ came to save his own, that is, those whom he had called and chosen from before the foundation of the world. This difference of opinion has gone by different names over the centuries, and there are many nuances that must be recognized, especially among those who think that the gospel is intended for everybody. Some of these may be universalists, which is to say that they think that everyone will be saved in the end, however much they resist or reject the gospel in this life. Such people are doubtless well-meaning, but there is no Biblical support for their position and much that argues against it. If they are right, then Jesus and the Bible are wrong, Christianity is false and the advocates of a universalist position ought to distance themselves from it as much as they can.

Others would be more cautious than this, arguing that the gospel is intended for everyone but that not everyone accepts it. Why that is so may be hard to say. Some would claim that it is a matter of free choice, and this is probably the most widespread view today. In many circles this position is now called 'Arminianism' after the sixteenth-century Dutch theologian Jacob Arminius (1560-1609) who expounded a version of it. Others would maintain that God himself restricts the application of a salvation that is in principle universal. That view is attributed to the French theologian Moise Amyraut (1596-1664) and so is called 'Amyraldianism', although, as recent research has demonstrated, it goes back to the teachings of a Scottish divine, John Cameron (1579?-1625), who went to France and taught Amyraut. It can also be found among certain Anglican theologians of the early seventeenth century, like John Davenant (1572-1641), John Preston (1587-1628) and James Ussher (1581-1656), in which case it is usually known as 'hypothetical universalism'. Scholars acknowledge that there were subtle differences among these men, but that need not concern us here. All of them, in their various ways, were trying to account for a salvation that was in principle offered to everyone but in practice was restricted to those who accepted it, whatever the ultimate cause of that acceptance may have been.

The opposite view, which is normally associated with Augustine of Hippo (354-430), Martin Luther (1483-1546) and especially, though somewhat unfairly, with John Calvin (1509-1564) is much more unified. It says that Christ came into the world to save his chosen people, that he died for them (and, at least by implication, not for anyone else) and that they alone are saved. To preach the gospel is to gather the elect into the kingdom of God. As Jesus might have put it, it is to go after the sheep which have gone astray and bring them back.[27] It is emphatically not an attempt to turn goats into sheep, or to broaden the membership of the flock to include goats as well. This is hard for many to accept, but it is what the Bible teaches and it is fundamental to our presentation of the gospel message. Unfortunately it has fallen into disrepute among some because of the fear that its advocates will use it as an excuse not to preach the gospel. Their logic is that if the elect are already saved, they will be gathered into the fold whether anybody evangelizes them or not, so why bother? That appears to be a logical conclusion to draw, but it contradicts the Biblical evidence just as much as the belief that there is no particular election at all. Paul would hardly have been languishing in gaol in Rome if he could have put up his feet in Tarsus and let God's plan fulfill itself!

As far as divine election is concerned, Paul's statement to Timothy could hardly have been clearer. He preached the gospel in order to save the elect. There is no indication that he knew in advance who the elect were, and we know from his lengthy exposition of the subject in Romans that he did not identify them with Israel, at least not if Israel is regarded as equivalent to the Jewish people. Physically the Jews had been chosen and set apart from the time of Abraham, but only those who believed as Abraham had believed were actually saved.[28] At the same time, Paul was not a universalist. Undoubtedly he believed that the sacrifice of Christ was adequate to pay the price for any human sin; nobody could argue that he could not be saved because Christ's blood was inadequate to cover his misdeeds. Christ, and only Christ, was the answer to the human dilemma, and that covered everything and everybody. But just as the sacrifice made by the high priest in the Jerusalem temple was sufficient to cover every sin, although it was made on behalf of the elect nation of Israel and applied only to them, so the sacrifice of Christ, our great high priest, must be understood in the same way.[29] The reason it did not cover everyone was not that it was somehow defective but that it was never intended to do so. As Paul made clear in this passage, Jesus died for the elect, and salvation was their particular inheritance; it was not the birthright of every human being.

Paul never saw any contradiction between the fact that Christ died for the elect and the fact that he had been appointed as a preacher of the

---

[27] Mt. 18.12-14; Lk. 15.4-7.
[28] Rom. 4.1-25.
[29] Heb. 4.14–5.10.

gospel who was charged with the task of bringing them into the fold. He saw himself as a servant whose duty it was to fulfill his master's commands without asking whether it was necessary for him to do so. He certainly did not regard himself as indispensable in God's eyes; he knew that if he did not do what God wanted him to, someone else would be called to do it instead. Indeed, Paul would not have written to Timothy to urge him to carry on the task, and train up others to do so, if he had thought that his own contribution was essential. Why God chose to work through him was a question that he could not answer, not for philosophical reasons but for moral and spiritual ones. He was a man who had persecuted the church of God and knew that he was unworthy of the task which had been assigned to him. It was for that reason that he did not understand why he had been chosen. The idea that if God did not need anyone to do his bidding he would not have chosen anyone to do it is something that apparently never crossed his mind. He marvelled at the way God worked but never questioned why he did it in the way that he did. He felt that he had received an inestimable privilege in being sent on the mission that had occupied him for most of his life, and that was good enough for him. The ways of God might be inscrutable, but to doubt them was a sign of unbelief that no Christian should ever fall into.[30]

The purpose of that mission was clear in his mind. It was so that the elect would obtain salvation in Christ Jesus. It was theirs by inheritance and divine appointment, but they had to be connected with it. Paul's mission was to turn theory into practice, to make real in the experience of the elect what was already theirs in principle. It was in this context that Paul was truly a minister of the Word. He did not invent the idea of the elect or their salvation, but was sent by God to link the one to the other.

Having made all this clear, Paul then added the somewhat curious phrase 'with eternal glory'. By itself, the meaning seems to be clear enough, but what is it referring to? Is it the salvation of the elect that is eternally glorious? Or will they become eternally glorious when they obtain it? Is 'eternal glory' something in addition to salvation, connected to it no doubt but conceptually distinct from it? All three readings are possible, but it seems most likely that it is the last of these that Paul had in mind. The eternal glory of the elect was the fruit of their salvation. Once they had obtained it they would enter into a life that would glorify them in and with the glory of God that had been manifested in Christ Jesus. It would not be a concealed salvation, something to be kept quiet out of humility or fear at offending others. On the contrary,

---

[30] Rom. 9.19-24.

it would be something that would shine out as evidence of the saving power of God and the magnificence of his grace. The elect would not glory in themselves, as if they had achieved something, but would reflect the glory of God in the gift that they had received from him. In other words, it was God's glory, and not theirs, that Paul was talking about here.

This understanding of 'eternal glory' chimes in with Paul's belief that the current state of mankind reflects a loss of the glory of God.[31] In that perspective, 'eternal glory' represents the glory that will be ours in eternity, in contrast to the sufferings that we are called upon to endure in the present. P. H. Towner expresses this as follows:

> What Timothy is to comprehend ... is that suffering is a normative part of the gospel ministry, as the lives of both Christ and Paul amply demonstrate. The picture stresses equally the mysterious paradox that makes human weakness the divine crucible from which ministry done in God's power may emerge. This fact alone makes enduring the hardest of afflictions worthwhile, and the completion of the elect's salvation is an urgent motive that Timothy himself must embrace.[32]

Paul went on from this to repeat what seems to have been a well-known saying, which he endorsed.[33] Sayings of this kind were popular in the early church, not least because few people could read and even fewer owned books. They had to commit their theological knowledge to memory, and simple verses like this one were one of the best ways to do that. This particular saying can be analysed into four phrases as follows:

| | |
|---|---|
| 1. If we die with Christ | We shall also live with him |
| 2. If we endure | We shall also reign with him |
| 3. If we deny him | He will also deny us |
| 4. If we are faithless | He remains faithful |

Each of the four phrases begins with a conditional clause and concludes with the effects which that condition will produce if it comes to pass. As is obvious from the content, the first two clauses were meant to encourage

---

[31] Rom. 3.23; 8.19-21. There may also be an echo of Jesus' prayer in John 17, especially v. 5, where he prays the Father to restore him to the glory which he had before his incarnation.
[32] Towner (2006), p. 506.
[33] Some have suggested that the saying may reflect an early Christian hymn, but that is uncertain and immaterial as far as interpreting it is concerned. See Johnson (2001), pp. 378-82, for a full discussion of the subject.

believers in their Christian life, whereas the last two were warnings of what would happen if they turned away from Christ.

To 'die with Christ' is a spiritual concept that Paul explained in Gal. 2.20, where he described himself as having been crucified with Christ but yet as alive in him.[34] This was not because he was still the same man that he had been before but because Christ had now transformed his life, giving him the hope of sharing in his eternal glory. It might be extended to include physical death, but that is not essential. For Paul, spiritual death and rebirth were primary, because once they had taken place, physical death would be of no real consequence. But to die physically without having first died spiritually would be a catastrophe, because there would be no way of coming back to life after death. Jesus was an exception to the rule, but only because as the Son of God he was sinless and so did not need to die spiritually. His physical death came about because he took on our sins, becoming a curse for our sake, so that by his death our sinfulness could be paid for and we could inherit the gift of new life that his resurrection brought.[35] The use of the past (aorist) tense for death indicates that it is something that should already have happened, and if that is the case it can only refer to our spiritual death, since its physical counterpart still awaits us. Paul was referring here to the basic identity that all Christians have – we have been born again in Christ. This is who we now are, and it determines everything that we think, say and do.

The second phrase speaks of endurance, or patience, which is expressed in the present tense – it is the life that believers are living now as children of God. The phrase that Paul quoted does not say whether this endurance involves suffering or not. We may take it that suffering is implied, or at least not excluded, but we must not press the sentence to the point of saying that if for some reason we do *not* suffer, we shall *not* reign with him. Suffering is not a necessary qualification for enjoying eternal glory, but endurance is. It may be that for some people endurance means simply hanging on through depression or discouragement, not 'suffering' in the classical sense of the term, but it is still not a pleasant experience! It may mean faithful fulfillment of routine daily tasks that seem boring most of the time but that are part of our service to God. Whatever the circumstances of any particular individual, it will always mean living as Jesus taught his disciples to do – one day at a time without worrying unduly about what might happen next.[36]

---

[34] The same image appears in Rom. 6.6-8, with reference to baptism, which underlines the spiritual nature of this 'death'.
[35] 2 Cor. 5.21; Gal. 3.13-14.
[36] Mt. 6.34.

The reward of enduring suffering in this life is that we shall reign with Christ in eternity. This is a theme that goes back to the teaching of Jesus himself, who told his disciples that when he took up his kingdom they too would sit on thrones and judge the twelve tribes of Israel.[37] The same idea occurs elsewhere in Paul's letters and is especially prominent in Revelation.[38] It was a stock theme of early Christian preaching, perhaps because the everyday reality than many Christians had to live with appeared to be so discouraging.[39]

The next line speaks of denial, which is obviously meant to be avoided. Translations read 'if we deny him', but the word 'him' is absent from the original Greek. No doubt it is a logical inference, based on Matthew 10.33, where Jesus said exactly this. But it may also be that there is a wider denial in view here – not just a rejection of Christ but of all God's works as well. It is what we would today call 'living in denial' by refusing to accept that Christ has any claim over our lives. If we fall into that trap, then he will deny us, not by ignoring us or claiming that we do not exist, but by excluding us from the benefits of a saving relationship with him. This is only fair; God will not impose himself on us if we do not want him, and we must not be surprised if he respects our decision to reject any connection with him. But at the same time we must understand that the practical result of that will be the loss of eternal life, which cannot be obtained apart from being faithful to him. John Chrysostom pointed out that although the phrase appears to express an equality of denial on both sides, in fact it is not so. In his words,

> we who deny him are men, but he who denies us is God; and how great is the distance between God and man, it is needless to say ... we injure ourselves, him we cannot injure.[40]

This reality was never far from Paul's thoughts, as we are reminded by his constant references to former disciples and colleagues who had fallen away and deserted the gospel mission. The temptation to renounce the faith was all the greater because Paul, the man who had done so much to propagate it, was now in prison awaiting probable death. It is unlikely that the apostle feared that Timothy would abandon him, especially given the warm commendation that the younger man received at the beginning of this letter, but others

---

[37] Mt. 19.28; Lk. 22.30.
[38] Rom. 5.17; 1 Cor. 6.2-3; Rev. 1.6; 3.21; 5.10; 20.4, 6; 22.5.
[39] Ambrosiaster (2009), pp. 146–7, added that we should bear our sufferings with out bitterness because the promised reward was so great.
[40] John Chrysostom, *Homilies on 2 Timothy*, 5.11 (NPNF, p. 492).

were more vulnerable and the likelihood of their falling away could not be discounted. What Paul said to Timothy wold have been heard by the whole church, and this was a message for them as much as it was for him.

The last line refers to 'faithlessness', which is similar to denial but not identical with it. The person who denies God is one who rejects him altogether, but someone who is faithless is one who disobeys or otherwise disappoints the God whom he has at some point agreed to serve. Faithlessness is failure in a relationship, not a complete rejection of that relationship's existence.[41] Like denial, it is something to be avoided, but notice how here the complementary part of the saying takes a different turn. In the previous three phrases there has been a direct parallelism – good has been matched by good, and bad by bad. In the final phrase, however, bad is matched by good. The reason for this is that although we can be (and indeed often are) unfaithful in our relationship with God because we are sinners, he cannot be unfaithful in his relationship to us, because he is sinless. As Paul put it, 'he cannot deny himself'. In a sense, both parties in the relationship are being true to character – we are naturally faithless and inconstant, whereas he is naturally faithful and trustworthy.[42] Thomas Aquinas saw in this an affirmation of Christ's omnipotence:

> to be able to fall pertains rather to impotence; for the fact that someone loses some being is due to the weakness of his power. But for Christ to deny himself would be to lose something of himself; consequently, the fact that he cannot deny himself is an aspect of his perfect power.[43]

It is in that that the assurance of our salvation lies. However far we may stray from him, God never gives up on us. He welcomes us back and restores us as the father in the parable restored his prodigal son.[44] Even denying him is not necessarily the end of the story, as the famous example of Peter reminds us.[45] There can be no greater sign of God's love for us that his willingness to forgive us and restore us to his fellowship. As Paul put it in Rom. 8.38-39, there is nothing that can separate us from that love. With God's promise we can know that when we repent of our faithlessness he will forgive us

---

[41] Marshall (2004), p. 741, echoed by Towner (2006), p. 513.
[42] Some commentators have taken Christ's faithfulness to mean that he will keep his word and pass judgment on apostates, but while that may be true in some sense, it is surely not what is intended here. See Marshall (2004), pp. 741-2, who rightly rejects this interpretation.
[43] Thomas Aquinas (2012), 2.2.57 (p. 369).
[44] Lk. 15.11-32.
[45] Mt. 26.69-75; Mk 14.66-72; Lk. 22.54-62; Jn 18.15-17. Only John (21.15-19) records Jesus' subsequent forgiveness and restoration of Peter.

and continue to bless us as he has promised he would do. The permanent faithfulness of God to his promises is amply illustrated by the history of Israel, the chosen people who were forever backsliding and turning their backs on him but whom he never abandoned. Paul even reminded his readers that despite their rejection of Christ, the Jewish people were still beloved and that once the work of evangelising the nations was completed, they too would be saved.[46]

For the Christian, the practical significance of this statement is that there is forgiveness for those who repent. However far we may stray from the path that God has prepared for us, there is always a way back. The lost sheep and the prodigal son can and will be reconciled to their shepherd and Father who will never abandon them.[47]

## 14-19. Working for God

*14. Remind them of this, and warn them before God that they are to avoid wrangling over words, which does no good but only ruins those who are listening. 15. Do your best to present yourself to God as one approved by him, a worker who has no need to be ashamed, rightly explaining the word of truth. 16. Avoid profane chatter, for it will lead people into more and more impiety, 17. and their talk will spread like gangrene. Among them are Hymenaeus and Philetus, 18. who have swerved from the truth by claiming that the resurrection has already taken place. They are upsetting the faith of some. 19. But God's firm foundation stands, bearing the inscription: 'The Lord knows those who are his', and 'Let everyone who calls on the name of the Lord turn away from wickedness.'*

After a fairly long digression, Paul now returned to the task that he had assigned to Timothy, which was the training of the next generation of teachers for the church. He asked Timothy to remind them of everything he had said, bearing witness before God 'not to quarrel about words' (*logomachein*), because that is useless and ruins those who hear the arguments, a policy that would inevitably lead to disaster (*katastrophē*). As Ambrosiaster perceptively noted,

> Argument inevitably twists matters, especially when many things are said which go against conscience, so that the person who appears to win on the outside actually loses spiritually on the inside. Nobody

---

[46] Rom. 11.23-32.
[47] Mt. 18.12-14; Lk. 15.3-7, 11-32.

lets himself be defeated, even if he knows that what he hears [from his opponent] is true.[48]

Here we come as close as Paul ever did to criticizing the kind of behaviour that was characteristic of the pagan philosophers of his time and possibly also of the rabbis he had known as a young man in Jerusalem. One of the main problems was that ancient philosophical schools generally lacked a fixed terminology, so people could either express the same idea in more than one way or else use the same words to mean different things. For example, words like 'being' and 'substance', which later became synonyms in Christian theology, were not necessarily so in the Greek intellectual world. What Christians understood by the term could be expressed philosophically as *ousia, to on, hypostasis, hypokeimenon* or even *hylē* ('matter'), depending on the preference of the individual teacher or school of thought. Whether one of these words was objectively preferable to the others was a matter of debate, and there were plenty of people prepared to indulge in that! Christians were by no means immune from this tendency, and in some ways it affected them more than it did the philosophers, because while they speculated about what ultimate reality might be, Christians had a specific world view and message to convey that was defined by the Hebrew Bible. It was therefore important for Christians to understand who and what God is, how he could become a man in Jesus Christ while remaining fully divine and how believers could experience his presence in their lives. What we now call the Trinity was inherent in Christian experience from the start, but it was not immediately clear how that belief could (or should) be expressed.

The church would take many centuries to work this out properly, and in some ways the task is not finished yet. But the experience of God that the words are meant to describe is the same today as it was in New Testament times. An agreed terminology is important in order to avoid possible misunderstanding, and in searching for this, theologians had to distinguish the substance of what they were trying to express from the various ways that it was being done in different parts of the church. In this very early period the process of definition had not gone very far, and Paul does not seem to have been addressing any particular debate, but his warning about the danger of getting entangled in words to no useful purpose would be needed in the centuries to come.[49] The church would be torn apart by arguments

---

[48] Ambrosiaster (2009), p. 147.
[49] Ironically, commentators argue about the precise meaning of the Greek phrase *ep'ouden chrēsimon*, translated here as 'to no useful purpose'. The general sense is clear enough, but there are differences of opinion as to whether it should be translated as 'good for nothing'

over whether the incarnate Christ had one 'nature' (*physis*) or two and over whether a 'person' (*persona*; *prosōpon*) was the same as a *hypostasis* or not. Modern scholars sometimes conclude that the various protagonists were not in fundamental disagreement with one another but needed to work out how what they were saying could be harmonized with the thought patterns of people who approached the same questions from different angles. Sometimes this worked, but often it did not, and the result was a series of schisms, some of which have endured to the present day.

Centuries later, John Calvin was aware of this danger and commented on it in his discussion of the Trinity, in which he accused those who rejected the standard theological terms ('person', 'substance', 'Trinity') of trying to smuggle in false teaching under the guise of strict Biblical 'accuracy'.[50] Even now, there are lively debates over theological terms which range from the supposedly 'sexist' use of masculine words like Father and Son to the more abstract question of whether it is still possible to speak of God as a 'substance'. These debates consume the energy of those who engage in them, but outsiders often wonder whether they really make much difference. Many conclude that theology is a waste of time and even potentially dangerous to the unity of the church because of the passionate disagreements that can arise over particular forms of expression. By taking things too far and creating controversies that need not exist, theologians have brought their discipline into discredit, to the great detriment of the church, which needs clear and sound doctrine in order to express its faith correctly. It can truly be said that Paul's fear that quarrels over words would lead to catastrophe has all too often been realized in the history of the church and is still a problem for us today.

Of course, it is possible for such debates to become a vehicle for introducing false teaching into the church, and Paul was very aware of that danger. He wanted Timothy to stick with the form of words which had been handed down to him and not to try to improve on them in the light of objections raised (or alternatives proposed) by people who did not appreciate what the gospel was. The ease with which that can happen, even with those who are well meaning, may be seen from the way in which the Greek term *psychikos anthrōpos*, which occurs in 1 Cor. 2.14, has been translated over the years. The meaning is clear enough – Paul was talking about unspiritual people whom he contrasted with the *pneumatikoi*, or spiritual ones. But many modern languages, including English, have no ready equivalent for *psychikos*, and in recent years translators have shied away from the generic use of 'man'

---

or 'to no useful result'. In practice, of course, it makes little or no difference. See Marshall (2004), p. 746.

[50] Calvin, *Institutio Christianae Religionis*, 1.13.3.

for *anthrōpos*, which can mean a human being of either sex. In the KJV, the phrase is translated 'natural man', which is a misreading of *psychikos*.⁵¹ But the ESV has retained 'natural' and altered 'man' to 'person', which is even worse. To say that the 'natural person' does not know the things of the Spirit of God is to deny that the members of the Godhead do not know themselves, because in theological usage the word 'person' is not synonymous with 'human being'. False teaching has thus crept in, although the intentions of the translators could not have been farther from that.

What Timothy was expected to teach to others he had to demonstrate himself. Paul tells him that he must 'study' (*spoudazō*) to present himself before God as one 'approved' (*dokimos*). The Greek word *spoudazō* implies effort and dedication, both of which are necessary if the goal is to be achieved. The indwelling presence of the Holy Spirit and the gift of God are essential prerequisites for success, but Paul knew that their work would manifest itself in an individual's life as a spiritual struggle against the 'flesh'. Paul did not use that word here, but the implication is clear. Anything that detracted from the service of God was to be avoided, and we know from what he said both here and elsewhere that the Christian worker would have to subdue his own desires before being fit to minister to others.

The familiar triadic pattern appears once more in the way Paul described what he wanted Timothy to be like. The word *dokimos* suggests that he will have been tried and tested. Approval of a worker does not come automatically, but only after he has been examined properly. The real training of a future minister lies in this testing. It is one thing to learn the facts and basic elements needed for ministry, but until these have been tried and refined by real-life experience, no one can know for sure how effective the minister will be in using the skills that he had been taught. Such testing may be a rude shock to the system, and it will certainly challenge anyone who thinks that Christian service is easy and straightforward, but it is the key to survival and to eventual success. Those training for ministry must realize this and accept that the struggles they have to face are essential preparation for the tasks that they will be called to perform.

The nature of Timothy's testing is made clear by what comes next. He has to show that he is a worker who is not ashamed or embarrassed (*anepaischyntos*) by the tasks that he has been given. Just as Paul had previously used the examples of a soldier and a farmer, so here again he compared Timothy to a 'workman' (*ergatēs*) rather than to a philosopher or a rabbi. Considering that the work he was being called to do was that of a

---

⁵¹ The Greek word for natural is *physikos*.

teacher, and that teachers would never have been described as 'workmen', the comparison is quite striking. 'Workman' is admittedly a fairly vague term, but it would be someone like a carpenter or a plumber, not a pen-pusher sitting behind a desk. In hiring such a person to do a job, we expect him to know what to do, and if he fails, it is embarrassing – not least to him. He must therefore be well trained and able to cope with whatever might turn up within his expected range of competence, which in Timothy's case was a tall order. As the chief pastor of an eclectic congregation he had to deal with a wide range of different people – Jews and Gentiles, old and young, skilled and unskilled. The gospel message was the same for everyone, but its practical application varied from one individual to the next. Paul could (and did) help out to some extent, but even he could not foresee everything that might happen, and so Timothy had to be prepared to cope with the unforeseen and the unforeseeable. As any modern pastor will be quick to affirm, nothing much has changed in the centuries since!

As a good workman, Timothy was called to 'rightly divide' (*orthotomō*) the word of truth. The image is that of a carpenter or a butcher, who is expected to be able to cut things up in the right way. It could be used of writing, because a *tomos* (literally a 'cut') is a volume, so what we have here might be described as a play on words.[52] The important thing was that Timothy should know how to apply the principles of his teaching in the right way. It was not enough to set out abstract ideas, even if they were true. Without the correct application, the theory would go over most people's heads and be discredited because nobody would know what to do with it. This is what often happens in modern sermons. The preacher may give a thorough and convincing analysis of his text but fail to indicate how it ought to be applied to the situation of his hearers. Some even justify this approach as the only 'objective' one; in their view, congregations ought to be able to apply the message to themselves without further assistance. Unfortunately, that is seldom true. Most people need to be walked through the meaning of a text and be given plenty of illustrations of how it might be used. It is obviously not possible for a preacher to foresee every situation and sometimes private guidance is needed, but at least he can put people on the right track and get them to ponder what the meaning of the message might be in their case. John Calvin expressed it very well when he wrote,

---

[52] For the many possible meanings of this word, see Marshall (2004), pp. 748–9. He concludes that the basic choice 'lies between right teaching and right living' but prefers the former because of the surrounding context. However, as so often in such cases, it is not necessary to choose. Right teaching and right living ought to go together.

Paul assigns to teachers the duty of carving or dividing the Word, like a father dividing the bread into small pieces to feed his children ... Some mutilate it, some dismember it, some distort it, some break it in pieces, some, as I have said, keep to the outside and never come to the heart of the matter. With all these faults he contrasts a right dividing, that is, a manner of exposition apt to edify. This is the rule by which we should judge every interpretation of Scripture.[53]

The meaning of the phrase 'the word of truth' (*ho logos tēs alētheias*) is somewhat ambiguous. It presumably refers to the message of the gospel, at least in some form, but it could also mean the Hebrew Bible, which Timothy was expected to interpret correctly. As so often in Paul's Epistles, where more than one option is available it is probably best to include both possibilities and to resist the temptation to choose one over the other. The gospel was proclaimed in the promises given through the prophets of the Old Testament, and rightly interpreting it would necessarily involve understanding what they were trying to say and not getting lost in superficial details or carried away by red herrings as the false teachers were doing. In the final analysis, of course, the 'word of truth' is Christ, who is both the *logos* and the 'truth', and 'rightly dividing' him is nothing other than rightly interpreting who he is and what he has done for our salvation.[54] Anyone who lost sight of Christ, for whatever reason, was failing in his duty to read the Scriptures and proclaim the gospel properly, and that was what Paul was mainly concerned about here.

This positive command contrasts sharply with what follows. After encouraging Timothy by pointing out to him what sort of person he must be like, Paul immediately went on to tell him what *not* to do. He was to avoid godless or irreverent 'babble' (*kenophōnia*, literally 'empty noise'), by which Paul appears to have meant false teaching more than anything else, though it would also include pointless speculation about genealogies and so on – the sorts of things he warned Timothy about in his first Epistle. The danger of indulging in such time-wasting babble is not just that it has nothing to offer but that it is liable to lead to something even worse. Paul was convinced that those who were attracted by such vanities were heading down the road of godlessness (*asebeia*) which was the exact opposite of the *eusebeia* that he was trying to promote. What we see here is the way in which false teaching, even if it is relatively minor and apparently harmless in itself, can develop into something far more serious and deadly. People who start off with a bad

---

[53] Calvin (1964), pp. 313–14.
[54] Jn 14.6.

grounding in the faith are unlikely to appreciate sound teaching, because it will not agree with what they have already learned. Instead, they will look for things that confirm what they already believe, and that can only lead them down the path of further error. Once that starts, the gangrene (*gangraina*) will spread and eventually destroy the body.

Two examples of people who had fallen into this trap were Hymenaeus and Philetus. We do not know who they were, though a Hymenaeus appears in 1 Tim. 1.6 and is probably the same person. In the earlier Epistle, Hymenaeus was accused of blaspheming, whatever that meant in the context, and if he was the same man as the one mentioned here, it would appear that his contrariness had borne poisonous fruit. Be that as it may, both men were obviously well known to both Paul and Timothy, and their ability to influence people in the church suggests that they were fairly prominent members of it. Whether they had any formal teaching qualifications is impossible to say, but they had certainly diverged from the truth and upset the faith of some believers. That indicates that they had been free to spread their ideas and that they had enjoyed some influence, if not any recognized authority, over others. Unusually, we are given some idea of what it was that they taught, but although we can easily understand why they were wrong, it is not clear how they arrived at their error in the first place. According to what Paul said about them, they believed that the resurrection had already happened! What could that possibly have meant, when it seems clear from simple observation that it cannot have been true?

At one level, it could be argued that the resurrection *of Jesus* had already happened, and perhaps they thought that he was the only one who would be raised from the dead in the literal sense. That went clear against the teaching of Paul, who on different occasions spoke clearly about the resurrection that was yet to come and that would embrace everyone.[55] Whatever Hymenaeus and Philetus were teaching, it cannot have been that, since it was so obviously false. Perhaps they understood 'resurrection' in a purely spiritual sense and believed that it had occurred to individual Christians at the time of their conversion.[56] If they had been 'born again in baptism', they assumed that there was then nothing more to look forward to.[57] From the way in which Paul described the effect that their teaching had on people, it is probably best to conclude that what they said was that any resurrection that was going to take place had already occurred. They would certainly include the resurrection of Jesus and possibly those of the others who were reported as

---

[55] 1 Cor. 15.35-58; 1 Thess. 4.13-18.
[56] Calvin (1964), p. 315, interpreted the phrase in this way.
[57] Rom. 6.3-5. See also Jn 3.5.

having come back from the dead when the tombs were opened on Easter Sunday morning.⁵⁸ The miracle of bringing new life out of death had already taken place and later believers would not experience it in the same way. That, of course, raised the whole question of what it meant to be a Christian in the first place. Without a bodily resurrection at the last judgment there could be no eternal life in the Christian sense and therefore no hope of genuine salvation for the believer.⁵⁹ Christianity would be reduced to being a moral code in this life, with the church as a fellowship of the like-minded and little else. In essence it would be no more than a support group, with little to offer other than companionship here and now. That was not unimportant, of course, but it was far less than the salvation promised to us by Jesus. Without the resurrection the gospel made no sense, and it was with this in mind that Paul called their teaching *kenophōnia*.⁶⁰

What Hymenaeus and Philetus actually taught is impossible to say for sure. Many commentators have thought that it was some form of gnosticism, but the vagueness of that term is such that it could cover almost anything. It may have had something to do with Paul's teaching on baptism, which he described elsewhere as a dying and rising again with Christ.⁶¹ If that were interpreted to mean that every baptized Christian had experienced a 'resurrection' in the act of professing Christian faith, then it could be claimed that there was nothing further to hope for. It might then lead to the view that believers can and should live a 'perfect' life here on earth, which might include ascetic practices that Paul had warned against in his first Epistle. In the words of P. H. Towner,

> The implication of such a teaching for the average believer would have been that the resurrection hope was completely spiritualized into some presently attainable mode of living. In essence, however, it meant the deflation of hope in a substantial resurrection, and meant that salvation became a totally spiritual (as opposed to material) affair. In any case, it marked a confusion of the relation of this temporal stressful existence and future perfection in salvation. For those in the community who could not quite see through the present curtain of distress to the traditional Pauline hope of resurrection, the doctrine of present resurrection offered a compelling substitute, but at the cost of the disruption to their faith.⁶²

---

⁵⁸ Mt. 27.53-54. Thomas Aquinas (2012), 2.2.68 (p. 372), referred to this.
⁵⁹ Mt. 25.31-46.
⁶⁰ 1 Cor. 15.17-19.
⁶¹ Rom. 6.3-8.
⁶² Towner (2006), p. 529.

This would appear to be closest to the truth, but we must be careful. John Chrysostom, for example, thought that Hymenaeus taught that the resurrection was past because he wanted to avoid judgment and retribution:

> if the resurrection is already past, not only do we suffer loss in being deprived of that great glory, but because judgment is taken away, and retribution also. For if the resurrection is past, retribution is also past. The good therefore have reaped persecutions and afflictions, and the wicked have not been punished, nay verily, they live in great pleasure.[63]

It is important to note that it was not so much the teaching that Paul wanted to condemn as the teachers who purveyed it. Perhaps he thought that the teaching was so obviously wrong that it did not need a rebuttal of the kind that he gave at some length in 1 Corinthians 15. Whether that was true or not, Paul's focus was clearly on the authority given to teachers, which must not be abused. Hymenaeus and Philetus may have gone astray, but in spite of that, there was a firm foundation (*themelios*) that remained and that can only be understood as divine election – the Lord knows who belongs to him because he has chosen and appointed them from the beginning. This verse is an allusion to Num. 16.5, where Moses tells the people that God will separate the true believers from those who have succumbed to the heresy of Korah. Paul did not dwell on that, but Korah's rebellion had a paradigmatic significance in the early church and it cannot have been far from Paul's mind when he thought of men like Hymenaeus and Philetus.[64] As far as Paul was concerned, this verse from the Torah set the seal (*sphragis*) on the truth of what he was saying and on the condemnation of the false teachers that followed on naturally from that. John Calvin interpreted this as follows:

> Both the word 'seal' and the clause that follows remind us that we are not to judge according to our own opinion whether the number of the elect is great or small. For what God has sealed he intends to be as it were a closed book to us: also, if it belongs to God to know who are his, it is not surprising that often a great number of them are unknown to us and that we should make mistakes as to who they are.[65]

The second part of v. 19 looks like another quote from the Old Testament, but although there is some resemblance to the LXX version of Isa. 26.13 it

---

[63] John Chrysostom, *Homilies on 2 Timothy*, 5.18 (NPNF 13, p. 493).
[64] See Jude 1.11.
[65] Calvin (1964), p. 316.

is hard to be certain about this. Perhaps Paul was alluding to Scripture in a loose way, as he sometimes did, or perhaps it was not intended to be a quotation at all but just his interpretation of the verse from Numbers. In that case, Paul's logic would be that because the Lord knows who belongs to him, those who call on his name must depart from their iniquity, since he is sure to see what they are doing and will reject them if they are not acting in a manner consistent with their profession. The expression 'who names the name of the Lord' has an obvious Old Testament ring to it, and the 'name of the Lord' can only be a reference to YHWH (Yahweh). The phrase means 'those who claim to belong to the Lord' which explains why they must cease from doing what is wrong. Those who belong to God must reflect his character in what they do, and if they fail in this they will be excluded from the kingdom when Christ returns in judgment. Jesus himself taught that there were many who called on his name but whose hearts were far from him, and he warned his disciples of the fate that awaited such people in the last judgment. Paul must have known that, and it seems that it was that that he was picking up on here.[66] Theodore of Mopsuestia saw this verse as a message of comfort for Timothy, expressing a rare appreciation in the Greek church for the doctrine of so-called 'double' predestination:

> Here there are two things to console you: first, that the straying away of others does not destroy the truth of the facts; second, that God long ago recognized those who are truly his own. And so God long ago knew that those you now see being led astray would be reprobates. Therefore, nothing strange is happening to bewilder you, but what is happening is what God long ago knew would happen.[67]

## 20-21. Worthy servants

*20. In a large house there are utensils not only of gold and silver but also of wood and clay, some for special use, some for ordinary. 21. All who cleanse themselves of the things I have mentioned will become special utensils, dedicated and useful to the owner of the house, ready for every good work.*

Paul's warning about the fate of Hymenaeus and Philetus is followed by an explanatory excursus that describes the nature of the church and the place of

---

[66] For a full discussion of the Old Testament allusions and their relevance to Timothy's situation, see Marshall (2004), pp. 755–9, and especially Towner (2006), pp. 529–37.
[67] Theodore of Mopsuestia (2010), p. 709.

its members within it. As he sometimes did, he picked up the image of 'a great house' (*megalē oikia*) to illustrate the situation of the church, a phrase that recalls the teaching of Jesus, who told his disciples that in his Father's house there were many 'mansions'.[68] In this text, however, Paul did not concentrate on the dimensions of the house but on the varied nature of its contents. In a big house there would normally be 'vessels' (*skeuē*) of different kinds. Some would be precious vases made of gold and silver, used for show and to impress guests when they came to visit. But there would also be vessels of wood and clay which were needed to do the dirty work, so to speak. They would mostly be hidden from view, especially if guests turned up, but they performed their own function which was necessary for the good management of the house as a whole.

The implication here is that the variety of people in the church is similar to the range of pots and pans that are to be found in a big house. There are precious members, the gold and silver vessels as Paul called them, who play a prominent part in its life and whose example is a shining light to the others. Then there are the others who are superficially less impressive but who were just as important for the proper functioning of the house as a whole. Elsewhere Paul made the same point by using the image of the body. Some parts of it are prominent and make a definite impression on those who see them. But other parts are kept covered, not because they are unnecessary but because they appear to be weaker and are regarded as less presentable.[69] We do not know exactly how Paul distinguished the more presentable parts of the body (or pots) from the less presentable ones, but that does not matter. What concerned him was not the nature of the body part or pot itself but the honour given to it, and it is here that the main difference between 1 Corinthians 12 and this passage lies. When he was discussing the supposedly dishonourable parts of the body, he was using the term not in a moral or spiritual sense but in the context of the use to which the parts were put. It is obvious that he was referring primarily to what we today call our 'private parts', which we use for two quite different purposes. The most common one is what might be described as 'waste disposal', which occurs on a regular basis. But the other is the procreation of the human race, less frequent perhaps but vitally important for our survival. Paradoxically, therefore, what is most dishonourable in one way is most precious in another.

The image of the pots works somewhat differently. In principle, the same pot can be used for a variety of different purposes. On the surface it might

---

[68] Jn 14.2. 'Mansions' here means 'rooms'.
[69] 1 Cor. 12.14-26.

appear that those made of finer substances would be put to a better use, but that is by no means guaranteed. A gold or silver vessel could be used for the most menial tasks, though it is not difficult to see what the result of that would be. People would see the incongruity between the inherent value of the vessel and the use to which it was being put and they would be scandalized accordingly. But in this case, it was not the way the pot was being used that Paul was calling attention to. Instead, he was more concerned with the pot's dignity. Its honour was not determined by its use but by its character. A believer who had cleansed himself from dishonourable habits and behaviour was ready for whatever work the Master might have in mind for him to do, including those menial tasks that in a house would normally be left to wood and clay vessels. In God's kingdom, the character of a believer is of primary importance, and he will not make use of someone who is not fit for his service.

This is not to say that God never makes vessels for dishonourable purposes. In Rom. 9.21 Paul wrote, 'Has the potter no right over the clay, to make out of the same lump one vessel for honourable use and another for dishonourable use?' The context there was different from this one, but the essential point is the same. Pots that in physical terms were identical were put to very different uses according to the wishes of the potter, who had consigned some to destruction and others to glory. Where human beings were concerned, the difference was evident in their faith or lack of it – unbelievers were destroyed but believers were glorified, whether they were Jews (children of the promise) or Gentiles. The way for a believer to be set aside for honour was by turning away from thoughts and deeds that reflect this world and embracing the things of God instead. The fact that this is possible shows that for Paul, the most important thing was that a believer is a 'vessel' (*skeuos*) which is not predetermined by its physical origin or nature but which can be transformed into something useful to God by the power of his Spirit. People who think that they are good for very little can be used for God's glory if their hearts and minds are pure. If his spiritual state is sound, then the believer will be sanctified (*hēgiasmenos*, from *hagiazō*) and made fit for the purposes of God's kingdom.

This sanctification is not a material change but a spiritual one, and it must be understood accordingly. Holiness is not a physical alteration or improvement in the condition of the one who receives it. Wood and clay do not become gold and silver by a process of transubstantiation, but if they are properly consecrated to God they can be used for the same purposes as a gold or silver vessel can be. For a gold vessel to be employed as if it were a wooden one seems wrong, but the reverse may be both surprising and impressive. Something we would never have imagined becomes possible because God has chosen humble things to shame the proud.[70] This is what the church is like. God's servants do not necessarily look the part in the way that the world judges such things, but if the heart is right, this will not matter, because it is in our weakness that his power is made strong.[71]

## 22-26. The character of God's servants

> *22. Shun youthful passions and pursue righteousness, faith, love, and peace, along with those who call on the Lord from a pure heart. 23. Have nothing to do with stupid and senseless controversies; you know that they breed quarrels. 24. And the Lord's servant must not be quarrelsome but kindly to everyone, an apt teacher, patient, 25. correcting opponents with gentleness. God may perhaps grant that they will repent and come to know the truth, 26. and that they may escape from the snare of the devil, having been held captive by him to do his will.*

From what Paul went on to say next it appears that he regarded the unsuitability of the dishonourable vessels as being at least partly due to their immaturity. This seems to be the implication of his command to Timothy to 'flee youthful passions' (*neōterikas epithymias pheuge*). He does not expound on what those passions might be, but young people are typically inclined to behave in ways that shock their elders and to be irresponsible in their behaviour.[72] They are often amused by things that are a complete waste of time and may be willing to experiment with drugs and so on, knowing in their minds that they are harmful but thinking that in their youth they are indestructible. They can always reform and settle down later, or so they imagine. Every once in a while, their escapades go terribly wrong and lead to the death of a young man or woman whose promise has been extinguished by a momentary act of foolishness that has cost them everything. Paul did not want Timothy to fritter his life away like that but rather to make the best use of his youthful energy by developing habits that would stand him in good stead for the future. This is particularly important for those called to Christian ministry. The quality of a pastor's devotional life, his sense of

---

[70] 1 Cor. 1.26-29.
[71] 2 Cor. 12.9.
[72] The general nature of Paul's warning is brought out by Marshall (2004), p. 764, supported by Towner (2006), pp. 543-4, who remarks, 'sexual lust does not seem to be the focus, and the plurality of the whole construction suggests a broad pattern of behaviour rather than a particular weakness.'

commitment and his general trustworthiness are of the utmost importance, not just for the impression he will give to others but for his own spiritual stability under stress. Too many pastors make shipwreck of their ministry because they have not heeded this advice, and Paul's counsel to Timothy is as valid for us today as it was for him.

John Chrysostom read these words in a way that applied them to everyone, whether young or old:

> Not only the lust of fornication, but every inordinate desire is a youthful lust. Let the aged learn that they ought not to do the deeds of the youthful. If one be given to insolence, or a lover of power, of rices, of bodily pleasures, it is a youthful lust and foolish. These things must proceed from a heart not yet established, from a mind not deeply grounded, but in a wavering state.[73]

Rather than associate with immature and irresponsible people, Timothy is advised to cultivate the company of those who 'call on the Lord from a pure heart'. There is an echo here of what Jesus said in the Sermon on the Mount, 'Blessed are the pure in heart, for they shall see God', but the sentiment is too general and too widespread for us to be able to say that it is a direct allusion to that.[74] What matters is that a person's heart should be pure before he or she prays or invokes the aid of God. This is vitally important and is too often overlooked. God is not an emergency rescue service whose job is to get foolish people out of trouble. He relates to those who relate to him in the right way. A pure heart is one that is free of all unworthy motives. We cannot use God to serve our own ends, or claim his support for things that we have done when we know they go against his will. A pure heart seeks only to obey God's commands to the best of its ability, whether it understands them or not. Trusting God is a matter of faith that he will keep his promises, whatever the circumstances and however much we may be tested along the way. Ulterior motives on our part must be peeled away and discarded, which is never easy to do, but which is essential if we expect God to hear us when we call on him.

Like those who have a pure heart, Timothy was commanded to pursue righteousness, faith, love and peace. Here Paul recalled what he had written in 1 Tim. 6.11. Three of the goals he mentioned (righteousness, faith and love) are the same, but this time he added 'peace' (*eirēnē*), which resembles the 'gentleness' (*praÿpathia*) of the earlier passage. This idea will recur in v. 25,

---

[73] John Chrystostom, *Homilies on 2 Timothy*, 6.22 (NPNF 13, p. 496). Calvin (1964), p. 319, said much the same thing but did not include older people in his remarks.
[74] Mt. 5.8.

but Paul's use of 'peace' here puts the emphasis more on outward relationships with the community than on the believer's own inner disposition. This may be connected with the fact that he has abandoned the usual triadic structure in favour of what appears to be a two-two contrast. Righteousness and faith are inner qualities that speak primarily of the believer's relationship to God, whereas love and peace, while they also draw on the believer's inner spiritual resources, are more likely to be seen in the way they govern his relationships with others.

To some extent this is an artificial distinction, but there is definitely a progression of thought from the internal to the external, from what is present in the heart to what is manifested in the church. The believer is called upon to be righteous above all, and the truly righteous person will be a man of faith. Out of his faith will flow love, which extends his righteousness to others, with peace becoming both the goal and the result of that.

Once again, Paul returns to a familiar theme, which is that of 'foolish and ignorant controversies' (*mōrai kai apaideutai zētēseis*). We do not know what these were, but by their nature they were probably ephemeral and inconsequential. That of course does not mean that they did not engage the energies of those who were involved in them. There are arguments that have to be fought because they involve matters of substance, but some people have a tendency to quarrel over trivialities or things that are of little consequence one way or another, and unfortunately their zeal for secondary matters may outstrip their concern for primary ones. What should the preacher wear in the pulpit? What version of the Bible should be preferred in the church? What hymns and/or style of music should predominate in worship? These things are important to many people and they may debate them with considerable passion, but in the larger scheme of things they hardly matter very much. The danger with distractions of this kind is that they will cause people to fall out with one another, the church will be divided and the gospel message will be lost in the process.

This is not the kind of situation that the Lord's servant (*doulos*) needs to be caught up in. He should not be an argumentative person but rather maintain benevolent neutrality when differences of opinion over non-essential matters arise and as far as possible adopt a common approach to everyone in the church. Disagreements there will be, but his duty is to smooth them over and try to make the various parts of the Lord's body work together in harmony. The qualities that ought to characterize him are as follows:

1. An ability to teach.
2. The patience to endure evil.
3. Gentleness in correcting his opponents.

The first of these is essential for every pastor and teacher, because it is the essence of his calling. There are always some people who have a great deal of knowledge and who may be brilliant in many ways but who cannot teach. It is simply not their gift. Of course it is important for a teacher to be teaching the right things; we do not want to learn from someone who is brilliant at conveying falsehoods! But the ability to teach is also necessary, because if the truth is not communicated effectively it will be lost, misunderstood or discredited. Teaching is a spiritual gift that must be respected as such, and it should never be assumed that just because someone has a doctorate, he or she will be able to do it well.

The servant of the Lord must also be *anexikakos*, another hard-to-translate Greek word that means something like 'impervious to the power of evil'. This is a quality that is seldom mentioned directly but that is of the utmost importance for any leader. People who hold high office in the church are exposed to attack more than the ordinary members are, because if they can be brought down the damage done to the witness of the gospel will be that much greater. They are also likely to be the object of personal attack from people who are taking their frustrations out on God in the persons of his servants. Anyone who has pastored a church is familiar with this phenomenon, and those who want to succeed in ministry have to develop a thick skin. Part of the secret is to have the emotional and spiritual detachment necessary to recognize that many of the people who do this kind of thing are deeply disturbed and in need of the help that the pastor ought to be able to give.

It also means that a pastor must have a clear conscience before God so that when he is attacked by others he will not be frightened or silenced by them. False accusations are often impossible to disprove, and those who try to do so will often arouse suspicion. Jesus was silent when he stood before Herod and Pilate, and his silence spoke volumes. So it should be with us. Being accused of bad behaviour is not by itself a matter for shame. Jesus told his disciples that they were blessed when that happened to them, because they were walking in the path of the prophets and gaining a great reward for themselves in heaven.[75] If there is no substance to the charges laid against us we have nothing to fear – sooner or later, the hollowness of the accusations will be revealed. This does not mean that the process will be painless, but it will fail to achieve its object. God is stronger than any accuser, and if we are 'impervious to the power of evil' we shall have nothing to fear.

---

[75] Mt. 5.11-12.

This may be the reason why Paul added that the servant of the Lord needs to be able to correct those who oppose him with gentleness (*praÿtēs*). After what Paul has said about the false teachers, it sounds odd to hear him speak like this, but for all his harsh words against those who pervert the truth and undermine the teaching of the apostles, Paul had the breadth of vision to see that those who did such things were not necessarily beyond redemption. If it was possible to put them right, then Timothy would be well advised to do so. There was always the chance, however remote it might seem to be, that God would grant them repentance. Repentance is never easy, particularly for leaders of the church who have gone astray, because pride gets in the way and prevents them from running the risk of losing face. They may be unwilling to withdraw earlier remarks, perhaps because they are afraid of what people might think if they did. Loss of face is a very powerful deterrent for many people and it often prevents the kind of restoration that Paul has in mind here.

The fruits of repentance are twofold. First, the repentant person will come to knowledge (*epignōsis*) of the truth. The Greek word is an expansion of the more familiar *gnōsis* and might best be translated as 'recognition'. There are plenty of unrepentant people who know the truth – the devil being foremost among them![76] It is not enough to have the facts; in order to guarantee repentance, there must also be a recognition of their importance and their authority over the way we think, speak and act. Knowing what is right is of no use if it makes no difference to anything we say or do; indeed, in that case the sinner's spiritual state will be worse than ever.

The second fruit of repentance is *ananēpsōsis*, another word that is hard to translate simply. It basically means something like 'coming to one's senses' and is to be understood as a healing and restoration of the mind. This is necessary because the sinner has been captured by the devil and ensnared to do his will. The dominion of Satan is not an external tyranny from which it is possible to remain internally pure in spirit. There are many cases where a foreign army has invaded a country but has been unable to subdue it, because it has remained spiritually resistant to the alien presence. Serious conquerors know that winning battles is not enough; it is also necessary to persuade the hearts and minds of the population so that they will willingly acquiesce in the situation. This is where Satan's victory over fallen man is most evident. Not only does he control the environment in which we live, but he has also trapped our will so that we do his bidding and not God's. Unbelievers do not engage in spiritual struggle the way Christians do, because they see no

---

[76] Jas 2.19.

conflict between what they want and what the devil has taught them to desire and expect. John Calvin was well aware of this and commented,

> Unbelievers are so intoxicated by Satan that in their stupor they are unaware of their misery. But, when God makes the light of his truth shine upon us, he wakens us out of that deadly sleep, breaks through the snares in which we were imprisoned, and having removed all the obstacles, forms us in his obedience.[77]

Paul knew that it was only when the sinner has 'come to his senses' and been set free from the power of Satan that he can begin to see what that is and fight against it. As he put it in his great epistle to the Romans, he knew what the right thing was but he was unable to do it, because his will on its own was incapable of resisting the power of sin.[78] It was only by the grace of God, given to him by the indwelling Holy Spirit, that he could he overcome this and live as a child of God in the world.

It is not clear from what Paul said here whether he was referring to a particular surrender to Satan on the part of the unbeliever nowadays or whether he was looking back to the primordial sin of Adam and drawing the logical consequences from that. The former interpretation seems to fit the context better, since not all sinners end up as false teachers and there does seem to be an inevitable correlation between these two things. But at a deeper level it does not matter very much whether we are talking about the recent or the distant past. The pattern of Satanic entrapment goes back to the garden of Eden and is a reminder to us that deliverance from his power is not attained by intellectual achievement alone. The idea that education is what is needed to dispel the clouds of ignorance is an Enlightenment conceit. It may be possible to get rid of a certain kind of wrongheadedness in that way, but there is no evidence that knowledge by itself will automatically lead to better behaviour.[79] In the mid-twentieth century no country was better educated or more scientifically advanced than Germany, but nowhere was the reign of evil more pronounced. What is true at a national level is also true of individuals – there is no one more dangerous than the 'evil genius'.

To be of sound mind is to have the right moral and spiritual compass, and this can only be acquired by being set free from the power of Satan. Evil is a spiritual force that can only be overcome by other spiritual forces that are more powerful than it is. The godless world does not understand

---

[77] Calvin (1964), p. 321.
[78] Rom. 7.15-25.
[79] Rom. 7.15-20.

this. Instead, it promotes learning and science as the answer to the human dilemma and tends to ignore the spiritual dimension altogether. Such a solution is inadequate and, in the end, it is a recipe for disaster. Repentance is in its own way a form of exorcism, though it seems strange to use that word to describe it. The reason for this is that it is a deliverance from spiritual forces beyond our control which results in a clear-headed understanding of what the human predicament really is. When that is understood, a new life in Christ becomes possible for the first time. The believer is delivered from his bondage and encouraged to make the most of his newfound freedom.

Whether Paul was thinking here of specific cases of people who had fallen into the snares of the devil is uncertain, though his naming of Hymenaeus and Philetus a little earlier suggests that he may have been. It seems that he thought that the deviations Timothy was forced to deal with were not so serious as to exclude the possibility of genuine repentance and restoration, as long as the right mixture of gentleness and patience was applied when teaching sinners the truth. Sometimes the greatest sinners turn out to be the ones who repent most deeply and sincerely – that is certainly how Paul saw himself![80] We should therefore avoid the temptation to develop theories about what Timothy's situation might have been and stick to the general principles that Paul outlined as a guide for him to follow. They remain the same, whatever the actual situation is, and are as valid for us today as they were for Timothy.[81]

---

[80] 1 Cor. 15.9; Gal. 1.13; Eph. 3.8.
[81] Thomas Aquinas (2012), 2.2.88 (p. 379), said of the devil, 'he gets only as much as he is permitted; but it is difficult to wrest from him what he has grasped.' Repentance and restoration were possible – but rare.

# 2 Timothy 3

## 1-9. The life and character of the godless

*1. You must understand this, that in the last days distressing times will come. 2. For people will be lovers of themselves, lovers of money, boasters, arrogant, abusive, disobedient to their parents, ungrateful, unholy, 3. inhuman, implacable, slanderers, profligates, brutes, haters of good, 4. treacherous, reckless, swollen with conceit, lovers of pleasure rather than lovers of God, 5. holding to the outward form of godliness but denying its power.*

*Avoid them! 6. For among them are those who make their way into households and captivate silly women, overwhelmed by their sins and swayed by all kinds of desires, 7. who are always being instructed and can never arrive at a knowledge of the truth. 8. As Jannes and Jambres opposed Moses, so these people, of corrupt mind and counterfeit faith, also oppose the truth. 9. But they will not make much progress, because, as in the case of these two men, their folly will become plain to everyone.*

In the third chapter of this Epistle, Paul gave an extended analysis of the godless characters who would infest the church before pointing to himself as a counterexample of the godly man whom he held up to Timothy as the right sort of person to follow. The theme of godlessness is one to which Paul had already alluded more than once in this Epistle, but now he let go with a list of vices, similar in some ways to the one in Rom. 1.29-31 but not quite as long. The list in Romans contains twenty-four different character types, whereas this one is limited to only nineteen! Both lists contain a number of unusual words, a few of which may have been invented for the occasion, but their meaning is unmistakable. The denunciation of vice was a stock theme of ancient rhetoric, so we should not be surprised to find Paul waxing eloquent on the subject, nor should we be concerned that the vices are not listed in any particular order, the way they appear to be in 1 Tim. 1.9-11, where there is a discernible connection to the Ten Commandments. It seems more likely that in this Epistle Paul just got carried away, as we would say today, and listed everything he could think of in the order that it came to him, without worrying about structuring the different types of vice in any logical sequence. Evil is evil after all, and it scarcely matters what order it comes in.[1] Having said that, there is a rhetorical effect that is noticeable when the words are read out loud, as they would have been in the early church. Many of them contain a *ph* sound, and there is a string of negatives beginning with *a*. In the mouth of a skilled reader, the list would have stuck in the minds of the hearers, and the message would have sunk in more effectively than it does today, when we are mostly reduced to reading it silently and in translation, where the effect is lost.[2]

Before launching into his catalogue, Paul prefaced it with an exhortation to Timothy, whom he urged to understand what was happening and why. Timothy had to realize that 'in the last days' (*en eschatais hēmerais*) 'distressing times' (*kairoi chalepoi*) would come. The theme of the 'last days' is frequently found in the prophetic literature of the Old Testament, where it usually refers to the culmination of God's plan and the fulfillment of his promises to Israel.[3] Elsewhere in the New Testament it is used to indicate the period since the coming of Christ, because it was in him that that plan and those promises were accomplished.[4] In that sense, the last days are right now, and Paul may have been referring to the present situation, as well as pointing towards the future.[5] This has led those who think the letter is pseudonymous to claim that the apostle was being portrayed as a prophet who was supposedly looking ahead to a situation that had come into being in the time of the pseudepigrapher, which may have been a generation or more later than the theoretical date of composition. I. H. Marshall, however, who does not accept Pauline authorship of the text in its present form, argues against the theory of a later pseudepigrapher:

---

[1] It should be noted, however, that Thomas Aquinas (2012), 2.3.93 (p. 382), divided the vices into three types. According to him, the first were sins against external things, the second concerned improper relationships to others and the third were sins against the self. The first three belong to the 'external' category, and the next six to the 'relational' one. They are subdivided into two groups of three – the first dealing with our attitudes towards superiors and the second with our attitudes towards our equals. Next come three more that are primarily directed towards the self. Unfortunately, the scheme seems to break down at that point and the last seven have no particular reference points.
[2] See L. T. Johnson (2001), pp. 409–10.
[3] This theme runs through Isaiah 40-66; Jeremiah 31–33 and Ezekiel 40–48.
[4] Heb. 1.2.
[5] Marshall (2004), p. 771, adopts this double perspective on the ground that Paul's verb usage shifts from the future to the present.

The writer gives the impression of quoting prophecy, but it is surely a natural enough device to say that we believe that in the last days certain things will happen, and indeed they already are! It is difficult to see why many commentators think that this is a sign of the mask falling as a second-century writer tries to preserve the fiction of Paul prophesying what would happen after his death and then cannot sustain the picture and so slips into the present tense.[6]

The position adopted here is that Paul was speaking of a time that had not yet come but that Timothy would live to see. That would seem to be the most obvious reading of the text as it stands, but if we opt for it, we must remember that the 'last days' stands for a spiritual reality more than for a temporal one and that it may be taking things too far to look for exact parallels to what Paul foretold in the life of the church of the next generation. On the other hand, there is no doubt that Paul thought that things would get worse before they got better and that Timothy had better be prepared for that. The 'last days' are portrayed, not as a time of ultimate triumph but as one of ever greater turmoil and trouble, and in that sense they are closer to the apocalyptic vision of Jesus than they are to the vision of a blessed fulfillment promised by the Old Testament prophecies.[7] That fact precludes us from interpreting the 'last days' in a purely eschatological sense, because chaos and disorder are not the end of the story. Destructive though they are, they are only the prelude to the final victory of Christ and his kingdom, which is already sealed in eternity but whose manifestation on earth we still await. It is from that perspective that we must approach what Paul revealed to Timothy here about what would come to pass before final consummation of God's victory over evil at the end of time.

It is in this context that we must understand the phrase 'distressing times'. The word used for 'times' implies 'seasons', that is to say, periods of time that may change or be interrupted. Things might be worse at one moment and better at others, or else an evil that is fundamentally constant might present itself in varying degrees of intensity and in different ways over an extended period of time. The situation at any given moment would be unpredictable and would not necessarily be explicable in terms of a single and inexorable decline. 'Distressing' is another word that is somewhat hard to define. At first sight we might get the impression that Paul was thinking about the spread of persecution or the emergence of widespread heresy, but that does not seem to have been the case. Paul appears to have been concerned primarily with

---

[6] Marshall (2004), p. 791.
[7] Mt. 24.5; Mk 13.5-6.

the moral and spiritual degeneration of particular individuals, though it is not immediately clear whether he was talking about members of the church or not. His categorizations are too general to be identified with any one group of people, and perhaps he had unbelievers in mind as well as Christians. But since there was not much that Paul or Timothy could do to influence those who were outside the fellowship of believers, we must assume that whatever the general population was like, members of the church were (or would become) equally bad, if not worse. They were Paul's primary concern, and it is in the context of church discipline that we must evaluate the force of his remarks. As John Calvin noted,

> He [Paul] does not attack or accuse external enemies who are openly opposed to the name of Christ, but people who belong to the family and wish to be reckoned among the members of the church. For God wishes to try his church to the point of letting her carry such pests in her own bosom, though she shudders at the thought of nurturing them. Thus if today there are mixed with us many whom we justly abhor, let us learn to groan patiently under that burden, since we are told that this is the lot of the Christian church.[8]

The corruption of God's people was nothing new, of course, and when Paul drew attention to Jannes and Jambres who had opposed Moses, he was tapping into an ancient tradition.[9] Israel had always contained dissident elements, and the church was no different. From the very beginning there were people who contested the apostles and their teaching, sometimes for financial gain.[10] The difficult times that Paul foresaw were therefore not very different from what had recurred periodically throughout Israel's history, and Paul was telling Timothy that such times had not ended with the coming of Christ. But in addition to interlopers who joined the church without really sharing its faith, there was the fact that even true believers are still sinful. The gospel is a message of salvation, but the grace of God does not transform people into something different from what they were before. What it does is offer us the strength to combat our sinful tendencies and make sure that they do not dominate our behaviour or the life of the church. The first step in this is to identify what the main character types are so that we can recognize our own failings and take appropriate steps to overcome them.

---

[8] Calvin (1964), pp. 322-3.
[9] See the remarks on v. 8 below.
[10] Acts 5.1-11; 8.18-24.

The first of the vices listed by Paul appears to be one that serves as an introduction to the others.[11] The people he was characterizing would be *philautoi*, 'self-centred' or 'lovers of self'. Everything else follows from that. Self-centredness is natural in one sense, because whoever else we are with at any given moment, we are never separated from ourselves. We are a constant presence in our own lives, and so it makes sense to recognize that and act accordingly. But God is also a constant presence in us and we cannot escape from him either. He is superior to us in every way and so deserves to take priority over our own self-interest. The problem with self-love is that it is wrongly focused. We are taught to love God first of all, and because we are created in his image, our love for him ought to be conducive to a proper love for ourselves that is based on that fundamental truth. In the context of this world, God-focused self-love understands that because we are sinners we cannot be the centre of our own mental and spiritual universe. We have to depend for survival on our fellow human beings, whom we must treat with the same consideration and respect that we have for ourselves. Above all, we must depend on God, who defines every other kind of love, including our self-love, and puts it in its proper place.

The lover of self who is not centred on God will probably also be a 'lover of money' (*philargyros*) if only because in any functioning economic system, it is money that makes our lives possible.[12] Without it we would be forced to beg and to live in reduced circumstances, and could not pretend to be the independent arbiters of our lives. Having enough to feed and clothe ourselves is a natural ambition and there is nothing wrong with it, but we can easily become obsessed by it and not know when to stop.[13] How much is enough? A family in the USA that has only one car and a black-and-white television set is regarded as poor, but in many parts of Africa and in the slums of India, such possessions would be luxuries. To have more money does not necessarily mean that we think we have too much and give the extra away. On the contrary, it usually seems to mean that we move into a higher income bracket and that our 'needs' expand to match. Grasping for money becomes an addiction; the more we have, the more we spend and the more we seem to need. Downsizing is not easy to do!

The next two vices belong together. A person who succeeds in this life is liable to become a 'boaster' (*alazōn*) and 'arrogant' (*hyperēphanos*). The first term implies a certain air of cockiness; the second, a sense of superiority. Whether people attribute worldly success to luck or to hard work, they enjoy

---

[11] See Marshall (2004), p. 772.
[12] See 1 Tim. 6.10, where Paul says that the love of money is a root of all evil.
[13] Jesus warned his disciples about this. See Mt. 6.19-21.

it when they get it and tend to think that they have deserved it. Today, even appeals to help the poor often assume something like this, because they ask us to contribute funds so that the people we are helping can have the comfort they *deserve*. Why do they deserve it? That is never explained, but the sense of entitlement which that expression conveys is now so pervasive that we no longer react to it. In the ancient world, boasting over one's prosperity was just as prevalent as it is today, although if we could be transported back in time we would just laugh at it. After all, even the Roman emperors did not live in the sort of comfort that most of us take for granted nowadays.

Arrogance is another vice that is easy to adopt, almost without thinking. If I am convinced that I have what I have because I deserve it, I am liable to think that I am better than others who are less well off. There is always a scale of relativity here, of course, because there are usually whole sections of society that are better off than we are. But there is always a certain type of person who will lick the boots of his superiors while at the same time kicking his inferiors down the steps, and that is the essence of what arrogance is. Needless to say it is highly destructive of social relationships, especially in the church where all members are equal, regardless of social or other worldly status. The equality of believers has never been easy to practise, and even in the early church there were differences of status that aroused the wrath of the New Testament writers.[14] Social inequality may be less visible today, especially in the Western world, but it is still there and it would be foolish to underestimate the power it has to distort the way members of the church interact with each other.

Self-importance and conceit will naturally tend to spill over into other things, and those who are arrogant are liable to be abusive to others (*blasphēmoi*). Nowadays we restrict the word 'blasphemy' to mean an offence against God, but in Greek it could apply to the abuse of other human beings as well. In essence, the phenomenon is an attitude common in relation to both God and man, because at its root it is failing to give others the respect that they should receive. It is more serious in the case of God, because the honour we owe him is so much greater than any deference that we ought to show to other people, but the principle is the same.[15] Abuse is particularly reprehensible when it is directed against parents, who in the ancient world especially, were always expected to be treated with the utmost consideration. 'Honour your father and mother' was the first commandment with a promise

---

[14] Jas 2.1-7.
[15] The possibility of a dual application of the word here is admitted by Marshall (2004), p. 773, and especially by Towner (2006), p. 556, though both commentators prefer the more general usage to one that is specifically directed against God.

attached to it and was doubly important for that reason.¹⁶ Those who did not submit to their parents (*goneusin apeitheis*) were destroying one of the most fundamental pillars of society by their indifference to the order of nature on which that society is based.

They were in fact being 'ungrateful' (*acharistoi*) which is the next category of vice. Ingratitude is one of the most widespread of sins and it touches people in every situation. Lack of appreciation for parents is the most fundamental form it can take, and once that is allowed anything becomes possible. People take what they can get and do not reflect on where it has come from or why. Even Jesus felt the force of it. On one occasion he healed ten lepers by telling them to go to the temple and wash themselves clean, but only one of them returned to say 'thank you'. If that could happen to him it can happen to anyone.¹⁷

Moving on from ingratitude, Paul mentioned those who are 'unholy' (*anhosioi*). He used the word *hosios* which emphasizes the human side of holiness more than the divine, perhaps because divine holiness (*hagiosynē*) is immutable and we either have it or not.¹⁸ Here it means an attitude that rejects any need to conform to the will of God or to orient our lives in a way that will be pleasing to him. Unholy people engage in activities that are inexpedient for the Christian, even if they are lawful. They have an unsavoury air about them which gives off an unpleasant spiritual odour. People like that are often very hard to deal with because they do not necessarily do anything wrong. Instead, they have a way of talking about things that are unedifying (to say the least) and of associating with people whose activities are not what one would expect of Christians. They may even justify this behaviour in the name of evangelism – they have to mix with the world in order to reach out to it! In fact, of course, it is the world that rubs off on them, not the other way round, and their pretensions are revealed for what they are. Christians cannot avoid ungodly people entirely, as Paul well understood.¹⁹ But there should be no tolerance for them in the church, which must draw a clear line between what is and what is not appropriate conduct for its members. The details of what this might be will vary from place to place, depending on local sensitivities, but the principle remains the same for all, and if there is a conflict between different interpretations of what is acceptable, Paul's advice

---

[16] Exod. 20.12; Eph. 6.2.
[17] Lk. 17.11-19.
[18] Jerome (2010), p. 300, explained the difference as follows: '"holy", which in Greek is expressed by *hosios*, signified more the idea of sanctity itself combined with religiousness. It is referred to God. For the one whom we call *holy*, the Greeks call *hagion*. But what they call *hosion* we can call pious towards God.'
[19] 1 Cor. 5.10.

was that believers should adopt the more restrictive approach so as not to cause unnecessary offence.[20]

Next come those who are 'inhuman' or 'heartless' (*astorgoi*). These are the people who are indifferent to the sufferings of others, who exact punishment without showing mercy and who demand from their debtors the very things that they seek to be excused from by their creditors. Jesus spoke about such people and condemned them in the light of the God who forgives the undeserving.[21] To be hard-hearted is the very antithesis of Christian love, and few people could be less indicative of what it means to be saved by grace through faith. The church is no place for heartless people, but neither can it become a 'soft touch' for the unscrupulous who will take advantage of the naive kindness of some believers. Jesus told his followers that they must be wise as serpents and harmless as doves, which in this case means that we must be discerning enough to spot frauds and resist them, but at the same time compassionate enough to recognize those who are truly in need and offer them all the help that we can.[22]

After the hard-hearted come those who are never satisfied, the 'implacable' (*aspondoi*). Some people seem to want everything and are not prepared to settle for anything less. They think that if they do not get their way they are not being properly respected – to say 'no' is to insult them! But life is seldom as absolute as that, and congregational life demands compromise. If one person insists on having his way all the time the community will soon grow tired of him and begin to disintegrate. What is the point of trying to share with others, if one individual insists on calling the tune for everybody? Worse still, giving such people what they want only increases their appetite for more. If their technique of blackmail has succeeded once, they reason, it will succeed again, and they will push the envelope (as we might say today) as far as they can. They are literally never satisfied! It is impossible to live happily with people like them because they have no consideration for others and do not respect anyone's interests but their own. Any community they are part of will be liable to fall apart if they are given free rein, and this is what we all too often see. Paul countered this in his letter to the Philippians, where he wrote that he had learned to be content with what he had been given and to make the best of his circumstances.[23] That is the spirit that every Christian should adopt, both for the common good and for his own peace of mind.

---

[20] 1 Cor. 8.1-13.
[21] Mt. 18.23-35.
[22] Mt. 10.16.
[23] Phil. 4.11.

Those who do not get their own way all the time are liable to turn against others and become slanderous (*diaboloi*). As far as they are concerned, everyone who opposes them is an enemy, and no words are too scurrilous to be used to defame them. It is no accident that Satan is the chief slanderer and that our word 'devil' is a corruption of the Greek term for this vice. Just as the devil created an inverted world in which innocent people are portrayed in the worst possible light, so human slanderers invent reasons for condemning others with little or no regard for the truth. It is easily done. Verbal accusations are often hard to prove and once a statement is uttered it cannot be retracted. Even people who are publicly declared to be innocent of a particular crime remained tarred with that brush, and sometimes it may be the only thing they are known for. The saying 'where there is smoke there is fire' is liable to be appropriated in such cases and cited to justify having a negative attitude towards the accused. The assumption is that they must be guilty of *something*, even if that cannot be proved or pinned down, and their reputation is ruined for no reason at all.

Slander is a crime, and in flagrant cases people can seek redress in the law courts, but that is an extreme scenario that seldom occurs in church life. Much more frequent are whispered comments behind people's backs, gossip that lacks any foundation in fact and a generally negative attitude towards others that is both attractive and repellent at the same time. It is attractive because there is a perversity in fallen human beings that likes to hear the worst about other people, but also repellent, because there is something unsavoury about the procedure and nobody really wants to be party to such behaviour. It is the divided mentality that keeps the tabloid press in business, but it has no place in church life. There are times when people have to be disciplined, but this should never be the result of accusations rooted in slander and gossip.

Another type of undesirable person was the *akratēs* ('un-self-controlled'), a word that has strong sexual connotations.[24] ('Chastity' is *enkrateia*.) It can probably be taken together with the next one, which is *anēmeros* ('brutal'). People who cannot master themselves but who act in ways that are injurious to others are an obvious source of discord in any community. Sex and violence may be the stuff of theatrical performance but they do not go down well in everyday life, and if they are allowed to run unchecked, society will dissolve into chaos. The ability to restrain oneself and guard one's strength for positive purposes is a mark of education and of maturity, both social and spiritual. It cannot be said that Christians are the only people who possess this virtue, but

---

[24] The NRSV translates this as 'profligates', the NIV and the ESV more accurately as people 'without self-control'.

they are certainly expected to manifest it as a sign of their faithfulness and dedication to the Lord.

After these come the *aphilagathoi* ('people who do not love good'). It is possible that Paul invented this word to fit the context, since it is not attested anywhere else, but its meaning is readily understandable. The 'good' (*agathon*) implies what is godly and pleasing to God, and is a more restricted concept than *kalos*, although the two terms are closely associated in classical literature, where the man who was *kalos k'agathos* was the ideal person that the philosophers longed for. Here Paul was talking not merely about those who have not attained that goal but about those who reject it and are put off by it. The people he had in mind were those who have turned against the 'good' in their minds and do not want it. There is, of course, a false piety which ought to be rejected, but that does not justify reacting against it to the point of despising goodness altogether. It remains a goal to be honoured and sought after, even when it cannot be achieved by human effort. Those who love it will be prompted to submit to the power of the Holy Spirit who can change their lives for the better; those who do not will remain in their state of lostness, unable even to recognize good when they see it.[25]

The *prodotai* ('treacherous') are another danger. These are the people who stab others in the back, who tell on them, often falsely, and who are completely unreliable. No church can survive if such people are tolerated in its midst because they cannot be trusted. They will betray confidences, blame others for things they have not done and generally discredit whoever they dislike and want to disparage. In some ways they resemble the next category, who are the 'reckless' (*propeteis*). The reckless are the ones who do not stop to consider the probable consequences of their actions. They do what they want, and if that works out the wrong way, then it is too bad for those who are caught up in the mess. Like the treacherous, they cannot be entrusted with anything. One of the reasons for such behaviour may be that those who indulge in it are conceited (*tetyphōmenoi*), and this is the next character trait that Paul condemned. Conceited people not only fail to see the effects of their actions but think that there is no need to consider them, because whatever they do must be right and therefore justified in itself. Nobody is perfect but the inability of so many to be self-critical is a real hindrance to progress in the church. Those who refuse to listen to others may get away with their audacity for a time but it will catch up to them in the end. For a pastor to fall into this trap is doubly dangerous, because he is liable to bring his congregation down as well as himself, and the latter state will be worse than the first.

---

[25] Mt. 23.37.

Finally, and in a sense summing up much of what has gone before, there are those who love pleasure (*philēdonoi*) rather than God (the *philotheoi*). What Paul has in mind here are people who have an appearance (*morphōsis*) of godliness on the outside but who deny its power (*dynamis*) in their lives and live for the pleasures of this world instead.[26] Of all the vices he has criticized so far, this is the one that is most particularly connected to the life of the church. The other character faults are shared in varying degrees with unbelievers, but this one is singled out because of the way that it contrasts with godliness, and godliness is a concept that is only meaningful in the context of a worshipping community. It could be applied to Judaism, and perhaps also to pagan worshippers, since 'godliness' or 'piety' (*eusebeia*) was known to them as well, but there can be no doubt that here it refers primarily to members of the church who 'talked the talk' but did not 'walk the walk', as we might say today.

Not surprisingly, Paul concluded his diatribe with the advice to 'avoid such people', but the position of the Greek conjunction *kai* ('and', 'also') suggests that it is these last ones that he has particularly in mind. The other vices are fairly obvious and it would not take much to steer clear of them, but Timothy might have been tempted to associate with those who were apparently godly. Among them he could at least speak and act like a Christian without any inhibition, and as the pastor of the church, he would probably be expected to do so. But this would be a misunderstanding and possibly even a form of deception on the part of the *philēdonoi*. While encouraging the pastor to be as godly as possible they would in fact be distancing themselves from him without saying so, and the end result would be the worst vice of all – hypocrisy. It is a common failing in the church, and Paul knew what he was talking about when he warned Timothy to avoid it.

Verse 6 indicates that some of these wicked people were active when Paul was writing. In particular, he was concerned about false teachers who had a way of worming themselves into individual households (*oikiai*) and captivating 'weak women' (*gynaikaria*). The 'households' were probably the places where Christian congregations met and where women enjoyed more freedom than they would have done elsewhere.[27] If the churches had congregated in a public place, it would have been difficult for outsiders to

---

[26] The word *morphōsis* may also mean 'training' or 'education' (cf. the French word 'formation'), but there is no real difference here. It is still a case of looking the part on paper but not corresponding to it in reality.

[27] We get glimpses of this from a number of New Testament texts. See, for example, the reference to 'Chloe's people' in 1 Cor. 1.11 and to the household of Lydia in Acts 16.14-15. Note that Lydia was free to invite Paul and his companions to stay with her – and they accepted!

wander in and start talking to women they did not already know. Nor is it very likely that there would have been groups like the one Paul described here that would congregate at random, even in somebody's house. It is much more likely that these women were part of a worshipping congregation, and that it was when they met for that purpose that these false teachers crept in. That they would gather together is not surprising, since probably the men and women sat separately, whether they were married or not. It may be that in many cases the women were there without their husbands, having become Christians (or at least developed an interest in spiritual things) on their own. We know that there were such people, and it is at least possible that some of them were widows, since they clearly had the freedom to meet in this way.[28] Quite how the false teachers, who were almost certainly men, were allowed to invade their gatherings is unknown, but it may be that the women invited them in to teach them, since Paul indicated that although they were always learning they never arrived at the truth. Passing statements of this kind give us an insight into what the early house churches must have been like, but as always, lack of evidence must make us cautious about coming to any firm conclusions about them.

It is obvious that Paul had a low opinion of these women, which is reinforced in the original text by the pejorative way in which he refers to them. They were *gynaikaria*, a neuter plural which when used to describe adult women was usually uncomplimentary, to put it mildly. In Latin, prostitutes were regularly referred to by using neuter words, and although Paul does not suggest that these *gynaikaria* were in that category, his hearers could easily have got a negative impression of them, which would only have been reinforced by the way he described them.[29] They were as follows:

1. 'Burdened with sins'.
2. 'Swayed by all kinds of desires'.
3. 'Always being instructed and never coming to a knowledge of the truth'.

There is a logical order in this triad. All three characteristics would have manifested themselves simultaneously, but Paul's analysis reveals their relative order of importance. First of all, these women were 'burdened' (*sesōreumena*)

---

[28] That women could be believers independently of their husbands is clear from Acts 17.4 and especially 1 Cor. 7.13-14.
[29] Ambrosiaster (2009), p. 150, was in no doubt that Paul's description fitted the Manichees perfectly. In his words, 'They seek out women who for vanity's sake want to hear something new, and by telling them some attractive things, they persuade them to accept wicked and unlawful ones.'

with sins.³⁰ This does not necessarily mean that they had committed a lot of sins that were weighing them down, either with guilt or with the consequences of their indiscretions. They were obviously not sinless but most likely they were not noticeably more sinful than anyone else. Perhaps they affected a sense of being burdened in this way in order to suggest that they were more spiritual than other members of the congregation, but if so, the opposite was true. Spiritually minded believers are always deeply conscious of their sinfulness, but they are not burdened by their sins, because they know that those sins have been forgiven by the blood of Christ and that they have been set free from them by the indwelling power of the Holy Spirit. There is all the difference in the world between being weighed down by a sense of guilt and being conscious that we are sinners saved by the grace of God. Those who are overwhelmed by sin have not heard the word of forgiveness and have not understood Christ in the way that they ought to. They may have been attracted to him as these women apparently were, but they have not been set free in the way that he wants them to be.

The sense of burden that these people felt was largely psychological and probably fictitious to a considerable degree. It would not be too much to suggest that they derived a perverse pleasure in feeling the way they did. It was a means of attracting attention, if nothing else, and gave them an excuse to waste their time in supposedly 'spiritual' pursuits, like studying the Bible for no apparent purpose. It is possible, as L. T. Johnson has suggested, that they were trapped by a social structure that offered no serious outlet to talented women. As he puts it,

> Women of position and means have often been seduced in just this fashion within patriarchal structures. In the twentieth century, the place and power of the monk Rasputin in the court of the czar owed everything to his capacity to captivate the czarina with his manner and message. The problem is obviously not the natural defects of women, but the artificial and culturally induced deficiencies of a society that systematically keeps certain categories of persons in a chronically undereducated and disempowered position, and therefore chronically in the posture of victims of unscrupulous manipulators of desperate human need.³¹

---

[30] The NRSV prefers 'overwhelmed by their sins', but 'burdened' is a better translation.
[31] Johnson (2001), p. 413. Johnson is clearly adopting the standpoint of a modern 'liberal' writer on women's affairs. Paul may have recognized the situation that he describes, but if so, he did not advocate what we would now call 'women's liberation' as the answer to the problem!

These women were governed by a wide range of feelings, and many of them were probably emotionally unstable. Their activities were a superficially respectable outlet for this, without providing a cure. The ESV translates *agomena* as 'led astray' but this is not necessarily implied by the text. It is not explicitly stated that they were being drawn into heresy, though that may be inferred from what follows in vv. 8-9. The fact that they were always studying but never arriving at any firm results suggests that they never got far enough to settle on a particular form of belief, whether it was heretical or not. They just flitted about from one thing to another, perhaps mixing truth with error but not noticing the difference. Their feelings ruled them but did not point them in any particular direction, which is why they were prime targets for unscrupulous false teachers.

The fact that they were 'always being instructed' suggests that they sought such teachers out. It is perfectly possible that if some of these women heard that a new teacher was in town they would gather around him and invite him to speak to them. Indeed, that is probable, since it would have been difficult for an unknown man to break into a female circle on his own initiative. These women made a habit of this behaviour, of course, which may have lessened the suspicions of the men and others in the church. If they had a reputation for that sort of thing they were probably left to get on with it, since trying to interfere would have caused more trouble than it was worth. That is certainly what tends to happen nowadays, and it may not be too fanciful to suppose that something similar was going on in the early church.

As with their sense of burden for sin, it is probable that they derived a perverse pleasure from this desire to learn and did not want any more than that. Their studying, like their sense of unworthiness, was not a means to an end but the end in itself. If they ever got what they were supposedly looking for their little game would be over, and they certainly did not want that! It is most unlikely that they were stupid. Some of them may have been a bit slow, but the relational dynamic that Paul was describing is too well known from other circumstances to allow us to explain their behaviour away like that. They were unable to come to the knowledge of the truth because they did not want to. They may be compared to children who are sent to piano lessons but never learn to play because they have no interest in it. No matter how many lessons they have, they never get anywhere, and the same seems to have been the case here.

It may be added in passing that the word for 'knowledge' is once again *epignōsis* rather than simply *gnōsis*, suggesting that what is involved is more than learning simple facts. What these women were failing to achieve was genuine understanding; they were simply not on the same wavelength as the material that was being put before them. The false teachers probably kept them going by flattering them, telling them that they were doing well when in fact they were getting nowhere. That would give the women a sense of achievement, make them invite the teachers back again and keep them useless as far as the rest of the church was concerned, which seems to be just what was happening.

Paul mentioned groups of women in a disparaging way, but is it fair to describe him as a misogynist? Could some men not have found themselves in a similar situation? First of all, it has to be said that Paul was not speaking about *all* women, but only about some. It is probably true that women were more gregarious than men and also more likely to be undereducated, so the situation he described here is by no means implausible. There were certainly men who sat around and discussed, and who were just as lost as these women apparently were, but they tended to be dignified as philosophers who were generally not very emotional or burdened by an inordinate sense of sin.[32]

But if, in the circumstances Paul was addressing, women came to the fore, it cannot be said that he thought that they were more prone to sinfulness than men were. After all, these women were being deluded by men, who may themselves have been deluded by others. Paul compared them to Jannes and Jambres, two men who opposed Moses, and blamed them for what they were doing to these women. Just as the sin of Eve was blamed on Adam, who should have known not to follow her into temptation, so here the behaviour of these women is blamed on the men who were leading them astray.[33]

Jannes and Jambres are apocryphal figures who may never have existed.[34] According to legend they had resisted Moses, and in Jewish folklore they were identified as the Egyptian magicians who tried to counter the plagues that Moses and Aaron inflicted on that country in an effort to persuade Pharaoh to let the Israelites leave.[35] They are mentioned in Targum Jonathan, and Origen (185?–254?) claimed that there was a book detailing their exploits, though it has not survived. Whether Paul believed that they were real people

---

[32] See Acts 17.21.
[33] Marshall (2004), pp. 777–8, makes this point forcefully, and even Johnson (2001), pp. 411–4, who is noticeably pro-feminist, agrees with him on this point.
[34] The names are probably corruptions of Hebrew originals. Jannes is thought to be connected with the Hebrew verb *'anah* ('oppose', 'contradict') in the form *Johana*, and Jambres may be a variation of *Mambres*, which actually appears in some ancient manuscripts and is supposed to derive from the Hebrew verb *marah* ('rebel'). See Marshall (2004), p. 778, and Towner (2006), pp. 563–4. The etymologies are uncertain but they have no bearing on the story itself.
[35] Exod. 7.11, 22.

is unknown and immaterial to his argument. They might best be compared to a figure like Merlin in the Arthurian legends. Everyone knows who he was but whether he existed historically is doubtful and is neither here nor there. So it was with Jannes and Jambres. Paul's readers knew who they were and understood what he was saying about them, and that was enough to validate his illustration in their eyes.

The sin of Jannes and Jambres was that they opposed Moses, the lawgiver of Israel and the voice of God to them. In exactly the same way, the sin of the false teachers was that they were opposed to the truth. This is interesting, because it tells us something about the structure of authority in the early church. The men who were misleading these weak women were not in the wrong merely because they were doing something that they had not been authorized or appointed to do. Paul would probably have commended them if they had been teaching the truth without 'official' approval, and it is clear that their apparent 'irregularity' was not the basis of his complaint against them.[36] Nor did Paul say that these men were opposing Christ, though that might have seemed the obvious contrast to make with Moses. No doubt he thought that they were, and since Christ was the truth, opposition to him would have amounted to falsehood, but even so, that was not the aspect of their behaviour that he concentrated on. Paul believed that it was the content of their message that was wrong, and it was because of their false teaching that he attacked them.

Paul described these men as 'corrupted in mind' (*katephtharmenoi ton noun*) and for that reason they were 'incompetent in matters of faith' (*adokimoi peri tēn pistin*).[37] Their problem was not one of inadequate education, as was the case of Apollos, who needed to be corrected in his views of baptism and repentance.[38] Rather it was that their minds were twisted and made unserviceable because the knowledge they had was corrupt. The difference may be compared to that between a car whose bodywork is rusted and a car whose engine has been ruined. The first kind of damage can be repaired, but the second cannot. So it was with these false teachers. Their faults were not superficial matters that could be put right with a little cosmetic surgery, as it were, but fundamental to their whole being. Even if everything they knew had been true in itself, it would have made no difference because their ability to process it had been fatally compromised. They were simply unable to

---

[36] Phil. 1.15-18.
[37] The NRSV paraphrases this as 'counterfeit faith' and the NIV describes them as rejected 'as far as the faith is concerned.' The ESV says that they are 'disqualified regarding the faith', which suggests that they have failed an examination!
[38] Acts 18.26.

connect with the truth as it had been revealed in Christ, and because of that they were unfit to teach anything regarding the Christian faith. Therefore whatever they learned and whatever they taught would have been skewed by their corrupt minds.

The only consolation Paul had to offer Timothy was that these false teachers would not get very far with their machinations. They might survive for a time, but sooner or later their madness (*anoia*) would become plain to everyone and they would fail, just as Jannes and Jambres had failed in their attempt to resist Moses. Falsehood can be made attractive and compelling for a time, but it lacks a solid foundation and eventually its weakness will be revealed. We see this in the church all the time. Just as in the first and second centuries, so today, false teachers appear for a time and gain a following, but when the bubble bursts their congregations collapse and before long it is as if they had never existed. Those who opposed the gospel in Ephesus must have seemed formidable to Timothy, but today we have no idea who they were and are only vaguely aware of what they taught, whereas Paul's words remain as vibrant now as they were when he first wrote them.

What we cannot know is why these men were led into their corrupt beliefs in the first place. The impression given by Paul is that it was not an accident of ignorance but a deliberate desire to refashion Paul's gospel for reasons that are not stated and impossible for us to reconstruct with any certainty. The closest we can get to what motivated them is a form of psychological speculation, as P. H. Towner has attempted. In his view, the false teachers may have

> found Paul's gospel insufficient or uncomfortable, probably because it did not affirm them as they wished to be affirmed, or protect the things that were most valuable to them. Perhaps because of its stress on equality or universality, those whose insecurities depended instead on affirmation of their uniqueness tended to resort to interpretations that underlined limitations and reinforced boundaries. Perhaps because of its stress on the unfinished nature of salvation and the pervasiveness of sin, those who were unsettled by a gospel that continually addressed immaturity and imperfection found it more comfortable to reshape the gospel into the proclamation of a finished salvation now.[39]

Perhaps ... that is all we can say for sure!

---

[39] Towner (2006), p. 567. Oddly, Towner goes on to claim that modern confessional orthodoxies are similar to the presumed errors of the false teachers because they have supposedly 'caged the gospel' and prevented it from being heard with its full force (p. 568).

## 10-17. The life and character of the godly

*10. Now you have observed my teaching, my conduct, my aim in life, my faith, my patience, my love, my steadfastness, 11. my persecutions and suffering the things that happened to me in Antioch, Iconium, and Lystra. What persecutions I endured! Yet the Lord rescued me from all of them. 12. Indeed, all who want to live a godly life in Christ Jesus will be persecuted. 13. But wicked people and imposters will go from bad to worse, deceiving others and being deceived. 14. But as for you, continue in what you have learned and firmly believed, knowing from whom you have learned it, 15. and how from childhood you have known the sacred writings that are able to instruct you for salvation through faith in Christ Jesus. 16. All Scripture is inspired by God and is useful for teaching, for reproof, for correction, and for training in righteousness, 17. so that everyone who belongs to God may be proficient, equipped for every good work.*

As he often did after a depressing account of sin and failure, Paul redressed the balance with a contrasting and positive message. This time, however, he did not tell Timothy what he should do to counteract the negative situation but praised him for what he had already done, and encouraged him to continue along the path he had marked out. Timothy had already distinguished himself in Paul's eyes as an authentic follower, someone who had understood his teaching, shared his attitude and accompanied him in his trials, if not physically then in spirit.

Paul introduced his theme with a list of the many ways in which Timothy had excelled. The essence of his success was that he had imitated Paul and based his ministry on that of the apostle. In commending him for this, Paul expounded his own life and ministry in three sets of triads, which may be set out as follows:

| | |
|---|---|
| 1. Paul's *teaching, conduct* and *aim* in life. | His purpose |
| 2. Paul's *faith, patience* and *love*. | His approach |
| 3. Paul's *steadfastness, persecutions* and *sufferings*. | His experience |

As is often the case, it is the first element in each of the triads that governs the other two, and the first triad that paves the way for the others. When we analyse what Paul said in this way we realize that it was his teaching that was the cornerstone of his ministry. This is only natural, since it was in order to safeguard and propagate that teaching that he was writing to Timothy in the first place. Without that foundation, the rest would have no meaning. Paul's doctrine can be summed up as Jesus Christ – who he is, what he has done and what he means for us. The rest is basically supplementary information and detail that fleshes out the wider implications of these basic principles. It is obvious, for example, that Paul believed that there was only one God, but this cannot be regarded as part of his 'teaching' in the sense that he was using the word here. It was a doctrine that everyone in the Jewish world already took for granted, and was not distinctive to him. When Paul spoke of *his* teaching he meant something that he could claim as his own, and that was the gospel. He could even speak of the gospel as if it were his personal possession, a message that had been specially entrusted to him for proclaiming to the Gentiles.[40] Of course, the other apostles taught the same thing, but as Paul had received it directly from the Lord he thought of it as in some sense uniquely his own.[41] For Timothy to follow Paul's teaching was therefore to preach Paul's gospel, and in the apostle's judgment, he had done that fully and fairly.

Next there came Paul's conduct, or behaviour (*agōgē*). There was a consistency between what Paul taught and how he lived that gave credence to his message. For Paul, the gospel was never an intellectual construct with little or no practical application. It was a new life in Christ that touched every aspect of his being. He recognized, as we all must, that he had not attained perfection in this life, but his goals had changed and he was determined to press on towards them.[42] His thoughts, his priorities and his everyday conduct were progressively being reoriented in order to conform more closely to the gospel, and he saw the same progression in Timothy. As John Calvin remarked,

> He [Timothy] is no ignorant raw recruit going forth into the arena, for Paul himself has already formed him by a long course of his own teaching. He refers not only to doctrine; for the other things he mentions are also of great importance ... he paints for us a lively picture of a good teacher, as one who shapes his pupils not only by his words but, so to speak, opens his own heart to them so that they may know that all his teaching is sincere ... such fundamental lessons had been imparted to Timothy in Paul's schools.[43]

---

[40] Rom. 2.16; 2 Tim. 2.8.
[41] Gal. 1.12.
[42] Phil. 3.12-16.
[43] Calvin (1964), p. 326.

The essential point Paul was making was that his behaviour, as well as Timothy's, was guided by his teaching. So often it seems to be the other way round – people act in a certain way and then justify it by concocting an explanation that will fit. But Paul was not like that. For him, it was the message of a new life in Christ that determined how he should behave in this world. That conviction often led to conflict, both inside the church and outside it, as he met various obstacles and prejudices that hindered his ministry. He was always in the spotlight, and those who wanted to discredit him lost no opportunity for doing so.[44] How he conducted himself was therefore of prime importance for his mission. Time and again, he was arrested and put on trial but the charges laid against him did not stick and he was set free. His message to Timothy was that honesty is the best policy – those whose behaviour is above board may be attacked but in the end they have nothing to fear.

This leads naturally to the third element in the first triad, which is Paul's aim in life (*prothesis*). His primary desire was to glorify God, something he could only do by obeying the divine mandate. In his case, the supreme command was his commission to preach the gospel to the Gentiles, and that is what he had done. He was determined to win others for Christ, to gather in the lost sheep of Israel, to offer new life and hope to those who were perishing in sin and ignorance. That aim had taken him across the world, had made him risk his life and had landed him in prison, but it had never changed. For Paul, life would not have been worth living if this aim had been abandoned, and he was convinced that as long as he remained faithful to it, things could only get better. However much he suffered, and even if he were to be put to death, it would all be for the sake of the gospel and his ministry would be fulfilled. In this too, Paul saw how Timothy was following in his footsteps and he rejoiced in that.

The second triad that Paul set out was the familiar faith, patience (*makrothymia*) and love, in which 'patience' may be taken as a variant for 'hope', since they both involve waiting on God for better things to come.[45] This triad comes second because it represents the means by which the goals of the first are realized. Faith, patience and love were all at work in the context of Paul's teaching, his conduct and his aim in life. It was by faith that the apostle dared to teach recalcitrant congregations, challenging them to accept unpalatable truths and to reform their lives in the light of them. It was with patience that he endured the many setbacks he was confronted with. Associates deserted him, converts lapsed into false teaching and his

---

[44] Acts 16.20; 17.6-7; 18.3; 19.26-27; 21.28-30.
[45] See 1 Cor. 13.13.

plans were thwarted by circumstances, but Paul pressed on regardless. He knew that the power of God is greater than anything we have or can claim for ourselves, and he was prepared to wait for him to act. God's timing is always right! Paul knew that in the end, the truth would triumph, and he trusted God to complete the good work that he had already begun. This patience he also saw at work in Timothy, who was learning by his own experience to take the long view in much the same way as Paul did.

Finally, there is love, the crowning glory of this triad of virtues and the one that connects faith and patience to pastoral practice. Paul had learned how to apply his beliefs to the people to whom he was ministering. With some he had to be gentle; with others he was forced to be direct and challenging. But whatever approach he took, it was always in love that he acted, because love was the fulfilling both of the law and of his mission. Of the three great virtues that undergirded his approach, love was the one that reached out to others, and it was for that reason that it was the greatest. Faith was directed towards God but in human terms it was internal to Paul himself and would not necessarily be apparent to others unless he taught them what it was. Patience likewise was directed towards God, but it was above all an internal virtue that other people would not immediately see. Love, by contrast, could not be hidden, even if some people misunderstood it. Like faith and patience, it was also directed towards God in the first instance, and it was with God's love for him that he loved others. But the fruit of this love was immediately visible to everyone, whether they appreciated it or not. In faith and patience he built himself up, but in love he built up the church. It was the crowning glory of his relationship both to God and to God's people, binding them together for his glory.

The third triad takes us from the spiritual attitudes that Paul adopted in the pursuit of his mission to the way it worked out in practice. This he characterized as 'steadfastness' (*hypomonē*). Steadfastness is a form of patience, but it is of a different kind from that represented by *makrothymia*. *Makrothymia* is the kind of patience that we often find in medical doctors. It begins as an approach to pastoral problems and reaches out to minister to those who suffer from them; it is an extension of Paul's love for the church and is best understood in that context. *Hypomonē*, on the other hand, is the patience that results from external attack. This was not something that Paul sought and in one sense it was quite alien to his mission, which was not one of stirring up conflict but of preaching the peace of God that passes understanding.[46] For him, his sufferings were part of his ministry and he

---

[46] Phil. 4.7.

understood that they would come to anyone who tried to live in a godly way, but he did nothing to invite them. At the same time, he did not strike back either, though when he was able to appeal to the law, he did so. Provincial officials did not have the right to beat Roman citizens, for example, and when that happened to Paul, he protested.[47] He also had the right to appeal to Caesar, which he did, and which explains why he was in prison in Rome.[48] But although he was not afraid to use the legal means of redress that were open to him, Paul never advocated the use of violence in response to the way he was treated. Just as Jesus told Peter in the Garden of Gethsemane to put his sword away,[49] so Paul told his congregations to arm themselves spiritually, not physically and to demonstrate by their steadfastness that theirs was the cause of truth.

When Paul spoke of persecutions in this context he meant those which he had suffered, not those that he had perpetrated against Christians before becoming one himself. The persecutions he had endured had led to considerable personal suffering. The two things are not necessarily connected, because it was always possible to exclude someone from the synagogue without pursuing and attacking him, as happened to Paul, but in practice they usually went together in his experience. Antipathy of this kind was something that he encountered almost everywhere he went, but in writing to Timothy he focused primarily on what happened to him on his first missionary journey, in Pisidian Antioch, Iconium and Lystra.[50] The story is told by Luke in Acts 13-14 and it is important for two reasons. First of all, it happened at the beginning of Paul's mission to the Gentiles and it set the tone for what was to follow. It is for that reason that Luke recounted these early persecutions in greater detail than he did those that occurred later on.

But secondly, it is important because it was on a return journey to Lystra that Paul came into contact with Timothy. We do not know whether Timothy was there when Paul first went to Lystra, but probably his mother and grandmother were fully aware of what was going on, even if Timothy was

---

[47] Acts 16.37-39; 22.25-29.
[48] Acts 25.11.
[49] Jn 18.10-11. See also Mt. 26.51-53; Mk 14.47-48; Lk. 22.50-51.
[50] A minor but telling point is that Lystra is neuter plural in Greek, not feminine singular, although Acts has the latter form three times (14.6; 14.21 and 16.1) and the former only twice (14.8 and 16.2). It was natural for neuter plurals of this kind to migrate to the feminine singular, and the curious duality of Acts, where the different forms occur in neighbouring verses, bears witness to this transitional uncertainty. But in 2 Timothy Lystra is (correctly) neuter plural – another argument against pseudonymity, since a later writer, and especially one who had never been there, would be more likely to make a mistake. Compare other Biblical examples – Myra (Acts 27.5) and Thyatira (Rev. 2.18), both of which are correctly recorded as neuter plurals.

not. It is therefore fair to say that Timothy's first experience of the apostle was against this backdrop of persecution. He knew what Paul had been through and had seen how God had rescued him from his tormentors, many of whom he would have known personally. Whatever the young Timothy understood of Paul's message, he must have been deeply impressed by what he had seen coming out of it. A man who is prepared to submit himself to the trials that Paul endured for the sake of his beliefs is someone who inspires respect and admiration, and it is quite possible that Timothy regarded him as a hero for that reason. We do not know that for sure, of course, but relationships often develop out of the circumstances in which they begin, and this one would appear to have been no exception. When Paul took the young Timothy with him, Timothy knew what to expect. Perhaps he felt a certain sense of adventure, as young men often do, but whether he did or not, there was never any doubt as to what he was letting himself in for.

To what extent did Paul believe that the persecutions which he endured were an integral part of his mission? The question is raised by what he said to Timothy in v. 12. In the apostle's view, everyone who wants to live a godly life in Christ will be persecuted. What does this mean? First of all, it should be said that Paul never sought the kind of opposition that he received. He endured rebuffs, but he did not ask for them nor did he regard his mission as a waste of time if they failed to materialize. After Christianity was legalized in the fourth century, there emerged a North African sect which taught that the church was not being itself if it was not suffering persecution. This sect is known to us by the name of one of its early leaders, a man called Donatus, who persuaded many people that a church that was at peace with the world was a church that had been corrupted by it. It was therefore necessary to stir up persecution in order to keep the church pure, and the Donatists made a public nuisance of themselves in order to pursue that aim.

Paul did not share that view. He focused on living for Christ and believed that if he did so, persecution would come of its own accord. Living as he did in the first generation of the church, he could not foresee what would happen when it was effectively outlawed for two and a half centuries. He himself was probably put to death by the Roman authorities in (or shortly after) the first official persecution under Nero (in AD 64), but that was still in the future when he wrote to Timothy, and there is no sign that he believed that death would be the inevitable consequence for everyone who bore witness for the faith. He had no theology of martyrdom, at least not in the sense that later generations would come to understand that, and we should not read his words with the benefit of that kind of hindsight.

Instead, we should see his remarks as referring to something more enduring and insidious that physical attack. Paul had not yet suffered death as a result of his persecutions, but he had stirred up opposition to his teaching and he knew that his enemies would do everything in their power to stamp it out if they could. As was the case in Pisidia and Galatia, the most determined opposition to his teaching would probably come from those who, from another perspective, were closest to it. The men who attacked him in places like Lystra were not pagans whom he had offended but Jews, some of whom were not above stirring up the local populace as part of their strategy for defeating Paul. In other words, it was those who in principle professed faith in the one true God, but who did not understand what that entailed in the light of Christ, who were the motivating force behind the persecution that Paul suffered.

This phenomenon has repeated itself throughout history. In the Middle Ages, attempts to reform the church were frequently rebuffed by the church authorities themselves, who did not want their boat to be rocked. Sometimes, as in the case of Francis of Assisi (1181?-1226), initial opposition was overcome and later generations came to see such reformers as saints. In other cases, like that of John Wycliffe (1328-1384), that did not happen, and their followers remained on the margins of the establishment. Often they were persecuted by the very people whose ideals they were trying to affirm, and much the same can be said of the Protestant Reformers who emerged in the sixteenth century. John Calvin was well aware that persecution can take many forms. As he put it,

> It is clear that there have been many godly men who have never undergone banishment or prison or sudden flight or any other kind of persecution. I answer that Satan has more than one way of persecuting Christ's servants ... it is absolutely necessary that all of them should endure the hostility of the world in some form in order that their faith may be exercised and their constancy proved. Satan, who is Christ's perpetual foe, never allows anyone a whole lifetime without disturbance, and there will always be wicked men to be thorns in our sides. In fact, as soon as a believer shows signs of zeal for God, the rage of all the ungodly is kindled, and though they may not have a drawn sword, they spue out their venom either by criticising or slandering or making an upheaval in some other way. Thus, although all are not faced with the same attacks and not involved in the same battles, they have a common warfare to wage and will never be wholly at peace and exempt from persecutions.[51]

---

[51] Calvin (1964), p. 327.

Today the church can no longer resort to such dramatic means as burning people at the stake in order to preserve a corrupt *status quo*, but persecution of would-be prophets and reformers has not ceased. They are still kept at arm's length by the establishment, and are ignored, if not actually attacked, by those in positions of power. In local congregations such people may be squeezed out because they appear to be a threat to the leadership. They may be gossiped about and slandered behind their backs in ways that they are barely conscious of and can do nothing to refute. Worst of all, those who attack them may think that they are performing a good work in the service of God, when in fact it is the devil whose bidding they are doing.

Meanwhile, while this is going on, genuinely wicked people, whom Paul called the *ponēroi* ('wicked people') and *goētes* ('imposters') carry on as if nothing can touch them. They go from bad to worse, deceiving others and being deceived themselves. They live in a curiously evil kind of fantasy world where lies are accepted as truth, and the truth is stamped out. It is an inverted spiritual culture, which is typical of a world that has forgotten God and set up idols for itself. This pattern is universal. It manifests itself in different ways at different times, but it is always present. In the modern world, wicked people present themselves as uniquely honest, tolerant and 'inclusive', while those who resist them are often unfairly denounced as racial or religious bigots (or both).

As he had done before, here again Paul slipped into a denunciation of those who had opposed him. But rather than continue down that line indefinitely, he stopped short and addressed Timothy directly. The world may be what it is, said Paul, but his young disciple was not to be misled by it. Instead, he was to remain firm in what he had learned and believed, recognizing from whom he had learned it. As so often in the Pastoral Epistles, we can detect a threefold pattern here too. Timothy had *learned* the truth, he had *believed* it and he *knew* where it had come from and trusted that source.

First of all, Timothy had been taught by people whom he knew were deserving of the highest honour and respect. His faith was not something that he had invented or modified to suit his own particular tastes. On the contrary, it was a comprehensive belief system that he had learned from men who knew what they were talking about, and not least from the apostle himself.

Paul did not use the language of orthodoxy or of systematic theology, but it is clear that it was that which he had in mind. There was a coherent pattern in what Timothy had been taught that would lead him to draw conclusions that were consistent with it when he met new ideas. To become a Christian is to be born again mentally as well as spiritually. It is to have a new understanding of reality and a new outlook on life. One of the great dangers that the church in Paul's day faced was syncretism, which was the temptation to assimilate Christian ideas to pagan ones that were already familiar and create a hybrid religion. The various Gnostic sects that appeared in the second century were examples of these. They used Biblical concepts and vocabulary but attached them to pictures of reality that were far removed from anything the Bible taught.

Today, we see the same thing in so-called 'postmodern' readings of the Biblical text. People take the words in front of them and reconstruct the ideas they are expressing in order to articulate their own vision of life, which is usually very different from anything the apostles would have recognized. The Bible is detached from its historical roots and allegorized to create an alien world view that is then used to subvert its true meaning. This was not what Timothy had learned from Paul, nor is it what Christians today have inherited from him and his fellow apostles. Every generation has to face this challenge anew, and Timothy had to guard the inherited deposit of truth just as much as we have to guard it today.

Second, Timothy's faith was not just what he had *learned* but also what he had *believed*. This complementary addition is essential if we are to understand the full implications of what Paul was saying to him. It was not enough merely to study the truth of the gospel; he also had to commit himself to it. There were many young Jews who had received the same education that Timothy had, and some would have gone further than he did. But without faith, their learning amounted to nothing and was actually dangerous, because it gave those who had it the feeling that they knew what they were talking about when in fact they did not. Timothy's faith was not a naive and untested belief but one that had been through the fires of controversy and come out strengthened and refined by the opposition of persecution. He had proved himself worthy of it by standing firm in the face of attacks, and it was this that Paul commended and urged him to build on.

Third, Timothy knew from whom he had learned his doctrine and he did not doubt their authority. His relationship with his teachers was one of respect and trust. Even if he sometimes had doubts about certain things, he could always recall the witness of those who had taught him. Paul did not say so explicitly, but this assertion was a covert reminder of how important it is for a teacher to demonstrate personal integrity. If the one who teaches does not live by the maxims that he inculcates in others, his teaching will be discredited, and master and disciple will perish together. A good teacher is not someone who just conveys information but someone who also demonstrates a pattern of life that corresponds to the message he wants to convey. This is one reason why Christians have always sought to establish schools where the faith can be taught and communicated in this all-round way. Distance or online learning is sometimes necessary, but it is no substitute for a situation in which teachers and pupils share a common life, where the lessons learned go far beyond what is written in books or preached from the pulpit.

Having said that, Paul's emphasis here was on what Timothy had learned all his life, and the substance of that teaching had come from the Hebrew Bible. From his childhood, Timothy had known the 'sacred letters' (*hiera grammata*) that are able to make a person wise in the understanding of salvation by faith in Christ Jesus. In saying this, Paul introduced us to a deeper appreciation of his teaching than can be found in anything he had said up to this point. This would be the foundation for Timothy's future ministry, just as it had always been for Paul's. There is no substitute for a good theological education, and by starting in childhood Timothy had absorbed the truth from the beginning. Here we see the immense value of a Christian upbringing, which we know Timothy had received from his mother and grandmother. They could not have known how God would use the education which they imparted to him, but they understood how important it was. Parents who teach their children very little, on the assumption that when they grow up they will be able to decide for themselves, are in fact disobeying the God who has told us that if we teach a child the way in which he should go, when he is old he will not depart from it.[52] Christian faith cannot be passed on automatically from one generation to the next, but the foundations for its transmission can and must be laid. Paul saw the benefits of this in the way that Timothy had been brought up, and we must heed his example.

The expression 'sacred letters' (*hiera grammata*) is intriguing. First of all, Paul did not call them 'holy' as we do now, but 'sacred'. There may not be much to choose between these terms in practice, but we must pay attention to the different usage because it reflects a sensitivity to liturgical and religious matters that is not always found in the church today. The 'letters' were 'sacred', not because they were qualitatively different from others but because they belonged to the world of the priests (*hiereis*) and the temple (*hieron*). The Scriptures were not written in an esoteric language that only experts could decipher, nor were they hidden in oracles or symbols that required a special hermeneutical key to be understood. We take this for granted nowadays, but we must see it against the backdrop of ancient religions in general. It was quite common for pagan priests to guard secrets that only they could interpret, and mysterious 'oracles' were a well-known feature of the ancient landscape. Like other nations round about them, Israel had priests, but they were a tribe rather than a caste. In other words, you could not earn your

---

[52] Prov. 22.6.

way into the priesthood, nor could you be chosen for it on the basis of some innate gift or intellectual ability. It was something that was inherited as part of belonging to the tribe of Levi, and therefore it embraced the full range of human talents and abilities – or lack of them. There was nothing special or different about the priesthood that distinguished it from the common run of humanity, but it was set aside for particular tasks that no one else in Israel was authorized to perform.

The same principle applied to the Scriptures. The language of the texts was not 'holy' in any objective sense. Biblical Hebrew must have sounded old-fashioned in the time of Jesus, rather like the King James Bible sounds to us today, but it was not incomprehensible to those who knew Aramaic. Most tellingly, it had been translated into Greek about three hundred years before Paul's time so that more people could understand it – a unique phenomenon in religious history up to then. When Paul said that Timothy had known the sacred letters from his childhood, we must assume that he had read them in Greek, not in the original Hebrew, which he probably did not know. That was not true of Paul, of course, but Paul was Jewish to a degree that Timothy was not. Furthermore, Paul had received his theological education in Jerusalem, where Timothy had not studied and had almost certainly never been. The important thing for us to note is that none of this mattered. Paul did not specify what text Timothy used or what language he read the Bible in because it did not matter to him. He did not think that it was necessary to sit at the feet of somebody like Gamaliel (as he himself had done) in order to understand what the Scriptures meant.[53] The message could be (and was) communicated through translation; it was meant to be understood by everyone. The modern preoccupation with the accuracy of minutiae in the text was foreign to Paul. He was concerned with the general sense of it and did not waste his time arguing about disputed points as if the message of the gospel hung on them.

The importance of this approach to the sacred writings of Israel must not be underestimated. Jews long preserved Hebrew as a religious language, though it has recently been revived as a spoken tongue as well. Muslims read their scriptures in classical Arabic, which has to be learned for the purpose, even by Arabs. Hindus and Buddhists rely on Sanskrit and on Pali, which was originally the spoken form of the artificial sacred tongue but is now just as ancient and sacred as Sanskrit is. Until recently, Roman Catholics worshipped in Latin, a language that has been 'dead' for over a thousand years, and most Eastern Orthodox Christians still use obsolete forms of their spoken languages – Koine Greek, Old Church Slavonic, classical Georgian

---

[53] Acts 22.3.

and Armenian, Coptic and Geʻez, to name but the most prominent ones.[54] The early Christians did not do that. They read the Scriptures in their everyday speech, and when it came time to write the New Testament, it appeared in the same form. Even the words of Jesus are almost all translations of what he actually said, and nobody has ever had any problem with that. The message is clear enough, and there is nothing esoteric about it that would make translation impossible.

What made the 'letters' sacred was not some oddity in their form or their archaic language but the fact that they had been set apart by the guardians of the religious traditions of Israel – the priests in the temple. For the most part they had not been written by the priests but had been collected and edited by them. Who originally wrote most of the Hebrew Bible is unknown to us. The five books of Moses (Genesis-Deuteronomy) may go back to him in some sense but he probably did not write much (or any) of them himself. Similarly, the prophets proclaimed their messages but seldom if ever wrote them down; that was the work of scribes and disciples who came later. Occasionally we know who they were – Baruch transcribed the teaching of Jeremiah, for example – but usually we do not.[55] What we do know is that the temple priests selected them and canonized them, as we would say today.

In essence, therefore, Paul used the word 'sacred' to express what we would now call 'canonical'. We do not know for sure how well defined the canon was in Paul's day, but that there was such a thing can hardly be doubted. At the heart of Jewish worship was the Torah, a basically untranslatable word that means both 'law' and 'teaching'. The Torah, or five books of Moses, constituted the foundation of Israel's religion and was the first port of call for anyone who claimed to read or study the Scriptures. It was the Torah that Jesus quoted more than anything else, and Paul's theological argumentation almost always started with it. This was normal Jewish practice, and we can assume that the education of the young Timothy followed that pattern.

Beyond the Torah it is harder to be certain about the extent of the canon that Timothy would have been exposed to. Probably he knew the prophets, or most of them, and almost certainly he read them in the LXX translation. He would also have known the Psalms. How many of the other writings would have been available to him in Lystra is impossible to say, but it is quite likely that he was familiar with most, if not all of the Old Testament as we know it.

---

[54] The tenacity of this tradition, and the problems it can cause, is well illustrated by the history of the translation of the Bible into Modern Greek. Despite several attempts to do this, beginning in the seventeenth century, an officially authorized translation did not appear until 1986, and it is still not used in public worship.
[55] Jer. 45.1.

We have no way of knowing to what extent he might have studied the 'extra' books that appear in Greek but not in Hebrew, though if the New Testament is any guide, it seems likely that any knowledge he had of them would not have affected his faith very much. These books, known collectively today as the 'Apocrypha' are never quoted in the New Testament, though there are some allusions to extra-Biblical Hebrew writings, including some that are *not* part of the Apocrypha as it is now generally received.[56]

Paul clearly regarded the Old Testament as capable of informing Timothy about salvation through Jesus Christ, and in this he was saying no more than what most early Christians believed. In Luke 24 we read of the famous encounter of the risen Christ with the travellers on the road to Emmaus, when Jesus opened the Scriptures to them and showed where they spoke about him.[57] In John's Gospel we find him telling the Pharisees the same thing and rebuking them for failing to see the message that the sacred text conveyed.[58] What is unfortunately not known to us is how Paul and his colleagues actually read and taught the Scriptures. There were certain proof texts which are recorded for us in the Gospels, where the coming of Christ was prophesied, and no doubt he and Timothy made full use of them. But whether they went through the Hebrew Bible systematically in order to interpret how it spoke about the coming Messiah we do not know. The closest that we come to this is in the account of the synagogue at Beroea, whose members searched the Scriptures diligently to see whether what Paul was telling them was true.[59] But where they looked and what they concluded we are not told.

Having commended Timothy for his knowledge of the Scriptures, Paul went on to explain what they were and why they were so important for the life of the church. All Scripture, he said, is 'inspired by God' (*pasa graphē theopneustos*). What these words mean has been the subject of a vast literature, and it is probably true to say that more has been written about them than about the rest of the Epistle combined.[60] Most of this literature has taken the phrase out of its context and used it to prove that the Bible is the inspired Word of God, and it must be admitted that claims have been made for the character of the text that go well beyond what the apostle actually wrote. Modern commentators have dealt with this problem in different ways.

---

[56] See for example, Jude 1.14-15.
[57] Lk. 24.25-27.
[58] Jn 5.39.
[59] Acts 17.11.
[60] For a summary of the different views that have been propounded, see Marshall (2004), pp. 790–5, and Towner (2006), pp. 581–90.

Some have defended the dogmatic use of the text, which can be supported by other New Testament references.[61] It goes without saying that almost all of these have been conservative theologians who have been influenced by their own confessional commitments, even if it is going too far to say that they have been misled by them.

At the other extreme, liberal scholars have done their best to reinterpret the text so that it does not mean what their dogmatically inclined colleagues have claimed. L. T. Johnson expresses a fairly moderate version of this position when he writes,

> The authority of the Bible does not rest on its inspiration, but on its canonicity, a status that each church confirms by the use of the Bible in every generation in liturgy and in decision making. The Bible functions within the process of revelation not as an exclusive textual source, but as an essential and normative resource for discerning and measuring God's self-disclosure within human existence and activity.[62]

Where this view falls down is in its failure to recognize that the canonicty of the Bible is due to its inspiration. The church did not establish a list of acceptable books and then claim that they were inspired. On the contrary, it received the Old Testament from the Jews more or less in its definitive form, which it regarded as inspired because Jesus taught that he had come to fulfill it to the letter.[63] The New Testament obviously did not appear until later, but it was not formally canonized until after the sixteenth-century Reformation, when that became necessary. However, its twenty-seven books had long been received in the church as a divinely inspired collection on a par with the Hebrew Bible, and it was on that basis that its canon was officially recognized.

That Paul thought of the Old Testament as divinely inspired seems clear from his use of the term *hiera grammata*, which gives us the key to interpreting *pasa graphē*. It is perhaps true, as P. H. Towner suggests, that the second phrase does not necessarily have to cover the entire Biblical text, but the context strongly suggests that it does and Towner eventually comes to that conclusion.[64] As I. H. Marshall puts it,

> what is the point of saying 'every inspired Scripture is *also* profitable'? Why mention inspiration at all? ... this interpretation might imply that

---

[61] Rom. 15.4; 2 Pet. 1.21.
[62] Johnson (2001), p. 422.
[63] Mt. 5.17-19.
[64] Towner (2006), p. 588.

some Scripture was not inspired, which is unlikely to have been a view held by either the author or his opponents. It is more likely that the reference to inspiration is part of what the author wants to affirm about Scripture in order to defend its universal usefulness.[65]

Here Marshall makes the important point that Scripture is useful because it is inspired by God, following the standard Biblical principle that the validity of what a person (or a thing) does depends entirely on what that person (or thing) is. As far as Paul was concerned, he would almost certainly have seen the matter in much the same way as 2 Pet. 1.21, where we are told that holy men were moved by the Spirit of God to write what we know as the Scriptures. Peter thought of inspiration as a spiritual gift that had been given to human beings; he did not believe that the Biblical text had come down from heaven already written, like the golden plates that supposedly contained the Book of Mormon. The word *theopneustos* used here by Paul suggests that their composition was the work of the Holy Spirit (*pneuma*), but that is not explicitly stated. More important is that inspiration extends to the whole of the Scriptural text as we have it now. It was not possible, in Paul's view, to find chaff in the wheat; there were no passages in the Hebrew Bible that had crept in and mixed the impure with the pure. Everything was equally inspired, including the genealogies that so intrigued those who were opposed to his teaching, and the entire text had to be read and venerated in the light of Christ and the salvation that he had brought.

John Calvin expressed the classical Christian view in very clear terms:

> This is the principle that distinguishes our religion from all others, that we know that God has spoken to us and are fully convinced that the prophets did not speak of themselves, but as organs of the Holy Spirit uttered only that which they had been commissioned from heaven to declare. All those who wish to profit from the Scriptures must first accept this as a settled principle, that the law and the prophets are not teachings handed on by the pleasure of men or produced by men's minds as their source, but are dictated by the Holy Spirit. If anyone object and ask how this can be known, my reply is that it is by the revelation of the same Spirit both to learners and teachers that God is made known as its Author ... it is not surprising that many should doubt the authority of Scripture. For although the majesty of God is

---

[65] Marshall (2004), p. 793.

displayed in it, only those who have been enlightened by the Holy Spirit have eyes to see what should have been obvious to all, but is in fact visible only to the elect.[66]

Whether the divine inspiration of the text, as opposed to its human authors, necessarily implies that the Scriptures are objectively true in what they affirm (or apparently affirm) is not a question that Paul ever addressed and so it is impossible to be sure what he thought about that. Did he believe, for example, that the world had been created in six 24-hour days? Did he think that Job and Jonah were historical figures? How did he understand the historicity of Genesis 1–11? These and other questions that have so exercised modern interpreters and apologists seem to have been of little interest to him. As far as we can tell, he took the Old Testament text 'literally', but what that meant in his case is another matter. As we have just seen, he apparently read the story of Jannes and Jambres 'literally', even though it is not in the Old Testament at all. The most we can say is that such questions did not particularly bother him. When dealing with Sarah and Hagar, for example, who most certainly were real people in his mind, he did not hesitate to allegorize them, so even when he understood them 'literally' he was not limited in his exposition to the historical facts alone.[67] The idea that he might go into the Arabian desert to see whether he could find traces of Hagar and Ishmael there never crossed his mind. Biblical archaeology is a modern discipline that has come into being in answer to questions raised by modern thinkers; it was unknown to Paul. We can safely assume that the need to read the texts in their original context passed him by almost completely. The Bible was important to him, not so much because of what it said (or did not say) about the distant past but because of what it is saying to us now about the new life that we have received in Christ. This does not mean that he denied what we would call the 'historicity' of the text but that he read it as a living word from God and not simply as a historical record.

We can see this from the way in which Paul explains why the inspired Scriptures matter. For him the Bible was 'useful' (*ōphelimos*) for 'teaching' (*didaskalia*), which in his mind seems to have consisted of three fundamental parts: 'reproof' (*elegmos*), 'correction' (*epanorthōsis*) and 'training' (*paideia*) in righteousness. In other words, it was a practical guide to the Christian life and so we ought to read it with that in the forefront of our interpretation. We should not be surprised by this approach. It was a basic tenet of all ancient education, Gentile as well as Jewish, that its purpose was to form morally

---

[66] Calvin (1964), p. 330.
[67] Gal. 4.24-31.

responsible human beings. Information was not valued for its own sake, and research, as we would understand the term, was often bracketed with curiosity and actively discouraged. Learning what the ancestors had passed on was far more important than discovering new things, and novelty was always suspect. The view generally taken was that if something was good it had been said or done before; if it was new, it was probably wrong and possibly harmful. Paul did not express himself on that subject to any great extent but from what he did say it is reasonable to conclude that he would have concurred in this assessment.

The Torah was believed to be superior to the pagan classics because it was much older than they were, and some people assumed that the Greeks had stolen their best ideas from the Hebrews. That would have been possible chronologically but we would now regard such a suggestion as so improbable that we would not take the theory seriously. But to ancient minds the antiquity of the Torah gave it a moral authority that surpassed even the epics of Homer, which formed the basis of pagan Greek education. It was assumed that because it originated at a period that was closer to the origin of the human race, it must have been less corrupted by the passage of time. Jews went further than that, of course. To them, the fact that the Torah had been inspired by God meant that it had not suffered any corruption at all, whereas the pagan classics, inspired as they had been by false gods, were full of errors and deceptions.

Something like this approach had already been adopted by Philo of Alexandria (d. AD 50), who was Jewish and the first man to write what we would now call commentaries on the Biblical text. Philo was not opposed to Greek philosophy; in fact, he was a major proponent of the idea that Plato had stolen his best ideas from Moses. His aim was to demonstrate that Greek thought could be harmonized with the Hebrew Bible, which he naturally assumed was truth in its purest revealed form. But even that had to be allegorized because God had chosen to explain some things to his people in story form, or in ways that were morally repugnant, at least to the superficial observer. There were also numerous references to the hand, the eye and the arm of God that make him sound like a glorified human being, and these passages likewise had to be allegorized away.

The remarkable thing about the New Testament is that it contains so little of this sort of thing. There is no sign of Philonic influence on it, despite the fact that Philo was a Diaspora Jew who was writing for just the kind of audience that Paul was trying to win for the gospel. The only time that Paul made any direct reference to pagan thought was when he was addressing the philosophers in Athens, and that hardly amounted to a sustained argument.[68]

---

[68] Acts 17.28.

His limited use of pagan Greek sources treated them favourably, it is true, but this was only because he quoted them selectively in support of an argument that was drawn entirely from the Hebrew Bible. As for claims to antiquity as a justification for its authority, Paul said nothing. Had he believed such arguments he might have used them, but he did not. We in the modern world live in a mental universe very different from Paul's, so we must be grateful that he did not lend his authority to speculations that we would feel obliged to disavow in the light of later historical knowledge.

But although Paul certainly believed in the objective character of the Scriptures as God's revealed Word, he also knew that they had been given to the chosen people for a purpose. In particular, as W. D. Mounce observes,

> Timothy is to make Scripture central in his ministry. He has learned the Hebrew Scripture from childhood, had known the character of those who had taught it to him, had come to understand experientially that it was true, had recognized that its source was the very breath of God, had understood it within the context of the early Christian proclamation of Jesus Christ, and therefore had become convinced that it and it alone was able to equip him fully for the task of ministry.[69]

What strikes us most about Paul's understanding of the Bible's purpose is how relevant it still is – his approach has stood the test of time and is as valid and applicable today as it was in the first century. The Bible is first and foremost a manual of moral and spiritual instruction, and it is from that perspective that we must learn to read it and apply its message to our lives today.

As Paul expounded the matter, the basic elements of the moral and spiritual education that we are meant to get from the Scriptures are three. The first of these is 'reproof', which corresponds to what Jesus called conviction of sin, which he taught was the first work of the Holy Spirit in the heart of a believer.[70] Rightly so, we might add. The gospel message is virtually unintelligible to people who have no idea, or who have the wrong idea, of sin. There is little point in offering salvation to those who see no need for it because the very concept is alien to them. To use a medical analogy, it is impossible to offer a cure to someone unless we first arrive at a proper diagnosis of the disease. For this reason, 'reproof' must be the first function of the Scriptures, because it is by this means that the essential human problem is revealed.

---

[69] Mounce (2000), pp. 583–4.
[70] Jn 16.8.

Reproof, however, is not enough. By itself, it is a word of condemnation, not of salvation, and if a preacher restricts his interpretation of the text to that, he will have no gospel to proclaim. It is therefore necessary to move on to 'correction' which is the logical corollary of reproof and gives the latter its purpose. Correction is putting right what has gone wrong, and it is the function of the Scriptures to point out how this is to be done. Finally, Paul spoke about the need for 'training in righteousness', which is the instruction believers must receive in order to live the Christian life. Both these things are just as essential as reproof, since there is no point in diagnosing a problem without trying to correct it, or in correcting errors if the people so corrected then either do nothing or are left to their own devices. In the first case, there would be no post-conversion life at all, which is nonsensical; in the second, the danger of falling back into sin would be enormous.

Paul's pattern of reading and applying the Bible is the same as the teaching of Jesus about the work of the Holy Spirit that we find in John 16. As we have already remarked, 'reproof' is the conviction of sin. Correction is the teaching of righteousness – the path that we ought to follow. Finally, the training is the judgment – the proof of the pudding is in the eating, as we might say today.

It is not difficult to see in this triad what later came to be known to theologians as the 'three uses of the law'. It is the law (Torah) which was the primary subject of Paul's exposition here, and although the idea that it has three uses is often associated with John Calvin and the Reformed tradition, it is actually intrinsic to the original text. By bringing that out, Calvin and his followers were merely following the guidance given to Timothy by Paul as to how he should interpret and apply the Scriptures.

Verse 17 sums up the goal of the instruction that Scripture is intended to provide. The man of God who follows its teaching will be 'proficient' (*artios*), having been 'made fit' (*exērtismenos*) for 'every good work' (*pan ergon agathon*). The Greek text uses the same word *artios* for the result as for the process, but it is difficult to capture this in translation.[71] We may assume that in the background there lies the image of the worker who is adequately prepared to do his job and who will not be embarrassed when he is faced with a circumstance that he has not previously encountered. This seems to be the force of Paul's concluding remark about 'every good work'. Study of God's word may equip some people for specific tasks, and of course there are always lessons to be learned from it that can be applied in particular situations. But

---

[71] It is hard for non-Greek speakers to see this because the verb form *exērtismenos* contains an 'augmented' *eta* instead of the *alpha* of *artios*.

speaking in general terms, as Paul did here, its primary purpose is to produce the right kind of person – a 'man (*anthrōpos*) of God'. This is someone, male or female, who is a qualified servant of the Lord, a servant of the truth who can be relied upon not only to do God's will but to do it in the right way and for the right reasons.

This is what we would now call a fully rounded education, and in the end it is more important than the kind of specialization in a particular field that is pushed so far nowadays as to make the specialist virtually useless outside his chosen discipline and often incapable of seeing the bigger picture. It also means that the man of God must reflect his calling in every aspect of his life. It is no good writing books on holiness, for example, without putting it into practice. Paul knew that it was possible for him to preach to others but lose his own salvation, and he was determined to avoid that.[72] This is ultimately what Paul believed that the Scriptures were there to do, and why he recommended them to Timothy, both for his own study and for the edification of those to whom he had been called to minister.

Before leaving this subject, it should be said that Paul's affirmation of the divine inspiration and consequent usefulness of Holy Scripture does not mean that other writings are necessarily false or useless. Thomas Aquinas was especially sensitive to this:

> how is it that not all writings are divinely inspired, since Ambrose says that every truth, no matter who utters it, proceeds from the Holy Spirit? I answer that God works in two ways: either immediately, as his own work, when he works miracles; or mediately, by using secondary causes, as in the works of nature ... And so in man he instructs the intellect both immediately by the sacred writings, and immediately by other writings ... there are four effects of Sacred Scripture, namely to teach the truth, to reject falsity, as far as the speculative intellect is concerned; to snatch evil and to induce to good, as far as the practical intellect is concerned. But its final effect is to lead men to the perfect good, for it produces not just any good, but the perfect good.[73]

Aquinas was thus able to reconcile divine inspiration with a particular function in a way that protected not only its truthfulness but also the possibility (and indeed the reality) that truth can be found in other places, albeit with a different purpose in view.

---

[72] 1 Cor. 9.27.
[73] Thomas Aquinas (2012), 2.3.126-128 (p. 393).

# 2 Timothy 4

## 1. The return of Christ

*1. In the presence of God and of Christ Jesus, who is to judge the living and the dead, and in view of his appearing and his kingdom, I solemnly urge you.*

The last chapter of 2 Timothy is a magnificent crescendo to everything that has gone before. In his parting words Paul summed up his commission to Timothy with particular passion, relating what he was saying both to his own situation and to that of his young disciple. The first verse introduces his theme in a particularly dramatic way. Paul spoke to Timothy not by himself, but in the presence of God and of Christ Jesus. In particular, he invoked Christ as the judge of the living and the dead, who would vindicate Paul's ministry when he returned to take up his kingdom. This was literally an ecstatic moment, when Paul was lifted up in his mind from the concerns of his human situation in prison and enabled to paint a panoramic vision of heaven and earth, of time and eternity. Thoughts which had been latent in his mind and which had shaped his approach throughout the Epistle were now expressed with a clarity and a concision that is truly breathtaking.

Paul underlined the solemnity of what he was saying by using the word *diamartyromai*, which the ESV translates as 'I charge', although that is only one aspect of its full meaning.[1] It is yet another example of a Greek word that cannot easily be rendered in another language because it includes so many distinct ideas. Paul was not merely telling Timothy what he must do, but he was bearing witness to it by professing it publicly and invoking the presence of God as the guarantee, both that he was telling the truth and that he meant what he was saying. His words have the character of a solemn oath. This was not just an opinion or a piece of casual advice but a message that was so serious that he laid it before God himself as the ultimate witness of what he was about to say.

---

[1] The NRSV 'I urge' is not strong enough. The NIV has a paraphrase but employs 'charge' as a noun within it.

More than that, Paul also laid it before Christ Jesus, demonstrating by that act that he regarded him as equal to God the Father. It is important to note that he mentioned Christ not because of what he had already done for the salvation of the world but because of what he was going to do in the future. In Paul's vision, Christ would come again to judge the living and the dead, a phrase that we are familiar with because it was picked up by the creeds of the early church and used by them as a confession of what the church would expect from his return in glory.

The belief that the same Jesus who went up to heaven would come back again with his holy angels dominated the thinking of the early church and was fundamental to the gospel message. It appears first in Acts 1, when Jesus was taken up to heaven, and is developed to its fullest extent in the book of Revelation.[2] Paul referred to it frequently, and it was a significant dimension of his preaching and teaching ministry.[3] Here we find it condensed into a single introductory sentence, which reminds us of how important it is for understanding what follows.

When Christ returns, he will come to be our judge. Objectively speaking, the judgment has already been given, but it still needs to be applied to each person individually. We are told that when he comes again, everyone who has died will be brought back to life. Once the dead have been resurrected, the sentence on them will be pronounced. Those who have done evil will be consigned to everlasting damnation, and those who have done good will be saved.[4] At first sight this sounds like salvation by works, but it is not, because those who have 'done good' are to be understood as those who have believed in Christ for salvation. Anyone who has tried to save himself by his own efforts will be rejected. This is because works done apart from faith are sinful, even if they appear to be good on the surface. There is no comfort here for those who think that if they do their best, God will look kindly on them at the last judgment. That judgment is in Christ and is determined by what he has done for us. Believe that and you are saved; reject it and you are condemned. This is the ultimate manifestation of the sovereignty of God and the death of human pride. The tragedy is that so many people will reject the promise of salvation because they cannot accept it as a free gift which they have done nothing to deserve. Perhaps the most galling aspect of this is that the same reward will be given to all, even to those who have come to Christ on their deathbeds and to those who have wasted their lives and abused what God has given to them.[5]

---

[2] Acts 1.11; Rev. 22.6-21.
[3] 1 Cor. 15.20-28; Col. 3.4; 1 Thess. 5.1-11; 2 Thess. 1.5-12.
[4] 1 Cor. 3.11-15.
[5] Mt. 20.1-16; Lk. 15.11-32.

Paul told the Thessalonians that those who are still alive when Christ returns will also be judged.[6] At his return, the distinction between the living and the dead will be abolished and every human being will be treated in the same way. The only difference is that those who are dead will be brought back to life, whereas those who are still alive will be 'caught up into the air', which means that they will be transformed in a way that will put them on an equal footing with those who have already died.[7]

The judgment will take place at Christ's appearing (*epiphaneia*). Today we use this Greek word to describe the moment when he was shown to the wise men shortly after his birth, but the 'epiphany' spoken about here is quite different from that. When Christ appears at the end of time it will be in his glory, and when that happens every knee will bow and every tongue confess that he is Lord.[8] The wise men knew that the baby they saw before them was destined to become the king of the Jews, but they soon realized that they had been given a revelation that was hidden from everyone else.[9] At the second coming of Christ, the revelation that came especially to them will be universal.

It is a basic theological principle that who Christ is is the foundation and justification for what he does, and we find this principle reflected here. When he appears in his glory his kingdom (*basileia*) will come with him. The kingdom of Christ is a major theme of the New Testament and was fundamental to Jesus' teaching about himself and his mission. Paul did not expand on its meaning in his charge to Timothy but he did not have to. Both men knew that when Christ comes his heavenly rule will extend to the whole earth and every element of opposition to it will be eliminated.[10] There will be no more sin and no more occasion of stumbling. The healing and saving power that Jesus revealed as the first fruits of the kingdom during his earthly ministry will be extended to cover everything and everybody who comes under his sway. The efforts made in the interim by Paul, Timothy and all of Christ's disciples will be ratified and brought to fulfillment as their ultimate purpose is finally realized.

It is important to understand that Paul saw his mission, as well as Timothy's, in this wider eschatological context. The apparent failures and setbacks that occurred from time to time were all relative to the eternal plan of God that was being worked out and that plan would not fail. The opposition

---

[6] 1 Thess. 4.13–5.10.
[7] 1 Thess. 4.17.
[8] Phil. 2.11.
[9] Mt. 2.1-12.
[10] 1 Cor. 15.25-28; Phil. 2.11.

that Paul encountered was counterbalanced by the knowledge that, above and beyond the particular circumstances of this life, the hand of God was guiding and governing events. Paul might be imprisoned and Timothy might be silenced, but those who did such things would be frustrated in the end. Christ's followers knew that they were working in a bigger context and they persevered for that reason.

The motivational dimension of Paul's statement must be emphasized. Timothy might get discouraged by Paul's imprisonment and death, but if so, he needed to get these apparent setbacks in perspective. As P. H. Towner puts it,

> Paul took firm hold on the future realities to which they pointed and reoriented present life around them. As Timothy hears the solemn commission, 'Christ's epiphany and kingdom' are not simply the temporal boundaries that mark the horizon or the end of his race. They are strong symbols of promise and power ... The motivational force of these 'promises becoming reality' is certainly to encourage, but also to bind him [Timothy] to his task.[11]

### 2-5. The preaching ministry

*2. Proclaim the message; be persistent whether the time is favourable or unfavourable; convince, rebuke, and encourage, with the utmost patience in teaching. 3. For the time is coming when people will not put up with sound doctrine, but having itching ears, they will accumulate for themselves teachers to suit their own desires, 4. and will turn away from listening to the truth and wander away to myths. 5. As for you, always be sober, endure suffering, do the work of an evangelist, carry out your ministry fully.*

After his majestic introduction, Paul launched into an equally striking summary of his commission to Timothy. Above all else, Timothy was to preach the Word and to persist in doing this 'in season and out of season' (*eukairōs akairōs*). Paul's order of priorities is significant. He might have advised Timothy to resist discouragements by continuing to hold worship services and to engage in his private pastoral activities. Those things were important and could not be neglected. In modern times persecuted churches have sometimes been allowed to carry on holding services as long as there

---

[11] Towner (2006), p. 599.

was no preaching or teaching attached to them. That was the case in the former Soviet Union and in some other communist countries, where public worship was tolerated to some degree because it was regarded as a harmless concession to people who might otherwise have been active in their opposition to the regime in power. There is not much that a church can do when the state imposes such a restriction, but when it is free to order its activities there is no excuse for holding services without preaching, as can sometimes happen today.

Preaching is the central and most important single act of ministry, and it governs everything else. If it is weak, the church is weak. If it is marginalized, the church suffers the consequences. There is no substitute for it and nothing must be allowed to upstage it. A minister of the gospel must devote himself to this task more than to anything else, because it is in this way that his message will be heard.[12] Today, as we know, there are many objections to preaching. Perhaps the most damaging of them is that it is often dull and uninspired. Many preachers seem to think that their primary task is to teach their congregations, and so they give them lectures that may be full of sound content but that are more appropriate to the classroom than to the pulpit. Often the sermon is derived from secondary sources and may be little more than the expression of the preacher's personal opinion, so it lacks the weight that attaches to the Word of God. Effective preaching certainly depends on good teaching, which is often weak or non-existent, but the two things are not the same. Teaching is primarily the conveying of information, whereas preaching goes beyond that to exhortation. It is not enough to know what the Bible says, essential as that is – we also need to be challenged to take its message to heart and apply it in our lives. That is what the preacher ought to be doing, and what is so often weak or absent from the modern pulpit.

The crisis of preaching in the modern church has many causes, one of which is the great change in the means and methods of communication that has occurred in the past hundred years. Before the invention of radio, oral communication depended almost entirely on public speaking which could not be artificially amplified. That meant not only that the acoustics of a room were of the utmost importance but also that the speaker had to be well trained in the art of rhetoric in order to get his message across. In that respect, little had changed since ancient times and the great preachers of the eighteenth and nineteenth centuries approached their task in a way that was not very different from the apostles and evangelists of the early church. Today, however, all that has changed. The shouting and histrionics

---

[12] Rom. 10.14-17.

that preachers in earlier times found necessary in order to be heard now come across as ridiculous and off-putting. Speaking into a microphone or facing a camera is a very different exercise from banging the pulpit. The art of rhetoric, taught and practised for centuries, has now declined to the point of oblivion. The result is that few people know how to speak in public and many potential listeners switch off because there is nothing in the presentation that retains their attention.

Unfortunately this failure in technique is frequently matched by lack of substance. How many preachers today have anything to say? The sermon, which ought to be the focal point of worship and the highlight of the believer's week, is all too often reduced to a short homily that is as likely to be crammed with jokes and banalities as with anything significant. The awful truth is that for many people, the sermon is the most boring part of the church service and the sooner it is over, the better! The word of God is silenced not by persecution but by the ignorance and neglect of those whose duty it is to proclaim it.

What exactly did Paul mean by the 'word' (*logos*)? Most modern commentators, and in particular those who take this injunction seriously, assume that he was referring primarily to the gospel message.[13] It is Christ, his life, death and resurrection above all else. The meaning of these events was explained by the Scriptures, on which Paul always based his preaching, and, of course, by 'Scriptures' he meant the Old Testament. Sometimes, especially in passages like the genealogies in 1 Chronicles, it is quite a challenge to see how the text relates to Christ, and modern preachers may think they are being more faithful to it by *not* mentioning him. Many Old Testament scholars would support that approach, not just in these difficult passages but more generally, on the grounds that Jews do not find Christ in their Scriptures and that the original authors could not have foreseen the Christian interpretation of them. In other words, faithfulness to the original intention of the author(s) is nowadays often believed to demand that Christ should not be mentioned in an exposition of any Old Testament text, except perhaps in those that were explicitly used by Jesus and the early Christians as evidence for the claims they made.

Arguments of this kind appear to be scholarly and they may convince many, but in practice the result tends to be that the Old Testament is often ignored in the church. Whereas preachers a hundred or two hundred years ago often worked their way through books like Leviticus and thought nothing of

---

[13] Calvin (1964), p. 332, interpreted *logos* to mean the Scriptures, which are the repository of the gospel message for later generations.

using Abraham, David or Elijah as examples for illustrating the Christian life, their modern successors are more reticent about this and many neglect the Old Testament altogether. They can argue, with some justification, that their forebears were prone to allegory and to fanciful interpretations that found Christ artificially in the texts they were expounding and brought the whole exercise into disrepute. It may be possible to draw spiritual lessons that are still valid for Christians out of some Old Testament texts, but to their minds, responsible exposition means sticking to their literal, pre-Christian context. Especially when it comes to a book like the Song of Songs, the luxuriant allegories of yesteryear are now eschewed, with the unfortunate result that the book has practically died as the Word of God for the church today.

What is wrong with this approach is that it ignores the situation of the early church which Paul was addressing. He and Timothy did not have the New Testament, though they understood the message it conveys and they preached it. Remarkably, from a modern point of view, everything they said came from their exposition of the Hebrew Bible, which they were convinced was sufficient for their needs. They did not hesitate to claim that the Old Testament spoke about Christ; indeed, he was the reason why it had been given in the first place. Everything in it pointed to him, and apart from him it could not be interpreted correctly.[14] To argue in the way that many modern commentators and exegetes do is to deny the witness of the early church, and therefore to fail to preach the Word, even when using the words of the Biblical text.

This is a hermeneutical question, and hermeneutics lies at the centre of the church's appropriation of the Scriptures. As far as the early Christians were concerned there was no doubt at all about the Christocentricity of the Bible. To their minds, even Jews who had never heard of Jesus should have understood that, which is why Jesus condemned them for failing to see him in it. They believed that the Bible promised them eternal life, and therefore they should have understood its Messianic bent, even before the coming of Christ himself.[15]

The modern church is committed to this Christian understanding of the Old Testament. If we worship Christ as our Lord and Saviour we must have his mind in us, and having that mind means having also a Christological understanding of the Hebrew Bible. It is not necessary to allegorize everything in it in order to justify this approach. The Protestant Reformers believed that it was possible to see Christ in the developing history of Israel, and to that

---

[14] Lk. 24.44-47.
[15] Jn 5.39.

end they expounded what came to be called 'covenant theology'. According to that hermeneutic, the Old Testament reveals a series of stages by which God spoke to his people about his plan for them. This was his covenant, given to Abraham, renewed by Moses and confirmed in the promises made to David. When Paul told Timothy to preach the Word, this is what he had in mind. Timothy was to proclaim the message that the covenant made with Israel had been fulfilled in Christ, and that people of every tribe and nation could be integrated into it by believing in him.

Paul nowhere suggested that his letters were Scripture, though it was not long before others recognized them as such.[16] The logic of the gospel demanded an expanded canon because the gospel was the fulfillment of the law and the promises given by God to Israel. If God had inspired the texts that recorded a message that had not yet been fully revealed, it is not hard to understand why Christians would have expected him to inspire other texts that explained how that revelation had come to pass in Christ. Paul did not hesitate to tell Timothy to copy his example, and he expected the church to receive his instructions as a word that had come to him from God. The fact that his letters were accorded the same authority as that of the Scriptures was regarded as evidence that they enjoyed the same inspired character. We should therefore not be surprised that it was not long before the church collected them, and other writings of the same kind, and regarded them as the Word of God on a par with the Hebrew writings that they had inherited from the distant past.

It may be added in passing that the preaching of the early church is the best evidence that we have that the so-called Apocryphal books of the Old Testament were not regarded as Scripture in the same way that the Hebrew texts were. The reason for this is that preachers required commentaries in order to help them understand and interpret the difficult parts of the Bible. From about the year AD 200 such commentaries began to appear in considerable numbers, but there is not a single one that is devoted to one of the Apocryphal books! The conclusion that we must draw from this is that those books were not preached in the church – they were not part of the 'Word' as this was understood by the apostles and their immediate followers. It was not until the fourth century and later that commentaries on the Apocrypha start to appear, and even then they were very few in number and not comprehensive in their coverage. The church has never relied on them for its message of salvation, and however important they may be for our understanding of the world in which Jesus and his disciples ministered, they

---

[16] 2 Pet. 3.16.

were not then, and ought not now, to be regarded as canonical Scripture on a par with either the Old Testament or the New.

It might be thought that such a wonderful message of salvation would be widely accepted and that even those who did not believe it would have no reason to object if others did so. But as the history of the early church reminds us, that was not the case. Far from being tolerant of the beliefs of others, those who disagreed with the gospel message were often moved to oppose it, sometimes with open persecution. There were others, of course, who accepted it and were converted. Among them, Paul and his colleagues were welcome to preach the Word whenever they wanted to and the congregation was eager to hear it. This is the difference between preaching 'in season' and preaching 'out of season'. The translation 'season' might suggest that there was a time of year when gospel preaching was more acceptable than at other times, but the Greek word *kairos* also means 'moment', or a defined period of time, whether or not it corresponds to a particular external or natural phenomenon. Today we sometimes have to break bad or unpleasant news to somebody but are advised to wait and do this 'at the right time', and that is the meaning of the word here. The difference is that Timothy was to preach the gospel whenever he got the opportunity to do so, and not to wait for the 'right time' for it, because that time might never arrive. People need to hear the gospel message whether they were eager and willing to receive it or not. Indeed, it could be said that they were in greater need of it when their ears were closed and it was 'out of season' as far as they were concerned. Timothy was not to follow the mood swings of his hearers but to challenge them at all times, whether they were prepared to listen to him or not.[17]

Paul also specified what the emphasis of Timothy's messages should be, and here we are taken back to what he said about the Scriptures in 2 Tim. 3.16. They had been given as teaching for the church, and it was that teaching that Timothy was commanded to preach. The content of his preaching could not be different from that of the teaching that he had received but had to be based on it. Timothy was called to teach the principles of the faith and to preach for their acceptance and application. The difference between the two

---

[17] Marshall (2004), pp. 800–1, understands this, but Towner (2006), pp. 600–1, who usually follows Marshall, seems to overlook it for some curious reason. John Chrysostom, *Homilies on 2 Timothy*, 9.4.2 (NPNF 13, p. 510), mistakenly regarded the phrase as referring to the preacher's circumstances rather than to the spiritual state of his congregation. Thomas Aquinas (2012), 4.1.134 (p. 397), misread it in another way. He wrote, 'if a man were to take advantage of an opportunity to speak only to those wh are willing to hear, he would benefit the just alone; but it is his duty to preach also to the wicked, that they may be converted; that is why he adds "out of season".'

things lies in the mode and purpose of the communication of the message, not in its content.

The triadic pattern found in 3.16 reasserts itself at this point as we read that Timothy was to 'convince', 'rebuke' and 'encourage' (NRSV) or better, 'rebuke', 'challenge' and 'exhort' (ESV) his hearers – three dimensions of preaching that correspond to the character of the teaching contained in Scripture. The first of these commands is a direct repetition of what he had said earlier. The *elegmos* ('reproof') of 3.16 now appears as the imperative verb *elenxon* and obviously has the same meaning as it did before. The fact of the matter is that the Bible and the gospel exist because human beings have gone wrong and need to be faced with their misbehaviour. The preacher is not called to deliver 'hellfire and brimstone' sermons that contain little or no mention of God's saving grace, but he is obliged to remind his hearers that the message he has come to proclaim is one that they need to hear because they are sinners in the sight of God. Those who have no conviction of their own sinfulness will be indifferent to a message that announces salvation from it for the obvious reason that they see no need for it.

The word translated as 'rebuke' (NRSV) or, better still, 'challenge' (ESV) is *epitimēson* in which we see the noun *timē* ('value' or 'honour'). Many different translations are possible, but in the context it is best to link it to what Paul previously called 'correction' (*epanorthōsis*), where the presence of *orthos* ('right' or 'straight') is analogous to *timē*. It is possible that the word appeals to the sense of shame that people ought to feel when they have done something wrong. If they sense that their honour is at stake, they may be more inclined to do something about it – to save face, as we might say. It was not Timothy's job to go around deliberately shaming members of his congregation in order to frighten them into repentance, a tactic that if he had tried it would probably not have worked for long. Instead, by pointing out what God's standards were, he was to make people see how far short of them they had fallen and to encourage them to draw the logical conclusion for themselves. That is why 'challenge' is a good translation here.

Thirdly, *parakaleson* ('entreat' or 'exhort') is the aim of all good *paideia* ('training'), and therefore of all good preaching as well. The force of the word is perhaps best grasped by recalling that the first person, present tense of the verb (*parakalō*) is the Greek way of saying 'please' or, more exactly, 'I beg you'. It is an appeal to the other person's conscience that is intended to elicit a favourable response. This is how Timothy was meant to 'entreat' his congregation, not beating them over the head like a tyrant but appealing to their own sense of right and wrong in order to persuade them to do the right thing.

In all these ways, Paul expected Timothy's preaching to reflect the purposes for which the Scriptures had been given. If it succeeded in doing that it would be truly expository and fulfill the task for which it was intended. The factual content of the Bible was a given that members of the church were expected to be familiar with already. The sermon was not the place to impart basic information like who Abraham was but to exhort them to learn from his example and apply it to their lives. Obviously they would need to know the story, but that was a preparatory exercise that was best carried out outside the worship context. The preacher's job was to build on a basic knowledge of the facts and challenge his hearers to put what they already knew into practice. Ignorance of the Bible was a barrier to the success of good preaching, as Paul discovered when he went to Athens. There he preached to intelligent men who had no idea what he was talking about, and so for the most part his message failed to communicate.[18]

Of course, the way in which Timothy exercised his preaching ministry would make all the difference to its eventual success. He was told to use all patience (*makrothymia*) and 'teaching' (*didachē*) as he went about his task. Patience is the hallmark of a good teacher, and its importance is readily understood by anyone who has tried it, but what did Paul mean by *didachē*? His normal word for 'teaching' was *didaskalia*, which stands for the content and application of the message being conveyed. *Didachē* can also mean that, but it seems unlikely that it is a synonym of *didaskalia* in this verse. This is not just because *didaskalia* appears in the next sentence with its customary meaning but because the coupling of *didachē* with *makrothymia* strongly suggests that it is to be understood as something more like that. It might therefore be best to translate it as 'educational skill'. Timothy was not only expected to be patient with his congregation but also to find the right way of getting the message across to them. He had to speak in a way that they would understand, use illustrations that they would relate to and apply the results in ways that made sense to his hearers. This was far more than simply conveying facts in the abstract, but it was essential if his message was to get across. John Calvin understood that very well:

> Reproofs either fail to have any effect because they are too violent or because they disappear into thin air, not being founded in sound teaching … We see examples of this in people who possess much zeal and great asperity but are not equipped with solid teaching. They wear themselves out, they shout at the top of their voices and make a great noise, but all to

---

[18] Acts 17.18-34.

no avail because they are building without a foundation. I am speaking of those who are in other ways good men, but have insufficient learning and too much emotional fervour.[19]

In v. 3 Paul elaborated on what he had in mind when he told Timothy to preach the Word 'out of season'. There would come a time, he said, when people would stop listening to the 'health-giving teaching' or 'sound doctrine' (*hygiainousa didaskalia*) and instead find teachers who would suit their own passions (*epithymiai*), because of their insatiable curiosity. Paul described this as 'scratching the hearing' (*knēthomenoi tēn akoēn*), an idiomatic expression that we translate as 'because they have itching ears'.[20] John Calvin thought that people like this got what they deserved when false teachers appeared on the scene and deceived them:

> The fact that false teachers so often abound and sometimes come forth in swarms should be ascribed to God's righteous judgment. We deserve to be overwhelmed by this kind of rubbish, since God's truth finds no place in us, or, if admitted, is immediately driven from possession.[21]

As so often with remarks like this, how we interpret them depends on what we think about the authorship of the Epistle. If Paul was the author, as we believe, he may have been thinking ahead to a time when the congregation would have lost its initial enthusiasm and would be casting around for something new to latch onto. But if there was a pseudepigrapher at work, he was probably describing a situation that had already arisen in the church and projecting it back onto Paul's presumed spiritual foresight. Since there is no objective evidence to help us decide this question either way, we are obliged to consider what the most likely conclusion is according to the standard internal criteria of evaluation. In favour of Pauline authorship, there is no indication of who these false teachers are, a vagueness that fits better with the earliest period of the church's existence than with a later time when there were well-defined schools of thought and heretics were called out by name. The emphasis here is placed not on particular false teachers but on the members of the church who would grow weary of what they were hearing every week and long for something new. Once they were in that frame of mind they would be tempted to go looking for teachers who

---

[19] Calvin (1964), p. 333.
[20] Marshall (2004), pp. 802–3, supports this interpretation of the phrase. Ambrosiaster (2009), p. 152, thought that Paul was predicting the later emergence of the Manichees.
[21] Calvin (1964), p. 335.

would satisfy their desires, and it mattered little who they were or what they actually taught.

The idea that a group of people would eventually get tired of the same old thing and look around for a change is too universal in human experience to force us to pin it down to a particular occasion; Paul's apparent 'foresight' in this case is no more than what we might expect from someone who understands human nature. There is therefore no reason to say that it cannot have been an authentic observation of his, and the hypothesis that there was a pseudepigrapher working from hindsight is not necessary to explain what the text says. If that were the case, we would expect him to home in on specific details, but there is no sign that the author had a particular agenda.

What would happen when weariness set in and the people started looking around for variety was perfectly clear, and Paul gave Timothy a straightforward assessment of what he could then expect. On the one hand, he could anticipate that his congregation would reject the hearing of the truth; on the other hand, he could probably assume that they would wander off into myths instead. There is something about the truth that people do not like. Sometimes it is too simple, and complex minds look for something more elaborate that they can grapple with. Often the truth is so obvious as to be humiliating. Most people are proud in one way or another, and to be brought low by the truth is an unpleasant experience. Given that Timothy was told that he must keep on rebuking his congregation and trying to correct them, we must not be surprised if sooner or later they would decide that they had had enough of that. Someone with a more comforting message would then be very welcome, even if what he said was untrue. The bearer of good tidings is always popular, whether the message he brings is accurate or not.[22]

It is when we are confronted with a situation like this that the temptation to turn to fantasy starts to make sense. Objectively speaking, myths do not correspond to reality and most people would naturally reject them. In the ancient world, intelligent men and women had no time for their inherited mythology and the philosophers generally despised it. But many found it impossible to live in the cold light of pure reason and turned for spiritual solace to the so-called 'mystery' religions that came from the East. These were becoming increasingly popular in Paul's day, and eventually even the philosophers would try to turn their beliefs into a religious system. That is what happened to Platonism in the early third century, and it explains the great popularity that it was to enjoy in late antiquity. Ironically, the creation of a new religion was the exact opposite of everything Plato himself had

---

[22] Compare Isa. 52.7 with Jer. 6.14.

stood for. His ideal society would have been governed by pure reason, and that would naturally exclude mythology, which Plato called *theologia*, a word he may have invented.

To the apostles and their disciples, Christianity was neither a rationalistic philosophy nor a mystery religion. It was a revelation of the truth about human nature, of the judgment that would come upon humanity because of its sinfulness, and of the way in which men and women could be saved from that and enjoy eternal life with God. It was reasonable without being rationalistic, and supernatural without being mysterious. Those who rejected it began by turning away from its reasonable explanation of the human predicament, and once they had done that, they sought out fantasies that would substitute for the genuine supernaturalism represented by divine revelation in Christ.

It is not difficult for us to appreciate this because similar things are very common today. There are many people in the modern world who have rejected the Christian explanation of human nature as outmoded and instead have claimed that human beings are fundamentally good. They have no concept of sin and believe that self-expression is to be encouraged, as long as it does not harm other people. This self-expression can take many forms. Some seek fulfillment in oriental religions like Hinduism or Buddhism, others create their own mishmash of mythology and dignify it with names like 'Celtic spirituality', 'new age' and the like. Often they believe in sacred stones, semi-magical potions, oracular mantras – almost anything in fact, as long as it is not the traditional gospel preached by the church. Even within the Christian world there are many who have rejected the Bible as out of date or otherwise unpalatable because it is 'patriarchal', 'hierarchical' or whatever other pejorative adjective they can come up with. Instead they reconstruct their own image of Christ which is based purely on what they want to find in him and not at all on what he has told us about himself. Once this happens, they can justify almost anything as being 'Christian', including same-sex marriage and similar aberrations that neither Jesus nor his disciples would have countenanced. Indeed, perhaps few things in 2 Timothy are more immediately recognizable today than this tendency to wander off into myths!

Having painted this bleak picture, Paul then turned from it in order to point out to Timothy how different he must be from people like the false teachers and fickle congregations he had been describing. Faced with such irrational behaviour, Timothy was called to 'stay sober' (*nēphe*), a common idiom that was used in both a literal and a metaphorical sense, as it can still be used today. Given that Timothy was unlikely to be driven to drink by the behaviour of his congregation, we must assume that it was the metaphorical sense that Paul had in mind here, and this hypothesis is confirmed by what follows. Paul outlined three ways in which 'sobriety', by which he meant a balanced approach to the challenges Timothy would face, ought to manifest itself:

1. He was to 'endure evil' (*kakopathēson*).[23]
2. He was to do the work of an evangelist.
3. He was to fulfil his ministry (*diakonia*).

As we have already seen on other occasions when Paul listed things like this, what appears to be simple and straightforward on the surface can look more complicated once we start to analyse what he intended, or may have intended, by his advice. First of all, what did it mean for Timothy to 'endure evil'? At one level this undoubtedly implied that he should be patient in his sufferings. As Paul had already indicated more than once, Timothy would have to endure opposition, persecution and rejection by his supposed followers. He might also have to suffer physically, as Paul did on several occasions, when he was beaten and thrown into prison.[24] It was all very well to protest at the injustice of this, but as Paul discovered, complaining about it did not stop the attacks from happening nor did it necessarily result in the dismissal of the accusations that had been brought against him. The whole saga of his journey to Rome to face trial was an injustice, but he had to undergo it and could not simply be set free on the grounds that there was insufficient evidence against him. The ancients believed that where there was smoke there was fire, and did not necessarily subscribe to the modern principle that a man is innocent until proved guilty. Timothy could therefore expect to suffer both physically and spiritually when he was attacked for his beliefs, and he had to prepare himself for that, so that when the time came he would endure it as a child of God and use it to bear witness to his faith in Christ.

Second, Timothy was called to do 'the work of an evangelist' (*ergon evangelistou*). To us the meaning here seems obvious. He was to preach the gospel, in season and out of season as Paul had just told him to do! But it is not clear that Paul was repeating himself here. We know from what he says elsewhere about the distribution of the spiritual gifts, that an evangelist was one of the categories of ministry that were found in the early church.[25] Evangelists no doubt did go around preaching the gospel, but so did the apostles, prophets and deacons, none of whom was distinguished in this

---

[23] The NRSV and ESV both translate this as 'endure suffering'; the NIV says 'endure hardship'.
[24] See Heb. 13.23.
[25] Eph. 4.11. Philip the deacon was also described as an 'evangelist' (Acts 21.8).

particular way. We also know that the Gospel writers were called 'evangelists', and it is possible that there was a group of people in the church whose main task it was to edit and safeguard the teaching that would eventually be canonized under the names of Matthew, Mark, Luke and John. These evangelists were the guardians and teachers of the sayings of Jesus that had to be preserved and passed on until they were eventually written down and codified.

Is that what Timothy was called to do? It is hard to say what Paul had in mind here. We do not know whether Timothy had a hand in the compilation of any of the four Gospels, nor can we say for sure whether he went about preaching to previously unreached people in the way that Paul did. It may be significant that Paul thought of himself as an apostle, not as an 'evangelist', and regarded his itinerant pioneering ministry in that light, but that does not mean that one activity excluded the other. Everything we hear about Timothy belongs to the category of 'follow up', whether it was by going on missions to places like Corinth and Philippi, or whether it was holding the fort for Paul in Ephesus. The difficulty in defining this role precisely is well stated by I. H. Marshall:

> Opinions are divided whether the term refers here to a particular type of church leader, occupying a position in time in between the apostles and the later bishops, or is simply a characterization of one of the tasks assigned to a church leader.[26]

Status or function? It is possible that the focus was on an itinerant ministry, and it may be that if Timothy was not at Ephesus when Paul was writing that he was engaged on a preaching mission somewhere in the interior. Paul certainly saw the spreading of the word to unreached areas and people as a prime goal of his labours, and it would not be at all surprising if he were here encouraging Timothy in a similar task.[27] But as P. H. Towner reminds us,

> hard and fast distinctions between, for example, evangelism and teaching or between local and itinerant ministries are not safely made, as the orbits of these activities would have overlapped to a significant extent. The safer distinction may be one of audience or intention, and

---

[26] Marshall (2004), p. 804. Calvin (1964), p. 336, interestingly if probably mistakenly, preferred the first option.
[27] Towner (2006), p. 608, suggests this as a possibility.

the ministry would have been carried out both within the church and outside of it.[28]

For Paul, preaching and teaching were always evangelistic, and he did not need a particular job description that would define what his tasks were. Most likely, he wanted Timothy to be evangelizing whatever he was doing and not to limit himself to one particular function, either inside or outside the church.

Finally, Timothy was told to 'fulfill his ministry'. Again, it is not entirely clear what this means. What exactly *was* his ministry? We have already argued that Timothy was probably not an elder or an *episkopos* in a local church, since he was expected to supervise them. Nor was he a deacon in the sense intended by Acts 6. There is no recognized category into which his ministry obviously fits, but he was fully occupied with the tasks that Paul had assigned to him and was clearly a key player in the mission of the early church. His main tasks were to teach and to discipline congregations that had been formed by Paul and to guard the deposit of faith that had been entrusted to him. These were very important, but how was anyone to know when they were 'fulfilled'? It is not as if there was a production quota that he had to reach or a particular goal that he had to attain in order to get the approval of his supervisor (Paul?). Given the context, 'to fulfill' his ministry probably means something like 'to be faithful' to it. In other words, Timothy was to stick to what he was supposed to be doing, to do it to the best of his ability and to pass it on to a successor more or less intact. It probably would not have mattered to Paul very much if Timothy had started with a congregation of a thousand and ended up with only three hundred or so, as long as those three hundred were stronger in their faith when Timothy left them than they had been when he first arrived.[29] Quality, not quantity, was what counted, though in the nature of the case, the expansion of the church was so remarkable that quantity was there whether he actively sought it or not. In fact, we might even go so far as to say that Paul's strategy was to insist on the highest quality in the church membership because that would then attract an increased quantity of members over time. Church growth was not an exercise in number-crunching but a serious desire to ensure that those who called themselves Christians were spiritually mature examples of the faith they claimed to profess. Paul certainly did not want a large congregation of lukewarm or unstable believers – the whole Epistle bears witness to his fear of ending up with just that!

---

[28] Towner (2006), p. 608.
[29] Think of the example of Gideon in Judg. 7.2-8.

## 6-8. Paul's hope

> 6. *As for me, I am already being poured out as a libation, and the time of my departure has come. 7. I have fought the good fight, I have finished the race, I have kept the faith. 8. From now on there is reserved for me the crown of righteousness, which the Lord, the righteous judge, will give me on that day, and not only to me but also to all who have longed for his appearing.*

Having given Timothy his instructions, Paul next turned to himself and described his own situation and prospects. On the surface, and from a modern perspective, we might say that Timothy's future looked bright whereas Paul's appeared to be increasingly bleak. To some extent, that was the inevitable result of his ever-increasing age. Old people usually have fewer options than young ones and cannot reasonably expect to have a ministry that will last as long. If Timothy could have kept going for another forty years or so, Paul knew that even if he were to be set free, he would probably have had less than half that time to fulfill his ministerial calling. Given the fact that he was in prison awaiting trial, the years available to him were likely to be far fewer. He understood that, of course, and his remarks on the subject show that he was preoccupied by his sense that for him at least, the end was near. He was no longer contemplating long missionary journeys to places like Spain but looking back on what he had done and evaluating it in the light of eternity.[30] Nothing is more characteristic of old age than that!

At the same time, we must not think that Paul was a resentful old man who was nursing his wounds and regretting the fact that his days were numbered. Nor was he determined to hang on to the bitter end. One of the worst characteristics of some people in ministry is that they cannot retire or hand things on to younger people. They are determined to carry on until they can do no more, however ineffective they may become and however frustrated their potential successors may be. Paul knew that the time had come for him to move on and he accepted it with a good grace, knowing that what awaited him was something far better than anything he could have constructed or worked out for himself. It was that expectation that governed his attitude and made his sense of resignation to what awaited him a blessing to those around him and not the unhappy embarrassment it might otherwise have been. The right note is struck by I. H. Marshall:

---

[30] Rom. 15.28.

The exhortation to Timothy is rounded off by a passage in which Paul is presented as being at the end of a lifetime of faithful service after which he can expect his heavenly reward. The purpose is threefold: to put an example before Timothy which he is to follow; to indicate that he (and others) must take the place now being vacated by Paul; and to hold out the promise of reward for faithful service. It is, however, the second of these three purposes which basically structures the passage.[31]

Verse 6 set the scene as Paul told Timothy that he was already being 'poured out' (*spendomai*) and that the time of his departure (*analysis*) had come. The language was somewhat euphemistic, making it difficult to interpret what he really meant, but the general drift is surely clear. The word *spendō* was commonly used of the ritual libations that preceded sacrifices in the ancient world, which is why the NRSV added the words 'as a libation' even though they are not in the text.[32] It has often been thought that this was a reference to the spilling of his blood which Paul anticipated, but libations were not themselves sacrifices and this interpretation may be taking things too far. On the other hand, to empty a jar of water or of wine is an act that can easily be interpreted as exhausting a resource, and it is not difficult to see why Paul would have used it to describe the withering away of his strength and stamina, whether he was headed for imminent execution or not.

Similarly, it has been suggested that the word *analysis* can also mean 'release' and that Paul was here anticipating the end of his imprisonment. In that case, he was expecting to be set free to continue his ministry and was not thinking about death at all, though that reading is hard to square with the tone of the text and is explicitly rejected by I. H. Marshall, with good reason.[33] The difficulty here, of course, is once again the fact that Greek words can often bear many meanings and the one to be preferred has to be deduced from the context. In this case, it is what follows in the next two verses that must determine our choice. Like many people today, Paul avoided using the word 'death', preferring other terms that expressed the same idea in a gentler way. There is no need to suppose that he foresaw his coming martyrdom in his use of *spendomai*, although perhaps he did. The main point is not that but rather that he knew that his active ministry was coming to an end, whatever form that end might take.

It was in those circumstances that he embarked on a self-analysis which he shared with Timothy in order to set an example before the younger man

---

[31] Marshall (2004), p. 805.
[32] The NIV and ESV both have 'drink-offering' for 'libation', which is the same thing.
[33] Marshall (2004), pp. 806–7.

and encourage him to follow it. The categories by which he measured himself were the same as the ones he had used earlier to tell Timothy what kind of minister he ought to be. We can reproduce his check list as follows:

1. Soldier: I have fought the good fight (tick).
2. Athlete: I have finished the race (tick).
3. Hard-working farmer: I have kept the faith (tick).

The first two are obvious; the third is perhaps more debatable, until we remember that farming involves sowing crops and then patiently waiting for them to produce fruit. Sowing the seed is what Paul had done all over the place, and he had kept the faith by trusting God to give the increase in response to the groundwork that he and others like Apollos and Peter had done.[34] He had not changed course halfway through, or adopted another technique because the one he was using seemed to be too slow in getting results. Nor was he ever tempted to copy the methods of others. He had done what he was commissioned to do and trusted that God would honour his faithfulness. So although the third analogy may not be as immediately obvious as the first two are, it nevertheless fits the overall picture that he was drawing of his life's work and achievement. John Chrysostom tells us how he wrestled with this passage before coming to understand what it means:

> Often, when I have taken the apostle into my hands, and have considered this passage, I have been at a loss to understand why Paul here speaks so loftily: 'I have fought the good fight.' Bu now by the grace of God I seem to have found it out ... He is desirous to console the despondency of his disciple, and therefore bids him be of good cheer, since he was gong to his crown, having finished all his work, and obtained a glorious end.[35]

After coming to terms with the past, Paul turned to the future. What remained for him now was the 'crown of righteousness' (*ho tēs dikaiosynēs stephanos*) which was laid up for him in heaven. The image recalls the rewards given to successful soldiers and athletes, and Paul's use of it was no doubt deliberate. Paul was not interested in worldly success, but he was not afraid to use it as a pale image to illustrate what really counted. The crown of righteousness would not be given as a reward for any righteousness that he might have earned, because of course, he had not earned any! Nor was it a means of

---
[34] 1 Cor. 3.5-9.
[35] John Chrysostom, *Homilies on 2 Timothy*, 9.4.7 (NPNF 13, p. 511).

obtaining righteousness, as if he would be getting something in and through the crown that he did not already have. The crown was waiting for him because it was already his, not by virtue of any achievement on his part, nor as a remedy for any lingering problems that he might have been dealing with, but as a sign that he had found favour with God and that the Lord would recognize that when the time came.

The underlying message is that it is God alone who is righteous, and that he was the one who would judge Paul, not Caesar or any other earthly authority. The irony here is that while Paul was innocent according to Caesar's law, it was quite likely that he would be punished by the state in some way, as indeed he already had been by his lengthy imprisonment. In the presence of God, on the other hand, Paul was guilty, because like everyone else, he was a sinner and deserved whatever punishment God might choose to give him.[36] But the divine judge is 'righteous' (*dikaios*) and would give Paul a share in his righteousness, not because Paul had done anything to deserve it but because God had loved him and chosen him for the honour. In that sense, God's sovereignty was greater than his justice because he could look at Paul, not as the sinner that he was in himself but as the saint that he had become in Christ.[37]

That fact was already a reality but it had not yet been fully revealed or come to public knowledge, as it would when he received the crown confirming his status in the heavenly kingdom. Paul told Timothy that he would receive it 'on that day' (*en ekeinēi tēi hēmerāi*), a phrase that is ambiguous. It could mean the day Paul died, or it could refer to the last judgment. The fact that he had just spoken of God as the 'just judge' suggests that it is the second of these two interpretations that is to be preferred, but it is hard to see that it makes much difference in practice. Paul knew that when he died he would go to be with Christ, and he looked forward to that. Once he was there, time would cease to exist for him and so 'that day' would no longer have any temporally

---

[36] In support of this suggestion, Towner (2006), p. 616, says, 'A possible polemical challenge to the imperial judgment handed down against Paul should not be discounted.' Marshall (2004), p. 809, also mentions this possibility, which he thinks may be implicit in Paul's insistence that God is a 'righteous judge', presumably in contrast to any human counterparts.

[37] Thomas Aquinas (2012), 4.2.151 (p. 402), wanted to have it both ways: 'it seems that eternal life is conferred because of grace ... Therefore, it is not a matter of justice. I answer that grace is involved inasmuch as it is the root of merit, and justice inasmuch as it is an act proceeding from the will.' John Calvin (1964), p. 338, also tried to reconcile grace and works, but in a different way. He wrote, 'Justification by free grace conferred upon us through faith is not at variance with the rewarding of works; the two are rather completely consistent – man is freely justified by Christ's grace and yet God will render to him the reward of his works.'

defined meaning. From the standpoint of those still on earth 'that day' would naturally lie in the future, but for him it would be a present reality because he would have passed from time to eternity.

That it was the final judgment that Paul had in mind here is confirmed by the last part of the sentence. His reward was not something that he would receive in isolation from anything or anyone else. He was not expecting to get a special gift that would not be given to others. On the contrary, he insisted that what was coming to him would be granted in due course to everyone who has 'loved his appearing', in other words, who was eagerly expecting the return of Christ in judgment. Theodore of Mopsuestia was struck by this:

> it is worthy of marvel that he [Paul] did not say 'to those who have toiled or suffered', but instead said 'those who love his coming'. This is because there is not always a time for contests and sufferings, but there is always time for love. If now even in time of peace someone should be eager to preserve love as he ought, he would not be defrauded of his reward, although a time for contests were by no means his lot.[38]

Those who are right with God love his coming and do not have to fear that event, as if there was a chance that they would be given a test at the end and fail it.[39] As Paul had said at the beginning of this Epistle, he knew whom he had believed and was persuaded that he was able to keep what he had committed to him 'against that day', and so in the words of the famous analogy used by Jesus, he was not afraid that he would be found wearing the wrong garment at the wedding feast of the Lamb.[40] This confidence is what we call 'assurance' and it is a gift given to all who have trusted in Christ, not just to those who have achieved the kinds of things that Paul had done.

It may be added as a conclusion to this section that here Paul underlined his conviction that Christ is fully and truly God, even though he did not say so in so many words. The 'Lord' is an ambiguous term, in that it was usually used of Jesus but could also apply to God the Father and was in fact the term that Jews usually substituted for the unpronounceable name of Yahweh (YHWH). Judgment belonged to God the Father, but is here executed by the 'Lord', and of course it was the Son, not the Father who would appear at the end of time. Paul glided from speaking about the Father to speaking about the Son without comment, attributing the acts of the one to the other

---

[38] Theodore of Mopsuestia (2010), p. 729.
[39] Calvin (1964), p. 339, makes this point and says that those who are afraid of Christ's return are not believers at all.
[40] Mt. 22.1-14.

because in reality they were all the work of the one God. The divinity of Christ is rarely stated openly in the New Testament, but in passages like these it shines through clearly and we cannot understand the work of Christ as it is described here without attributing the fullness of the divine being to him.

## 9-15 Personal relationships

> 9. Do your best to come to me soon, 10. for Demas, in love with this present world, has deserted me and gone to Thessalonica; Crescens has gone to Galatia, Titus to Dalmatia. 11. Only Luke is with me. Get Mark and bring him with you, for he is useful in my ministry. 12. I have sent Tychicus to Ephesus. 13. When you come, bring the cloak that I left with Carpus at Troas, also the books, and above all the parchments. 14. Alexander the coppersmith did me great harm; the Lord will pay him back for his deeds. 15. You also must beware of him, for he strongly opposed our message.

At the end of his Epistle Paul turned, as he often did, to personal relationships and news of his friends and acquaintances. It is interesting to note that 2 Timothy is much more detailed in this respect than 1 Timothy (which has no comparable section at the end) or Titus, where only a small number of his colleagues are mentioned. This may have been because Paul had not seen Timothy in a long time and needed to bring him up to date on what was happening in the circles in which they both moved. When he wrote 1 Timothy Paul had only recently left Ephesus, was planning on going back there soon, and was apparently not in contact with any mutual friends or acquaintances in the meantime. He was further removed from Titus, but again not so far as to make a long account of other people and their relationships important or necessary. But here in 2 Timothy he thought he had to say more, and most of the rest of the Epistle is taken up with the news of the comings and goings of various mutual friends and associates.

Another reason why Paul may have felt the need to tell Timothy what was going on was that he had apparently missed him when he had last been in Ephesus and was expecting him to come to Rome in the near future. If that was the case, he probably thought that Timothy ought to know what to expect when he arrived. Paul wanted Timothy to do his best to come to him 'as quickly as possible' (*tacheōs*). In practical terms that could have meant anything up to a year's delay from the time of writing. This is because it would have taken three or four months for the letter to have reached Timothy in Asia Minor, and then Timothy would have had to make preparations for the journey. Winter would probably have intervened at some point, adding another four months or more to the time it would have taken him to travel to Rome, although Paul was hoping that Timothy might be able to get to him beforehand (see v. 21). Both men must have known that by the time Timothy arrived, things could have changed in any number of ways and Timothy would surely have brought news that had not yet reached Paul. From our standpoint, it is possible that Paul died before Timothy got this letter, and it may even be that it was still waiting to be sent when he passed away, either from natural causes or through martyrdom. We simply do not know and must be cautious about drawing conclusions that cannot be substantiated for lack of evidence. What is certain is that we hear no more about either man after this and must therefore regard these parting words as the last ones in their long mutual relationship, whether they actually were or not.

What follows is a progress report that is as up to date as Paul could make it. Demas, who was still with Paul when he wrote to Philemon and the Colossians, had deserted him and gone to Thessalonica, out of 'love for this present world' (*agapēsas ton nyn aiōna*).[41] The usual interpretation of this is that Demas had given up his Christian faith and that may be right, though it may be that although he had abandoned the Pauline mission, perhaps out of fear that it might lead him to his death, he had not given up on his faith.[42] It should be noted that Paul said that Demas had deserted *him*, not that he had renounced *Christ*, and he also knew where Demas had gone. It is hard to believe that Demas would have been in Thessalonica for long without the church there getting wind of his presence. He might have come from Thessalonica in the first place, and perhaps the church there was able to get hold of him and straighten him out. We do not know the full story and must be careful about drawing conclusions that may not be justified, though it is abundantly clear that Paul was not happy about what Demas had done.

Crescens had gone to Galatia, though who he was and why he had gone there are both unknown.[43] We may surmise that he had set out to visit Paul's churches in that province, but we do not know for sure. Titus had likewise

---

[41] Phlm. 1.24; Col. 4.10-12. We learn from the second passage that Demas was a Gentile, who may have come from Thessalonica, as ancient commentators generally assumed, but we cannot know that for certain.

[42] See Marshall (2004), pp. 815–16, who admits this possibility. Towner (2006), pp. 622–3, goes further and comments, 'There is ... no reason to think that his desertion from the Pauline team, as serious as that was in Paul's eyes, indicates his rejection of the faith or even necessarily his retirement from Christian service.' Calvin (1964), pp. 339–40, was of the same opinion.

[43] This is the only mention of him in the New Testament. Both Theodore of Mopsuestia (2010), p. 731, and Theodoret of Cyrrhus (Cyrus) (2001), p. 138, thought that 'Galatia' meant 'Gallia', that is, 'Gaul' because that is how it had been referred to in ancient times, but why Crescens would have gone there is a mystery.

gone off to Dalmatia, again, probably to visit Paul's churches there, but we do not know that for certain either.[44] Of his main companions, only Luke was still with him in Rome. Whether Luke was writing his Gospel and Acts at that time we cannot say, but there are similarities between the Pastoral Epistles and Luke that make some literary collaboration between them at this time possible, if not certain. Some people have suggested that Luke was the author of the Pastorals, and it may be that they used the same amanuensis, but although this theory fits the evidence to some extent, it cannot be regarded as conclusive. As so often in such matters, all we can do is offer suggestions as to what might have been the case and plead ignorance.

More interesting in some ways is what Paul had to say about Mark, who must have been somewhere in the neighbourhood of Ephesus at this time, or had been there when Paul last heard about him. Early in his missionary journeys, Paul had fallen out with Barnabas over Mark, because the young man had been unwilling (and in Paul's eyes too immature) to accompany them on the mission.[45] Timothy must have been aware of that, because he had met both Paul and Barnabas in Lystra and had been in contact with Paul ever since. It is even possible, though this is nowhere stated, that Paul had originally seen Timothy as a substitute for the unsatisfactory Mark! Whatever the case, things had clearly changed for the better, because now Paul regarded Mark as very useful (*euchrēstos*) for his ministry. It is rare and therefore heartening to see such a reconciliation, and it must count as evidence against the likelihood that the Epistle was written by a pseudepigrapher. If all that was known about Mark's relationship with Paul was what we read in Acts 15, it is most unlikely that someone would have invented such a positive commendation. It is much easier to believe that there had been a genuine reconciliation between the two men and that Paul was perfectly sincere in his request to Timothy.

What we do not know is *how* Mark was useful to Paul. What had he done to deserve such a recommendation? We hear from Papias, a second-century Christian writer, that Mark was close to Peter and transcribed Peter's memoirs, which have become Mark's Gospel,[46] but there is no corresponding information about the relationship between Mark and Paul, nor is it possible to reconstruct a relative chronology of events. Had Mark already written his Gospel at this point, or did that come later? Did Peter arrive in Rome around this time? Yet more questions that we cannot answer!

---

[44] That Paul had preached in the region is known from Rom. 15.9.
[45] Acts 15.37-39.
[46] Eusebius of Caesarea, *Historia ecclesiastica*, 3.39.15.

Tychicus has already been sent to Ephesus, but this remark also raises questions. He had gone there at Paul's command, but what does that tell us (if anything) about the departure of Crescens and Titus? Did they leave without Paul's blessing? And where was Timothy at this time? If he had been in Ephesus, he would surely have known of Tychicus' arrival without having to be told, and Tychicus could even have taken the letter. Another mystery!

Wherever Timothy was at this point, he must have been somewhere in Asia Minor, because Paul seems to have assumed that he would at least pass through Ephesus on his way to Rome. He also assumed that it would be possible for Timothy to stop in Troas, near the Dardanelles and almost on the site of ancient Troy, where Paul had left a cloak, books and loose parchments with a man called Carpus.[47] When was that? How long had those things been there? Was Timothy going to collect them on his way to Rome from Ephesus, or on his way to Ephesus from wherever he was? And what was in those books and parchments that made them so desirable for Paul to have? The effort of bringing them would have been considerable, but Paul evidently thought it was worthwhile – why? More questions that we would like to have the answers to but which are hidden from our eyes.

The gaps in our knowledge and the apparent incongruity of the information that we have been given have allowed those who argue for pseudepigraphy to claim that this is a prime example of it – the author knew enough about Paul to mention these people but had no way of knowing where they were or what they were doing at any particular time. He put together enough to make it all seem plausible but did not worry too much about loose ends. A contrary argument of course is that a pseudepigrapher would have made sure that he did not say things that were implausible or that others could disprove. In fact, it is hard to see why a pseudepigrapher would bother with all this unnecessary information. If 1 Timothy has nothing similar and Titus is much briefer, why could he not have done the same with 2 Timothy? By giving so many details he was just opening himself up to detection by those who knew the facts, but nobody ever questioned them until the nineteenth century. We may just as well conclude that the apparent loose ends are genuine and that we simply lack the additional information that we would need to fit the jigsaw together.

---

[47] Most commentators assume that Paul wanted his cloak because of the onset of winter, but Ambrosiaster (2009), p. 153, took it to mean a toga and thought that Paul needed it in order to make a court appearance as a Roman citizen. That explanation was taken up by Haimo of Auxerre and included by Thomas Aquinas (2012), 4.3.158 (p. 406), in his commentary.

In v. 14 we meet Alexander the coppersmith, who may be the same man that Paul mentioned in 1 Tim. 1.20, though it is impossible to say for sure. Alexander was a common name, after all, and Paul evidently felt that he had to identify the man according to his profession so as not to get him confused with others. Alexander was clearly opposed to what Paul and his associates were teaching and he had done Paul great harm, but where and when that was we do not know. It seems that Timothy had not come across him before, so he was probably not from Ephesus, in which case it is hard to identify him with the man mentioned in 1 Tim. 1.20. Maybe he was from Troas, since Paul mentioned him immediately after Carpus, though of course we do not know that either! If so, Paul was probably warning Timothy to watch out for him when he got to Troas himself, because Alexander might be lying in wait to attack him too.

## 16-18. Paul's rescue

*16. At my first defence no one came to my support, but all deserted me. May it not be counted against them! 17. But the Lord stood by me and gave me strength, so that through me the message might be fully proclaimed and all the Gentiles might hear it. So I was rescued from the lion's mouth. 18. The Lord will rescue me from every evil attack and save me for his heavenly kingdom. To him be the glory forever and ever. Amen.*

At this point Paul paused in his catalogue of people and events to mention the opening stage of his trial. Whether this happened during the two years that he stayed in his own hired house in Rome or afterwards we do not know. If we think that Paul was set free the first time round and was then rearrested, we cannot say for sure whether this incident took place during his first imprisonment or the second one. In any case, we know that it was over by the time he was writing, that he survived the experience and that nobody had stood by him in court. Why was that? Where was Luke, for instance, when this was happening? Perhaps only Roman citizens could have accompanied him and stood by him during his trial, and if that was so, then it may be that the others whom he mentioned were not Romans. In any case, he named no names, so we cannot tell one way or the other.

What we do notice is that Paul bore them no grudges. He did not want their desertion to be held against them, perhaps because he knew that the disciples had deserted Jesus when he had been on trial, and Jesus had forgiven them. With a precedent like that, how could Paul have done otherwise? Perhaps he knew that they might have been charged with guilt by association, and so he understood why they had disappeared. Roman law courts generally functioned in an upright manner, but if somebody had decided to arrest Paul's companions, neither he nor they could have done much about it. Rome was not a democracy, and as we know from the careers of men like Nero, who was emperor at this time, civil rights then were not what we would recognize by that name today.

Whatever the truth of the matter was, Paul knew that he was being supported and protected by the Lord, whose presence he felt at every moment of his ordeal. Whether he was speaking here of God the Father or of Christ, he knew that he was being defended by a power that no human force could oppose and that as events unfolded, he was being given the strength to proclaim the gospel in its fullness to all who were present. Seen in that light, Paul's trial gave him a major platform to preach the Word, particularly to people who would not otherwise have heard it. We have no idea what they made of it, of course, but the fact that Paul said that he had been 'rescued from the lion's mouth' suggests that his words earned him the sympathy of the judges. The image here recalls Daniel, who had been thrown into the lions' den, and we must assume that the consequences were the same in both cases.[48] But we must also note that it reflects the LXX reading of Psalm 22 (21 in the Greek version), which is, of course, the psalm that Jesus quoted on the cross.[49] Whether Paul was consciously putting himself in the place of the crucified Christ is uncertain, but possible, since he did so elsewhere.[50] If that was the case, then Paul's emphasis was subtly different – where Jesus cried out that God had abandoned him, Paul stressed that he had been delivered from the mouth of the lion.

Whatever interpretation we adopt, there is no doubt that the experience had taught Paul that he could trust the Lord for the next stage in his trial and whatever might follow from that. He had the confidence that he would be rescued from all the evil that other human beings might attempt against him and that in the end he would be brought safely into the heavenly kingdom. What that would mean in terms of his subsequent fate is impossible to say. Legend tells us that he was martyred in Rome, and if so, the trial did not turn out in his favour. Perhaps he was released, but he was not really expecting that, and it is safer to conclude that he never emerged from his prison. He may have died there of natural causes, of course, and later been reckoned as a martyr because of the circumstances of his death. We do not know

---

[48] Dan. 6.1-23.
[49] Mt. 27.46; Mk 15.34.
[50] Gal. 2.20.

what actually happened and it is useless to speculate. All we can say with reasonable certainty is that this is the last we hear of Paul.

It is therefore entirely appropriate that his parting words to us were to give glory to God for ever and ever. Paul's priorities were always firmly fixed on Jesus, his gospel, his promises and his glory. As Paul took his leave of this world, that was the note that he sounded, and we may be sure that it was with those words on his lips that he entered into the heavenly kingdom and received the crown that he knew was waiting there for him.

## 19-22. Final greetings

*19. Greet Prisca and Aquila, and the household of Onesiphorus. 20. Erastus remained in Corinth; Trophimus I left in Miletus. 21. Do your best to come to me before winter. Eubulus sends greetings to you, as do Pudens and Linus and Claudia and all the brothers and sisters. 22. The Lord be with your spirit. Grace be with you.*

The last few verses are a kind of appendix to the Epistle that consists of the usual greetings to various people who were known to both Paul and Timothy. First come Prisca (Priscilla) and Aquila, who were presumably in Ephesus at this time. We know that they travelled from Rome to Ephesus and Corinth and then back to Rome again, so we are not surprised that they should have been in Ephesus at this time.[51] Onesiphorus was from Ephesus, and Paul asked Timothy to greet his household, which may mean that Onesiphorus was still in Rome or perhaps that he had died.

Paul's mention of the fact that Erastus remained in Corinth and that he left Trophimus in Miletus suggests at first glance that he was talking about something that had happened on his journey to Jerusalem, where he was arrested and eventually sent to Rome. But it appears from the account in Acts that Trophimus did not stay in Miletus at that time but made it to Jerusalem where he was spotted in Paul's company.[52] This makes it unlikely that Paul could have been referring to that journey, and it is hard to believe that a pseudepigrapher could have made such a crass mistake and not been spotted. The more likely scenario is that Paul was referring to another and more recent occasion. Trophimus was from Ephesus and it is quite likely that after Paul was arrested in Jerusalem, he made his way back there since it would

---

[51] Acts 18.1; Rom. 16.3.
[52] Acts 21.29.

have been pointless for him to have stayed in Palestine for upwards of two years.[53] If that was what happened, Paul could have met up with him again after being released from prison in Rome, and Trophimus may have agreed to accompany him on his journey but fell ill at Miletus.

As for Erastus, he was most likely the same man who was (or had been) the treasurer of Corinth, and he stayed home when Paul left for Troas.[54] Paul may have felt a need to tell Timothy that since the two men had worked together and Timothy might have wondered why he did not travel to Ephesus with Paul.[55] The details are obscure but they do not support any theory of pseudepigraphy. Why would someone have bothered to invent such a detail, which adds nothing to the Epistle and serves no purpose on its own?

The chronology of Paul's movements later in life is impossible to reconstruct with any degree of precision, but this passage is the best evidence we have that he may have been released from imprisonment in Rome and allowed to travel again. If we accept that possibility, it is relatively easy to make sense of the details which can be understood as follows:

1. Paul left Rome for Corinth, taking Erastus and possibly Trophimus and others with him.
2. Erastus stayed at Corinth (his home) and Paul moved on with Trophimus to Miletus, where Paul left him because he was ill.
3. Paul passed through Ephesus on his way to Troas, but Timothy was not there for some reason. He may have lodged with Onesiphorus and his household during his stay in the city.
4. On arriving at Troas, Paul was attacked by Alexander the coppersmith in an altercation that may have led to his rearrest.
5. On leaving Troas for Rome, Paul deposited his belongings with Carpus. It may also have been that it was in Troas that Demas abandoned Paul and returned to Thessalonica, which was not far away.
6. Paul was taken back to Rome and given a preliminary hearing, which did not lead to the case against him being dismissed. This may have been because he was caught up in the aftermath of the great fire of Rome (19–26 July AD 64), which Nero blamed on the Christians.
7. Paul had time to send Crescens to Galatia, Titus to Dalmatia and Tychicus to Ephesus. He also thought it possible for Timothy to come to Rome, bringing the belongings he had deposited at Troas with him.

---

[53] Acts 21.29.
[54] Rom. 16.23.
[55] Acts 19.22.

If we prefer the hypothesis that there was only one imprisonment in Rome, the chronology has to be shorter, and there are difficulties in harmonizing some of the details. A reconstruction would then have to look something like this:

1. Paul left Erastus at Corinth, on his way to Jerusalem *via* Macedonia and northern Asia Minor.
2. Paul reached Troas and left his possessions there with Carpus. He may have had an altercation with Alexander the coppersmith at this point.
3. Paul went to Ephesus, but Timothy was not there. If Alexander was the same person we read about in 1 Tim. 1.20 (who may have been the same man who appears in Acts 19.33), then an altercation between him and Paul may have taken place in Ephesus.
4. Paul went from Ephesus to Miletus, but did he leave Trophimus there because he was ill? That seems to be unlikely, because Trophimus reappeared in Jerusalem when Paul finally got there.[56] Since Paul never went back to Miletus, he must have despatched Trophimus there at some later point, but this does not fit the text very well. Why would Paul send someone who was ill on a journey like that and describe the whole incident in ambiguous and misleading terms? In the sixteenth century, Theodore Beza emended the text to read 'Melita' (Malta) which would mean that Paul left him there on his way to Rome, but that is pure speculation and unlikely.[57]
5. Paul reached Rome with several of his entourage, whom he then sent off on various missions. Demas, however, feared what might be coming and deserted Paul before being sent anywhere.
6. Onesiphorus eventually heard of Paul's travails and found out that he was in Rome, where he located him after a diligent search. This must have happened about three years after Paul left Ephesus, which is a long time.
7. Paul wrote to Timothy towards the end of his two-year stay in Rome but probably died before Timothy could get there to see him. Whether his death was from natural causes or martyrdom is not known, though every tradition regarding Paul says that he was put to death for his faith. All we know is that he had been through his first defence and was still in prison when he wrote to Timothy, which means that he was not released at that time.

---

[56] Acts 21.29. John Chrysostom, *Homilies on 2 Timothy*, 10.20 (NPNF 13, p. 515), was also puzzled by the reference to Trophimus and dd not know how to resolve the difficulty.
[57] See Marshall (2004), p. 827.

Both these scenarios have a large number of uncertainties attached to them, but the two-imprisonment theory is easier to make sense of. Of course, if the letter was written by a pseudepigrapher, no reconstruction of events is necessary, since he could have made it all up. However, as I. H. Marshall maintains, the closing lines of the Epistle are the ones most likely to have come from Paul himself, even if they were subsequently reworked and integrated into a composite whole after the apostle's death.[58] Certainty is impossible, but if we are to maintain the authenticity of the Epistle as a genuine Pauline letter, then it must be said that the two-imprisonment hypothesis is the more plausible one.[59]

The Epistle's final sentence contains the names of four people who were with Paul in Rome and who appear to have been members of the church there. We know nothing about them other than what is said here, although Linus may have been the man who is supposed to have succeeded Peter as the second 'bishop' or 'pope' of Rome.[60] Whether there is any substance to that story is unknown, but at least this Epistle tells us that there was a Christian called Linus in the city at that time, so he had historical existence even if we know nothing about his subsequent life or career. What is interesting about this is that it tells us that Paul was still in contact with the local church. He mentioned that all the brothers sent their greetings to Timothy, so there must have been a general awareness in the community of what Paul was doing. This in turn reminds us that when Paul wrote that he had been deserted and left alone, he was talking about his close companions and associates. He was certainly not in solitary confinement!

One point that might be mentioned about the names that appear in this chapter is that there seems to be a fairly even division between Greek and Latin ones, but none that can be regarded as Semitic or Eastern in origin. The list is as follows:

| Greek | Latin |
|---|---|
| Demas | Crescens |
| Luke | Titus |
| Tychicus | Mark |
| Carpus | Prisca (Priscilla) |

---

[58] See Marshall (2004), p. 812.
[59] It was first put forward by Eusebius of Caesarea, *Historia ecclesiastica*, 2.22.2-3.
[60] According to Irenaeus, *Adversus omnes haereses*, 3.3.3, and Eusebius of Caesarea, *Historia ecclesiastica*, 3.2.13.

| Greek | Latin |
|---|---|
| Alexander | Aquila |
| Onesiphorus | Pudens |
| Erastus | Linus |
| Trophimus | Claudia |
| Eubulus | |

The two women in the list both have Latin names, which is interesting. We know that Prisca was the wife of Aquila, and it is possible that Claudia was the wife of Linus, but we cannot be sure about that. Paul lived in a world in which men and women mixed reasonably freely, and although men predominate in this passage, that can be explained by the circumstances. Paul did not travel with women, as far as we know, and they may not have had access to him in prison. Prisca (Priscilla) was in Asia Minor and was always associated with her husband Aquila, so not much can be made of that. The Greek names call for no special comment, but the Latin ones betray an influence in the circles in which Paul moved that was not reflected by any corresponding use of the Latin language. Were these people Roman citizens? Did they have Latin names because their parents liked them and gave them to their children, much in the way that many people in Africa have Western names in addition to local ones? Each individual case is probably different, but the cumulative evidence suggests that the fusion of Greek and Roman culture that made up the empire was in full swing at this time and that other nationalities were more or less excluded, at least on the surface.

There is much that we do not know, but it is at least possible that what we see here is the steady progression of the church away from the Jewish circles in which it was born towards a more complete identification with the Gentile world. That transition was mediated by men like Paul (a Latin name) who was also Saul in Hebrew, though after his conversion that name seems to have faded out of the picture. Was this conscious, or did it just happen without much awareness on anyone's part? Perhaps it was a bit of both, but whatever the case, by the time Timothy was an old man the transition was well underway, and the Jewish-Christian world in which Paul had lived and worked was rapidly becoming a thing of the past.

The Epistle closes with the personal salutation: 'The Lord be with your spirit', a version of which appears also in Philemon, but not in 1 Timothy or in Titus. The final 'Grace be with you (*hymin*)' adds a plural dimension to what is otherwise an intensely personal letter, and it is possible that it was added by a later scribe in imitation of 1 Timothy. It hardly matters, because however personal 2 Timothy originally was, it has survived as a letter to the whole church, and it is as members of the body of Christ that we read it today – not as somebody else's mail, but as a communication directed to us as well as to Timothy, our brother in the faith and fellow disciple of the apostle who wrote it.

# Titus

## Chapter 1

- 1-4   Greeting
- 5-9   The character of an elder
- 10-16   The character and behaviour of the wicked

## Chapter 2

- 1-8   The behaviour of church members
- 9-10   Slaves
- 11-13   The grace of God in the life of the believer
- 14   The work of Christ
- 15   Paul's charge to Titus

## Chapter 3

- 1-3   The character of a Christian
- 4-8   The nature and effect of the gospel
- 9-11   The divisive person
- 12-15   Final greetings and advice

# Titus 1

## 1-4. Greeting

*1. Paul, a servant of God and an apostle of Jesus Christ, for the sake of the faith of God's elect and the knowledge of the truth that is in accordance with godliness, 2. in the hope of eternal life that God, who never lies, promised before the ages began – 3. in due time he revealed his word through the proclamation with which I have been entrusted by the command of God our Saviour. 4. To Titus, my loyal child in the faith we share: grace and peace from God the Father and Christ Jesus our Saviour.*

The third of the Pastoral Epistles is the shortest one and in some respects the most mysterious. In both subject matter and style, the epistle to Titus is noticeably closer to 1 Timothy than it is to 2 Timothy, and the common assumption that they were written at more or less the same time is plausible, though not certain. Neither of them is a prison epistle, and the general impression we get from both is that Paul was pursuing his missionary vocation unhindered by the state authorities. Opposition to his activities, such as it was, came mainly from false teachers and recalcitrant or unruly church members. There is also the fact that in both Epistles Paul seems to have been on a journey that took him through Macedonia to Nicopolis in Epirus (or the extreme south of Illyricum), though he does not appear to have been in either place when he wrote these Epistles.[1]

Like 1 Timothy, Titus is concerned with church order. But although there is a certain amount of overlap in subject matter between the two letters, it is not very likely that one of them was copied from the other. The epistle to Titus is specifically geared to the situation in Crete, and although Paul's advice regarding the qualifications of elders and *episkopoi* is fully consonant with what we find in 1 Timothy, it is not exactly the same. The need to establish a durable form of church government is a preoccupation in both Epistles, but the problems in Crete seem to have been internal to the congregations

---

[1] He mentioned Macedonia in 1 Tim. 1.3 and Nicopolis in Tit. 3.12.

themselves to a greater degree than was the case at Ephesus. The false teachers who appear in Titus resemble the Judaizers who were troubling the Ephesian church, but Paul did not dwell on them to the extent that he did in 1 Timothy and it seems that the real problem was the immaturity of the Cretan Christians who needed to be warned about them, whereas in Ephesus they had to be rooted out.

Compared with Timothy, about whom we learn quite a bit in the two Epistles addressed to him, Titus barely figures in his Epistle at all. He was Paul's assistant, left in Crete to do a job, and the advice given to him is for the most part quite businesslike in its tone. Most of what Paul said to Titus could have been said to anyone, which may help to explain why the Epistle has been preserved as part of God's word to the universal church. It is a blueprint for mission, and as such it is more comprehensive than either 1 or 2 Timothy, despite the fact that it is shorter than either of them.

Paul's main concern in writing to Titus was the need to appoint good pastors, with men like Titus setting a good example, and to encourage sound teaching and good behaviour among the local converts in order to further their spiritual growth and that of the churches. Respectability would come in handy when dealing with outsiders, a consideration that figures prominently in 1 Timothy, but in Titus it was the edification of the believers themselves that appears to have been Paul's main priority.

The Epistle opens with the customary salutation, though it is more elaborate than that found in the apostle's other letters. This immediately raises the question of pseudepigraphy, with the usual double-edged response. On the one hand, those in favour of a post-Pauline provenance argue that the salutation is not typical of Paul and therefore must have been composed by someone else. On the other hand, those who argue for Pauline authorship say that a pseudepigrapher would have followed the apostle's normal practice and not produced something as unexpected as this. Neither of these arguments is conclusive, but it seems likely that if the letter were not genuine, critics in the early church would have pointed to the atypical salutation as evidence of its inauthenticity. Nobody did, however, and the universal willingness of the ancients to accept it as Pauline in spite of such oddities surely ought to count in its favour.

Paul began his greeting in a familiar way, although with some interesting touches that make it different from that found in either 1 or 2 Timothy. In the other Epistles he called himself no more than an apostle of Christ Jesus, but here he started off by saying that he was a servant (or slave) of God, before going on to say that he was an apostle of Jesus Christ.[2] Yet again we

---

[2] The reversal of the order of the Saviour's names is perhaps significant, especially as it is continued throughout the Epistle (in contrast to both 1 and 2 Timothy).

are faced with the dilemma – does this difference support the view that the Epistle is pseudepigraphal, or the opposite? Deviation from the Pauline norm on a symbolic matter like this would surely have been noticed and remarked upon, but it was not. It is particularly hard to explain it if we think that 1 Timothy and Titus were written by the same man at the same time. Why would he employ a typically Pauline usage in his two letters to Timothy, supposedly written at different times and in quite different circumstances, but not in the one to Titus, which might have been penned at about the same time as 1 Timothy was? Paul himself would not have felt that he had to copy himself; he could have written whatever he liked! Perhaps he deliberately avoided the form 'Christ Jesus' here because he was writing to an exclusively Gentile church that would not have grasped the significance of what to them would have been the reversal of the normal order, but that is only a guess. What is certainly true is that the opening salutation is far more extensive in its outline of theological principles than what we find in Paul's other letters, which may reflect a need he felt to spell out the fundamentals of the gospel to a church that was still trying to absorb them.

In reminding Titus that he was first and foremost a 'servant of God' Paul was establishing his missionary credentials by stating them in the right order.[3] It was because he was a servant that he became an apostle, not the other way round. The same order can be observed in Phil. 2.5-11, where it was because the Son of God was a servant that he became a man. In both cases, not only did their status determine the formation of the subsequent mission and its nature, but those who were sent had to humble themselves before being exalted to the position reserved for them. This principle is vitally important and permeates all Christian thinking. Nowadays, for example, even the pope calls himself 'the servant of the servants of God' (*servus servorum Dei*) in order to indicate that as head of the Roman Catholic Church he is not its master but its supreme servant. Jesus taught his disciples the same thing – the last shall be first and the first last; he who would be great in the kingdom of heaven must first become the servant (slave) of all.[4] Words like 'minister' and 'deacon' mean 'servant', and although they now stand for particular offices in the church, their names continue to reflect what is expected of them, both in relation to God and to their fellow believers. Paul's self-designation here may

---

[3] The Greek word *doulos* can mean 'slave' as well as 'servant', but since most servants in ancient times were indentured labourers of one sort or another, that distinction was less apparent than it would be today. Marshall (2004), pp. 116–18, prefers 'slave' but he slips into using 'servant' from time to time as well!

[4] Mt. 20.26; Mk 9.35; 10.44.

be unique in the New Testament, but in theological terms there is nothing surprising or unusual about it at all.[5]

Paul did not specify whether 'God' was to be understood as 'God the Father' though the coupling of the name with Jesus Christ would suggest that as the most likely interpretation. In practical terms it makes little difference, since Paul was a servant of all the persons of the Trinity, whether he spelled that out or not. The point was that he was a man under authority and that he was responsible to God for his mission, not to another human being. The designation 'servant of God' establishes his place in the cosmic hierarchy. In spiritual terms he was bound to do the will of the sovereign Almighty God and could only be his servant. But because he was directly commissioned by God to be an apostle of Jesus Christ, he had an authority on earth that no man could challenge. In other words, his power as a preacher and teacher of the church was the result of his submission to God as his Lord and Saviour, a pattern which he regarded as paradigmatic and which he taught to others, if not explicitly, then by his self-description and practical example.

All Christians are called to be servants of God, but not all are commissioned as apostles of Jesus Christ. This difference was expressed by Martin Luther as follows:

> Not only does he [Paul] know that he serves God and that he speaks the Word of God, but also that he has been sent and commissioned by God and that an obligation to teach has been laid upon him. To know the Word of God and to teach it are two different things. He who has the Word of God does not immediately teach it unless he is called.[6]

The main part of the salutation is grammatically complex but theologically rich. It can be analysed in the familiar triadic way as follows. Paul was appointed an apostle

1. in relation to the faith of God's elect.
2. in relation to the knowledge of the truth that accords with godliness.
3. in the hope of eternal life.

---

[5] Marshall (2004), pp. 116–17, and Towner (2006), p. 666, both note that Paul normally referred to himself as a 'servant of Christ' and not as a 'servant of God', a title that in the Old Testament was given to the very greatest Israelites like Moses (Ps. 105.26), David (2 Sam. 7.4) and some of the prophets (Jer. 7.25; Amos 3.7; Hag. 2.23). Was Paul putting himself on the same level with them? Perhaps, but the term is sufficiently general not to require such an interpretation.
[6] Luther (1968), p. 5.

The third element in this triad is then further broken down as follows:

1. God promised this hope before time began.
2. God revealed this hope at the right time in his Word and through the preaching (of it).
3. God had entrusted Paul with this message (of hope).

First there comes the faith of God's elect. God has chosen a people to serve him. There is no human explanation for this choice. God's people have no identity apart from him and there is nothing intrinsic to them that would make them special or superior to other human beings. Nobody can choose to belong to the elect, nor can anyone resign from their number. The nature and implications of election are made clear by the history of Israel. From the very beginning, there was something mysterious about it. The Israelites did not doubt that God had chosen them and called them to serve him, but they had difficulty when they tried to explain why. As Moses told them,

> You are a people holy to the LORD your God. The LORD your God has chosen you to be a people for his treasured possession, out of all the peoples who are on the face of the earth. It was not because you were more in number than any other people that the LORD set his love on you and chose you, for you were the fewest of all peoples, but it is because the LORD loves you and is keeping the oath that he swore to your fathers[7]

At the heart of Israel's election was the love of God for his people, a love that has no explanation beyond the character of God himself. It was something that Israel experienced in its collective life but that could not be understood without knowing God. Jews believed that they were chosen because they were descended from Abraham, but important though that was, it was not enough to ensure that they would reap the benefits of belonging to God. For that, faith was required. God demonstrated his faithfulness to Israel by preserving them in spite of their sins and foolishness, but if the Israelites did not respond to this by a faith of their own, they would experience their blessings as a curse. As Paul explained at length in his letter to the Romans, this was the fate that had befallen the Jews of his own time. By rejecting Christ, the supreme manifestation of God's love and faithfulness towards him, they had incurred God's wrath, not because he had stopped loving them but because they had shown themselves incapable of loving him. It was their lack of faith, not

---

[7] Deut. 7.6-8.

God's unfaithfulness, that had led to their rejection and had deprived them of the salvation that Paul was proclaiming to the Gentiles.[8]

Members of the church have been grafted into the body of the elect, but only because of their faith. Unlike Israel, they have no ancestral claim to the love and faithfulness of God. Their relationship to Abraham, and thus to the promises made to him, is established not by their blood but by their faith, a criterion that changes what it means to be elect. Faith cannot be artificially created nor is it confined to intellectual belief in a set of doctrines, important though that is. Faith is the result of a meeting with God that has been initiated by him and which is so powerful and overwhelming that we cannot doubt who he is and what he has done for us. Paul knew that from his own experience. He never wanted to become a Christian and certainly did not 'choose' Christ as his Lord and Saviour. It was very much the other way round. Jesus met him when he was on his way to persecute the church and the experience was such that he could never again doubt it, even if it took him some time to be able to articulate it properly and even longer to preach and teach it to others.[9]

At the time of his conversion Paul was already theologically well educated, but he knew that it was not this learning that had led him to faith. On the contrary, it was his faith in Christ that had given him the knowledge of the truth that he needed in order to understand what true godliness was. The word we translate as 'godliness' or 'piety' (*eusebeia*) described what was expected of both Jews and pagans who observed the rites of their respective religions. In one sense, Paul saw nothing wrong with that. He, too, wanted to be 'godly' (*eusebēs*), but Christian godliness was something different from its Jewish equivalent. It was not the correct performance of certain rituals, even those that had been mandated by God in the law of Moses, that made a person 'godly', but a spiritual rebirth that could only come from a personal encounter with God by faith in Jesus Christ. He is the truth, and by knowing him the elect come to understand what true godliness is – submitting to his lordship and obeying his commands.

The goal of godliness is the hope of eternal life. In knowing Christ by faith, the elect are already in possession of that life, even though it has not yet been fully realized. Paul was speaking in terms of this world and the Christian life as believers know it now. But no sooner had he done this than he introduced the eschatological hope of eternal life and put the whole question into a wider context. The life that we are called to hope for in this world had been proclaimed in eternity by the God who cannot lie (*apseudēs*). Once again we

---

[8] Rom. 4.1-25; 9.1–11.36.
[9] See Acts 9.1-30; Gal. 1.15-23.

see that Greek has a word for this that cannot be easily or exactly translated. In practice, 'unlying' is much the same as *pistos* ('faithful'), but the emphasis is different. When Paul said that God is 'faithful' he was putting the emphasis on the fact that God would fulfill what he has promised, however long it might take and however unfaithful his people might be in the meantime. But when he said that God cannot lie, the emphasis falls more obviously on what God has already said and done; it is a word oriented more to the past than to the future, to the promises he had made to Israel more than to the way they would eventually be fulfilled in Christ. In the context of this Epistle, it also stands in sharp contrast to the reputation that Cretans had of being congenital liars. As P. H. Towner points out, this even extended to the claim that Crete housed the tomb of Zeus:

> This claim, according to Callimachus, was a lie, and it could be introduced as evidence (along with the particular view of the gods that went with it) of the accuracy of the widespread assertion that 'Cretan are always liars.' Paul's language calls up this background by echoing the retort of Callimachus, who said: 'It is speaking without lying (*apseudēs legōn*)' to say that the Cretan tomb is empty. Consequently, when Paul describes God as 'unlying', he uses loaded language. With it he makes his claim about God's veracity on the surface level, while it also raises the spectre of the ancient critique of the flawed Cretan religion and morality.[10]

God's revelation of eternal life is the revelation of his Word (*logos*) 'through preaching' (*en kērygmati*) 'at the right times' (*kairois idiois*). As we have already noted, the 'Word' that God has spoken has many different aspects to it. It is speech, which has been recorded for us in Scripture. It is Christ, the word made flesh and the object of all divine revelation. It is also an organized plan – the *logos* is a coherent thought with a purpose that will be fulfilled in the final judgment, the end of time and the transformation of the world. When that happens, the hope of eternal life that has been given to Christians will become a reality in their experience. This was the aspect of the *logos* that Paul was stressing when he mentioned that it had come 'through preaching'. The importance of preaching for understanding the unfolding of God's plan was fundamental to Paul's thought. Without the preaching of the Word, nobody would have come to faith.[11] Preaching was the means chosen by the Old Testament prophets to communicate their message. The content

---

[10] Towner (2006), p. 671. See R. M. Kidd, 'Titus as *Apologia*: Grace for Liars, Beasts and Bellies', *Horizons in Biblical Theology* 21 (1999), 185–209.
[11] Rom. 10.14.

of that message was later written down, but the Scriptures are a record of oral communication and they were read and expounded orally. The written form was important because it preserved the message intact, but it had little effect unless it was preached.

It was to this task that Paul had been called and appointed. The divine Word, in the sense of the message of God's eternal plan and purpose, had been entrusted to him 'according to the mandate of God our Saviour', a phrase which is paralleled in 1 Tim. 1.1, though without the addition of Christ as our hope. The reason for this apparent omission was probably that Paul had already mentioned the hope of eternal life and would go on to call Christ our Saviour in the next sentence. There is no difference of doctrine or even of emphasis between the two Epistles but only one of style. As for calling 'God', that is to say, the Father, our Saviour, John Calvin explained this as follows:

> He [Paul] gives the same title both to the Father and to Christ, since each of them is indeed our Saviour, but in a different way. The Father is Saviour because he has redeemed us by the Son's death that he might make us heirs of eternal life: but the Son is our Saviour because he shed his blood as the pledge and price of our salvation. Thus the Son brought us salvation from the Father, and the Father bestowed it through the Son.[12]

In addressing the letter to Titus, Paul described him in the same terms that he used to address Timothy. Like Timothy, Titus was Paul's 'loyal (*gnēsios*) child in the faith we share'.[13] Some people have interpreted Paul's salutation as evidence that Titus had heard the gospel through Paul's preaching and had been converted as a result of his ministry, but although that is possible, it is not required by the text, and given our lack of further information, it must remain uncertain. On the other hand, it is safe to say that Titus was a prime example of the sort of Christian that Paul wanted to promote in the church. He was a Gentile believer who, despite not having the same advantages as Jewish Christians, had studied the Scriptures and mastered their contents. He was therefore capable of assuming an important leadership role and was not to be considered inferior to a Jewish Christian. That may be why Paul put

---

[12] Calvin (1964), p. 355.
[13] Jerome (2010), p. 285, recognized that it was impossible to translate the Greek word into Latin because of its many-sided meaning. He also claimed that Paul was singling Titus (and by extension, Timothy) out from his many other 'sons', whom he did not regard as 'genuine' in the way that they were. There is, of course, no evidence to support that assertion!

a special emphasis on the 'common faith' (*koinē pistis*) which he and Titus shared, whereas in his letter to Timothy he mentioned only 'faith'.[14] Given that Timothy was half-Jewish by birth and had been brought up in a Jewish way, it may be that Paul did not need to specify that the faith they shared was 'common', since most people would have assumed that his beliefs and Timothy's were identical. The same could not have been so easily said of a Gentile, and so Paul had to stress that they were indeed on the same spiritual wavelength.

Timothy was a well-known companion of the apostle Paul, the two men were very close for many years and it is not at all surprising that Paul should have written to him more than once. Titus, on the other hand, is a more shadowy figure, and although he too was part of the Pauline mission there is little sign that the two men were similarly intimate. But if Paul had a more businesslike relationship with Titus, he nevertheless regarded him as his 'child in the faith' just he did Timothy. Titus was with the apostle at key moments in his missionary career and played a significant part in it almost from the beginning. We know, for example, that he accompanied Paul on his journey to Jerusalem fourteen years after the latter's conversion, when he went there to confer with the apostles who had been disciples of Jesus. We also know, more significantly, that as a Gentile, Titus was not required to be circumcised – an important point, considering the controversy on that subject that was a major bone of contention between Paul and the Jerusalem church.[15]

Later on, Titus was the man who, along with two others who are unnamed, was entrusted with delivering Paul's second epistle to the Corinthian church.[16] Paul described him as his 'partner and fellow worker' which suggests that Titus was one of his inner circle, whereas the other two men did not seem to have any particular relationship with him, despite their fame as preachers and evangelists. When Paul was imprisoned in Rome, Titus had gone to Dalmatia, perhaps to follow up church-planting work that Paul had undertaken there.[17] Paul had been prevented by his arrest from returning to the Adriatic province and it is possible that he had sent Titus in his place. If so it would confirm what we know of him from this epistle – Titus was a man whom Paul could trust to continue the missionary work that he had left unfinished.

---

[14] The NRSV needlessly obscures the Greek by translating this as 'the faith we share'. Jerome (2010), p. 286, thought that Paul and Titus shared a faith that was not common to others, because they were of one mind while others were not, even if they were also Christians.
[15] Gal. 2.3.
[16] 2 Cor. 8.16-24.
[17] Rom. 14.19. Illyricum and Dalmatia were different names for what was essentially the same Roman province.

In this Epistle, it appears that Titus had been 'left' in Crete in order to consolidate the apostle's evangelistic work there, but we do not know when that had taken place. The Acts of the Apostles mentions Crete only in chapter 27, when it records that Paul and he and his military escort stopped there briefly on their way to Rome. They had intended to winter on the island but were blown off course and ended up in Malta, so there would have been little chance that Paul could have ministered there at that time.[18] (There is also no indication that Titus was with him on that journey or could have been left behind at that time.)

That leaves one of two options, if we believe that the Pauline mission to Crete actually took place. He could have gone there during one of the times when he was residing in Corinth or Ephesus, which would place the mission sometime in the 50s, or else he could have preached in the island along with Titus after being released from his first imprisonment in Rome, assuming that he had enough time to do that before being rearrested. Either scenario is possible, but neither can be supported by external evidence. Everything we know about Paul's missionary journey to Crete is contained in the Epistle itself.

Perhaps the easiest reconstruction of events is to say that Paul and Titus went to Crete from Ephesus, but that Paul returned to that city on his own, in order to plan his next journey to Macedonia and Illyricum. If that was the case, then both 1 Timothy and Titus were written when he was on that journey, which took place in AD 55 or 56. Working on that assumption, Paul would have spent one of those winters, probably AD 56-57, at Nicopolis in Epirus (now in northwestern Greece), where he wrote his second letter to the Corinthians. Titus met him there as planned, and together with his two anonymous companions, he took the letter to Corinth, paving the way for Paul to return to that city in person as he promised in his letter that he would do.[19] Nicopolis is not all that far from Corinth and Titus could have made the journey there overland (and thus in winter), sending word back to Paul that the way was clear for him to come as soon as he could. Paul then went to Corinth himself, where he wrote his Epistle to the Romans, recounting his recent adventures and outlining his plans for the foreseeable future.[20]

What happened to Titus after that is uncertain. He was not among the party that set out for Jerusalem, though it seems that he was in Rome for at least part of the time that Paul was imprisoned there.[21] Most likely he spent

---

[18] Acts 27.7-28.1.
[19] 2 Cor. 13.1.
[20] Rom. 15.18-28.
[21] Acts 19.3-5; 2 Tim. 4.10.

the intervening years somewhere in Greece, ministering in the churches and perhaps planting new congregations, but there is no record of that. We can only speculate about what he was doing, but it is reasonable to suppose that wherever he was, he was active in furthering the Gentile mission associated with Paul.

The salutation 'grace and peace' is a commonplace of Paul's letters and of ancient Christian writings in general and requires no special comment. What is different about this one is that Paul referred to Christ Jesus as 'our Saviour' rather than as 'our Lord' as he commonly did elsewhere. This was a direct and doubtless deliberate repetition of what he had just said about the mandate that he had received from 'God our Saviour' and a clear indication that Paul thought of Jesus as God. The context recalls that this divine salvation was planned in eternity, long before the incarnation of the Son in time and space. That in turn reminds us that Paul's believed in the eternal pre-existence of Christ and was convinced that his apostolic mandate had come from both the Father and the Son, in accordance with a foreordained divine plan.

## 5-9. The character of an elder

> 5. *I left you behind in Crete for this reason, so that you should put in order what remained to be done, and should appoint elders in every town, as I directed you:* 6. *someone who is blameless, married only once, whose children are believers, not accused of debauchery and not rebellious.* 7. *For a bishop, as God's steward, must be blameless; he must not be arrogant or quick-tempered or addicted to wine or violent or greedy for gain;* 8. *but he must be hospitable, a lover of goodness, prudent, upright, devout, and self-controlled.* 9. *He must have a firm grasp of the word that is trustworthy in accordance with the teaching, so that he may be able both to preach with sound doctrine and to refute those who contradict it.*

Verse 5 takes us into the substance of the letter. We are told that Paul and Titus had been on an evangelistic mission together in Crete but that Paul had not stayed there long enough to settle the churches as he wanted to. That was why he had left Titus on the island, certainly for a few months and possibly for longer. How long Titus had been there when Paul wrote to him is impossible to say, but it is clear from the text that he expected Titus to depart before too long, in order to be able to join him at Nicopolis before winter. Could Titus have completed his missionary task in the few weeks that would have been left to him? Did Paul envisage that Titus would return to Crete the following year and stay there for some time? We do not know. It is at least possible that Titus went back to Crete for a few years and then made his way to Rome when Paul was imprisoned there. It is even possible that he found out that Paul had passed through Crete briefly, on his way to Rome, and that it was after that that he made plans to go to the capital himself.

There is much that we are ignorant of, and it is fruitless to speculate about what might have happened. What is certain is that Paul left Titus in Crete with a lot of unfinished business, which is probably how we would best translate the words 'ta leiponta'. The most important aspect of this was the need to appoint elders 'in every city' (*kata polin*), which we know that he had done at the end of his first missionary journey in Galatia and which was probably his standard practice.[22] His failure to do this in Crete may be an indication that he had to leave the island in a hurry, or that the task was too complicated to have been carried out in a short time. Just as in Galatia, it appears that in Crete, too, churches had been started in more than one location and putting them in order required a further round of visits that must have taken several weeks, if not months, to complete.

Unfortunately Paul did not say where the Cretan churches were located, so that it is impossible to know how he reached the island or where he went when he got there. Crete had been the home of a great prehistoric civilization, but by Paul's time it had long been a backwater in the Greek world. The Romans attached it to Cyrenaica, in what is now eastern Libya, and governed it from Gortyn, a city which they built on the southern side of the island. There is an ancient tradition which says that Titus was bishop of Gortyn, but we have no way of knowing whether it is accurate or not. Most likely Paul went to Crete from the north, which suggests that the cities he evangelized were also there (as the major Cretan cities are today) but as with everything else concerning his mission, that can be no more than speculation. It is even possible that there were churches on the island before the apostle got there, since there were Cretans in Jerusalem on the day of Pentecost and they may have taken the new faith home with them.[23] If so, those churches must have been very informal, lacking structure and solid teaching, which may explain not only Paul's emphasis here but also his apparent confidence that enough elders could be found to minister in them.

Titus' task was to set up elders (*presbyteroi*) in every city where there were Christians. That suggests that the original mission had been fairly widespread, but we cannot tell whether Paul intended each place to have several elders or not. When he came to give a detailed description of the kind of people he

---

[22] Acts 14.23.
[23] Acts 2.11.

had in mind, he resorted to the word *episkopos* which he always used in the singular, so perhaps he imagined that each church would have only one of them. It is possible that many of the Christian congregations were small and that there were few people in them who would have been willing or able to perform the functions of an elder. If that was the case, Titus might have been relieved to find someone who could hold the church together and so ended up with no more than one elder in some of the smaller places where he went.[24] This possibility is strengthened by the fact that Paul made no mention of deacons, which suggests that their role would have been fulfilled by the elders, if only because there was nobody else available for diaconal work.

What does seem clear is that in this case 'elders' and 'overseers' were the same people, but whether this synonymity was deliberate or accidental we cannot say. Perhaps the ideal was a body of elders with a single overseer who acted as their executive officer, so to speak. In that case, every church would have had an overseer with the number of elders determined by the size and ability of the members to supply them. If there was only one such person, he would have been obliged to fulfill both roles, which would then have merged. However, there would always have been the possibility that more *presbyteroi* could have been appointed in due course without their necessarily becoming *episkopoi* as well. Here we are reduced to speculation, but the balance of opinion is that there was no effective difference between the two terms. *Presbyteros* described a status; *episkopos* explained the function which those who has the status were expected to perform. Only later, and gradually, did a monarchical episcopate emerge.[25] That development may have been natural in the circumstances, but it cannot be allowed to intrude on our interpretation of what Paul was saying to Titus. John Calvin was very clear on this point:

> For my own part I find no fault with the custom which has prevailed from the very earliest days of the church whereby each assembly of bishops has one man as moderator. But to take the title of the office which God has given to all and to transfer it to one man and deprive the rest of it is both unjust and absurd. Besides, to pervert the language of the Holy Spirit so as to make the very words have a different meaning from the one he has chosen, smacks of excessive and unholy temerity.[26]

---

[24] Towner (2006), p. 680, mentions this possibility.
[25] That was the view of Jerome (2010), pp. 288–90, who expounded it at some length, apparently because his contemporaries did not know the history and doubted his assertion that at the beginning the two words had described the same people.
[26] Calvin (1964), pp. 359–60.

The next few verses are taken up with the qualities that an *episkopos/presbyteros* ought to have and the list is similar to the one found in 1 Tim. 3.1-7, though by no means identical to it. A comparison of the two gives the following criteria for whoever was expected to take up the office.[27] The *episkopos* must be as follows:

| 1 Timothy 3 | | Titus | |
| --- | --- | --- | --- |
| 1. Above reproach (*anepilēmptos*) | (1) | 1. Above reproach (*anenklētos*) | (1) |
| 2. Husband of one wife | (2) | 2. Husband of one wife | (2) |
| 3. Sober-minded | | 3. With believing children | (12) |
| 4. Self-controlled | (12) | 4. Above reproach (again) | |
| 5. Respectable | | 5. Not arrogant | |
| 6. Hospitable | (10) | 6. Not quick-tempered | |
| 7. Able to teach | (17) | 7. Not a drunkard | (8) |
| 8. Not a drunkard | (7) | 8. Not violent | (9) |
| 9. Not violent but gentle | (8) | 9. Not greedy | (11) |
| 10. Not quarrelsome | | 10. Hospitable | (6) |
| 11. Not a lover of money | (9) | 11. A lover of good | |
| 12. Good household manager | (3) | 12. Self-controlled | (4) |
| 13. Not a recent convert | | 13. Upright (*dikaios*) | |
| 14. Well thought of by outsiders | | 14. Holy (*hosios*) | |
| | | 15. Disciplined | |
| | | 16. Faithful | |
| | | 17. Able to teach | (7) |
| | | 18. Able to refute false teaching | |

The list in Titus is longer than that in 1 Timothy, though it is broken into two sections.[28] If that is taken into account, the second section in Titus has fourteen required characteristics, the same number as in 1 Timothy. Nine of them are shared by the two lists, though not always using the same vocabulary. In 1 Timothy the *episkopos* had to be able to manage his household well and

---

[27] The numbers in parentheses indicate the corresponding quality in the other list.
[28] The theory that there were originally two lists, one for the *presbyteroi* and another for the *episkopos*, which were then merged into one, cannot be sustained. See Marshall (2004) 149, 170–81, for a detailed refutation of this hypothesis.

control his children; in Titus the children must be *pistoi*, which may mean either loyal or believers. What is particularly noticeable is that the order is not the same, which makes it unlikely that there was a recognized checklist of qualities or that Paul was copying one list from the other. It is much easier to suppose that in both cases he was listing desirable attributes more or less as they came to his mind. That there should be some overlap between the lists is understandable and to be expected. What is surprising is how different they are from each other, especially considering that they cover the same subject matter and are addressing the same question. It is particularly noticeable that when Paul was writing to Titus he said nothing about choosing as an *episkopos* someone who was not a recent convert. This may have been because there was little choice in Crete, where everyone in the church would have come into that category.[29] In this Epistle Paul also put greater stress on the elder's teaching ability, including an aptitude for refuting opponents, which may have gone some way to compensating for their relative newness in the faith. If that interpretation is correct, the need to teach the rudiments of the gospel and defend it was more pressing in Crete than in Ephesus, where the church was larger and more deeply rooted. P. H. Towner is uncompromising in his assessment of the situation:

> in comparison with 1 Timothy 3, the requirements and extra attention given to ministry reflect a church situation in Crete that is primitive, harsh, and verging on crisis. Vices are listed that should not need to be discussed in a Christian church, and the reference to dishonest gain draws on the Cretan stereotype ... in the Cretan setting, where (as tradition told) the civilizing influence of Hellenistic culture had failed to establish a beachhead and the Christian faith was in the very early days, ethical formation needed to begin at the ground floor.[30]

As always we are reduced to speculation when trying to explain things like this, but if it is impossible to say why the two lists differ in the way they do, at least they do not contradict one another! In many ways the Titus list covers the same ground as the one in 1 Timothy, only in greater detail, and it seems reasonable to suggest that that may reflect the newness of the churches in Crete, which had not yet settled down to a regular pattern of ministry.

Given the basic independence of the two lists, it is interesting to note that in both of them Paul put the same two items first. An *episkopos* must be

---

[29] Marshall (2004), p. 146, alludes to this possibility but does not develop it.
[30] Towner (2006), pp. 693–4.

'above reproach, the husband of one wife'. The first of these sets the tone for the rest of the list and everything else follows directly from it. There must be no cause for complaint in the way an *episkopos* lives or in what he teaches. If he falls down in some way the whole church will be affected, not only because, as a public representative of the congregation, he will bring the rest into disrepute if he misbehaves, but also because he will be unable to exercise the ministry to which he is called. If a congregation is deprived of the right teaching and discipline, it will fall apart, and so the character of its teacher(s) is of the utmost importance.

This character is manifested first and foremost in the private life of the *episkopos*, who is called to be the husband of one wife.[31] Paul never thought in terms of a female *episkopos*, but he did allow a male one to be married, and we know from other evidence that in the household culture of the time, the wife of an elder would have a considerable role to play in the life of the church. As far as we can tell, Timothy and Titus were single and celibate, as Paul himself was, but that was not a requirement for ministry in the local church. Some people might be tempted to interpret Paul to be saying that an *episkopos* had to be married, but that is reading too much into the text. Most likely, in the village culture that he was addressing, almost every adult male would have been married in any case, so the question would not have arisen, but it is hard to believe that a man would have been passed over for the eldership merely because he was single. Nor is anything said about whether an *episkopos* could marry after his appointment, or whether a widowed one could take another wife. In later times, an ordained *presbyteros* or *episkopos* would not be allowed to remarry after the death of his wife and celibacy would be imposed on one who was ordained as a single man, but there is no hint of that here.[32]

The complications that could arise from widowhood were well understood by Jerome, who reminded his readers:

> It is not that we are to think that every monogamous man is better than the one who has been married twice ... For let there be some young man who has lost his spouse, and overcome by the necessity of the flesh has taken a second wife, whom he also immediately loses. Then he lives continently. But let there be another man who was married to an older woman and made use of his wife ... which of the two seems better to you, chaster, more continent? Surely it is the one who was unhappy (*infelix*)

---

[31] On the NRSV translation of this as 'married only once', see the remarks on 1 Tim. 3.2.
[32] Those prohibitions were enacted at the Council *in Trullo*, held in 691–2.

even in the second marriage and afterward lived chastely and piously, and not the one who was separated from his wife's embrace [only] in old age.³³

It is possible to read the verse as forbidding polygamy, and no doubt it does that, but since polygamy was generally not practised in the Graeco-Roman world, it is unlikely that Paul was thinking primarily about it.³⁴ It must be divorce and remarriage that he has in view more than anything else, and that was what was forbidden. An officer of the church was expected to model the marital relationship that God had established in the Garden of Eden and that Jesus had insisted upon.³⁵ Failure to do so was a disqualification for ministry, quite apart from the disruption it would have caused in a close-knit society. Husband and wife were in the service of the church together, and their relationship was one of the fundamental building blocks undergirding the community of the elect.

To make his point even more strongly, Paul added that the children of an *episkopos* must be 'faithful', an ambiguous term that could mean either that they must be loyal to their parents or Christians themselves. The context suggests that it is the former of these that Paul has in mind and that interpretation is supported by the parallel verse in 1 Timothy 3. He may well have thought that the children should also accept their parents' faith as part of their filial duty, but that was not his main concern here.³⁶ More important was that they should not bring shame on the family by their misbehaviour. If they were open to the charge of debauchery (*asōtia*) or if they were insubordinate (*anhypotakta*), the parents would be disgraced and the results for the family's reputation could be catastrophic. It is very possible that Paul had in mind the infamous case of Eli, the high priest whose sons betrayed him and brought down destruction both on themselves and on him.³⁷ Here there is an ideal of virtue that Jews and Gentiles shared, and for Christians to be seen not to respect it would have done great harm to the cause of the gospel.

---

³³ Jerome (2010), pp. 291–2.
³⁴ This is generally agreed today, but Calvin (1964), p. 358, was of a different opinion. For some strange reason he wrote, 'Polygamy was so common among the Jews that the depraved custom had almost turned into a law'. Where he got that idea from is unknown.
³⁵ Mt. 19.3-12.
³⁶ For a different view, see Towner (2006), pp. 682–3. He says, 'As a reflection on the father's reputation as a householder, the religious convictions of the children would be expected to conform to those of the master/father'.
³⁷ 1 Samuel 2–4.

It is difficult for modern minds, especially Western ones, to appreciate how deep this feeling went.[38] We are told that when Jesus was twelve his parents took him to the temple, where he went missing for several days. When Joseph and Mary eventually found him he explained that he was about his Father's business, but even so, Luke recounts that he obeyed them and submitted to their will.[39] We may also recall that Jesus is recorded as having learned filial obedience in the school of suffering, and that he went to his death because it was his Father's will that he should do so.[40] The fact that believers are adopted as children of the same heavenly Father puts us under a similar obligation to obey him, though it is fair to say that the implications of that obedience would have been more obvious to the first generation of Christians than they are to most of us today. We live in a world where it is assumed that children will grow up and leave home, and that once they are adults they no longer have to obey their parents. We also think that for a parent to demand obedience to the point of death would be excessive and cruel. Certainly anyone who tried to insist on that today would be in serious trouble with the law and would probably have their children removed from their care! The patriarchal power of the father is no longer what it once was, and so we must pay careful attention to what Paul had to say about its implications. We know from what he said elsewhere that he expected parents to behave responsibly towards their offspring – Christian faith was not an excuse to justify child abuse.[41] But children had obligations to their parents that went beyond what many people today, especially in the developed world, would accept. In the early church, as in the ancient world generally, family ties mattered, and there was a clear hierarchy stretching down from the eldest to the youngest that everyone was expected to respect.

There is also the possibility that Paul was guarding against a pagan accusation that people who became Christians were rejecting their ancestral gods and therefore dishonouring their parents. If that was the case, a break with the past was inevitable, but if Christianity was not an ancestor cult, neither was it a license for breaking up the family unit. In 1 Corinthians 7 Paul dealt with that question directly, reminding the church that its members were not to seek to leave their unbelieving spouses or be unaware that their own profession of faith had brought immense blessing to their entire household.[42]

---

[38] Towner (2006), p. 683, makes this point.
[39] Lk. 2.49-51.
[40] Heb. 5.8.
[41] Eph. 6.4; Col. 3.21.
[42] 1 Cor. 7.12-16.

In v. 7 Paul repeated his earlier remark that an *episkopos* must be 'above reproach'. Various explanations have been given for this. Some have claimed that in vv. 5-6 he was talking about *presbyteroi* (in the plural) whom he regarded as being of a lower ecclesiastical order than *episkopoi*. In other words, the distinction between bishops and presbyters (priests) that emerged in later times is held to have existed in the first century and to have been of apostolic origin. Alternatively, the same argument has also been used as evidence for pseudepigraphy – the pseudepigrapher was reading back into apostolic times a system of church order that did not then exist. In fact, however, the text cannot bear either interpretation because as 1 Timothy 3 tells us, the qualifications for presbyteral ministry outlined here are the same as those for an *episkopos*. If there is any distinction to be made between them, it is that the qualities given in vv. 5-6 are preconditions for appointment to the office of *episkopos/presbyteros*, whereas what follows concentrates more on the behaviour to be expected of the man who has been chosen for that position.

That is made clear by the definition of *episkopos* which Paul gives. He is the *Theou oikonomos*, 'God's steward', a reminder of the importance of his work but also of the true nature of his appointment. Titus was called to seek men out for the position, but he was really only giving visible expression to the choice that had already made by God. The *episkopos* was not ultimately answerable to Titus or to Paul, but to God himself, which is why his character and behaviour had to imitate the divine as closely as possible. Paul outlined what this meant, first of all by telling Titus what the *episkopos* must *not* be like. There were five things that he must not be:

1. Arrogant (*authadēs*)
2. Quick-tempered (*orgilos*)
3. Addicted to drink (*paroinos*)
4. Violent (*plēktēs*)
5. Greedy (*aischrokerdēs*)

Once again, the wealth of the Greek language is on display here as Paul used a variety of words to describe what he had in mind and many of them are difficult to capture in translation. *Authadēs* is literally 'full of self' or 'self-centred' and it is used to mean 'overbearing', 'arrogant', 'domineering' and the like. A man who puts himself first and demands that others treat him as if he is more important than anyone else has made an idol of himself and is unfit to serve God. The essence of being a Christian is to die to self, and a Christian leader must demonstrate that quality even more than ordinary believers.[43] In

---

[43] Gal. 2.20.

the church it is not the ones who are the most outstanding in human terms who are to be honoured but those who have surrendered their lives most fully to Christ. A congregation that is governed by someone who is failing to do this is being corrupted from within by a relationship between pastor and people that does not reflect the true status of either in the sight of God. Sadly, many congregations, even large ones, develop a personality cult of the pastor which he might not encourage but which he does nothing to deflect either. After he leaves, those who were there because of him leave too, and sometimes a local church falls apart because of that. It is a reminder to us that arrogance has a passive as well as an active form, and the wise minister of the gospel will be on guard against it.

The man who is *orgilos* is also unfit for ministry. The word derives from *orgē* ('wrath') and can be understood as someone who gets angry easily. A person who is constantly irate can do nothing but alienate others, who are bound to become the objects of his wrath whether they deserve to be or not. The next three negatives pick up what Paul said in 1 Tim. 3.3 and follow the same order as they do there. All three represent distortions that are liable to cause imbalance in relationships and lead to trouble. A man who is always drunk cannot be trusted. His mind and his judgment will be affected by his physical state and he will be reduced to foolishness and impotence in his dealings with others. Jerome added another dimension to drunkenness:

> wherever there is overabundance and drunkenness, there lust is in control. Look at the belly and the genitals, the arrangement of the members [has] in view the nature of the vices. I will never regard a drunken man as chaste. Even if he is lulled to sleep by the wine, nevertheless he could have sinned through the wine.[44]

No church leader can afford to fall into a trap like that.[45] Violence, too, must be avoided because it is another form of loss of self-control. It is easy to react in extreme ways to provocation, and some people are known to encourage this in others, often in the hope of discrediting them.

Greed is another sin that reflects a disordered judgment. What will it profit a man if he gains the whole world but loses his own soul in the process?[46] The love of money is a root of all evil, as Paul said to Timothy.[47] The Bible is full

---

[44] Jerome (2010), p. 296. Luther (1968), p. 27, thought that carousing was a particular sin of the Greeks and that this was why Paul included it in his list!
[45] Paul may have been thinking of the shame of Noah and its consequences. See Gen. 9.18-27.
[46] Mt. 16.26; Mk 8.36.
[47] 1 Tim. 6.10.

of warnings of this kind, and few things distort perceptions more than bribes and other such inducements. Those who want something badly enough will often be prepared to pay for it, but they will expect something in return. A church run by people like that is obviously in great danger, because all sense of fairness disappears before the lure of gold, or 'filthy lucre', as Paul called it in 1 Tim. 3.3. Then as now, this is one of the greatest temptations of all and there must be no sign of it in a Christian leader.

The list of 'don'ts' is immediately followed by its opposite, as was customary with Paul. The *episkopos* is called to be hospitable, a lover of what is good, wise, just, holy and chaste. The first of these requires no comment, because it was a staple virtue in the ancient world. A person who was not hospitable was regarded by both pagans and Christians as deeply antisocial. In a world where there was little or no public welfare and where travellers could not draw money out of the local bank to pay their way, hospitality was an essential quality for individuals to possess. The Bible stresses this over and over again. It even points out that some found themselves entertaining angels, without realizing it.[48] Those who refused to welcome missionaries who had sacrificed everything in order to preach the gospel were warned that they would be given a taste of their own medicine on the day of judgment.[49] One way or another, the duty of hospitality was inculcated into believers, and anyone who wanted to be a leader of the church had to demonstrate this quality above all. Failure in this would soon be noticed, and the reputation of the congregation would suffer as a result.

An *episkopos* must also be *philagathos*, a 'lover of the good'. The meaning is clear although the precise application is left somewhat vague. What constitutes the 'good' may vary according to circumstances, but the important thing is always to have the right attitude and to look for the best in everything. A man with a genuine love for what is good will be respected for that and forgiven if he gets it wrong or if his trust is betrayed by others who are less high-minded than he is. It is a valuable quality to be cherished in leaders of the church. The use of the word *agathos* for 'good', instead of *kalos*, implies that the *philagathos* was someone who prized moral and spiritual goodness over everything else. *Kalos*, by comparison, might be thought to include outward goodness, or beauty, which was both superficial and potentially deceptive.

The same *episkopos* must also be *sōphrōn*, another Greek word with many possible meanings. Here it probably ought to be translated as 'wise' or 'discerning' rather than as 'self-controlled', even if self-control is an obvious

---

[48] Heb. 13.2.
[49] Rom. 12.13; Heb. 13.2; 3 Jn 1.5-11.

aspect of wisdom. The man who is wise will know how to approach every situation and deal with it in the right way, finding a good solution without unduly antagonising those involved. It is a precious gift and correspondingly rare, but it reflects the mind of God perhaps more clearly than the other qualities listed here do.

An *episkopos* must also be *dikaios*, a word which can be translated as 'just' or 'righteous' and which in this case probably means something close to what we would describe as 'fair'. The *episkopos* cannot be righteous in himself, but he can minister the justice of God in a way that is fair, and it is the ministry rather than the inner quality that Paul is emphasizing here. Likewise he must be 'holy' (*hosios*), that is to say, he must live in a way that accords with the kind of behaviour that God expects of us. He may be theoretically free to do whatever he wishes, but his desire to please God and not to offend others will lead him to adopt certain patterns of conduct that reflect this.[50] Human 'holiness' in this sense is not to be confused with the divine gift of holiness (*hagiosynē*) which is freely bestowed by God's grace and is not to be regarded as the fruit of works. It is something that we can do to conform our lives to God's will, but it cannot reflect the nature of God himself. That kind of holiness is a gift of the Holy Spirit that is given to all believers, whether they are *hosioi* or not. Holiness in the sense intended here is a response to that gift, an attempt to apply its consequences in our everyday lives and not a desire to substitute our own righteousness for that which can only come from God.

Finally, the *episkopos* is expected to be 'chaste' or 'continent' (*enkratēs*), a word that is often translated as 'disciplined'. This is a possible interpretation, but it lacks the sexual dimension which is clearly present in the Greek and which ought to be retained. The minute that sexual desire enters into the work of a minister, his ministry is liable to be ruined. There are too many cases of pastors falling in love with their parishioners and allowing their feelings to get out of control for us to pass this over in silence. In the Christian church, where the *episkopos* is serving his brothers and sisters in the Lord, that kind of thing amounts to spiritual incest, with all its attendant horrors. Paul does not forbid matrimony if two people fall in love and want to get married, but if this gets in the way of ministry, it is to be avoided. If one or both of the parties are already married to someone else, it is to be condemned. It is not necessary to go to the extreme of lifelong celibacy to appreciate the importance of this for effective Christian service, and Paul did not hesitate to add it to his list of essential qualifications for an *episkopos*.

---

[50] 1 Cor. 10.23-29.

Verse 9 moves on from the personal qualities that an *episkopos* is meant to exhibit to the role that he is expected to play in the life of the church. In order for him to minister as he should, he must first of all hold fast to the 'faithful word' (*pistos logos*) that he has received 'according to the teaching' (*kata tēn didachēn*). The meaning here is clear enough to those who understand the context, but translations tend to obscure it. The ESV, for example, speaks of 'the trustworthy word as taught', and the NIV says 'the trustworthy message as it has been taught', neither of which captures the true flavour of Paul's teaching. The NRSV comes closer. What Paul meant was that there is a faithful, reliable word that has been communicated by the teaching of the apostles, which Titus had absorbed from Paul and which he now had to communicate to the churches he was setting in order in Crete. The *logos* is the gospel, the word of God that has been revealed in Scripture and incarnated in Christ. It is 'faithful' (*pistos*) because it does what it promises to do. It gives new life to those who believe, forgiveness of sins to those who repent and hope to those who suffer in this world. It is the transforming power of God. Furthermore, it has been given to the church in a particular way, which Paul calls the *didachē* or 'teaching'. This teaching is that the Son of God has become a man in Jesus Christ, has paid the price for our sins by his death on the cross and has risen again to fulfill the promises of God. He is now seated at the right hand of the Father and will come again in judgment. We who believe are servants of this heavenly king who is also our earthy Saviour. In him we are connected to God and enjoy the first fruits of eternal life. Anything that downplays this – for instance, by thinking of Jesus as no more than a man who has set us a good example of how to live, or by denying the hope that we have of eternal life in heaven – is a lie. The *episkopos* must have a firm grip on this message, so that he knows what it is and also what it is not. If he gets that right, then he will be able to exercise the two complementary aspects of his ministry that Paul proceeded to outline in this passage.

First of all, the well-prepared *episkopos* will be able to instruct others in the saving (or health giving) teaching that he himself has embraced. Here the word for 'teaching' is not *didachē* but *didaskalia*, which puts the accent on the process of inculcating the truth rather than on its basic content, which is of course assumed. But the effective *episkopos* will also be able to control (*elenchein*) those who object to it. What this means is that he will be able to prevent them from taking over the church with their own message and leading believers astray. The *episkopos* must be the good shepherd who protects his sheep from the ravenous wolves who would try to devour them.[51]

---

[51] Jn 10.1-18.

This can only be done properly by someone who recognizes the danger when he sees it and who knows how to counteract it. The enemy we face is subtle, and therefore this quality is all the more important for the faithful *episkopos* to master. Feeding the sheep on sound doctrine and keeping them out of harm's way – this is what the good shepherd must do, and this is the model for the true *episkopos* in the church of God.

## 10-16. The character and behaviour of the wicked

> *10. There are also many rebellious people, idle talkers and deceivers, especially those of the circumcision; 11. they must be silenced, since they are upsetting whole families by teaching for sordid gain what it is not right to teach. 12. It was one of them, their very own prophet, who said: 'Cretans are always liars, vicious brutes, lazy gluttons.' 13. That testimony is true. For this reason rebuke them sharply, so that they may become sound in the faith, 14. not paying attention to Jewish myths or to commandments of those who reject the truth. 15. To the pure all things are pure, but to the corrupt and unbelieving nothing is pure. Their very minds and consciences are corrupted. 16. They profess to know God, but they deny him by their actions. They are detestable, disobedient, unfit for any good work.*

The particular problem that Paul focused on in his letter to Titus was that of false teachers who were not only leading entire households astray by their message but demanding payment for it as well. This phenomenon was not unknown in the ancient world, and where people were hungry for learning, it was relatively easy for those who were seemingly educated to offer their services in this way. They had been a problem for Socrates and Plato nearly half a millennium before and had been denounced by them as 'sophists'. There was a strong sense in the ancient world that knowledge was public property; the notion of copyright was unknown and what we call 'plagiarism' was commonplace – and accepted as legitimate. Philosophers were expected to be above worldly concerns and not to worry about such trivial things as having food to eat and clothes to wear. Jesus also told his disciples not to concern themselves with matters of that kind, not because he believed in an ascetic lifestyle, but because he taught that God would provide for his disciples' needs.[52] The aversion to sophism thus ran deep, both in pagan and in Christian circles.

---

[52] Mt. 6.19-24.

We know that there was a revival of sophism in the second century AD and it may have begun before that, so the false teachers whom Paul was denouncing would not have appeared unusual or out of place.[53] From what we can gather, Paul was attacking Judaizing tendencies more than anything else, and most likely the false teachers he mentioned were communicating the same kinds of myths and genealogical studies that he censured in 1 Timothy. The main difference here is that Paul spelled out to Titus their Jewishness in a way that he did not do when he wrote to Timothy, though why he did so is uncertain. Perhaps the fact that both Titus and the members of the churches he ministered to were Gentiles made him think that it was necessary for him to be more specific, since they would probably have been less familiar with Jewish aberrations, but we have no way of knowing that for sure.[54]

In some ways Paul's censure of these Judaizers recalls what he wrote to the Galatians.[55] Shortly after his departure from those churches false apostles arrived, telling the people that they had to be circumcised and adopt Jewish customs in order to be Christians. That had led to a major controversy within the church, in which Paul had been forced to stand up against Peter and others in Jerusalem who either thought like that themselves or who failed to speak out against the activities of these people. As a result of that debate, it was agreed that Gentiles could become Christians without having to become Jews as well, but there could be no escaping the fact that Christianity was of Jewish origin, and it is likely that Jews with a knowledge of the Old Testament and other Jewish traditions enjoyed considerable prestige among newly converted Gentiles.[56] They were people who understood the background to the gospel message, as we would say today, and who could resolve difficult questions about it that people without that learning might stumble over.

There is, however, no suggestion here that the false teachers were saying that Gentile converts ought to become Jews. Circumcision is mentioned, but only as a means of identifying those who were Jews already, not because it was being promoted as something that was necessary for Gentiles to become Christians. Paul did not say where these false teachers had come from, though probably they were Jewish Christians who had not accepted

---

[53] See Towner (2006), p. 698, who develops this theme.
[54] There was a sizeable Jewish community in Crete but whether the Gentile converts knew much about it is unknown. There is no indication that the churches contained a mixture of Jews and Gentiles, which is surprising given Paul's usual evangelistic strategy of preaching in the local synagogues first. Perhaps he followed his usual practice and the false teachers were local Jewish converts. We do not know.
[55] Gal. 1.6.
[56] Acts 15.1-29. It is not certain how the events recorded in Acts 15 are related to Paul's letter to the Galatians, but it is clear that the problem was the same in both cases.

the apostolic decisions regarding the inclusion of Gentiles in the church and who were doing their best to make them as Jewish as possible. Circumcising them might have been a step too far, but immersing them in Jewish folklore was potentially more dangerous because it would take the Gentile converts' minds off the centrality of the gospel, give them a permanent sense of their own inferiority in the church, and incline them towards keeping the law of Moses, which they would then have accepted willingly.

In describing what kind of people the false teachers were, Paul employed one of his standard triadic formulas, in which the first element governs the others. As we have already seen with the officers of the church, he was more concerned with the character of these false teachers than with their message. This was because who they were and what they were like would determine the authority of whatever they might say. Right teaching and knowledge came from the apostles, to whom the rest of the church had to submit. Failure to appoint the right people would inevitably result in teaching that was not solidly grounded, and if that happened, it would be no more than empty talk. Even if some of what the false teachers said was true, as it probably was, it would serve no purpose because it was not given according to the pattern of sound words inherited from the apostles.[57] Isolated facts without a framework in which they should be interpreted were of no use and might easily incline those who were persuaded by their truth to dispense with the need for a coherent system of thought. If that were to happen, isolated 'truths' would become a vehicle of error – the subtlest and most dangerous form of heresy.

The false teachers were 'insubordinate' (*anhypotaktoi*) and it was this insubordination that made them 'empty talkers' (*mataiologoi*) and 'deceivers' (*phrenapatai*). The logic here is simple. Insubordination is disobedience and means that the false teachers were not following the content of the gospel message that they had heard and had apparently accepted. Like so many people then and since, they believed that they could do better than their teachers and they proceeded to demonstrate that by constructing an intellectual framework which they regarded as an improvement on what the apostles had taught them. From the context we can deduce that this 'improvement' consisted mainly of providing a Jewish context into which the gospel message could be fitted, whether it belonged there or not. Superficially at least, this was a plausible approach because Christianity was undoubtedly of Jewish origin. Its followers also claimed that it fulfilled the promises made in the Old Testament, so what better thing could be imagined than to study

---

[57] Cf. 2 Tim. 1.13.

what those promises were? That this so-called study passed through a filter of myths and speculations did not worry the false teachers, who may have thought (or at least taught!) that they were revealing secret mysteries hidden behind the apparently simple words of Jesus and his disciples.

The result of such an approach was that the false teachers were empty-talkers. They had made it all up! Their theories had no redeeming value and made no difference to anybody's spiritual state. Those who listened to them were not only being treated to meaningless verbal constructions, but they were also being led astray. The empty talk was not harmless but deeply damaging to the minds and lives of those who fell for it.

That this was probably what the false teachers were doing is supported by the word 'deceivers' (*phrenapatai*) which literally means 'those who deceive the mind' (*phrēn*). The most effective form of deception is misapplied truth. For example, the false teachers could have said that the law of Moses is a schoolmaster leading us to Christ, which is true, and then say that imitating the schoolmaster was the only way to get to the Saviour.[58] In itself, this sounds unobjectionable and quite logical, but it is a twisted logic that, if followed, would lead people away from Christ and not bring them closer to him. We do not know whether these false teachers actually said this, but it is an example of the kind of argument they could have used to make their case and win support from those who were unable to see beneath the surface argument and examine its deeper implications.

The techniques of these false teachers were probably pretty much the same everywhere, but Paul apparently thought that they would have particular success in Crete because of the nature of the local inhabitants, who were exceptionally susceptible to such people and their way of teaching. Unusually, he quotes the ancient poet Epimenides, a Cretan himself, who wrote that 'Cretans are always liars, evil beasts, lazy gluttons.' The quotation is interesting, not least because it is one of only two surviving examples of it in the original Greek.[59] Epimenides was a semi-legendary poet who lived sometime around 600 BC. According to one story, he fell asleep in a cave where he remained for fifty-seven years before emerging as a seer with the gift of prophecy. After that, he was supposed to have helped Solon reform the laws of Athens and to have prophesied at Sparta on military affairs. How he died is unknown, but one account said that he was put to death by the Spartans who captured him when

---

[58] Cf. Gal. 3.24.
[59] The other is in Callimachus, *Hymn to Zeus*, 8. See Towner (2006), pp. 700–1, and for a full discussion of the problems surrounding the attribution of the quotation to Epimenides, Marshall (2004), pp. 199–203. Theodoret of Cyrrhus (Cyrus) (2001), p. 254, knew only of the citation in Callimachus.

they went to war with Cnossos. At any rate, his tattooed skin was supposedly preserved in Sparta, perhaps as a good luck charm.

The verse Paul quoted comes from a lost work known as the *Cretica*.[60] The context is preserved for us in a ninth-century Syriac commentary on the Acts of the Apostles, written by Isho'dad of Merv, which was discovered, edited and retranslated into Greek by Professor J. Rendel Harris.[61] In the original poem, the words are those of the Cretan King Minos, and are addressed to Zeus:

> They fashioned a tomb for you, holy and high one,
> Cretans, always liars, evil beasts, idle bellies.
> But you are not dead; you live and abide for ever,
> For in you we live and move and have our being.

The last line is familiar to us because by coincidence the original Greek has been preserved elsewhere in the New Testament. Paul quoted it in his dialogue with the philosophers of Athens and we must assume that both he and his audience understood the reference.[62] There is no indication in the New Testament that Paul was deeply familiar with ancient Greek literature. He never quoted any of the classics, and apart from this verse of Epimenides, he cited only a single line from the Hellenistic poet Aratus, which is also found in Acts 17.28. It may be significant that both his quotations are from Greek poetry, partly because poetry is easier to retain in the memory than prose and partly because in ancient Greece poets were regarded as divinely inspired. That Epimenides should be a prophet was a perfectly natural assumption, and it is as such that Paul remembered him here.[63] The fact that he did not mention him by name is insignificant. That was a standard literary practice in antiquity, when readers were expected to be well versed in the classics and to know their sources well enough to identify them without being told what they were. In any case, the heavy hint that this prophet was himself a Cretan would have been enough for Epimenides to spring to mind, especially as he was virtually the only one who was widely known outside his native island.

---

[60] Jerome (2010), pp. 304–6, knew it as *Peri chrēsmōn* ('On oracles'). He knew that the first line was also found in Callimachus and that the latter had borrowed it from Epimenides. On the other hand, though he attributed the last line of the quotation to Aratus, *Phaenomena*, he was unaware that it too had originally come from Epimenides.
[61] Harris published his findings in *The Expositor* (Oct. 1906, 305–17; Apr. 1907, 332–7).
[62] Acts 17.28.
[63] Calvin (1964), p. 363, drew this conclusion.

More important for our purposes is the relevance of the context of the quotation. Did Paul simply pick it up as a memorable way of describing the bad habits of the Cretans, or did he have a deeper theological purpose in mind, as he certainly did when he quoted the same text in Acts 17.28? This is important, because what Epimenides was saying is that the Cretans of Minos' time had proclaimed the death of Zeus and even built a tomb for him, when Zeus was generally supposed to be eternally alive and the source of all human life.[64] In Acts 17.28 Paul did not hesitate to identify Epimenides' Zeus with the God of the Bible, and seen in that context, what the Cretans were doing was denying his existence. This was why they were liars, evil beasts and idle bellies. If that was what Paul had in mind, his criticism of the Cretans was not due to their secular habits of behaviour so much as to their false theology. Was Paul saying that this was what the problem was? If so, we may conclude that the Cretans, in Minos' time as well as in his, were people who wanted to deny God. Nor would that be surprising. Unbelief and atheism are by their nature forms of denial, and although the details vary from one situation to another, denial is basically what these people's problem was.

It might even be possible to draw a direct parallel between what Epimenides said and Paul's description of the false teachers. The latter were insubordinate, claiming to teach the truth which they did not know, but this defect seemed to fit the Cretans, who were habitual liars.[65] The false teachers made no sense; they were like dumb and wild beasts. Finally they were deceiving people who were in any case lazy gluttons, always claiming to desire the truth but not willing to put in the effort needed to attain it. That is speculation, of course, but the description fits the Cretans quite well and may explain why Paul used a phrase that in other respects seems strangely out of place. It is hard to see why he would have singled out Cretans for special moral condemnation; at that level, the words of Epimenides could surely have applied to almost everyone. Cretans were not noticeably worse than anyone else, and even if these vices were typical of them, they were probably not universal. Yet Paul swore that Epimenides was right, and this in the context of their willingness to listen to false teaching. It seems preferable therefore to regard his statement here as a reference to the Cretans' penchant for false theology and not as a slur on their everyday behaviour. The Cretans appear to have been so limited in their understanding that they lied

---

[64] John Chrysostom, *Homilies on Titus*, 3.1.12 (NPNF 13, p. 528), knew this and commented, 'The poet said that the Cretans were liars for saying that Jupiter was dead.'
[65] Luther (1968), pp. 38–9, claimed that all Greeks were habitual liars but that the Cretans were the worst. He based his prejudice on the ancient Romans and quoted Vergil, *Aeneid* 2.65, in support of it!

to themselves by denying the eternity of God and were reduced to the state of wild animals because of it. Whether they were exceptionally bad in this respect is impossible to say. Titus was going to Crete and one of their native poets had written this about them, so it seemed natural to Paul to put the two things together and advise his deputy accordingly. There is no need to suppose that he found the Cretans abnormally difficult – probably he would have said the same thing about most people, whether there was a poet to back him up or not!

In any case, it was the susceptibility of the Cretans to false teaching that made Paul warn Titus that he must deal firmly with them. He had to rebuke them sharply, so that they would be sound in the faith. There is a slightly concealed reference here to surgical practice. The diseased mind of the Cretans had to be cut out so that they could be healed by the truth of their faith. Their error was like a cancer that was destroying the whole body and unless it was removed it would only spread and get worse. The harsh tone that Paul adopted was explained by John Calvin as follows:

> One of the most important parts of the tact and wisdom needed by a bishop is the ability to adapt the manner of his teaching to the character and habits of his people. He will not deal with the stubborn and insubordinate in the same way as with the meek and teachable. To the latter we should show a mildness suited to their teachableness, but the stubbornness of the former must be corrected with severity, for as they say, it takes a hard wedge to remove a hard knot. He [Paul] has already given the reason why Titus is to be sharp and unbending in rebuking the Cretans – they are wicked brutes.[66]

The errors that Titus had to look out for and avoid are clearly stated. First there were the 'Jewish myths', followed next by the commands of men who had turned away from (and therefore corrupted) the truth. By now it is clear that the false teaching was fundamentally Jewish in origin, but its actual content remains obscure. The Jewish myths that Paul was referring to may be the sort of folkloric tales associated with people like Enoch, Abraham and Joseph, to name but a few. There was a fashion for such stories in New Testament times, particularly in the diaspora, where Jews felt the need to explain their national peculiarities by references to myths that would justify them to their Gentile neighbours. As for the 'commands of men' our minds naturally turn to the criticisms that Jesus made of the Pharisees, who substituted their own

---

[66] Calvin (1964), pp. 364–5.

rules for the plain teaching of the law and in the process found themselves getting further and further away from the underlying truth which that law represented. The circumstances in Crete were doubtless very different from what prevailed in Judaea, where the proximity of the temple and the presence of the Jewish establishment would have given the problem of Jewish mythology a particular intensity, but the principle is surely the same. Anything that added to the revelation of God was a departure from the truth, even if it was originally a well-intentioned attempt to explain and apply it.

That the commands being taught had something to do with the laws of Jewish ritual purity seems to be clear from what Paul said next. He laid down the principle that to the pure (*katharoi*) everything is pure. This was the teaching of Jesus, expressed in a more abstract and succinct form. Jesus taught his disciples that it was not what a man ate that defiled him but what came out of his heart and mind.[67] In other words, uncleanness was a spiritual matter rooted in the soul of a man and this could not be affected by external considerations. This was a fundamental teaching of Christianity and it set the church apart from any form of Judaism. Jews believed that they ought to protect themselves by a series of rituals and observances that cut them off from other people. Even if the things in themselves had no spiritual value, they nevertheless insisted on them as a sign of their faithfulness to God. Circumcision and the food laws were of particular importance because they touched directly on the body and drew a clear line between Jews and Gentiles. Jews were not unaware of the deeper implications which these things had, but they could not imagine fulfilling the weightier demands of the law if its simpler and apparently more superficial commands were ignored.

Christians rejected this way of thinking and insisted that the law only made sense to those who were spiritually prepared to receive it. Defilement was not a ritual matter but a question of faith – those who were unclean were in that state because they were unbelievers. To people like them, nothing was pure, because their minds and their consciences were already corrupted. Paul's teaching here is of exceptional spiritual importance, not just because it places the responsibility for sin on the inner life of the individual but because it teaches that it is possible for the mind (*nous*) and the conscience (*syneidēsis*) to be corrupt. If we have been taught the wrong things from the beginning we shall be sensitized to them, and when they are denied or disregarded our consciences will react accordingly. This was the problem faced by Jewish Christians when they encountered Gentiles who happily ate meat that had been sacrificed to idols. To Jewish minds, sacrifice to a false god was evil and

---

[67] Mt. 15.11; Mk 7.15.

they might become nauseous just thinking about it. They would have the same reaction to non-kosher food of any kind, but the fact that it had been sacrificed to an idol would have added insult to injury. The vision that Peter had before he went to visit Cornelius is clear testimony to the power of this attitude and the difficulty that even someone who had been as close to Jesus as he had been would have in trying to shake it off.[68] It is no accident that Luke spent so long on an incident that must seem fairly trivial to most people today; the physical revulsion that such a breach of conscience could produce was very real indeed to those who were directly involved.

The psychological problem faced by many Jewish converts was a real one, but it could not be allowed to deflect Gentile believers from the true nature of the Christian faith. The only way to solve this dilemma was by clear teaching about the nature of purity, and that is what Paul was trying to do. In John Calvin's words,

> In the first clause of the verse he [Paul] asserts our Christian freedom, declaring that nothing is unclean to believers, and at the same time he indirectly attacks the false apostles to whom that inner purity, which alone has value with God, was of no importance. In this way he rebukes their ignorance in not understanding that Christians are pure, quite apart from legal ceremonies.[69]

At the same time, there is also a warning here not to deify either the mind or the conscience. Many people today tend to assume that if something is rational it must be good, and they may think that religious scruples that suggest otherwise are nothing but relics of ancient superstition. That is by no means impossible, of course, but it is not universally true and the idea that the mind is the measure of all truth is mistaken. Our minds are finite, which makes it impossible for us ever to know the whole picture about anything, and they are also corrupted by sin, which is a spiritual, not a rational, problem. As the terrible example of Nazi Germany reminds us, some of the most brilliant people alive were capable of the most evil thoughts and deeds, often in the name of their science. That experience alone should warn us against ever trying to deify the mind.

It is a similar problem with the conscience. If our consciences are rightly formed then they will act in the right way, but if not, they will be dulled to the point where they will no longer be able to function as an inner guide to the truth. Murderers, thieves and adulterers may start with a sense that

---

[68] Acts 10.1-33; 11.5-18.
[69] Calvin (1964), p. 366.

what they are doing is wrong, but as they progress along their chosen path their consciences are hardened and they cease to feel any guilt about what they are doing. Some may even go so far as to persuade themselves that their actions are justified, either by circumstances that leave no real alternative or by such maxims as 'might is right', 'the survival of the fittest' and so on. There are too many examples of this kind of behaviour in the modern world for anyone to feel complacent about their chances of avoiding this, and we must be constantly on our guard against the temptation to let our wounded and anaesthetized consciences be our guide to the way we behave. Like everything else, our minds and our consciences must be captive to the word of God if they are to function as they should, and Christians must never appeal to them as their authority outside that controlling context.

The people Paul was talking about here claimed to know God but they denied him by their behaviour. This is a constant problem for any religious person, but it is particularly acute for those who are tied to a Scriptural authority as the principal justification for their actions. The Jews who observed the letter of the law were doing what to them was the right thing, and they could well claim to have the authority of the text on their side. The problem, as Paul knew from his own experience, is that it was possible to be a master of the written law, as he had become during his years as a student in Jerusalem, and yet not know God. He could make sense of the law and argue his case from it, but he did not know the mind of its author and therefore his starting point was wrong. The result was a skewed argument that ultimately falsified the law by not expounding its true meaning.

It was only when Paul met with God in the person of Jesus Christ, on the road to Damascus, that his mind was set free and that he was given the grace to understand the law from the stand point of the lawgiver. This is a constant problem in any legal culture, since the 'original intention of the author', important as it is, is often unknown. Modern Biblical scholars, for example, will often argue that it is necessary to know what the author had in mind before attempting to interpret (let alone apply!) a given text, but they are thinking of the human writer, who is often unknown to us and whose conscious intentions are difficult, if not impossible to fathom. An obvious case of this is the Song of Songs in the Old Testament. Who wrote it, what was his (her?) intention and how should we read it today? To say that nobody has a definitive answer to those questions is an understatement, and the vast array of possible readings is ample testimony to the difficulty we face in interpreting it correctly.

Paul, of course, was not interested in the human author so much as in the God who had inspired him to write. To know God is to possess the hermeneutical key to the interpretation of his word, and the right application of it follows naturally from that. The false teachers claimed the former, but their failure to carry through with the latter belied that claim. They did not adhere to the teaching of the apostles but set themselves up as independent authorities, giving themselves a licence to teach on the basis of their assumed knowledge of Jewish folklore, not the Christian gospel. Secondly, and just as bad in Paul's eyes, they charged for their services. Paul never did that. Of course he believed that those who worked for the mission deserved their reward, but he left that up to the generosity of the congregations. Those who had benefitted from his teaching would reward him out of the goodness of their hearts if they could, and if they could not, they were still welcome to benefit from his ministry. The grace of God cannot be bought or sold, and the fact that the false teachers crossed that line showed just how spurious their claims were.

Finally, Paul concluded his remarks about the false teachers by summing them up as 'destestable' (*bdelyktoi*), 'disobedient' (*apeitheis*) and 'unfit' (*adokimoi*) for anything worthwhile. Once again, he used a triadic schema to convey what these people were like and what the consequences of that were. First of all, and most important, they were detestable. Their insubordination and their greed combined to make them thoroughly dishonourable in the eyes of any genuine Christian minister. The instinctive reaction of any true believer was one of revulsion, and it was this that the apostle focused on first. Having established that, he then went on to explain why Christians reacted to them in the way they did. First of all, the false teachers were disobedient because they refused to submit to apostolic authority. That in itself was a serious cause for alarm in the church, because its testimony to the world was built on the foundation laid by the prophets and apostles and held together by Christ himself.[70] To disregard that was to undermine the very principles on which faith in the Saviour was based, and the effect could only be one of disintegration and destruction, which every believer feared above all else.

Even if the false teachers somehow ended up doing the right thing on occasion, the circumstances in which that happened were accidental and therefore of no lasting value or importance. Those who believed them because of such flukes were deceived, whereas anyone who failed to see their true nature was in an even worse situation than they were. As far as Paul was concerned, saying or doing the right thing had no redemptive value if it was said or done in the wrong way, that is to say, if it was the fruit of disobedience rather than of submission to the authority given to the apostles by God.

---

[70] Eph. 2.20.

Lastly, people like the false teachers were 'unfit for any good (*agathon*) work'. Paul did not think of these works in purely objective terms, as if they could stand on their own, apart from the spiritual state of those who did them. What he was thinking of were 'pious' works, works done to the glory of God and deriving their spiritual value from that. The false teachers were not on that wavelength and were therefore incapable of achieving what they set out to do. In the final analysis they could not be trusted, and it was that, as much as anything else, that made them unfit for the ministry to which they thought they had been called.

# Titus 2

## 1-8. The behaviour of church members

*1. But as for you, teach what is consistent with sound doctrine. 2. Tell the older men to be temperate, serious, prudent, and sound in faith, in love, and in endurance. 3. Likewise, tell the older women to be reverent in behaviour, not to be slanderers or slaves to drink; they are to teach what is good, 4. so that they may encourage the young women to love their husbands, to love their children, 5. to be self-controlled, chaste, good managers of the household, kind, being submissive to their husbands, so that the word of God may not be discredited. 6. Likewise, urge the younger men to be self-controlled. 7. Show yourself in all respects a model of good works, and in your teaching show integrity, gravity, 8. and sound speech that cannot be censured; then any opponent will be put to shame, having nothing evil to say of us.*

After denouncing those who had perverted the ministry of the gospel, Paul turned to the positive instruction and encouragement of his own emissary. The apostle never hesitated to condemn wrong behaviour, but he was careful not to leave matters there. It was not enough for him to rail against what he found unacceptable; he also had to focus on what ought to take the place of such wickedness. In this, he was acting like the good pastor that he was, and his approach sets an example for church leaders in every generation and situation. In the words of P. H. Towner,

> Paul urges Titus to teach the Cretan believers in such a way that their commitments and behaviour will be on an entirely different level from those of the opposing teachers and from Cretan society. This will be achieved through the integration of godly ethics and sound theology.[1]

---

[1] Towner (2006), p. 718.

Paul began his task by telling Titus to teach whatever accorded with 'sound doctrine' (*hygiainousa didaskalia*), a phrase which clearly refers to the life-giving message of the gospel. This dimension is unfortunately obscured in translation because there is no ready equivalent for the Greek word *hygiainousa*. As the related English word 'hygiene' reminds us, there is an element of health-giving present in the term, which is difficult to capture adequately. The teaching of the gospel is not just solid in itself; it is the means by which God brings his people to a healthy spiritual life. That is the effect of the present participle of the verb which is used here as a reminder that the teaching has an active and transforming effect on those who receive it. Somewhat unusually, Paul did not go on to expound that theme any further but instead turned to an analysis of the types of people to whom Titus was called to minister and explained what his hopes for them were. The underlying reason for that was surely that sound doctrine has to be applied to real people in actual life situations, and it is when we see how it changes them for the better that we come to realize how health-giving the teaching they have received is. If there is no improvement in their condition, then the doctrine has something wrong with it, even if it appears to be true in itself. John Calvin picked up this aspect of the matter and went further:

> He [Paul] distinguishes two parts of sound doctrine. The first is that by which God's grace in Christ is commended to us, so that we know where to look for salvation; the second that by which our life is trained to the fear of God and to innocence. But although the first, having to do with the faith, is by far the more important and so is to be impressed upon us with far greater zeal, Paul in this letter to Titus was not careful about observing the proper order.[2]

Paul's pastoral approach was the mark of an experienced teacher who knew that the same message would be heard in different ways by different groups of people and that the desired goals of the instruction were not necessarily the same for each group. The teacher must know how to categorize his people and target each of them according to their most typical needs. Of course, generalizations can never be comprehensive or exclusive. For example, when Paul insisted that the old men should be 'sober-minded', he does not mean to imply that sober-mindedness was not required of others as well, nor should it be understood to mean that old men are especially prone to lack this quality. It is also possible, and perhaps even probable, that there were a number of

---

[2] Calvin (1964), p. 368.

old men in the church who were already models of what the apostle expected, so we cannot interpret his remark here as a blanket condemnation of group behaviour. What Paul was saying was that sober-mindedness is something we ought to look for in old men and expect to find in them because of who and what they are. What he was implying was that if this characteristic was not evident in the old men, Titus' ministry to them would have failed. In writing this way, Paul was giving his colleague a goal to aim for and a standard by which his ministerial success might be measured.

Paul analysed the congregations which Titus was called to serve according to age first and then sex, following established customs of respect but without being rigid about them. It was natural for him to start with the old men, but the fact that he then moved on to the old women, rather than to the younger men, shows that age was a more important consideration in his mind than sex. It is also interesting to note that he moved from the old women directly to the younger ones, leaving the young men to last, which may be taken as evidence that while he respected the norms of society, he was not bound by them. It may also reflect a certain sense that the conduct of the younger men was of crucial importance. If anyone in the church was likely to step out of line it would have been them, with their high testosterone levels and willingness to take risks by defying the leadership, and so he may have wanted to emphasize his advice to them by putting it last, so that it would be remembered.

Paul dealt with slaves as a separate category, no doubt because of the special conditions that applied to them. The distinctions that he drew when dealing with free people were to some extent irrelevant to those in bondage. They had to follow certain rules of behaviour regardless of their age or sex – a reminder to us of the dehumanizing effect that the institution of slavery had.

As in 1 Timothy, Paul made no mention of children, which presumably means that he did not expect Titus to minister directly to them. Children were in the care of their parents and it would not have been appropriate (or acceptable) for Titus to have interfered with that arrangement. Paul was not indifferent to the upbringing of children, to which he referred in some of his other epistles, but they were not Titus' responsibility and so he did not mention them in his instructions for the other members of the church.[3] More surprisingly, and in obvious contrast to 1 Timothy, there is no mention of widows as a separate category either. Probably many of the old women were widowed, but there is no sign of any younger widows of the kind who were causing such problems in Ephesus. Arguments from silence are never

---

[3] For Paul's view of children, see 1 Cor. 7.14; Eph. 6.1-4; Col. 3.20-21. In every case, his words about them were directly connected to the role he expected their parents to play.

satisfactory, but probably the social structure of the Cretan villages was such that no widow problem existed in the churches. In a big city like Ephesus, it is quite likely that there were a number of unattached widows, with no immediate family on whom they could rely. But in a village, widows would have had families to take them in and to care for them. They probably had the same freedom to circulate and to congregate with other widows that those in the big cities had and possibly more, but they would not have led independent lives in the way that urban widows could have done. Perhaps there were exceptions to this rule – there usually are – but if so, they were not common enough to merit special comment and the Cretan congregations seem to have been spared the difficulties that Timothy had to face in Ephesus.

## The old men

As in 1 Timothy, Paul did not say where the boundary lay between 'old' and 'young'. He may have been thinking in terms of Titus' own age, reckoning that people older than he was were 'old' and those who were younger were 'young', but this is far from certain. In any case, we do not know how old Titus was, although he was presumably older than Timothy, whose relative youth was a matter of special comment. The most that can be said about this is that people would probably have known what category they belonged to and would have fallen naturally into the appropriate group. Wider patterns of socialization would have been at work here, as they are in almost all societies, and there was no need for rigid definitions of who belonged where.

One interesting point that is often missed in translations is that whereas in 1 Timothy Paul used the word *presbyteros* to mean both 'elder' and 'older man', making it sometimes unclear as to who he was talking about in any given context, he did not do this in his letter to Titus. Instead he used the absolute form *presbytēs* for 'old man' and reserved *presbyteros* for 'elder' in the church sense. In outlining what he expected to find in the old men, he used two triads, of which the first appears to be more concentrated on the inner qualities of character that he wanted them to exhibit and the second on the kinds of behaviour to which he assumed that those qualities would naturally lead.

In the first triad we find that old men were expected to be 'temperate' or 'sober-minded' (*nēphalioi*),[4] 'serious' or 'dignified' (*semnoi*) and 'prudent'

---

[4] Martin Luther (1968), p. 52, had a rather strange take on this. He said, '*Temperate* means wakeful, not lazy or snoring. They should bestir themselves and not be overly devoted to sleep. Those who are drunk sleep a great deal, but those who are wakeful are able to arise in the morning and are sober.' Calvin (1964), p. 369, also interpreted it in relation to strong drink, but he did not go further than that.

or 'self-controlled' (*sōphrones*). The first of these qualities sets the tone for the other two, which have to be understood in relation to it. As is generally the case in Greek, the full meaning of these adjectives is almost impossible to convey in a single word. This means that although the translations describe some aspects of what Paul meant, they do not capture the whole meaning. A *nēphalios* was a man who exercised sound judgment based on a dispassionate consideration of the facts and circumstances. He was not the kind of person who would be swept away by his own passions or inclined to show favouritism for unworthy motives. A *semnos* was someone whose conduct matched his profession of faith. This was a man who did what was expected of him, who played his part in a way that earned general respect and who did not behave in ways that were inconsistent with his standing in the community. Customs differ from place to place, of course, and what might be acceptable in one time and place would not be well received elsewhere. A good example of this is that today we would think nothing of it if an old man were to play Santa Claus at a Christmas party, but that sort of thing would not have been considered dignified in ancient Crete! Paul laid down the principle to be observed, but wisely left the detailed application of it to common sense and the judgment of the congregations concerned.

Finally, an old man had to be *sōphrōn*. This impossible-to-translate word was an essential virtue in ancient Greece and one of the main goals of all education. It certainly involved 'self-control', which is how it is often translated, but it was more than that. A *sōphrōn* was someone who was wise in a practical way and balanced in his behaviour. He knew how to deal with every situation without compromising himself. He maintained his cool in the most trying circumstances, was slow to react and eschewed judgments based on emotion rather than on reason. He was not deceived by appearances or swayed by personal preferences that might cloud his decisions and make him appear erratic or biased in the eyes of others.[5]

Old men also had to bring sound spiritual leadership to the congregation by their faith, their love and their patience (*hypomonē*). The verb used here is often translated by the adjective 'sound', but while this is certainly accurate as far as it goes, it neglects the active force which the original implies. The old men are not merely to be upright in themselves but also to act as a steadying influence on the community, bringing their soundness to the aid and service

---

[5] John Chrysostom, *Homilies on Titus* 4.2.2 (NPNF 13, p. 531), had an interesting take on these qualities. He said, 'There are some failings which age has that youth has not ... it has a slowness, a timidity, a forgetfulness, an insensibility, and an irritability ... there are ... among the old, some who rave and are beside themselves, some from wine and some from sorrow. For old age makes them narrow-minded.'

of others. They had to do this, first of all, by their faith (*pistis*), which in this context probably meant something like 'commitment'. Not only did they have to believe the right doctrine, but they must also demonstrate by their constancy that they were committed to the church and to the mission of the gospel. Being old, they would have seen many things in life, some of which may well have knocked their self-confidence and made them cynical, if not bitter.[6] That is not the right attitude for a leader of the church. Those who are called to set an example must not only be believers themselves but also be able to give others the confidence to be believers in their turn. Their faith must be an encouragement and an inspiration to others who lack their experience and who may be inclined to give up the quest for godliness if they meet with setbacks along the way.

The fundamental attitude of faith that Paul enjoined on all Christians manifests itself in two ways. The first of these ways is love. Love is not an abstract ideal, nor can it be confined to the inner, spiritual life. An individual can have faith, but unless there are others around him, he cannot be said to have love as well, because there is nobody for him to love.[7] Only in relationships with others can love show itself, and that love must be the practical application of the confidence that grows with and out of faith. Finally, an old man needs patience. In theory that ought to be the fruit of long experience, but there is also the phenomenon of 'an old man in a hurry', someone who knows his time is running out and wants to achieve his goals before passing away. It is also not uncommon for old men to lose patience with younger people who in their eyes cannot do something nearly as well as they can (or could). Few people really admire those who succeed them in a job, and the temptation to be critical of them can sometimes be overwhelming. Letting others make their own mistakes and learn from them is not easy, and it is not unknown for fathers to dismiss their own sons as 'useless' because they have not mastered something that to the old man seems straightforward and obvious. Just as faith has to be demonstrated in love, so love can only mature if it is patient and kind, as Paul reminded the Corinthians.[8]

There is no shortcut in the life of godliness. The old men of the Cretan congregations were expected to demonstrate how a lifetime of experience could (and should) produce a spiritual maturity that would justify their

---

[6] Thomas Aquinas (2012), 2.1.52 (p. 435), was aware of this danger and urged old men to combat it in themselves.

[7] Thomas Aquinas (2012), 2.1.52 (p. 435), said of this: 'among the old there is little friendship, since love is nourished by being together. But no one wishes to stay long with those who are sad. And old people are sad, with the result that they have no friends.'

[8] 1 Cor. 13.4.

position of honour in the church and demonstrate to others what being more Christlike meant. The health of the church depended ultimately on the quality of its leadership, and in the nature of things, much of that would inevitably have fallen on the behaviour of the old men. In many ways they were the key to the edification of the body of Christ and it was with that in mind that Paul dedicated so much attention to expounding in detail what he expected from them.

## The old women

After dealing with the old men, Paul turned to the old women, whom he described here by using the absolute form *presbytides* rather than the more ambiguous comparative *presbyterai*, just as he did with the men.[9] In his scheme of pastoral government, the old women were to play a role that was every bit as important as that of the old men, and in some respects even more so. Not only were they expected to maintain the same high spiritual standards as their menfolk, but to them was entrusted the responsibility of training up the next generation of women in the ways of godliness. As always, this task is not to be understood in exclusive terms, as if nobody else in the congregation had any say in the matter, but is to be seen as a special charge given to the older women because they were the ones most likely to perform it in an effective manner.

Above all else, the old women were instructed to be 'reverent' (*hieroprepeis*) in their way of life (*katastēma*). Yet again we are confronted here with untranslatable Greek words that convey more nuances than most modern equivalents are capable of. To be *hieroprepeis* was to behave in a way that reflected the sacred character of the life they were called to live as members of the church. The church is a 'sacred space' (*hieron*), not in physical but in social terms. There were no buildings set aside for the worship of God, but the community that gathered for that purpose had a spiritual character that its members were required to respect and promote. What was sacred was the gathering itself, and it is that context that we must understand Paul's advice to Titus regarding the old women. The second element of the word (*prepeis*) means 'appropriate' or 'consistent with', so that those who were *hieroprepeis* were prepared for the ministry of sacred things. As for *katastēma*, this word could have a wide range of meanings including 'situation' and 'business', in the sense of owning a shop. The translation 'way of life' gives some sense of this breadth, which includes outward behaviour as well as inward disposition.

---

[9]  It is possible that *presbytera* would have meant the wife of a *presbyteros*, as it did in later times (and still does today). Paul's intentions here were much broader in scope.

The latter led naturally to the former, but it was the external appearance that others would see, and the old women had to make sure that they were giving the right impression to others.

As experienced managers of their households, in many of which the church would have gathered, the old women set the tone for much of what went on in the Christian community. They did not preside over worship, but they created the atmosphere and their conduct might easily determine whether a congregation would survive and grow in a healthy state or deteriorate and eventually disappear. This is why Paul went on to say that these all-important old women should not be 'slanderers' (*diaboloi*). Paul understood how they could easily have lapsed into the kind of gossip that would spread false rumours, and how critical they could be of others, not least towards other women like themselves. For whatever reason, women do seem to be more prone to this kind of thing than men, though of course a man who did such things would not have been tolerated either!

Next there comes the rather interesting phrase 'not addicted to much wine'. The Greek word for 'addicted' is 'enslaved' (*dedoulōmenai*), and the meaning is clear enough. Drinking was a common feature of ancient society, and men normally indulged it in their *symposia*, a word that means 'drinking together'. Of course, as the word 'symposium' indicates, this was part of a social life that involved discussion, often of a philosophical or political nature, and it was generally controlled by what we would now call 'group dynamics'. Men did get drunk, but they usually did so in company and within the framework of recognized social activities. Drunkenness as we understand it was severely condemned, and a man who could not hold his drink was generally despised by his peers. It was not an ideal situation, to be sure, but there were checks and controls that operated to prevent it from getting too far out of hand.

With women the situation was different. They were not prevented from drinking, but they did not socialize in the same way that the men did. For them, there was no social structure to keep the drink under control, and in any case their bodies were not able to consume as much alcohol as the average man could. Those who drank probably did so in the privacy of their own home, quite likely in the kitchen, where wine would have been kept on hand for cooking and other purposes. It would have been very easy for women to take a little sip here and there, and to become addicted without realizing it. Older women may have found this a particular temptation, especially if they could persuade themselves that it was all to help the rheumatism! It is a fact that the aging female body is more prone to suffer from weak bones and bad circulation, and in a world where wine was often the only tranquilizer available, it is not surprising that it should have been resorted to more than was wise.[10] Paul did not say that these women should not drink at all, and we know from his advice to Timothy that he appreciated wine's helpful effects if it was consumed in moderation, but he also knew that this was a potentially undesirable situation that required careful monitoring and advised Titus accordingly.

The old women were also called to be *kalodidaskaloi*, a word that can mean both 'good teachers' and 'teachers of what is good'. Despite the assertions of some commentators, it is not necessary to choose between these meanings, because both apply in this case.[11] Neither Paul nor Titus would have known how a 'good teacher' could teach what was not good; to them a person who was skilled in the techniques of teaching but who used them for the wrong purposes was the worst teacher of all. What this good teaching consisted of is the subject of the rest of the sentence (vv. 4-5).

The old women were charged with the responsibility of teaching the younger ones how to live. They were in effect the grandmothers who helped their daughters with their tasks and gave them advice when they needed it. This is a pattern that replicates itself in every society and is still familiar today. Paul did not suggest that the old women should babysit while the younger ones went out to work, though that may have happened from time to time. More important to him was the need to pass on social skills from the older to the younger generation. When a young woman married, her life changed more dramatically than her husband's did, and she would find herself burdened with responsibilities that she might previously have been unaware of. Most likely she would be moving into another household and acquiring a new set of relationships, with perhaps only limited support from her own family. In most cases, therefore, we are probably dealing here with mothers and daughters-in-law rather than with mothers and daughters as might be the case today.

### The young women

The context is set for us at the beginning because Paul told Titus that he must counsel the old women to teach the younger ones how to love their husbands. The use of the verb *sōphronizō* for 'teach' is a reminder of the complex nature of this task. It was not a case of learning a few basics, like what the man liked to eat and so on, but of developing a new relationship of

---

[10] John Chrysostom, *Homilies on Titus*, 4.2.3 (NPNF 13, p. 532), was aware of this and commented on it.
[11] For example, Towner (2006), p. 724, opts for the former meaning but Marshall (2004), p. 246, for the latter.

which the younger woman had no previous experience. The need for this was all the greater considering that most of these women had probably married in their teens, had never been away from home and may never have met, let alone socialized with, men outside their immediate family. A number of the husbands would also have been considerably older than they were and had higher expectations than might have been the case with men of their own age. Romantic love, as we understand it, existed in ancient society, but it was regarded as dangerous because it upset the social order by introducing an irrational passion into everyday life. People in New Testament times did not normally marry for love but for what to us would be essentially business reasons. A woman would bring a dowry and be expected to produce heirs for her husband's family, and considerations like these would determine how the parents (and not the couple themselves) would arrange the marriage.

Such a system seems strange in the developed world today, but it is still the norm in many places and it cannot be said to create more unhappiness than the free choice alternative that we are accustomed to does. There were certainly mismatches and those sometimes led to tragedy, but there was not the widespread divorce that we encounter in the modern West. One of the main reasons for this was that it was accepted that the wife's first duty was to learn how to love her husband, and that if she succeeded in this, he would respond by loving her in return. It was in fact a way of creating a bond between 'equals' in a society where few people believed that men and women were truly equal and where men were expected to form a relationship with girls who might be young enough to be their daughters. That being said, the principles are still valid; the main difference is that Paul's advice would nowadays be applied just as much to the husband as to the wife, given that the circumstances of each are more likely to be similar today than they were two thousand years ago.[12]

After learning to love their husbands, the next task facing the younger women was the need to learn to love their children also. This is obvious and in some ways was probably much easier, since the maternal instinct is so strong, but loving children is a more demanding task than loving a spouse. Husbands would not expect to be followed everywhere and waited on hand and foot, but children require that degree of attention, especially in

---

[12] Towner (2006), pp. 726–8, gives great credence to the theory that there was such a thing as a Roman 'new woman' who was exploring sexual freedom in a radical challenge to ancient cultural norms. There may have been some women like that in aristocratic circles in Rome, but it is hard to imagine them getting very far in a Cretan village, nor does the text lead us to suppose that there was a 'new woman' phenomenon in the local churches that had to be countered.

their younger years. It is also necessary for parents to learn when to let go; some mothers 'protect' their offspring for years after that is necessary, and in those cases true love means letting them find their own way in life. But most important of all was the need for mothers to teach their children. Jerome saw this very clearly:

> Now they love their children ... if they educate them in the instruction of God. But to be unwilling to cause them grief by teaching what is good, and to give them licence to sin, this is not to love children but to hate them.[13]

Permissiveness, as we would call it today, was not the recommended course for a truly caring parent. Things could get even more complicated when there were (as was often the case) many children in the household, of different ages and with different needs. Keeping them all going at the same time was not easy, and as many children can testify from experience, the wise eye of a grandmother can often make a positive difference to a child's education.

Having established that, Paul moved on to the basic qualities that he expected the old women to inculcate in the younger ones. As with everyone else in the community, they were to be *sōphrones*, knowing what to do, how to behave and how to act in every situation. Of all the qualities Paul mentioned it is *sōphrosynē* that he applied equally to all. It may have worked itself out in different ways, but the same attitude and approach was meant to be common to the whole church. It was the practical expression of the pattern of relationships that God wants his people to have and that best reflect his own mind. It is a kind of wisdom that does not come naturally but that can be learned by precept and example, and it is for this reason that *sōphrosynē* is essential for good relationships to develop and for a healthy community to expand and grow in the way that God intended.

The next quality that Paul singled out was chastity. The younger women were to be *hagnai* ('chaste'), giving no cause for suspicion on sexual grounds. Here again, the social context of the time has to be understood. A young woman of marriageable age would not normally have gone about unchaperoned or have been allowed to talk to male strangers on her own. Nor would any sign of flirting have been tolerated. These customs were not specifically Christian; they applied to the whole of society. Christians might regard one another as brothers and sisters within the church, but in public they could not afford to acquire a reputation for loose living, especially as

---

[13] Jerome (2010), p. 320.

it would almost certainly have been undeserved. The modern mind might be tempted to suggest that any fault in this area would lie equally with both sexes, but while that may be true as a matter of objective fact, it was not perceived like that in ancient times. Of course Paul did not permit men to look at women in the wrong way, but he could only dictate to those who were Christians. The problem he was dealing with here was that women who were too free with their behaviour might attract the attention of non-Christian men, who would then assume that the women were easy targets for their illicit desires. By demanding chaste behaviour of the young women, Paul was protecting them from such unwanted attention and defending the purity of the church at the same time. A woman whose honour was compromised might easily have been forced to marry a non-Christian man in order to protect her family's reputation. In a village context, such considerations would probably always have outweighed loyalty to the church, and so Paul had a double reason for being cautious in this respect.

The younger women also had to learn to be 'homemakers' (*oikourgoi*). It is a sign of the political correctness of the modern age that this word is no longer readily used or even understood. The ESV translates it as 'working at home' (as opposed to working in the office?!) and the NIV says that they should be 'busy at home', which is closer to the original sense but still not altogether clear. The meaning, however, is perfectly obvious. Women had to learn to keep a good house, so that the many duties of hospitality that were incumbent on ancient families could be carried out properly. If the church met in her home, the place had to be fit to receive it. The fact that the household was often the centre of economic life also made its upkeep of prime importance. Women might be engaged in what we would now call 'cottage industries' like spinning and so on, and there was nothing wrong with that, but that was not the main thrust of Paul's teaching. For him, the home had to be a place of welcome, a showcase of what the Christian life was all about, and in some undefined sense, a foretaste of heaven. It was the job of the women to ensure this, and when we appreciate the many dimensions of their calling, we realize just how important their ministry was in the life of the church as a whole.

Women were also called to be 'good' (*agathai*), a word that in this context is often translated as 'kind' and expresses that indefinable quality of godliness and serenity that is the mark of a homemaker who is in control of her household. It might in fact be best to take it not as a distinct adjective but as part of the meaning of *oikourgoi* – as 'good homemakers' (*oikourgoi agathai*) they would be doing exactly what Paul expected of them.

Finally, the younger women were to be 'subject to their own husbands'. In one sense this meant that they were expected to obey their husbands and do as they were asked, something that was important for the standing of the man in the community and may have been perfectly natural if he was considerably older than she was. It probably also meant that they were to obey their own husbands and not those of others. This may seem strange at first sight, but in an extended family a younger woman might be called on to submit to her father-in-law as the head of the household. No doubt, if she were subject to her own husband and he were in turn subject to his father, there would be little difference in practice, but there is an important Biblical principle at stake here that must be taken into consideration.

Paul insisted that a woman should obey her *own* husband because otherwise the word of God might be blasphemed, and the word of God made it plain that when a couple married, they were to leave father and mother and become one flesh.[14] Economic circumstances might complicate matters in practice, but the principle nevertheless had to be maintained. A daughter-in-law was not an extra daughter, and still less a slave. She was the son's wife, and it was to him, not to his father, that she was primarily responsible. Here we have an interesting example of how the gospel could subtly undermine social traditions not by removing them altogether but by substituting a higher ideal for them. Commentators often claim that this is how Paul viewed slavery – he accepted the reality he found around him but imposed conditions on it that in the long term would serve to transform the institution from within. Whether that is true or not, what we find here may be a similar phenomenon with regard to the family unit. Paul could not break up the extended family and probably did not want to, but he could establish boundaries within it that would eventually bring about a profound transformation of the way it worked. The nuclear family, as we call it today, was the desired Biblical norm, and Paul expected to see it worked out even in the rather different social and economic context that he had to deal with.

In summing up the advice Paul gave to Titus concerning the way the old women should inculcate their values in the minds of the younger ones, I. H. Marshall has this to say:

> The qualities are largely those which would be recognized and approved by contemporary ancient society. The first pair, stressing love for husbands and children, is often mentioned on commendatory epitaphs. The second pair stress the basic qualities of self-control and moral purity which are a central concern of the writer, and which are specifically applied to the sexual morality of women. Their proper way of life is

---

[14] Gen. 2.24; Mt. 19.5; Eph. 5.31.

summed up in the third pair as managing their households and doing so in a spirit of kindness. The final instruction to be submissive to their husbands suggests that there was a danger of Christian freedom and equality leading to behaviour with which the ancient world found it hard to come to terms.[15]

In sum, Christian women were not to scandalize the wider society in which they lived. The reputation of the church and its freedom to preach the gospel were more important than whatever rights and liberties women might claim as part of their salvation in Christ.

### The young men

After a lengthy exposition of the roles of both the older and the younger women, with its detailed list of what he expected of the younger ones in particular, Paul turned to the young men. Putting them last (after the women) was unusual, but he had very little to say about them beyond what he said to everyone – they must be *sōphrones* in all things, just like everybody else. Perhaps there was no need for him to say more, since the young men would be spending most of their time with the older ones and learning from them how to behave in wider society. But appearances are deceptive, as I. H. Marshall notes.[16] Paul no doubt sensed that the younger men were best instructed by example, rather than by precept, as befits a class of society that tends to congregate in clubs and teams more than other groups do.

If that was what he was thinking, it would help to explain what he went on to say next. Titus was closer to the younger men than to any of the others Paul mentioned, and for that reason he was better able to present himself to them as a model (*typos*) of 'good works' (*kala erga*). As so often, the apostle stated his principle in general terms, making it broadly clear what he wanted but leaving the details up to individuals to work out in each particular situation. Titus was to set an example, but not in the sense of being what we would call a 'role model' today. The reason for that is that there was a defined limit to the extent to which Titus' example could apply. The younger men in Crete were not all expected to follow him into a full-time ministry, though perhaps some of them would. Their imitation of him was more a matter of spiritual principle than of practical application, because most of them would have

---

[15] Marshall (2004), p. 246.
[16] Marshall (2004), p. 251.

been tied to their family farms or businesses and would remain so. But that did not stop them seeking to be like Titus in their character and behaviour, and if Titus succeeded in producing young men of that stamp he would have done more for the church in Crete than he would have achieved by preaching a thousand sermons.

The reason for that is simple. People notice when lives are changed. Men especially are expected to act in certain ways and can easily be rejected from social groupings to which they do not conform. Women and older people are often more sedentary, and this was especially true in ancient times. The downside of this was that if a gang of young men decided they were going to spend an evening drinking in the local taverna and topping it off with a visit to the temple prostitutes, it could take considerable courage for a dissenter to refuse to go along.[17] But if a significant number of men turned away from such things, they could have provoked a social revolution in the village. In group dynamic terms there might not be all that much to choose between a riotous night out and an evening of prayer and Bible study, but we may be quite certain that the effects would have been very different. Young men like a challenge, and if they are challenged to memorize the Ten Commandments instead of to break as many of them as possible at one sitting, the transformation will be electric. This is what Paul wanted to see and why he instructed Titus in this way.

## Titus as teacher and role model

What Paul meant by 'good works' is as vague and comprehensive as the rest of his advice. It could (and probably did) include a wide range of things, from all-night prayer vigils to helping old people do their housework. There was not a certain type of activity that was 'good' in itself; anything could be included in that category if it was done in the right spirit and for the honour and glory of God. Paul expected great things of these young men and had every confidence in Titus' inspired leadership, but he let the basic principle work itself out in its own way, as the Holy Spirit would guide them according to their circumstances and needs.

Titus was expected to demonstrate his leadership qualities both by his behaviour and by his teaching, which underlay it and ought to be entirely consistent with it. Nothing would harm his ministry or discredit the gospel more than if he were to say one thing and do another, or else teach what others ought to do but take no disciplinary action if they failed to live up

---

[17] Towner (2006), p. 730, thinks that this sort of behaviour was the norm in Cretan society.

to expectations. In developing this theme, Paul returned to the triadic pattern and described Titus' teaching in the following terms. It was meant to demonstrate the following:

1. Integrity (*aphthoria*)
2. Gravity (*semnotēs*)
3. A sound, irreproachable message (*logos hygiēs akatagnōstos*)

Once again we are faced with untranslatable words. Today we think of 'integrity' primarily in personal and moral terms, so that to teach with integrity would now be understood as applying mainly to the sincerity and upright behaviour of the teacher. Paul would never have denied that, of course, but that was not the focus of his command to Titus. For him, to teach with *aphthoria* was to teach without corrupting the message, hence with 'integrity' as the word is often rendered in translation. It assumes that the content being taught has been received by the teacher as a complete package, which (in this case) is what we would call 'the apostolic deposit of faith'. Titus' duty was to convey that message in its fullness, leaving nothing out, emphasizing what needed to be emphasized in the right proportions and ensuring both a balanced presentation and application of the teaching in the circumstances in which he was placed.

Consistency and faithfulness to the content of the teaching had to be backed up by a proper sense of its importance, which Paul described as *semnotēs*, 'dignity' or perhaps 'seriousness'. The teacher must respect the significance of what he was teaching and not betray it by a flippant attitude towards it or by a lack of preparation that left the impression that what he was saying did not really matter. In the modern world there is a strong tendency to 'dumb down' instruction, to make it user-friendly and enjoyable by adding large doses of humour and so on. These things can be helpful if they are kept under control, but if teaching turns into entertainment and little else, its seriousness is liable to be lost. The sad fact is that for a long time now, churches have maintained a Sunday School level of instruction that never moves on from the milk of the word of God to its more substantial meat.[18] As a result, children often leave the church when they get to adulthood because they perceive that they have outgrown the teaching they have received and think that there is nothing more for them to learn. The duty of the true teacher is to produce the exact opposite effect – people should go away wanting to learn more, and sensing that they must do so for the good of their own souls. This is what the apostle

---

[18] Heb. 5.11-14.

meant by 'seriousness', and it is an essential ingredient of the message being taught in the church.

Finally, and in close conjunction with this, what the teacher says must be true, consistent and irreproachable, in the sense that it must be able to stand up to any counterargument that might be raised against it. Christian leaders are often exposed to the charge of hypocrisy by people who claim that what they do does not correspond to what they say and that what they say does not make sense. Paul knew this and told Titus that he needed to think through what he was teaching and to present it in a way that nobody could find fault with. There would always be some who would disagree with the message and reject it, but they must not be given any opportunity to tear it apart from within. A word (*logos*) that claims a person's entire life and allegiance must have the consistency or 'integrity' that such a claim deserves. Jerome understood this very well. Commenting on this passage and focusing on the need for *semnotēs*, or 'continence' as he put it, he had this to say:

> One should also know that continence is necessary not only in respect to deeds of the flesh and desires of the mind but in all affairs. Let us not seek honours we do not deserve. Let us not be set on fire by greed; let us not be overcome by any passion ... It is not profitable for someone to be trained in teaching, and to have sharpened his tongue for orating unless he teaches more by example than by words.[19]

Paul did not specify any particular kind of opponent here, and it is safe to say that his observation was a general one.[20] Controversialists often try to pick holes in the arguments of others and believe that if they can do so, those arguments will fall to the ground. Anti-Christian apologists do the same, but their accusations can (and must) be shown to be without foundation. It is astonishing how many modern atheists use arguments that were common to second-century pagan critics of Christianity, like Celsus the philosopher who was refuted at length by Origen.[21] The details of such arguments vary over time but their substance is remarkably similar – the Bible is mythical, much of its teaching is immoral and it contradicts itself. The Christian expositor must present his material in such a way as to show that criticisms of this kind are false and that those who make them have not understood the basic

---

[19] Jerome (2010), p. 322.
[20] Marshall (2004), p. 256.
[21] Origen, *Contra Celsum*, trans. H. Chadwick (Cambridge: Cambridge University Press, 1953).

## 9-10. Slaves

*9. Tell slaves to be submissive to their masters and to give satisfaction in every respect; they are not to talk back, 10. not to pilfer, but to show complete and perfect fidelity, so that in everything they may be an ornament to the doctrine of God our Saviour.*

Having covered the main categories of church members, Paul next turned to the slaves, who formed a distinct group of their own that cut across all the others. Modern abhorrence of slavery makes it difficult for us to appreciate the true import of Paul's teaching here. He was not defending the institution as such and certainly not recommending it as a way of life.[22] Human bondage can take many forms, of course, and in the ancient world it was often closely connected with economic realities that still exist but that are now handled in a different way. One of these is the need for contractual labour, which was more acute in a pre-industrial and pre-technological society than it is today. Another is the question of debt and indebtedness; some people sold themselves into bondage as a way of paying off their debts, a defined purpose which mitigated the moral aspect of the question which we would have at the forefront of our minds today.[23] Then, too, there was the question of what we would now call 'social security'. In a world without public welfare, slavery was often a way of surviving. Slave owners did not normally kill or even seriously mistreat their property, because it would have been foolish to do so, and those on the receiving end knew that they would be fed and housed as long as they were in bondage. In many cases, there were ways of buying freedom, and manumission for faithful service, especially in the will of a master at his death, was far from uncommon. Bad as slavery was in principle, it was not as unremittingly oppressive as we now imagine, and owners were under obligation to their slaves almost as much as those whom they owned were subject to them.

We have to understand this in order to appreciate what Paul said to the slaves, especially since much of it can be applied to any modern employee. First of all, it was the duty of the slave to do his master's bidding. Obedience

---

[22] See Marshall (2004), p. 257, who puts the whole question of slavery in context.
[23] See Lev. 25.39-46 for the rules that governed slavery in ancient Israel.

is the first test, and sometimes the most difficult. We have grown used to the idea that an employee ought not to do his employer's bidding if he knows that it is immoral, and the frightening example of prison guards sending innocent Jews and others to their deaths because they were 'only following orders' haunts us every time this subject comes up. Jerome, who lived in a slave society and understood this problem, made it clear in his commentary on this verse that a slave was called to obey his master in 'all things' provided that they were not contrary to God or Holy Scripture. If a slave were asked to do something that went against his faith or conscience, he was to obey his master 'more in spirit than in body', in other words, he was not to rebel openly but was to find a subtler way not to accomplish what he had been asked to do.[24]

In reality, few of us are ever placed in a situation that is clearly and radically evil. Much more common is the possibility that we may be asked to do things that we personally dislike and disagree with but are expected to do as part of our job. It is at this point that the test of loyalty comes. Paul's argument was that a slave was better off doing as he was told, however disagreeable it might be at the time, because in the longer term it was that loyalty that would earn him respect and reward, not a contrary spirit of the kind that is always raising objections to whatever is being suggested. It is interesting to note that Paul envisaged that sort of rebellion as a real possibility; the slaves he knew evidently did not always lie down and be quiet! The fact that they could make objections at all tells us that their relationship with their masters was more complex than we now imagine.

Perhaps more important still was the need for the slave to be honest in his dealings. Stealing from one's employer is a widespread practice and can take many forms, most of them seemingly petty. Some people steal by taking longer lunch breaks than they are entitled to; others use company property or facilities for private purposes. The abuse of business expense accounts is now so routine that people are sometimes advised to play fast and loose with the rules because otherwise they stand to lose out! In the household economies of the ancient world, pilfering was common, as it still is wherever domestic servants are employed. Most masters must have known this and factored it into their costs. From the slave's point of view it could be justified on the ground that since slavery was wrong to begin with, stealing was merely repayment for the injustice. Many people think that if they are being treated unfairly and have no other recourse but to act in this kind of way that they are justified in doing so, and it is easy to have some sympathy for that view.

[24] Jerome (2010), p. 324.

Nevertheless, Paul did not believe that two wrongs make a right. Neither he nor Titus was in a position to end the institution of slavery, which would have required a social revolution of major proportions and was probably a practical impossibility in the circumstances, but they could try to put a stop to the wrongs that emerged in response to it. A slave could not set himself free, but he could lead a life that was consistent both with what was expected of him by his master and with what he was obliged to do as a Christian. In effect, the slave could liberate himself spiritually by applying the standards imposed on him by God to his circumstances and by being honest in all his dealings. His master would soon notice that things had changed and would probably be impressed, since it was so unexpected and so unusual. No doubt he would want to know why the slave was behaving better, and this would give the latter an opportunity to explain the gospel and the way it which it had transformed his life.

It is impossible to know how a master would have responded to something like that, and no doubt the reactions that actually occurred varied enormously according to the different cases. Paul could not predict that one way or the other, but influencing the slave's master was not his primary concern. What he wanted to ensure was that the teaching of God our Saviour would not be compromised by the behaviour of those who claimed to have been saved by him. A master who knew that he could depend on his slave because his slave was a Christian might not become a believer himself, but neither would he have been able to discredit the gospel by claiming that it was the last refuge of hypocrites who used it as an excuse for evading their responsibilities. The first duty of the slave was not to his earthly master but to his heavenly one, and by obeying the former he was in fact honouring the latter. This was the dimension of reality in which Paul was operating and it was with that perspective in mind that he gave this advice to the slaves in the church.

The state of the slave in the household was a paradigm of the spiritual position in which all human beings find themselves, and that is what Paul went on to deal with next. Physical bondage was a limited picture of the spiritual condition that affects us all until we are set free by our Saviour Jesus Christ. The special gift given to the human slave was that he could demonstrate this truth in an open and obvious way by changing his behaviour even without acquiring his freedom. A slave who had been manumitted without experiencing this spiritual change (as many no doubt were) would not easily unlearn the habits acquired in servitude and would probably be just as grasping and self-seeking in freedom as he was before. There is no shortage in the modern world of freedom fighters who have won their independence only to become dictators in their turn, living off the spoils of the land in which they had previously claimed to be the slaves of some colonial or other master. Jesus told the story of the dishonest steward who begged for mercy from his master but then turned on his own debtors, and the phenomenon is too well known to need further comment.[25]

Paul's message was that there is no place for this kind of thing in the Christian life. Whatever our early status or condition may be, we all serve a heavenly master and are accountable to him for our behaviour. The gospel of salvation that he has revealed to the world is worked out in the lives of each one of us, and it is our duty to present it in the best possible light. There will be opposition to it, but that opposition should not have the opportunity to attack the message on the ground that those who preach it do not adhere to its principles. The Greek verb *kosmō*, related to our word 'cosmetic', implies that what we do is a decoration of the gospel, not a modification or an addition to it. Just as a product is more likely to sell well if it is presented in an attractive way, so Christians are called to put their best foot forward in the proclamation and spread of the message of salvation.

Did Paul accept the cultural norms of his time without challenging them, or was his teaching subtly designed to undermine slavery from within and lead to its eventual collapse? This is a modern debate, occasioned by the near-universal hostility to the institution in our time and our desire to exonerate Paul from charges that modern people would lay against him.[26] Unfortunately there is no way that this question can be answered satisfactorily. Most likely Paul regarded slavery as something that existed in the fallen world and that would not be eradicated until the return of Christ. In his view, that event would occur sooner rather than later, and it was best to prepare for it and not worry too much about a social reform that, even if it were achieved, would have little time to result in any positive effect. In later times, however, Christians often defended what seems to us to be an unjust social order. Thomas Aquinas, for example, had this to say:

> the faith of Christ did not come to set aside the order of justice, indeed, the faith of Christ preserves justice. But justice requires that some men be subject to other men, although such servitude is limited to the body. For through Christ we are now set free of the servitude which binds the soul, but not from the servitude or corruption of the body; but in the future we shall be set free even from bodily servitude and corruption.[27]

---

[25] Lk. 16.1-13.
[26] See Towner (2006), pp. 735–40, who argues that Paul was laying foundations for the eventual overthrow of slavery.
[27] Thomas Aquinas (2012), 2.2.64 (pp. 440–1).

In other words, deliverance will come in the *eschaton*, but for now justice demands the continuance of the present order, however corrupt and inadequate it may be, as a reflection of God's glory and ultimate intention for his people.

### 11-13. The grace of God in the life of the believer

> *11. For the grace of God has appeared, bringing salvation to all, 12. training us to renounce impiety and worldly passions, and in the present age to live lives that are self-controlled, upright and godly, 13. while we wait for the blessed hope and the manifestation of the glory of our great God and Saviour, Jesus Christ.*

Having dealt with particular pastoral questions, Paul next turned to the more general principle that underlies the existence of the church as a community and provides the rationale for the exhortations to changed behaviour that he had just given. He reminded Titus that the body of believers had come into existence because the saving grace of God had appeared to all people (*anthrōpoi*), not just to Jews.[28] The grace (*charis*) of God is any act of favour that he has shown towards his creation, and in principle, it is not visible. Grace is not a thing that God has made but a spiritual attitude, so when Paul says that it has 'appeared' what he means is that its effects have been seen. In this case, it is the acts by which we have been saved that he was talking about, and in these few words we find comprehended the entire life, death, resurrection, ascension and heavenly reign of our Lord Jesus Christ, as well as the sending of the Holy Spirit at Pentecost. Furthermore, as I. H. Marshall puts it,

> God's grace has an educative transforming effect on people which enables them to turn away from godlessness, to live lives of positive goodness, and to look forward to the final revelation of God's glory in which they will share.[29]

---

[28] John Calvin (1964), p. 373, interpreted this in the light of what Paul had just said concerning slaves. In his words, 'He expressly declares that salvation comes to all men, having especially in mind the slaves of whom he has just been speaking. He does not mean individuals, but rather all classes of men with their diverse ways of life, and he lays great emphasis on the fact that God's grace has condescended even to slaves. Since God does not despise even the lowest and most degraded class of men, it would be extremely foolish that we should be slow and negligent to embrace his goodness.'

[29] Marshall (2004), p. 263. Towner (2006), pp. 740–5, wants to see this passage as the climax of Paul's critique of a specifically Cretan mythology, related to that of the wider

In the present context the most important aspect of this grace is that it has been given 'to all people'. This does not mean that everyone has been saved but that the message of salvation is not confined to Israel. It has been announced to the Gentiles, too, and they have been given the opportunity to enter into the kingdom of God. This is a great favour, but it also creates a special obligation on them that did not exist before. In the time of the old dispensation, the word of God had not been preached to the Gentiles and so they could not be blamed if they did not hear and obey it. Indeed, as Paul pointed out in Romans 2, many Gentiles instinctively understood the mind of God and did what they knew to be right even without the revelation that had been given to Israel, something which redounded to their credit.[30] But once the revelation was opened up to everybody, the need to respond to what it entails was also imposed on everyone. Gentiles now had no excuse; they too, must hear and obey what God has said to them.

The 'saving' (*sōtērios*) grace of God can and must be distinguished from other manifestations of divine grace. The preservation of the world in spite of human sin is a work of God from which believers and unbelievers both benefit, but it does not bring salvation. Saving grace is not an alternative to preserving grace but something in addition to it. Every human being is preserved in this life but not all are saved in eternity. God's saving acts were neither random, nor did they flow naturally from one to another. They were all manifestations of the foreordained purpose of God, which was ordained by him from the beginning.

Another difference between preserving and saving grace is that those who have been saved by grace are called to live in the world not just as people who have been preserved from divine wrath, but according to the light which they have received as a consequence of their salvation. The practical effect of this is that those who have been saved continue to enjoy all the blessings of the created world but that they approach it with a mind that is different from that of those who have been preserved from destruction without being saved. In effect, believers are called to live in the world according to the principles and intentions of the God who has saved them but also condemned the disobedience of those who have sinned against him. They can do this without any sense of incongruity, because the created order is their proper inheritance just as much as the kingdom of heaven is. Those who have been saved are strangers not to the creation as God made it but to the state of rebellion into which it has fallen.

---

Graeco-Roman world but not identical with it. However, there is nothing in the text itself that would necessitate such an interpretation.

[30] Rom. 2.12-16.

The saving grace of God operates in us in order to train us how to live in the way we should. It has the function of a teacher and guide that will prepare us for the eternal destiny to which we have been called. In practical terms, it manifests itself in two distinct but complementary ways. First, it appears objectively in the law of God, given to Moses, interpreted by the prophets and fulfilled in Christ. Then it comes to us subjectively as the inner working of the Holy Spirit, who applies the principles of God's revelation to our lives in a way that prepares us for eternal life with God. This work of teaching and preparation makes two complementary demands on us. First, we must *deny* ungodliness (*asebeia*) and 'worldly desires' (*kosmikai epithymiai*) and then we must *live* in the present age in a way that pleases God and that reflects our new standing with him.

To deny ungodliness means that we must first recognize what it is and reject it. There are many people who are dissatisfied with their lives but who do not perceive them as being ungodly because they do not know what ungodliness is. It is by the Holy Spirit that we are given both the ability to identify ungodliness and the strength to turn away from it. Ungodliness is anything that opposes or detracts from our relationship to God and it can take many forms. 'Worldly desires' are a large part of it, though there is more to it than that. It is possible to be ungodly above and beyond any worldly desires we may have, and so it is best to think of those desires as particular instances of ungodliness rather than as the chief (or only) way in which it is revealed.

The difficulty we face here arises because we are called to live as saved people in a world that is controlled by powers that are in rebellion against God. The desires that we have may not be wrong or harmful in themselves; indeed, they may be necessary for our survival. There is nothing sinful in wanting food to eat, clothes to wear, a place to sleep and so on. But as Jesus told his disciples, God knows that we need these things and will provide for them.[31] It is not his purpose to shortchange us or to make us think that feeling miserable and deprived is part of his plan for our salvation. The problem does not lie in our desire for the things we need but in an approach to the blessings of this life that turns them into idols and ends in themselves.

The minute our minds are distracted from the things of God and turned towards created things, we have fallen into the trap of ungodliness. If we look to them for happiness, and even for some kind of salvation, we shall be bitterly disappointed, and the good that we could and should have derived from the creation will be contaminated by our wrong attitude towards it.

---

[31] Mt. 6.25-34.

When it came to instructions about how the saved should live in this present age, Paul employed his customary triadic pattern and expresses it by using three adverbs. This device works well enough in Greek but is hard to translate exactly. Most versions say something like 'to live self-controlled, upright and godly lives', introducing a non-existent substantive ('lives') and rendering the adverbs as if they were its adjectives. In fact, the criteria he outlines are attached to the verb, which gives them a more dynamic application. It is not the lives of the saved that must be self-controlled, upright and godly, but the way they live. The difference in meaning is that Paul did not envisage an objective standard of what saved people ought to be like but rather demanded that they should think and act in ways that were compatible with their calling. He did not prescribe whether believers should be celibate or married, whether certain professions (like military service) should be barred to them, or how many children they should have. These things matter in individual cases, of course, but they must be worked out according to the principle that lies behind godly living and not predetermined by an artificial standard that provides precise guidelines as to what godly living is.

The first of the adverbs is already familiar to us from what Paul said to the different groups of people in the church, and in many ways it represents the foundation of the Christian life as he presented it in this Epistle. Christians are expected to live wisely (*sōphronōs*), applying their sanctified common sense in every relationship which they have and to every situation that may come their way. Self-control is, as always, essential to this, but it is only one aspect of a bigger picture. It is a prerequisite to the exercise of this spiritual gift of wisdom, but the gift is not limited to it.

The Christian is also expected to live 'justly' (*dikaiōs*). In everyday terms this will mean that he must be honest in his dealings, which is probably why it is often translated as 'upright', but there are other dimensions to it that should not be neglected. The man who lives justly is the man who thinks rightly, who does not form opinions about others without proper knowledge, who is not prejudiced in his dealings and who seeks the good of everyone, not just of himself. This will involve giving proper consideration to the best use of resources, for the right way to care for the poor and the needy, and so on.

The Christian is also called to live in a godly way (*eusebōs*), another theme that recurs in this Epistle and represents an attitude towards life that Paul saw as being fundamental to the believer. The heart of godliness is that we should be turned towards God. We are free to devote ourselves to many different activities, but whatever we do, we must please him and not ourselves. The way we use the blessings we have been given must correspond to the nature and will of the God who has given them to us. *Eusebeia* is the response demanded of the believer to the grace that he or she has received. This grace has been given to us so that we might consecrate our gifts to the Giver and so enjoy them as we ought.

Finally, Paul specified that all of this is intended for our life 'in the present age' (*en tōi nyn aiōni*). When describing 'worldly desires' he used the word *kosmos*, referring to the created order. In this verse he employed a less material term, *aiōn* ('age', 'eon'), which refers primarily to time but is used to describe the dispensation in which we have been called to live rather than a fixed number of years. In the plural it is frequently employed to mean 'for ever and ever', implying a reality that transcends the boundaries of time, and its adjectival form (*aiōnion*) is the standard word for 'eternal'. We ought therefore to think in terms of a state of being rather than a limited amount of time, although, in this case, the addition of the word 'present' (*nyn*) emphasizes the fact that the condition in which we now find ourselves will not last for ever. But although that is true, it is where we are at the moment, and we are responsible for the way we live in the world as it is. Salvation in and through Jesus Christ is not merely the hope of something to come in the future but that cannot be experienced in any meaningful way right now. On the contrary, it is a relationship with him that we can and must work out in the context in which we now find ourselves, so that our hope for the future is realized, we shall be ready, willing and able to enter into our inheritance.

The eschatological dimension of our calling should determine the behaviour of the Christian, and this is what Paul was preparing believers for. We are to live in this world with the help of the grace of God because we are hoping for the appearance 'of the glory of our great God and Saviour Jesus Christ'. This phrase has provoked an enormous amount of comment. Was Paul speaking of two persons or of one? Is this verse evidence that Jesus was already being called God in New Testament times? That the word 'Saviour', normally applied to Christ, could be used of God the Father as well is clear from the opening verses of the Epistle (1.3-4), and it may be that the two persons of the Godhead have been run together here. Commentators are divided in their assessment, motivated, one suspects, more by their own prior theological commitments than by strict impartiality in the face of the textual evidence. It is highly unlikely that any consensus view will be arrived at, but I. H. Marshall's assessment deserves to be pondered. After examining the arguments on all sides of the debate, he concludes,

> the Epistles demonstrate a strong functional equality, if not identity, between God [the Father] and Christ which makes the transfer of the

title fully possible. It is difficult to see why the One in whom God is fully manifest should not thereby be entitled to the title of God.[32]

P. H. Towner, on the other hand, rejects this and argues that the 'great God and Saviour' refers to one person – God (the Father) – and that Jesus Christ, 'in his eschatological epiphany, is the blessed hope'. Towner concludes from this that Jesus Christ is not equated with God but with God's glory, of which he is 'the embodiment and full expression'.[33] Is it necessary to choose one over the other? It is hard to see how Jesus Christ could be the expression of God's glory without being God, since anything less would not be expressing the divine at all.[34]

Paul called the hope we have in Christ 'blessed' (*makaria*) because it is a gift from God himself. Those who are not believers live without hope in the world, either because they are in despair or (more usually) because they prefer not to think about it.[35] They live one day at a time, do what they can and await whatever comes their way. Those who are optimists by nature may hope for the best, having no idea what that might be, while those who are pessimists may sink into despair if they start to think about what might happen to them next.

In contrast to both of these, the Christian knows what is coming and focuses his life on that. He is aware that whether this life brings him good times or bad, the end result will be the same – the glory of God will be revealed in him. The positive nature of Christian hope, it should be said, goes against all natural wisdom. Scientists tell us that the world is winding down and that in several billion years from now the sun will burn out. Social commentators tend to think that the human race will disappear long before that. The threat of self-destruction through nuclear warfare is a very real one and it could happen any time. The breakdown of traditional family and other structures proceeds apace and is bound to have very negative effects sooner or later. The pace at which we are exhausting the world's resources is such that many people calculate that if worldwide prosperity were ever to be achieved we would run out of them in a few years, if not weeks. Doomsday scenarios of one kind or another proliferate, with no obvious solution in sight. Of course there are people who try to point in the opposite direction, hoping against hope that a world of peace and universal brotherhood might somehow

---

[32] Marshall (2004), p. 282. For the full discussion, see pp. 276–82.
[33] Towner (2006), p. 758.
[34] Compare Heb. 1.1-3.
[35] Eph. 2.12; 1 Thess. 4.13.

emerge, but the facts are against them. It is not for nothing that such rosy views of the future are labelled 'utopian', because that is what they are.

The Christian vision does not promise a gradual resolution of human problems, but neither is it a message of despair. It recognizes that this world is passing away and condemns as foolish the attempts that are made to prop it up artificially. Salvation is not to be looked for in the right application of the present world's resources or in the correction of the abuses to which they have been put, important though those things are in their context. Our only hope is the appearance (*epiphaneia*) of God's glory; when time will come to an end, the world we know will be wound up and the kingdom of God will be ushered in in its fullness.

Paul has told us that it is the *glory* of our great God that will appear, and this for two reasons. The first is the theological fact that God is invisible and will always remain so. He does not and will not appear to us as a definable being. In the Old Testament, Moses saw God's glory on the mountain, and the disciples of Jesus beheld it in the word made flesh.[36] The second reason is that God's glory is external to him (in so far as such a statement makes sense). It is not the inner essence of the divine being that will appear to us but the culmination of the self-revelation that he has made over time and that appeared in its fullness in Jesus Christ. It will therefore be the return of the Christ who went up to heaven that will be the appearing of the divine glory, and it is that which we are called upon to await.[37]

We know from other parts of the New Testament that the coming of Christ in glory will bring about the general resurrection of the dead, which in turn will be accompanied by the judgment, after which those who are condemned will go to hell and those who are saved will enter into heaven.[38] But although this was known and understood by the early Christians, it is not what Paul was focusing on here. He did not present the blessed hope as the realization that justice will be done, that the enemies of God will get what they deserve and that the righteous will have the satisfaction of seeing the ungodly burn in eternity. There have been people down through the ages who have thought in such terms, and even today it is tempting to think that injustices will be righted at the end of time by punishing the wicked who have perpetrated them. That is true, of course, but it is not what Christians should be looking forward to. What we want to see is the fullness of the glory of God who will reveal himself in us and through us proclaim his salvation to the entire creation.

---

[36] Exod. 33.20-23; Jn 1.14.
[37] Acts 1.11.
[38] 1 Cor. 3.13-15; 15.12-28; 1 Thess. 4.13-17.

## 14. The work of Christ

*14. He it is who gave himself for us that he might redeem us from all iniquity and purify for himself a people of his own who are zealous for good deeds.*

At this point Paul comes to the very heart of the gospel message, which he expounds more fully and more clearly here than anywhere else in the Pastoral Epistles. Why this should have been so we can only speculate. He was certainly not saying anything new, and his words have an echo of his preaching that must have struck a chord with Titus and the Cretans who first read this Epistle. Fundamental to the message is his assertion that our Saviour Jesus Christ, the one who will reveal the glory of the great God at the end of time, is also the one who gave himself 'for us' (*hyper hymōn*). The man who was sinless became sin for us.[39] The innocent one took our curse upon himself so that by paying the price for our sins we could be set free and admitted into his eternal presence.[40] In these few words, the grandeur and the mystery of the gospel are fully revealed. Why did the Son of God do this? The answer must be that it was because his Father wanted to save his people, and the only way that could be done was by someone paying the price for the sin that cut them off from his grace. There was no human being who could accomplish that, because we have all inherited the sin of Adam and are guilty before God for the alienation from him which resulted from that.

In order to overcome the abyss that separates fallen humanity from its Creator, the Son of God voluntarily submitted himself to the Father, became a man and died for us on the cross.[41] What had previously been pictured by the annual sacrifice of a spotless lamb in the temple now became reality as the divine-human Lamb of God took away the sins of the world. He did not do this by finding the perfect sacrifice, in the way that the high priest of Israel went looking for a lamb that was worthy to be slain, but by becoming the sacrifice himself. Priest and victim are united in him – 'he gave himself'. Furthermore, he gave himself 'for us', taking the place that would otherwise be ours.[42] Nothing is more central to the Biblical doctrine of atonement than what theologians call 'penal substitution'. The punishment that we cannot bear ourselves, God has borne for us in Christ. This is the heart of the gospel proclamation, the key element that makes sense of all the rest. To deny it is

---

[39] 2 Cor. 5.21.
[40] Gal. 3.13.
[41] Phil. 2.6-8.
[42] Heb. 5.1-10.

to deny Christ and reject the salvation that God the Father has granted to us in the gospel.

This self-giving of Christ has two aspects to it that Paul brings out here. The first is that he gave himself in order to redeem (*lytrō*) us 'from all unlawfulness (*anomia*)'. The basic idea is clear enough – we have been set free from sin – but the words used to describe it demand some comment. First of all, there is the verb translated as 'redeem' or 'ransom'. This brings to mind the image of a payment that is made in order to obtain the freedom of those who have been made captives. This normally happens in war or following a kidnap, but in this case it refers to the human race, which has been seduced by Satan and made captive to his will. Does this mean that God has made the payment to Satan in order to get him to let his people go free? In the early church there were those who thought that. According to them, Satan was tricked into letting his prisoners go, only to find that when he took the bait offered by the Father in the form of his Son, he was powerless to resist him. The Son of God had entered his dwelling place ('descended into hell' as the creeds put it) and had overthrown his power. That scenario seemed logical, but it struck many people as immoral and unworthy of God, who owed Satan nothing. The theory was soon abandoned, but the question of who received the payment remained to be answered. One possible interpretation was to say that the language being used here is metaphorical. In other words, although there was no financial transaction of the kind implied by the verb, the early Christians adopted the imagery as a way of explaining how God's people were set free from the power of sin.

That explanation sounds good and no doubt it contains an element of truth. All human explanations of a divine activity must be to some extent metaphorical, because the language of earth is not able to express the fullness of the mind of God. But although we must allow for that, we also have to say that the verb chosen to describe what happened was not selected at random. It conveys a reality that is inherent in what Christ did, and that aspect must not be forgotten. The redemption was indeed a payment, not to the devil, who was not entitled to receive it, but to God, whose righteousness had been offended by the sin of Adam. God does not (and cannot) ignore our sin as if it was of no great importance. Our sinfulness matters to him because we matter to him. What we do is important in his eyes, and if what we do is wrong, then it must be taken seriously and put right. To be cut off from God by disobedience is to be cut off from the source of our life – it is death. The only way to put that right is to pass through death and overcome it, which is what the Son of God did in his crucifixion and resurrection.

The nature of the captivity from which we have been delivered is described by Paul as 'unlawfulness' (*anomia*), a word that is also, though less helpfully, translated as 'lawlessness'. *Anomia* does not mean 'lawlessness' in the sense of anarchy, doing without any law at all, but 'unlawfulness', in the sense of going against a well-established order. It is true of course that Adam and Eve did not have the law of Moses, but they had a relationship with God that was written in their hearts and they knew what they could and could not do. They could also observe the creation over which they had been given dominion and recognize how God's law was written in it.[43] By succumbing to the temptation of Satan the first human beings had fallen away from the law that was written on their hearts and thus found themselves in the state of *anomia*. The law of Moses was only a pale reflection of the law that Adam had transgressed, a reminder to the chosen people of what God required of them and of how far short of his will they had fallen. *Anomia* could not be cured by introducing order into a world of disorder, because that was not the problem. Adam and Eve may have disobeyed God, but the law of creation remained inviolate. By their sin, their inheritance was turned into a hostile environment that led to their deaths instead of to the eternal life that God wanted them to enjoy. Even within the realm of *anomia* there was an order of sorts, but it was the order of Satan; it was rebellion *against* God and not merely separation *from* him. Human beings do not live in a no man's land, caught between the forces of God and the devil, but in territory controlled by the latter. To be set free from this is therefore not to be set free from morally neutral anarchy and chaos but to be delivered from sin and disobedience. It is to change sides in the spiritual warfare being waged between good and evil, and not simply to be protected by one side so as not to fall into the clutches of the other.

The second aspect of Christ's self-giving sacrifice on the cross was that by it, he intended 'to purify for himself a people for his own possession'. As usual, the Greek words mean more than what any one term can convey in translation, and so it is necessary to look at them carefully. The word used for 'purify' is *katharizō*, which normally implies some kind of cleansing. Purification could theoretically take many forms. It might be achieved by amputation, as in the case of a gangrenous limb. It might happen by spraying the air, something that in ancient times could be accomplished by incense or some other perfume. There were various forms of ritual purification that did not involve any physical substance at all but were achieved by prayer, fasting or some other such means. In this case, however, it is clear that the purification was by cleansing the soul from the spiritual corruption of sin. The only cleanser that could achieve this was the blood which Christ shed at

---

[43] Ps. 19.1-11; Rom. 2.14-16.

Calvary, not because it had any intrinsic power in itself but because it was a sacrifice that was acceptable to God. It was effective because God recognized the character and intention of his Son. His character was determined by the fact that he was also God and therefore perfectly sinless. His intention was determined by his obedience to his Father's will, not just in his divinity but more importantly in his humanity as well. It was as a man that Jesus Christ submitted to God and it was because of that, and not because there was anything especially virtuous in Christ's human blood, that his sacrifice had the power to take away sin.

The Son of God did his Father's will, not for some purely objective purpose, as if sin was a kind of cosmetic blemish that did not matter to him personally, but for a very specific reason. He wanted to create a people for himself, who would belong to him not only by default (as creatures) but also by choice (as the elect). If this desire to establish his own kingdom were attributed to anyone else it would sound selfish, but in the case of the Son who is the Creator and Redeemer God, it was both natural and appropriate. As his creatures we already belong to him whether we have been cleansed or not; what he wants to do now is to change the nature of that belonging from something that can only lead to our condemnation to something that will make us fellow workers with him in the kingdom of God the Father.

The people whom God was calling to himself was called to be *periousios*, an unusual Greek word whose meaning is unclear. Even Jerome was puzzled by it:

> Though I have often pondered what the word *periousion* means and have questioned the wise men of this world in the hope that they may have read it somewhere, I was never able to discover anyone who could explain to me what it meant. For this reason I was forced to consult the Old Testament from which I thought the apostle had taken what he had said.[44]

Jerome found the term in two Old Testament texts, Deut. 7.6, which is almost certainly the source for Paul's use of it here, and Psalm 135.3-4.[45] In both

---

[44] Jerome (2010), p. 329.
[45] Jerome (2010), pp. 330-1, also mentioned that Symmachus, a Jew who made a more exact translation of the Hebrew text than the usual LXX version, rendered the word as *exhairetikon* ('excellent'). He also noted that *periousion* is virtually synonymous with *epiousion*, the word somewhat unhappily translated as 'daily' in the petition for bread contained in the Lord's Prayer. Jerome knew that the word came from the Hebrew *s'gullah*, but it was Martin Luther (1968), p. 67, who translated it correctly as 'private property' or 'own possession', as it is normally rendered today.

cases, what is meant is that God's people were to be set apart for him in a special way, that they were to be given particular blessings and charged with exceptional tasks, so that his glory would be revealed to the nations. In the Christian context, the revelation of that glory would include, and even be dominated by, the preaching of the gospel. Where Israel would impress the surrounding nations, the church would seek to convert them and integrate them into the promises made to the chosen people from the beginning.

This explains why Paul finishes his remark with the statement that his chosen people will be 'zealous for good works' (*zēlōtēs kalōn ergōn*). Those who have been redeemed by the blood of the Lamb who was slain for them are not stored up in heaven as trophies gracing the palace of the king. On the contrary, they are raised to a new life so that they can become profitably active for the first time. The person who is truly saved will not only do what is right but will also be eager to do it. The Christian is someone who ought to be excited about doing good. Paul did not go into details about what the nature of that good might be – he left it open because in objective terms, it could be almost anything. What counts in the sight of God is the willingness of those who have been saved to do what is right and the preparedness for it that is revealed in their zealousness. Once that new spirit has been implanted in a believer, then its application will follow as a matter of course in whatever way is appropriate. The Christian life is not the mechanical performance of certain rituals but the outworking of a desire to serve the Saviour in whatever place and in whatever way he directs. All that is needed from us is the eagerness to serve.

## 15. Paul's charge to Titus

*15. Declare these things; exhort and reprove with all authority. Let no one look down on you.*

The second chapter of Titus concludes with a brief but important summary of what Paul had said so far. In it he reminded Titus that these were the things that he had to preach, insist upon and enforce with a clear sense of the authority that the apostle had given him for his mission. The familiar triadic pattern is employed once again here in order to guide Titus through the three stages of exhortation, beginning with the mildest form of it and working up from there to its most intense manifestation.

In the first stage, Titus must simply declare what needs to be said. The verb Paul used was *lalō*, a common word for speaking. Titus had to begin with communicating his message, because unless people understand what is required of them there is no reason to expect them to do it. It is only fair that they should know the rules before being asked to keep them! But Paul also knew that information, important though it is, is not sufficient by itself. The good teacher must become a preacher by turning his words of instruction into exhortations to put it into practice. He knows the difference between teaching and preaching, which unfortunately is not always well understood today. Some pastors preach without really teaching their people much. In other words, they tell them what to do but do not give them adequate reasons why they should do it. Others fall into the opposite trap. They inform their hearers at great length about what God has said and done in the past but they make little or no effort to apply those lessons today. The unfortunate result of that is that a congregation can know all about Abraham, David or Paul, but if it is not exhorted to learn the lessons those men have taught us and submit to the commands that arise out of that knowledge, the teaching is of little practical use.

This is why Paul moved from speaking to exhortation (*parakalō*).[46] Whereas teaching is the objective communication of facts, preaching adds the subjective note of personal request and involvement in it. Titus must urge his hearers to do something about what they know and not just sit back and wait for the next round of instruction. It is only by putting each lesson into practice that its true meaning will be grasped, and that is the message that he must convey to the congregations to which he is being called to minister.

Finally, and most intensely, Titus must insist that his teaching and preaching should take effect. Here Paul used the word *elenchō*, a verb that implies taking control of the process and making sure that it brings the right results. It can be translated as 'rebuke', as it often is, but it is more than that. It is not simply a condemnation but also a correction of what has gone wrong. Paul was not concerned to insist that Titus should tell people off for not doing what they were told. What he wanted to see is the teacher guiding the pupil's hand and leading him along the way, especially if and when the pupil is unable or unwilling to go by himself. Titus had the right to do this because of the mandate (*epitagē*) which he had received from God, operating through Paul as his agent. It is hard to convey this other than by using the word 'authority' which expresses the meaning but tends to obscure the fact that Titus' authority did not come from his own character or from Paul, but from God.[47]

---

[46] It is no accident that *parakalō* is also the Greek word for 'please', which could be translated as something like 'I beg you'.
[47] We owe this translation to Calvin (1964), p. 375. Erasmus had rendered it as 'diligence' and John Chrysostom as 'severity' (against sin), but Calvin appealed to the immediate

It is easy to forget this. Many people think that a pastor is being arrogant if he tells them things they do not want to hear, or exhorts them to do things they do not want to do. It is true that some pastors get carried away with a sense of their office and act as if others owe them obedience because of who they are, but this is an abuse of their authority and not the proper exercise of it. Other pastors take the easy way out and decline all responsibility for the welfare of those in their charge; rather than upset anyone, they prefer to be nice to everybody and end up saying nothing that might cause the slightest offence, or instill in them any desire to change their behaviour. The pastor needs to remember that he has a mandate from God to rebuke and instruct his people. Of course he has to ensure that what he says does not represent his own preferences and prejudices but is a faithful transmission of the word of God. In the end it is to God that he will answer for his commission, because it is from God that he has received it, and it is only with that conviction that he can legitimately go out and proclaim the message that has been entrusted to him.

Finally, Paul told Titus that he was not to allow anyone to ignore him or disregard his message. When he said the same thing to Timothy he mentioned Timothy's youth as a possible reason why others might not respect him, but that does not seem to have been a problem with Titus, who was probably an older man.[48] Even so, there would always have been some people who would refuse to listen to what he had to say. Paul knew that there were people who ignored him, and he was an apostle, so how much more likely would they be to disregard a mere delegate like Titus? It was a long way from a Cretan village to wherever Paul was, and Titus could not easily contact him for instructions about what to do with obstreperous characters. He had to claim his authority on the spot and insist that his message was for everyone. There was no room in the church for those who thought they knew better than the appointed representative of the apostle; anyone who thought like that had to be sent away from the congregation. We are not told whether there were such people in the Cretan churches, and it does not seem that Paul had anyone particular in mind when he wrote this. But he knew enough from his experiences elsewhere to realize that whether this was a current problem for Titus or not, people like that could easily turn up and Titus would have to deal with them in order for his authority to be accepted in the church as a whole. Forewarned is forearmed, and that is what Paul wanted Titus to be.

---

context and rejected both those readings. He has been followed in this by almost all modern translators and commentators.

[48] See 1 Tim. 4.12.

# Titus 3

## 1-3. The character of a Christian

*1. Remind them to be subject to rulers and authorities, to be obedient, to be ready for every good work, 2. to speak evil of no one, to avoid quarrelling, to be gentle, and to show courtesy to everyone. 3. For we ourselves were once foolish, disobedient, led astray, slaves to various passions and pleasures, passing our days in malice and envy, despicable, hating one another.*

In the final chapter of this Epistle, Paul concentrated on the behaviour that he expected from the members of his churches. He gave his reasons for this emphasis and discussed at some length the nature of the change that the coming and work of Christ had brought about. As he saw it, the task now was to make that change a reality in the lives of those who had put their faith in it. He began by giving Titus an extensive checklist of what he wanted each Christian to be like. Then he contrasted this ideal with the state of moral and spiritual bankruptcy that characterizes people in this world and from which believers had been rescued by their conversion. Titus was charged with reminding his congregations of what they should be aiming for, so what he had to say was not new – it was exactly the same as what Paul himself had taught when he had been there in person.

Paul included his pre-Christian self in this exhortation, which is a reminder that the characteristics that he mentioned were general statements about the kind of mental atmosphere and social universe that unbelievers live in and are susceptible to, whether they are personally culpable of these failings or not. His point was not to condemn miscreants but to remind believers that although we have been rescued from the consequences of mankind's rebellion against God, we have nothing to be proud of. We are cut from the same cloth as the rest of humanity and the fact that we have learned through the teaching of the gospel that a better way of life is possible must not let us forget where we have come from or lead us to condemn others, whose blindness to their faults we once shared. The Christian life is not a transformation from sinfulness to perfection but an awakening to the seriousness of sin that must then produce in us a determination to overcome it.

There are seven traits that Paul mentioned as antidotes to seven failings that he censured as the bad habits of the past. It may not be immediately obvious, but there is a definite, if sometimes fairly loose, connection between them as follows:

| What Paul recommended (vv. 1-2) | What Paul censured (v. 3) |
| --- | --- |
| 1. Submission to secular rulers | 1. Foolishness |
| 2. Obedience | 2. Disobedience |
| 3. Readiness for good works | 3. Going astray |
| 4. Speaking evil of no one | 4. Slavery to passions |
| 5. Avoidance of quarrels | 5. Malice and envy |
| 6. Gentleness | 6. Attracting hatred from others |
| 7. Courtesy towards everyone | 7. Showing hatred towards others |

It is hard to see any particular logic in the order of what is mentioned in this list, although in general terms it covers matters dealing with the relationship of church members to the wider community. There is no mention of anything that would be restricted to the inner life of the church – like devoting special times to prayer and fasting, or gathering together on a regular basis or of hearing the word of God preached. The emphasis is not on individual piety or on corporate worship, important though those things undoubtedly were, but on matters that would have a negative effect the church's witness to the outside world. As always in such lists, the first thing mentioned sets the tone for what follows, and so it is somewhat surprising to find that the apostle began with a reminder that believers must submit to the 'ruling authorities' (*archai exousiai*), by which he meant the organs of secular government. This is a theme that he developed elsewhere, notably in Rom. 13.1-7 and in 1 Tim. 2.1-2; it was fundamental to his conception of the relationship between the church and the state. There is no sign in this Epistle that Paul thought that the authorities might one day persecute Christians or that any trouble had arisen between them, which suggests that it was probably written before the great fire of Rome in AD 64. Paul seemed to be more concerned that believers might use the excuse that they were citizens of the kingdom of heaven as a means of avoiding their responsibilities on earth, and he was determined to avoid a situation in which rebellion against the state could be seen as the natural corollary of the coming of Christ's kingdom.¹

In practice, submission to the authorities meant little more than paying taxes, which could sometimes be onerous, and cooperating with the municipal councils in the different cities that were charged with keeping law and order. Since this was in everyone's interest it is unlikely that there would have been serious opposition to Paul's exhortation. Probably most Christians gave little thought to the state and had almost no contact with it most of the time. Crete was not a frontier province, so the presence of the Roman army there would have been minimal, and rebellion against the empire was pointless for an island that was surrounded by it. The church benefitted from a *pax Romana* to which it contributed almost nothing, and Paul believed that Christians ought to acknowledge that by being good citizens and subjects of Rome. Apparently he did not have to consider what Christians should do if the state demanded acquiescence in something that went against their faith, which shows that the official persecution of the church had not yet begun. However, there was no doubt in the mind of Theodoret of Cyrrhus (Cyrus), who commented,

> And since those in power at that time were godless, he [Paul] was obliged to add the distinction, 'to be ready for every good work'; one need not be obedient to the rulers in everything – only pay the tribute and the tax, and accord the due respect, but show public opposition should they give any godless order.²

Martin Luther, speaking just over a millennium later, had a rather different view. Speaking in a context where the church had secured exemption for its clergy froms ecular jurisdiction, he said,

> The magistrate ought to be honoured in order that he may realize that this doctrine [Christianity] is sound. This is a noteworthy passage which

---

¹ We should bear in mind that rebellion against the Romans was frequently urged by radical Jews. This letter was written before the outbreak of the Jewish revolt in AD 66, but that was brewing for some years before it actually happened. Christians left Jerusalem to avoid becoming entangled in the struggle, which destroyed the semi-autonomous Jewish state that had existed under Roman suzerainty for more than a century. Jerome (2010), p. 334, refers to Jewish rebellions associated with false Messiahs, and Calvin (1964), p. 377, said that the Jews 'were for ever rebelling and raging'.
² Theordoret of Cyrrhus (2001), pp. 256-7.

ought to shake up the disobedient clerics so that they are not subject to Christian magistrates in external jurisdiction, even though Paul subjects himself and all Christians to profane magistrates. When they brought it about that they were not subject to the laws of the emperor, a good part of Christian life perished. It is a great accomplishment to know that one is doing something that is pleasing to God, no matter how ordinary it is. Even if the command came from magistrates who are foolish and cruel and I did not obey it, I would be sinning; I would certainly obey it just as if it came from an angel.[3]

On the other hand, Luther subsequently qualified his remarks when commenting on 'being ready for any honest work'. There he said, 'I want you to obey the government, but to the extent that it commands yo to do good things; for it happens that some men administer the government unjustly. A Christian distinguishes between a good and a bad command of a prince'.[4] So in the end, he was closer to Theodoret that he seemed to be at first sight.

The fact that Paul wanted the church to take a position regarding its relationship with the state is significant, because it established the principle that the secular authorities were legitimate powers that were entitled to act within the sphere of competence assigned to them. This mattered, because those authorities saw themselves as sacred and maintained that what they did was part of the worship due to a pagan god or gods. Religion and public life were not separate in the ancient world, and Christians could not submit to the governing bodies that were placed over them if that involved participating in the worship of pagan gods. Part of the fear that non-Christians had of church members was that they would be politically subversive because of this, and it was hard for them to understand the distinction between faith and citizenship that Paul was advocating. This incomprehension would soon lead to persecution, but Christians were told not to bring that on by their own actions. As far as they were concerned, the line between what belonged to Caesar and what belonged to God was clear, and by their obedience to each in his own sphere they were called to demand respect for their approach from the world at large.[5] In Paul's view, the submission of Christians to the authorities was meant to be the prelude to a transformation of the common cultural understanding of who those authorities were and what their power rested on.

---

[3] Luther (1968), p. 71. His twentieth-century German followers would pay a heavy price and lose a good deal of their credibility for following him on this point.
[4] Luther (1968), p. 73.
[5] Mt. 22.21; Mk 12.17; Lk. 20.25.

The next thing that Paul mentioned was obedience, which he expressed in general terms and which we must take to be much the same as the submission to the laws of the state that he had just advocated. If this adds anything to it, it may be that Paul expected the church to demonstrate an active willingness to cooperate with the secular authorities and not just a passive acceptance of what was dictated by them. That interpretation is strengthened by what follows next, which is that Christians should be 'ready for every good work'. In the context Paul's words seem to refer primarily to social projects intended for the good of the community, which might range from ordinary policing to poor relief, road repairs and a number of other similar things that local councils would undertake for the benefit of everyone. The very open-endedness of what Paul was saying makes it possible to extend his command to cover almost any kind of legitimate public work, and he seemed to think that believers ought to play a prominent part in civic activities, even though they were not directly related to the church.

The important thing was that Christians were expected to be *ready* to contribute to the common good. In ancient times public works were usually funded by wealthy individuals, a burden that could bankrupt even the rich, and that discouraged many from playing their proper part in public life. Few Christians would have been men of such means, but in the absence of a single benefactor it was possible for groups of people to work together for the common good. Paul did not say that believers should necessarily take the initiative in this, and if they were not citizens of their local city that would probably have been impossible in any case. But he did think that they should be prepared to pitch in and help when the opportunity arose. Christians were to gain the reputation of givers rather than takers, of people who were an asset to society and not a drain on its resources. In this sense, a readiness to take part in good works was an important means of gaining and retaining a good reputation in the unbelieving world. We can perhaps compare his approach to that of the Salvation Army today, where evangelism and social work go hand in hand. Salvationists may be regarded as somewhat peculiar in the way they behave, but they are widely respected and supported even by people who have no understanding of the gospel they proclaim. That seems to have been what Paul wanted his churches to be like.

Moving on from the relations that church members ought to develop with the wider community, Paul turned to consider the behaviour that they should exhibit to individual members of it in their everyday encounters and transactions. First of all, they were to 'speak evil of no one'. The word he used here is *blasphēmein*, which gives us some idea of what he had in mind. The reputation of others and the honour due to them was to be respected, because even if they were not Christians, they were still humans who had been created in the image and likeness of God. Christians were to regard other people as spiritual beings and treat them accordingly, whether they agreed with them or not. It is easy to turn against unpopular people, and especially in a village culture, there are occasionally incidents in which the entire community does this.[6] Individuals who do not fit in for one reason or another can be stigmatized and expelled, as of course can rich landlords who are accused of extortion and prominent people who have fallen out with the authorities and perhaps been deprived of public office as a result. Christians were not to join in such madness but to refuse to say anything about others that might prove harmful to them.

Instead of that, Christians were to set an example to others by their positive behaviour towards them. To start off with, they were to be 'unquarrelsome' (*amachoi*), a word that is easy to understand but hard to translate. They were not meant to go around picking fights with others, causing trouble for no reason and using petty excuses in order to disrupt the peace. Most societies have people like that and have to find ways of dealing with them. It is well known, for example, that many lawsuits are initiated by a small number of litigious people and that a disproportionate number of complaints to various authorities come from a few self-appointed watchdogs who have an axe to grind. In ancient times there were fewer intermediaries between the citizen and the state that could intercept and deal with them, and troublemakers were more likely to resort to direct action. It was only too easy for one provocation to lead to another, but Christians were told to stay out of such things as much as they could.[7]

Rather than stir up trouble, Christians were called to be peacemakers by being considerate (*epieikeis*) of others and showing complete 'courtesy' (*praÿtēs*) towards everyone. They were called to become known for this approach, so that others would see that this was the fairest and most efficient way of resolving problems without harming the social fabric in the process. The word *praÿtēs* means 'meekness', a term that is seldom used nowadays but that suggests a calm, cool and collected approach to the difficulties of social interaction. Christians are not to charge into public affairs demanding their own rights but to stand back from the debates going on and think about the common good. In this way they would make a contribution to the welfare of

---

[6] This happened, for example, when Jesus went to preach in Nazareth and told people there who he was and what he had come to do. They chased him out! See Lk. 4.16-30.

[7] It was not always possible for them to avoid trouble, however. One notable incident was what occurred in Ephesus, where Paul's preaching provoked a riot (Acts 19.21-41), and similar incidents occurred in other places as well.

society as a whole and commend the gospel which they proclaimed and to whose principles they adhered.

Paul's motive for being so accommodating towards the secular authorities of his time must be understood in the context of mission, which to him was all-important. The freedom to preach the gospel without hindrance was uppermost in his mind, and as long as he could secure that without religious compromise he was prepared to accept the established order of his time. Nevertheless, it is probable that he had a deeper, more long-term aim in view. As P. H. Towner puts it,

> we may rule out the thought that respectability or public image was held to be an end in itself. While the fuller church-in-world theology detectable in Romans is perhaps only anticipated here ... the fact that this text is set into a missiological bracket and so, thoroughly grounded in eschatological realities, suggests that the church's subjection to the state, worked out in public Christian service, has the redemption of creation as its goal, not simply peaceful co-existence with the secular power structure.[8]

Having given a fairly extensive list of the things that he wanted to see, Paul then went on to remind the church's members of where they had come from. The problems which he expected them to grapple with as believers were common to the world of unbelief, and those who had turned to Christ ought to recognize that they too had once been enslaved to them. That awareness should keep them humble and give them some sense of compassion for those with whom they were dealing. A superior attitude towards others was the last thing that Christians needed to exhibit, not only because it was unjustified but also because it could do nothing to cure the difficulties that they had identified in the behaviour of others and that they wanted to tackle.

The first of the problems of the ungodly was that they were 'foolish' (*anoētoi*) as we believers also were before we heard and accepted the word of God. Yet again, we are faced here with a Greek term that cannot be easily translated. The man who is *anoētos* is someone who is not in his right mind (*nous*), not because he is insane but because he is not being guided by the right principles. The human mind is structured according to the purpose and plan of God, and if it is functioning as it should, it will reflect his will and his law for the created order. But sinful human beings have rejected this and

---

[8] Towner (2006), pp. 771–2. His suggestion that Romans, written about AD 57, contains a more developed version of this way of thinking supports the view put forward here that this Epistle was written a year or so before that.

become 'foolish', wanting to establish their own laws and ignoring what God has decreed. The state authorities exist partly in order to correct this error and to make it possible for people to go on living in the world even though they are no longer in tune with it. This is why secular rulers are agents of God, rewarding those who do good and punishing those who do not, even when the said rulers do not acknowledge the source of their authority. The *anoētos* will often refuse to submit to them because he has already rebelled against God in his heart. The idea that the state is the enemy, that the law is to be ignored and that taxes are to be avoided if at all possible is a common one among the *anoētoi*, and it is destructive of human life and the social order. We do not have to go back to the days of the Roman Empire to see this; it is a widespread phenomenon in the world today and virtually the norm in many countries, especially in those that have recently experienced corrupt or tyrannical regimes.

This 'foolishness' of the ungodly is the root of the problem that has produced disobedience, which is the second thing that Paul mentions in his list of bad habits that the believer has been delivered from. A corrupt way of thinking naturally leads to rebellious behaviour, which is what Paul was censuring here. Once that starts we are soon led astray (*planōmenoi*) because the markers that set us on the right path have been removed. Far from being ready for every good work, as we ought to be, we are instead left to wander off to no good purpose and to waste our intellect and resources on false pursuits. This is the tragedy of the fallen human race. Adam and Eve did not become lesser beings when they sinned against God; they retained all the capacities that he had given them at their creation. What they lost was their sense of purpose and direction, with the result that their many gifts were either misused or rendered null and void. Instead of being a help and support to the unfolding of God's plan they became a menace because of the virtual certainty that their great gifts would be developed and used in the wrong way.

The practical effect of this of course is that fallen human beings are enslaved to 'various desires and pleasures' (*epithymiai kai hēdonai poikilai*), physical and emotional impulses that have no direction and are out of control. Those who are in this condition are all too likely to speak evil of others, particularly of those who stand in the way of their own enjoyment or advancement. Putting the self first is the most assured way of thinking badly of other people, because sooner or later they are bound to become a nuisance and a hindrance to us. Those who are enslaved to their own desires do not care about the harm they may be doing to the wider community, as long as they get what they want for themselves. Christians are called to discern this evil in the world, to recognize that they too were once subject to it, and to avoid it at all costs.

Those who are wrapped up in their own desires are especially prone to 'malice' (*kakia*) and 'envy' (*phthonos*) in their relationships with others. The former results from a suspicion that somebody else has what I want and has probably acquired it by underhanded means. The ultimate object of course is to surpass them or, if that is not possible, to deprive them of enjoying their ill-gotten gains. If rumours can be spread about how they obtained what they have, their reputations may suffer and, in extreme cases, they may find it easier to divest themselves of their targeted asset rather than see their fortunes sink any further. Any opportunity to do them down in some way will be seized upon in a spirit of envy, which is the very opposite of the mentality that seeks to build peaceful and cooperative relationships. Selfishness is always harmful to a community and we must not be surprised to see it doing its destructive work wherever it can.

The last two characteristics of the unbeliever that are at work in wider society are complementary. On the one hand, those who are only interested in furthering their own interests make themselves 'abominable' (*stygētoi*) and hate each other. Hate, rather than love, is the force that governs their lives and is the exact opposite of what is expected of Christians. Paul did not tell church members to love those outside the fold, but he did advise believers to be considerate and kind towards them, which amounts to the same thing. The gospel message is that we should learn to love our enemies and do good to those who hate us, not repay them in kind.[9] Here Paul emphasized that believers know what it is like to be far away from God, because they have been in that position themselves. This should give them not only a deeper sympathy for those who had not yet seen the light but also a stronger desire to see them turn to Christ.

There are two ways in which we may be hated by others that must be carefully distinguished from each other. First of all, there is the hatred that believers suffer because of their faithfulness to the teachings of Christ. Jesus was hated by those who discovered that their shallow piety was upstaged by his more penetrating demands on them and who responded in the only way they knew. This kind of hatred will come to believers from the outside world, and it is to be expected. Christians are seldom guilty of provoking this, although there is no cause for any believer to respond to it in kind. The other kind of hatred is the one Paul is referring to here. This is the reaction that

---

[9] Lk. 6.27.

people bring on themselves by their behaviour. A selfish and inconsiderate person will soon be spotted as such and detested, even by people who do much the same thing themselves. Those who behave like that will generally be avoided and isolated from the rest of the community because people do not want to have to deal with them. They will be treated like lepers because they demand everything from society but give nothing in return.

Unfortunately, in a world governed by self-interest, people who make themselves abominable by their excesses are unlikely to be cured of their problem, because even those who see what is wrong are to some degree infected with the same disease. Quite literally, as Paul states, they 'hate one another' (*misountes allēlous*). When there are only so many resources to go around, competition can become fierce and the willingness to give way to the needs and interests of others declines proportionately. There are many examples of how people who have been put under terrible pressure lose their civilized veneer of politeness and deference and resort to an 'every man for himself' approach. We may even end up using the language of justice and fairness to all in order to condemn those who we feel have received an undue advantage and begrudge the success of others, especially if we are convinced it was obtained by some kind of fraud.

The picture that Paul painted of this kind of behaviour is not a pretty one, but he did it in order to press home to us just how wicked the human heart is. Those who have been saved by grace ought to understand this better than others because as God's light reaches further into the depths of our souls, the true extent of the corruption that lies in us is exposed in ways that unbelievers never perceive. The more we realize this, the more we shall turn away from it and take refuge in the mercy of the God who has saved us from its consequences. The closer a Christian draws to his Saviour, the more the horror of evil becomes both apparent and repugnant, and the more distasteful it is, the more we are likely to avoid it.

## 4-8. The nature and effect of the gospel

*4. But when the goodness and lovingkindness of God our Saviour appeared, 5. he saved us, not because of any works of righteousness that we had done, but according to his mercy, through the water of rebirth and renewal by the Holy Spirit. 6. The Spirit he poured out on us richly through Jesus Christ our Saviour, 7. so that, having been justified by his grace, we might become heirs according to the hope of eternal life. 8. The saying is sure. I desire that you insist on these things, so that those who have come to believe in*

*God may be careful to devote themselves to good works; these things are excellent and profitable to everyone.*

As he often did, Paul moved immediately from a description of the depths of human depravity to its exact opposite. For him, convicting people of their sin was only the prelude to announcing the grace and mercy of God who has come to take it away from us and to give us a new life in Christ. Paul never left his hearers in despair but always provoked them to have hope and to do good works by reminding them of the seriousness of their own sins and encouraging them to see the wonder and the grandeur of their salvation in Christ. Verses 4-7 constitute a kind of refrain that may have been memorized by church members as a reminder to them of what their salvation meant. It is one of the most concise and carefully structured presentations of the gospel to be found anywhere in the New Testament, and it develops further the thought already expressed in 2.13-14. The overall pattern may be sketched out as follows:

1. The goodness and love of God our Saviour have appeared
2. Not because of our works, but because of his grace
3. He saved us

   - by the washing of the new birth
   - by the renewal of the Holy Spirit
   - whom he poured out richly on us
   - through Jesus Christ our Saviour

4. We have been made righteous by that grace
5. We have become heirs according to the hope of eternal life

Paul's main focus in this section was quite clearly on the work of salvation that had been brought about by our Saviour according to the detailed analysis outlined in point 3 above. Before he got to that, he talked about the spiritual preparation for salvation and the conditions under which it has been given. After that, he went on to talk about its consequences – the benefits that have come to us as a result of what Christ has done on our behalf.

To begin at the beginning, Paul saw the work of salvation as ultimately dependent on the character of God. He did not speak in this instance of a divine plan, though he certainly thought that there was one, but located the source of God's work in his 'goodness and lovingkindness' (*chrēstotēs kai philanthrōpia*).[10] As usual in such cases, the translation hardly does justice to the meaning. In classical Greek this concept had referred primarily to the usefulness or serviceability of something – a good sword, for example, or a good plough was so called because it performed the task for which it was designed and did so in the most efficient manner. Used of human beings, it came to refer to someone who acted in a way that was consonant with his gifts and character. A man could be physically and morally 'good' (*kalos k'agathos*) in an objective sense, someone to be admired from a distance, but that did not necessarily mean that he would be of any practical use in everyday affairs or use his qualities for the common good. For that he had to be honest in his dealings, brave in battle and merciful in dealing with his enemies. In other words, *chrēstotēs* was not an abstract quality but something that revealed itself in practical activity.

In the case of God, this was really the only kind of 'goodness' that mattered as far as human beings were concerned. God was obviously good in himself, since he defined what goodness was in others, but as his nature is unknowable this made very little difference in practice. If anything, it was merged into the concept of holiness, a term that stressed the distance between God and his creation and the unattainability of his character. But the Christian claim is that God's goodness is something that he has revealed to us and that has been manifested in what he has done on our behalf. It has appeared not as an abstract quality but in a series of acts that demonstrates not only what he is like but also what difference he makes in our lives. Paul had already spoken about the 'saving grace' (*charis sōtērios*) of God and now he explained what that means in practical terms. God's grace is *chrēstē*, because it reveals how good and kind he is in the way that he approaches his people. To experience his grace is to understand his divine nature, not in itself (since that is hidden from our eyes) but in its redeeming effects on us.

The New Testament writers did not have a developed vocabulary of personal relationship in the way that we have today, but this is essentially what the apostle was saying to the church here. In a strictly objective sense, it might be possible to imagine God saving us without our knowledge. He could presumably have destroyed Satan while we slept and whisked us off to heaven before we knew what had happened to us. His sovereign power would have guaranteed the efficacy of such an action and we would have played no part in it. But God has chosen to deal with us in the context of a

---

[10] John Calvin (1964), p. 380, seems to have misunderstood Paul's intention here, because he felt he had to explain that the goodness and lovingkindness of God had been experienced by the Israelites before the coming of Christ as well as afterwards. Paul was not denying that, of course, but the question is irrelevant to his discussion.

relationship that he has revealed to us, explained to us within the limits of our understanding and expected us to accept, so that we might reign alongside him in his kingdom. We are not mute objects of his affection but participants in the outworking of his glorious plan, which he has revealed to us in Christ. This is what his *chrēstotēs*, or practical kindness, entails.

In addition to this there is his *philanthrōpia*, or 'love of humanity', which explains the context in which his kindness operates. God could have chosen to save the world; presumably he could also have chosen to save Satan and the fallen angels if he had desired to do so. But the particular wonder of his saving grace is that it arose out of his love for the human race, the people whom he had created in his own image and likeness and whom he continued to cherish even after their disobedience and fall. God's innate kindness is perhaps fairly easy to understand as a natural offshoot of his inner nature, but his love of humanity in particular is harder to grasp. Why would God have gone out of his way to save creatures who had shown no regard for him or his laws? Why would he have gone to the extent of sending his own Son to identify himself with us, taken our sins upon himself and died for our redemption? This is the mystery of the gospel and the true grandeur of the divine love. We have nothing to offer him that he does not already have. In order to make us what he wants us to be, he has to put himself out in a way that is entirely voluntary and brings no obvious benefit to him. We have no claim on his goodness, but he has loved us and in the end that is all that matters.

John Calvin made an important distinction between the incarnation of Christ and the revelation of the gospel, in which the goodness and lovingkindness of God was revealed. As he put it,

> At Christ's first coming Paul was not renewed, for although Christ was raised in glory and salvation in his name had shone upon many not only in Judaea but in neighbouring lands, Paul, blinded by unbelief, was still labouring to extinguish this grace by every means in his power. His meaning is therefore that God's grace appeared to himself and to others when they were enlightened in the knowledge of the gospel.[11]

What was true of the apostle's personal journey of faith is true more widely also. The incarnation was the necessary preliminary to the atonement and resurrection, but it was the latter, buttressed by the subsequent ascension and descent of the Holy Spirit, that reveals the saving grace of God and makes the proclamation of the gospel possible.

---

[11] Calvin (1964), p. 380.

Paul rammed this message home in the qualifications that he put on the action of the goodness and lovingkindness of God. Translations often obscure the sentence order because they tend to insert the main verb at this point rather than follow the rhetorical development of the Greek, which admittedly sounds somewhat awkward when it is translated literally. Nevertheless, it is important to get the order right because it is part of the logical build-up to the crescendo which the main verb represents. Before anything else, Paul insisted that it was not because of works done by us in righteousness that God has shown his saving grace towards us. We have not been rewarded for our good deeds, which do not count in his eyes.

Paul did not deny that human beings can do what is good and right in the sight of God. It is not clear what he meant by the term 'righteousness' (*dikaiosynē*) in this context, but it could be something akin to 'in good faith' or 'with the right attitude'. There is no suggestion that he meant 'self-righteousness', that is to say, a mistaken belief in the essential goodness of the actions in question, though that unlikely possibility cannot be totally excluded. What can be said for certain is that it does not matter either way, because in whatever spirit our works are done, they do not influence the operation of God's saving grace. That may sound unfair to some people, but in fact it is a great blessing. First of all, even the most diligent and innocent of human high-achievers could not begin to cross the abyss that sin has created between us and God. The scale on which our good works are evaluated is totally different from the one that has been established by God and there is no common measure between them.

Secondly, even if there were some way in which our works could be calculated in line with the divine plan, there would be differences of degree between them and therefore different kinds of salvation on offer. It would then become possible to measure the grace of God on a scale of success, an exercise that would create a works-righteousness culture that placed more emphasis on the value of our work and less on the miraculous nature of the reward that we would receive, since the extent of that would in some sense depend on our achievements.

Instead of this, our salvation is the fruit of the mercy (*eleos*) of God himself. It is because he has decided to reach out to us that we receive his benefits. This mercy is in no way a response to any activity or prayer on our part but stems entirely from the love of God, which is why Paul described it as 'his own mercy'. In revealing this to us God was revealing himself and establishing the relationship with us which is the basis of everything that he does in our lives. His mercy is the practical outworking of his 'goodness' (*chrēstotēs*) and his love of humanity (*philanthrōpia*), and it is in this form that these divine qualities are revealed to, and experienced by, those who have put their trust in him.

Having laid the groundwork, Paul now reached the climax of his exposition. 'He saved us.' From beginning to end, salvation is a work of God, prepared by his grace, applied by his mercy and worked out by what follows. Most important, it is a true deliverance from the power of sin and evil. God has not merely reprieved us. He has not forgiven us for the sins that we have committed in the past but with no guarantee that he will do the same in the future. Salvation is not a process that began with the coming of Christ into the world and that remains to be progressively worked out over time. Instead, it is a once-for-all event, a single action revealed by the death and resurrection of Jesus, that is valid for all times, places and people. Those who have received it have received a new life, and that cannot be withdrawn – once saved, always saved. There can be no greater blessing than this.

The first step in this work of salvation is what Paul calls 'the washing of regeneration' (*loutron palingenesias*), an intriguing term that suggests many things without clearly indicating a preference for any one of them. First of all, it suggests that the passage from a life in sin to the saving grace of Christ is a kind of cleansing, something that Paul had already hinted at in 2.14. Sin is compared to dirt on the body, though of course it is a spiritual thing and cannot be reduced to something so crudely material as that. However, in the Jewish temple rituals there were many ceremonial washings, and our minds turn naturally to baptism, which is associated with the regeneration brought about by Christ.[12] There must certainly be an allusion to that here, but the interesting thing is that baptism is not specifically mentioned in the text, which is odd if it was the means by which rebirth and renewal would occur.[13]

The answer to this must be that just as sin is not to be reduced to physical dirt, so its removal cannot be achieved by physical cleansing in baptism. Baptism may be used to symbolize the washing away of sin, of course, but the rite must not be confused with the reality that it represents. Rebirth, or regeneration, is a spiritual experience that can only be had by spiritual means. Furthermore, as the sentence is constructed, it is the spiritual rebirth that does the cleansing, not the cleansing that produces the rebirth. If it were that, then our salvation would be a work done in our righteousness and not a gift of God. We would be able to claim a human act as evidence that a spiritual transformation has taken place, an understanding of the relationship

---

[12] Rom. 6.3-4.
[13] See Marshall (2004), pp. 317–18, who insists that baptism is neither mentioned nor implied in this text.

between matter and spirit that is of the very essence of idolatry. John Calvin struck the right balance here. He allowed that baptism was alluded to in the text but was careful to distinguish the physical rite from the work of God:

> The power and use of the sacraments are rightly understood, when we connect sign and thing signified in such a way that the sign is not made vain and unefficacious, and when we do not for the sake of exalting the sign take from the Holy Spirit what belongs to him. Although ungodly men are neither washed nor renewed by baptism, yet it retains its efficacy as far as God is concerned, for although they reject God's grace, it is still offered to them. But here Paul is addressing believers in whom baptism is always efficacious and is therefore rightly spoken of in connection with its reality and effect. By this way of speaking we are reminded that if we do not wish to make holy baptism null and void, we must prove its power by newness of life.[14]

The true meaning of this verse is spelled out by what follows. The washing of regeneration is the same as 'the renewal of the Holy Spirit' (*anakainōsis Pneumatos Hagiou*). There are some who would claim that the presence and work of the Holy Spirit invariably accompany the right administration of baptism, but that is a misunderstanding of the way God works. What Paul was saying here recalls nothing so much as the conversation between Jesus and Nicodemus recorded in John 3. Jesus told Nicodemus that he must be born again of water and the Spirit, and that the Spirit blows where he wills.[15] The water represents the cleansing and the Spirit stands for the new life, but although the two things are closely connected they are nevertheless distinct. Jesus did not offer to baptize Nicodemus on the spot for the simple reason that that was not what was required at that point. Before he could be baptized, Nicodemus had to open his heart and mind in order to understand how the Holy Spirit works in the lives of those whom he has chosen. If he could get that far, then the Spirit could have come into his life and done what is necessary. Baptism would then follow as the sign and seal of the Spirit's work in his heart.[16] If the Spirit was not present, all the water in the world would have made no difference to his spiritual state. As I. H. Marshall puts it,

---

[14] Calvin (1964), pp. 382–3.
[15] Jn 3.8.
[16] This was the normal pattern for an adult convert, which Nicodemus would have been. The children of believers could be baptized because the promise was made to them as well (1 Cor. 7.14). They were no longer unclean but holy, though the rite of water baptism was no guarantee that they would make a personal profession of faith as adults.

while the rite of baptism might celebrate, illustrate or commemorate the work of the Spirit and therefore be immediately called to mind or alluded to by such a statement ... this is not a proof text for baptismal regeneration and sacramental salvation.[17]

This is exactly what Paul was saying here, as can be seen from the way in which his argument proceeds. It is not the water of baptism that is poured out on the believer (though the image is preserved) but the Holy Spirit himself. Obviously the Holy Spirit cannot be reduced to water (or to any other material substance) and the metaphor must be respected for what it is. Paul did say that the outpouring is 'rich' (*plousiōs*, the adverb), a description that is open to differing interpretations. Is it 'rich' in quantity or in quality, or in both? The Spirit cannot be quantified nor does he vary in quality, so the adverb can hardly be applied to him. The richness of the outpouring is rather a question of the degree to which we participate in him, and through him in Christ, and that is an indication of the measure of our faith, not of the Spirit's power.[18]

On the other hand, it is probably fair to say that Paul was not here referring directly to the gift of the Spirit. Elsewhere he talked about receiving the gifts of the Holy Spirit, and he urged Christians to seek the higher ones, evidently on the assumption that a greater outpouring of the Spirit is both possible and desirable.[19] Most probably the distinction that we make between quantity and quality is irrelevant to this. It may be possible to speak endlessly in tongues (quantity) but unless there is a use for that (quality), it is pointless to do so and Paul told the Corinthian church that those who had that gift must learn when to *stop* using it![20] He clearly preferred the gifts that had a deeper quality about them because they would be of use for the edification of the church. But he knew that the highest gift of all, the apostleship, was not

---

[17] Marshall (2004), p. 322. Martin Luther (1968), pp. 81–2, had an odd take on this. He believed that these verses were all about baptism, but while he agreed that the outward rite had no saving power in itself, he was convinced that 'in baptism there is not holy mere water, because there is present here the name, or all the divine power joined through the Word in baptism, and God himself is the one who baptizes ... Baptism bears the Word of God by which the water is sanctified, and we are sanctified in the water'. He compared this with the incarnation of Christ: 'If the humanity of Christ were without the Word, it would be a vain thing. But now we are saved through his blood and his body, because the Word is joined to it.' Luther did not appreciate that there is a world of difference between the unique incarnation of Christ and the repeated acts of baptism (or the Lord's Supper) which could not claim the same divine presence in them.

[18] See Towner (2006), pp. 782–6, who discusses this in detail and comes to the conclusion accepted here.

[19] 1 Cor. 12.28-31.

[20] 1 Cor. 14.26-33.

open to church members who had not seen the risen Christ, and so there was a natural restriction placed on it that in time would lead to its disappearance as a living ministry in the church.

What is clear is that Paul believed that the Holy Spirit has been poured out richly on all believers, whatever gifts particular individuals may have received. There is no distinction among us because we are all one in Christ Jesus. As he outlined it here according to the familiar triadic pattern, the outpouring of the Holy Spirit is the following:

1. The gift of God our Saviour through Jesus Christ our Saviour.
2. The evidence that we have been justified by grace.
3. The promise of adoption leading to eternal life.

The inner relationship of the persons of the Trinity is expressed here more clearly than perhaps anywhere else in the New Testament. The Holy Spirit is the gift of God our Saviour. Paul did not include the word 'Father' here but the context is such that it is impossible to understand it in any other way. Both 'God' and Jesus Christ are called 'our Saviour', which underlies their essential unity, but they are also distinguished from one another, because 'God' sends the Spirit *through* Christ. The sender must therefore be someone else, and logic forces us to conclude that this can only be the Father. W. D. Mounce sums it up beautifully:

> God's goodness and love through his mercy have brought salvation, which consists of a cleansing and an empowering by the Holy Spirit, who is given through Jesus Christ. As a result, having been justified by God's grace, believers now have an inheritance, a hope, which is eternal life. Throughout the process there is a threefold presentation of the Godhead, God the Father initiating the process, made possible through the work of the Son and actuated by the Holy Spirit.[21]

What we see here is an explanation of the way in which God reaches out to us and reveals himself in three ways simultaneously, but it was an explanation that was in need of an adequate theological terminology to describe it. Paul could refer to God without qualification and be understood to mean the Father because nobody has raised the question of how Christ could also be called God. Later on there would be those who would say that a verse like this proves that Jesus cannot be divine, and when that happened the church had

---

[21] Mounce (2000), p. 455.

to tighten up its terminology. The idea that Paul might have thought along similar lines is excluded by the way in which he applies the term 'Saviour' to both Father and Son indiscriminately and (in this case) side by side. If we ask who our Saviour is – God or Jesus – it immediately becomes clear that there is no real distinction between them. They have undertaken a common work which effectively underlines the divinity of the Son, alongside that of the Father.

The theological question at stake here can be explained like this. There is no theoretical difficulty with the idea that God should be our Saviour, since no creature is capable of doing the work that salvation requires. But if God is above and beyond his creation, it is hard to see how he can connect with it. What was required was the payment of the price for human sin, and God in his transcendent glory could not have done that. Somehow he had to become a man, take on sin and put it to death, all without ceasing to be himself. This apparently impossible task was accomplished by Jesus Christ, whom it would have been blasphemous to call 'our Saviour' if he were not also God, and yet there is only one God. It is to explain this apparent paradox that the doctrine of the Trinity was developed.

It is a Trinity of three persons and not a binity of two because of the outpouring of the Holy Spirit. The effects of the saving work of God and Christ are felt only when the Spirit comes into the heart of a believer, but if they are to be a genuine experience of the divine presence the Spirit must also be God. What Paul said here is outlined in much greater detail in John 14, but the inner dynamic of their relationship and the need for all three persons of the Godhead to act together is obvious. Without that, there would be no real salvation because neither the plan nor the work of the Saviour could be effectively applied to those who were supposed to be saved.

In the light of historical theology it is interesting to note that Paul stated that God (the Father) poured out the Holy Spirit *through* Jesus Christ. This is relevant to a controversy over the so-called 'double procession' of the Holy Spirit which originates from the interpretation of Jn 15.26, where Jesus told his disciples that he would send them the Spirit 'who proceeds from the Father'. The question then becomes, what is the relationship between the Son and the Holy Spirit? Since the time of Augustine (354–430), the Western (Latin) church has asserted that the Holy Spirit proceeds from the Father and from the Son on the grounds that he must do so if the Father and the Son are equal in every respect. This conclusion has been resisted by the Eastern churches, which have claimed that the Father alone is the 'source' (*pēgē*) of divinity. They have never pronounced on the precise nature of the relationship between the Son and the Spirit, but one possible explanation of this is that the Holy Spirit proceeds from the Father through the Son, and at different times that has been suggested as a possible solution to the problem. The words of Paul here would certainly seem to support such a conclusion, though Paul is speaking only of the mission of the Spirit in the world and not of his eternal relationship to the other persons in the Godhead.[22]

What is certain is that the Holy Spirit can be known and experienced only in and through Jesus Christ. Whether Christ is the source of the Spirit alongside the Father or not, he is certainly the only channel through whom the Spirit has been given to the world. The implications of this are several. First of all, as Jesus told his disciples, no one can come to the Father except through him.[23] The Holy Spirit does not bear witness to anyone else. Secondly, there can be no genuine experience of the Spirit that is not focused on Christ. To receive a supernatural gift, like that of prophecy, for example, that does not glorify Christ is to receive something that has not come from the Holy Spirit of God. We are warned in the New Testament that there are other spirits at work in the world and that we must be on our guard against them.[24] Finally, and this is the point that Paul went on to develop in this Epistle, there is no work of the Spirit that goes beyond what Christ has already accomplished. It is the Spirit's task to secure that work in our hearts and to allow us to enjoy it to the full, not to add something new to it.

In v. 7 Paul explained that we have been justified by the grace of Jesus Christ, an act which we are meant to understand took place before the outpouring of the Spirit.[25] He did not discuss the question as to whether this justification can be connected directly to the election of the saved in eternity, but whether it can or not, it is certainly tied to the atoning death of Christ. By paying the price for our sins, Jesus has made it possible for us to stand in the presence of God the Father, clothed not in our own righteousness but in his. Whatever good there may be in the things that we do, it is swept aside by the overwhelming power of God's grace at work in the sacrifice of the Christ

---

[22] This has to be stated because the longstanding disagreement between the Eastern (Greek) and the Western (Latin) churches over the procession of the Holy Spirit makes this distinction. Both churches agree that the Holy Spirit proceeds from the Father *through* the Son, but the Western churches insist that this means that he proceeds from both, a conclusion that the Eastern churches reject.

[23] Jn 14.6.

[24] 1 Jn 4.1.

[25] Many commentators have argued that the meaning of justification here is different from what appears in Romans, making it probable that Titus is pseudepigraphal and that the author had misunderstood the apostle. Much of the argument hinges on the fact that this text does not mention 'by faith', though how this differs from 'the grace of Christ' is hard to tell. After all, as Paul said in Eph. 2.8, we have been saved by grace through faith! For a discussion of these arguments and a refutation of them, see Marshall (2004), pp. 323–5.

who took our place on the cross. Our standing before God is therefore not the result of any achievement on our part but is entirely due to his grace.

The outpouring of the Holy Spirit is the natural outcome of that penal substitution on our behalf. Having justified us by the sacrifice of Christ, God the Father sends his Spirit so that we may become 'heirs' (*klēronomoi*). This concept of inheritance is one that is found throughout the New Testament and especially in the writings of Paul. It is a way of expressing how we can legitimately claim possession of something that does not properly belong to us and that we have done nothing to earn. Inheritance presupposes a relationship that Paul assumed without stating it explicitly. This is that we have become children, or more specifically 'sons' (*hyioi*) of God by being adopted in and through the Spirit. What Christ the Son is by nature we have become by grace, and it is that standing, given to us by the indwelling presence of the Holy Spirit, that allows us to be 'heirs'.[26]

Inheritance also allows for the possibility that we have a standing before God that has not yet been fully realized. In human life there are often conditions placed on inheritance. Normally it cannot be claimed until the one who has given it has died, though sometimes there are additional stipulations as well, such as that the heir must have attained a certain age. In the case of our spiritual inheritance, the death of the testator Jesus Christ has made it possible for us to claim it in one sense, but in another sense it remains something that we have not yet fully received. It is in this second sense that Paul used the term here, because as he put it, our inheritance is 'according to the hope of eternal life'.

At this point we have reached the key to the interpretation of the Christian life, and therefore also of most of this epistle, which deals with different aspects of that subject. The new life that we have received in Christ is spiritual and eternal, but it is obvious not only that we have not yet died and gone to heaven. The life we are now living in the flesh is not one that will continue in its present form for ever, but at the same time there is a real link between what we are and do now and what we shall be and do in heaven. I am expected to live on earth with the perspective of someone who belongs in heaven, even though I have not been there yet. That does not mean trying to bring heaven down to earth, as was the case, for example, when the medieval Western church imposed celibacy on its clergy, claiming as its justification that that is how the angels live in heaven and so the institutional church on earth ought to model that. But neither does it mean ignoring the parameters of a dimension of experience that is not bound by the time and

---

[26] Rom. 8.15-17; Gal. 4.6.

space creation. How we apply the principles derived from eternity in the circumstances thrown up by time is the fundamental challenge that we face, and it is this that constitutes the essence of the Christian life.

One element of it that is easily forgotten but gives it a meaningful purpose is the sense of hope (*elpis*) which undergirds it. Hope is the conviction that whatever happens to us in the present, the future will be better. The sufferings we endure now will bear fruit in ways that we cannot yet imagine. Christians must be focused on the future, which will culminate in the appearing of Christ at the end of time, and we must govern our lives accordingly. To most of Paul's hearers that must have come as quite a surprise. The ancient world was heavily focused on the past, on the preservation of the values of the ancestors who represented the golden age before things started to go wrong. Many people lived only for the present – eat, drink and be merry, for tomorrow we die. The future was the great unknown and many people dreaded it. In human terms it could only lead to old age and the loss of our physical powers. What lay beyond the grave was a mystery, though different theories about it proliferated.

It was into this world of doubt and uncertainty that the Christians came preaching a message of hope. It was worth working for the future because the future would merge into eternity as we pass from this life to the next. That is the hope of the Christian and the ultimate justification for the lives that we are called to live here on earth as we wait for the promise to be fulfilled.

Paul made this point in his concluding remarks in v. 8. First of all, he told Titus that the history of salvation that he has just rehearsed can be relied on – it is the truth. That is why Titus must continue to insist on the principles that Paul has laid down, because unless people understand what the big picture is they will not be able to focus their own lives within it. In particular, it is essential that those who have professed faith in God should concentrate on doing good works. Good works are not the justification for our salvation but they are the inevitable result of it. A Christian who does not manifest his faith in his behaviour towards others is living a lie and betraying the beliefs that he claims to uphold. This pattern is intrinsic to the gospel message. Jesus told his disciples to love God first and then to love their neighbours as themselves.[27] James wrote that faith without works is dead.[28] There has been a persistent tendency in some circles to claim that Paul's aversion to 'works righteousness' stands in contradiction to this, but of course it does not. It is not good works that Paul condemned, but reliance on them as giving those who perform them some claim to deserve salvation as their reward.

---

[27] Mt. 22.37-40.
[28] Jas 2.26.

On the contrary, Christians are obliged to demonstrate the meaning of the salvation we have already received by acting in a way that is consonant with the life and character of God. Paul did not define what he meant by 'good works' though a similar reminder in v. 14 suggests that their primary focus ought to be to help people in need. Deciding what that need was could be left to circumstances and the judgment of the church. We almost automatically think in terms of poor relief, and that was probably part of it, but there could have been any number of things that would qualify under such a heading. For example, people would be expected to rally round if someone's house were burnt down, a not unknown phenomenon in ancient times. They might also be called to help in times of sickness, and to offer hospitality to strangers.

The only explanation we are given is that the works concerned are good in themselves and therefore worth doing for their own sake, but at the same time they are also 'helpful' (*ōphelima*) to other people. Paul did not say whether works are helpful even if the recipients do not appreciate them, or whether it is the helpfulness of the deeds that makes them 'good', but we can probably assume that common sense would have prevailed most of the time. The purpose of the good works Christians were called to do was to commend the gospel, and that would hardly have been the result if they were performed against the will of those receiving them.

As always in such matters, context and relationships must have counted for a good deal in the way the principles enunciated here were worked out in practice. What is more striking, given the context, is that although these works were meant to commend the church and its teachings to others, there is no hint that they were intended to serve a proselytizing or evangelistic purpose. Perhaps there would be people who would turn to Christ because of the behaviour which they observed in his followers, but Christians were not expected to do good works with that aim in view. Their good deeds were not a means to an end, a kind of bait to trap the fish (as it were) but an end in themselves. For that reason they were to be offered to everyone, because everyone could and should reap the benefits they would bring. Believers were naturally expected to take care of their own, but they were not to restrict their caring to those to whom they had a special obligation. In all things they were to remember that they were working primarily for God and in order to please him, and with that perspective in view, the rest would take care of itself.

## 9-11. The divisive person

*9. But avoid stupid controversies, genealogies, dissensions, and quarrels about the law, for they are unprofitable and worthless. 10. After a first*

> *and second admonition, have nothing more to do with anyone who causes divisions, 11. since you know that such a person is perverted and sinful, being self-condemned.*

In sharp contrast to the good works that Titus was told to encourage were a number of other activities that were the exact opposite and to be avoided at all costs. Paul mentioned four in particular that he thought were of special importance in the church at that time. Some of them were expressed in such general terms that it can be said that they still recur today, while others are less familiar to us. Nevertheless, the underlying principle is clear and the examples we have been given are enough to enable us to apply it to our own circumstances.

The four things to be avoided are

1. 'Stupid controversies' (*mōrai zētēseis*)
2. 'Genealogies' (*genealogiai*)
3. 'Arguments' or 'dissensions' (*ereis*)
4. 'Legal disputes' (*nomikai machai*).

In the first category we might put disagreements about things that are unknown and probably unknowable. For example, what was God doing before he created the world? That kind of question intrigues some people, but there is no answer to it, or at least not one that is accessible to us. What happens to those who die without ever hearing the gospel? Again, an interesting question for some, but not one that can be resolved on the basis of our present knowledge. It is possible for Christians to spend an enormous amount of time in trying to solve problems like these, and some have been known to do so. Churches can be divided over the precise details of how and when Christ will return again, even though nobody really knows the answer and we are not meant to.[29] Many secondary matters can arise in congregational life that appear to be important but which do nothing but distract congregations from preaching the gospel and divide them. Knowing what questions are 'stupid' and what ones need to be answered is the business of the teacher, and that is what Titus was called to be. Thomas Aquinas wrote,

> In regard to the first point it should be noted that the burden of satisfying those who raise questions of doctrine falls on the teacher, who should answer some of these questions himself. Furthermore, the teacher should

---

[29] Acts 1.7.

argue with those who resist, and indicate the question to be avoided. In the other sciences no wise man is expected to answer every question, but only those which pertain to his science. Consequently, the teacher of truth ought not to answer every question.[30]

The inclusion of 'genealogies' in this list recalls what Paul told Timothy in 1 Tim. 1.4 and is interesting because it helps us to understand better what the problem with them was. Many Jewish people paid a great deal of attention to their ancestry, and some of them were very fond of claiming descent from important people in their nation's past. The witness of the Old Testament and the stories of the birth of Jesus lent a certain plausibility to this kind of activity, but of course, the discussions concentrated on what was *not* revealed by the Bible, not on what was. Legitimate interpretation of the historical record thus became the springboard for wildly unjustified speculation which was of no practical use to anybody. In fact, Christians, even Jewish Christians, soon ceased to bother maintaining their family trees, and today nobody can trace their ancestry back to the Bible, with the result that debates of this kind no longer take place in the church. For whatever reason, Paul's advice has been heeded and we are none the worse off as a result. In the Jewish world, however, interest in the subject remained lively for a long time. Jerome came across this on several occasions and testified,

> I myself heard one of the Hebrews, who pretended that he believed in Christ, in Rome raise a question about the 'genealogies' of our Lord Jesus Christ, which are written in Matthew and Luke, namely that from Solomon to Joseph they do not agree with one another either in number or in the equivalence of the names. This man perverted the hearts of the simple as if he were announcing certain kinds of solutions, as it seemed to himself, from sanctuaries and by oracle, though he should have sought the justice, mercy and love of God.[31]

Following the genealogies come 'arguments' or 'dissensions', a broad category that could include almost anything. We have no way of knowing what Paul had in mind here, and perhaps there was nothing in particular that he was aiming at. It is a fact of life that people like to quarrel and that left to their own devices they will soon find something or other to argue about. Churches can be split over forms of worship, structures of church government, the kind

---

[30] Thomas Aquinas (2012), 3.2.99 (p. 455).
[31] Jerome (2010), p. 343.

of music that will be played – almost anything in fact. Everybody knows this from experience, and the bad feeling that is stirred up because people react strongly to things they do not like often does considerable harm to the life of a church community. Whatever the outcome, the animosity engendered by such things is simply not worth it and Christians are told to avoid being trapped like this.

The Jewish flavour of many of these problems is brought out by the last of the four things that Paul mentioned – 'legal disputes', by which he meant quarrels about the right interpretation of the Jewish law.[32] We find something similar to this elsewhere in the New Testament. Some people, we are told, observe particular days of fasting and prayer, whereas others do not. Some people emphasize particular traditions which they associate with the right observance of their faith, whereas others ignore them. Most famously of all, there were some people who ate meat that had been sacrificed to idols on the ground that idols do not exist and that therefore nothing had happened, whereas others thought that perception was part of the reality and that practices like this, that might cause confusion, ought to be avoided.[33] As Paul said on other occasions, there is no simple 'right' or 'wrong' answer in cases like these. People must do what they think is right and at the same time avoid criticizing others who disagree with them. Endless arguments over secondary matters that cannot be resolved to everyone's satisfaction are a distraction that weakens the church and for that reason they must be avoided.

Paul summed this up by contrasting these negative activities with the good works that he insisted on. The latter were 'helpful' (*ōphelima*) whereas these were 'unhelpful' (*anōphelē*). The latter were 'good' (*kala*) whereas these were 'vain' or 'worthless' (*mataia*). The difference could not be clearer, and Paul wasted no time in expressing which of the two types of behaviour he preferred to see in the lives of believers.

Before concluding this section on things to be avoided, Paul added advice as to how to deal with those who were causing such trouble. Quarrels do not arise out of nowhere. They have to start with the people who engage in them, and although some may be caught up in them accidentally, others are not. Unfortunately there are those who like nothing better than to cause division, whatever their reasons may be. It is not always possible to tell who has got trapped in an argument accidentally and who is deliberately stirring one up, but close observation over a period of time is usually enough to enable us to make this distinction. Some people get a reputation for being troublemakers,

---

[32] Marshall (2004), p. 334, comments, 'it is hard to see what other kind of law could be meant'.
[33] Rom. 14.1-23.

and when that happens something must be done about them. The approach that Paul recommended might now be called 'three strikes and you are out'. The first time a person was accused of being divisive he was to be taken aside and reasoned with. This is the meaning of the Greek word *nouthesia* ('mind-setting'), which is usually translated as 'warning'. It was not simply a matter of telling the person what would happen to him if he did not desist but of trying to straighten him out. He must know not only *that* he was being divisive but also *why*, and what the right attitude and approach he should adopt ought to be. As the Greek word says, his mind must be properly recast, since otherwise the warnings would fall on deaf ears.

If this process did not work the first time, then it must be tried again. The guilty person must be given an opportunity to repent of his actions and it must be clear to everyone that he was not being persecuted by jealous members of the church who were just looking for an excuse to be rid of him. But if the problem recurred a third time, then the offender must be excluded from the fellowship. It would be clear by then that the problem would not be resolved and it could not be allowed to fester and destroy the church. At that point, Titus had to accept that the person in question had condemned himself because his mind had been warped and he had fallen into sin.

The translations generally paraphrase the original text here, because it is difficult to convey the logic of Paul's thought. The fact that the offender had failed to mend his ways after two opportunities to do so was an indication that on the third count he had effectively condemned himself because he had ignored the instruction that he had been given. His thinking was therefore skewed and his behaviour was wrong. The behaviour could not be corrected because it proceeded from a warped way of thinking, but that could not be dealt with either, because he had already rejected the advice given to him.

Of course we must also understand what it means to be a 'divisive person' (*hairetikos anthrōpos*) in the first place. Some people would apply this term to anyone who is critical of the leadership, whether the criticism is justified or not. Admittedly there are always fault-finders who will never be satisfied with anything, but there are also people who in good conscience object to what they see going on around them because they know that it is wrong. Paul himself could be classified among these second types, and many of his epistles would never have been written if he had just been prepared to go along with whatever was happening in the church. There has to be a place for legitimate concerns to be expressed and nobody should be branded as a troublemaker for doing so when the need arises. The temptation to suppress uncomfortable truths is always there and it must be resisted.

In Paul's mind, a divisive person was not one who was uncovering unpalatable truths but someone who was leading people astray by preaching what amounted to false doctrine. Modern interpreters resist the obvious temptation to connect *hairetikos* with 'heretical', but there is a link between divisiveness and heresy that cannot be overlooked. The gospel message was based on truth and whatever detracted from it was to that extent false. It is perfectly possible to find churches today where questions like the divinity of Christ or the legitimacy of same-sex marriage are ruled out of order because they are likely to be divisive, even though the result of such apparent fairness is that the truth of the Christian faith is diluted. Division cannot be avoided when truth is at stake, painful though the consequences may be. Knowing when to stand up for what is right and when to paper over the cracks is not always easy, but the temptation to do one at the expense of the other must be avoided, and the only way to do that is to base all such judgments on the doctrine taught by the apostles and preserved in the New Testament. On that there can be no compromise, and those who stand up for the truth of Christ do not fall into the category of the *hairetikos anthrōpos* whom Paul censured here. This was very clear to Ambrosiaster, who wrote,

> Heretics are those who attack the meaning of the law by using the words of the law to do it. They give their own meaning to the words of the law in order to promote the corruption of their own mind by the authority of the law. Ungodliness knows how important authority is, and so invents deception under cover of it, so that it will be commended by the good reputation of the name, since an evil thing will not be accepted on its own. It is therefore essential that such people should be disciplined[34]

It is interesting to note here that Jerome was aware that the Greek word *hairesis* does not mean 'division' but 'choice' and described heresy as occurring when 'each one chooses for himself what seems better to him'.[35] Thomas Aquinas picked this up and went further. To him, 'a heretic is a selector who obstinately clings to some sect that he has chosen'. He then went on to explain,

> Hence it should be noted that every heretic is in error; but not the converse, for two reasons. First, by reason of the matter in which he errs; for example, if the error is not about the end of human life or not about faith and morals, the one who errs is not a heretic. But if he is in error about matter, pertaining to the end of human life, then he is a heretic ...

---

[34] Ambrosiaster (2009), p. 160.
[35] Jerome (2010), p. 345.

for example, if a person were to maintain that God is not triune and one, or that fornication is not a sin, he would be a heretic.[36]

John Calvin also commented on this question and did so in a way that still commands our attention for the care that he took to make the proper distinction between false teaching and legitimate difference of opinion:

> There is a familiar and well-known distinction between a heretic and a schismatic which in my view Paul here disregards. For by heretics he does not only mean those who embrace and defend known error or some pernicious doctrine, but in general those who do not assent to the sound teaching which he has just laid down ... But we have to exercise moderation in not immediately making a heretic of everyone who does not agree with our opinions, for there are some matters on which Christians may disagree among themselves without being divided into sects. Paul himself makes this point elsewhere when he bids them wait in unbroken harmony for the revelation of God (Phil. 3.15).[37]

## 12-15. Final greetings and advice

*12. When I send Artemas to you, or Tychicus, do your best to come to me at Nicopolis, for I have decided to spend the winter there. 13. Make every effort to send Zenas the lawyer and Apollos on their way, and see that they lack nothing. 14. And let people learn to devote themselves to good works in order to meet urgent needs, so that they may not be unproductive. 15. All who are with me send greetings to you. Greet those who love us in the faith. Grace be with all of you.*

The last four verses form an appendix to the main letter and resemble similar notes that can be found in many other Pauline epistles, though interestingly, not in 1 Timothy, which is in many ways the one that is closest to Titus. If this letter was the work of a pseudepigrapher then these last verses could be ignored, since they would be purely cosmetic and would have no known relationship to historical fact. But if it is genuinely Pauline, as we believe that it is, then they give us precious information about Paul's activities at a

---

[36] Thomas Aquinas (2012), 3.2.102 (pp. 456-7). Thomas also added that if someone who made the wrong choice was willing to be corrected, then he would not be a heretic, because he acted from ignorance and not from malice.

[37] Calvin (1964), pp. 387-8.

point in his life that is otherwise obscure. The difficulty, of course, is trying to decide *what* point in his life it represents, whether it is a time in the mid-50s or after his supposed release from his first imprisonment in Rome.

The picture we get from these verses is that Paul was actively at work in a mission hub, as we might say today. Around him were at least four co-workers, two of whom (Tychicus and Apollos) are well known from elsewhere and two others (Artemas and Zenas) who are unknown apart from this text. Paul did not say where he was, but he did mention that he was on his way to Nicopolis, where he intended to spend the winter. It is not certain which Nicopolis he meant, but there are three possible candidates – a city in Cilicia, one in Thrace and another in Epirus. Of these the one in Epirus is the most likely, since we know that Paul visited that area at some stage and had mission connections there.[38] If he had gone to Cilicia he might as well have gone back to his home city of Tarsus, which was not far away, and the Thracian Nicopolis seems to have been too far off his beaten track to be considered a serious possibility.[39]

To get to Nicopolis in Epirus he would probably have had to go through Corinth, which is where he was most likely to have been residing at this point. Tychicus and Apollos both had connections with that city, which was also a major centre for ships sailing to Crete. Although this must remain speculation, it makes the most sense of the data that we have. Artemas is otherwise unknown, although early church tradition said that he was the first bishop of Lystra. That might be true, but even if it is, it makes no difference to our interpretation of Titus.

Tychicus is better documented. He was a native of Asia Minor and the brother of Trophimus, both of whom accompanied Paul on his third missionary journey to Macedonia and Achaia.[40] He was with Paul during his imprisonment in Rome and was sent from there to Ephesus.[41] It is possible that he and Trophimus were the two brothers associated with Titus in collecting money for the churches in Judaea, though we cannot be certain of that.[42] In any case, he was an experienced co-worker of the apostle's and would have made an excellent replacement for Titus in Crete, if Paul ever did send him there. Since we know that he sent Tychicus to Ephesus, it is

---

[38] Rom. 15.19. Marshall (2004), pp. 341–2, accepts this as the only reasonable choice, as does Towner (2006), p. 800. Jerome (2010), p. 347, located it correctly, noting, 'Nicopolis itself was named after Augustus' victory, who had defeated Antony and Cleopatra there.' The battle of Actium, as it is known to us, took place in 31 BC.
[39] However, John Chrysostom, *Homilies on Titus*, 6.12, preferred it, as did Theodoret of Cyrrhus (Cyrus) (2001), p. 258, though he may have been copying Chrysostom.
[40] Acts 20.4.
[41] Col. 4.7-8; Eph. 6.21-22; 2 Tim. 4.12.
[42] 2 Cor. 8.16-24.

most likely that it was Artemas who went to Crete, allowing Titus to set out to meet Paul at Nicopolis. All we can say for sure is that it must have been a last-minute decision on the apostle's part, since at the time of writing he had not yet made up his mind.

The letter carriers probably included Zenas and Apollos along with Artemas, although we cannot be absolutely certain of that. Zenas, a name that is short for Zenadorus, is described as a 'lawyer' (*nomikos*), which implies that he was well educated and able to make and defend a case, but unfortunately we do not know what kind of lawyer he was. He may have been trained in Roman law, in which case he was probably a Gentile, but he may also have been educated in Jewish law, and if so he would certainly have been a Jew.[43] He seems to have accompanied Apollos on the journey to Crete and it appears that the two men were passing through on their way to somewhere else, but more than that we cannot say. Apollos was a native of Alexandria, and if he were on his way from Corinth to his home town, Crete would have been a natural stopping-off point. If Zenas was going there with him, he may also have come from (or been connected to) the large Jewish community in the city, which would increase the likelihood that he was a doctor of Jewish law, but we can say no more than that.

Titus was told to show Zenas and Apollos hospitality and send them on their way with whatever they needed. Helping them seems to have been one of the good works that Paul wanted to see 'our people' (*hoi hēmeteroi*) engaged in, but the precise meaning of this description is not clear. Perhaps he thought that Zenas and Apollos were 'our people' and that they should be involved in good works just as much as the Cretans. The phrase is ambiguous and we do not have any evidence that would incline us to interpret the phrase one way in preference to another.

The final verse is a fairly standard closing salutation though it is without an exact parallel in any other New Testament epistle. Everyone who was with Paul, and the implication is that there must have been quite a number of helpers in his entourage at this point, sent their greetings to Titus, who was in turn asked to greet those who loved them in the faith, in other words, all the Christians who remembered Paul and his companions. The last line is unexceptional and indicates only that the Epistle, though sent to Titus personally, was intended for a wider audience, which we must assume was

---

[43] John Calvin opted (probably correctly) for the second option, but did so on unusual grounds. To his mind, the fact that Zenas was poor and needed outside help proved that he could not have been a Roman civil lawyer and must therefore have been a doctor of Jewish law. Given that Calvin had himself been trained in the law, he was in a good position to know such things.

the Christian community in the various churches in Crete. More than that, we cannot say. Paul's words were preserved for us because they demonstrated the character of the Word of God, active and life-transforming in Christian communities far beyond the island of Crete. For us, the original circumstances of its composition remain unclear and will probably never be known with any degree of certainty. But the message that Paul conveyed to Titus, and through him to the Cretan church, still resonates with believers today, and through this Epistle we learn once more what the communion of the saints in every age means in practice. Paul's mission to Crete was short-lived, but its legacy is still with us and in that sense it continues to bear fruit, as he would have wished, in the life and spiritual growth of those who follow Christ.

# Select bibliography

## Pre-modern commentaries

References to PG and PL are to the editions of Jacques-Paul Migne, *Patrologia Graeco-Latina* and *Patrologia Latina* (Paris, 1844–).

Alcuin of York, *Tractatus super sancti Pauli ad Titum epsitolam*, PL 100, cols 1007–26.

Ambrosiaster, *Commentarius in Epistulas Paulinas*, ed. H. J. Vogels, 3 vols, Wien: Hoelder-Pichler-Tempsky, 1966–9.

Ambrosiaster, *Commentaries on Galatians-Philemon*, trans. G. L. Bray, Downers Grove, IL: Inter-Varsity Press, 2009.

*Ancient Christian Commentary on Scripture. New Testament IX: Colossians, 1–2 Thessalonians, 1–2 Timothy, Titus, Philemon*, Downers Grove, IL: Inter-Varsity Press, 2000.

Anselm of Laon, *Epistolae ad Timotheum et ad Titum*, PL 114, cols 623–42.

Anton of Vercelli, *Epistolae ad Timotheum et Titum*, PL 134, cols 663–720.

Bede, *Excerpts from the Works of Saint Augustine on the Letters of the Blessed Apostle Paul*, Kalamazoo, MI: Cistercian Publications, 1999.

Bruno of Cologne, *Epistolae ad Timotheum et ad Titum*, PL 153, cols 423–84.

Cajetan, Thomas de Vio, *Epsitolae Pauli et aliorum apostolorum ad Graecam veritatem castigatae*, Paris: Apud Iod. Badium, 1532.

Calvin, John, *The Second Epistle of Paul the Apostle to the Corinthians and the Epistles to Timothy, Titus and Philemon*, trans. T. A. Smail, Edinburgh: Oliver and Boyd, 1964.

Calvin, John, *Sermons of M. John Calvin on the Epistles of S. Paule to Timothie and Titus*, trans. L. T., London: G. Bishop, 1579.

Calvin, John, *Sermons on 1 Timothy*, trans. R. Van Neste and B. Denker, 2 vols, Jackson, TN: Union University Press, 2016.

Calvin, John, *Sermons on Titus*, trans. R. White, Edinburgh: Banner of Truth, 2015.

Chrysostom, John, *Homiliae in Epistolas ad Timotheum et Titum*, PG 62, cols 501–700.

Chrysostom, John, *Homilies on the Epistles to Timothy and Titus*, Nicene and Post-Nicene Fathers, First Series, Buffalo: NY: Christian Literature Publishing Company, 1889, vol. 13, pp. 407–543.

*Critici sacri, sive annotata doctissimorum virorum in Vetus ac Novum Testamentum, quibus accedunt tractatus varii theologici-philologici*, 9 vols, Amsterdam: Henricus et Vidua Theodori Broom, 1698.

Dionysius the Carthusian, *Opera omnia in unum corpus digesta ad fidem editionum Coloniensium*, 42 vols, Monstrolium, 1896–1913.

EphraimSyrus, *Commentarii in Epistolas D. Pauli*, Venezia: Typographia Sancti Lazari, 1893.
Erasmus, Desiderius, *In Noveum Testamentum annotationes*, Basel: Johann Froben, 1519.
Florus of Lyons, *Expositio in epistolam I ad Timotheum, II ad Timotheum et ad Titum*, PL 119, cols 397–410.
Grotius, Hugo, *Annotationes in Vetus et Novum Testamentum*, Amsterdam, 1641.
Haimo of Auxerre, *Expositio in Divi Pauli Epistolas*, PL 117, cols 783–814.
Hervé de Bourg-Dieu, *In epistolas ad Timotheum et ad Titum*, PL 181, cols 1403–1506.
Hugh of St Victor, *In epistolas ad Timotheum et ad Titum*, PL 175, cols 593–608.
Jerome, *Commentarium in Titum*, PL 26, cols 555–600.
Jerome, *Saint Jerome's Commentaries on Galatians, Titus and Philemon*, trans. T. P. Scheck, Notre Dame, IN: University of Notre Dame Press, 2010.
Lanfranc of Bec, *Commentarii in omnes Pauli epistolas*, PL 150, cols 345–72.
Luther, Martin, *Lectures on First Timothy*, in *Luther's Works*, 55 vols, St Louis, MO: Concordia, 1973, vol. 28, pp. 217–84.
Luther, Martin, *Lectures on Titus*, in *Luther's Works*, St Louis, MO: Concordia, 1968, vol. 29, pp. 4–90.
Melanchthon, Philipp, *Enarratio epistolae primae ad Timotheum et duorum capitum secundae, scripta et dictata in praelectione publica*, Wittenberg: Crato, 1561.
Melanchton, Philipp, *Epistola Pauli ad Titum*, Erfurt: Mattheus Maler, 1519.
Nicholas of Lyra, *Postilla super epistolas Pauli*, Mantova: Paulus de Butzbach, 1478.
Oecumenius of Tricca, *Pauli Apostoli ad Timotheum et ad Titum epistolae*, PG 119, cols 133–262.
Pelagius, *Commentarius in Epistulas D. Pauli*, PL 30, cols 875–900.
Peter Lombard, *In epistolas ad Timotheum et ad Titum*, PL 192, cols 325–394.
Rabanus Maurus, *Expositio in epistolam I ad Timotheum, II ad Timotheum et ad Titum*, PL 112, cols 580–692.
Sedulius Scotus, *In epistolas ad Timotheum et ad Titum*, PL 103, cols 229–250.
Theodore of Mopsuestia, *In Epistolas B. Pauli Commentarii: The Latin Edition with Greek fragments*, vol. 2, *1 Thessalonians-Philemon*, ed. H. B. Swete, Cambridge: Cambridge University Press, 1882.
Theodore of Mopsuestia, *Commentary on the Minor Pauline Epistles*, ed. R. Greer, Atlanta: GA: SBL, 2010.
Theodoret of Cyrrhus (Cyrus), *Commentary on the Letters of St Paul*, 2 vols, trans. R. C. Hill, Brookline, MA: Holy Cross Press, 2001–10.
Theophylact of Ochrid, *Epistolarum Divi Pauli ad Timotheum et ad Titum expositio*, PG 125, cols 9–172.
Thomas Aquinas, *In omnes Sancti Pauli Apostoli commentaria*, 2 vols, Torino: M. E. Marietti, 1924.

Thomas Aquinas, *Commentaries on St Paul's Epistles to Timothy, Titus and Philemon*, trans. C. Baer, South Bend, IN: St Augustine's Press, 2007.

Thomas Aquinas, *Latin-English Edition of the Works of St Thomas Aquinas*, Lander, WY: The Aquinas Institute for the Study of Sacred Doctrine, 2012, vol. 40, pp. 239–458.

## Modern commentaries

Bauer, B., *Kritik der Paulinischen Briefe*, Berlin: Hempel, 1850–2.
Baumgarten, M., *Die Ächtheit der Pastoralbriefe*, Berlin: Dehmigke, 1837.
Baur, F. C., *Die sogenannten Pastoralbriefe*, Tübingen: Fues, 1835.
Beckhaus, M. J. H., *Specimen observationum de vocabulis hapax legomenois et varioribus dicendi formulis in primam epistolam at Timotheum obviis*, Linga, 1810.
Bengel, J. A., *Gnomon Novi Testamenti*, Tübingen: Fues, 1855.
Bernard, J. H., *The Pastoral Epistles*, Cambridge: Cambridge University Press, 1899.
Collins, R. F., *1 and 2 Timothy and Titus*, Louisville, KY: Westminster John Knox Press, 2002.
De Wette, W. M. L., *Kurze Erklärung der Briefe an Titus, Timotheus und die Hebräer*, Leipzig: Weidmannische Buchhandlung, 1844.
Dibelius, M., and Conzelmann, H., *The Pastoral Epistles*, Philadelphia, PA: Fortress Press, 1972.
Eichhorn, J. G., *Einleitung in das Neue Testament*, 3 vols, Leipzig: Weidmannische Buchhandlung, 1812.
Fee, G. D., *1 and 2 Timothy, Titus*, Peabody, MA: Hendrickson, 1988.
Fiore, Benjamin, *The Pastoral Epistles: First Timothy, Second Timothy, Titus*, Collegeville, MN: Liturgical Press, 2007.
Guthrie, D., *The Pastoral Epistles*, London: Tyndale Press, 1957.
Hanson, A. T., *The Pastoral Epistles*, Grand Rapids, MI: Eerdmans, 1982.
Hendriksen, W., *New Testament Commentary: Exposition of the Pastoral Epistles*, London: Banner of Truth, 1959.
Holtzmann, H. J., *Die Pastoralbriefe kritisch und exegetisch behandelt*, Leipzig: Engelmann, 1880.
Johnson, L. T., *The First and Second letters to Timothy*, New York: Doubleday, 2001.
Kelly, J. N. D., *The Pastoral Epistles*, London: Adam and Charles Black, 1963.
Knight, G. W., *Commentary on the Pastoral Epistles*, Grand Rapids, MI: Eerdmans, 1992.
Köstenberger, A., *Commentary on 1–2 Timothy and Titus*, Nashville, TN: Broadman and Holman, 2017.
Long, T. G., *1 and 2 Timothy and Titus*, Louisville, KY: Westminster John Knox Press, 2016.

Maier, J. A., B. D. *Pauli Antonii exegetische Abhandlung der Pastoral-Briefe Pauli an Timotheum und Titum*, Halle: Orphanotropheus, 1753.
Marshall, I. H., *The Pastoral Epistles*, 2nd edn, London: T&T Clark, 2004.
Matthies, C. S., *Erklärung der Pastoralbriefe, mit besonderer Beziehung auf Authentie und Ort und Zeit der Abfassung derselben*, Greifswald: Mauritius, 1840.
Michaelis, J. D., *Introduction to the New Testament*, 4 vols, Cambridge: J. Archdeacon, 1793–1801, vol. 4.
Mounce, W. D., *Patoral Epistles*, Nashville, TN: Nelson, 2000.
Planck, H., *Bemerkungen über den ersten paulinsichen Brief an den Timotheus*, Göttingen, 1808.
Schleiermacher, F., *Über den sogenannten Ersten Brief des Paulus an den Timotheus: Ein kritisches Sendschreiben an J. C. Gass*, Berlin: Realschulbuchhandlung, 1807.
Schmidt, J. E. C., *Historisch-kritische Einleitung ins Neue Testament*, Giessen: Tasche und Müller, 1804.
Spicq, C., *Les Epîtres pastorales*, Paris: Gabalda, 1948.
Towner, P. H., *The Letters to Timothy and Titus*, Grand Rapids, MI: Eerdmans, 2006.
Wegschneider, J. A. L., *Der erste Brief des Apostels Paulus an den Timotheus neu übersetzt und erklärt, mit Beziehungen auf die neuesten Untersuchungen über die Authentie desselben*, Göttingen: Apud Röwerum, 1810.
Wiesinger, A., *Biblical Commentary on St Paul's Epistles*, trans. J. Fulton, Edinburgh: T&T Clark, 1851, pp. 147–256.

## Other works

Cartwright, S. R., *A Companion to St Paul in the Middle Ages*, Leiden: Brill, 2013.
Holder, R. W., *A Companion to Paul in the Reformation*, Leiden: Brill, 2009.
Köstenberger, A. J., and Wilder, T. F., *Entrusted with the Gospel: Paul's Theology in the Pastoral Epistles*, Nashville, TN: Broadman & Holman, 2010.
Sirilla, M. J., *The Ideal Bishop: Aquinas' Commentaries on the Pastoral Epistles*, Washington, DC: CUA Press, 2017.
Thornton, D. T. *Hostility in the House of God: An Investigation of the Opponents in 1 and 2 Timothy*, Winona Lake, IN: Eisenbrauns, 2016.
Young, F., *The Theology of the Pastoral Letters*, Cambridge: Cambridge University Press, 1994.

# Index of Scripture References

**Old Testament**

Genesis

| | |
|---|---|
| 1 | 220, 421 |
| 1.26–27 | 332 |
| 1.28 | 172 |
| 2.24 | 511 |
| 3.1–6 | 292 |
| 3.5 | 330 |
| 3.15 | 170 |
| 3.16–19 | 334 |
| 3.22 | 330 |
| 4–11 | 88 |
| 5.24 | 334 |
| 9.18–27 | 482 |
| 9.22–27 | 104 |
| 14.17–20 | 74 |
| 25.21 | 171 |
| 28.10–22 | 199–200 |
| 30.1 | 171 |
| 39.6–20 | 195 |

Exodus

| | |
|---|---|
| 3.2 | 307 |
| 3.14–15 | 332 |
| 7.11 | 403 |
| 7.22 | 403 |
| 20.12 | 395 |
| 30.19–21 | 164 |
| 32.1–10 | 214 |
| 32.8 | 214 |
| 33.19 | 115 |
| 33.20–23 | 526 |

Leviticus

| | |
|---|---|
| 18.6–23 | 106 |
| 25.39–46 | 516 |

Numbers

| | |
|---|---|
| 16.5 | 378 |

Deuteronomy

| | |
|---|---|
| 4.10 | 32 |
| 7.6 | 530 |
| 7.6–8 | 467 |
| 9.10 | 32 |
| 10.18 | 247 |
| 12.25 | 144 |
| 12.28 | 144 |
| 13.19 | 144 |
| 17.6 | 261 |
| 18.16 | 32 |
| 19.15 | 261 |
| 21.9 | 144 |
| 24.17 | 247 |
| 25.4 | 259 |
| 31.30 | 32 |

Joshua

| | |
|---|---|
| 2.1–21 | 108 |

Judges

| | |
|---|---|
| 7.2–8 | 443 |
| 11.29–40 | 109 |
| 20.2 | 32 |

Ruth

| | |
|---|---|
| 1.16–17 | 249 |

1 Samuel

| | |
|---|---|
| 1.5–20 | 171 |
| 1.21–2.11 | 201 |
| 2–4 | 479 |

| | | | |
|---|---|---|---|
| 2.12–36 | 187 | 127.3–6 | 171 |
| 17.47 | 32 | 135.3–4 | 530 |
| | | 139.7–12 | 305 |

2 Samuel

Proverbs

| | | | |
|---|---|---|---|
| 7.4 | 466 | | |
| 7.12–16 | 358 | 20.3 | 300 |
| 11.1–12.23 | 105 | 22.6 | 415 |

1 Kings

Isaiah

| | | | |
|---|---|---|---|
| 8.14 | 32 | 1.17 | 247 |
| 11.36 | 358 | 7.14 | 170 |
| | | 26.13 | 378–79 |

2 Kings

| | | | |
|---|---|---|---|
| | | 40–66 | 390 |
| | | 52.7 | 439 |
| 2.9–10 | 296 | 54.1–17 | 171 |
| 2.11–12 | 334 | 55.8–9 | 331 |
| 4.14–17 | 171 | | |
| 11.4–21 | 237 | Jeremiah | |

2 Chronicles

| | | | |
|---|---|---|---|
| | | 6.14 | 439 |
| | | 7.25 | 466 |
| 13.5 | 358 | 29.7 | 139 |
| 23.1–11 | 237 | 31–33 | 390 |
| | | 33.17 | 358 |
| Job | | 45.1 | 417 |

| | | | |
|---|---|---|---|
| 1.21 | 291 | Ezekiel | |

Psalms

| | | | |
|---|---|---|---|
| | | 40–48 | 390 |
| 19.1–11 | 529 | Daniel | |
| 19.9 | 205 | | |
| 22 | 454 | 3.9 | 137 |
| 34.8 | 193 | 6.1–23 | 454 |
| 34.10 | 290 | 6.21 | 137 |
| 36.1 | 101 | 7.25 | 214 |
| 51.4 | 205 | | |
| 89.20–37 | 358 | Amos | |
| 91.11 | 265 | | |
| 104.15 | 269 | 3.7 | 466 |
| 105.26 | 466 | | |
| 106.48 | 136 | Obadiah | |
| 110.4 | 74 | | |
| 113.9 | 171 | 1.10–14 | 87 |

# Index of Scripture References

| Micah | | 10.10 | 260 |
|---|---|---|---|
| | | 10.16 | 396 |
| 6.8 | 264 | 10.33 | 368 |
| | | 11.19 | 205 |
| Haggai | | 12.31 | 158 |
| | | 12.42 | 359 |
| 2.23 | 466 | 13.1–9 | 148, 354 |
| | | 13.18–23 | 148, 354 |
| Malachi | | 13.20–21 | 215 |
| | | 15.3–6 | 249 |
| 1.3 | 331 | 15.11 | 493 |
| | | 15.24 | 228 |
| **Apocrypha** | | 16.23 | 214 |
| | | 16.24 | 328, 360 |
| 2 Maccabees | | 16.26 | 482 |
| 3.24 | 305 | 17.1–13 | 307 |
| 3 Maccabees | | 18.12–14 | 364, 370 |
| 5.35 | 305 | 18.23–35 | 396 |
| | | 19.3–9 | 105 |
| **New Testament** | | 19.3–12 | 479 |
| | | 19.5 | 511 |
| Matthew | | 19.9 | 105, 186, 252 |
| | | 19.16–22 | 116 |
| 1.1–17 | 87 | 19.16–30 | 309 |
| 1.20 | 205 | 19.28 | 368 |
| 1.20–23 | 170 | 20.1–16 | 428 |
| 2.1–12 | 429 | 20.21 | 208 |
| 2.1–18 | 137 | 20.26 | 465 |
| 4.1–11 | 214, 291 | 22.1–14 | 448 |
| 4.11 | 205 | 22.21 | 538 |
| 5.8 | 92, 383 | 22.37–40 | 556 |
| 5.9 | 300 | 23.37 | 398 |
| 5.11–12 | 338, 385 | 24.4–12 | 214 |
| 5.13–16 | 141 | 24.5 | 391 |
| 5.16 | 271 | 24.40 | 350 |
| 5.17–19 | 419 | 25.31–46 | 228, 377 |
| 5.17–48 | 97 | 26.14–39 | 254 |
| 5.21–26 | 104 | 26.39 | 75, 100 |
| 6.5–6 | 164 | 26.42 | 75 |
| 6.19–21 | 309, 393 | 26.51–53 | 410 |
| 6.19–24 | 291, 456 | 26.69–75 | 369 |
| 6.25–34 | 291, 522 | 27.46 | 454 |
| 6.34 | 367 | 27.53–54 | 377 |
| 7.16 | 271, 345 | 28.2 | 205 |
| 7.23 | 99 | 28.19 | 206, 337 |
| 10.6 | 228 | | |

## Mark

| | |
|---|---|
| 3.29 | 113, 158 |
| 7.8–13 | 249 |
| 7.15 | 493 |
| 8.36 | 291, 482 |
| 9.2–13 | 307 |
| 9.35 | 465 |
| 10.4 | 208 |
| 10.44 | 465 |
| 10.45 | 156 |
| 12.17 | 538 |
| 13.5–6 | 391 |
| 13.22 | 214 |
| 14.47–48 | 410 |
| 14.58 | 201 |
| 14.66–72 | 369 |
| 15.34 | 454 |
| 16.5–7 | 205 |

## Luke

| | |
|---|---|
| 1.26–35 | 170 |
| 1.26–38 | 205 |
| 2.25–35 | 126 |
| 2.25–38 | 201 |
| 2.27–35 | 235 |
| 2.41–51 | 237 |
| 2.49–51 | 480 |
| 3.23 | 248 |
| 3.23–38 | 87 |
| 4.16–30 | 540 |
| 6.27 | 543 |
| 7.29 | 205 |
| 7.35 | 205 |
| 9.23 | 324, 360 |
| 9.28–36 | 307 |
| 10.7 | 260 |
| 11.31 | 359 |
| 15.3–7 | 370 |
| 15.4–7 | 364 |
| 15.11–32 | 369–70, 428 |
| 16.1–13 | 519 |
| 16.19–31 | 291 |
| 17.10 | 330 |
| 17.11–19 | 111, 395 |
| 17.26–37 | 350 |
| 20.25 | 538 |
| 22.30 | 368 |
| 22.42 | 75 |
| 22.50–51 | 410 |
| 22.54–62 | 369 |
| 23.34 | 115 |
| 23.39–43 | 116 |
| 24.4 | 205 |
| 24.25–27 | 418 |
| 24.44–47 | 433 |
| 24.44–49 | 357 |

## John

| | |
|---|---|
| 1.9–11 | 207 |
| 1.14 | 203, 526 |
| 1.45–46 | 284 |
| 2.19 | 201 |
| 3.5 | 376 |
| 3.8 | 550 |
| 3.16 | 91, 350 |
| 3.19 | 288 |
| 4.17–18 | 252 |
| 5.39 | 418, 433 |
| 8.1–11 | 116 |
| 8.32 | 197 |
| 8.44 | 161 |
| 8.56 | 331 |
| 8.58 | 333 |
| 10.1–18 | 485 |
| 13.1–17 | 254 |
| 14.2 | 380 |
| 14.6 | 151, 282, 375, 554 |
| 15.26 | 553 |
| 16.8 | 234, 423 |
| 16.8–10 | 283 |
| 17.5 | 366 |
| 18.10–11 | 410 |
| 18.15–17 | 369 |
| 18.36 | 358 |

| | | | |
|---|---|---|---|
| 19.15 | 138 | 16.2 | 410 |
| 19.26-27 | 244, 249 | 16.14 | 253 |
| 20.12-13 | 205 | 16.14-15 | 399 |
| 20.24-29 | 206 | 16.16-18 | 215 |
| 21.15-19 | 369 | 16.20 | 408 |
| 21.25 | 357 | 16.31-34 | 277 |
| | | 16.37-39 | 410 |
| Acts | | 17.2-3 | xiii |
| | | 17.4 | 400 |
| 1.6 | 208 | 17.6-7 | 408 |
| 1.7 | 558 | 17.11 | xiii, 418 |
| 1.8 | 206, 337 | 17.14-15 | 22 |
| 1.11 | 428, 526 | 17.16-21 | 283 |
| 2.8-11 | 206 | 17.18-34 | 437 |
| 2.11 | 474 | 17.21 | 403 |
| 5.1-11 | 392 | 17.22 | 136 |
| 5.34-39 | 113 | 17.28 | 422, 490-1 |
| 6 | 197 | 18.1 | 14, 455 |
| 6.1 | 247 | 18.2-3 | 14, 167 |
| 6.1-6 | 181 | 18.3 | 408 |
| 6.1-7 | 191 | 18.12 | 13 |
| 7.1-53 | 191 | 18.18 | 14 |
| 8.1 | 11 | 18.18-19 | 167 |
| 8.18-24 | 392 | 18.24-26 | 213 |
| 8.26-40 | 191 | 18.24-28 | 345 |
| 9 | 116 | 18.26 | 14, 167-8, 404 |
| 9.1-19 | 12 | 19.1-7 | 213 |
| 9.1-30 | 468 | 19.3-5 | 472 |
| 9.3 | 307 | 19.21-41 | 139, 142, 540 |
| 9.23-31 | 12 | 19.22 | 456 |
| 9.30 | 319 | 19.26 | 101 |
| 10.1-33 | 494 | 19.26-27 | 408 |
| 10.34 | 112 | 19.33 | 129 |
| 11.5-18 | 494 | 20.4 | 564 |
| 12.7-11 | 206 | 20.17 | 181 |
| 13-14 | 410 | 20.28 | 181, 190 |
| 14.6 | 410 | 21.8 | 441 |
| 14.8 | 410 | 21.9 | 168 |
| 14.21 | 410 | 21.10-14 | 126 |
| 14.23 | 474 | 21.28-30 | 408 |
| 15.1-29 | 487 | 21.29 | 455, 457 |
| 15.37-39 | 14, 451 | 21.39 | 11 |
| 16.1 | 410 | 22.3 | 11, 416 |
| 16.1-3 | 21 | 22.25-28 | 11 |

| | | | |
|---|---|---|---|
| 22.25–29 | 410 | 8 | 344 |
| 25.11 | 410 | 8.1 | 84 |
| 25.13–26.32 | 137 | 8.3 | 156, 204 |
| 26.4–21 | 319 | 8.7 | 157 |
| 26.14 | 319 | 8.15–17 | 222, 555 |
| 26.27–29 | 143 | 8.19–21 | 366 |
| 26.32 | 140, 262 | 8.26–27 | 327 |
| 27 | 274 | 8.34 | 157 |
| 27.5 | 410 | 8.38–39 | 305, 341, 369 |
| 27.7–28.1 | 472 | 9.1 | 161 |
| 28 | 46, 66 | 9.1–5 | 319 |
| 28.11–16 | 13 | 9.1–11.36 | 468 |
| | | 9.13 | 331 |
| Romans | | 9.15 | 115 |
| | | 9.19–24 | 365 |
| 1.1–7 | 113 | 9.21 | 381 |
| 1.3–4 | 205, 359 | 10.5–17 | 206 |
| 1.4 | 204 | 10.14 | 469 |
| 1.29–31 | 389 | 10.14–17 | 431 |
| 2–4 | 35, 89 | 10.14–18 | 337 |
| 2.11 | 112 | 11.1 | 319 |
| 2.12–16 | 99, 145, 521 | 11.1–24 | 207 |
| 2.14–16 | 529 | 11.13–24 | 161 |
| 2.16 | 110, 407 | 11.23–32 | 370 |
| 3.18 | 101 | 11.26–32 | 144 |
| 3.21–26 | 122, 145 | 11.29 | 324 |
| 3.23 | 306, 366 | 12.2 | 329 |
| 3.27–31 | 144 | 12.6–8 | 182 |
| 3.28 | 97 | 12.13 | 253, 483 |
| 4.1–25 | 364, 468 | 13.1–7 | 125, 138–9, 306, 536 |
| 4.25 | 204 | | |
| 5.8 | 350 | 13.9 | 109 |
| 5.12 | 334 | 14.1–23 | 124, 560 |
| 5.12–14 | 170 | 14.8 | 331 |
| 5.12–21 | 155 | 14.19 | 471 |
| 5.17 | 368 | 15.4 | 419 |
| 6.3–4 | 549 | 15.9 | 451 |
| 6.3–5 | 376 | 15.18–28 | 472 |
| 6.3–8 | 377 | 15.19 | 26, 46, 564 |
| 6.6–8 | 367 | 15.20 | 337 |
| 7.7 | 97 | 15.28 | 444 |
| 7.12 | 95 | 16.1 | 245 |
| 7.15–20 | 387 | 16.3 | 14, 167, 455 |
| 7.15–25 | 387 | 16.6 | 227 |

| | | | |
|---|---|---|---|
| 16.7 | 16, 319 | 8.12 | 128 |
| 16.11 | 319 | 9.16–17 | 110 |
| 16.21 | 22 | 9.20 | 161 |
| 16.22 | 15 | 9.20–22 | 21, 33 |
| 16.23 | 46 | 9.27 | 121, 425 |
| | | 10.13 | 291 |
| 1 Corinthians | | 10.23–29 | 484 |
| | | 11.3–16 | 169 |
| 1.11 | 253, 399 | 11.5 | 165 |
| 1.11–17 | 46 | 11.6 | 166 |
| 1.20–25 | 162 | 11.7–10 | 170 |
| 1.23 | 336 | 11.10 | 265 |
| 1.26–29 | 382 | 11.11–12 | 171 |
| 2.2 | 336 | 11.13 | 165 |
| 2.6–15 | 92 | 11.23 | 310 |
| 2.8 | 115 | 12 | 286 |
| 2.8–16 | 37 | 12.4–6 | 216 |
| 2.14 | 372 | 12.4–11 | 182, 234 |
| 2.14–16 | 35, 329 | 12.14–26 | 380 |
| 2.16 | 288 | 12.27 | 201 |
| 3.1–2 | 223 | 12.28–31 | 551 |
| 3.5–9 | 337, 446 | 12–14 | 37, 344 |
| 3.11–12 | 309 | 13 | 91, 123 |
| 3.11–15 | 428 | 13.1 | 230 |
| 3.13–15 | 526 | 13.1–13 | 92 |
| 4.15 | 79 | 13.4 | 504 |
| 5.10 | 395 | 13.13 | 171, 408 |
| 6.2–3 | 368 | 14.20–33 | 163 |
| 6.9 | 106 | 14.26–33 | 551 |
| 6.11 | 122 | 14.27–31 | 164 |
| 6.19 | 201 | 14.33–35 | 167, 169 |
| 7.5 | 218 | 14.40 | xiv, 101 |
| 7.12 | 17 | 15.1–28 | 125 |
| 7.12–16 | 480 | 15.5–9 | 357 |
| 7.13–14 | 400 | 15.6 | 16 |
| 7.13–16 | 102 | 15.8 | 72 |
| 7.14 | 322, 501, 550 | 15.8–11 | 113 |
| 7.14–16 | 141 | 15.9 | 388 |
| 7.21–22 | 278 | 15.10 | 227 |
| 7.36 | 218 | 15.12 | 95 |
| 7.40 | 17, 76 | 15.12–19 | 71, 357 |
| 8.1–13 | 21, 92, 124, 396 | 15.12–28 | 526 |
| 8.7 | 128 | 15.14–17 | 336 |
| 8.10 | 128 | 15.17–19 | 377 |

| | | | | | |
|---|---|---|---|---|---|
| 15.20–28 | 428 | 1.12 | 407 | | |
| 15.22 | 155, 170 | 1.13 | 388 | | |
| 15.25–28 | 429 | 1.13–16 | 113 | | |
| 15.27–28 | 36 | 1.15 | 159 | | |
| 15.35–58 | 376 | 1.15–16 | 72, 147, 245 | | |
| 15.42 | 155 | 1.15–23 | 468 | | |
| 15.50 | 154, 226, 334 | 1.16–19 | 12 | | |
| 15.51–55 | 341 | 1.20 | 161 | | |
| 15.53–54 | 335 | 1.21 | 12 | | |
| 16.10–11 | 22, 229 | 2.1–3 | 19 | | |
| 16.16 | 227 | 2.3 | 471 | | |
| 16.19 | 167 | 2.4 | 16 | | |
| | | 2.7 | 110 | | |
| 2 Corinthians | | 2.7–10 | 72 | | |
| | | 2.8 | 12 | | |
| 1.1 | 80 | 2.11–14 | 16 | | |
| 1.15–24 | 337 | 2.12 | 95 | | |
| 3.4–5 | 319 | 2.20 | 156, 334, 359, 454 | | |
| 4.1–6 | 113 | | | | |
| 4.4 | 207 | 2.20–21 | 71 | | |
| 5.21 | 156, 367, 527 | 3.1–2 | 73 | | |
| 6.2 | 332 | 3.1–3 | 215 | | |
| 8.16–24 | 471, 564 | 3.1–6 | 35 | | |
| 10.12 | 95 | 3.7–11 | 95 | | |
| 11.1–15 | 16 | 3.13 | 156, 527 | | |
| 11.13 | 73 | 3.13–14 | 367 | | |
| 11.21–33 | 12, 316 | 3.19 | 265 | | |
| 11.22 | 319 | 3.24 | 489 | | |
| 11.23–33 | 338 | 3.28 | 33, 88, 117, 277 | | |
| 11.31 | 161 | 4.4–5 | 156 | | |
| 12.6 | 161 | 4.6 | xv, 84, 222, 327, 344, 555 | | |
| 12.9 | 382 | | | | |
| 13.1 | 261, 472 | 4.11 | 227, 441 | | |
| 13.10 | 17 | 4.24–31 | 421 | | |
| 13.14 | 84 | 5.3 | 330 | | |
| | | 5.9 | 268 | | |
| Galatians | | 5.16–26 | 106 | | |
| | | 5.17 | 292 | | |
| 1.6 | 487 | 6.9 | 325 | | |
| 1.6–9 | 73 | 6.17 | 360 | | |
| 1.7 | 95 | | | | |
| 1.11–15 | 330 | Ephesians | | | |
| 1.11–24 | 316 | | | | |
| 1.11–2.10 | 16 | 2.2–3 | 207 | | |

| | | | |
|---|---|---|---|
| 2.8 | 554 | 4.6 | 133 |
| 2.12 | 71, 102, 525 | 4.7 | 84, 409 |
| 2.18 | 84, 306 | 4.11 | 396 |
| 2.20 | 323, 496 | | |
| 3.7–8 | 113 | Colossians | |
| 3.8 | 388 | | |
| 3.8–10 | 206 | 1.1 | 80 |
| 4.1–6 | 35 | 1.24 | 328 |
| 4.3–6 | 216 | 1.27 | 71 |
| 4.8–10 | 343 | 1.29 | 227 |
| 4.11 | 441 | 2.8–15 | 35 |
| 5.31 | 511 | 3.4 | 428 |
| 6.1–4 | 243, 501 | 3.20–21 | 243, 501 |
| 6.2 | 395 | 3.21 | 480 |
| 6.2–9 | 278 | 3.22–4.1 | 278 |
| 6.4 | 480 | 4.1 | 274 |
| 6.9 | 274 | 4.7–8 | 564 |
| 6.10–20 | 353 | 4.10–11 | 52 |
| 6.11–12 | 207 | 4.10–12 | 444 |
| 6.11–13 | 301 | 4.16 | 15 |
| 6.11–20 | 338, 352 | | |
| 6.21–22 | 564 | 1 Thessalonians | |
| Philippians | | 2.4 | 110 |
| | | 2.5 | 289 |
| 1.15 | 95 | 4.3 | 329 |
| 1.15–18 | 404 | 4.13 | 525 |
| 1.19–22 | 334 | 4.13–17 | 341, 526 |
| 1.21 | 341 | 4.13–18 | 376 |
| 1.21–23 | 79 | 4.13–5.10 | 429 |
| 2.5–11 | 328, 465 | 4.17 | 429 |
| 2.6–8 | 527 | 5.1–11 | 428 |
| 2.7–8 | 156, 337 | 5.12 | 227 |
| 2.8 | 327 | 5.17 | 135 |
| 2.11 | 429 | | |
| 2.12 | 102, 271, 341 | 2 Thessalonians | |
| 2.16 | 227 | | |
| 3.4–11 | 113 | 1.5–12 | 428 |
| 3.5 | 87 | 2.3–12 | 214 |
| 3.5–6 | 319 | | |
| 3.8 | 340 | 1 Timothy | |
| 3.10–11 | 71 | | |
| 3.12–16 | 407 | 1.1 | 44 |
| 3.15 | 563 | 1.1–2 | 71–85 |

| | | | |
|---|---|---|---|
| 1.2 | 51 | 6.6–10 | 289–95 |
| 1.3 | 463 | 6.7 | 44 |
| 1.3–7 | 85–95 | 6.9 | 51 |
| 1.4 | 52 | 6.10 | 393 |
| 1.8–11 | 95–110 | 6.11–12 | 295–302, 383 |
| 1.9–11 | 389 | 6.13–16 | 303–8 |
| 1.9 | 52 | 6.15 | 51 |
| 1.12–17 | 111–26 | 6.16 | 51 |
| 1.18–20 | 126–31 | 6.17–19 | 308–9 |
| 1.20 | 29 | 6.20 | 44, 52, 338 |
| 2.1–2 | 536 | 6.20–21 | 310–12 |
| 2.1–4 | 133–50 | | |
| 2.2 | 44, 52 | 2 Timothy | |
| 2.5 | 52 | | |
| 2.5–7 | 150–162 | 1.1–2 | 315–18 |
| 2.8–15 | x, xi, 162–76 | 1.3 | 11 |
| 2.11 | 100 | 1.3–5 | 318–22 |
| 2.11–15 | 54 | 1.5 | 20 |
| 2.15 | 57 | 1.6 | 236 |
| 3.1 | 53 | 1.6–8 | 322–8 |
| 3.1–7 | 177–90, 476 | 1.7–8 | 52 |
| 3.2 | 252, 478 | 1.8 | 254 |
| 3.3 | 482 | 1.9–10 | 328–36 |
| 3.4 | 100 | 1.11–14 | 336–45 |
| 3.8–13 | 191–198 | 1.13 | 488 |
| 3.12 | 252 | 1.15 | 29 |
| 3.14–16 | 198–209 | 1.15–18 | 345–8 |
| 3.15 | 34, 52 | 2.1–7 | 349–56 |
| 4.1–5 | 211–21 | 2.3 | 52, 254 |
| 4.2 | 52 | 2.8 | 407 |
| 4.3 | 52 | 2.8–13 | 356–70 |
| 4.6–10 | 221–8 | 2.11 | 44, 52 |
| 4.11 | 280 | 2.12 | 44 |
| 4.11–16 | 229–40 | 2.14–19 | 370–9 |
| 4.12 | 243, 553 | 2.17 | 29, 129 |
| 5.1–2 | 241–6 | 2.20–21 | 379–82 |
| 5.3–16 | 246–57 | 2.22–26 | 382–8 |
| 5.7 | 280 | 2.25 | 44 |
| 5.10 | 184 | 3.1–9 | 389–405 |
| 5.14 | 186, 252 | 3.10–17 | 406–25 |
| 5.17–22 | 257–68 | 3.16 | 361, 435 |
| 5.18 | 283 | 4.1 | 427–30 |
| 5.23–25 | 269–71 | 4.2–5 | 430–43 |
| 6.1–2 | 273–81 | 4.6 | 52 |
| 6.3–5 | 281–9 | 4.6–8 | 444–9 |

## Index of Scripture References

| | | | |
|---|---|---|---|
| 4.7 | 127 | Hebrews | |
| 4.9 | 29 | | |
| 4.9–15 | 449–53 | 1.1 | 310 |
| 4.10 | 23, 26, 44, 46, 131, 472 | 1.1–3 | 525 |
| | | 1.2 | 214, 391 |
| 4.10–11 | 52 | 1.3 | 124 |
| 4.11 | 18 | 1.5–14 | 152, 358 |
| 4.12 | 564 | 2.14 | 156 |
| 4.13 | 27, 47 | 4.14–5.10 | 364 |
| 4.14 | 129, 323 | 4.15 | 358 |
| 4.15 | 291 | 4.16 | 358 |
| 4.16–18 | 453–5 | 5.1–10 | 527 |
| 4.19 | 167 | 5.6–10 | 74 |
| 4.19–22 | 455–60 | 5.8 | 327, 480 |
| 4.20 | 47 | 5.8–9 | 100 |
| | | 5.11–14 | 514 |
| Titus | | 5.12–14 | 223 |
| | | 6.4–6 | 250 |
| 1.1–4 | 463–73 | 6.20–7.21 | 74 |
| 1.5 | 181 | 7.17 | 157 |
| 1.5–9 | 473–86 | 11.1–40 | 89, 320 |
| 1.7 | 181 | 11.31 | 108 |
| 1.10–16 | 486–97 | 11.32 | 109 |
| 1.15 | 92 | 12.2 | 352 |
| 2.1–8 | 499–516 | 12.14 | 300 |
| 2.5 | 100 | 13.2 | 253, 483 |
| 2.9 | 100 | 13.8 | 333, 362 |
| 2.9–10 | 516–20 | 13.23 | 22, 302, 441 |
| 2.11–13 | 5, 520–6 | | |
| 2.13–14 | 545 | James | |
| 2.14 | 527–31 | | |
| 2.15 | 531–3 | 1.27 | 247, 249 |
| 3.1 | 100 | 2.1–7 | 394 |
| 3.1–3 | 535–44 | 2.10 | 330 |
| 3.3–5 | 52 | 2.19 | 386 |
| 3.4–8 | 544–57 | 2.26 | 556 |
| 3.9 | 300 | 3.9 | 300 |
| 3.9–11 | 557–63 | 3.18 | 300 |
| 3.12 | 27, 46, 463 | 4.4 | 157 |
| 3.12–15 | 563–6 | | |
| | | 1 Peter | |
| Philemon | | | |
| | | 1.1 | 17 |
| 1.1 | 80 | 2.5 | 199, 201 |
| 1.24 | 450, 459 | 3.11 | 300 |

| | | | |
|---|---|---|---|
| 3.18 | 145 | Jude | |
| 4.9 | 253 | | |
| | | 1.11 | 378 |
| 2 Peter | | 1.14–15 | 88, 418 |
| | | 1.17–23 | 300 |
| 1.1 | 17 | 1.18 | 214 |
| 1.16–18 | 72 | | |
| 1.21 | 85, 419 | Revelation | |
| 3.3 | 214 | | |
| 3.15–16 | 18 | 1.6 | 368 |
| 3.16 | 434 | 1.8 | 333, 362 |
| | | 1.10–13 | 206 |
| 1 John | | 2–3 | 315, 346 |
| | | 2.1–7 | 24 |
| 1.5–7 | 335 | 2.1–3.22 | 206 |
| 2.16 | 292 | 2.6 | 25, 212 |
| 2.18 | 214 | 2.10 | 301 |
| 3.4 | 99 | 2.15 | 25, 212 |
| 4.1 | 554 | 2.18 | 410 |
| | | 2.20–22 | 169 |
| 2 John | | 3.21 | 368 |
| | | 5.10 | 368 |
| 1.1 | 82, 183 | 13.8 | 333 |
| | | 17.14 | 305, 307 |
| 3 John | | 19.16 | 307 |
| | | 20.4 | 368 |
| 1.1 | 183 | 20.6 | 368 |
| 1.5–6 | 253 | 22.5 | 368 |
| 1.5–8 | 184, 253 | 22.6–21 | 428 |

# Index of Ancient and Medieval Writings

This list does not include commentaries on the Pastoral Epistles written in ancient and medieval times. They are indexed by author with Names and Places.

*Apostolic Constitutions* 53
Aratus
  *Phaenomena* 490
Athenagoras of Athens
  *Legatio* 32 52
Augustine of Hippo
  *Confessions* 11.12 160
  *De doctrina Christiana* 4.16 53

Callimachus
  *Hymn to Zeus* 8 489
Chrysostom, John
  *De sacerdotio* 4.8 53
Clement of Alexandria
  *Exhortatio* 52
  *Paedagogus* 52
  *Stromateis* 52
    2.11 44

Eusebius of Caesarea
  *Historia ecclesiastica* 2.22.2–3 458
    3.2.13 458
    3.39.15 451

*Glossa Ordinaria* 57, 59

Ignatius of Antioch
  *Epistles* 179
Irenaeus of Lyons
  *Adversus omnes haereses* 52
    3.3.3 458

Justin Martyr
  *Apology* 1.4 301

Pliny the Younger
  *Epistles* 10.96 142
Polycarp of Smyrna
  *Epistle to the Philippians* 44, 294

Seneca
  *De beneficiis* 3.3.1 279

Tertullian
  *Adversus Marcionem* 5.21 7, 52
  *Apologeticum* 50.1 139, 143
  *De praescriptione haereticorum* 33 52
  *Scorpiace* 13 52
Theophilus of Antioch
  *Ad Autoclytum* 3.14 52

Vergil (Virgil)
  *Aeneid* 2.65 491

# Index of Names and Places

Achaia 564
Alcuin of York 56
Alexander 29, 129–31
Alexander the coppersmith 29, 129, 456–7, 459
Alliluyeva, Svetlana 104
Ambrose of Milan 56
Ambrosiaster 54–6, 94, 96, 115, 122, 127, 140, 146, 153, 167, 173, 189, 194, 200, 213, 226–7, 231–2, 246, 255–6, 260, 293, 308, 317–18, 368, 371, 400, 438, 452, 562
Amyraut, Moise 363
Anselm of Laon 56–7
Antioch, Pisidian 410
Anton of Verceil 57
Anton, Paul 49
Apollos 26, 213, 564–5
Aquila 14, 455, 459
Aquinas, Thomas 58–9, 97, 120, 182, 186, 194, 369, 377, 388, 390, 425, 435, 447, 452, 504, 519, 559, 569
Aratus 490
Arius 151, 153
Arminius, Jacob 363
Artemas 564–5
Asia (Minor) 345–7, 449, 452
Athanasius 151
Athens 31–2, 361, 422, 437, 489–90
Augustine of Hippo 20, 53, 56, 160, 289, 322, 363
Augustus Caesar 564

Barnabas 14, 451
Bauer, Bruno 64
Baumgarten, M. 65
Baur, Ferdinand Christian 31, 63–5
Beckhaus, M. J. H. 65
Bede 53, 56

Bengel, Johann Albrecht 61
Bernard, J. H. 43
Beroea xiii
Beza, Theodore 457
Britain, Great 361
Bruce, Frederick Fyvie 6
Bruno of Cologne 57

Caesar, Julius 138
Cajetan, Thomas de Vio 60
Callimachus 469, 489–90
Calvin, John 60–1, 83–4, 86, 91, 97–8, 112, 115, 123, 127, 134–5, 141, 149, 158–9, 164, 166, 168, 170, 174, 178, 185, 189, 194, 200–1, 205, 213–14, 224, 228, 239, 257, 269, 271, 280, 290, 300, 302, 304, 310–11, 321, 335, 340, 342, 348, 353, 359–60, 363, 372, 374–6, 378, 383, 387, 392, 407, 412, 421, 432, 438, 442, 447–8, 450, 470, 475, 479, 490, 492, 494, 500, 502, 520, 532, 537, 546–7, 550, 563, 565
Cameron, John 60, 363
Carnegie, Andrew 291
Carpus 452, 456–8
Casaubon, Isaac 60
Cassiodorus 55
Castellio, Sebastian 60
Celsus 515
Chrysostom, John 53–4, 75, 83, 117, 149, 152, 177, 182, 194, 318, 368, 378, 383, 435, 446, 457, 491, 503, 507, 532, 564
Churchill, Sir Winston 231
Claudia 459
Clement of Alexandria 44, 52
Cleopatra VII 138, 564
Corinth 13, 46

## Index of Names and Places

Crescens 450, 452, 456, 458
Crete 25–6, 28–9, 38, 463–4, 472–4, 477, 485, 487, 489–93, 499, 502–3, 533, 537, 564–6
Cyprian of Carthage 52

Dalmatia 26, 46, 451, 456, 471
Davenant, John 363
Dawkins, Richard 284
Demas 29, 131, 450, 456, 458
De Wette, Wilhelm 63
Diogenes Laertius 290
Dionysius (Denys) the Carthusian 59
Donatists 411
Dublin 361

Eichhorn, Johann Gottfried 63
Elizabeth II 137–8
Ephesus 13, 22–3, 25, 28–9, 38, 46, 61, 81, 86, 90, 137, 139, 147, 211–13, 241, 259, 312, 345–8, 449, 452, 455, 464, 502, 531, 540
Ephrem (Ephraim) Syrus 53
Epimenides 489–90
Epirus 463, 472, 564
Erasmus of Rotterdam 60, 532
Erastus 46, 456–7, 459
Eubulus 459
Eunice 20, 321–2
Eunomius 153
Eusebius of Caesarea 451, 458

Fee, Gordon D. 95
Florus of Lyons 56
Francis of Assisi 412

Gallio 13
Gamaliel 11
Germany 8, 279, 326, 387, 494
Gray, John x
Gregory of Nyssa 157
Grotius, Hugo 60
Guthrie, Donald 65

Haimo of Auxerre 57, 452
Harris, J. Rendel 490
Hermogenes 29
Hervé de Bourg-Dieu 58
Hippolytus of Rome 52
Hitler, Adolf 104, 326
Holtzmann, Heinrich Julius 64, 66
Homer 422
Hugh of St Victor 57–58
Hymenaeus 29, 129–31

Iconium 410
Ignatius of Antioch 43, 179
Illyricum 26, 46, 85, 463, 471–2
Ireland 361
Irenaeus of Lyons 45, 52
Isho'dad of Merv 490
Israel xiii, 32–3, 73–4, 87, 103, 146–7, 199, 249, 274, 331, 358, 362–4, 368, 370, 390, 408, 415–16, 433–4, 467, 521

Jannes and Jambres 403–4, 421
Jerome 55, 57, 395, 470, 475, 479, 482, 490, 509, 515, 517, 530, 537, 559, 562, 564
Johnson, Luke Timothy 5–7, 44, 46, 48–9, 52–3, 61, 64–5, 67, 90, 175, 194, 205, 247, 257, 295, 309–10, 320, 340, 348, 366, 390, 401, 403, 419

Kidd, R. M. 469
Köstenberger, Andreas J. x–xi
Kreglinger, Gisela H. 269

Lanfranc of Bec 56
Lightfoot, John Barber 182
Linus 458–9
Lois 20, 321
Lombard, Peter 56
Long, Thomas Grier x–xii, 1–2, 4, 145–6

Luke 11, 14, 18, 451, 453, 458
Luther, Martin 31, 60, 71, 83, 93, 97, 127–8, 130, 134, 140, 149, 154, 158, 164, 166, 168, 170, 185, 189, 194, 205, 219, 227, 243, 279, 294, 363, 466, 482, 491, 502, 530, 538, 551
Lystra 20–1, 47, 79, 236, 321, 323, 410, 451, 564

Macedonia 22, 463, 472, 564
Maier, J. A. 49
Manichees 213, 400, 438
Mark 451, 458
Marcion 7–8, 44, 63, 213
Marshall, Ian Howard 4–5, 7, 48, 90, 103, 110, 118–20, 131, 139, 141, 143–7, 150–1, 156, 160, 163–4, 169, 177, 181, 184–5, 189, 193–4, 197, 201–4, 214, 225, 227–8, 232, 236, 248, 253–5, 258, 260, 269, 281, 290, 295, 300, 305, 310–11, 316, 320–1, 329, 340, 348, 359, 369, 371–2, 379, 382, 390–1, 393–4, 403, 418–20, 435, 438, 442, 445, 447, 450, 457–8, 465–6, 476–7, 489, 507, 512, 515–16, 520, 524–5, 549, 551, 554, 560, 564
Matthies, Conrad Stephanus 65–6
McLean, Don 129–30
Melanchthon, Philip 60
Merlin 404
Michaelis, Johann David 61
Minos 490
Monica 322
Mounce, William D. 4–5, 8, 29, 48, 78–9, 119, 169, 179, 191–2, 194, 200, 214, 240, 275, 423, 552
Murphy-O'Connor, Jerome 315

Napoleon 157
Nero 13, 47, 139, 411, 456
New Zealand 87, 286
Nicholas of Lyra 59
Nicodemus 78

Nicopolis 39, 463, 472–3
Novatian of Rome 52

Oecumenius of Tricca 56
Onesimus 277
Onesiphorus 46–7, 345–8, 455–6, 459
Origen of Alexandria 52, 157, 403, 515

Papias 452
Patricians 213
Pelagius 55–7
Peterson, Eugene H. 269
Philetus 29, 129–31
Philo of Alexandria 422
Phygelus 29
Pilate, Pontius 139, 302
Planck, Heinrich 65
Plato 33, 106, 439–40, 486
Pliny the Younger 142
Poland 287
Polycarp of Smyrna 43–4, 52, 294
Preston, John 363
Primasius 55–7
Prior, Michael 315
Priscilla (Prisca) 14, 455, 458
Pudens 459

Rabanus Maurus 56
Reiss, Michael 284
Rensberger, D. K. 53

Schleiermacher, Friedrich 62, 65
Schmidt, J. E. C. 62
Scultetus, Abraham 60
Sedulius Scotus 57
Seneca 47, 278–9
Silas (Silvanus) 14–15, 22, 26
Simon Magus 45, 204, 311
Socrates 290, 356–7, 361–2, 486
Solon 489
Somalia 87
Sparta 258, 489–90
Spicq, Ceslas 48

## Index of Names and Places

Stalin, Josef 104
Stephen 11, 191
Symmachus 530

Tatian 44
Tertius 15
Tertullian 7, 138–9, 143, 301
Theodore of Mopsuestia 27, 54, 82, 86, 96, 119, 133–4, 163, 170, 178, 185, 189, 204, 213, 236, 333, 359, 379, 448, 450
Theodoret of Cyrrhus 54, 96, 109, 125, 134, 153, 163–4, 170, 181, 185, 189, 213, 311, 333, 359, 450, 489, 537, 564
Theophrastus 99
Theophylact of Ochrid 56
Thessalonica 450
Thomas of Chobham 234
Thornton, Dillon 1, 29–30, 45, 94–5, 119, 190, 211, 214, 225
Tiberius Caesar 139
Timothy 10, 14–15, 19–25, 79–82, 126–31, 234–5, 237, 323–8, 413–18, 440–3, 471, 502, 533
Titus 10, 19–27, 450–1, 456, 458, 470–4, 502, 512–16, 533, 565
Towner, Philip H. 3, 5, 7, 46, 48, 76, 80, 88, 90, 92, 98, 103, 109, 128, 131, 133, 141, 144, 147, 150, 161, 165, 169, 177, 190, 193–4, 205, 214, 227, 231, 233, 241, 251, 253, 255, 258, 260, 267, 279, 300, 304, 320, 322, 328–9, 340, 359, 366, 369, 377, 379, 382, 394, 403, 405, 418–19, 430, 435, 442–3, 447, 450, 466, 469, 475, 477, 479–80, 487, 489, 499, 507–8, 513, 519–20, 525, 540, 551, 564
Trophimus 47, 455–7, 459, 564
Tychicus 15, 452, 456, 458, 564

Ussher, James 363

Valla, Lorenzo 59–60
Vergil 491

Wegschneider, J. A. L. 65
Wiesinger, Albert 66
Wilder, Terry L. x–xi
Winter, Bruce William 165
Wycliffe, John 412

Young, Frances x–xi

Zenas 564–5
Zeus 469, 490–1

# Index of Subjects

angels 77, 151–2, 203–6, 264–5, 334,
    428, 483, 555
asceticism, false 42, 211–21

Christ, Jesus
    eternal purpose of God in
        73, 328–36
    Mediator 150–62
    resurrection of 30
    return of 137, 427–30
    union with 356–70
    work of 34, 74, 527–31
church
    as household of God 30–1, 34, 89
    government of 31, 35–8, 40–1
    members 31–5, 42, 162–76,
        241–6, 499
    mission of 133–50
conscience, good 92–3, 128

deacons 191–8
demons 213–17
discipline, self- 229–40, 269–71
doctrine, true and false 41–2

elders 42, 181–3, 236, 257–68, 473–86

faith 93, 118, 128, 230, 295–302
faithfulness 345–56

genealogies 85–90, 357–8, 558–9
Gnosticism 38, 45, 64, 77, 90, 414
God
    Creator 77, 124, 152, 170, 220,
        298, 309
    nature of 111–12, 123–4,
        305–9, 329–32
    Saviour 144–50, 152, 473,
        525, 552–3

Trinity 124–5, 137, 371–2, 553–4
godlessness 98–109, 389–405,
    486–97, 522
godliness 41, 198–209, 221–8, 370–9,
    406–25, 523–4, 535
gospel 109–10, 145, 335–7, 342, 344,
    357, 359–60, 363–4, 375, 377,
    432, 544–57
grace (of God) 331, 430, 349–50, 392,
    500, 511, 520–8, 531, 546

Holy Spirit 84–5, 109, 113, 158, 199,
    202–5, 215–16, 225, 264,
    306, 326–8, 344–5, 349, 373,
    398, 420, 423–5, 520, 522,
    550–1, 553–5
    gifts of the 35, 37, 234–5, 286,
        322–8, 484
hope 444–9, 525–6, 556

justification 31

law, Mosaic 32, 34, 41–2, 74, 94–110,
    199, 212–13, 219, 330, 343,
    424, 488–9, 560
love 91–4, 118, 230, 260, 298–9, 327,
    393, 409, 467, 508–9, 522, 529

matrimony 185–6
men
    old 241–4, 502–5
    young 244, 512–13

overseer (bishop) 81, 177–90, 475–86

Pastoral Epistles
    authorship of 1–3, 7–15, 24, 62–8,
        71–2, 119, 197–8, 315–16, 320,
        438, 452, 465–6

date of 1, 43–8, 66
genre and style of 48–51
greetings and salutations in 71–85, 310–12, 315–18, 455–60, 463–73, 563–6
interpretation of (historical) 51–68
unity and diversity of 39–43, 49–51

Paul
apostleship of 12, 15–19, 71–3, 110, 160
confession of 227–8, 318–22, 336–45
conversion of 12, 111–26
co-workers of 19–29, 38, 40, 449–53, 563–6
example of 336–45
future plans of 38, 43
mission(s) of 12–13, 39, 46, 364–5, 408, 429, 463, 471–2, 474
opposition to 28–30, 42, 45, 345–7, 411–12
trial of 13, 453–5
prayer 133–5
preaching 360, 430–43

Roman Empire 124–5, 137–144, 148–9, 537–8

salvation 153–5, 329–33, 336, 343–4, 377, 392, 470, 548–9, 556–7
assurance of 362–70

order of 77–8
Satan 77, 100, 129–31, 156–7, 161–2, 170, 189, 194, 214–16, 256, 264–5, 280, 292, 330, 334, 338, 343, 386–8, 397, 412, 528–9, 546–7
Scripture, Holy
inspiration of xii–xiii, 35, 416–24
interpretation of 432–5
public reading of 232–3
service, Christian 370–88
sin 155, 330, 542–3, 548
origin of 100, 120, 529, 542
sinners, types of 99–109
slaves 107, 273–81, 501, 511, 516–20

teachers, false 16, 21, 25, 41–2, 85–95, 211, 281–9, 343, 345, 355, 378, 399, 403–5, 438–40, 464, 486–97
Ten Commandments 103–9, 243, 389, 394–5, 513

wealth 289–95, 308–9
women 105–6, 136, 164–76, 185–6, 194–5, 261, 321–2, 351, 399–403, 459
old 241, 244–5, 505–7
submission of 165–76
widowed 246–57
young 245, 507–12

www.ingramcontent.com/pod-product-compliance
Lightning Source LLC
Chambersburg PA
CBHW051330230426
43668CB00010B/1214